GULF WAR

THE COMPLETE HISTORY

Thomas Houlahan

Schrenker Military Publishing

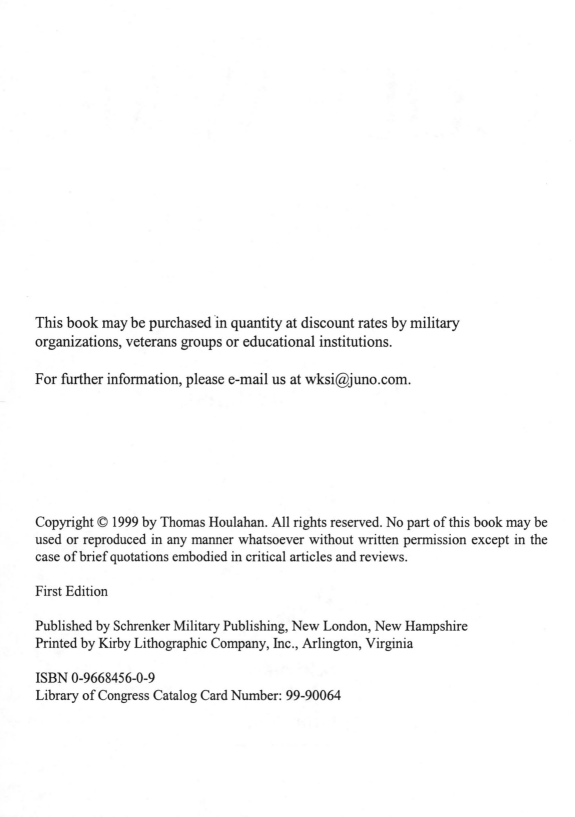

This book may be purchased in quantity at discount rates by military organizations, veterans groups or educational institutions.

For further information, please e-mail us at wksi@juno.com.

First Edition

Published by Schrenker Military Publishing, New London, New Hampshire
Printed by Kirby Lithographic Company, Inc., Arlington, Virginia

ISBN 0-9668456-0-9
Library of Congress Catalog Card Number: 99-90064

Table of Contents

Acknowledgements

This book would not have been possible without the patient cooperation of the officers and NCOs I interviewed (they are listed on page 453). Very few interviewees got off with only one interview. Most were interviewed several times and spent hours answering my questions. The book would be neither complete nor accurate had they not been willing to put up with all of those questions.

A special thanks is due to those who were interviewed regarding friendly fire incidents. They provided honest answers about an extremely sensitive topic. Because of that honesty, I have been able to unravel some lingering mysteries. Because confusion about these incidents in many cases led to erroneous official findings immediately after the war, some in the press have been inclined to charge cover-up. Had these officers been motivated by a desire to cover up, they would certainly have refused to cooperate with me, and would have thrown a brick wall in my path. Had they done so, I would almost certainly have failed in my attempt to find out what caused these incidents. Instead, these officers offered full cooperation, even in cases where it became apparent that the answers they were giving were implicating units that they had commanded. They were as intent on getting to the bottom of what happened as I was. This level of integrity was refreshing.

Author's Notes

Readers of this book may find it a bit unusual. Most readers of military history are accustomed to reading books written from the small unit perspective or from the perspective of division or corps level. Either the reader gets a taste of the nature of the fighting from small unit anecdotes or he gets a general idea of how the battle or war was fought.

I found that neither perspective provided the information the reader needed to really understand this war. Though this book does examine significant small unit actions, heavy reliance upon small unit anecdotes cannot produce a coherent picture of a major battle, or of a war. And, though Allied division and corps commanders did a creditable job, the nature of the fighting was determined largely by the decisions of brigade and battalion commanders. I have therefore written the book largely from their perspective.

Military purists may object to the lack of military graphics in this book. I decided to use simple, reader-friendly diagrams so that nonmilitary readers could understand them.

Purists may also object to the way I have designated rank. Different countries and services abbreviate ranks differently. For instance, a major general in Britain may be referred to in writing as "Maj.Gen. Smith." A U.S. Army major general would be MG Smith. A U.S. Marine major general would be MajGen Smith. I decided to use the most commonly accepted designations of rank throughout the book.

I reserve the right to be inconsistent, however. In terms of unit designation, most countries or services abbreviate battalions which are part of a regiment with dashes. For instance, the 5th Battalion of the 16th Infantry Regiment would be written "5-16th Infantry." That is the format I used throughout the book, with one exception. The U.S. Marine Corps is rather insistent that slashes be used instead of dashes. So, when referring to Marine battalions, I used slashes. Almost all nations and services (including the U.S. Marines) use slashes to abbreviate a battalion's subordinate companies. For example, D Company, 5th Battalion, 16th Infantry Regiment would be written "D/5-16th Infantry." So, like most of the rest of the world, I use slashes for companies. One caveat, though. When writing out company designations, most countries or services write the letter first (D Company), but the U.S. Marines have the letter last (Company D). Again, in the Marine sections, I did it the Marine way.

Introduction

With war, there is always a gap between what happens and how the history is written. This being the case, no one can ever write a perfect history of any war. The question is how much one can close the gap between his writing and the reality of his subject. That question is ultimately determined by how much time, money and effort an author is willing to put into chasing down facts, and the length of time his publisher is willing to wait for the finished product.

I decided to go whole hog on this subject. I felt that the best way to close the gap between history and reality would be to follow every Coalition maneuver battalion through the war and piece together what I found. So, I read every published Gulf War narrative I could get my hands on, then I went to the men who were there. With army, corps, division, brigade, and battalion commanders, I worked out the details of the fighting. In the extremely rare instances where a commander wouldn't talk, I went to his operations officer. When more detail was required, I talked to company commanders and platoon leaders. It sounds like a lot of work, and it was, but there is no getting around the fact that to put a puzzle together one needs all of the pieces.

Before I began writing this book, I knew that what I found would not completely match the perception of the war that the public had at the time. I had no idea how wide the divergence would be.

The public has been given the impression that the ground war was merely a cleanup operation. After Coalition air forces had bombed the Iraqi Army to pieces, ground forces rounded up the survivors, who by then were eager to surrender.

Instead, I found that air power had not performed as advertised. At the time, CENTCOM estimated that fixed-wing kills of Iraqi armored vehicles numbered around 2,600. I found that the actual kill total was around 600. In the final analysis, fixed-wing air power claimed slightly over 10% of all Gulf War armored vehicle kills.

Perhaps this explains why I found that there was a lot more fight in the Iraqis than we have been led to believe. We know that the low-grade Iraqi units on the Saddam Line disintegrated. We have all seen footage of soldiers surrendering to any non-Iraqi who happened to be around on the day the ground offensive began. What we did not see was that the morning after this footage was shot, the Marines had to beat off a series of desperate armored counterattacks. We also did not see VII Corps at work in the west. Almost every unit VII Corps encountered in Iraq had to be destroyed in combat.

VII Corps represents one of the war's biggest perception gaps. Our perception of that unit's activities has been shaped largely by the statements and writings of CENTCOM's wartime commander, Gen. H. Norman Schwarzkopf. One is left with the impression of the corps dithering under an indecisive commander while Maj.Gen. McCaffrey's 24th Infantry Division swept all before it. In fact, VII Corps accounted for about three-fifths of all Iraqi armor destroyed in the Gulf War. This is not to belittle the 24th ID's performance, merely to provide perspective. Three of the four divisions the VII Corps' commander had under his command on G-Day, and the corps' cavalry regiment, claimed more armored vehicle kills than the 24th ID. Both Marine divisions, whom many assume were just rounding up prisoners, also had more armored vehicle kills.

We have also been led to believe that because of VII Corps' dithering, the Republican Guard escaped with most of its combat power. Two of the Republican

Guard's three heavy divisions fought VII Corps. Both were wiped out. One armored division did escape the war in relatively good shape. However, as I will explain in the book, it had been stationed so close to a safe haven that neither VII Corps nor any other unit could have caught it once it left its positions. Three Republican Guard motorized divisions and a commando division were also overrun during the war. The Republican Guard was dealt a blow from which it has never fully recovered.

The biggest perception gap has been in the nature of the ground operations. The maneuvers of the 100 Hours may have been made to look easy, but they were not. Virtually every maneuver battalion in the Coalition ran into at least one situation which could have, or even should have, stopped it cold. On these occasions, adjustments and improvisations were made, and the drive continued.

There was a lot more to the Gulf War than has so far been recounted. I've found it an interesting subject to research and write about. Hopefully, you will find this book as interesting to read.

Thomas Houlahan
5 April, 1999

Part I

Saddam's Big Gamble

"The major difference between myself and Saddam Hussein is that I have a conscience and he doesn't."

—Gen. Norman Schwarzkopf

1

Kuwait Has Ceased to Exist

Just after midnight on August 2, 1990, Kuwaiti Army radar operators picked up a large formation of vehicles moving south from the Iraq–Kuwait border. Three Iraqi Republican Guard divisions, two armored and one mechanized, were invading Kuwait. This was not totally unexpected. The Kuwaiti Army had been on alert since 17 July in response to an Iraqi buildup along the border. The royal family was roused and the Kuwait City garrison called to its battle stations. At 2 a.m., the residents of the capital awoke to the sound of jet engines and helicopter rotors as Iraqi warplanes and helicopter gunships attacked strategic targets within the city.

The emir made his way to his helicopter, which lifted off and headed for Saudi Arabia. Minutes later, an Iraqi helicopter gunship unleashed a torrent of rockets into the emir's palace, while two battalions of Republican Guard Special Forces troops landed by helicopter and began attacking strategic points around the capital. Within the hour, they were joined by Republican Guard armored units, which swiftly occupied communications facilities, government buildings and the central bank. Meanwhile, seaborne commandos had landed south of the city, cutting the coastal road to Saudi Arabia. Desperate pleas for outside help went out over Radio Kuwait. Kuwait City's garrison fought admirably, at long odds, but by the end of the day, Kuwait City had fallen.

Kuwait's army consisted of fewer than 16,000 men and 250 tanks, 450 armored personnel carriers and fewer than a hundred artillery pieces. Many more tanks and APCs had been purchased from Yugoslavia, but these vehicles had not arrived yet. The emir's air force was tiny, with 30–40 strike aircraft, two transports and no bombers. Even worse, to avoid antagonizing Iraq, the emir had sent a large part of his army home on leave. He had hoped that the reduction of force would ease tensions. It did not. The move turned out to be an open invitation to the Iraqi Army, and the understrength Kuwaiti Army was left so badly outnumbered that members of Kuwait City's police force had to join in the fighting.

Still, Kuwaiti forces put up a fight. Over a dozen Iraqi warplanes were shot down by Kuwaiti ground fire. A dozen Kuwaiti planes were lost in a series of valiant attacks against Iraqi armored units. At about noon on 3 August, further attacks on Iraqi forces became impossible when Ahmed al-Jaber Airfield, the Kuwaiti Air Force's southernmost base, was overrun. Kuwait's few serviceable aircraft flew to bases in Saudi Arabia. What remained of Kuwait's army, about 5,000 men and 40 tanks, crossed into Saudi Arabia. Kuwait had ceased to exist.

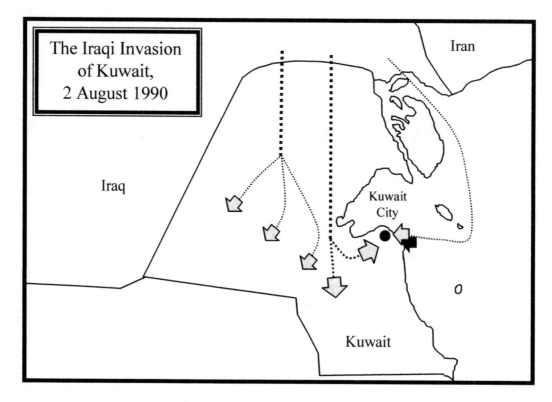

The Iraqi Invasion of Kuwait, 2 August 1990

Iraq's threatening gestures toward Kuwait were nothing new. Iraq first threatened to occupy Kuwait in 1952, while it was still essentially a British colony. The British threatened to use armed force against Iraq. Iraq backed down. A more serious incident occurred when Kuwait gained its independence in 1961. Iraqi troops piled up on the border. A few British regiments deployed on the Kuwaiti side. Again, Iraq backed down, but the tension remained. In 1973, Iraqi troops occupied a small part of Kuwait, and left only after a substantial Kuwaiti cash payment to Baghdad. In 1975, Iraq again threatened to invade Kuwait, but was faced down by about 15,000 Saudi soldiers sent to aid the emir. Iraq's reconsideration had less to do with fear of Saudi soldiers than with fear of Saudi economic clout.

In late July of 1990, when Iraq accused Kuwait of stealing oil from its Ar Rumaylah Oilfields, experts assumed it was just more Iraqi bluster. Kuwait was accused both of drilling diagonally from its small portion of the oilfields into Iraqi territory, and taking more than its allotment from the oilfields. Saddam Hussein demanded $2.4 billion, the value of the extra oil. Although the Kuwaitis denied the diagonal drilling charge, they had never denied that they were exceeding their allotment. As far as the Kuwaiti government was concerned, Iraq owed Kuwait money for loans made during Saddam's war with Iran, and Kuwait was taking payment in the form of oil.

Saddam demanded that Kuwait cancel Iraq's war debt. He reasoned that since Iraq had fought to save the Arab world from Iranian fundamentalism, the Gulf oil states should help pay for the war. The emir felt that Kuwait owed Iraq nothing, and was angered at what he saw as Iraqi ingratitude for Kuwaiti support during the war. Kuwait's position was that: (1) no one had asked Saddam to attack Iran in the first place, and (2) Iraq had not fought for moderate Arabs. Iraq had fought to grab disputed territory from Iran.

Iraq also made groundless charges that Kuwait had taken several hundred square miles of Iraqi territory during the Iran–Iraq War. In addition, Iraq claimed that Kuwait was exceeding its OPEC quotas, overproducing oil in a conspiracy to keep world oil prices down, and Iraq weak. With these claims came a demand for $14 billion in reparations, as well as an 80% hike in OPEC crude oil prices. In response to the Iraqi demands, Kuwait, which had been exceeding its OPEC quota, cut back its oil production, offered to share revenues from the Ar Rumaylah Oilfields and offered Saddam more guaranteed loans. Kuwait refused to pay reparations or cancel the debt, however.[*]

The situation was tense, but the ruling families of Kuwait and Saudi Arabia saw no particular danger. They had experienced Iraqi brinkmanship before. The emir doubted that Saddam would launch a new military adventure so soon after ending a long, costly war with Iran. Even as Republican Guard divisions massed on Kuwait's border, the governments which would soon find themselves at war with Iraq were relatively sure that Saddam was bluffing.

Saddam had never been this desperate before, however. Military spending had put his economy in dire straits. The war with Iran had kept Iraq on a war footing, and the development of the civilian economy suffered. As a result, when the war finally ended, Saddam had a difficult time demobilizing his army. There were few jobs for soldiers to come home to. This created pressure to maintain a large and expensive standing army.

Iraq's 1990 military budget was $12.9 billion. That figure represented over 99% of the previous year's oil revenues. That figure also represented roughly $1,400 per Iraqi wage earner, in a nation where the average annual income was $1,950. The oil revenues were needed to run the country, and Saddam could not demand 72% of every paycheck in Iraq and hope to stay in power, so he borrowed.

During the war, Iraq had borrowed about $90 billion from a number of countries, and most of that money had not been repaid. Iraq owed Kuwait over $15 billion, and another $25 billion to other Gulf states. Iraq also owed over $40 billion to the non-Arab suppliers of its military equipment. Saddam could not pay these creditors, so they began to cut him off.

Another problem was Iraq's inflation rate, which was about 40%. By July, Saddam had decided that the only thing that would save his economy (and his military machine) was an immediate and significant rise in crude oil prices. It was simply impossible to put Iraq's economy in order or pay its $80 billion national debt while crude oil prices were down. Desperate men do desperate things, and Saddam Hussein was a very desperate man.

Saddam Hussein was born in 1937 in the village of Tikrit in northern Iraq. His father, a poor peasant, died shortly before he was born. Saddam was sent to live with

---

[*]Agreeing to Iraqi demands would not have helped anyway. Senior Iraqi officers captured during Desert Storm revealed that by that point, the decision to invade had already been made.

Khairallah Talfa, a maternal uncle. Khairallah, Saddam's future father-in-law, probably had a greater influence on Iraq's future dictator than any other individual. An ardent Arab nationalist, Khairallah's promising career as an army officer was cut short in 1941, when he was involved in an unsuccessful coup attempt. The plotters had intended to drive the British Army out of Iraq. Khairallah passed his passionate hatred for Jews, Iranians and the West on to Saddam.

Young Saddam showed disrespect for any form of authority. On one occasion, he threatened the life of a teacher who had recommended his expulsion from school. The recommendation was withdrawn. After failing the entrance examination for the Baghdad Military Academy in 1956, Saddam joined the *Ba'ath* (Renaissance) Party as an enforcer. In 1959 he was chosen to take part in the attempted assassination of Iraq's dictator, Gen. Abdel Karim Kasem. After taking power, Saddam would portray himself as the leader of the group, but in fact he was a junior member of the hit squad. Saddam sustained a minor leg wound in the failed attempt, and fled to Egypt. There, he enrolled in the law program at Cairo University, but soon became wrapped up in the frenzy of Gamal Abdel Nasser's Pan-Arabism. The adulation he saw showered upon the Egyptian president was a major influence on Saddam's aspirations.

In February 1963, Ba'athists assassinated Kasem, and the world got its first glimpse of the Ba'ath Party's innovative public relations techniques. Kasem's corpse was propped up and shown to a national television audience. Public displays of Ba'athist brutality would be a party trademark when it came to total power. After the assassination, the Ba'ath Party set up a government with the military, whose cooperation had made Kasem's assassination possible. Less than a year later, however, the army capitalized on splits within the party, outmaneuvered the Ba'athists, and took power. Saddam, by then an important party member, was jailed soonafter.

Prison gave Saddam two years to reflect on what had gone wrong. His future actions indicated that he had taken three major lessons to heart. First, he decided that power sharing was a bad idea. The Ba'ath Party would never become involved in another power sharing arrangement if Saddam had anything to say about it. Second, he had seen how squabbling within the Ba'ath Party had weakened its power base. He would never allow internal bickering again. Dissent would be met with an iron fist. Third, he realized that the support of the army held temporary advantages but contained mortal dangers. The army had to be kept out of politics.

In 1968, the Ba'ath Party rode to complete power on a tide of Arab nationalism. Iraq's military government had not committed fully to the Arab cause during the 1967 war with Israel. Aside from one strafing run on an Israeli coastal town, Iraq did nothing. The government sent a small expeditionary force of one armored and three infantry brigades to Jordan, but despite pleas from King Hussein, the Iraqi force stood by while Jordanian forces where overwhelmed by the Israeli Army. Even after the Israeli Air Force attacked a base inside Iraq, destroying 20 Iraqi planes, the government was unmoved. The government lost face, and serious popular unrest eventually led to its downfall in a bloodless coup on July 17, 1968.

The new government was headed by President Ahmed Hassan al-Bakr, Saddam's cousin, who put Saddam in charge of internal security. Saddam did not take long to bring the party's message to the people. Public hangings of suspected plotters became commonplace. Saddam used the security apparatus to purge the party of thousands of his political opponents. He then purged the security apparatus and restocked it with his own henchmen.

Saddam created three separate security forces, of which the *Mukhabarat* was the most powerful. The Mukhabarat was the Ba'ath Party's main security organ. It watched over all other organizations, including the other security organs, the police and the armed forces. The *Estikhabarat* was in charge of military espionage and surveillance of Iraqi dissidents abroad. It also carried out political assassinations when necessary. The *Amn* (pronounced: AH-min) *al-Khass* was responsible for internal security.

Saddam soon emerged as Iraq's number-two man. In the early 1970s, he began to push for the top spot. Saddam moved to deal with the armed forces, his main obstacle. The Defense Minister, former Air Force chief Hadan al-Tikriti, went from being an al-Bakr favorite to exile after being undercut by Saddam. He was then assassinated in Kuwait by the Estikhabarat. More than a dozen senior officers were imprisoned or executed. Al-Bakr never saw the end coming. He thought he could trust Saddam because he was a relative, and felt that Saddam, a young man, would be willing to wait for power. He was wrong on both counts. Saddam methodically replaced al-Bakr's supporters with his own until July 17, 1979, when al-Bakr resigned "for health reasons."

At a special party meeting a few days later, Saddam claimed knowledge of a conspiracy by an Iraqi *ayatollah* to replace Ba'athist rule with a fundamentalist regime. The names of the "conspirators" were read aloud, one by one, giving each delegate time to sweat in terror. As Saddam calmly puffed on a cigar, 68 party members were led out of the hall. None have been heard from since, and at least 22 were publicly shot on 8 August. A videotape of the meeting was shown later on national television.

Much of what Saddam did both politically and militarily over the next twelve years seems to have been motivated by Iraq's military inferiority to Iran and Israel, and Saddam's hatred of those two countries. When he assumed power, he had a small book that his uncle had written in the late 1940s printed and widely distributed. The title of the book was: *Three Things God Never Should Have Created: Persians, Jews and Flies.*

Iraq's relations with Iran during the 1970s were unequal. Under the Shah, Iran dominated the Persian Gulf region. When the Ba'ath Party took control, Iraq began to make claims on international waterways and dispute territory held by Iran. The most important of these claims was on the *Shatt al-Arab* (Arab River) waterway, through which oil tankers passed on their way to and from Iranian oil facilities.

The Iraqi claims only irritated the Shah. He became so irritated that in November 1971, he seized three islands on the approach to the Straits of Hormuz. The islands were actually taken from the United Arab Emirates, but in Iranian hands they represented a greater loss to Iraq. Iraqi tankers needed to pass through the straits and past the islands to get oil out to sea. Iraq severed diplomatic relations, but was too weak to take military action. Frustrated, the Iraqi government increased its aid to Kurdish insurgents inside Iran. The Shah retaliated by furnishing aid to Kurdish rebels inside Iraq. The insurgency inside Iran was never a threat to the Shah. The insurgency inside Iraq drained the Iraqi government financially and militarily.

In February 1974, the Shah seized more territory and stepped up aid to Iraqi Kurds. By May, the al-Bakr government was forced to give in. The Algiers Accord, signed on March 6, 1975, gave Iran half of the Shatt al-Arab in return for withdrawal of the Shah's aid to Iraq's Kurds. It was a humiliating political defeat for Iraq, and must have been especially galling to the man who was sent to sign for Iraq —Saddam Hussein. In all likelihood, Saddam would have gotten rid of al-Bakr eventually, but the inability of al-Bakr to deal forcefully with Iran probably hastened his removal.

Iraq's experiences with Israel during the 1970s had also been unhappy. After Egypt and Syria had achieved a measure of success at the beginning of the 1973 War, Iraq joined in. However, by the time Iraq's armored expeditionary force reached the scene of the fighting, Israel had turned the tide. The Iraqis arrived just in time to take part in the Syrian retreat. Iraq lost over 150 armored vehicles with only a handful of disabled Israeli tanks to show for it. Twelve Iraqi planes were shot down, including four accidentally downed by the Syrians.

During the Kurdish insurgency, Israeli military advisors served with Kurdish rebels inside Iraq. The Israeli government did very little to hide its involvement. It did not have to. Iraq lacked the ability to retaliate effectively against Israel. In addition, since Iraq had never signed a peace treaty following Israel's 1948 War of Independence, the two nations were (and still are) technically at war.

Immediately upon taking power, Saddam attempted to alleviate Iraq's military inadequacies. The Shah was gone, Iran was in chaos and Saddam had a chance to make Iraq the dominant power in the region. He believed that he could use his country's oil wealth to build an army powerful enough to unite the Arabs, destroy Iran and Israel and drive Western influence from the Gulf. This was the first overt manifestation of Saddam's megalomania. Saddam embarked upon a crash building program for the army. For the next decade, 40%–50% of Iraq's GNP would be spent on the military.

Saddam misjudged the vulnerability of Ayatollah Khomeini's regime, however, and attempted to settle accounts with Iran before the buildup was even fully underway. In 1980, Iran was reeling. Teheran was fighting a civil war against Iranian Kurds. The religious fundamentalists had purged the army. The United States had suspended all trade with Iran, so the Iranian Army could get no spare parts for its American-built equipment. Saddam felt that the time was right to seize some territory.

The war started off well. The disorganized Iranians retreated before the Iraqis and their Soviet equipment. However, instead of exploiting his army's success against an army in shambles, Saddam called a halt to the Iraqi offensive after only a week of operations. He felt that a short, limited offensive would bring Iran's leadership to the negotiating table on terms favorable to Iraq, but the Iranian Army, saved from a decisive defeat, used the respite to regroup and gather strength. When Iraq finally resumed the offensive, the chance for victory had passed. The war would end after eight years of bloody stalemate. A decade later on the border of Saudi Arabia, Saddam would make another major miscalculation.

Since the Gulf War, many have wondered why Saddam did not take Saudi Arabia in August, when he had the chance. Why did he allow Coalition forces a place to land, and time to gather strength? The most likely answer can be found in Saddam's war aims. His primary goal was to deal with his debts. Occupying Kuwait, then stopping, appeared the most rational means to that end. This would leave him in a position to force a major increase in the price of oil, by seizing the Kuwaiti fields and menacing the other kingdoms. The other kingdoms could also be cowed into canceling his debts. More oil for Iraq, higher prices for it, and instant forgiveness of half of Saddam's debt would have gone a long way toward solving Iraq's financial problems.

Saddam did not believe that the United States, or any other country, would go to war to rescue Kuwait. This was certainly a reasonable assumption. After the invasion, a significant proportion of the American public and most of President Bush's advisors felt that the nation should not go to war over Kuwait. Even many of the generals who would

8

eventually be charged with driving Saddam out of Kuwait were not enthusiastic about the idea at the outset. On the other hand, Saddam had every reason to believe that invading Saudi Arabia would force the United States and Great Britain to fight. So, having gone a long way in solving his economic woes by taking Kuwait, he would face the virtual certainty of an expensive war with Western powers and the significant risk of losing Kuwait, by attacking Saudi Arabia. At the time, stopping at the border seemed the smart play.

The Iraqi Army began its occupation of Kuwait with a systematic looting of banks and jewelry shops. According to Iraqi reasoning, Kuwait was now part of Iraq, so this was not really looting. Auto dealerships were also a priority target. Iraq's army was very short on transport vehicles, so cars were stolen for use by the occupation forces. While occupation forces were stealing cars, the Iraqi government stole 15 jetliners from Kuwait International Airport.

Outrages against Kuwaiti citizens were relatively uncommon during the early days of the occupation. The first Iraqis in Kuwait were Republican Guardsmen. They were generally well-disciplined and well-behaved, and usually paid for goods. It was obvious that there would soon be problems, however. The troops were not well-supplied, and were forced to knock on doors and ask for handouts from Kuwaiti citizens. Relations between Kuwaiti citizens and their Iraqi occupiers were tense, but not yet violent. Resistance during this period usually took the form of refusal to work.

The occupation soon took a dark turn. The guardsmen were joined by undisciplined units made up mostly of over- or underage soldiers. When these soldiers got hungry, they simply broke into houses and took food.* There were plenty of abandoned houses to loot. Saddam, happy to see as many Kuwaitis as possible leave, had left the borders more or less completely open, and some 360,000 Kuwaitis had left. When soldiers eventually ran out of abandoned houses to loot, they robbed occupied houses at gunpoint. Ultimately, 170,000 houses and apartments would be looted. Iraqi soldiers also developed a taste for the finer things, such as televisions and stereos.

Saddam trotted out the new government of Kuwaiti "resistance" fighters in whose name the invasion was supposedly undertaken, but few Kuwaitis were willing to collaborate with the new government. Within days, Saddam reversed himself, and claimed Kuwait as Iraq's "19th province." The "resistance government" was no more.

Foreign embassies operating in Kuwait City were ordered to leave, since as far as Iraq was concerned, Kuwait was no longer a country. Kuwaiti citizens were ordered to exchange their Kuwaiti currency for Iraqi dinars and to exchange their Kuwaiti license plates for "19th province" plates. The word "Kuwait" was removed from everything. Pictures of the emir were replaced by pictures of Saddam.

The occupation really got rough when about 7,000 agents of Iraq's Mukhabarat arrived and set up torture centers. The first victims were Kuwaitis found to be displaying the emir's picture. Accused resistance fighters came next, and received much worse. At first the Mukhabarat relied on simple tortures, like removing fingernails, but before long, barely living bodies were being delivered to Kuwaiti hospitals with a variety of imaginative wounds. Drill holes through joints were common, as were acid burns, severed ears and noses, missing eyes, and ax wounds. In one case, a woman had the top

---

*Knowing that any food found in a Kuwaiti vehicle would be immediately confiscated, some Kuwaitis drove through checkpoints intentionally, with parcels of food mixed with rat poison.

of her skull removed while she was conscious. Often, the bodies of victims were dumped in front of their homes for their families to see.

The truly disgusting abuses were perpetrated by the Mukhabarat. However, the Iraqi soldiers who garrisoned Kuwait City, according to many in the West only luckless pawns in Saddam's power play, were hardly innocent. The bodies of naked Kuwaiti women, victims of gang rape, began showing up in garbage dumpsters. Filipino maids also received the attention of Iraqi occupiers. Many Iraqi soldiers seemed to take unbridled delight in the act of killing. Perceived insults often ended in summary execution. Between the soldiers and the Mukhabarat, the Iraqis would kill over a thousand Kuwaiti civilians.

Some killing was utterly senseless. Housepets were slaughtered. In one case, at a kennel, dogs were slit open, and the Iraqis placed bets on which one would drag itself the farthest before it died. The bodies were left to rot. "As near as I can figure it," one Green Beret would say after the war, "the Iraqis just liked to kill anything that couldn't kill back." The animal population of the Kuwait City Zoo would be virtually wiped out during the occupation.

2

Bush Responds

The morning after the invasion, President Bush met with his top advisors. Military, intelligence and civilian policy officials all expressed their regrets over what had happened to Kuwait, but most advised the president not to intervene militarily. Their chief concern was the Iraqi Army, the region's largest. However, Bush had all but made up his mind that the United States had to intervene. He was primarily concerned about the long-term implications of allowing Iraq's aggression to succeed. Iraq had just seized 15% of the world's oil reserves. If allowed to remain in Kuwait, Saddam could overrun Saudi Arabia at will, although he did not need to. The threat of invasion would allow him to dictate terms to the kingdom. Over half of the world's oil wealth would then be influenced or controlled by a brutal and unpredictable dictator.

Saddam's intentions regarding Saudi Arabia were a major concern. According to *Newsweek*, he had once proposed a military alliance between Iraq, Egypt, Syria and Jordan to President Hosni Mubarak of Egypt. The plan was to attack and carve up Saudi Arabia and Kuwait. In return for his cooperation, Mubarak would have received $25 billion for Egypt. Mubarak declined. Saddam had also offered Yemen two southern Saudi provinces and offered Jordan the western part of Saudi Arabia in return for their cooperation in an attack. These areas are mostly barren desert. Most of Saudi Arabia's oil is in the northeast, which Saddam had reserved for himself under his plan. Thus, these were not considered particularly attractive offers, and were not given serious consideration by Jordan or Yemen. While these schemes came to nothing, they were an indication of hostile intentions.

Even more frightening was a report by the CIA that Republican Guard units had consolidated their hold on Kuwait and were massing on the Saudi border. The CIA felt that Saddam intended to take over Saudi Arabia, and could do so easily against the kingdom's tiny armed forces.

Saddam was also bent on the development of chemical, biological and nuclear weapons. That development was directed toward two purposes: domination of the region and the destruction of Israel. Another consideration was other dictators who used fear as a bargaining tool in international diplomacy. They would surely be encouraged by a weak American response.

Finally, while top advisors worried about the prospect of another Vietnam, Bush was haunted by the specter of another Munich. If Britain and France had had the will to stop Hitler in 1938 they could have easily done so. They had not, and millions of people, including over 300,000 Americans, lost their lives. Bush concluded that one way or another, the Iraqi Army had to leave Kuwait.

British Prime Minister Margaret Thatcher had already been scheduled to meet with the president on 2 August at the ranch of Henry Catto, then United States ambassador to Great Britain. Thatcher was unpacking at the ranch when she learned of Saddam's takeover of Kuwait. She immediately condemned the invasion, and spent most of the day with Bush monitoring developments. Thatcher made it clear to Bush that whatever his response to the invasion was, he could count on the unqualified support of the United Kingdom.

Meanwhile, Secretary of State James Baker was in Siberia with Soviet Foreign Minister Edvard Shevardnadze. When the foreign minister was first told of the invasion by Baker, he did not believe it. Saddam had even taken his friends by surprise. Baker told Shevardnadze that while he too found it hard to believe, he had reports, and the reports were accurate. As soon as the Soviets were satisfied that Saddam had indeed attacked Kuwait, Shevardnadze joined with Baker in calling for an immediate world-wide arms embargo of Iraq.

Bush knew that American troops had to be sent, but whether or not King Fahd of Saudi Arabia would accept a large scale American presence in his country was another question. During previous crises the United States had responded feebly. After the Shah's overthrow for instance, the United States had sent one squadron of unarmed F-15s to Saudi Arabia. The king was worried that an insignificant force would only encourage Saddam, and might be withdrawn the minute real fighting started. He sent Prince Bandar bin Sultan to meet with Secretary of Defense Dick Cheney and Joint Chiefs Chairman General Colin Powell. As a military man (an ex-fighter pilot), the prince understood the military issues involved.

Bandar relayed the royal family's concerns to Cheney and Powell, who showed him satellite photos of Iraqi troop movements and plans for an American military response to an Iraqi invasion. Bandar indicated that the royal family would probably accept an American presence, but only if the United States was committed. The prince was told by Powell that the American force would total over 100,000 troops. When Bandar left the meeting, he was sold on the U.S. government's determination to ensure the territorial integrity of Saudi Arabia.

The king still was not convinced. A call from the president to the king was followed by a high level mission to Saudi Arabia to brief King Fahd on the Iraqi threat, and the U.S. government's plans to counter it. That 7 August briefing, by Secretary Cheney and General H. Norman Schwarzkopf, settled the issue. The king was told that there was no guarantee that Saddam would invade Saudi Arabia. However, if Saddam did invade, and there was no substantial American force on the ground, the United States would be unable to land a significant force in time to save the kingdom. One of the king's advisors recommended that he wait until Saddam showed clearer signs of an intention to attack. The king reminded him that the Kuwaiti government had waited for clear signals from Saddam, and it was now in exile in hotel rooms in Saudi Arabia. "The Kuwaitis delayed asking for help, and they are now our guests," he said. "We do not want to make the same mistake and become somebody else's guests." King Fahd agreed to an American military presence. Cheney relayed the news to the White House and received authorization to deploy forces immediately.

King Fahd was not the only one concerned about the U.S. government's resolve. Once President Bush decided that the military would play a role, Gen. Powell prevailed upon him to deploy a massive expeditionary force, one capable of winning and winning quickly if war became necessary. Powell, a veteran of the Vietnam conflict, also wanted no more Vietnams. He wanted to ensure that the United States used the power at its disposal to achieve a satisfactory outcome if war did break out. The 54-year-old general had served two tours of duty in Vietnam, where he earned a Bronze Star, a Purple Heart, a Soldiers' Medal, and a passionate dislike for fighting with one hand tied behind his back. "We have a toolbox that's full of lots of tools," he would say later, "and I brought them all to the party."

Unlike other commands, U.S. Armed Forces Central Command (CENTCOM) existed largely on paper. Formed in the early 1980s, CENTCOM's responsibility was planning for and reacting to crises in the Middle East. Its active strength before the Iraqi invasion consisted of Gen. Schwarzkopf and 700 staff members working out of MacDill Air Force Base in Tampa, Florida. CENTCOM's strength would eventually reach more than a half-million Americans and almost a quarter-million Allied troops.

While other commands regularly ran large scale maneuvers, political constraints had made large scale CENTCOM exercises impossible. Middle Eastern nations are extremely sensitive about foreign military activity in the region. With the exception of the U.S.–Egyptian "Bright Star" exercises, no American training operations were permitted in the region. Most of the units assigned to CENTCOM during the Desert Shield deployment had therefore never worked together before, or operated in the desert for any significant period. Time, training and coordination would be required before the force was ready for combat.

No time would be required to bring CENTCOM's planners up to speed, though. CENTCOM had kept a careful eye on Iraq. When the war with Iran was over, Saddam had continued to build his army. To CENTCOM planners, this was an indication of intentions that were not purely defensive. They began to develop strategies to counter a possible Iraqi invasion of Kuwait, Saudi Arabia, or both. When Saddam began piling up men and equipment on the Kuwaiti border, the CIA, the Defense Intelligence Agency, and the State Department concluded that there was little possibility of an actual invasion. CENTCOM, on the other hand, was fairly sure that invasion was imminent, and was already examining its contingency plans.

Though CENTCOM had been unable to conduct maneuvers in Saudi Arabia, it had been allowed to maintain stockpiles there. The U.S. Air Force had pre-positioned about $1 billion worth of equipment in Saudi Arabia during the 1980s. The Saudis had not wanted a foreign military presence, but they knew that their oil resources made them an attractive target for a country like Iraq, and that foreign intervention might eventually become necessary. With that possibility in mind, the kingdom had built several air bases with hardened aircraft shelters, and had stockpiled fuel supplies. There had also been U.S. Air Force AWACS (Airborne Warning And Control System) planes stationed there for surveillance purposes.

CENTCOM's commander, General H. Norman Schwarzkopf was born in Trenton, New Jersey, on August 22, 1934. His father, a West Point graduate and World War I veteran, joined the New Jersey State Police after the war, and eventually led the investigation into the kidnapping and murder of the Lindbergh baby. When the United States entered World War II, the elder Schwarzkopf rejoined the Army, was quickly promoted to brigadier general, and was sent to Iran to organize and train the Shah's national police force. When the war ended, Brig.Gen. Schwarzkopf's family joined him in Iran. After completing his schooling in Iran, Italy, Germany and Switzerland, the younger Schwarzkopf attended the Valley Forge Military Academy before attending West Point, where in 1956 he graduated 42nd in a class of 485.

Schwarzkopf was especially well-suited to the dynamics of coalition warfare. During the Vietnam conflict he had been an advisor to a South Vietnamese airborne unit. He received the first of his three Silver Stars (the Army's third highest award for valor behind the Medal of Honor and the Distinguished Service Cross) as the senior advisor attached to a force of about a thousand Vietnamese paratroops that relieved a trapped Special Forces unit after two weeks of savage fighting. His second Silver Star and first Purple Heart came after a particularly bloody assault on a position held by the Vietcong. He was wounded four times during the assault, but refused medical attention until the position had been taken and his wounded soldiers were evacuated. He developed a reputation for frugality with the lives of his soldiers, even when those soldiers were not Americans. This reputation made him a commander with whom even the most tentative members of the Coalition could be comfortable.

As a battalion commander in the U.S. 23rd "Americal" Infantry Division, Schwarzkopf received his second Purple Heart and gained unwelcome personal experience with landmines. In mid-1970, part of one of his companies became trapped in a minefield. As he attempted to guide them out of the minefield, one of his soldiers stepped on a landmine. The blast wounded Schwarzkopf. As his men prepared to enter Iraqi minefields almost 21 years later, Schwarzkopf saw to it that they were fully prepared to deal with the mines.

The first ground troops to arrive in Saudi Arabia were strictly defensive and lightly equipped. Col. Ron Rokosz's 2nd "Falcon" Brigade of the 82nd Airborne Division arrived in Saudi Arabia from Fort Bragg, North Carolina on 8 August, and took up positions behind the Saudi task force that guarded the Saudi–Kuwaiti border. This force represented the "line in the sand." It was just large enough to make it clear to Saddam that an attack on Saudi Arabia would be considered an attack on the United States. The brigade was equipped with its own 56 Humvee-mounted TOW (Tube launched, Optically tracked, Wire guided) anti-tank missile launchers and 14 Sheridan light tanks from B Company of the 82nd's 3rd Battalion, 73rd Armor Regiment. Until the 24th Infantry Division showed up with its Abrams tanks, Sheridans would have to do. These tanks were about one-third the size of the Republican Guard's T-72s, but their crews were excellent, and they were the only American tanks available on such short notice. The Falcons also had support from 48 F-15C fighters from the 1st Tactical Fighter Wing, which deployed from Langley, Virginia to bases in Dhahran and Riyadh. By the end of August, the F-15s would be joined by more than 200 ground attack aircraft.

Another important deterrent was a regiment of Egyptian Rangers. A single regiment of soldiers, however well-trained or spirited, did not amount to much strategically. But, like the Falcon Brigade, these Rangers had a major power behind them. Egypt had one of the most powerful armies in the region, and a leader who had entirely lost his patience with Saddam Hussein. As his army prepared to invade Kuwait, Saddam had assured President Hosni Mubarak that he would not attempt to settle his differences with Kuwait by force. Mubarak had taken him at his word, and had relayed Saddam's assurances to Kuwait. Mubarak, a proud man, had been lied to and used by Saddam.

Many Egyptians also felt that they had a score to settle with Saddam. During the Iran–Iraq War, when virtually all able-bodied Iraqi men had been swept into the Iraqi war machine, unskilled Egyptian workers had flocked to Iraq in search of opportunity. Most found only harsh conditions and cheating employers. At the end of the war, many Iraqi soldiers were demobilized, only to find Egyptians in their former jobs. Hundreds of Egyptians were murdered. Few of their murderers were prosecuted. In a final outrage, the Iraqi government expelled the workers, most with only the clothes on their backs and without whatever pay they were owed. Many Egyptian soldiers felt that their nation had been shamed, and were itching for a showdown with Iraq. Undoubtedly, Saddam knew that even a minor brush with Egyptian Rangers could bring one of the region's largest and most experienced armies down around his neck.

Whether or not Saddam would have attacked Saudi Arabia was a topic of some debate. Some senior American military officers were certain that he would. Gen. Powell was almost certain that he would not. War with Kuwait was one thing. War with the United States and Egypt was another. Powell was sure that Saddam would think twice before engaging American forces. Still, many intelligent people had tried to predict Saddam's actions before, and had been wrong. At this point, no one knew for sure what he was going to do, and no one was taking any chances.

In the meantime, while Saddam was using the world's media to scare the American public, CENTCOM was using the media to intimidate Saddam. Gen. Schwarzkopf was heartened by American press reports that consistently overrated the American presence. He knew Saddam was watching. Schwarzkopf made sure that news crews had no trouble filming the beehive of activity at Dhahran Airfield. The Pentagon made sure that the news media knew of every division in the Gulf. The media did not necessarily know that many divisions were represented only by skeleton crews awaiting their main body.

About that time, the American public was receiving another scare. Army doctors in the Gulf were reporting that their field hospitals were woefully underequipped, and would be unable to handle the heavy casualties they expected to treat in the event of an Iraqi assault. However, the absence of medical equipment was not an oversight, but the result of a decision based on CENTCOM's recognition of reality. Medical equipment was simply a lower priority than troops and tanks. At that point, space on transports was reserved almost entirely for combat soldiers and equipment. Combat divisions were not even bringing over their own support battalions yet. CENTCOM realized that medical equipment would not help much if the front line units could not hold the Iraqis. On the other hand, soldiers and tanks in sufficient numbers might make the Iraqis decide not to attack in the first place, making the medical equipment unnecessary.

A strong defensive force might keep the Iraqi Army out of Saudi Arabia, but it would not force it to leave Kuwait. For that, at a minimum, sanctions would be necessary. Among the sanctions sought by President Bush was the closing of the pipelines that allowed Iraqi oil to pass through Turkey and Saudi Arabia. Although Turkey needed the hard currency the pipeline brought in (over $200 million per year), the Turkish government was willing to comply, but Saddam saved Turkey the trouble. Perhaps thinking that Turkey's dependence on the pipeline fees would force her government to distance itself from the Coalition, Saddam cut off the pipeline. Turkey stood her ground, and the pipeline stayed dry.

Saudi Arabia was another matter. Turkey had a strong standing army. Turkish soldiers are renowned for their toughness and fighting spirit. Turkey was also a member of NATO, and an attack on Turkey would be an attack on NATO. Saddam would not dare invade Turkey, but Saudi Arabia was a juicy target, and the Saudi government knew it. Since the invasion of Kuwait, the Saudis had taken great pains to avoid provoking Saddam. Saudi forces even pulled back 20 miles from the border with Kuwait to avoid the appearance of hostile intent toward Saddam's forces. Now the king was being asked to make a decidedly provocative move. If Saudi Arabia was not already on Saddam's target list, cutting off the pipeline would probably put the kingdom on it. Realizing that the future of his country was at stake, King Fahd made one additional request of President Bush. If war did break out, he did not want to deal with a wounded and angry Saddam later on. He wanted Iraq's offensive capability completely destroyed. Bush was not prepared at that point to make such a promise. A restatement of his guarantee of the defense of Saudi Arabia's territorial integrity was all the president could offer. King Fahd agreed to cut off the pipeline.

Bush had worries of his own. Saddam had taken 20,000 Western hostages and had sent 56 American, 27 French and 137 British citizens to key military installations throughout Iraq and Kuwait, to act as "human shields." Saddam believed that this would forestall any American military action. "Americans react pathologically to hostages," he confided to an aide. However, Bush had no intention of sharing the fate of former President Jimmy Carter. He made it clear that he would not be the prisoner of a hostage crisis, and that this action would not affect American policy. To reinforce his point, Bush went through with his planned vacation in Kennebunkport, Maine. Publicly, the president said little about the "foreign guest" issue, except to point out that whatever these civilians were called, they were being used as hostages, and the Iraqi government would be held responsible for their safety.

In late September, on the floor of the House of Commons, Prime Minister Thatcher issued a challenge to Saddam's manhood. She said that it was curious in her view, that someone who portrayed himself as a modern Arab knight would hide behind women and children. Saddam immediately recognized that this challenge —by a woman, no less, had seriously damaged his image in the eyes of the Arab world. He responded by releasing all foreign women and children within days of Thatcher's speech.

By late September, the two active duty brigades of the 24th Infantry Division, the 101st Airborne Division (Air Assault) and a Marine brigade were in defensive positions. That amounted to about 50,000 troops with almost 300 tanks. Meanwhile, Saddam sent more troops to the Saudi border. Iraq was also moving warplanes toward the border and there was evidence that Iraqi forward bases were stocking up on bombs. Saddam did not seem to be getting the message.

In October, Saddam began to extend his line westward, until it had doubled in length. That fact, and the belief that an overwhelming combat force would make the

16

success of a Coalition attack more certain and keep casualties down, prompted CENTCOM to ask for more troops. Schwarzkopf requested two more armored divisions and an armored cavalry regiment from Germany, as well as an armored division from the United States. He forwarded his preliminary plans to Powell, who had gathered a small planning team of senior officers. When they were done, Powell submitted the request to Cheney. In addition to Schwarzkopf's requests, the team's plan called for a battleship, three carrier battle groups and the equivalent of a division of Marines to be sent. On 31 October, President Bush approved the revised plan, but decided not to make the plan public until after the November 6th congressional elections.

CENTCOM continued to align all of its forces along the Saudi–Kuwaiti border, arrayed directly opposite the strongest Iraqi positions. These preparations for what appeared to be a frontal assault diverted Iraqi attention from the possibility of a flanking movement. On 15 November, CENTCOM attempted to conduct the highly publicized "Operation Imminent Thunder," an amphibious training exercise. Rough seas prevented effective training, but the planned exercise had focused Iraqi attention on the possibility of an amphibious assault. In anticipation of possible landings, the Iraqis built extensive defenses and stationed large numbers of troops along the coast. Though the Iraqis were clearly deceived, Imminent Thunder was more than a deception. There was a possibility that an amphibious landing might become necessary at some point. If it did, CENTCOM wanted to be ready.

Congress and the public began to sense the gravity of the situation in mid-November as the two sides moved closer to hostilities. Congressional and public concern began to grow. The original American force of 210,000 had swelled to 430,000 and had the equipment to take offensive action if necessary. Iraq refused to budge. Public hearings were held by the Senate Armed Services Committee. A steady stream of experts on foreign policy, intelligence and military affairs presented a gloomy picture of what could be expected if fighting broke out. Most of them significantly overestimated the capabilities of Saddam's military machine and counseled patience. Former Joint Chiefs Chairman Admiral William Crowe predicted that the United States would prevail in a land war, "but at a terrible price."

While many members of Congress felt that the economic sanctions should be given more time, President Bush did not have a great deal of confidence in them. He believed that in the end, the Iraqi people would have been the real victims of the embargo. Saddam, his Revolutionary Command Council and the Republican Guard would have received adequate food and supplies. There was also a great deal of concern as to how well the embargo would hold up once Western television viewers began seeing pictures of starving Iraqi children each night.

In late November, events moved beyond the control of Congress. Secretary of State Baker had spent most of November lining up support for the United Nations resolution authorizing the use of force. The representatives of every nation on the U.N. Security Council were contacted by the State Department. A combination of reason and American economic leverage was employed. The discussions had the desired effect. On the 29th, the United Nations approved a resolution authorizing the use of force to remove Iraqi troops from Kuwait. The resolution set a deadline of 15 January for Iraqi forces to leave. After that, they would be fair game. Of the nations on the Security Council, only Cuba and Yemen voted against the resolution. All American aid to Yemen was cut off the next day.

Unfortunately, the resolution reinforced the American public's fear of a major land war. Fears deepened when Saddam test fired three Scud missiles at targets inside Iraq. To soothe those jitters, Bush invited Iraqi Foreign Minister Tariq Aziz to Washington and offered to send Secretary of State Baker to Baghdad. In what had become a public relations war, Saddam attempted to go Bush one better. He agreed to release his remaining "foreign guests." Western public opinion had turned sharply against Saddam on the hostage issue. Press and citizenry alike had been appalled by his parading of hostages in front of television cameras. This had provoked not fear, but anger. By early December, Saddam had begun to sense that his hostage gambit had failed. He judged from Bush's behavior that hostages would offer no security in the event of an attack, but concluded that their release might have propaganda value.

The ray of hope sparked by Bush's offer quickly vanished. Saddam continued to insist on redrawing Iraq's borders with Kuwait and linkage between the situation in Kuwait and Israel's occupation of the West Bank. Without new boundaries and an international conference on the Palestinian issue, Iraq would not budge. In Washington, the recognition of a border redrawn by military force was unthinkable, and linkage was seen as another of Saddam's smokescreens. Like the "Arab solution" Saddam claimed to seek, linkage was seen as an attempt by Saddam to portray himself as the champion of the Arab masses. Finally, Saddam refused to receive Baker until three days before the deadline. Bush saw this as a transparent stalling tactic.

By Christmas, Bush had run out of patience. He decided that if Saddam refused to leave Kuwait on his own, he would be driven out, even if it meant heavy American casualties. Bush had read the Amnesty International report on atrocities in Kuwait and had concluded that the issue boiled down to good versus evil. "If we have to go," he warned, "it's not going to matter to me if there isn't one congressman who supports this, or what happens to public opinion. If it's right, it's gotta be done." Saddam was not going to be allowed to remain in Kuwait, a sword hanging over the heads of the region's oil kingdoms. The United Nations, with the United States in the lead, would offer Saddam Hussein two options: get out of Kuwait, or be driven out by military force. In Gen. Powell's words, the Iraqi Army could "move it or lose it."

Bush made one last attempt to secure a peaceful Iraqi withdrawal from Kuwait. He sent Baker to Geneva for a meeting with Tariq Aziz. Baker presented Aziz with a letter from Bush to Saddam Hussein. Aziz refused to accept the letter. After meeting for several hours and accomplishing nothing, the two diplomats returned to their capitals. On 12 January, as the members of Iraq's Revolutionary Command Council watched on CNN, Congress authorized the use of force by a vote of 52–47 in the Senate and 250–183 in the House.

The United Nations' embargo of Iraq was having a marked effect on the Iraqi economy. Iraq was losing over $1 billion in oil revenues each month, and monthly industrial output had dropped 30%–40%. Still, Saddam showed no intention of withdrawing from Kuwait peacefully. Between the invasion of Kuwait and the 15 January deadline, Saddam quadrupled the number of troops in Kuwait and southern Iraq and increased the number of tanks in the theater tenfold. Saddam understood nothing about the West, its citizens or its technology. Aside from a short trip to France in 1972, he had never been to a Western nation. He accepted as gospel the stereotype of the West as decadent, self-indulgent and weak. He was confident that the prospect of heavy casualties would cause the West to back down. The Iraqi buildup continued until the first bomb fell.

Part II

Aerial Avalanche

"All those precision weapons and gadgets and gizmos and Stealth fighters are not going to make it possible to reconquer Kuwait without many thousands of casualties."

—Edward Luttwak,
Center For Strategic and
International Studies,
Georgetown University
(December 1990)

3

Air War: The Strategic Phase

Perhaps the most memorable aspect of the Gulf conflict was the air war, which helped pave the way for the stunning success of ground operations six weeks later. The air campaign was masterminded by Air Force Lt.Gen. Chuck Horner. Horner had racked up 4,500 flying hours on the Air Force's most advanced fighters in his 33 years of service and had flown 111 combat missions in Vietnam. Many of his combat flights had been electronic jamming or radar destroying missions like those which would be so crucial to the conduct of air operations in this war.

Horner was well-suited to working with Gen. Schwarzkopf, since he was in no way intimidated by Schwarzkopf's periodic displays of temper. When, before bombing began, Schwarzkopf saw that he planned to use B-52s largely to hit strategic targets instead of concentrating on Republican Guard divisions, he began shouting at Horner and threatened to fire him. Horner calmly told Schwarzkopf he was free to do so. Schwarzkopf regained his composure, and the B-52 raids went in as Horner had planned them.[*]

Strategic targets were Horner's first priority. Attacks on strategic targets represented a relatively small percentage of the total missions flown, but they had a significant impact on the war's successful outcome. The strategic phase of the air campaign involved the destruction of Iraqi command and control centers (including telephone exchanges), nuclear, biological and chemical facilities, Scud missile sites, the Iraqi Air Force and its airfields, air defense systems (including early warning radars), power facilities and vital war industries.

----

[*]This proved wise. When B-52s did attack the Republican Guard, damage was slight. B-52s were useful as a platform for cruise missiles, or for scattering large numbers of mines quickly. They were also an effective terror weapon. However, while extravagant destruction claims (80 or 100 Iraqi armored vehicles in a single raid) were made at the time, B-52s probably accounted for fewer than a dozen destroyed Iraqi armored vehicles in the course of the war.

Finding targets was not a problem. The "Lacrosse" satellite produced radar images, and could identify objects a yard long through a sandstorm or any other type of adverse weather. Among other things, the Lacrosse was used to produce the precise terrain information which was then digitally coded and loaded into the electronic "brains" of the Tomahawk missiles that struck Iraq during the opening hours of the war. There were also two "Mentor" signal intelligence satellites which allowed the Allies to monitor Iraqi radio traffic. Finally, since Iraq had contracted with French companies to tie its command and control centers into a unified system, the Coalition had easy access to information about the network.

During the Vietnam War, the Air Force, in Lyndon Johnson's words: "couldn't bomb an outhouse without my approval." Limitations on American pilots were severe, and in many cases absurd. The most glaring absurdity was that during Johnson's presidency American pilots were not allowed to attack the surface-to-air missile batteries that were shooting down American planes. Johnson, afraid such attacks might kill Soviet advisors and increase tension with Moscow, opted to make life riskier for his pilots.

There would be no such political interference during Desert Storm. In this war, targets were selected and approved by CENTCOM in Riyadh. Only two targets were removed from the target list by Washington. A massive statue of Saddam Hussein and the Iraqi War Memorial had originally been targeted. The War Memorial is a sixty foot high bronze arch comprised of two crossed Arab swords held by huge reproductions of Saddam Hussein's forearms. At the base of each forearm was a large net containing the bullet-riddled and shrapnel-torn helmets of thousands of dead Iranian soldiers. Saddam had used the arch for his military parades. The Air Force felt that the destruction of these two symbols would make a statement. Secretary of Defense Dick Cheney thought it was overkill. Meanwhile, CENTCOM had become convinced that a command and control center was being run out of the basement of the al-Rashid Hotel in Baghdad. However, when the al-Rashid became a headquarters for foreign journalists, CENTCOM had to take it off the list. "We don't hate journalists that much," joked one officer.

Once targets were agreed upon by CENTCOM, the weaponeers were called in. Weaponeers are experts in destructive power. Commanders give weaponeers targets and tell them how much and what kind of damage they want to do. Weaponeers tell the commanders what type of, and how many, bombs or missiles will be necessary to carry out the mission. They already had voluminous information on many targeted structures. The companies that had built them for Iraq provided blueprints for CENTCOM showing how the structures were built, with what materials, and what areas were vulnerable. By the time the air war began, the Air Force knew as much about these installations as the Iraqis did, in some cases more.

With such a wealth of intelligence information, specific targets could be analyzed extensively by computers, like those at the Naval Strike Warfare Center in Fallon, Nevada. Precision was paramount, especially for Iraq's nuclear facilities. Hitting a reactor risked the possibility of large scale nuclear contamination. Pilots needed to hit reactor buildings in such a way that the buildings collapsed on the reactors and entombed them. Just hitting targets would not be enough in this war.

The finished product of all this planning was the Air Tasking Order (ATO). An ATO is a highly detailed document that contains the mission of each aircraft in a command, from fighter-bombers to air refueling tankers. Horner's original ATO covered the first 48 hours of the war and was some 300 pages in length.

Before the war, many believed that Iraq's air defense system would be more sophisticated than anything encountered during the Vietnam War. Baghdad was defended by 60 anti-aircraft missile batteries and 3,000 AA guns. Only Moscow had a denser concentration of anti-aircraft weapons. American experience had led planners to expect that sustained operations against such a system would claim about 3% of the planes sent on each mission during the early stages of the air war. A 3% chance of each combat sortie being "one-way" does not seem like much, but with thousands of combat sorties to be flown, losses were expected to be high.* There were critical differences between attacking targets in Vietnam and attacking targets in Iraq, however.

It is a lot easier to hit targets in the desert than in the jungle. In addition, new bombing equipment and techniques had made bombing more accurate since Vietnam, so pilots in the Gulf War could deliver their payloads from higher (and safer) altitudes, and with greater accuracy. The bombs had also improved. Over 6,500 tons of guided munitions were dropped during the war, about 8% of the total.

Vietnam-era U.S. warplanes had to come in relatively close to their targets to deliver their ordnance. This made them vulnerable to anti-aircraft artillery, known as "triple A" by pilots. Over 80% of the U.S. aircraft lost over North Vietnam were shot down by guns. Since their bombs were less accurate, Vietnam-era planes had to attack their targets more often, and get shot at more often, than their Gulf War descendants.

Iraq used much the same equipment that the North Vietnamese had used twenty years before. In that time, however, Western aircraft had become a lot harder to hit. Many analysts had believed that Iraq's radar system would compensate for the shortcomings of her anti-aircraft weapons. It did not. Iraq's air defense system was dependent on centralized direction. If command and control could be interrupted or knocked out, the system would be paralyzed. Coalition aircraft would expend some $300 million worth of ordnance during the first 24 hours of the war. Most of it would be aimed at the command and control network.

The components of Iraq's air defense system were not particularly durable. The system could not operate under any appreciable strain or for any length of time without experiencing system failure. The Iraqis faced a dilemma. Either they could train extensively and realistically with their radar equipment and ruin it, or they could keep it shut down most of the time and tolerate a low standard of operator training. They chose the latter. A hint of this low standard of training was evident in 1981, when Israeli warplanes destroyed the Osirak nuclear facility. That a relatively large force of strike aircraft, however skillfully flown, could have penetrated the air defenses of a nation on a war footing so easily said a great deal about the quality of the defenses.

When the air war began, most of Iraq's major radar systems were turned off. In the months preceding the outbreak of hostilities, Allied fighter-bombers often raced toward the Iraqi border in attack formation. Iraqi radars tracked them. At the last moment the planes would break off and head for home. This allowed Coalition reconnaissance planes to locate radar and communications systems by monitoring their signals. To avoid giving the Coalition any more information about their air defenses, the Iraqis shut most of their radars off, gambling that they would get enough warning of an impending attack to turn them back on in time. The gamble did not pay off.

---

*Each plane's individual air mission is called a "sortie". The term applies to all air missions, including refueling and other support missions. Well over half of the sorties flown during the war were combat missions.

Iraqi ground radar directed not only the surface-to-air missile system, but the air force as well. Ground radar was more important to Soviet-style air forces than it is to Western-style air forces. Soviet-built planes were not equipped with the comprehensive array of radar systems that Western aircraft are. Iraq also had no equivalent to the AWACS, which directed Coalition planes from the air. Iraqi pilots depended on ground radar for direction. Without ground radar, there was no direction.

Iraq had about 300 SA(Surface-to-Air)-2 and SA-3 missile launchers for use against high and medium altitude aircraft. These systems were over thirty years old. Both were obsolete. In its heyday during the Vietnam War, it took an average of 50 SA-2s to knock down each American aircraft. By 1968, the U.S. Air Force had adjusted, and it took over a hundred missiles to knock down each aircraft. By 1990, the SA-2 was virtually useless against modern aircraft. SA-2s are also completely immobile. SA-3s are mobile, but even less effective. The Soviets were phasing out SA-2s and SA-3s, so they sold them to countries like Iraq.

Iraq also had more than a hundred improved Hawk anti-aircraft missiles. These had been sold to Kuwait by the United States, and had been captured. The "I-Hawks" were not a major factor, however. The Iraqis had not had enough time to train crews on the effective use of the I-Hawks. Also, since they were American missiles, it was a fairly simple matter for the U.S. Air Force to employ countermeasures. Within three days of their arrival in Saudi Arabia, all Air Force combat planes had their jamming systems upgraded to deal with I-Hawks.

The ideal condition for modern high-tech bombing is pitch-black, moonless night. Anti-aircraft gunners have no illumination to work by, while infra-red and laser guidance systems enable pilots to see and hit targets in complete darkness. January 15–17 was moonless, and gave the Allies a window of opportunity.

At 2:20 a.m. on 17 January, two teams of helicopters (Task Force Normandy) commanded by Army Lt.Col. Dick Cody, crossed the Iraqi border.* Each team consisted of two MH-53 Pave Low helicopters (from the Air Force's 20th Special Operations Squadron) packed with high-tech navigation gear and four Apache attack helicopters (from the 1st Battalion of the 101st Airborne Division's 101st Aviation Regiment) armed with laser-guided Hellfire missiles. There were also four mechanics and a small supply of spare parts traveling with the assault force in a Blackhawk cargo helicopter, in case there were any mechanical breakdowns.

The Pave Lows guided the teams to the targets, which the Apaches leveled. Both attacks followed the same pattern. First, the electrical generating plant which provided power for the station was knocked out. Next, the communications equipment was destroyed, then the radar itself. Several anti-aircraft guns were also destroyed before they had a chance to fire. The two Iraqi radar installations were completely demolished, opening a radar-free corridor about eight miles wide for attack aircraft to pour through.

At 2:41 a.m. (Baghdad time) on 17 January, 17 minutes before Task Force Normandy hit its targets, an F-117A Stealth dropped the first of 88,500 tons of bombs that would fall on the Iraqis in the six-week war. At 3:01, Iraqi Air Force headquarters was hit. At 3:09, an attack on an important telephone exchange caused CNN anchorman

---

*There had originally been three teams, but only days before, one radar station had been shut down by the Iraqis and had been dropped as a target.

Bernard Shaw's video feed to go dead. In the first minutes of the attack, 20 air defense, command and control, and electric facilities around Baghdad were struck. Another 25 sites were hit during the first hour.

There were 10 Stealth aircraft in the first wave over Baghdad and 20 in the second wave, which hit 1½ hours later.[*] The air attack on Baghdad was flown by the 37th Tactical Fighter Wing, which had deployed a total of 42 F-117As in the Gulf. Stealths carry two 2,000 lb. guided bombs which they are able to deliver with extreme accuracy, but they have no guns for defense. Their only defense is their computer designed, radar defeating shape, which allows them to avoid detection until they have done their damage. The Stealth is not the most aerodynamic plane in the world, though. Like many of the high-tech aircraft in the American inventory, the Stealth has to be controlled by a computer. Were the computer to fail, the plane would crash instantly.

There are no 90 degree angles on the Stealth, as right angles produce a pronounced radar signature. In addition, anything on the plane which opens or closes has zig-zag edges. On a conventional aircraft, the edges along which the canopy and the fuselage meet produce a radar signature, as do the meeting edges of conventional bomb bay doors. On the Stealth, edges interlock like shark's teeth, minimizing radar reflection. Between its shape and coatings which absorb rather than reflect radar, the Stealth produces one-thousandth the radar signature of an average fighter.

Even after Stealths have done their damage, they are not easy to hit. In addition to being virtually immune to radar-guided missiles, they are not particularly vulnerable to heat-seeking missiles. These missiles home in on engines or jet exhausts. The F-117A's engines are buried deep within the fuselage, and cool air from outside is constantly vented across the engines and into the exhaust, cooling both. The Stealth also has no real jet exhaust signature. On the F-117A, exhaust is channeled through two series of vents in the rear of the aircraft, 12 on each side of the tail, referred to as "platypus exhausts." Instead of offering a significant heat source (and target) at the rear of the plane, the heat fans out over a wide area and mixes with cooler air quickly. The exhaust vents are also not metal (which stays hot). They are made of ceramic tile.

Iraqi anti-aircraft guns were also not a problem. The Stealths' bombing accuracy allowed them to bomb from altitudes well beyond the range of Iraqi AA guns. Remembering that over 80% of the U.S. aircraft lost in Vietnam were downed by AA guns, CENTCOM had decided that high altitude bombing was preferable to risking lucky hits by Iraqi AA guns. As awe inspiring as videotapes of F-117A bomb strikes were, the knowledge that Baghdad was bombed from 25,000 feet makes them even more impressive. The guns were not a problem even when F-117As flew within their range. EF-111A Raven electronic warfare aircraft were used to put false targets on Iraqi radar shortly before scheduled Stealth attacks. Batteries threw up savage barrages of AAA fire at empty sky. By the time the Stealths showed up for their runs, many AAA batteries were either low on ammunition or allowing their overheated gun barrels to cool.

The design of the Stealth and its accuracy gave the F-117A a degree of protection enjoyed by no other aircraft. In over 1,200 sorties flown during the war, not one Stealth was even scratched, though they flew against Iraq's toughest targets. One-third of all Stealth sorties were flown over Baghdad. "If I had gone where I went in a conventional aircraft, I would have died," one pilot said later.

---

[*]Though the F-117A's official designation is "Night Hawk," it is almost universally referred to as the "Stealth."

Stealths provided air planners with an opportunity for unprecedented economy of force. Because the F-117A is virtually undetectable to enemy radar, the Stealth does not need as much support from electronic warfare planes and fighters as non-Stealth bombers, although EW aircraft did support Stealth missions. In general, it takes 38 support planes just to get four bombers over one target. In contrast, 21 F-117As attacked 38 targets on the first night, with support only from tankers and a handful of electronic warfare aircraft. The use of Stealths freed many aircraft to perform other tasks during the critical first wave.

The Stealth's accuracy also meant that fewer bombs needed to be dropped, so fewer sorties were required to drop them. In one instance, 16 F-16 fighter-bombers and 40 supporting aircraft attacked a nuclear reactor near Baghdad. The attack was only partially successful. The next night, eight Stealths launched a clean-up attack on the reactor, supported by two refueling tankers. The reactor was completely destroyed.

As a British television correspondent peered over the railing of his sixth floor balcony, he saw a Tomahawk cruise missile streak by on its way to Iraq's defense ministry. Two American correspondents watched in awe as a Tomahawk executed two 90 degree turns to avoid the al-Rashid Hotel, then sped on toward its target.

At about 1:30, the USS *San Jacinto* had fired the first Tomahawk of the war from the Red Sea, headed for Baghdad.* That night, eight high explosive Tomahawks (TLAM-Cs) smashed into the presidential palace. Another six wrecked Ba'ath Party headquarters. Thirty more hit a large missile complex at Taji, destroying it.

Sea-launched Tomahawk cruise missiles could be launched from 5–600 miles out in the gulf, and delivered 1,000 lb. warheads with great accuracy, without risking the loss of Allied pilots. The Tomahawks, also known as TLAMs (Tactical Land Attack Missiles) were guided to their targets by topographic maps stored in their electronic brains. The missile scans the terrain in front of it and compares what it sees against digitally coded topographic information preloaded by the Defense Mapping Agency.

Tomahawks are difficult for anti-aircraft batteries to bring under effective fire. At a speed of about 550 mph, they are relatively fast, and since they are able to fly along the contours of the terrain, they can fly close to the ground, to avoid radar detection. Of the 288 Tomahawks launched at the Iraqis, at least 233 scored hits. Eight malfunctioned after launch, 45 missed their targets and only two were shot down.

For attacks on targets in the open, the warhead can be programmed to explode a few feet above the target, crushing it beneath the force of the blast. Another version of the Tomahawk (the TLAM-D) flies over its target and drops 166 individual bomblets. Since this version can be programmed to drop its bomblets in spurts at intervals, it is well-suited to attacking missile sites, fuel depots or aircraft spread out on an airfield.

For attacking key power facilities, CENTCOM had another version of the Tomahawk, a variation on the TLAM-D. However, instead of releasing bomblets, it releases tiny filaments which drift downward and drape themselves across power lines, short-circuiting them. This variation, known as the TLAM Kit-2, wreaked havoc on Baghdad's power grid.

Eighteen months after their use, the Navy would reveal that a fourth variety of Tomahawk was fired on the first night of the war. A total of 106 Tomahawks were

---

*The ship reportedly received this honor because the president had flown off another USS *San Jacinto* during World War II.

launched on the first day of the war, and another 110 on the second. Some of them (the Navy still refuses to say how many) carried a new variety of warhead, the High Power Microwave Warhead, designed to produce electro-magnetic pulse (EMP).

EMP's military significance is in its effect on high-tech equipment. It occurs when the immediate release of energy from a blast alters the properties of the electrons in the atmosphere around the blast. The result is a field of intense electrical and magnetic activity. The power surges produced by the electrical disturbances can burn out electronic circuitry in radar systems, computers or communications equipment. The phenomenon is similar to the lightning strike on a house which causes the television and the appliances to burn out. The magnetic activity is capable of erasing the memory banks of key computerized military hardware.

EMP also tends to linger, causing sporadic interruptions in equipment function long after the initial surge has passed. Until now, it has only been a concern in the study of nuclear warfare, since EMP is a by-product of a nuclear explosion. This was the first recorded wartime instance of significant levels of EMP being produced by a conventional warhead.

To supplement the Tomahawks launched by the Navy on the first night, a flight of seven B-52Gs dropped ALCMs (Air Launched Cruise Missiles). Although ALCMs are manufactured by Boeing, and Tomahawks are made by General Dynamics, the two missiles perform essentially the same function. The ALCMs that were dropped on the first day were originally part of the Air Force's nuclear weapons arsenal. They had been converted, their nuclear warheads replaced by high explosive warheads, at a cost of almost $400,000 per missile.

The B-52Gs, from the 8th Air Force's 2nd Bomb Wing, stationed at Barksdale Air Force Base in Louisiana, flew directly from Louisiana to Saudi Arabia. It was the longest combat bombing mission in history. The bombers covered 14,000 miles, air-refueled four times, twice in each direction, and were in the air for more than 35 hours.

B-52s are known largely for their ability to "carpet bomb" with conventional ordnance, but they can carry up to 20 ALCMs each, six under each wing, and eight on a rotary launcher inside the bomb bay. The bombers that hit Iraq were traveling relatively light. Some carried five ALCMs, some six. To preserve operational security none were carried on the wings. Thirty-five of the thirty-nine ALCMs carried by the flight were launched at power stations and communications facilities inside Iraq. The missiles were launched from Saudi territory, just beyond the Iraqi air defense networks. At least 30 scored direct hits.

With the opening of the radar-free corridor by Task Force Normandy at 2:58, non-Stealth jets from bases all over Saudi Arabia, as well as four aircraft carriers in the Red Sea and two in the Persian Gulf, headed for their targets in Iraq. While the Stealths, Tomahawks and ALCMs were striking, the more conventional "strike packages" were completing their in-flight refueling.* In-flight refueling was done just before the packages entered hostile airspace. This vastly extended the striking range of Coalition aircraft. It also dramatically increased the number of bombs that could be carried. Full fuel tanks mean that a plane can carry fewer bombs before it reaches its maximum takeoff weight. With the availability of in-flight refueling, Coalition warplanes could

---

*The term "strike package" refers to any force designated to attack ground targets. In the Gulf War, a strike package could consist of a single Stealth, or more than 70 aircraft.

take off with extremely light fuel tanks and heavy bomb loads, then refuel in the air. There were reportedly 160 tankers in the air on the first night. The largest were modified Boeing 707s carrying over 70 tons of fuel. During the war, some 46,000 warplanes would refuel in flight, receiving about 13,750,000 gallons of fuel from the fleet of some 230 tankers.

During the war, radar suppression missions accounted for about 4% of all USAF sorties. In those sorties, Wild Weasels and Ravens largely removed Iraqi radar as a serious threat. Traveling at the head of a package, Wild Weasels flew within about 10 miles of the targeted radar sites and let loose their High Speed (flying at twice the speed of sound) Anti-Radiation Missiles, or HARMs. The term "Wild Weasel" usually refers to the F-4G, a Vietnam-era Phantom jet fitted with an array of sensors and armed with HARMs. Forty-eight of these aircraft flew from bases in Bahrain. Twenty more F-4Gs based in Turkey paired up with F-16s to form "hunter-killer" teams. In these teams, the F-4G detected the radar, and the accompanying F-16 fired HARM missiles at it.[*]

Over 200 HARMs were fired on the first night. HARMs are fired in the general direction of enemy radars. If a radar is turned on, the missile homes in on the beam, rides it back to its source and destroys it. Most HARMs destroyed their targets. In some cases, Iraqi operators had time to shut down their radars and the HARMs self-destructed, but this still removed their radar as a factor in the battle.[†]

Supplementing the roughly 2,000 HARMs fired during the war, the British fired 123 ALARM anti-radar missiles. The ALARM is a bit more sophisticated than the HARM. Like the HARM, it can be used to attack targets directly. Unlike the HARM, it can "loiter" over a target and attack it after the plane has left. In these indirect attacks, the ALARM climbs to 40,000 feet after launch, deploys a parachute and descends slowly, while its seeker searches for targets. When it finds one, it jettisons the parachute and glides into its target. Sometimes radar operators are alerted by the attacking aircraft and shut down. Once they are sure the aircraft has left, they turn the radar back on. That is when the ALARM strikes.

Wild Weasels cannot attack every single radar station, so they are supplemented by EF-111A Raven jamming aircraft. The EF-111A is designed to blind enemy radar over a wide area, neutralizing radars which have not been directly attacked. During the war, 18 Ravens would fly over 900 missions. They flew holding patterns about 100 miles from their targets and caused Iraqi radar screens to white out or saturated them with electronic clutter and false targets. False targets were produced by recording Iraqi radar signals, then projecting them from several different places, making each plane look like several.

Whatever Iraqi radar stations were operational often could not network with other stations or gun batteries because of the activities of the Coalition's EC-130H Compass Call aircraft. Specially equipped C-130 cargo planes designed to jam ground communications, Compass Calls were especially useful in jamming communications between radar stations and missile batteries. There were nine Compass Calls on duty in the Gulf.

---

[*]F-16s are usually called "Fighting Falcons." However, when they carry HARM missiles and are used in an anti-radar role, like the F-4Gs, they are referred to as "Wild Weasels."

[†]Radar emissions from the air defense network would drop off by 95% by the sixth day of the war.

Before a package began bombing, reconnaissance planes took pre-strike photographs of the target. These photos were taken by another version of the Phantom, the F-4C. This model is equipped with the KS-127 camera, which can take detailed photographs from 50 miles away. The photos would later be compared against photographs taken after the smoke cleared to help Air Force analysts make a battle damage assessment, or BDA, to determine what was actually achieved by the strike.

Next came the bombers. In addition to their anti-radar role, F-16s were used extensively as bombers. F-16s got an intense workout during the war. They flew an average of 54 missions each, well over a mission per day, the highest sortie rate of any combat aircraft.[*] Most of these missions were flown in daylight, since only 72 of the 249 F-16s deployed to the Gulf were equipped for night bombing.

F-15E Strike Eagles were used to deliver guided bombs, usually from 15–20,000 feet, comfortably beyond the range of Iraqi anti-aircraft weapons. The F-15E was a recently developed two-seat fighter-bomber version of the F-15. It was so new that when Iraq invaded Kuwait, there were only two squadrons of F-15Es in the Air Force. Worse, the targeting pods for the plane were still under development, and there were only enough to equip half of the force. As a result, when delivering laser-guided bombs they worked in pairs, with one carrying a full load of bombs, and the other carrying a light load of bombs and a laser designator to provide guidance for the bombs.

The 48 Strike Eagles deployed to the Gulf flew an average of 45 missions apiece. The Air Force would lose two F-15Es to Iraqi fire during the war, but in 2,200 sorties, the Strike Eagle force would account for the destruction of 23 communications centers, 36 bridges and numerous armored vehicles.

The most effective of the non-Stealth bombers was the F-111F Aardvark bomber. F-111Fs were designed to bomb in all types of weather, day or night. They swept in toward their targets below enemy radar and delivered their bombs to devastating effect. Aardvarks were able to bomb effectively at night and in bad weather because of LANTIRN (Low Altitude Navigation and Targeting Infra-Red system for Night), which illuminated targets at night using infra-red light beams. F-111Fs dropped 3,650 tons of bombs during the war. Almost 60% of the guided bombs that hit targets during the war were dropped by Aardvarks.

F-111Fs struck a dozen targets on the first night. One of their targets was Saddam Hussein's summer palace in Tikrit. The job was assigned to four bombers from the 48th Tactical Fighter Wing.[†] As the Aardvarks approached the target, an Iraqi MiG-29 fighter approached the formation. The four jets dropped to 200 feet and increased speed in an attempt to outrun the MiG. Eventually, the Iraqi warplane became a threat to the last bomber in the flight. The F-111F abandoned its mission and drew the fighter away from the formation. Taking evasive action, it eventually shook the Iraqi fighter off its tail. The remaining three Aardvarks flattened the palace with twelve 2,000 lb. bombs.

In addition to the attack on the summer palace, F-111Fs attacked several Iraqi air bases, destroying hardened aircraft shelters or dropping CBU-89 "Gator" area denial munitions. CBU-89s scatter 600 landmines over a 200 by 300 meter area, denying defenders access to critical areas. On the first night, the Allies were aided by Iraqi carelessness. In the early hours of the attack, many airfields still had their runway lights on, making them easier for Coalition pilots to find.

---

[*] Five F-16s were lost in combat during the war.

[†] F-111Fs from the 48th TFW had bombed Qaddafi's headquarters in Libya in 1986.

Not all targets were strategic. During the first two days, 289 sorties were flown against the Republican Guard. The Tawakalna, Hammurabi and Medina divisions received visits and some 1,700 tons of bombs, from 214 F-16s, 36 F/A-18s, 31 B-52s and 8 F-15Es. Another 150 A-10 attacks went in against troops in the area where Iraq, Kuwait and Saudi Arabia come together.*

Navy strike packages made extensive use of decoys in their attacks. A TALD (Tactical Air Launched Decoy) is 7 ft. 8 in. long, weighs about 400 lbs. and is carried by attacking aircraft to a release point about 50 miles from an enemy radar installation. When the TALD is dropped, its wings deploy and it flies a few minutes ahead of the strike package. On a radar screen, a TALD looks like an attacking aircraft. This causes the enemy to waste surface-to-air missiles on pilotless drones. Iraqi batteries may have fired as many as ten missiles at each drone that came up on their radar screens. The "jets" that the Iraqis reported shooting down in the early hours of the war were actually decoys. In many cases, SAM crews had fired the missiles from their launch racks at drones and were in the process of reloading when real bombers showed up. The TALD also forces enemy radar in the sector to track it. While the radar is tracking it, Wild Weasels can pinpoint the radar's location and mark it for destruction. The TALD fleet was supplemented by waves of ground-launched decoys from bases in Saudi Arabia.

Carrier-based Navy strike packages used slightly different aircraft and techniques than their Air Force counterparts. The dynamics of carrier warfare are different than air operations conducted from land bases. Maintaining a wide variety of planes makes sense for the Air Force, but it makes less sense for the Navy, which is concerned mostly with ships. In addition, even if the Navy had the desire and capacity to maintain numerous aircraft models, it could not make effective use of them all. An aircraft carrier can only carry about 85 planes. There is simply no room for narrowly specialized aircraft. The Navy therefore relies upon a few basic airframes that can be used in several different roles. These airframes tend to be older and less sophisticated than many Air Force models, but when employed effectively, they can still hit hard.

An example of this airframe versatility was the A-6 Intruder, which provided the basis for a long range medium bomber, an electronic warfare plane and an in-flight refueling tanker. The A-6 was originally fielded in 1963. This meant that a lot of the people who flew A-6s during the war were younger than their airframes. On the inside, however, the A-6 was a completely different plane than it was when it came off the assembly line 28 years earlier.

The A-6E Intruder, used for long range (over 1,000 miles fully loaded with 15,000 lbs. of bombs) medium bombing, had a state-of-the-art terrain following radar system which allowed the plane to fly at low levels at night or in bad weather. It also had a computerized bombing system which allowed Intruders to drop the most advanced guided bombs and missiles.†

Intruders dropped over a hundred GBU-15 guided bombs and launched over a hundred TV-guided 500 lb. Walleye II missiles during the war. Seven SLAMs (Standoff Land Attack Missiles) were also fired during the war, most of them from A-6Es. The

---

*Though its official designation is the "Thunderbolt II," the A-10 is almost universally referred to as the "Warthog."

†The A-6E has since been replaced by the F/A-18.

TV-guided SLAM missile, which had just finished its final testing before the war broke out, carried a 500 lb. high explosive warhead and flew at just below the speed of sound. One launch of only two SLAMs completely destroyed an Iraqi hydro-electric plant.

The EA-6B Prowler is an electronic warfare configuration which can either jam, or using HARM missiles destroy, enemy radar systems.* It can also jam communications systems. The Prowler is little more than an Intruder with all of its attack electronics removed and replaced with a jamming system. Though the system saw combat in the late stages of the Vietnam War and 27 saw extensive action in Desert Storm, no Prowler has ever been lost in combat.

The frame also serves as a fuel tanker (KA-6D). The KA-6D can carry about 10½ tons of fuel and can be used to ferry fuel from air bases or larger KC-135 tankers to the carrier itself. This allows the carrier to maintain air operations without having to come into port. This saves time and keeps the carrier beyond the range of shore-launched anti-ship missiles. KA-6Ds also served as refueling tankers for Navy strike packages.

Another Navy jack-of-all-trades is the F/A-18 Hornet. It is both an effective bomber and a lethal dogfighter. The F/A-18 can carry about 6½ tons of assorted bombs, missiles and sensors. As a fighter, it badly outclassed all of what the Iraqi Air Force had to work with. An illustration of this came on the first night of the war. On the way to a target, two Hornets from the USS *Saratoga* ran into two Iraqi MiG-25s. The Hornets had two 2,000 lb. bombs hanging from each wing, increasing the weight of each plane by one-third and severely limiting their speed and mobility. Nevertheless, the heavily laden Hornets still retained enough speed and manueverability to make short work of the MiGs, claiming the only two Navy air-to-air kills of the war.

Flying escort for the bombers were U.S. Air Force F-15C fighters. The typical strike package was escorted by four F-15Cs. There were 120 F-15Cs deployed. At 3:10 a.m., Capt. Jon Kelk of the 33rd Tactical Fighter Wing recorded the first kill of the war, a Soviet-made MiG-29.† Fourteen minutes later, Capt. Robert Gaeter, also of the 33rd TFW, shot down two French-built Mirage fighter-bombers. Thirty minutes later, Capt. Steve Tate of the 1st TFW recorded the fourth air-to-air kill of the war. The Iraqis lost nine jets in the first 24 hours of the war.

Shortly thereafter, the Air Force recorded what may have been the first destruction of a fighter by an unarmed aircraft in its history. A Raven jamming aircraft from the 390th Electronic Combat Squadron was flying a mission in western Iraq when an Iraqi Mirage F-1 fired an air-to-air missile at it. The pilot, Captain James Denton, released a cloud of chaff, thin strips of foil designed to clutter the enemy's radar systems. He also released flares, in case the missile was heat-seeking. Denton then went into a steep dive, both to avoid the missile, and make it difficult for the Mirage pilot to lock on for another shot. As Denton pulled out of the dive, he looked over his shoulder just in time to see his adversary, unable to pull out of his dive, slam into the ground.‡*

---

*Though most associated the HARMs with Air Force Wild Weasels, over 61% were actually fired by Navy aircraft.

†Ultimately, the 33rd TFW would record 14 kills, the highest victory total of any unit.

‡During the encounter, an F-15C fired an air-to-air missile at the Iraqi warplane. Though the missile impacted after the Iraqi had already crashed, the F-15C was given credit by the Air Force for the kill.

As if losing a fighter plane to an unarmed electronic warfare plane was not embarrassing enough, an Iraqi fighter was lost to another Iraqi fighter that night. During a six-plane F-15E strike on Iraq's H-2 Airfield, an Iraqi MiG-29 was about to take a missile shot on an F-15E when it was destroyed by another MiG-29. Iraqi pilots tended to fly into combat with their missiles already armed, and their triggers depressed. This saved them a few important seconds during an engagement, but it also meant that as soon as the missile locked on to something, it fired, whether the target was friend or foe. This was believed to be the cause of this friendly fire incident.

These were some of the few instances where the Iraqi Air Force, the world's sixth largest, put up any fight at all. On the first night, only 24 Iraqi fighters took to the air. Most left the combat zone, then came back in the morning when the Americans were gone. Those that did not run were shot down.

At a briefing a day and a half into the air war, Lt.Gen. Horner showed a videotape of guided bombs slipping through the open doors of a Scud missile storage bunker and exploding. Another showed a laser-guided bomb floating down the airshaft of Iraqi Air Force Headquarters, then exploding.

Guided bombs are about four times as expensive as regular bombs, and the equipment necessary to deliver them is also expensive, but they are much more efficient than regular bombs. Only 8% of the Coalition's total bomb tonnage was guided, but these bombs accounted for almost one-third of the destruction inflicted on the Iraqis by fixed-wing aircraft. Guided bombing is less susceptible to cancellation for bad weather than conventional bombing, since planes equipped with sophisticated guidance systems can fly in bad weather. During the first two weeks of the air war, when miserable weather forced the cancellation of almost half of all bombing missions, these specially equipped planes were able to keep flying.

Guided bombs differ from guided missiles in that they have no propulsion. Once dropped, they glide to their targets. Most guided bombs were 1950s vintage general purpose bombs with cameras or infra-red sensors installed in their noses and steerable fins. There are basically two types of guided bombs. Laser-guided bombs (LGBs) home in on laser light reflected off a target. The Weapons System Operator (WSO) rides in the back seat, and is responsible for the bombing, while the pilot evades enemy groundfire. The WSO does not have to steer the bomb. He just reflects laser light off the target, and the bomb guides itself to the target, making the WSO's job much simpler. Electro-optically guided bombs (EOGBs) have either a TV camera (for daylight raids) or an infra-red sensor (for night operations) in their noses, and are guided onto the target by the WSO, who uses a joystick.

The success of the first day of the air war exceeded the Air Force's most optimistic expectations. It had been projected that as many as 150 aircraft could be lost by dawn on the 17th, but all returned safely. Iraq's air force was not fighting, and therefore was not shooting down Coalition planes. On the night of the 17th, however, things soured a bit. A Navy F/A-18 Hornet was hit by an Iraqi SAM as it returned to the aircraft carrier *Saratoga* from a Scud hunting mission. In that incident, Lt.Cmdr. Michael Speicher became the first American killed by enemy fire in the war.

---

*On the 19th, the Iraqis would lose another plane in the same fashion, when Capt. Caesar Rodriguez of the 33rd TFW used his F-15C to maneuver a MiG-29 into the ground.

Another chastening experience was the attack on H-3 Airfield in western Iraq. An important Scud launching site, H-3 was bristling with anti-aircraft defenses, eight SAM launchers and about 150 AA guns. Four Navy A-6Es attacked the airfield at low level. One was shot down and another had to jettison its bombs and struggle to an emergency landing in Saudi Arabia after a SAM explosion damaged an engine. The plane could not be salvaged. Two planes out of four had been destroyed. Two fliers out of eight had been captured. Thereafter, Navy planes would be restricted to bombing altitudes of 16,000 feet or higher.

In the early minutes of 18 January, Air Force F-15Es ran into trouble. Six Strike Eagles targeted an oil refinery southwest of Basra. Worried about the many SAM batteries in the area, the jets flew low and over a swamp, since the Iraqis could not position SAM launchers in a swamp. There were two problems. First, the Navy had hit the oil refinery earlier, and the flames lit up the night sky, silhouetting the Strike Eagles and making them better targets. Second, while there were no SAM launchers in the swamp, almost an entire Republican Guard division (with its AA systems) was camped beside a road that ran along the swamp. The division's gunners, alerted by the earlier Navy strike, shot down a Strike Eagle, killing both crewmen.

Only ten Italian combat sorties had been scheduled during the first two days. All but one had to return to base because only one pilot had mastered the art of in-flight refueling. The lone Tornado was shot down. Its pilot and navigator were captured and later shown on Iraqi television. The Italian air contingent made the necessary adjustments, and in the more than 200 combat sorties flown by the Italians during the rest of the war, no additional planes were lost.

Even with these losses, the air campaign was a stunning success. By 19 January, over 4,000 sorties had been flown, with the loss of only six American, two British, one Free Kuwaiti and one Italian aircraft. This represented a loss-per-sortie rate of less than a quarter of one percent.

The Coalition was pulling out all the stops to keep aircraft and pilot losses down. About 19 miles inside Kuwait was the al-Abraq SA-2 missile site. Al-Abraq was a threat because it was located along a key Air Force flight route into Kuwait. Forty-two minutes after midnight on the 18th, a VII Corps artillery unit launched an ATACMS battlefield missile at the site. Two minutes later, the missile broke open over the site, disgorging 950 bomblets. The al-Abraq site was completely destroyed. This was the first battlefield missile strike in the history of the U.S. Army and the first shot fired by VII Corps in combat since World War II.

The Air Force experienced more bad luck during a night attack on 20 January, when 70 planes, including 56 F-16s, headed for a nuclear research facility in Baghdad. One-fourth of the package had to return home after the formation was broken up by Iraqi anti-aircraft fire, and the planes could not find the main flight again in the foul weather. The first group of F-16s dropped its bombs without incident. Unfortunately, Iraqi anti-aircraft activity was heavier than expected, and the Wild Weasels had to expend all of their HARM missiles. When the second wave of F-16s came in, there was no anti-radar support and two were shot down by SAMs. Air planners had learned another lesson. For the rest of the war, only Stealth fighters would bomb targets in Baghdad.

The British RAF contingent suffered the highest losses during the first 96 hours relative to its total size. Two of its 36 Tornado strike aircraft had been lost. British Tornados, which accounted for only 4% of the Coalition's air strength ultimately suffered 26% of its losses. Tornado pilots had the most hazardous task, swooping down on enemy airfields at low levels to deliver cratering ordnance.

The Tornado's agility made it an ideal choice for low level attacks on enemy airfields. Tornados used the JP 233 cratering system to disable Iraqi airfields. The JP 233 is made up of two dispensers. Each carries 30 cratering bombs designed to break up the pavement of runways and 215 area denial munitions set to explode at various intervals for 12 hours after an attack to make life difficult for cleanup and repair crews trying to clear the runways and fix the craters.

The Tornados did not target runways. They concentrated on the taxiways between the hardened aircraft shelters and the runways. A disabled taxiway is just as crippling as a disabled runway, since a plane that cannot make it to the runway cannot take off. Taxiways are also softer than runways and are safer to attack because the approaches to them are less well-defended than approaches to runways.

On the first night of the air war the British had help from the U.S. Air Force in the airfield denial mission. Twelve B-52s attacked five airfields in southeastern Iraq with cratering and area denial munitions at 400 feet. Five more B-52s attacked two air bases in northern Iraq. After the first night however, the Tornados were on their own. B-52s are big, slow targets. Using them at low levels against Iraqi airfields with the element of surprise was one thing. Using them against alert defenders would have been suicidal.

Anti-airfield operations went almost without a hitch for the first 24 hours. One Tornado did experience problems after it collided with a large bird, damaging the leading edge of one of the plane's wings. After the first day, the Iraqis began to throw up walls of AAA and machine-gun fire in front of the onrushing Tornados, making delivery more difficult. As dangerous as it all sounds, the skilled Tornado pilots made it look relatively simple. Over 60 runway denial sorties were flown by the British. Only two deliveries were partially off target due to evasive maneuvering. While five Tornados were lost in 450 sorties in week one, only one of the downed aircraft had been on a cratering mission. That aircraft crashed on the way back to base, after it had delivered its ordnance. It was not believed to have been destroyed by enemy fire. Another was destroyed accidentally when one of its eight bombs exploded immediately after release. Two others had been downed by Roland SAMs while on conventional bombing runs.

Iraq had acquired 100 Roland systems from France before the war. The Roland is a twin missile system mounted on a light, tracked chassis. It can destroy planes as low as 1,500 feet, or as high as 18,000. The French had sold Iraqis Roland 1 systems, which are only effective in daylight and in clear weather. This weakness notwithstanding, the Roland 1 was a dangerous weapon, as the crews of the two Tornados discovered.

It is a minor point, but the JP 233s did not do quite as much damage as Allied planners had hoped. The sand beneath the runways and taxiways absorbed some of the shock of the explosions, so the concrete did not fracture as badly as expected. Nevertheless, the runway denial missions did succeed in shutting down the airfields.

By the end of the first week, the British had finished with the airfields and shifted their attention to bridges. By the war's end, British Tornados had dropped over 4,200 unguided bombs, 950 guided bombs and 31 ALARM anti-radar missiles in addition to the cratering munitions.

Much of the credit for the success of the air war goes to the Air Force AWACS planes that controlled it. AWACS made it possible to choose the best possible aircraft for each mission. This economized on lost planes and lives as well as return trips for missed targets. One AWACS, a modified Boeing 707, can control about 100 friendly aircraft at a time. It can also monitor almost ten times as many hostile aircraft. An AWACS can pick up high altitude attack aircraft from as far as 375 miles away and low flying aircraft from almost 200 miles.* The typical AWACS has a crew of four and 13–17 operators monitoring nine consoles. During the Gulf War, each AWACS usually carried an extra set of operators, since missions generally ran upwards of sixteen hours, two full shifts.

As devastating as the air offensive was, it could have been worse for the Iraqis. The worst weather in fourteen years made target identification difficult or impossible. As a result, many bombing missions had to be canceled. Without positive identification of targets, mistakes would have been made, and civilian casualties would have resulted. Forty percent of the primary bombing targets were passed by during the first ten days of the war. In addition, during this period, some 15% of all combat sorties were diverted to hunting Scud missile launchers. These two factors set back the bombing schedule by one to two weeks and delayed the start of the campaign against Iraqi ground forces. This gave Iraqi units extra time to spread out and dig in deeper. It would therefore take more ordnance to destroy each weapon, and attack planes would have to fly more sorties.

Before the war, Iraq was thought to have at least 400 Scuds, though Iraq's actual holdings were slightly over 200. The Allies were not sure what Iraq's Scuds could deliver. Soviet Scuds were capable of bursting 1,200 lbs. of lethal VX nerve agent over a target. For airfields, they could deliver forty 25 lb. runway penetrator submunitions, producing a damage radius of about 150 meters. For troop concentrations they could scatter 11 lb. anti-personnel fragmentation bomblets over a 250 meter radius. Luckily, Saddam had been embargoed by the Soviet Union for much of the 1980s during his war with Iran. While Iraq received considerable quantities of materiel from the USSR when not under embargo, the Soviets had always been leery about sharing their latest technology or their most effective weapons with a loose cannon like Saddam.

The Scud was originally designed by the Soviets to deliver small nuclear warheads onto NATO targets such as supply depots and airfields. It had a range of about 190 miles and a Circular Error Probable (C.E.P.) of about 500 meters. This means that a Scud had a 50% chance of landing somewhere within 500 meters of its intended target. That is not particularly accurate, but since the Soviets were planning on using Scuds with nuclear warheads, near misses would have been acceptable. The limited range did not bother the Soviets either. They had intercontinental ballistic missiles for the long shots.

The limited range did bother the Iraqis, who bought over 800 Scuds from the Soviet Union. Iraq was fighting a war with Iran, and a 190 mile launch would fall about 150 miles short of Teheran, so Iraq developed the al-Hussein missile. Al-Husseins were produced by modifying the Scuds. The Scuds were enlarged by about 10%, and the size of the explosive warhead was reduced from about 2,200 lbs. to about 1,100 lbs. The extra room was then used for fuel. Although a 400 mile range allowed al-Husseins to reach Teheran, the damage caused by the missiles that hit the city was slight. About 2,000 civilians were killed, but this is not much to show for some 190 missile strikes. The al-Hussein was also less than half as accurate as the original Scud.

---

*The Navy had its own smaller, carrier-based version of the AWACS. The "Hawkeye" has a crew of two and can track as many as 2,000 hostile aircraft and direct 40 friendly aircraft within a radius of 300 miles.

Iraq had tried to make an even longer range rocket by removing even more explosive. The al-Abbas could fly about 550 miles, but it only had a 660 lb. warhead. The al-Abbas program was abandoned, however, because the rocket was only about one-third as accurate as the al-Hussein and less than one-sixth as accurate as the Scud. The Iraqis saw more promise in upgrading the motor and propellants used on the al-Hussein.

The al-Hussein's performance during the Gulf War was disappointing. Several exploded shortly after launch. Those that did not had a tendency to fall apart on the final approach to their targets. This is to be expected with a rocket that is essentially the product of jerry-rigging. Jerry-rigging something that is going to be shot almost 100 miles into the air at high velocity and subjected to tremendous stresses during a flight of a few hundred miles is a recipe for disappointment.

The military insignificance of the al-Hussein becomes clear when it is contrasted with the American F-111F bomber. The Aardvark could carry about 37½ times more explosive payload (41,260 lbs. of bombs against the al-Hussein's 1,100 lb. warhead), and the Aardvark could deliver it accurately. The range of the al-Hussein was about 400 miles. The F-111F has a range of 3,000 miles, and this can be extended greatly by in-flight refueling. Finally, F-111Fs do not fall apart while they are delivering their payload, and you can use them again and again.

Scuds are launched from large, eight-wheeled trucks, called MAZ-543s. The Iraqi Army had about 60 prepared launch sites from which Scud launchers could fire their missiles from fortified shelters. During the first day, the 30 sites which CENTCOM had pinpointed were destroyed or heavily damaged. CENTCOM knew that there were at least 36 mobile launchers. There may actually have been as many as two hundred. Attacking these was a more difficult proposition. MAZ-543s are capable of driving cross country at speeds of up to 45 mph. Thus, by the time satellite intelligence about a Scud launch had been relayed to the battlefront, 12 hours later in some cases, the Scud launcher could be long gone. Worse, while American surveillance aircraft had no trouble spotting vehicles, a Scud launcher is virtually indistinguishable from a large cargo or fuel truck. The Iraqis also employed decoy launchers. As a result, how many Scud launchers (if any) were destroyed by air attacks may never be known.

With no Scud firings in the first 24 hours of the war, there was hope that Iraq's Scud force had been dealt a decisive blow, but early on the 18th, Tel Aviv sustained the first of eight Scud strikes that Israel would receive that morning. Other Scuds hit in the vicinity of Haifa and Ramallah. Early news reports indicated that one Scud had released nerve agent and that a hospital in Tel Aviv had received about 20 chemical victims. In fact, the Scuds had leaked some of their noxious rocket fuel, the fumes of which had much the same effect as tear gas on unprotected onlookers. In addition, a few Israelis, believing that they had been infected with nerve agent injected themselves with the atropine antidote that was issued with their masks. Atropine works on people who have actually been infected by purging their systems of nerve agent. If injected when there is no nerve agent in the system, it will make its user dehydrated and violently ill.

The Scuds killed no one, but four elderly Israelis and one small child died of heart attacks or suffocated as a result of poorly fitted masks. Twelve other people were injured. Israeli intentions now became a source of concern to Allied planners. While President Bush and British Prime Minister John Major prevailed upon Israel not to retaliate, U.S. warplanes went looking for Scud launchers.

While Israel was under attack that Friday morning, air raid sirens were going off in Dhahran, Saudi Arabia. A Scud began its downward arc. Patriot missiles rose to meet it. The Scud exploded in mid-air, showering debris over the ground below. It was the first time that an incoming missile had ever been destroyed by a defensive missile.

The Patriot missile system was designed to destroy high flying (as high as 72,000 feet) aircraft, but recent modifications had given it anti-missile capability. Each Patriot battery has eight launchers. On each launcher is a pod containing four missiles. The system is highly sophisticated. It takes a year and eight months just to train a crew.

One of the most impressive features of the Patriot is its radar system. Conventional radar systems emit a constant radar beam. This is why life was so difficult and dangerous for Iraqi radar operators. At best, their radar alerted Allied pilots and allowed them to take evasive action. At worst, HARM missiles rode the radar beams back to their sources, destroying the radar and killing the radarmen. Patriot crews do not have this problem. The Patriot uses a "phased-array" radar system. A phased-array radar does not emit a constant beam. It shoots beams rapidly at different points in the sky in a computer generated pattern. Each beam is only thousandths of a second in duration, so the radar cannot be tracked. All of the individual images produced by the beams are then consolidated by computer to form a single radar picture in the Patriot's control station.

The Patriot's state-of-the-art radar system also combines several functions. The radar, in conjunction with a computer control unit, searches the sky, acquires the target, fires the missile (which can also be launched manually), tracks the target, and guides the missile. This eliminates the need for several different units performing several different functions, all requiring coordination. When the missile is in the vicinity of the incoming enemy missile, its 150 lb. warhead explodes, and the fragmentation damages or destroys the enemy missile.

Since the end of the war, it has become fashionable to question the Patriot's reported success rate. In fact, no one ever knew what the Patriot's actual success rate was. The best that anyone in the Defense Department could do was offer their best guess. Many people have the image of missiles that launched, smashed directly into the nose of falling Scuds and blew them up, but this is not the case. The Patriot is a proximity weapon. It gets to the vicinity of an incoming missile, then blows cube-shaped metal fragments all over the place. If everything works right, the fragments will cause the missile's warhead to explode prematurely, or will rupture a fuel tank, causing an explosion. This outcome is referred to as a "catastrophic kill."

Sometimes the explosions damaged the Scud's warhead so that it failed to detonate when it impacted with the ground. This is referred to as "dudding the warhead." Some dudded warheads were found with Patriot fragments in them. A Patriot explosion may also do so much damage to the structure of a missile that its course is altered, causing it to miss its target. The damage may even be sufficient to cause a missile to break up in mid-air, its warhead impacting far short of its intended target. When a Patriot causes a missile to miss its target, it is referred to as a "mission kill."

Damage assessment was problematic even in cases of catastrophic explosion. Most of the Scuds that hit Israel were of the jerry-rigged al-Hussein variety. Since the al-Hussein had a tendency to fall apart on its final approach, no one could ever be sure whether an al-Hussein broke up by itself, or if the Patriot caused it to break up. In fact, the al-Hussein's fuel tanks often ruptured by themselves on the missile's downward arc. Sometimes the rupture was severe enough to cause a catastrophic explosion. So, even when a Scud exploded in mid-air, no one could ever state with absolute certainty that it was a Patriot that caused the explosion. On the other hand, if a Patriot exploded a considerable distance from the Scud, but the Scud burned up, no one could say that the Patriot did not cause it to burn up, since only one or two hot metal fragments through the Scud's thin skin and into its fuel tanks could cause a fiery explosion. With Patriot vs. Scud confrontations, even if the engagement is on videotape, what happened is almost never absolutely certain. One thing is certain, though. Apartment damage from Scuds was cut in half after the deployment of Patriot missiles in Israel, even though three times as many Scuds were then being fired.

The following morning brought three more Scud attacks in the skies over Tel Aviv. Again, no one was killed, but another dozen civilians were injured. Secretary of Defense Cheney, fearing Israeli retaliation, called Israel's defense minister, Moshe Arens, on a hot line that had been established before the war began. Arens informed Cheney that 12 Israeli F-16s were already in the air and were prepared to strike into western Iraq. Arens requested the "friend or foe" recognition codes that would identify them as friendly aircraft when challenged by Coalition fighters. If the codes could not be provided, Arens told Cheney, he would be satisfied with a four-hour cessation of Allied air operations over western Iraq. This would give the Israeli warplanes time to hit Scud launchers without fear of being accidentally shot down by Coalition aircraft. Other requests included American pressure on Jordan or Saudi Arabia to allow Israeli jets to fly over their territory on their way to Iraq. Arens also had plans for operations in western Iraq involving hundreds of Israeli paracommandos. Cheney told Arens that he did not have the authority to grant any of the requests, but would forward them immediately to the president.

The president phoned Israeli Prime Minister Yitzhak Shamir. He expressed his condolences and offered Shamir two batteries of Patriot missile launchers and their crews. Shamir, sensitive to the presence of foreign soldiers on Israeli soil, grudgingly accepted. Bush assured Shamir that all necessary steps would be taken to protect Israel from further Scud strikes.

During the war, it was reported that Israel had been offered Patriots before the war, but had declined the offer. This was not exactly accurate. Israel had been offered the Patriot PAC I, which is only effective against aircraft. Had Israel accepted the initial offer, the system would have been unable to knock down Scuds. The Patriot PAC II upgrade, which included the software which allowed Patriots to engage incoming missiles, had not been offered, largely because the U.S. Army was not even equipped with it yet. When the first Patriot batteries were sent to the Gulf, there were only three PAC II systems in the entire Army. These were sent to the Gulf, along with the other PAC I batteries. As the upgrades and the software became available, they were sent directly to the Gulf. By the time the air war started, the systems had all been upgraded and the crews hastily trained on the new features.

After the arrangements for the Patriots were made, Cheney called Arens to tell him that the launcher batteries were on the way and would be in place and working that evening. He also told him that Allied Special Operations Forces (SOF) were on their way to western Iraq on search and destroy missions, and that hundreds of bombing missions had been diverted to hunting Scuds.

The ad hoc special operations organization tasked with Scud hunting was made up of members of the U.S. "Delta Force" and the British Special Air Service (SAS). The unit was supported by A-10 ground attack planes. Small groups of commandos were dropped off by helicopter behind enemy lines to destroy the command and control centers from which the Scuds received their targeting orders. They also attacked the storage sites that supplied the launcher batteries.

At the same time, mobile units roamed western Iraq looking for the launchers themselves. Each mobile team consisted of three or four men in heavily muffled dune buggies. When they located a launcher, they fixed its position using PLRS (Position Location and Reporting System), a hand-held device that tells the user his location to within a few yards. Air strikes were then called in by AWACS.

The commando operations were not without loss. During the air war, a dune buggy overturned while searching for Scud launchers, seriously injuring one of its crew of three commandos. His comrades radioed for a helicopter medical evacuation, or "medivac" and a Blackhawk helicopter assigned to Task Force 160 responded. On the return flight, the Blackhawk crashed, killing both pilots and their two crewmen as well as all three Delta commandos.

Night-capable F-15E fighter-bombers were also sent out on patrol over western Iraq. Whenever a launch plume was sighted, the position of the launch was cluster bombed. In addition, the roads used by Scud launchers to get to their launch sites were targeted. B-52s flew along the roads, dropping bombs more or less at random, chewing up the roads and making travel along them more difficult.

The countermeasures worked. In the first week of the war, there were 35 Scud launches. In the second week, the number of firings dropped to 18.[*] In addition, because the air patrols forced missile crews to launch hastily from unsurveyed ground, many Scuds landed in open spaces or in the sea.

As each day passed, Coalition intelligence analysts doubted more strongly that Saddam would use his Scuds to deliver chemical warheads. His purpose in launching Scuds at Tel Aviv was to bring Israel into the war. The Scuds launched at Dhahran were an attempt to disrupt the air base. Chemical-carrying Scuds probably would have achieved both ends. High explosive Scuds achieved neither. They did not inflict enough damage to justify the hazard of launching them. There was every reason to believe that if Saddam was going to use chemical-carrying Scuds, he would have done it by the end of the second week. CENTCOM planners began to relax.

---

[*]Some 80–90 Scuds were launched during the war. After the war, the UN destroyed 44 Scuds and certified that the Iraqis had destroyed 78 more.

4

Air Interdiction

The first naval engagement of the war took place on 18 January. On the previous day, Navy warplanes had been fired upon by Iraqis on offshore drilling platforms as they returned to their carriers. The destroyer USS *Nicholas* was sent to silence the anti-aircraft guns. On the second night of the war, attack helicopters from the destroyer rippled 2.75-inch rockets into two drilling platforms, sending defenders leaping into the water and detonating ammunition that had been stacked on the platform. Sporadic fire was received from several other platforms. One by one, they were silenced by the *Nicholas'* deck guns. Twenty-three Iraqis were picked up from the platforms or fished out of the water. Six had been killed. One American medic was wounded.

On 23 January an Air Force F-16 was hit by ground fire and went down two miles off the Kuwaiti coast. The *Nicholas* sent a helicopter full of Navy SEAL (SEa, Air, Land) commandos to recover the pilot, who had bailed out before the crash. After a 35-minute rescue operation, the pilot was returned safely to the ship.

At the end of the first week, the Navy recaptured the first piece of Kuwait. The Iraqis had established a listening post on the island of Qaruh. At about noon on 24 January, Navy helicopters were trying to rescue 22 Iraqis whose minelayer had just been sunk near the island, when they were fired on by Iraqi forces on Qaruh. The American guided missile frigate USS *Curts*, part of the *Midway* carrier group, maneuvered toward the island and opened up on the Iraqi positions with its deck guns. SEALs aboard the USS *Leftwich* boarded helicopters and headed for Qaruh. The island was reclaimed by late afternoon. The Navy captured 67 Iraqis, a minelayer that had been docked at the island, and detailed information on the whereabouts of Iraqi anti-ship minefields in the area.

On 29 January, the 13th Marine Expeditionary Unit conducted Operation "Desert Sting," a raid on the Iraqi-held island of Um al-Maradim. The 13th MEU found the island abandoned. But the Iraqi occupiers had left behind large quantities of equipment, ammunition and supplies, which the Marines destroyed.

One of the less glamorous endeavors of the Coalition's naval effort was minesweeping duty, but aside from aircraft carriers, the minesweepers had the most work to do. Coalition minesweepers picked up and disarmed over 600 of the 1,167 sea mines laid by Iraq after the invasion of Kuwait.

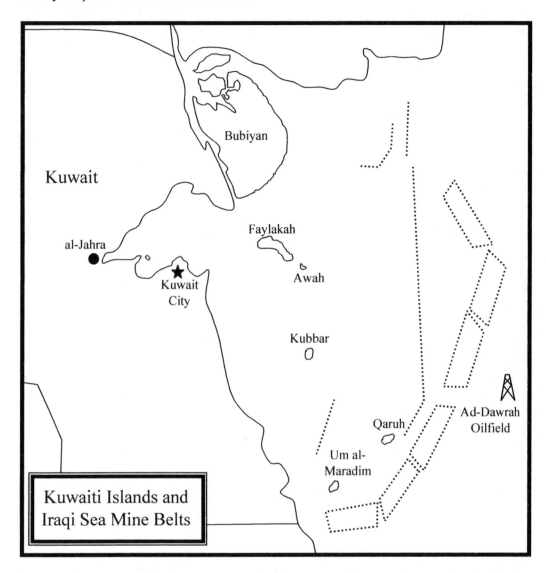

As the air war moved from the strategic phase toward the tactical phase, the Allies began to knock out the bridges and supply lines that ran from Baghdad to southern Iraq and Kuwait. Thirty-three of the thirty-six bridges on the Baghdad to Kuwait City supply route were hit. Truck traffic along the route was cut by an estimated 90%. The destruction of bridges also disrupted communications. Iraqi signalmen had been seen stringing fiber-optic cables for military communications across them. When the bridges went down, so did the communications lines.

Such positive reports sparked skepticism in the media, though. When news correspondents divided the total number of sorties flown against the bridges by the number of bridges hit, they calculated that it took several sorties to destroy each bridge. Some took this as a sign that the military was lying about the accuracy of guided bombs.

Actually, the high sortie to destroyed bridge ratio had nothing to do with guided bombs, which were working exceptionally well.

Many of the bridge attacks were not guided bombing sorties. Early in the war, most Allied warplanes were not equipped to drop guided bombs. Those that were had more important targets to hit. Brig.Gen. C. Buster Glosson, CENTCOM's chief targeteer, and the commander of all Air Force wings in the Gulf, initially believed that less sophisticated aircraft using modern bomb sights could deliver unguided bombs with sufficient precision to destroy bridges. He had ordered 180 sorties against bridges in the first three days of the war, and all had failed. As soon as aircraft capable of dropping guided bombs became available, they were directed against the bridges.

Another problem was that the bridges had been reinforced against earthquakes, so one hit was often not enough to destroy a section of bridge. In addition, in cases where there were civilians in close proximity to a bridge, and near misses on the ends of the spans might have killed innocent people, pilots usually targeted the center of the span. Damage from a center span hit is much easier for engineers to repair. After these bridges were repaired by Iraqi engineers, more bombing missions were required.

Another factor pushing up the sortie rate was the need to attack most bridges with two different planes to ensure destruction, with one bomb at each end of the span. In attacks by the Royal Air Force, three sorties were required for most bridges. Tornados were not designed to carry laser designators, although a few were upgraded and rushed to the Gulf. On bridge-destroying missions, a Buccaneer bomber had to provide laser designation while two Tornados dropped laser-guided bombs.*

Iraqi forces in the KTO (Kuwaiti Theater of Operations) were becoming increasingly isolated. Just under a quarter of all Coalition sorties during the war were directed at Iraqi supply bases and supply routes. Before the bombing began, about 20,000 tons of supplies per day were reaching Iraqi forces in the KTO. After two weeks of bombing, it was down to about 2,000.

The Iraqi Air Force proved no obstacle during the bombing campaign. Before the war, Iraq had about 275 interceptors, many of which were in poor shape. The best of Iraq's warplanes, MiG-29s, were no match for the F-15Cs that patrolled the skies looking for them. Iraq also had very few top-caliber pilots. Iraqi pilots had gained virtually no experience in air-to-air combat during the war with Iran. The lack of durability of their Soviet-built planes had also limited their flying time, and training had suffered. The USAF pilots they faced in combat had been under no such constraint.

The Iraqi Air Force was also a neglected stepchild, starved for parts and armament due to Saddam's acute distrust of his air force. This was not unusual among Third World leaders. The technical nature of modern air combat requires the recruitment of a higher proportion of well-educated people for an air force than for other services. In the Third World, these pilots usually have to travel abroad for training at some point in their careers, bringing them into contact with other ideas, cultures, and lifestyles. High I.Q.s and foreign travel combine to make air force officers a politically unreliable group. Almost anywhere there have been coups in the Third World, air force officers have figured prominently.

---

*During the war, Buccaneers mounted 24 attacks on bridges and another 15 on airfields. All 24 bridges were either destroyed or damaged beyond further use. During the war Buccaneers flew 216 sorties, guided in 169 bombs from Tornados and dropped and guided 48 of their own.

This fact was not lost on Saddam, who kept a close eye on his air force.[*] Saddam never forgot that Air Force officers had been his most bitter opponents during his rise to power in the 1970s, and he maintained an air force which was no threat to him. Unfortunately, it was even less of a threat to Allied planes.

The Iraqi Air Force was a dismal failure against the Allies in air-to-air combat. In the first three days, 15 Iraqi planes were shot down by the Coalition without the loss of a single Allied plane. Seven more Iraqi warplanes met the same fate by the end of the first week. No Allied warplanes were attacked by Iraqi fighters after 24 January.

On the 24th, two Iraqi Mirage F-1s were spotted by an AWACS. The AWACS directed a Saudi F-15C piloted by Capt. Ayehid al-Shamrani toward the Mirages. Saudi pilots were well-trained and eager to prove themselves. They had run regular patrols, but they had almost given up hope of ever seeing an Iraqi plane in the air. Now, as the two Mirages prepared to fire Exocet missiles at ships in the Gulf, Ayehid locked on and fired. Saudi Arabia had a national hero, and Iraq had two fewer warplanes.

What was left of the Iraqi Air Force began to hide in its shelters. Though many Iraqi planes could not have gotten into the air if they had wanted to due to extensive cratering and unexploded ordnance on taxiways and runways, CENTCOM wanted them destroyed. The Allies, armed with manufacturers' blueprints showing the vulnerable areas, started bombing shelters on 23 January with laser-guided 2,000 lb. bombs.

The Iraqi Air Force had felt secure in the belief that its hardened shelters were impenetrable. CENTCOM had opted to use the GBU-10 instead of its most lethal penetration bomb, the GBU-27. Air Force planners believed that although it could not penetrate as well as the GBU-27, the GBU-10 could get the job done. They were wrong. Stealth fighters dropped some 30 GBU-10 bombs, none of which penetrated the shelters.

The failure of the GBU-10s turned out to be a bit of good luck for the Coalition. Now thoroughly overconfident, the Iraqis moved even more planes into the shelters. Unfortunately for the Iraqis, USAF planners, having learned their lesson, switched to GBU-27s. The GBU-27s smashed through the reinforced concrete of the shelters and exploded inside, destroying aircraft and killing groundcrews. In some cases, bombs sliced through the tops of shelters, penetrated the floors, and blew planes into the air, smashing them against the ceilings like toys.

The Iraqi Air Force collapsed almost instantly. On 26 January, Iraqi planes began flying to Iran. That day, 29 Iraqi planes headed for the border. Many speculated that this was part of an arrangement between Iran and Iraq, until Iranian air defenses destroyed two of these planes and heavily damaged another two.

By 28 January, 69 Iraqi planes had escaped to Iran. Many of those that remained were towed into heavily populated areas because the Iraqis knew that these areas would not be bombed. This may have saved the aircraft, but it meant that the planes were no longer even a minor threat, since they could not take off from crowded neighborhoods.

The flights to Iran stopped on 31 January. There was some worry that the remaining planes might be saving themselves for suicide attacks against Coalition ground forces. The fear was groundless. With the Allies in total control of the skies, there could be no such attacks. In addition, many of Iraq's pilots had never even practiced ground attack missions and there was no time or opportunity for practice now. In any case, by

---

[*]The first Armed Forces Day parade after the Iran–Iraq War was cancelled because Saddam feared bombing and strafing runs on his reviewing stand.

the end of the second week, only 5 of Iraq's 66 airfields were showing any activity at all. Most of Iraq's remaining planes had been hidden.

The simple truth was that Iraqi aircraft had stopped flying to Iran because their escape route had been cut off by aggressive U.S. Air Force patrolling of the Iranian border. Patrolling continued for four days with no sign of Iraqi aircraft. With no Iraqi planes heading to Iran, the border patrols were suspended.

At that point, the high sortie rate was causing severe crew fatigue. Overworked pilots were now relying heavily on stimulants to get them through missions, and sleeping pills to help them get a few hours of sleep after missions. Chemical dependency was becoming a major concern. Another concern was the fact that sometimes even chemical stimulants were not enough to keep fliers going. In one case, all four crewmen of a two-plane flight of F-15Es fell asleep for 45 minutes on the way to their target. The planes were on auto pilot and there were no crashes, but incidents like this caused concern among Air Force planners.

Unfortunately, as soon as the border patrols stopped, Iraqi flights to Iran resumed. On 5 February, over 30 Iraqi planes headed for internment. On 6 February, CENTCOM was forced to resume patrolling. Seven fleeing Iraqi planes were shot down in the next two days. The pilots of this last wave of would-be escapees took no evasive action even after they knew that they had been locked on by Coalition aircraft. The few planes which got to Iran crashed. American pilots now had an accurate measure of their opponents —not very competent. The border patrols stopped the flights to Iran for good.

Iraq had begun the war with about 550 combat planes. There were now 121 Iraqi combat planes in Iran. About 120 more had been destroyed on the ground or wrecked in the more than 300 hardened aircraft shelters that had been bombed.[*] Iraq's air-to-air losses stood at 35. Twenty-nine more combat planes would be captured and destroyed during the ground campaign.

Desperate to stop the bombing, Saddam tried the "human shield" tactic once more. Again, it backfired. Thirteen captured pilots, eight Americans, two British, two Italians and one Kuwaiti were paraded before Iraqi television cameras. In what were obviously coerced statements, they condemned "American aggression against the peaceful people of Iraq." Saddam refused to allow the POWs, some of whom were in bad physical condition, to be examined by the International Red Cross. Worse, Iraqi radio vowed that they would be used as human shields at strategic targets. Both the coerced statements and the use of prisoners of war as hostages were gross violations of the Geneva Conventions. They were also utterly ineffective. The air war did not slacken at all, even when Radio Baghdad reported falsely that one of the hostages had been killed by an Allied bomb dropped on a government building. The sight of injured fliers only served to unite the citizens of the Coalition nations against Saddam.

Many of the pilots were badly mistreated by the Iraqis. After being turned over to Iraqi troops by Bedouin, Major Jeffrey Tice sustained a ruptured eardrum and a dislocated jaw as the result of an Iraqi beating. Electrodes were placed at various points on his head, and finally, an interrogator put a loaded pistol to his head and threatened to shoot him if he did not participate in the making of the videotape.

Not all Coalition pilots downed behind Iraqi lines were captured. In the early morning of Monday, 21 January, a Navy F-14 pilot bailed out in northwestern Iraq. After

---

[*]Ultimately, 375 of Iraq's 594 hardened aircraft shelters would be wrecked.

44

eight hours he was located by search aircraft. Two A-10s were dispatched to the area to provide cover while an MH-53 Pave Low helicopter made its way toward the downed pilot. While waiting for the helicopter, an A-10 piloted by Capt. Paul Johnson destroyed an Iraqi Army truck moving toward the downed flier. The Pave Low made its pickup, and the first air rescue mission of the war had been accomplished. Another mission rescued a downed Navy A-6E pilot on the following night.

Some downed airmen escaped through the Kuwaiti underground. In the first week of the war, a downed Free Kuwaiti pilot was picked up by Kuwaiti resistance fighters and smuggled out of Kuwait through an E&E (escape and evasion) network which had been set up by the resistance and the CIA before the bombing began. These resistance fighters had a cellular phone link with CENTCOM which they also used to report the results of Allied air missions.

During the second week, the world witnessed the dawn of "ecoterrorism." In what may have been either an attempt to sabotage Saudi desalination plants or frustrate amphibious landings, Saddam created what was, at the time, the largest man-made environmental catastrophe ever.[*] The Iraqis opened the valves of Kuwait's Sea Island terminal and began pouring millions of gallons of oil into the Persian Gulf. The terminal is Kuwait's main supertanker loading facility, about 10 miles off the shore of Kuwait's largest refinery at Mina al-Ahmadi. The flow of oil was stopped when F-111F bombers destroyed the pumps that fed the terminal. Two Aardvarks dropped electro-optically guided bombs from 20,000 feet while the weapons officer of a third guided the bombs in by joystick. The slick never reached the desalination plants. It was originally believed that as many as 11 million barrels of oil had poured out of Sea Island. While the true extent of the spill, about 1.1 million barrels, was much less shocking, it nevertheless represented a spill well over four times as large as that produced by the *Exxon Valdez*.

In week three, the Allies turned up the pressure on Iraqi forces in Kuwait in preparation for the ground war. Although targets like runways, roads and bridges were revisited as the Iraqis tried to rebuild them, this phase was dedicated to softening up the Iraqi Army for the coming ground offensive. Fuel and ammo dumps, tanks, artillery pieces, armored personnel carriers (APCs) and bunker complexes, which had already seen limited bombing, now received special attention.

The French Air Force was a frequent visitor at installations in Kuwait and Iraq. By the end of the war, the French had flown 2,884 sorties, suffering only four damaged aircraft. Most of the air-to-ground attacks were flown by Jaguars. The 28 French Jaguars flew a total of 615 sorties. Jaguars launched a total of 30 laser-guided missiles at key Iraqi targets, with an 80% hit rate. They also made extensive use of Belouga cluster bombs. Each Belouga is designed to be dropped at low level and contains three types of bomblets: armor piercing, fragmentation and delayed action. Each bomb can be set to dispense its 151 bomblets in one of two patterns, 40 meters wide by 121 meters long, or 40 meters wide by 242 meters long.

No French pilots were killed or captured on these missions, although one received minor wounds from ground fire on the first night of the war. Though there were

---

[*]He would break his own environmental damage record later in the war, in the oilfields of Kuwait.

no French losses, the French attacks were quite dangerous. In one attack on Ahmed al-Jaber Airfield in Kuwait, four of twelve attacking planes were damaged by ground fire, and one pilot received a bullet hole in his flight helmet.

British Jaguars were also active in the skies over Iraq and Kuwait. In 618 sorties, Britain's 12 Jaguars dropped 750 high explosive bombs and almost 400 cluster bombs. They also fired over 600 unguided rockets and over 9,600 rounds of 30mm cannon ammunition at Iraqi ground forces. No British Jaguars were shot down or damaged.

On 4 February, a battery of Iraqi BM-21 multiple rocket launchers opened fire on Marine positions. The battery's location was pinpointed, and a Marine Harrier strike was called in. Within moments, the battery was destroyed with CBU-87/B Combined Effects Munitions (CEM). The Harriers also jumped an Iraqi convoy, destroying 24 armored vehicles.

While Harriers carry only about 9,200 lbs. of bombs, those they carry are fairly lethal. Each CBU-87/B contains 202 3½ lb. bomblets, each with its own parachute. After the canister breaks open, the bomblets float toward their target. These are called combined effects munitions because each bomblet serves several different functions. The bottom of each bomblet is a high explosive shaped charge, capable of penetrating the top of any APC. The parachute guarantees that the bottom hits the target first. The main body of the bomblet explodes into lethal steel fragments, effective against soft-skinned vehicles and dismounted troops. Each bomblet also containes a small incendiary device.

Marine air missions were some of the most dangerous flown by American pilots. Eight Marine aircraft, including four Harriers, were lost. Marine losses per mission were more than twice as high as Navy losses and 3½ times as high as those sustained by the Air Force. This stems in part from the fact that Marine missions were often flown at low levels. The Harrier is also a dangerous plane to fly. Its engines are center line on the airframe. When a Harrier's engine is hit by a heat-seeking missile, the plane is almost guaranteed to go down.

By using sound tactics, Marine pilots were able to limit their losses somewhat. Harrier pilots found that when approaching a target from low level, they were visible to the enemy from several miles. However, when they dove on their targets at a steep angle from high altitudes, they were virtually invisible to their victims until after they had dropped their bombs. Over 150 Harriers took part in Operation Desert Storm, unleashing about 10,000 tons of ordnance on Iraqi ground forces.

In flying missions against Iraqi front line positions, Allied airmen faced air defense systems that appeared a lot more formidable than they actually were. These Iraqi systems were outdated and in short supply. The SA-6 was the primary Iraqi anti-aircraft missile system for the protection of the front lines. Though mounted on a tracked chassis, the SA-6 is not very mobile in practice, since the system takes several hours to set up again after a move. There are three SA-6 launchers in a battery, and three missiles on each launcher. In the 1973 Arab-Israeli War it took an average of over 50 SA-6 missiles to score each hit. In the two decades since then, Western electronic countermeasures had raised the number of missiles required for each hit to over a hundred.

Lenin once remarked that quantity had a quality of its own. An air defense using outdated anti-aircraft missiles can still be dangerous if there are enough missiles. Iraq may have had as many of 16,000 AA missiles of all types. Even at a success rate of one percent, these missiles could have been a problem for Allied pilots, but Iraq was short on battlefield launchers. A first-line Soviet division had 42 SAM launchers. The Iraqis probably had around 300 operational battlefield SAM launchers in their entire army. Launching missiles was also dangerous, because Coalition warplanes were hunting for launchers. Radar-guided weapons were Iraq's most lethal, but they were also the easiest to track down and destroy because of the radar signals they emitted.

Iraqi soldiers in the trenches were finding out about another of the unpleasant aspects of fighting for a dictator. Most dictators are obsessed with their own self-preservation, so they tend to surround themselves with soldiers and weapons that could be better used elsewhere. Saddam kept about one-third of his anti-aircraft weapons in and around Baghdad. This may have made Saddam feel safer, but it didn't do much for his soldiers at the front, who were being harried relentlessly by Coalition air power.

By the end of the third week, Iraqi units were virtually defenseless in the face of Allied air power. SAM crews, fearful of HARM missile strikes, turned off their radars and fired their missiles blind, or did not fire at all. Wild Weasel aircraft, tasked with the destruction of SAM systems, were reporting that they were encountering no radar activity at all on 80% of their missions.

CENTCOM planners divided Kuwait into "kill boxes." These were areas about 400 miles square. An F-16 would cruise over a given box. When it spotted a target, it fired white phosphorous rockets into the area, sending up a cloud of thick white smoke. F-16s with bombs (known as "Killer Bees") were then directed to the area. With their targets already marked, it should have been just a matter of collecting the kill.

Actually destroying Iraqi armor proved to be a problem, however. Although F-16s were used more extensively than any other combat aircraft during the war, they inflicted comparatively little damage. F-16s did not carry smart bombs or laser designators, so they were limited to dropping unguided bombs or cluster munitions. They were also restricted to higher altitudes by CENTCOM for their own safety. F-16s have only one engine and are not heavily armored, so they do not stand up particularly well to hits from anti-aircraft weapons. While the missile threat may have been largely gone, the Iraqi Army still had AA guns on the battlefield, so low altitude runs were dangerous. Although the absence of laser designation was offset somewhat by a sophisticated aiming device in the F-16, accuracy dropped off sharply at higher altitudes. Iraqi tanks were also widely dispersed, and hitting single tanks from altitudes of over 10,000 feet was difficult. The vast majority of the bombs dropped from these altitudes exploded harmlessly in the sand. Though F-16s enjoyed a high degree of success when firing HARM missiles in the anti-radar role, the aircraft was a dismal failure as a bomber. There is no evidence to indicate that the Iraqis lost more than two dozen armored vehicles to F-16 strikes.

Infra-red devices provided an effective answer to the problem. Since sand cools faster than metal, at night, tanks contrast sharply with surrounding sand. This led Air

Force planners to believe that dug-in Iraqi tanks would be easy prey for F-111F bombers with sophisticated night vision equipment and guided bombs. The notion was tested in an experimental, or "concept validation," raid by two Aardvarks on the night of 5 February. The raid was a success. Now, even dug-in tanks were not safe, and kill rates rose sharply. Using this tactic, Aardvarks would destroy about two hundred armored vehicles during the war. With the success of the F-111Fs in "tank plinking," other planes, like F-15Es and carrier-based A-6E Intruders, began using the tactic.

Often referred to as "Whispering Death" because most of the jet's noise is projected rearward of the aircraft, giving AA gunners little advanced warning of an impending strike, F-111Fs were in demand for other missions as well. During the war they destroyed 245 hardened aircraft shelters, 158 buildings, 113 bunkers, 90 troop assembly or logistics sites, 32 chemical facilities, 25 anti-aircraft sites, 19 warehouses, 13 runways, 13 aircraft hangars, 12 bridges (seriously damaging another 52), 9 communication lines, 9 towers, 5 pumping stations, 4 aircraft on runways, 4 mine entrances and 2 ships. All of this destruction was done in only 2,417 sorties. That was a lot of work for only 66 planes, especially since 25 man-hours of ground crew maintenance are required for each hour flown, but the workload did not cause any significant maintenance problems for the F-111F fleet.

Air Force commanders found that A-10s, which hunted by day, were also effective at night. The A-10 carries over 15,000 lbs. of bombs, which it can deliver accurately. It also has a seven-barreled gatling-type gun (the GAU-8), capable of firing 35–70 30mm rounds per second. The 30mm rounds contain super-hard depleted uranium, and are fired at the top of a tank, where the armor is thinnest.

Warthogs are not designed for night fighting, but they carried Maverick missiles, which have infra-red night vision imagers in their noses. The pilot could see what the imager saw by watching a small monitor in the cockpit. Thus, pilots could use their missiles as TV cameras. That gave them the ability to fire their 30mm guns while looking through their infra-red Maverick imagers. Once the Mavericks were fired, the pilot was blind and had to return to base, but by then, the damage was done.

A total of 144 Warthogs saw action in the Gulf. Before the war, it was widely believed that the A-10 was too slow for modern war, but the A-10's toughness made up for its lack of speed. The titanium armor surrounding the pilot's compartment is capable of stopping rounds of up to 23mm. Almost every vital component of the aircraft has a backup system. The Warthog's self-sealing fuel tanks can absorb hits without catching fire or exploding. Its twin engines are also heavily armored. Equally important, they are located high on the rear of the aircraft's fuselage. On most fighter aircraft, the engine exhaust comes out directly below the tail of the aircraft. Since SAMs home in on exhaust, a hit will generally blow the tail off, making the plane impossible to control. A direct hit on an A-10 engine would knock it out, but would probably leave the other engine and the tail structure intact. At least 70 A-10s were piloted back to base after sustaining battle damage, 15 with serious damage. One A-10 returned to base with 378 holes in it, including 45 in the armor surrounding the right engine, and 15 in the left engine's armor. Both engines kept running. In 8,100 sorties, only five A-10s were shot down, one for every 1,620 trips.

Target detection in the hunting phase of the air war was aided by an airborne radar system known as JSTARS (Joint Surveillance Target Attack Radar System). The JSTARS is somewhat similar to the AWACS. Both radar systems are operated from modified Boeing 707 airplanes, but while AWACS directs air activity, JSTARS directs ground activity. Using its downward looking radar, the JSTARS can locate and identify targets in any weather. Its radar can operate in one of two modes. On the wide area setting, it can scan an area of about 16 by 12½ miles. On the detailed setting, it can scan an area of about 3 by 2½ miles.

JSTARS was not due to be deployed for several years. There was concern about possible flaws in the system. Other concerns centered around the effect that early revelation of the technology might have on the system's value in future conflicts. In addition, Gen. Schwarzkopf simply did not see a pressing need for its deployment. Lt.Gen. Frederick Franks, commander of the VII Corps, which would be doing most of the fighting during the ground offensive, did see a need for it. He had used JSTARS in Europe on an experimental basis and had been impressed with its capabilities. Franks was determined to employ whatever technology was available to keep his casualties to a minimum. Though the system had flaws in it, an imperfect JSTARS would be of more use to his troops than none at all. At a briefing for civilian Department of Defense officials, Franks pressed the point. Air Force planners could not justify withholding technology from a present conflict to preserve its secrecy for a future conflict that might never come within the useful lifetime of the system. JSTARS was sent to the Gulf.

Though it contributed to the success of the air war, JSTARS had its problems. In at least one instance, during the Battle of Khafji, JSTARS directed a massive B-52 strike on what appeared on radar to be an Iraqi armored column. The "column" turned out to be a long stretch of densely packed barbed wire. On a few occasions, reports of Iraqi activity turned out to be herds of sheep. Far more serious, during the ground war, JSTARS showed what appeared to be a retreat from the Republican Guard's main line of defense. In fact, the line was being reinforced by armored and mechanized units whose movement JSTARS operators had failed to spot. The system's shortcomings notwithstanding, intelligence provided by JSTARS was useful to the Air Force in its search for Iraqi ground targets, and to the Army, which used the information in planning for the coming ground offensive.

Life in the Iraqi trenches was made almost unbearable by Coalition air power. With Iraqi ground radar silent, larger SAM systems were no longer a major threat. Iraq's 4,000 or so anti-aircraft guns became the primary Iraqi battlefield air defense system. AA guns are not particularly efficient. Experience has shown that it takes about 10,000 AA gun rounds to shoot down each plane. Iraqi AA guns were also vulnerable to cluster bombing, since they depended on firing large numbers of shells, which were stored near the guns. The number of serviceable Iraqi AA guns dwindled with each airstrike.

Each Iraqi front line division had about twelve self-propelled AA guns. Iraq had two types of self-propelled AA guns. One, the ZSU 57-2 (57mm, two barrels) was obsolete because of its low rate of fire (4 rounds per second) and lack of radar, and saw virtually no action in the war. The other, the ZSU 23-4 (23mm, four barrels), or "*Shilka*," is not effective against low flying aircraft. The rapid return of the gun's radar signal from low flying aircraft clutters the radar screen and confuses the operator.

The Iraqi Army's Shilkas were not effective on anything else, either. The Shilka's 3,200 to 4,000 round per minute rate of fire was not as impressive as it sounded. Since Shilkas only carry 2,000 rounds, it would only take 30 seconds at full tilt to exhaust the entire ammunition supply. In practice, they are limited to two-second bursts. In addition, the crews of Shilkas which had not yet been destroyed by anti-radiation missiles followed the lead of the missile batteries and shut off their radars, firing blind. There was no question of using the radar only for short periods during an attack. Either a crew uses the radar or it does not, because the radar takes two minutes to warm up after it is turned on.

ZSU 23-4 Shilka. (Photograph: Thomas Houlahan)

About 60% of Iraq's AA guns were of the much less effective towed variety. The S-60, a single-barreled, 57mm gun, was the most common of these pieces. With a 70 round per minute rate of fire and no radar, it was almost useless. Iraq also had a non-radar-equipped, twin-barreled, towed version of the Shilka. It could only fire 2,000 rounds per minute, and was only effective in clear weather.

Iraqi soldiers at platoon- and company-level did have shoulder-launched SAMs (SA-7s). These missiles only have about a 10% hit rate, and they tend to damage, rather than destroy, their targets.* For each Israeli plane shot down by an SA-7 during the 1973 Arab–Israeli War, fifteen were hit but survived to fight another day.

The history of the SA-7 is one of the best illustrations of the never-ending battle between those who develop weapons, and those who develop equipment and tactics to frustrate the weapons. The first models of the SA-7 had a tendency to home in on heat sources other than jet exhaust, like the sun. If the missiles were launched at low flying targets in desert conditions, they sometimes homed in on heat reflected off the ground, and nose-dived into the sand. Western planners also learned that attack planes could release flares to frustrate heat-seeking missiles. The flares were hotter than a jet's exhaust, so missiles homed in on the flares instead of the exhaust. To eliminate these problems, the Soviets designed a seeker for the missile that homed in on the second hottest source, so that the missiles would ignore the flares and hit the exhaust. Western planners simply designed a system that dispensed flares of different intensities. Now, the missiles ignored the hottest flares, but often homed in on slightly less hot flares.[†]

Morale in the trenches was deteriorating rapidly. Soldiers in the KTO had not heard from their families since they got to Kuwait, and this was contributing to psychological depression on a wide scale. Physical deprivation was a fact of life. Many units were running out of food. Water, though strictly rationed, was rapidly running out. These factors had a devastating impact on morale.

Allied leaflets were the only item that was not in short supply. Some 30 million were dropped on the Saddam Line, encouraging Iraqi troops to surrender, and instructing them on how to do so. In addition, Coalition radio broadcasts featured religious messages and testimonials from contented prisoners of war. Total Coalition mastery of the air allowed the Allies to broadcast many of their daily bombing targets as well. Iraqi soldiers found it hard to resist the temptation to tune in and find out whether or not they were going to be bombed. Many Iraqi defectors said that they had been influenced by broadcasts, even though in many instances, unit commanders had banned the use of transistor radios in an attempt to hide the true extent of the war's disastrous developments from their men. Iraq's grotesquely unconvincing response to the Coalition psychological warfare operations ("Psyops") blitz was "Baghdad Betty," who produced not depression, but laughter among Allied soldiers, especially when she claimed that while American soldiers were in Saudi Arabia, their wives were sleeping with Bart Simpson (a cartoon character).

---

*Harriers are particularly vulnerable to destruction by SA-7s. Because their engines are in the center of the aircraft, an SA-7 strike will usually destroy enough vital components to bring down the plane. All combat Harrier losses in the Gulf War were inflicted by SA-7s.

[†]The sun is still a problem for the SA-7. Newer models of the SA-7 will not turn and home in on the sun on their own, but if a pilot has an SA-7 chasing him, he can maneuver his plane so that the missile is pointed at the sun, then turn sharply away. Often, the missile will continue to fly toward the sun.

The residents of the Saddam Line were getting more than leaflets dropped on them. Iraqi units tended to keep their soldiers bunched tightly together, so their leaders could keep an eye on them. This made them good targets for Coalition air power. The Allies had several munitions capable of exploding in mid-air and showering bomblets into the trenches. The munition of choice for attacking dug-in infantry is the 750 lb. CBU (Cluster Bomb Unit)-52. Each CBU-52 splits open in mid-air and spills out 665 one pound "Sadeye" fragmentation bomblets. Each Sadeye consists of about 11 ounces of TNT surrounded by 600 steel shards. Generally, about one-third of the Sadeyes explode at 30 feet and rain down hot steel. Another third explode on impact with the ground or objects on it. The remaining third are set with delayed action fuses. They go off intermittently for a few minutes. This is demoralizing, as soldiers in the trenches can not be sure when the explosions are finished.

Iraq's soldiers were not prepared for the unprecedented ferocity of the air and artillery strikes launched against them. Artillerymen and anti-aircraft gunners stopped firing, while infantrymen cowered in their trenches. Survival, not Kuwait, was their main concern now. Iraqi soldiers found themselves incapacitated by fatigue. Constant air and artillery strikes were keeping Iraqi soldiers awake, and lack of sleep degrades individual performance. If deprived of sleep for long enough, any soldier can become combat ineffective.

Such misery gave rise to thoughts of surrender, a fact of which Iraqi military leaders were aware.[*] Commanders regularly lied to their soldiers about their proximity to Allied lines. In some cases, soldiers who were within a few miles of Allied lines were told that they were several days march away to discourage surrender. It worked, but it also lulled many Iraqi soldiers into a false sense of security which was shattered when Allied artillery began to fall on them.

Soldiers were also reminded by their commanders that the safety of their families might depend on their performance at the battlefront. Many tried to desert anyway. A few deserters were caught and hanged by roving execution squads, their bodies left hanging as a grim reminder to other soldiers about the risks inherent in deserting. Most deserters were not caught, however.

The war saw the dropping of the world's largest conventional bomb, the 15,000 lb. BLU-82, or "daisy cutter." The term "daisy cutter" comes from its original use. In Vietnam, the BLU-82 was used to clear tracts of jungle for helicopter landing zones. The BLU-82 is not particularly high-tech. The BLU-82's explosive content is made up 12,600 lbs. of ammonium nitrate (fertilizer) and aluminum powder. Ammonium nitrate is extremely explosive, and aluminum powder burns fiercely.[†] The BLU-82 creates a

---

[*]By the fifth week of the war, some 250 Iraqi soldiers had picked their way through their own minefields to give themselves up.

[†]Some have mistakenly referred to the BLU-82 as a "fuel-air explosive." Fuel-air explosives burst in mid-air, creating a large ball of highly flammable mist which is then ignited by a secondary explosion. The BLU-82's main ingredients are not fuels, and it is set off when its 6 foot long probe makes contact with the ground.

fireball and a shock wave five times greater than an equal amount of TNT. When the bomb explodes, the force of the blast pushes the air in front of it. The air becomes compressed, and is pushed outward at six times the speed of sound. This fast moving, compressed air is what is referred to as the shock wave.

The pressure of a shock wave is usually measured in pounds of pressure per square inch. Eardrums begin to rupture at 5 lbs./psi. At 15 lbs./psi, eardrums shatter, chests can cave in and lungs can collapse. A 50 lb./psi shock wave will kill half of the people it hits. The BLU-82 creates an overpressure of 1,000 lbs./psi.

The shock wave is referred to as a "primary" blast effect. The BLU-82 also produces significant secondary and tertiary effects. Secondary effects occur when sandbags, rifles, shovels and other items lying around the target area are picked up and hurled through the air at extremely high velocities, crushing, decapitating or impaling anyone unfortunate enough to be in their path. When live bodies are lifted off the ground and propelled into stationary objects with sufficient force to kill or maim, it is referred to as a "tertiary" effect. A BLU-82 explosion also uses up massive amounts of oxygen instantaneously. Enemy ground troops close to the center of the blast may actually have their lungs sucked out after they have been crushed to death by the shock wave.

The BLU-82 is delivered by a specialized version of the C-130 cargo plane (called the MC-130 Combat Talon) in a decidedly low-tech operation. When the plane is over the target, the rear cargo ramp is lowered, and the bomb is shoved out the back of the plane. A parachute then deploys, and the bomb floats toward its target. Because an MC-130 downed by AA fire would almost certainly experience a crew fatality rate of 100%, it was deemed necessary to release the bombs from 18,000 feet.

The dropping of the bombs was largely a scientific endeavor. Critical questions had to be answered about the bomb's effects. It had been expected that the BLU-82, designed to knock down trees, would direct most of its blast horizontally. The Air Force had nevertheless hoped that there would be enough downward blast force to blow gaps in minefields before G-Day.

There were also questions about the BLU-82's accuracy. The bomb had never been dropped from 18,000 feet before. With no knowledge of critical factors like the degree of drift that could be expected from that height, there was no way to accurately calculate a release point. There could be no question of using the bomb on the minefields or on front line Iraqi positions if there was a chance that it would drift south of its target and land on or near American forces in their staging areas. Without aiming data it also would not have been much use against armored formations behind the front lines. Though the BLU-82 is devastating to anyone or anything within its blast radius, its blast radius is limited. Because these units had spread out, a high degree of precision would have been required if a bomb was to inflict significant damage.

In the early morning of 7 February, two MC-130s dropped two BLU-82s. The results were disappointing. Air Force planners had hoped for large craters. None could be found. A second drop days later also produced no craters. Finally, a drop on Faylakah Island left only a modest crater in the island's loose sand. The results of the three drops made it clear that the BLU-82 would be practically useless against mines.

The drops also did nothing to solve the accuracy problem. The first two bombings produced no craters, so Air Force analysts could not determine where any of the four bombs had landed. The impact point of the Faylakah bomb was evident, but one bombing result was not enough to produce data that would allow the bomb to be delivered safely or effectively. Plans for combat use of the BLU-82 were dropped.

The Allies received an unexpected benefit from the first BLU-82 strike, however. The two massive explosions appeared to the Iraqis to be the beginning of a major attack. Iraqi radars were hastily turned back on, allowing the Coalition to find and destroy them. A frenzy of Iraqi radio traffic provided Allied ground forces with even more information about their enemies.

At the end of week five, CENTCOM estimated that Iraq had lost about 1,685 tanks, 925 APCs, and 1,450 artillery pieces. Inter-agency rivalry began to rear its ugly head, as the CIA disputed those numbers. Some CIA analysts claimed that CENTCOM's destruction claims were twice as high as they should have been. This prompted Pentagon officers to joke that if a CIA man saw a tank on one side of the river and its turret on the other side, he would report "possible damage." When the CIA estimates seemed to have little impact on military planning, CIA personnel leaked their estimates to the press, annoying military planners. "Weren't they [the CIA] the guys who told us that the Iraqis only had thirty-six mobile Scud launchers?" one Army officer asked.

The man responsible for the CENTCOM estimates, Brig.Gen. John Stewart, Jr., was inclined to err on the side of caution. As bombing began, Stewart developed a conservative formula for estimating bomb damage on Iraqi armor. All kill reports which were backed up by gun camera video or other imagery were counted as confirmed kills. Of kills reported by A-10 pilots, half were credited.

About halfway through the bombing campaign, the formula was modified to make it even more conservative. A-10 pilot claims were reduced in weight from one-half to one-third. Gun video confirmations were reduced from 100% to 50%. The modifications were a response to the fact that Coalition aircraft were beginning to hit some vehicles which had already been knocked out. In addition, like most Soviet-trained armies, the Iraqi Army was fairly well-drilled in "*maskirovka*" (loosely translated: deception tactics). The Iraqis had begun to take measures like setting off burning tires on tanks to make it look like vehicles were destroyed when in fact they were not. There was also the problem of decoys. During the air war, an Egyptian brigade commander cautioned a British brigade commander that a lot of what the Air Force was claiming as kills were probably decoys. "We did the same against the Israelis," he said. "They are looking for strikes, give them strikes. A few barrels of petrol inside your decoys, and it makes a very nice explosion."

Even with the conservative targeting criteria, the CENTCOM estimates (and the CIA's for that matter) turned out to be high. CENTCOM estimated that by G-Day, over 2,600 Iraqi armored vehicles had been destroyed by fixed-wing air attack. In all likelihood, however, only about 600 Iraqi armored vehicles were knocked out by air attack before G-Day. Most of the kills went to A-10s and F-111Fs. One Iraqi armored brigade in the British attack zone had been destroyed by air attacks. Singled out for special attention by Lt.Gen. Franks, the VII Corps commander, it was caught in exposed positions and its armor was virtually wiped out. However, when the ground forces attacked on G-Day, they would find that most Iraqi armored or mechanized brigades had lost less than 10% of their armored vehicles to air attack. Many Iraqi tanks were abandoned when ground forces arrived, and in many cases this was the result of air attacks scaring the crews away, but actual bombing damage was relatively light.

Iraqi casualty estimates were also overblown. The main reason for the low casualty rates was that in raids against heavy units, the U.S. Air Force targeted armored vehicles and artillery pieces, not troops. Most Iraqis stayed well away from their armored vehicles or guns during bombing raids. As a result, though air attacks were extremely effective in demoralizing Iraqi troops (most captured line unit commanders indicated that their units were disintegrating as G-Day approached), they produced few casualties. For instance, the armored brigade that was stripped of most of its armor at Lt.Gen. Franks' behest only sustained a 6.5% casualty rate.

Air raids against dug-in infantry units produced surprisingly few casualties. This war proved that it is still difficult to kill properly dug-in troops. After the ground war, the two U.S. Marine divisions would find through interrogations of captured Iraqi officers that the most heavily bombed Iraqi divisions in their zone of attack had suffered an average casualty rate of about 1.5% during the air war. In the 101st Airborne Division's sector, a three-hour airstrike on a position holding over four hundred Iraqis produced five casualties, none of them fatal. In VII Corps' sector, there was a somewhat higher loss rate, but many of those casualties were inflicted by the massive Multiple Launch Rocket System strikes which had taken place in that sector.

MLRS strikes proved a far more efficient killer of troops than air strikes, because in many cases the rockets were launched at Iraqi artillery batteries in the act of firing at Allied forces. Because the guns were manned when they were hit by counterbattery fire, the destruction of a gun battery might produce forty casualties. The destruction of a gun battery by air would usually produce few, if any, casualties. In the vast majority of these cases, the crews were in their shelters during the bombing, well away from their guns.

Though estimates of Iraqi soldiers killed by bombing ran as high as 15,000 at the time, it is probable that fewer than 1,500 were killed by fixed-wing air attacks. Perhaps as many as a thousand more were killed by artillery fire, helicopter gunships, or armored raids during this period.

The failure of air power to live up to its billing cannot be attributed to any failing on the part of Allied pilots, who, man for man, were among the best that the nations of the Coalition had ever produced. There are simply limits to the damage that aircraft can inflict against dug-in troops and equipment from high altitudes.

The failure cannot even be blamed on the senior officers who produced bomb damage assessments which turned out on further review to be inflated. The BDAs were made in good faith. However, unless an analyst has before and after photos of every square kilometer of a given battlefield, he will be forced to some degree to rely on pilot reports. Again, these pilots were bombing from extremely high altitudes, where it is difficult to evaluate the results of a given strike. During the war, the media created the impression of an all-seeing, unblinking eye in the sky over Kuwait and southern Iraq. The Department of Defense did nothing to discourage this portrayal. In fact, aerial reconnaissance assets were in limited supply, so most of the battlefield went unmonitored and unphotographed most of the time.

While reconnaissance assets were scarce, intermediate range imagery was virtually nonexistent. Intelligence analysts basically had access to two types of aerial photographs during the war: wide-angle area photographs, and high resolution close-up photos. There was virtually no in-between. Wide-angle photos could be used to determine Iraqi dispositions, but their the resolution was not high enough to determine conclusively whether or not a vehicle was still serviceable, or, for that matter, that it was in fact a vehicle and not a decoy. Close-up photographs had the resolution to make these determinations, but they did not cover much area, so they provided little perspective. Brig.Gen. Stewart would later liken the situation to that of a television viewer attempting to figure out what was going on in a football game when he was only being offered blimp shots of the stadium and the surrounding city and close-ups of individual players.

Pilots and analysts could only form their opinions of the effects of bombing on the Iraqi Army based on the limited information at their disposal at the time. That limited information led them to conclude that there would not be much serious fighting for the ground forces to do during the coming ground offensive. Events would prove otherwise.

Part III

The Countdown

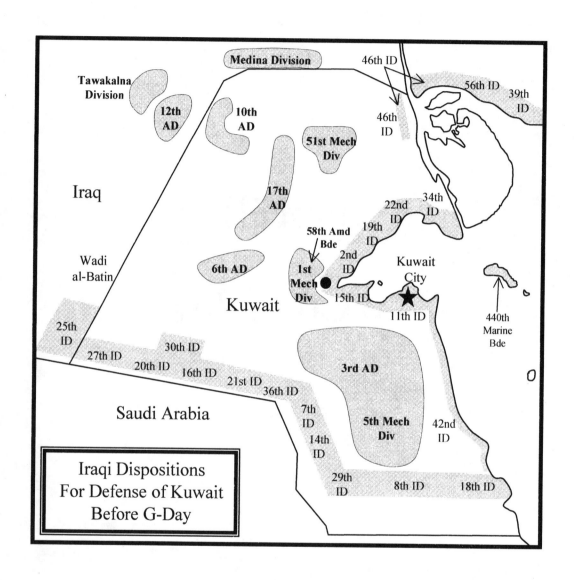

Medina Division

46th ID

56th ID

39th ID

Tawakalna Division

12th AD

10th AD

46th ID

51st Mech Div

Iraq

17th AD

22nd ID

34th ID

19th ID

58th Amd Bde

2nd ID

Kuwait City

Wadi al-Batin

6th AD

1st Mech Div

15th ID

11th ID

440th Marine Bde

Kuwait

25th ID

27th ID

30th ID

20th ID

16th ID

21st ID

36th ID

3rd AD

Saudi Arabia

7th ID

14th ID

5th Mech Div

42nd ID

29th ID

8th ID

18th ID

Iraqi Dispositions
For Defense of Kuwait
Before G-Day

5

Inside the Iraqi Army

Good hype about a nation's armed forces is mainly useful in helping that nation bluff other nations into letting it have its way without a fight. Inevitably, there are instances when the other side is not scared off. When that happens, the bluffing nation can back down, or it can fight. If it fights, and there is a significant gap between the hype and its military capabilities, the nation may see its armed forces destroyed, as Iraq's would be in this war.

Hype about Islamic fanaticism and Iraq's "battle-hardened war machine" raised fears of a bloodbath in the impending ground war. However, when the ground assault came, Iraq's army proved largely rhetorical, long on bluster and short on combat capability. An explanation for its dismal performance can be found in the society that produced the army. Armies tend to exhibit the characteristics of, and reflect the limitations of, the societies from which they are raised. A society's problems will usually show up in its army. If the society is undereducated, underdeveloped, and socially fragmented, it is a good bet that its army will not be much better off, fancy weaponry notwithstanding. Saddam bought equipment. He could not buy an army.

Before the war, many analysts assumed that the Iraqis had an edge in terms of morale. Iraq's army was often viewed as a mass of religious fanatics who would fight to the death for Allah. Much of this belief came from watching the Iranian Army in action. However, there were critical differences between Iranian soldiers and Iraqi soldiers. The Iranian soldier comes from a religious country and the Iraqi soldier does not. Iran is a theocracy, ruled by clergy. Iraq is a single (Ba'ath) party dictatorship. Ba'athism is a form of secular socialism. While Ba'athism has always paid lip service to Islam, its commitment to it has always been superficial. The main goal of the Ba'ath Party is to modernize Iraqi society to better cope with the influence of Western powers. Islam, especially the fundamentalist variety, is seen by the party as reactionary and an impediment to this goal. Religion does not play a central role in Iraq as it does in Iran. This was most apparent in the physical appearance of women in Iraq. Most wear Western dress, not black robes and veils.

There was also large degree of religious unity in Iran, where 93% of the population is Shi'ite. Iraq, where 60% of the population is Shi'ite, is ruled by a small group of Sunni Muslims. Only about 25% of Iraq's population is Sunni. Shi'ites and Sunnis in the Middle East do not get along well. Iraq's leadership has been insensitive to Shi'ite traditions and beliefs, and this has fueled religious discontent. The fact that Saddam had invaded Shi'ite Iran didn't help.

Ethnic discontent was another problem. Iraq's population was about 15% Kurdish. There were strong separatist feelings in the northern part of the country, where most Iraqi Kurds lived. The genocidal manner in which Saddam dealt with Kurdish opposition only intensified Kurdish hatred.

The Iraqi Army was not immune to ethnic and religious grumbling. Saddam's insistence on maintaining a huge military machine forced the army to rely heavily on politically undependable elements of the Iraqi population. Sunnis were well-represented in the officer and senior NCO ranks. The privileged Republican Guard was largely Sunni. However, there simply were not enough Sunni Muslims in Iraq to stock an army of some 400,000 men.[*] The problem was exacerbated by the fact that Sunni males found it easier to obtain draft deferments owing to better access to Iraq's decision-making elite. As a result, while 75% of Iraq's population was Shi'ite or Kurdish, almost 90% of the soldiers on the Saddam Line came from these unreliable ethnic groups, which helps explain their lack of fighting spirit. These men had little stake in their government, and none at all in keeping Kuwait. Iraq's soldiers were resigned to the reality of the coming conflict, but they had no zest for it.

The Iraqi Army was held together primarily by fear. Soldiers did as they were told basically because they were afraid of their leaders. Leadership through intimidation is fatally flawed as a doctrine. Intimidation can work for a while, often a long while. However, men who are compelled to fight primarily by fear of their commanders will give up, run away, or shoot their leaders the first time they have to face something that scares them more than their commanders. This helps explain why during the war with Iran, significant numbers of Iraqi soldiers were absent from their units without leave at any given time, and why the problem was even worse against the Coalition.

Iraqi soldiers had a great deal to be afraid of. The bombing campaign brought a terror for which no Iraqi soldier could have adequately prepared. When the ground war came, it was equally terrifying. Iraqi soldiers were subjected to the ravages of Coalition artillery. After the smoke cleared, they did not even have the satisfaction of testing themselves against Coalition soldiers on anything like even terms. For Iraqi infantrymen, this was a war pitting Iraqi men against unstoppable Allied machines. Soldiers in tank or mechanized units found no comfort in their armor, which was a generation out of date and no match for Coalition hardware. If either side's soldiers were psychologically suspect, it was Iraq's.

The advancing Allies would find many leaderless units. One Iraqi doctor in Kuwait City was astonished to find that: "When the land war began, the officers fled in their cars and left us behind." Leadership is what holds an army together in battle, and the Iraqi Army found itself at a disadvantage in that area. For starters, Coalition soldiers

---

[*]At the time, due to the number of divisions in the Iraqi Army, Saddam was believed to have a "million man army." However the divisions were significantly understrength.

60

found it a lot easier to fight for generals who had been in life-threatening situations before, and had distinguished themselves, than their Iraqi counterparts did to fight for political appointees, who were in most cases unproven and in many cases cowardly. Leadership by example was not a hallmark of the Iraqi Army.

As a dictatorship, Iraq was at a grave disadvantage because it had to select and evaluate its officers based upon their political reliability rather than their military or technical skill. The bedlam that resulted was similar to that which would afflict the U.S. Army if its officer corps was restricted to members of the president's party who had either contributed heavily or organized extensively during his campaign. While much was made of Iraq's "heroic defensive efforts" against Iran, less was made of the fact that the relief of officers for cowardice or incompetence was commonplace during that war.

When a regime like Saddam's stumbles upon the odd competent officer, it does not retain him for long, since such people tend to become too popular for their own good. Iraq is a cult of personality —Saddam's personality. Overachievers are viewed as a threat. There is only room for one hero. Many of Iraq's best leaders from the Iran–Iraq War had met with fatal "accidents" or fallen victim to Stalinesque purges by the time the Gulf War started. Within a year of the end of the Iran–Iraq War, at least four senior Iraqi military leaders with successful war records had died in mysterious helicopter crashes. At least three more were relieved between the wars. Not surprisingly, the Iraqi Army was badly outgeneralled by the Coalition.

Leadership was no better in the enlisted ranks. Here, Iraq faced another dictatorship disadvantage. Life in the Iraqi Army was exceptionally harsh. As soon as a soldier was allowed to leave the service, he generally did. This made it extraordinarily difficult to develop a cadre of competent, experienced NCOs. The noncommissioned officer corps is the backbone of most armies. Officers set training standards, and NCOs see that those standards are met. In many armies, like that of the United States, strong NCOs are also instrumental in the training of junior officers. The poor quality of the Iraqi Army's NCOs guaranteed poorly trained soldiers and junior officers.

Even if the Iraqi Army had possessed a strong NCO corps, training its soldiers would have been a daunting challenge. Saddam was obsessed with acquiring vast quantities of military hardware. That obsession caused him to ignore deficiencies in the men who had to use it. Many of Iraq's conscripts were illiterate. School was only mandatory to the age of ten in Iraq. Saddam's soldiers were therefore severely limited in the amount of training they could absorb. When American soldiers outperformed their Iraqi counterparts by a wide margin, it should have surprised no one. If one country spends vast amounts on education and another spends comparatively little, when those two nations come together in conflict, the outcome should be predictable. The Iraqi Army took substandard conscripts and provided them with substandard training, weapons and leaders. The idea that religious passion would make up the difference was a fantasy.

The Iraqi Army entered the Gulf War with an overconfidence that was rooted in the Iran–Iraq War. The Iranian Army had been its own worst enemy. The lack of planning and imagination that went into Iranian offensive movements was shocking. The Iranians consistently launched suicidal human wave attacks against prepared, dug-in Iraqi positions without close air support, and without effective artillery preparation. Worst of all, the attacks almost always took place in broad daylight, and involved no sophisticated tactical maneuvers. Thanks to the Iranian Army's general ineptitude, the

Iraqi Army's deficiencies never hurt it. This resulted in a misplaced faith both in the value of defensive operations and in the abilities of the Iraqi Army.

Whenever the Iraqis got the best of an engagement, it was almost always because the Iranians had lost, not because the Iraqis had won. Even so, against Iran, the Iraqi Army was unable to exploit the tremendous advantages it possessed. Iranian offensives were generally preceded by public calls for volunteers, which should have alerted the Iraqis, who also had complete control of the air, and should have seen any attack developing. However, the Iraqi Army always seemed genuinely surprised by Iranian offensives.

The Iraqis were also slow to react to attacks when they came. Often, Iranian attacks enjoyed significant success before they were repulsed. This had much to do with the hazards of being a military officer in a dictatorship. Iraqi commanders were slow to inform their higher-ups, who did not handle bad news well, about setbacks. When higher commanders finally learned of Iranian breakthroughs, they were slow to commit their reserves aggressively, because failed counterattacks often had fatal consequences for commanders in Saddam's Iraq.

Before Desert Storm, Western analysts tended to marvel at how the Iraqi Army had managed to fight the larger Iranian Army to a standstill. The real marvel was that even with the benefits of air superiority, poor Iranian tactics, and, by 1987, overwhelming materiel superiority (4½:1 in tanks, 4:1 in other armored vehicles and 2½:1 in artillery), Iraq could only manage a draw.

The war with Iran had bled Iraq significantly, a point overlooked by most Western analysts. Some 110,000 Iraqi soldiers had been killed and about 210,000 wounded during the war with Iran. Though Iran lost more than twice as many men as Iraq during the war, the losses had less of an impact on Iran, which had three times Iraq's population. Iraq also suffered serious losses among its combat leaders. In addition, many Iraqi officers died at the hands of their own army. In the fall of 1982, for instance, when Iranian human wave attacks threatened to overwhelm Iraqi forces, Saddam executed almost 300 senior officers. By the time the Gulf War started, most of Iraq's best combat leaders were dead.

The experience gained by the Iraqi Army in that war was in no way worth the price the army paid for it. Combat experience is a double-edged sword. There is a fine line between being battle-hardened and being combat-fatigued. The Iraqi Army had crossed that line. No army can fight a major war for a decade without suffering serious losses and widespread psychological trauma.

Western armies break units into combat gradually. Western doctrine calls for units to be withdrawn from combat when their casualties reach 10%–30%. Combat missions are also generally shared by a large number of units. That way, experience will be spread around, and no unit will be completely wiped out. Iraq sent units of green troops into savage combat. When 70%–85% of them had been killed or maimed, the unit was replaced. Survivors, who by that time weren't good for much psychologically, were sent to other units.

Combat experience is only useful if soldiers live to take advantage of it. Many of Iraq's combat experienced soldiers did not survive their experience. Many lived, but were ruined by their experiences. Of the approximately 800,000 soldiers who served in the "hot" sectors of the front during the Iran–Iraq War, about 110,000 were killed (almost 14%), and some 50,000 (more than 6%) received wounds so extensive that they were physically unfit for further military service. Thus, about one-fifth of the soldiers actively engaged were taken out of service permanently by the Iranian Army.

There is also no guarantee that combat experience will improve a soldier. If that experience involves seeing 20% of his comrades killed or maimed, or receiving non-crippling wounds (as about 160,000 Iraqi soldiers did), it can cause a soldier to hate the idea of ever putting on a uniform again. About 40% of the Iraqi soldiers in the active combat zone had become some kind of physical casualty by the time the war ended.* There is no accurate count of Iraqi psychological casualties, but it can be safely assumed that the Iraqi soldier's combat experience had not made him eager for more.

Iraq had an extremely inefficient system of manpower allocation, which guaranteed a shortage of good unit-level leaders throughout the army. The best men were concentrated in a few units, and the rest of the army was deprived of potential leaders. The Republican Guard was the living embodiment of this gross inefficiency. During the war, men who could have been sergeants or even junior officers in the regular army were serving as privates in the Republican Guard.

Originally known as the Presidential Guard, the Republican Guard began its life as Saddam Hussein's personal bodyguard. In the beginning, the Presidential Guard consisted of about 15,000 men recruited on the basis of political reliability. All had been born and raised in Tikrit, the village of Saddam's birth. In the mid-1980s, the Presidential Guard began to grow. By the end of the war with Iran, it had grown to a strength of eight well-armed, well-equipped divisions, and it was known as the Republican Guard. The most promising soldiers were sent to these units. They were better paid and received more privileges than their regular army counterparts, and they enjoyed an elite status within the Iraqi Army.

The Republican Guard also enjoyed a reputation in the Western media that it did not deserve. The Guard had some limited success during the war with Iran, but most of the battles that Iraq won during the war were won by the regular army. In fact, even in the Guard's victories there was a consistent pattern of regular army units shedding the blood, and the Guard entering the battle in the late stages and taking most of the credit.

The Guard's soldiers did seem to fight with a greater degree of spirit than their regular army counterparts during the Iran–Iraq War, but even this was misleading. Regular army units were subjected to life in a meat grinder day in and day out. Such conditions dampen morale. The Republican Guard was usually kept safely in reserve, away from the battle. Not surprisingly, when Guardsmen were sent into combat, their morale was a good deal higher than it would have been if they had experienced the daily bloodbath with their regular army comrades.

Guard units were by far the best equipped in the Iraqi Army. A Republican Guard battalion had an authorized strength of 44 tanks, nine more than a regular army battalion. A Guard tank division was authorized 312 tanks and 180 armored personnel carriers. A Guard mechanized infantry division had an authorized strength of 224 tanks and 252 APCs.

Guard units also got the best tanks and APCs, as well as the heaviest self-propelled artillery. Guard infantry platoons had far more combat power than regular infantry platoons. Each Guard platoon had three RPG(Rocket Propelled Grenade)-7 anti-

---

*Two weeks after he invaded Kuwait, to buy a measure of peace on his eastern border, Saddam returned the territory his army had taken from Iran at such great cost.

tank projectile launchers and three light machine-guns.* Regular platoons had only one of each weapon.

The Guard suffered from a serious lack of mobility, however. There were two Republican Guard tank divisions and one mechanized division. Though four of the other five divisions had one battalion of tanks and one battalion of armored fighting vehicles (the Special Forces division had no armor), the soldiers of the other Guard divisions walked or rode in soft-skinned vehicles. This was a problem throughout Iraq's army. Trucks offer almost no cross country capability. Truck-borne soldiers are dependent on roads and bridges to get where they need to go. If the roads are cratered and the bridges are destroyed, the soldiers walk, and have to leave much of their ammunition and heavy equipment behind. In addition, Allied air superiority meant that even if roads and bridges had remained intact, truck convoys would have been bombed and strafed to pieces before they reached their destination. A wheeled column, forced to travel by road, makes an easy target. Once Allied bombing began, there was no way for these Guard units to move without being mauled.

The motorized units also suffered from the manpower distribution system. Within the Republican Guard, the best officers and men went to the three heavy divisions. The Special Forces Division, the mission of which included the defense of sensitive areas like airfields, got the pick of the rest. What was left went to the motorized divisions. This showed in the performance of individual divisions during the Gulf War. The three heavy divisions spearheaded the conquest of Kuwait, supported by Special Forces units, but there was little looting or other criminal behavior by the soldiers of these units. Soldiers from the motorized divisions were involved in looting. The heavy units maintained their cohesion during the ground war. In the case of two of them, cohesion was maintained right up to the moment they were destroyed by VII Corps. Where Special Forces units were encountered, they fought fiercely. The motorized divisions in the path of the 24th Infantry Division offered little resistance, and essentially evaporated. Though thoroughly outclassed, the soldiers of the heavy divisions and the Special Forces Division showed basic tactical and technical competence during the ground war. The soldiers of a motorized unit fighting the 1st Armored Division did not even arm their rocket-propelled grenades before firing them. Finally, many officers and NCOs in the motorized units abandoned their troops, a phenomenon virtually unheard of in the heavy divisions.†

In addition to the Republican Guard's armored forces, Iraq had six regular army tank divisions (3rd, 6th, 10th, 12th, 17th, and 52nd) and three mechanized infantry

---

*The RPG (Rocket Propelled Grenade)-7 is a simple, shoulder-launched weapon that is not very effective against modern tanks, but can be devastating against more thinly armored vehicles. It consists of a light (15 lb.), three foot long cylindrical launcher, onto the end of which a soldier loads a 5 lb. cone-shaped, high explosive, 85mm anti-tank grenade containing rocket propellant. The projectile, which can be launched with impressive accuracy within 300 meters, is capable of penetrating 16 inches of steel.

†After the bombing began, the Iraqi Army began raising five more Republican Guard motorized divisions. None saw action, or were even fully equipped by the war's end. Three (the al-Abed, Mustafa and al-Nidah divisions) were fully manned with untrained soldiers. Two were staffed by cadre, without soldiers. Four of the five divisions were subsequently disbanded. Only the al-Nidah Division was still active as of 1999.

divisions (1st, 5th and 51st) in the Coalition's path. A regular armored division had an authorized strength of 252 tanks and 180 APCs. A regular mechanized division had an authorized strength of 180 tanks and 252 APCs.* These units did not have much of an impact on the fighting during the ground war. While light Iraqi infantry units were overrun and destroyed immediately and almost without a fight, mobility and firepower merely allowed these units to escape destruction for a few hours, and put up minor opposition to Coalition forces.

Though the Iraqi regular army's heavy units ultimately proved little more than a speed bump to advancing Coalition forces, it was a regular army mechanized unit which scored the Iraqi Army's only success of the war. The 5th Mechanized Division's short-lived success at Khafji was the only bright spot in a sea of military disaster. However, the dreadful beating sustained by the unit at Khafji left it without enough combat power to play a significant role during the final Coalition assault. What was left of the division would be destroyed in a series of courageous but futile attacks aimed at closing the 1st Marine Division's breach.

Unlike their Coalition adversaries, who had designed tanks, trained for and developed tactics to combat a Soviet tank threat, Iraq's armored forces had never faced a serious armored threat in their war with Iran. Against masses of badly led Iranian infantry, charging over open ground in broad daylight with no air support, even the poorest units could perform well. Since the Iraqi Army never felt a pressing need to develop its regular armored forces, it accorded them a low priority.

Just as an army cannot afford to have all of its best men concentrated in a few units, it cannot afford to have all of its best equipment concentrated in a few units. Iraq's best tanks and APCs were concentrated in Republican Guard armored and mechanized units. The regular armored and mechanized units were forced to make do with inferior models. Some units acquitted themselves reasonably well by Iraqi standards, their poor equipment notwithstanding. These units might have made better use of the newer equipment than the Republican Guard did.

The underequipment of these units was due partly to a shortage of modern tanks and partly to Saddam's paranoia. Distrustful of the officers in regular tank and mechanized units, he wanted them equipped well enough to inflict some damage on the enemy, but not well enough to turn on him.

The term "Special Forces" was a cause of confusion for many. In the accepted usage of most modern armies, the term denotes hand-picked troops specializing in commando operations, demolitions and guerrilla warfare. Iraqi Special Forces soldiers received no special training. They were simply an expedient response to a difficult problem.

The Iraqi system of manpower distribution ensured that very few quality soldiers would reach infantry units. The Iraqi Army's unarmored infantry units received the lowest caliber of soldier. The cream of Iraq's conscripts went to the Republican Guard. The mechanized and armored units had the pick of what was left. What remained after the supply of quality soldiers was nearly exhausted went to the infantry.

Forced to make do with what amounted to human leftovers, Iraqi infantry units faced serious readiness problems. Units with a low caliber of manpower are neither

---

*The 1st Mechanized Division fought the war with one armored and one (instead of two) mechanized brigade.

aggressive on offense nor steadfast in defense. To solve that problem, infantry division commanders began to select the best men in each division and form them into companies directly answerable to the division commander. Any armored personnel carriers the division had went to these companies. The Iraqi Special Forces were born.

The combat role of Iraqi Special Forces during the Iran–Iraq War was similar to the historical use of shock troops. In defense, these mobile troops worked in conjunction with the division's reserve tank battalion to plug holes in the line as they appeared. On offense, these troops and their tank support exploited holes in the Iranian line as they appeared. The Iraqi Army had never mastered the art of battlefield reconnaissance. It simply threw low quality infantry troops at the enemy. When, after considerable slaughter, these troops stumbled upon an enemy weak point, the reserve task force was called in. The idea worked reasonably well, and by the end of the war with Iran, some divisions had a full battalion of Special Forces troops.

Though there were 40 of them in the Iraqi Army, the regular army's unarmored infantry divisions contributed little in terms of combat power. In addition to low troop caliber, they had almost no firepower to speak of. Infantry divisions were especially short on artillery. With only 54 guns each, these divisions had fewer artillery pieces than Republican Guard and regular armored or mechanized units had. Most of these pieces were smaller caliber (122mm) guns. Iraq's best artillery was not on the Saddam Line.

Each Iraqi motorized or foot-propelled division was supposed to have a reserve tank battalion with 35 tanks. In practice, most divisions never had their full complement. Most infantry divisions began the war with 15–25 tanks. In addition, once the bombing started, units on the Saddam Line lost many of their tanks. For example, the 48th Infantry Division would lose 18 of its 25 tanks to air attack. The 27th Division would lose 8 of 17. Though these units were supposed to have 36 APCs, most infantry divisions had none.

The low caliber of Iraq's line divisions resulted in the backfiring of a perfectly sensible precaution exercised by the Iraqi Army. Soviet doctrine held that offensives or counteroffensives should be conducted by fresh units. It also held, wisely, that unless it was absolutely necessary, front line troops in defensive positions should never play a significant role in an offensive or counteroffensive. To bring these units into such an operation risked its compromise, due to the proximity of these units to the enemy. The Soviets felt that whatever these units might contribute to such an attack was not worth taking a chance on attack plans or soldiers (who might reveal plans or key information under interrogation) being captured in raids. As a result, front line units were kept in the dark about offensive operations as a matter of doctrine.

The Iraqi Army felt the same way, and though the armored and mechanized units backstopping the Saddam Line in the U.S. Marine sector had extensive counterattack plans, front line soldiers knew nothing about them. As a result, faced with violent Marine attacks, and with no reason to believe that help was on the way, the men of these units surrendered en masse. Counterattacking units then moved to their attack positions, only to find U.S. Marines waiting for them.

6

The Battle for Khafji

The morning of 21 January saw the beginning several days of Iraqi probes along the Kuwaiti border. At a Marine observation post known as "OP 6" seven Iraqi soldiers, including two lieutenants, surrendered, telling the Marines at the outpost that 50–60 more Iraqis would be defecting later that night. Since 47 Iraqis had given themselves up at the outpost over the previous three weeks, nothing seemed out of the ordinary. However, this surrender would prove to be part of a ruse.

The OP was located in the small town of Hamaltyat, which had been evacuated a week earlier. At 11:05 that night, atop the most prominent feature at the outpost, a two-story concrete building, Marine sentries spotted 20–25 Iraqis coming toward them. Just before 11:30, when the group was within loudspeaker range, they were ordered to halt. One of the Iraqis shouted to a Marine interpreter that the group wanted to surrender but was concerned about minefields, and needed to know where they were. Suspicious, the Marine NCO in charge of the post had the interpreter tell the Iraqis that they had five minutes to surrender. Seconds later, the Iraqis launched an assault on the OP from three directions with machine-guns, assault rifles and rocket-propelled grenades.

The OP's garrison of eight Marines responded, and after a violent 15-minute firefight, the Marine interpreter heard some of the Iraqis shouting orders to rally at an assembly area. The Marines took advantage of the Iraqi disorganization to make good their escape shortly after midnight. At 2:30 a.m., with the eight men of the OP 6 garrison acting as guides, a Marine light armored infantry company entered the OP and found it abandoned. The Marines would learn from prisoners several days later that the Iraqi force had been a commando company from the 36th Infantry Division and had numbered 115 men, five of whom had been killed in the firefight.

Farther west, the U.S. Army made contact with the Iraqis on the 22nd, when a Saudi border patrol called for help after running into a platoon of Iraqi infantry. A platoon of Bradleys from Col. Douglas Starr's 3rd Armored Cavalry Regiment responded to the call, accompanied by Starr. In the exchange, which marked the combat debut of the Bradley Fighting Vehicle, the Iraqis were driven off after losing several dead and six prisoners. The fighting cost the Saudis three wounded and the Americans two wounded.

Meanwhile, north of Khafji, three Iraqis claiming to be defectors made their way to a Marine outpost on the coast, and told their captors that all of their officers had deserted them. CENTCOM was deeply suspicious. Its intelligence indicated that units directly to the north were in good order. There was no sign that the units were leaderless. CENTCOM began to strongly suspect that the Iraqis were up to something.

On 26 January, there was a radio intercept proposing a commander's conference in the Iraqi III Corps sector. The exact location was not given in the transmission, and the meeting was to take place in two hours. Back in Washington, analysts grabbed every bit of photo imagery they had on the area and frantically looked for a site that might be suitable for such a meeting. Finally, they found a photo of a large building and guessed that this might be the place. Targeting instructions were immediately phoned to Air Force targeteers in Riyadh as the photo was sent by fax. Luckily, the targeteers had two F-111Fs in the area, fully loaded with bombs. The bombers overflew the building at high altitude. They found it lit at one end and surrounded by military and civilian vehicles. This looked like a meeting. The bombers swooped down and destroyed the building and many of the vehicles surrounding it. Unfortunately, the III Corps' commander was not at the meeting, but several of his most important officers had been killed in the strike.*

As it turned out, III Corps was planning an offensive. Staggered by the devastation visited upon his armed forces, Saddam Hussein had ordered his army to launch an offensive while it still had the means to do so. Saddam reasoned that if his army could inflict a defeat on Coalition ground forces, he might reap benefits out of proportion to the size of the victory. Perhaps, stung psychologically from an embarrassing defeat, Allied forces might think twice about launching an invasion of Kuwait or Iraq, and would negotiate a settlement on Saddam's terms. Or, perhaps they would react to their humiliation by attempting to launch their invasion prematurely. Either way, Saddam would benefit. Even if the offensive failed, Saddam surmised, he might bag a few hundred prisoners to use as hostages. At least the army he had built and maintained at such vast expense would be doing something other than getting bombed.

What became known as the "Battle of Khafji" was actually a number of separate engagements involving U.S. Marines and Saudi and Qatari forces from 29 January to 1 February. The Iraqis were supposed to begin a coordinated attack on the night of 29 January. The Republican Guard was too far away from Coalition forces to mount an attack, and Saddam was saving it for later. The only heavy units that were in position to attack Coalition forces immediately were the 5th Mechanized and the 3rd Armored divisions from III Corps. Elements of the 3rd Armored Division would hit the Marines in the west while units from the 5th Mechanized Division launched an assault in the east. Unfortunately for the Iraqis, Coalition air power disrupted the plan. The destruction of command and control facilities (like the III Corps meeting site) made it difficult for orders to be disseminated throughout the attacking units. Bombing and strafing also made it difficult for Iraqi armor to assemble. Only parts of the forces which were supposed to attack were ready to do so at H-Hour.

The main Marine engagements were fought between nightfall of the 29th and dawn of the 30th. On 29 January, the Marines still had no major troop concentrations

---

*On 31 January, Kuwaiti resistance reported that another high-level meeting was taking place in a building at a former Kuwaiti military base near the coast. At about 7:30 p.m., two Marine Intruders attacked the building with laser-guided bombs. The III Corps' commander was apparently killed.

along the border with Kuwait, only a screening force. They established nine observation posts (OPs), numbered 1 through 9. The OPs were manned by reconnaissance teams, and OPs 1 through 8 were backed by two battalions of mobile Marine light armored infantry. OP 9, outside the Marines' western boundary, was the U.S. Army's responsibility. The lightly defended OPs were essentially an early warning system for the main body, still well to the south. OPs 4, 5 and 6 on the western end of the Marine line were the responsibility of the 1st Marine Division. OPs 1, 2, 3, 7 and 8 belonged to the 2nd Marine Division.* The men on the OPs were alerted to the possibility of a night attack by Iraqi attempts to jam their radios at dusk on the 29th.

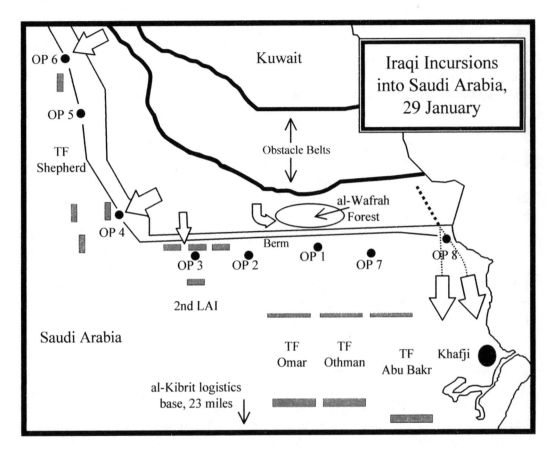

A series of probes was launched across the Saudi–Kuwaiti border, about 30 miles west of Khafji, to the west of the cultivated area known as the "al-Wafra Forest." This area was defended by the 2nd LAI (Light Armored Infantry) Battalion, under the command of Lt.Col. Keith Holcomb.

At 10:50 p.m., Company C, 2nd LAI, covering OP 2 on the battalion's right flank, reported that it had fired upon a force of about 30 Iraqi armored vehicles at long range. The force had been attempting to enter Saudi territory to the company's northeast. After taking fire from Company C, the Iraqi force withdrew.

---

*OPs were referred to by number in radio traffic. The Marines, though relatively sure that the Iraqis could not intercept and decrypt their messages, could not take this for granted. The OPs were therefore not consecutively numbered. That way, if the Iraqis somehow discovered the designation of one or two OPs, they would not be able to deduce the designation of the rest.

At OP 3, shortly before midnight, Corporal Edmund Willis of Company A, 2nd LAI, scored the 2nd Marine Division's first hit of the war, disabling a T-62 with a TOW missile from over 3,000 meters as it emerged from a gap in the berm that ran along the Saudi–Kuwaiti border. The tanks accompanying the stricken tank fled. Just before two, a group of about 20 vehicles appeared. Willis spotted an Iraqi tank moving in the same area as the disabled tank. Another of Willis' TOW missiles scored another direct hit. Willis thought he had killed a second tank. In fact, it was a second strike on the same tank, which the Iraqis had been attempting to recover. As soon as the Iraqis began to tow the tank away, the second TOW impacted on the crippled tank's front slope. The remainder of the Iraqi force withdrew.

Iraqi activity in this area was a cause of serious concern to the Marines. It appeared that the Iraqis might be attempting to raid and destroy the al-Kibrit logistics base, at which the Marines had been stockpiling supplies for the coming attack on Kuwait. The possibility was dealt with by calling in air attacks on the al-Wafra Forest to break up the Iraqi attacks before they formed. Meanwhile, a company of tanks from the 1st (Tiger) Brigade of the Army's 2nd Armored Division was sent to bolster the force defending the al-Kibrit base.

The rest of the night passed without any more Iraqi probing of the berm in 2nd LAI's sector. The only direct fire the 2nd LAI took came just after 1 a.m. on the 30th, when Saudi forces began firing over the battalion's positions. This was reported to the 2nd Marine Division's Operations Officer, Col. Ronald Richard. After a quick call to the Saudis, order was restored.

On the 30th, the division would stiffen the defenses in front of the al-Kibrit base by moving two mechanized battalions, the 1st Battalion, 6th Marines and the 2nd Battalion, 2nd Marines (1/6 and 2/2) and an artillery battalion into positions behind 2nd LAI.* The only major excitement that night would be a warning of an imminent Iraqi chemical strike which never materialized. There were no ground encounters with the Iraqis in the Wafra Forest, who would sustain two days of periodic Marine air attacks.

The largest Marine battles were fought to the west, by Task Force Shepherd, which consisted of two companies from the 1st LAI Battalion and two companies from the 3rd LAI. The Marines had recently turned up the pressure on Iraqi units in the area. On the 26th, the 1st Division had launched a combined arms raid on an Iraqi brigade headquarters at an abandoned border police post. Two Marine artillery batteries dropped Dual Purpose, Improved Conventional Munition (bomblet) rounds on the headquarters, killing several Iraqis, destroying three soft-skinned vehicles and driving off two others. One of these vehicles took a wrong turn and was destroyed by Marine light armor screening for the artillery. The artillery then wiped out an Iraqi artillery battery, while F/A-18s dropped Rockeye cluster bombs on the police post to ensure its destruction. Though no Marines were killed by Iraqi fire during the operation, there were three deaths resulting from a vehicle accident.

OP 4, located at "the elbow," about 50 miles west of Khafji, was the most strategically important of the three observation posts under 1st Division control. Formerly the As-Zabr Police Post, OP 4 was a small compound consisting of a brownstone main building with two towers, a small, white concrete out-building which housed the power generator, and a water tower. It was manned by 2nd Platoon, Company

---

*The terms "6th Marines" and "2nd Marines" refer to Marine regiments.

A, 1st Reconnaissance Battalion. The platoon leader and six Marines occupied the main building. There were also two eight-man observation posts, one about 200 meters to the north of the complex and another about 300 meters to the south.

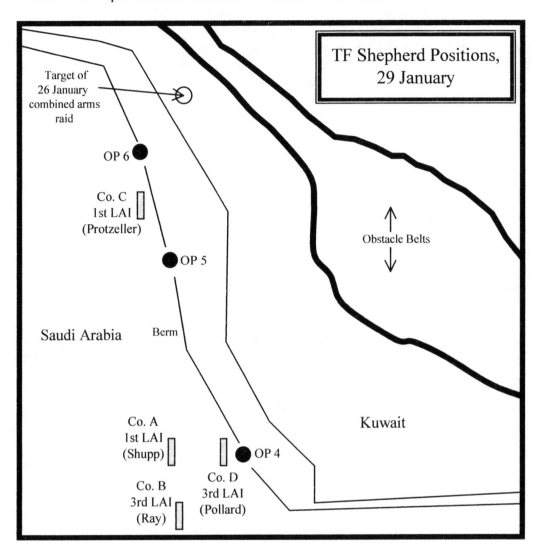

Backing up OP 4 were three companies of Marine light armored infantry. Directly behind the station was Company D, 3rd LAI. The company had just arrived on its position that day, having moved from behind OPs 5 and 6. After coordinating with the Marines at OP 4, Capt. Roger Pollard, Company D's commander, moved his 20 Light Armored Vehicles (thirteen mounting 25mm cannon and seven mounting TOW missile launchers) to a slight rise in the terrain, behind the compound. After being relieved at its position behind OP 4 by Company D, Company B, 3rd LAI Battalion, commanded by Capt. Eddie Ray, was ordered to take up positions to the south. Capt. Michael Shupp's Company A, 1st LAI Battalion was posted about two miles west of OP 4.

Neither Maj.Gen. Myatt, commander of the 1st Marine Division, nor Lt.Col. Clifford Myers, commander of the defending force, dubbed "Task Force Shepherd" had any intention of trying to stop a major Iraqi thrust at the border. In such an event, Myers wanted his four companies (Company C, 1st LAI Battalion was covering OPs 5 and 6) to make a fighting withdrawal. Using their TOW missiles and 25mm chain-guns, supported by aircraft and artillery, they would buy time for the main force to arrive.

The Battle for OP 4 began just before 8 p.m. on 29 January. Following a fairly successful Iraqi jamming effort, five T-62 tanks approached the compound, followed by several BMPs.* The five tanks were the lead element of a force of 30–50 armored vehicles. The tanks were attacked by an F/A-18 without effect and continued their advance on the compound. When they were within small arms range of OP 4's forward eight-man observation post, they were engaged with rifle-launched grenades and 66mm LAW (Light Anti-tank Weapon) rockets. Two hits from LAW rockets immobilized one tank.†

The Iraqis responded by firing main gun rounds into the main building. Luckily for the Marines inside, the ill-trained Iraqi tank gunners fired solid-shot penetrator rounds instead of high explosive anti-tank (HEAT) rounds. While the solid-shot rounds ripped through the walls and caused small chunks of masonry to fly about, HEAT rounds would probably have killed most of the building's occupants.

Three T-55s now joined the fray. With the Iraqi tanks on the very edge of the compound, and the Marines out of LAWs, the platoon leader decided to withdraw his troops. The platoon pulled back and huddled behind a horseshoe-shaped berm to the rear of the compound as Iraqi tank rounds ripped into the berm or whizzed over their heads.

Company D raced to the rescue. Capt. Pollard had seen that the Iraqi fire had pinned down the recon platoon. He decided to attack the Iraqis before they had a chance to finish off the platoon. When the Light Armored Vehicles were within chain-gun range of the Iraqis, they opened up with a hail of 25mm fire, followed by a volley of TOW missiles, which destroyed an Iraqi tank. Company D's counterattack knocked the Iraqis off balance, and gave the recon platoon a chance to make its escape.

Once the recon platoon was clear, Pollard consolidated his vehicles and took stock of the situation. One of his own LAVs had been mistakenly engaged and destroyed by a TOW from another LAV. As a result of the accident, he temporarily suspended further launches of TOW missiles. If any more Marine vehicles were going to be hit, they would be hit by far less lethal 25mm chain-gun rounds. For the time being, Pollard used his TOW LAVs as spotters.

When A-10s arrived to make strafing runs, the Iraqi assault began to peter out. Some Iraqi crews stopped where they were. Others panicked. Two tanks came under air attack, ran into the berm and became bogged down. After an A-10 laced the engine of one of the vehicles with 30mm rounds, both crews abandoned the tanks.‡

Several Iraqi tanks attempted to sneak around Company D's right flank. Pollard's LAVs opened fire as he called for more air support. Two A-10s set a course for his position. At 10:30 p.m., the pilot in the lead plane radioed ahead, saying that due to poor visibility, he would drop a flare while the second plane made its run. Unfortunately,

---

*Throughout the fighting in the west, no radio communications would be received from higher headquarters because of the jamming. Myers would find out later that division headquarters had been barely able to monitor Shepherd's transmissions and follow the fighting, but had been unable to get its transmissions through to Shepherd.

†The LAW rockets did not destroy the tank. It was finished off later by an A-10.

‡Near one of the tanks was a dead Iraqi with a gunshot wound in his head. He had been executed by one of his fellow crew members.

when the flare was dropped, it landed behind a Marine LAV-25. The second pilot took aim at what he thought was an Iraqi armored vehicle and released a Maverick heat-seeking air-to-ground missile. The missile hit the rear of the vehicle. Seven of the eight Marines inside the vehicle were killed instantly. Despite suffering their second friendly fire incident of the night, the men of Company D kept up their fire and drove the Iraqi tanks off. By 10:50, the fighting was over —temporarily.

Company C, 1st LAI Battalion, under Capt. Thomas Protzeller, had taken up positions overlooking OPs 5 and 6, which were situated north of OP 4. At 1:10 on the morning of 30 January, Iraqi high explosive and illumination rounds began bursting on and over the abandoned OP 6. A half-hour later, two sections of Iraqi APCs, totaling about a dozen, approached the OP. As Capt. Protzeller watched through his night vision goggles, the troops from the two units dismounted and engaged in a firefight with each other in the darkness. After about 10 minutes, in which apparently no Iraqis were killed, the Iraqi commander regained control of his soldiers and the Iraqis occupied OP 6 as the APCs withdrew to the desert to await the expected American counterattack.

Air strikes were immediately called in on the APCs, which fled to the north. As the aircraft chased the Iraqi APCs, Company C moved to within 700 meters of OP 6 and began hammering the Iraqi occupiers with direct fire. Soonafter, the company came under attack by about 20 Iraqi armored vehicles. The Marines responded with 11 TOW missiles, destroying 11 Iraqi vehicles. The dismounted occupiers of OP 6 withdrew, as surviving Iraqi vehicles fled north, chased by the Air Force. Thus ended the battle at OP 6, in which Company C sustained no casualties.

Back at OP 4, Company D had been ordered to withdraw following the destruction of the second LAV. Lt.Col. Myers moved Company A toward OP 4 to take its place. On the way, Capt. Shupp's men would also search for survivors from the two stricken LAVs. Movement was slow and careful. Company A, not wanting to be mistakenly attacked by American aircraft or artillery, spent a great deal of time coordinating with air and artillery as it moved. This turned out to be wise, as either A or D companies were mistakenly reported as a possible enemy force a total of five times by Company B, which was monitoring the developing battle. Had the coordination been less careful, it is possible that one of these sightings would have resulted in a fratricidal air or artillery strike. After two hours, at about 1 a.m., Company A established a defensive line in Company D's former position.

Slightly after 4 a.m., Iraqi activity picked up again. As Company A continued to search for survivors from the two wrecked LAVs, Iraqi shells began to impact around OP 4. The fire was inaccurate, and lasted only 10 minutes. During the barrage, Shupp's men found the LAV which had been destroyed by the A-10. Miraculously, the driver was still alive.

While Company A's medics treated the driver (who would fully recover), the Iraqis began massing for another attack. A volley of TOW missiles and an attack by a Marine Cobra destroyed three more tanks and stopped the Iraqi thrust before it could form. As the Iraqis were dodging missiles, one of Capt. Shupp's search teams found the remains of the other Company D LAV. From the condition of the wreckage, it was obvious that none of the four crewmen had survived.

For the next hour and a half, as Cobras arrived at the position, Shupp directed their attacks on the Iraqis to the north of the OP. By 7 a.m., three more Iraqi tanks had been disabled, and the last of the Cobras headed for home. As soon as the last section of Cobras left, however, 18 more Iraqi tanks showed up. Capt. Shupp decided to effect a fighting withdrawal beyond the range of the Iraqi tank guns. As Company A pulled back, four A-10s and two F/A-18s arrived, and began to bomb and strafe the Iraqi force. For the next hour, the combination of air attacks and LAV-launched TOW missiles kept the Iraqis well away from OP 4. At about 8:30, the attack broke and the Iraqis headed north. They were not allowed to leave quietly. Companies B and D joined Company A, and over the next two hours, all three companies launched TOW missiles and called in artillery on the fleeing Iraqi tanks.

By 10:30, all was quiet around the three OPs. The Iraqis had lost 22 tanks and another dozen APCs. Two other tanks had been abandoned intact. There were about 100 Iraqi casualties, and a few dozen Iraqis were captured, including the force's commander. The commander revealed that he had ordered another unit to follow his advance, but that the unit had run away from the battle. Over the next few days, several hundred more Iraqi foot soldiers, abandoned by their armor, made their way toward the Marines to surrender.

While the Marines were fighting in the west, an Iraqi mechanized infantry brigade crossed the border north of Khafji. On the beach, about a mile south of the border, stood OP 8. About a mile south of the ANGLICO (Air-Naval Gunfire Liaison Company) and Navy SEAL teams in the OP was a desalination plant manned by Navy SEALs, members of Marine Recon and Green Berets from the 5th Special Forces Group. Between observers at OP 8 and the garrison of the desalination plant, there were 34 Americans north of Khafji. Also in the border area were scouts from the 2nd (King Abdul Aziz) Saudi Arabian National Guard (SANG) Brigade.

The area north of Khafji had been active since 17 January. As soon as the Coalition started bombing Iraq, Iraq started shelling Saudi Arabia. At 2:45 on the morning of the 17th, the 1st Security Reconnaissance Intelligence Group at OP 8 reported that it was being shelled intensely. A flight of five Marine helicopters, four Cobras and a UH-1B Huey scout, responded. After the Huey had located the positions of the Iraqi forward observers, the Cobras attacked. Flying through descending Iraqi artillery rounds, the Cobras directed a stream of rockets at the Iraqi positions, killing several observers and causing the rest to stop spotting and seek shelter. Now without spotters, the Iraqi fire tailed off sharply. Eventually, the Iraqi gunners were themselves spotted by an OV-10A Bronco observation plane, which directed the Cobras and a flight of Marine Harriers onto the offending batteries. With the guns silenced, the rest of the night passed quietly on OP 8.

The next day, Cobras attacked and destroyed another observation post. They then turned their attention to an Iraqi mortar position, destroying it, its ammunition stockpile and the trucks supplying the position.

On 20 January, the Marines hit back again. During the first days of the air war, the Marines on OP 8 had noticed that each afternoon, Iraqi officers would sit drinking coffee and tea on the balcony of a beachside hotel just inside the border, as Allied attack planes flew over them, headed for other targets. On the 20th, the team manning the post directed an air strike against the hotel while the Iraqis were gathered on the balcony. A cluster bomb wiped out the tea drinkers.

The Iraqis responded by sneaking a battery of ASTROS (Artillery SaTuration ROcket System) II multiple rocket launchers toward the border that night and shooting a few rockets at the desalination plant. The battery tried the same thing on the following night. This time the Marines were ready. The spotters on OP 8 had artillery standing by, and when the Iraqi battery moved forward just after midnight, it was destroyed by Marine artillery.

On the 26th, the same team of spotters directed a Marine Harrier strike on an Iraqi barracks. Cluster bombs wrecked the building. Then, as Iraqi soldiers pulled corpses from the rubble, another Harrier strike went in. In the two raids, the Iraqis lost over a hundred dead and wounded. Two days later, Marine artillery followed up with another raid on Iraqi troops 10 miles inland.

Also on the 28th, two batteries of towed 155mm howitzers from the 2nd SANG's field artillery battalion conducted a raid. Firing Rocket Assisted Projectiles (RAPs), the 12 Saudi guns destroyed an Iraqi air defense site.

The 29th saw a marked increase in Iraqi activity in the coastal area. The occupants of OP 8 noted a good deal of traffic along the coastal highway, and on the east–west road which ran into the al-Wafra Forest. When some two dozen heavy equipment transporters were destroyed by Harriers along the east–west road, Iraqi soldiers cleared the road under fire. The incidents along the road convinced the commander of the forward surveillance force, Marine Lt.Col. Richard Barry, that the Iraqis were mounting a major operation that night. The traffic along the road had been a hint. The Iraqis exposing themselves to Marine ground attack aircraft to clear the road indicated a pressing need to keep the road open, and was a dead giveaway.

As if more confirmation was needed, at 8 p.m., the Iraqis fired illumination rounds over the desalination plant, the first time that had happened. Barry had concluded that the al-Wafra attack would be a feint, and the main Iraqi effort would be toward Khafji. The illumination rounds were an indication to Barry that the main effort was about to begin, and that it was time for him to get his men out. Barry led his force to a fallback position, a police station to the south.

Almost as soon as the force reached the police station, it saw Iraqi tanks from a flanking force rumbling past it in the distance. This armored force seemed to come out of nowhere. In an impressive display of tactical ability, the Khafji assault force had picked its way through the border defenses, with no headlights and in almost total radio silence. It had then split, with one half of the force making for Khafji down the coastal road and the other flanking the town to the west. The Marines, Green Berets and SEALs made a hasty retreat as bullets and tank rounds flew over their heads.

The lack of coordination in the attack turned out to be a lucky break for the Iraqis. When the Iraqi attack kicked off in the west at about 8 p.m., it appeared to be an assault on the al-Kibrit logistics base. As a result, Lt.Gen. Walter Boomer, I MEF commander, diverted most of his fixed-wing air assets to the west, leaving very little air support available for the defense of Khafji when it was attacked later. The Air Force also believed that the attack on Khafji was a feint, and that the town was in little danger. It therefore had most of its assets employed elsewhere. Without air support, the Saudis and Americans had no choice but to abandon Khafji.

Khafji, a Saudi resort town six miles from the border, controlled the main coastal highway running between Kuwait City and northeast Saudi Arabia. The town's 45,000 residents had been evacuated on 17 January to keep them out of Iraqi artillery range.

The four Saudi task forces of the Eastern Province Area Command (EPAC) were also stationed out of Iraqi artillery range. Task Force Omar, the westernmost, consisted of the 10th Royal Saudi Land Forces (RSLF) Mechanized Brigade with an Omani infantry battalion. It was stationed well inland, on the right flank of the Marines' screen line. To its right was Task Force Othman, which was made up of the 8th RSLF Mechanized Brigade with attached companies of Bahraini and Free Kuwaiti infantry. Guarding the coast was Task Force Abu Bakr, the 2nd Saudi Arabian National Guard (SANG) Mechanized Brigade and a Qatari mechanized infantry battalion. The coastal road south of Khafji was blocked by Task Force Tariq (two Saudi Marine battalions, a Moroccan infantry regiment and two Senegalese infantry companies).[*]

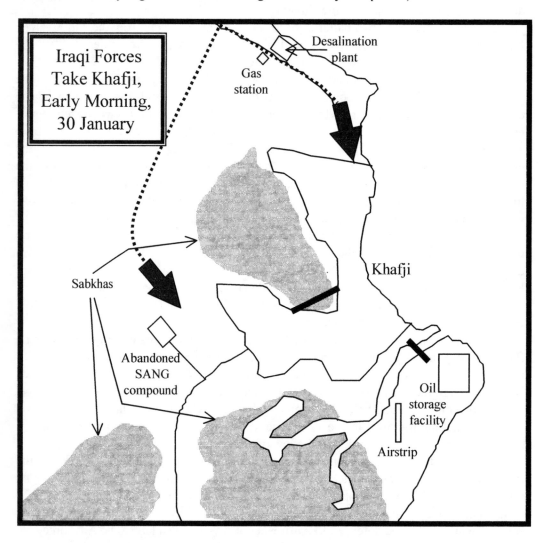

The Saudis reacted quickly to the Iraqi incursion. The Saudi forward commander, Maj.Gen. Sultan 'Adi al-Mutairi, gathered an armored reconnaissance force, taking a tank company from Task Force Othman and a Qatari tank company and anti-tank missile platoon from Task Force Abu Bakr.

The force, personally led by Maj.Gen. Sultan, might have been destroyed before it reached the town if not for the good judgment of a Marine Cobra squadron

---

[*]Abu Bakr, Othman and Omar were the three successors to the prophet Mohammed as leaders of Islam. Tariq bin Ziyad was the Moorish conqueror of Spain.

commander. Lt.Col. Mike Kurth, in a Huey outfitted with special night vision equipment, had arrived over the town with eight Cobras. In the confusion that characterized that night's activities, Marine air controllers, unaware of Sultan's mission, had told Kurth that there were no friendly forces in Khafji, and that his Cobras were cleared to fire on any formation they saw in or around the town. Looking for an extra measure of certainty before authorizing an attack, Kurth flew close enough to Sultan's force to recognize that the tanks were American-made M-60s, which the Iraqis did not have.

Meanwhile, unaware that the Iraqis had taken Khafji, the Saudis and Qataris were headed straight for the town. Kurth was able to make contact with the force, and inform Sultan that the Iraqis were in possession of Khafji. Sultan adjusted his tactics accordingly.

The reconnaissance force probed the northern approaches to the town just before dawn on the 30th, encountering a column of about a dozen armored vehicles. After four Iraqi tanks were destroyed in a six-minute exchange with the Qataris, 21 Iraqis abandoned their vehicles and surrendered. The Saudis were told that there were two Iraqi battalions in Khafji, one armored and one mechanized.

Shortly after the contact with Sultan's recon force, Kurth's Cobras attacked a column on the northwest approach to Khafji, destroying six vehicles. Realizing that the Iraqis were trapped, that his Cobras were not well-equipped for night fighting, and wishing to avoid unnecessary losses, Kurth discontinued gunship attacks for the night.

Fixed-wing aircraft then took over the battle. Throughout the 30th, Coalition air power was active north of the border. Coalition aircraft dropped tons of anti-armor mines to slow Iraqi armor down. B-52s cruised roads, looking for convoys to bomb.* Then, carrier-based aircraft dropped cluster and guided bombs. Close behind were Air Force jets firing Maverick missiles and dropping more cluster bombs. The follow-on forces abandoned their attempt to reinforce the Iraqis in Khafji.

That night, the Air Force lost an AC-130 Spectre gunship. There is only one Spectre Gunship squadron in the Air Force, the 16th Special Operations Squadron, which operates out of Hurlburt Field in Florida. Four Spectres from the 16th S.O.S. saw service during the Gulf War. Three were involved in the Battle of Khafji.

The Spectre is a modified C-130 cargo plane that packs a devastating punch. Each gunship carries a crew of five officers and nine enlisted men. It also carries two 20mm gatling-type miniguns. Each 20mm fires at a rate of about 2,500 rounds per minute. In practice, however, the miniguns are fired in 8–10 second bursts, since firing continuously for one minute would waste ammunition and cause the guns' barrels to overheat. There is also a 40mm gun, which is basically a modified rapid fire World War II vintage anti-aircraft gun. It fires 100 rounds per minute. The Spectre also carries a 105mm cannon that fires 33 lb. shells at a rate of about six per minute. This is by far the heaviest gun carried on any aircraft in the world.

The slow-flying Spectre is too vulnerable to ground fire to be operated safely during daylight. The Spectre is therefore used almost exclusively at night, and it carries a

---

*Though tons of bombs were dropped, little damage was done by the B-52s. They dropped their bombs from extremely high altitude, and accuracy suffered. In addition, many of the bombs were dropped on false targets picked up by JSTARS. For example, in one instance, the reported destruction of a column of 80 armored vehicles during this period was found after G-Day to have been a raid on a long stretch of densely packed concertina wire.

variety of sophisticated night vision devices and sensors. The Spectre is accurate because its gun systems work with a ballistic computer, which adjusts sights automatically to allow for things like speed and wind drift. The Spectre is also usually required to fight at low altitudes, to support small groups of soldiers in close contact with the enemy without endangering those troops, so it usually fires at its targets from point-blank range.

In combat, the Spectre often circles its target in a counterclockwise direction. All of the plane's guns are on the port (left) side of the aircraft, so when it circles, all of the Spectre's weapons can fire continuously on the target in the center of the circle. There is one hazard in this maneuver, however. A circle is a predictable pattern. If the plane circles one time too many, an anti-aircraft weapon that the Spectre crew does not see can hit it.

The Spectre that was lost had been engaging targets along the coastal road, paying particular attention to mobile anti-aircraft weapons. It had just completed its final engagement shortly before dawn on 31 January, and was turning to head for its base when it was shot down by an SA-8 missile over the coast of Kuwait, with the loss of all fourteen crewmen. It is almost impossible for crewmen to exit a stricken AC-130, so there are generally no survivors when one crashes.[*]

Meanwhile, Khafji's Iraqi occupiers were too busy looting the town to notice that they were being watched. Hidden in the upper floors of an apartment building were twelve Marine artillery spotters who had been trapped in Khafji. For the next day and a half, they would radio back information about Iraqi troop movements and call in artillery strikes on Iraqi armor.

When the Iraqis first took the town, the spotters had no artillery to call upon. Taken by surprise, most U.S. Marine units were too far south to respond immediately to the Iraqi attack. The nearest infantry unit, the 3rd Marine Regiment, was a dismounted unit, and lacked the transport to move it north immediately. The artillery unit supporting 3rd Marines did have transport, though. With 5-ton trucks to tow its 155mm guns, the 1st Battalion, 12th Marine Regiment had the transport it needed to get it into the battle. The battalion's commander, Lt.Col. Robert Rivers, immediately went forward to scout out positions for his guns, then ordered his unit north.

The first guns to arrive were those of C Battery, commanded by Capt. Stephen Morgan. Morgan's battery, after picking its way through retreating Saudi forces along the coastal highway, was directed by Rivers to positions about four miles south of Khafji. There, it established radio contact with the trapped Marine spotters.

Lt.Gen. Prince Khaled bin Sultan, commander of the Saudi Armed Forces (as well as all other Arab forces in the Gulf War), became aware of the plight of the two Marine teams on the afternoon of the 30th. He immediately directed Maj.Gen. Sultan to retrieve the spotters and retake the town. Most of the fighting would be done by the men of the 2nd (King Abdul Aziz) Brigade of the SANG under Colonel Turki al-Firmi.

Unlike members of the National Guard in the United States, Saudi National Guardsmen are full-time soldiers. In Saudi Arabia, there are two military establishments, the SANG and the MODA (Ministry of Defense and Aviation), of which the RSLF is the ground forces arm. The National Guard is primarily an internal security force with a

---

[*]After this shootdown, Spectre flights over enemy-held territory were suspended until the ground war was almost over.

secondary combat mission. The capital is garrisoned by National Guardsmen, as is every major industrial or oil installation in the country. Until Iraq invaded Kuwait, only SANG troops were stationed in the Eastern province, where most of the kingdom's industry and oil resources are located.

The National Guard does its recruiting exclusively among the descendants of the nomadic Bedouin, the kingdom's spiritual equivalent to the cowboys who roamed the American west. Therefore, National Guardsmen have more of a "rough rider" image than their RSLF counterparts.

For most of the kingdom's modern history, smugglers and internal nuisances have been more of a problem than the threat of invasion by a neighboring country. As a result, the National Guard has traditionally been the more important of the two ground establishments. With 56,000 men, it has also been the larger of the two organizations. The RSLF's peacetime strength was about 35,000, though during the crisis it had grown to over 50,000. With just over 5,000 men, brigades in the Saudi National Guard are relatively large. They contain four maneuver battalions instead of the three usually found in Western brigades. The 2nd SANG Brigade was made up of the 5th, 6th, 7th and 8th battalions.

The SANG's basic combat vehicle was the Cadillac-Gage V-150 armored car, which comes in 12 different variants, including TOW missile launcher, 90mm gun and APC versions. These wheeled vehicles are fast, maneuverable and mechanically reliable. However, the V-150 is not particularly well-armored, so it is not a vehicle to be used in armored charges. If casualties are to be kept down, V-150s must be employed skillfully.

Just after 4 p.m. on the 30th, Lt.Col. Hamid Moktar, commander of the 7th Battalion, 2nd SANG, received orders to retake the town. Surrounding the town were a number of large *sabkhas*, areas of salt marsh which will not support vehicular traffic. The sabkhas limited the number of avenues by which the Saudis might attack the town, giving the Iraqis an advantage.

For the attack, Hamid's battalion would be reinforced by two companies of Qatari tanks. The attack plan called for two of Hamid's companies to attack along the road into the western part of town while his third company stood by in reserve. Each of the attacking companies would be supported by a company of Qatari tanks.

At 11 p.m., Hamid's task force attacked. As it approached the edge of the town over open ground, the task force was met by a hail of bullets, which flattened the tires of several V-150s and stopped the attack in its tracks. The intensity of the Iraqi fire came as a complete surprise to Hamid's men. The 2nd SANG's commanders and staff officers were still under the impression that there was slightly more than a company of Iraqis in the town. The RSLF had been aware since that morning that a significant Iraqi force had occupied Khafji, but in the confusion, that information had not been passed on. The two forces engaged in a violent firefight until 3:20 in the morning. Because of the tremendous volume of ammunition expended during the firefight, the task force was forced to break off the engagement and pull back for ammunition resupply. Hamid ordered his force to fall back to the SANG compound, which had been abandoned during the early weeks of the air war.

Unfortunately, the convoy carrying the ammunition missed its link-up point and wandered toward Khafji. Though the force miraculously escaped without sustaining any casualties, two vehicles were destroyed, with the loss of over 50 TOW missiles, before the convoy reversed and linked up with Hamid's task force.

By this time, the Iraqi inhabitants of Khafji had consolidated, but their situation was becoming more and more tenuous. JSTARS had already reported the virtual cessation of Iraqi activity north of the border, telling the Marines and the Saudis that the Iraqis in Khafji were on their own. By dawn on the 31st, the Iraqis had also begun to realize that they were alone, and their morale began to sag. All they could do at that point was await the next Allied assault.

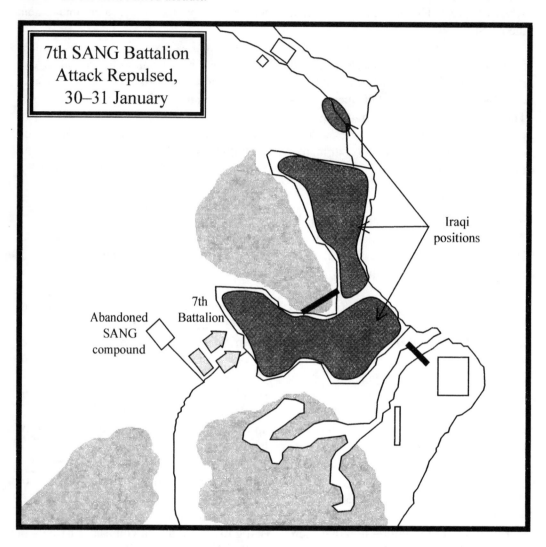

7th SANG Battalion
Attack Repulsed,
30–31 January

Iraqi positions

Abandoned SANG compound

7th Battalion

Now aware that there was a significant Iraqi force in Khafji, Col. Turki ordered the 6th and 8th battalions to assign one company each to the 7th Battalion. Further reinforced, Hamid's force was ordered to renew its attack on the morning of the 31st. The attack was to be coordinated with attacks by the 5th SANG Battalion to the north of the town, and an RSLF tank battalion which was to drive into the town on Hamid's northern flank. Meanwhile, the 8th Battalion, 2nd SANG, reinforced by a Qatari tank company and anti-tank missile platoon from the 6th SANG Battalion, would drive northward, push into the town, then take its place on the 7th Battalion's southern flank.

The attack would begin with a 15-minute Marine artillery barrage, and Marine attack helicopters would cover the assault, but on the ground it would be an entirely Arab operation. Marine ground units were available to assist them, but the Saudis and Qataris considered the recapture of the town a matter of national honor, and insisted on retaking the town themselves.

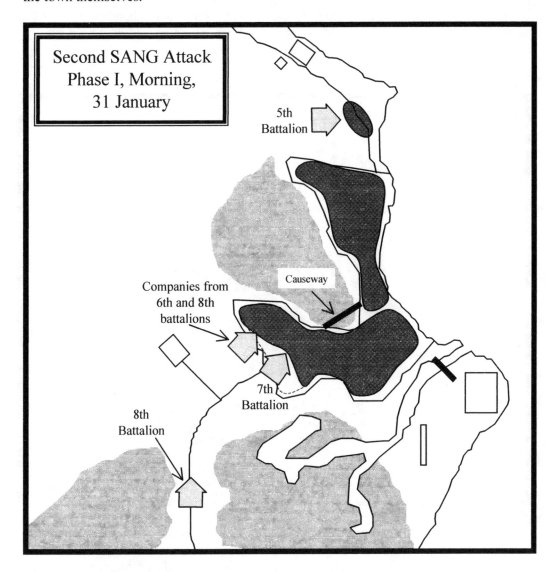

The assault started off badly. Hamid had planned on attacking with his own three companies and the attached Qatari armor, keeping the two attached companies from the 6th and 8th SANG battalions as a reserve. However, the RSLF tank battalion was not ready to attack when the assault force moved out. Hamid was forced to assign its mission to his reserve companies.

At ten, the 5th Battalion hit a company-sized element of Iraqi armor on the coastal road north of Khafji. In the ensuing half-hour firefight, the Iraqis lost 13 armored vehicles destroyed and another six captured without inflicting a single casualty on the Saudis. Some of the tanks had been fitted with Iraqi-manufactured add-on armor. However, since the armor was nothing more than large, heavy blocks of steel, it did little more than weigh down the vehicles. TOW missiles were able to knock out these tanks with relative ease.

When the Iraqis attempted to fall back and regroup, they were hammered by air and artillery strikes. After sustaining heavy losses and losing 116 prisoners, the remainder of the force fled. Unfortunately, a handful of Saudi vehicles gave chase and lost two men killed and five wounded when they were accidentally bombed by a mixed package of U.S. and Qatari fighter-bombers. After rounding up its prisoners and evacuating its wounded, the 5th Battalion pulled back to positions north of the SANG compound.

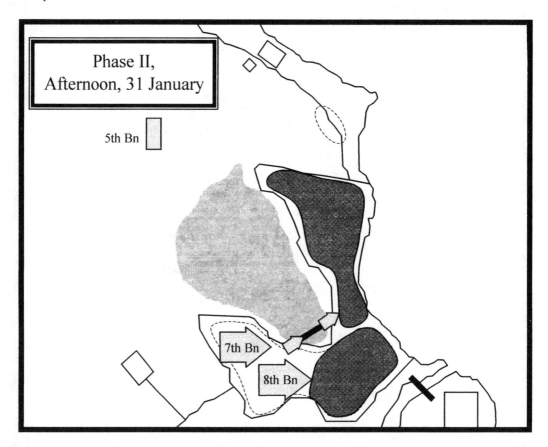

The ultimate outcome of the battle was no longer in doubt. However, Iraqi soldiers still occupied most of Khafji, and National Guardsmen had to root them out. The Iraqis resisted fiercely as the attack turned into a series of confused, street-to-street and house-to-house firefights. Around noon, the Iraqis mounted a counterattack, which caught a National Guard company in the middle of evacuating its wounded, destroying two ambulances (one, a V-150 armored ambulance) before being beaten off by the Saudis and Marine SuperCobra helicopter gunships. The Saudis also lost a V-150 to friendly fire during the counterattack when it was accidentally hit by a TOW from a Cobra. The driver was killed. The gunner, vehicle commander and several infantrymen in the back were wounded.

Two other V-150s were lost later in the battle. One APC exploded after being hit by an RPG-7 fired by an Iraqi in a building. The V-150 was hit and burst into flames. The driver and commander survived the explosion, only because they were blown out of their open hatches and clear of the vehicle by the blast. The four soldiers riding in the back of the APC were killed. An American advisor ran to a nearby Saudi armored vehicle and banged on it with his helmet. When a crewman opened the hatch, the advisor pointed to the building and shouted: "TOW, TOW!" The crewman nodded, and a few seconds later, a TOW missile was on its way toward the building. After a large explosion, a stream of Iraqis left the building waving white cloth. Later, a V-150 equipped with a turret-mounted 90mm gun was hit by a 100mm round fired by an Iraqi tank. All four of the vehicle's crewmen were killed.

While the firefight was going on, a reinforced company of Iraqi Type 63 APCs was assembling on the street near the hotel where a team of Marine spotters was hiding. A volley from every gun in 1/12 was called in on the Iraqis, destroying 17 Iraqi APCs. Many of the vehicles, which were packed with ammunition, erupted in secondary explosions as the company's surviving dismounted infantry fled down the street. The spotters shifted the artillery fire, and another volley killed or wounded many of the fleeing Iraqi infantrymen.* Shortly afterward, the two Marine spotter teams, which had taken advantage of the confusion to make their way through the town, linked up with the attached 8th Battalion company.

By 2 p.m., the 8th Battalion had arrived from the south and linked up with the 7th Battalion. The attack continued, with the 8th Battalion on the southern flank and the 7th Battalion on the northern flank. As soon as the 7th Battalion reached the causeway across the sabkha, it was met by a wall of machine-gun fire from the other side. Seemingly oblivious to the Iraqi fire, Hamid's men raced across the causeway, gained a foothold and unleashed their own wall of fire on the Iraqis. At 6:30 p.m., the attack was suspended because of darkness, with the 8th Battalion remaining in place and the 7th Battalion returning to the SANG compound to rearm.

The Saudis launched their final assault on the following morning at 7:30. At this point, there were about 20 Iraqi armored vehicles and 200 Iraqi soldiers in Khafji. The 7th and 8th battalions attacked on line at first, then split, with the 8th Battalion clearing the southern half of the town and the 7th Battalion driving northward, clearing the rest of the town, and ultimately retaking the desalination plant.

During the final assault, the SANG battalions found that their foes were utterly dispirited. Most Iraqi soldiers surrendered as soon as they were engaged. Others were keen to avoid being engaged. Several vehicles were destroyed by Saudi TOWs or Marine Cobras as they tried to escape to the north. By 3 p.m., the town and the desalination plant were in Saudi hands.

With an authorized strength of 420 armored vehicles, and an actual strength of around 400, at Khafji the Iraqi 5th Mechanized Division had lost about a quarter of its strength. A total of 23 tanks and 43 APCs had been destroyed and 9 tanks and 21 APCs had been captured intact. Two self-propelled 122mm guns were also destroyed as were about a half-dozen soft-skinned vehicles. This wasted combat power would be sorely missed when the Coalition went over to the attack on G-Day. Some 60 Iraqis were killed and 463 were taken prisoner (of which 35 were wounded). The Saudis lost 18 killed and 32 wounded, as well as two Qatari tanks (which were later repaired) and seven V-150s.

The fighting would undoubtedly have been more costly had the Iraqis been more organized. The Saudis would ultimately conclude that the Iraqi force had not been one

---

*Whether the Iraqi company was forming to launch a counterattack or leave Khafji remains unclear.

distinct unit, but elements of three different battalions. Bringing the diverse clusters of armored vehicles under centralized control was made difficult by a lack of communications equipment. Because of the lack of a coherent command structure, the Iraqi defense of the town was uncoordinated.

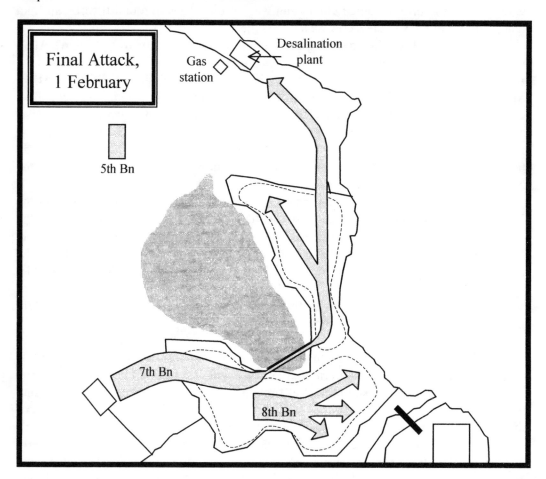

The fact that no one seems to have been in charge of the Iraqi force helps explain why the force's most effective weapons were never employed. Numerous Iraqi APCs were found with 82mm recoilless rifles inside them. Though not particularly effective against tanks, they would have been extremely effective against Saudi V-150s. A significant number of extremely dangerous French-made Milan missiles were also found inside Iraqi APCs. Though they would have been lethal to Saudi APCs and Qatari tanks, none were used. Finally, though Marine attack helicopters savaged the Iraqi defenders, not one of the many available SA-14 shoulder-launched anti-aircraft missiles was fired.

Failure to use their weapons was not something the SANG could have been accused of. The Saudis responded to every instance of Iraqi resistance with torrents of fire. More than 400 TOW missiles were fired during the fighting. One Iraqi T-55 was hit by ten TOWs. It was not unusual for heavily engaged units to finish a day's fighting with virtually no ammunition remaining. Indeed, most of the damage done to the town was done by the Saudis who retook it. Again, Lenin's dictum about quantity having a quality all its own proved true. Though Saudi fire was often inaccurate, the sheer volume of it kept the Iraqi defenders off balance and pinned down, minimizing Saudi casualties.

The Saudis also helped minimize their casualties by learning quickly from their mistakes. During the early fighting, SANG soldiers tended to stay in their armored vehicles. This meant that fewer infantrymen were out looking for Iraqis, and that increased the chances that unobserved Iraqis could get close-in RPG shots at the thinly armored V-150s. It also meant that if one of those shots hit the vehicle, it would make casualties of an entire squad, rather than just a driver and a gunner. After an entire infantry squad was killed in the back of a stricken V-150 early in the fighting, the Saudis learned to dismount and spread out in built-up areas.

In one final setback for the Iraqis, British aircraft spotted 15 fast patrol boats attempting to land troops near Khafji. British naval attack helicopters sank two boats with missiles and drove the others off. Coalition aircraft gave chase, sinking or severely damaging 10 of the remaining 13 boats.

The Saudis spent the next week combing the town, looking for Iraqis in hiding. About three dozen were captured. Though there was no resistance from the Iraqi stragglers, there were casualties. In a preview of a problem that would plague the Allies later in the war, over 30 Coalition soldiers were killed or wounded by unexploded bomblets in and around Khafji in the weeks following the town's recapture.

The series of battles collectively referred to as "The Battle of Khafji" convinced CENTCOM that the Iraqis would not fight well in the coming ground offensive. They had proven themselves unable to work effectively as units or hold up to mobile counterattacks. Iraqi artillery had been touted as among the world's best, but at Khafji, Iraqi gunners had not even been able to perform simple missions like shifting fire. Coalition commanders began to sense that the impending ground war might not be as costly as they had anticipated. Gen. Schwarzkopf would say later that Khafji was the time when he really began to think: "We are going to kick this guy's tail," and that the Iraqi Army was "a lousy outfit."

Khafji proved that the Saudis could fight. This was the first major battle that the Saudi military had ever fought. At the beginning of the battle, the Saudis were easily rattled, but as they became accustomed to combat conditions and gained confidence in their weapons, they settled down. After a few early mistakes, they began to show a solid grasp of tactics. They had also experienced adversity and overcome it. When Saudi APCs were hit by Iraqi anti-armor weapons, they burst into flames with their occupants inside them. Among the wounded had been some serious cases, even triple amputees. Instead of becoming demoralized or overcome with fear, the Saudis kept the pressure on the Iraqis until Khafji was recaptured.

The Saudi performance at Khafji also convinced the Saudi government that its army could fight. This was perhaps the most far-reaching consequence of the battle. Before Khafji, the Saudi government planned to use its forces only to defend Saudi Arabia. Now it decided that its forces should take part in the coming offensive to liberate Kuwait.

7

The Gathering Storm

Before dawn on 13 February, a laser-guided bomb from a Stealth slammed into the top of a bunker in the Baghdad suburb of al-Amiriyah. The bunker had been identified as an Iraqi command and control center, and the explosion of the bomb blew a hole in its roof. A second guided bomb slipped through the hole and detonated inside. It seemed to be a textbook operation against a command and control target, until CENTCOM learned that the bunker had been filled with almost 400 civilians.

The Pentagon claimed that the bunker had been used as a command and control center, but that the Iraqis had recently moved out and removed the evidence. There had been reason to believe that the bunker had been used by the military. It was much harder than the average civilian shelter, fresh camouflage paint had been applied and there were several satellite photos of military vehicles parked around it. In early February, CENTCOM began picking up military radio intercepts from the vicinity of the bunker.

While we may never know exactly what happened, it is clear that most of the civilians in the shelter had important government connections. It is also clear that key government officials and military officers worked out of the bunker. Apparently, some had brought their friends and families with them, believing that they would be safer in the hardened shelter than in their homes.

The bunker bombing was the second civilian bombing incident of the day. Earlier, British Tornados, with Buccaneer bombers providing laser guidance, attacked and destroyed the road and railway bridges over the Euphrates River at Fallujah. Unfortunately, during the attack, one of the bombs failed to guide, landed in the town itself, and caused several civilian casualties. Though great pains were taken to avoid civilian casualties, some 2,300 Iraqi civilians would be killed by bombs during the war.

Saddam could have capitalized on these incidents, but his responses to the bombing were clumsy. Baghdad radio warned of "devastating surprises" for the Allies. This only made people forget about the bunker and remember Saddam's fondness for Scuds and poison gas. His attempts to arouse sympathy were contrived. The most memorable scene to come out of the coverage of civilian damage was a middle-aged woman in a sweatsuit, raging at an American camera crew. She was immediately recognized by U.S. government analysts as an official of Iraq's foreign ministry. In fact, she had been interviewed for television at the ministry about two weeks earlier. She was later found to have given the same performance before a French camera crew.

An even worse blunder was Saddam's attempt to make it appear that the Coalition had bombed a mosque. The day before he was to make his accusations, the Pentagon released evidence in the form of satellite photos, which indicated that Saddam's combat engineers had blown up the mosque. With the failure of this public relations gambit, any hope of aid or comfort from moderate Islamic states vanished.

A great deal of ground activity had gone unreported while the world's attention was focused on the air campaign. In the first week of the war, the border between Kuwait and Saudi Arabia heated up. Marine raids tormented Iraqi border units along a broad front. Known as "ambiguity operations," these raids were designed to confuse the Iraqis as to the positions and intentions of Coalition ground units.

Artillery figured prominently in the raids. The first two raids were artillery missions fired by 1st Battalion, 12th Marines along the coast, in front of OP 8 on January 21st and 24th. Sure that the Iraqis' attention was fixed on the coast, Maj.Gen. Myatt ordered 5/11 to conduct artillery missions on the western end of the Marine line. There, the battalion fired two missions, on the 26th and 29th, before the Battle of Khafji put a temporary hold on the operations. On the 26th, Marine gunners bombarded a brigade command post, destroying two police posts and a battery of 122mm guns.

For that raid, Lt.Col. James Sachtleben, commander of 5/11, decided to use 155mm self-propelled howitzers. They did not have the range of 8-inch (203mm) guns and their shells did not have the same explosive payload, but with no definitive intelligence on Iraqi counterbattery capabilities, they were considered a bit safer. Ultimately, the Iraqis would only respond to the raid with a few mortar rounds, but in planning the raid, Sachtleben had to assume that his opponents were capable. The 8-inch guns took longer to set up, and would take longer to remove if something went wrong and they were targeted by Iraqi counterbattery fire. They also lacked armored overhead protection for the gunners, which would prove valuable if there was return fire.

On the 29th, in what would be described as a "drive-by shooting," Task Force Shepherd's LAV-25s pelted a border observation post with 25mm chain-gun fire while the unit's mortarmen dropped shells on it. During the attack, 5/11 isolated the post by suppressing Iraqi units behind it with both 155mm and 8-inch howitzers. The Iraqis did not fire a shot in return.

The battalion did not take an active part in the battles around the Marine OPs. Lt.Col. Myers and Lt.Col. Sachtleben realized that Iraqi jamming would make coordination between TF Shepherd and 5/11 difficult or impossible. Sachtleben's guns would be vulnerable, but not necessarily useful. After the first night's fighting, Maj.Gen. Myatt ordered the battalion southward to less exposed positions. Unfortunately, there was a friendly fire incident during the movement. A Marine Intruder mistook a column of self-propelled 155mm howitzers for attacking Iraqi armor. A 500 lb. bomb struck the gun barrel of a howitzer, killing the driver and wounding two other crewmen.

As soon as the Khafji battles were over, 5/11 resumed its raiding. On the night of 3–4 February, 8-inch guns were used to destroy an Iraqi radio intercept station and some ground surveillance radars to the west of OP 5. By this time relatively sure that Iraqi artillerymen could not put effective fire on his guns, Sachtleben had no hesitation in using his 8-inch howitzers.

Four days later, the Marines set out to locate and destroy two batteries of extremely dangerous ASTROS II multiple rocket launchers located about 13 miles from the border. This would be the deepest of the 12 targets engaged by Marine artillery during the ambiguity operations. The 155mm guns could be used on this raid, but only with Rocket Assisted Projectiles (RAPs). RAPs are simply standard rounds with a rocket booster at the base of the round. A 155mm RAP will travel just as far as an 8-inch shell, but at 155mm it produces a smaller explosion, and RAPs are slightly less accurate than regular rounds.

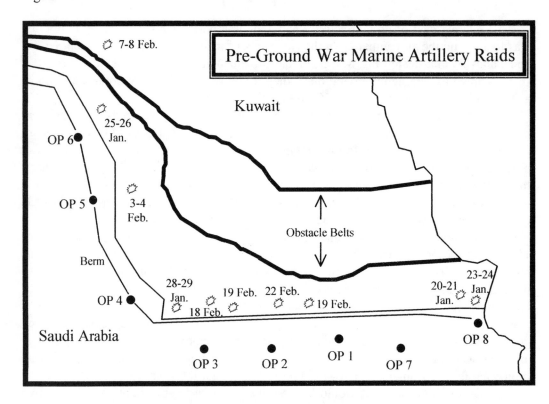

Neither of these disadvantages would be a problem for Lt.Col. Sachtleben, who decided to use his 155mm guns. He believed that he would not need shells with a large payload, and that a little inaccuracy would not hurt, since on this mission, his guns did not have to destroy the Iraqi rocket launchers. They just had to stay in position, firing shells until they drew Iraqi counterbattery fire. At that point, F/A-18s would spot the rocket flashes, swoop down and destroy the MRLs. The mission came off without a hitch. There were no Marine casualties, and two batteries of ASTROS IIs were destroyed by Rockeye cluster bombs.

When it became clear that the Iraqis' attention was focused on the coast and on the western end of the Marine line, the Marines ceased their activities in those areas. They shifted their attacks to the area in the center of the southern border of Kuwait, launching artillery raids there on 18, 19 and 22 February.

As the bombing and shelling continued, so did the massive movement of troops and supplies to the west. A total of 300,000 troops, 6,000 tracked vehicles and 60,000 wheeled vehicles would move hundreds of miles inland. Along with the combat units shifting west went many thousand tons of fuel, ammunition, spare parts, water and food.

CENTCOM wanted to ensure that there was a 60-day stockpile on hand, in the event that a battle of attrition developed.* Toward that end, 30,000 tons of supplies were flowing into Saudi Arabia each day.

The task of moving all of these supplies fell upon Saudi brigadier generals Salem al-Uwaymer (supporting Arab forces) and Abd al-Aziz al-Hussein (supporting Western forces), as well as CENTCOM's chief logistician, Maj.Gen. William "Gus" Pagonis. At the beginning of the deployment, CENTCOM's top priority was to get as many combat troops as possible into Saudi Arabia. As a result, there was a desperate shortage of American transportation personnel. However, there were a large number of migrant truckers available, mostly from India, Pakistan, and the Philippines. Pagonis quickly hired as many of them as he could, and formed an ad hoc transportation unit. This unit served with distinction for the duration of the conflict, ferrying supplies to units on the front lines. The Saudi government played a crucial role during this period, contracting for 4,000 civilian drivers and 22,000 trucks.

The main supply routes took on an American flavor. In August, immediately after arrangements were made for waste disposal, steps were taken to ensure that American troops could get American food. Mess tents serving such staples as pizza, chicken and hamburgers sprang up. Pagonis, the son of a short order cook, set up six truck stops where drivers could eat, use the latrine and get back on the road. For the troops who could not make it to the food, the food came to them in trucks.† Again, Saudi support was crucial, as the Saudi government paid for the feeding of all Coalition troops.

By the time the ground offensive began, the Allied armies had been supplied with about a hundred million meals, another hundred million gallons of fuel, 175 million gallons of water, and had stocked up on about a quarter-billion tons of ammunition, with the Saudi government paying for all transportation costs. Pagonis, his Saudi colleagues and their staffs had made it look easy.

The most obvious (to the Iraqis) avenue along which the Allies might launch their assault was through the Wadi al-Batin, which was essentially a heavily rutted canyon that ran along Kuwait's western border with Iraq. To help cultivate this belief by the Iraqis, Brig.Gen. John Tilelli, Jr.'s 1st Cavalry Division moved into positions at the southern end of the Wadi, and did little to conceal its presence.‡

The division's leaders had another reason for wanting the Iraqis to know that the 1st Cav was there. There had been some concern that Iraqi units just east of the Wadi al-Batin might launch a preemptive attack southward to disrupt the ongoing westward movement of Coalition troops and supplies. Awareness of the 1st Cav's presence would make the Iraqis think twice before launching such an attack.

The division soon made contact with Iraqis along the border. On 5 February, a patrolling Cobra attack helicopter from 1st Squadron, 7th Cavalry Regiment received small arms fire from Iraqi soldiers in or near an observation tower. The Cobra responded with five 2.75-inch rockets, two of which hit the tower, but did not destroy it.

---

*The logistical requirements of an armored division on the offensive are about 2,500 tons of ammunition, 12–18,000 tons of fuel, 125 tons of spare parts, 300,000 gallons of water and about 40 tons of food per day.

†For each U.S. Army combat soldier, there are 6–7 soldiers supporting him.

‡Tilelli was promoted to major general shortly after the war ended.

Forty feet high, the tower afforded Iraqi observers a view of almost 20 miles into the American rear. Letting the Iraqis know that the 1st Cav was in the area was one thing. Allowing the Iraqis to monitor the division's activities was another. The tower had to be destroyed.

At 1:25 p.m. on the 7th, helicopters from 1-7th Cavalry spotted two Iraqis entering the tower. At 1:38, 1st Battalion, 82nd Field Artillery Regiment, six miles to the south, fired a single 155mm "Copperhead" projectile. One of the helicopters directed a beam of laser light at the tower, and the Copperhead guided in on it. The round pierced the roof of the tower and exploded, destroying the tower and killing the two Iraqis inside.* Several more Iraqi soldiers were killed when the truck they attempted to flee in was hit by a TOW missile fired by one of 1-7th's Cobras. Seconds later, a shower of bomblets from 32 Dual Purpose Improved Conventional Munition (DPICM) rounds from 1-82nd FA impacted on the target, killing and wounding Iraqi soldiers in the vicinity.

On 10 February, the division continued shelling Iraqi positions in the Wadi with conventional artillery. The following day, the division began reconnoitering Iraqi positions. Within 24 hours, it had collected 126 prisoners.†

At 3:41 on the afternoon of 13 February, forward units of Col. George Harmeyer's 1st Brigade spotted four Iraqi trucks driving near the border. A barrage of 132 DPICM rounds from VII Corps' 2-29th FA Battalion's 155mm self-propelled howitzers destroyed the four vehicles.

February 13th also saw the first use of the Multiple Launch Rocket System (MLRS) against Iraqi positions in southern Iraq, courtesy of the 1st Cavalry Division. A Battery, 21st Field Artillery Battalion, the division's only MLRS battery, and three batteries of launchers from VII Corps' 1-27th FA Battalion moved cautiously toward the border.‡ Three batteries would move forward and engage their targets. They would then race back toward their lines, while the fourth battery monitored its artillery-spotting radars, waiting for Iraqi batteries to fire back, giving away their positions.

The AN/TPQ-37 radars used by the Coalition could pinpoint ten Iraqi firing positions simultaneously, to an accuracy of 10 meters. The AN/TPQ-37 detects enemy shells in flight, analyzes their trajectory by computer, and by extrapolation, pinpoints their launch point. The enemy's coordinates are then fed to computers which direct counterbattery fire, which can be on the way in under a minute.

At 6:17 p.m., A/21st FA fired the first of 216 rockets the batteries would send at Iraqi positions. Nine targets (eight artillery sites and an infantry company) were hit with 24 rockets each. The impact of over 139,000 bomblets devastated all nine targets, and caused secondary explosions of vehicles and ammunition stores which would continue throughout the night. The Iraqis did not fire back, so at 6:45, the fourth battery fired 36 rockets at three more previously identified Iraqi targets.

The raids became more regular, and still there was no Iraqi response, largely because Iraqi guncrews were terrified of Allied counterbattery fire. As it became apparent that Iraqi retaliation was not a serious concern, the MLRSs stayed longer and

---

*A Copperhead can hit a target from 17 miles. About 100 were fired during the war. About 75% destroyed their targets.

†By G-Day, the 1st Cav would take 1,800 Iraqi prisoners.

‡A/21st FA had ten MLRS launchers instead of the usual nine.

fired more rockets. Still there was no retaliation, so most available artillery was moved to the border. The bombardments became more intense with each strike.

There were of 127 Coalition MLRS launchers arrayed against the Iraqis along the front. They would fire 4,900 227mm rockets into Iraq before G-Day.[*] Eight MLRS launchers were capable of delivering roughly as much explosive weight in one volley as the 900 artillery pieces of General (later Field Marshal) Montgomery at El Alamein.

The MLRS is mounted on a Bradley chassis, so it can go anywhere armor goes. It can accurately fire rockets almost 20 miles. The rockets can be fired two at a time, or in 12-round ripples. Each rocket contains 644 half-pound bomblets, which are released in mid-air and rain down on the target —ideal for attacking entrenched positions.[†] One launcher can kill or wound half of the soldiers in a 100 by 700 meter area with one volley. Nine launchers can saturate an area the size of 36 football fields with over 72,000 bomblets, one every 2½ meters. This is why MLRS crews call their weapon "the grid square removal system." Iraqi units were decimated before they had a chance to take cover. Prisoner interrogations revealed that MLRS strikes terrorized Iraqi soldiers in the front lines more than any other Allied tactic. MLRS barrages were referred to as "steel rain" by Iraqi prisoners. Many of these prisoners cited these strikes as the major factor in their decision to surrender.

There is more to the MLRS than incredible destructive power. MLRS rockets are extremely accurate, due to the computerization of much of the system. Hitting a target is a matter of getting a rocket or shell from point A (the firing point) to point B (the target). A guncrew therefore needs accurate information about what point it is firing from, and what point it is firing at.

One of the biggest problems artillerymen face is locating themselves on the map. Distance and direction to a target are calculated from the point where a guncrew thinks it is. If the crew is actually somewhere else, the calculations will be off and there is no way the ordnance will land on the target. MLRS crews do not have to figure out where they are on the map. A navigation computer does it for them. This is ideal for modern, high tempo offensive operations. At the beginning of a mission, the battery moves to a known spot, and the computers are set. From then on, the computer keeps track of where the vehicle is. Human map reading error has thus been eliminated as a factor.

Targeting has also become almost foolproof. Innovations like the Global Position Locating System allow forward observers to obtain much more accurate target location data than they would by trying to place the target on a map. When the position of a target is relayed back to the MLRS battery by an observer, the MLRS's computer calculates the distance and direction from its location (which it knows precisely) to the target location (which it knows more or less precisely). All that remains is to fire the rockets.

When even more destructive power or greater range was required, there was the Army Tactical Missile System (ATACMS), which can send much larger rockets over 80 miles, and can do it with stunning accuracy. ATACMS rockets are fired from the same platform as MLRS rockets, but carry 950 half-pound bomblets, which are scattered over an area a quarter-mile in diameter. The Army estimates that one ATACMS rocket will do as much damage as a barrage of 300 conventional high explosive shells.

Thirty-two ATACMS rockets were launched during the Gulf War. Entire radar and air defense sites deep inside Iraq were wiped out by single ATACMS rockets. The

---

[*]There would also be 14,000 rounds of conventional artillery fired during this period.

[†]Some 10,000 MLRS rockets were fired during the war.

missile did have limitations, though. It contained conventional fragmentation bomblets, not the armor piercing variety, so while it was a good weapon for destroying soft-skinned vehicles or shredding radar antennae, it was of little use against armor. In addition, because of the ATACMS' expense, too few were available to do extensive damage. Launching the missiles also required elaborate airspace clearance procedures, so they were not a weapon that could be used as an immediate response to an unforeseen threat.

The BM-21, often referred to as the "*Katyusha*" (Little Kate), was the most common multiple rocket launcher (MRL) in the Iraqi Army. Six BM-21s can fire 240 122mm rockets within a few seconds, and can saturate a relatively large area. The major drawback of the BM-21 is that since it is truck-mounted (unlike the MLRS, which is tracked), it cannot handle rough terrain. It also has to be within about 10 miles of its target to deliver its rockets. Even if a battery could have gotten that close to American positions, it would probably have gotten off only one volley before it was targeted and destroyed by warplanes or counterbattery fire, since BM-21s throw up huge clouds of dust when they fire. BM-21s are also wildly inaccurate. Of every 40 rockets fired at a target, generally 20 will not even land within 120 meters of that target.

The Iraqi Army was also short on MRLs. Every mechanized or armored division was supposed to have eighteen. All infantry divisions were supposed to have six. By those standards, the Iraqi Army that was destroyed by the Coalition should have had about 400 multiple rocket launchers. It had about half that. Those it had went primarily to Republican Guard or to regular armored or mechanized units. These units were too far behind Iraqi front lines for the MRLs to be brought to bear effectively on Coalition forces. Front line infantry units usually had no MRLs.

Iraq had about 60 Brazilian-made ASTROS II MRLs. This was Iraq's best MRL. The Brazilian Avibras company had developed the system at Iraq's request, and Iraq put it to good use against Iran. Like the BM-21, the ASTROS II was wheeled, and not particularly accurate, but it was extremely versatile. It could fire thirty-two 127mm rockets 19 miles, sixteen 180mm rockets 22 miles, or four 300mm rockets 38 miles.* The rockets came in self-contained rocket pods. The larger rockets could carry bomblets. The 180mm rockets contained 20 bomblets. The 300mm contained 65, and these bomblets had armor piercing capability. If a commander wanted to fire 300mm rockets instead of 127mm rockets, he just changed pods. Unlike most of Iraq's other equipment, the ASTROS II was not a system to be taken lightly. Luckily for the Allies, Iraq was short of ASTROS rockets. Iraq did not manufacture the rocket pods, Avibras did. When the UN imposed its embargo, stocking up on rocket pods became impossible. This probably explains why only 18 ASTROS launchers were deployed during the war. Iraq had around 40 more available, but probably did not have rockets for them.

Iraq's primary battlefield rockets (since the Scuds were being misused as strategic rockets) were the Soviet-built FROG(Free Rocket Over Ground)-7 and a locally produced version of the FROG-7 called the Laith. FROG-7s are inaccurate, with only a 50% chance of landing within 1¼ miles of their intended target. They do not carry bomblets and only have a range of about 45 miles. The Laith had the same accuracy as the FROG-7 and a range of about 55 miles. Unlike the FROG-7, the Laith carried bomblets, and that made it somewhat dangerous. Neither the FROG-7 nor the Laith

---

*A 300mm rocket with a high explosive warhead makes a crater about twelve feet wide and three feet deep.

would be a factor in the Gulf War, however. Iraq had a few hundred of these missiles, but there were only 20–30 launchers, and most of the launchers, like the MRLs, were too far from the front lines to be a factor, although one FROG-7 wounded eight Senegalese troops on 21 February.

The 1st Cav's artillery attacks drew the Iraqi High Command's attention to the Wadi. The division's bombardments appeared to be the softening up that usually precedes a major attack. In addition, two weeks before the ground war started, there suddenly seemed to be a significant amount of Marine activity to the east, south of the al-Wafra Forest. Several of the 11th Marines' artillery raids were also fired from this area. The activity was an elaborate fake. Task Force Troy, under the command of Brig.Gen. Tom Draude, an assistant commander of the 1st Marine Division, consisted of 460 Marines equipped with dummy tanks and artillery pieces and a loudspeaker system to broadcast the sounds of tank engines. Supporting Troy was a fleet of helicopters, which made frequent trips to and from the base without ever dropping off or picking up anyone.

The main feint was in the Wadi al-Batin, however. On the night of 16 February, in an operation dubbed "Red Storm," three batteries of 155mm howitzers and three MLRS batteries from 42nd Field Artillery Brigade, as well as A/21st Field Artillery's MLRSs saturated an area 1¼ miles square with shells and bomblets. The barrage destroyed all Iraqi air defenses within the box, including a radar site, and allowed a formation of Apaches from Lt.Col. Terry Branham's 2-6th Cavalry Squadron of the VII Corps' 11th Aviation Brigade to fly into Iraq on their mission, dubbed "Bugle," unimpeded. About three miles into Iraq, the 18 Apaches fanned out into an attack line nine miles wide. As artillery secured the attack lanes by pounding the Iraqi defenses to the left and right of the Apaches, the gunships opened fire. Five minutes of sustained punishment left the target, a line of observation towers and communications buildings, in ruins.

On the 19th, Gen. Schwarzkopf instructed Brig.Gen. Tilelli to drive into the Wadi the next day. As the division's 1st Brigade was stationed to the west of the Wadi, and the 2nd was at its base, it would be the 2nd Brigade which conducted the attack. The brigade's mission was as delicate as it was important. Schwarzkopf wanted to get the Iraqis' attention, but he also wanted the 1st Cav at or near full strength on G-Day, in case it was needed to assist the Egyptians in their attack. Col. Randolph House, the brigade's commander, was therefore ordered by Tilelli not to allow his brigade to become engaged in a pitched battle or risk high casualties.

The 1st Cav was less able than other Coalition divisions to sustain large numbers of casualties. While other Army divisions in the Gulf had three maneuver brigades, Tilelli's division only had two. The Army had always planned that, if deployed, the division would be rounded out with a National Guard brigade. However, that brigade had not been fully combat ready when the crisis broke, so the Army had sent the 1st ("Tiger") Brigade from the 2nd Armored Division as the 1st Cav's third brigade. It seemed a perfect fit, since, like 1st Cav, the 2nd Armored Division was stationed at Fort Hood, Texas. The Tiger Brigade had been assigned to the 2nd Marine Division, however, to add firepower to its advance, leaving the 1st Cav a maneuver brigade short.

The Iraqis would be ready for the attack. To supplement the artillery attacks, the division had been conducting "berm busting" raids. In these raids, House would hammer sections of the berm with artillery to ensure that they were clear of Iraqi soldiers, then send units forward to those sections to punch holes in the berm. To the Iraqis, this activity seemed to confirm their suspicion that the Wadi would be the site of the main Allied attack. Based on this belief, they had moved several more units and dozens of additional artillery pieces into the Wadi.

Bradley Fighting Vehicle. (Photo: Sgt. Randall Yackiel)

The raid into the Wadi would be made by Lt.Col. Mike Parker's Task Force 1-5, made up of two tank and two Bradley companies. Before the war, the brigade's battalions had been organized into mixed armor-infantry formations on a permanent basis as an experiment. One of 1-5th Cavalry Battalion's infantry companies had been given to each of the brigade's armored battalions. In return, each of the armored battalions, Lt.Col. John Burch's 1-8th Cavalry and Lt.Col. Jim Methred's 1-32nd Armor, had assigned a tank company to Parker's unit.

Because the 1-5th Cavalry was nicknamed "The Black Knights," the Wadi attack was dubbed "Operation Knight Strike." The task force's goal was to plow through the first line of defense and into a bunker complex beyond, eliciting a response from the enemy before breaking off the attack and returning to its starting line. The Iraqis' response would provide valuable information about the nature of the defenses and the quality of the defenders.

Two Vulcan AA guns of 4th Battalion, 5th Air Defense Artillery Regiment were attached to Task Force 1-5 for the attack. The Vulcan is a six-barreled, gatling-type gun that fires large volumes of 20mm ammunition and is usually mounted on an M-113 armored personnel carrier. It is basically designed to throw a wall of bullets in front of attacking enemy aircraft. By this time, however, it had become apparent that Iraqi aircraft would not be a threat to Coalition ground forces. This left anti-aircraft units with little to do, so the Vulcans were employed in bunker busting. A Vulcan has two rates of fire, 1,000 and 3,000 rounds per minute. It is fired in bursts of 10, 30, 60, or 100 rounds.

The occupants of a bunker riddled by its 20mm bullets will usually not survive the experience.

Vulcan anti-aircraft gun mounted on an M-113 APC. (Photo: Thomas Houlahan)

The task force's mission began simply enough. After crossing its line of departure at noon, the task force advanced slowly northward, with its scout platoon forward and the rest of the task force in a diamond formation. A Company (Bradleys), which had conducted a thorough route and area reconnaissance of the first 1½ miles past the berm on the previous night, took the point, with tank companies to its left and right rear. Another company of Bradleys brought up the rear.

About 7½ miles into Iraq, just after 1:00, the battalion's scouts made contact with a battalion-sized Iraqi position, a network of trenches and bunkers in a reverse slope defense. This was an ambush tactic, and a standard Iraqi response to superior American weaponry. Sited on the rear side of high terrain, the Iraqis could not take long range shots at the Americans as they approached, but the ground offered both concealment and protection, mitigating much of the Abrams' main guns' range advantage.

In the center of the diamond, Col. House monitored developments through his binoculars and over his radio. As the scout platoon leader came under intense enemy fire, House was surprised by the composure of his subordinate leader, who seemed oblivious to the Iraqi fire as he gave his reports. "I could see his track [vehicle] getting all shot up," said House. "And he was talking like he was at the beach or something."

Like clockwork, the scouts moved to the side and A Company moved forward, dismounted and deployed its infantry, then began peppering the Iraqi positions with 25mm chain-gun and 7.62mm coaxial machine-gun fire. Iraqi resistance was more stubborn than expected. When a few of the defenders in the forward outposts found that they had been overrun and tried to give themselves up, they were fired on by other Iraqis farther back. About a thousand meters behind the forward edge of the fighting, House watched a Bradley commanded by A Company's executive officer, Lt. Christopher Robinson, put itself between the surrendering Iraqis and their more stubborn comrades. As the Iraqis were rounded up and sent to the rear, a Vulcan behind House was hit by an anti-tank round, killing the vehicle's commander, Staff Sergeant Jimmy Haws.* Seconds later, Robinson's vehicle was also hit, killing his gunner, Sergeant Ronald Rendazzo.

The fire was coming from six T-12 100mm anti-tank guns under cover on the side of the Wadi. These guns could fire four different types of shell, any of which could easily destroy a Bradley. They could also fire their 35 lb. shells at a relatively high rate, usually about one every eight seconds. The guns were dug-in and so well-concealed that the Americans did not spot them until they opened fire on A Company.

As the Bradleys continued to lay a base of fire and develop the situation, the M-1A1s on the flanks were ordered forward. The tanks picked off the half-dozen or so armored vehicles supporting the Iraqi positions, then destroyed most of the T-12s. Stripped of much of their heavy weaponry, many Iraqis began to abandon their defensive positions, only to be cut down by 25mm or machine-gun fire as they tried to escape.

House called in a fire mission from the division's MLRS battery, the only artillery unit within range of the Iraqis. As American bomblets began to impact in the vicinity of the Iraqi guns, another Bradley, under the command of Staff Sergeant Christopher Cichon, pulled up behind Robinson's Bradley. As Cichon began to evacuate casualties from the stricken Bradley, his gunner, using Robinson's Bradley as cover, fired at Iraqis over its front slope.

Unknown to Col. House, Lt.Gen. Franks, the VII Corps' commander, had been monitoring the battle on his radio. House received a call from the rear, telling him that Franks had made an offer of 40 A-10s. House quickly accepted the offer. Within minutes, the first of 10 flights of four Warthogs was on station. After dropping their payload of bombs from high altitude, the A-10s swooped down on the Iraqi complex, firing their 30mm rotating guns. When their supply of ammunition was exhausted, the next flight would arrive and begin pounding the Iraqi positions.

As medics tended to the wounded from Robinson's vehicle, Iraqi mortar and artillery rounds began to impact. Private First Class Ardon Cooper was attempting to render first aid to a wounded comrade when the rounds came in. Using his body to shield the wounded soldier, Cooper was mortally wounded by shrapnel. For this, PFC Cooper would receive the Silver Star. Seconds after Cooper was hit, Cichon's Bradley was hit in the turret by an anti-tank round, blowing its TOW missile racks off. Incredibly, no one inside the Bradley was killed.

After almost 40 minutes of fighting, the combination of direct fire from the ground units, MLRS strikes and the constant drumbeat of ordnance from successive waves of A-10s had loosened the defenders' grip on the kill sack. Iraqi artillery fire, the last serious threat to Parker's task force, was the next problem to be dealt with. As Iraqi forward spotters were killed or wounded in the continuing pounding of the defenses, Iraqi artillery barrages became less accurate, then thinned out as batteries were targeted and destroyed.

Just before 2:00, TF 1-5 began making its way back to its own lines behind a smoke screen provided by the division's artillery. The raid had killed some 200 Iraqis and netted 18 prisoners at a cost of three dead and nine wounded. On the way back, an Abrams was disabled when it ran over an anti-tank mine. No one inside the tank was killed or seriously wounded, and the tank was towed to the rear.

The next day, 1st Cav's artillery was joined by artillery from the 1st Armored Division for two heavy MLRS strikes on known and suspected Iraqi positions in and

---

*Haws thus became the first American soldier to be killed by Iraqi fire in the Gulf War.

around the Wadi. A noon raid of 312 rockets was followed at 3 p.m. by 276 more rockets. To the Iraqis, the combination of TF 1-5's attack and the massive artillery strikes seemed to confirm their suspicion that the main Coalition effort would be up the Wadi.

The 1st Cavalry Division would return to the Wadi at the beginning of the ground war. At 3 p.m. on 24 February, the 2nd Brigade pushed up the Wadi in a wedge formation, with TF 1-5 in the lead, and task forces 1-8 and 1-32 to its left and right rear. The brigade advanced several miles into the Wadi, destroying four Iraqi T-55 tanks and a ZSU 23-4 with Copperhead artillery rounds. The brigade's advance created the illusion that it was the lead element of a major assault force and caused the Iraqis to light their fire trenches.

Fighting in the Wadi continued on the 25th, with the brigade engaged in a fairly intense firefight. While ground units were fighting with the Iraqis, Col. House sent attack helicopters after two large defensive complexes in the back of the Wadi. The brigade's artillery launched a short barrage to suppress Iraqi air defenses on the position. Artillery bomblets rained down on Iraqi anti-aircraft defences, leaving the vehicles and artillery pieces around them almost completely defenseless.

After the barrage, Apaches arrived to destroy armored vehicles, trucks and bunkers with Hellfire missiles. When the supply of Hellfires was exhausted, the Apaches went after softer targets with 30mm cannon fire. Apaches were the perfect weapons for missions like this. While artillery is good at destroying large anti-aircraft weapons, barrages often leave shoulder-launched, heat-seeking anti-aircraft missiles intact. The Apache is heavily armored for crew protection, and has two engines, both of which are heavily shrouded to reduce their heat signatures. Without these design features, the hovering Apaches would have been dangerously vulnerable in areas of heavy combat.

No Apaches were destroyed by Iraqi air defense weapons, but an Apache was hit by a round fired by a T-12 anti-tank gun. The gunship was completely destroyed. However, its crew members attached their harnesses to weapons pod mounts on another Apache by means of a *carabiner*, a locking clasp used in mountain climbing, and were lifted to safety.

The ground element continued to move forward, pushing through minefields, destroying defensive positions and cutting up Iraqi units. However, Iraqi defenses were getting progressively tougher. There was no soft spot through which 1st Cav would be able to drive into Iraq. At noon on the 25th, Brig.Gen. Tilelli was ordered to suspend offensive operations. Its mission accomplished, 1st Cavalry doubled back and raced to join VII Corps for the attack on the Republican Guard.

The 1st Cav's activities in the Wadi had drawn Iraqi attention away from the main breach areas. The division had thus played a key role in keeping Allied casualties down during the crucial early hours of the ground war. In combat, it had destroyed 34 tanks, 14 APCs, 75 wheeled vehicles, 44 artillery pieces and 10 AA systems. After the war, it would scuttle 12 tanks, 29 APCs, 120 trucks, 24 artillery pieces and 51 AA weapons it had captured during the fighting.

Initially, General Schwarzkopf had little enthusiasm for special operations. He was not alone in his thinking. Some senior Army officers regarded "commando types" as shady, flaky loose cannons. In fact, there has always been method to their madness. Success in a major commando operation can save thousands of lives once the conventional fighting starts.

Those who volunteer for such duty are among the most dedicated soldiers in the Armed Forces. There are no illusions about what will happen to these men if they are captured. The approximately 9,500 special operations soldiers who took part in the Gulf War were acutely aware that the Iraqis were not terribly concerned with adherence to the rules of the Geneva Conventions.

Contrary to popular myth, "Rambo types" do not last long in commando units. "Rambo was a serious M.U.(malfunctioning unit)," said one Special Forces veteran. "I'm not going to sit here and tell you that every single Green Beret is absolutely stable, but we do weed out most of the wackos." Col. Arthur "Bull" Simons, one of the most legendary Green Berets, once told a zealot: "I don't feel like getting hit with a stray round when you take on their entire army with a knife and a pistol."* "Death was Patrick Henry's second choice," is another favorite commando saying.

Allied commando teams were active from before the start of the air war to the conclusion of the ground campaign. Early on, a few recon teams were dropped off in Kuwait and Iraq by helicopters painted with Iraqi Army markings. Just before the bombing began, there were reports that four Iraqi helicopters had flown into Coalition airspace and that their crews had defected. In fact, these four helicopters were carrying special operations teams returning from a reconnaissance mission.

Beginning on 7 February, commando activity picked up in preparation for the ground offensive. Teams infiltrated deep into Iraq to destroy strategic targets. In one case, a platoon of heliborne U.S. Army Rangers raided a strategic communications complex near the Jordanian border, knocking over a 350 foot microwave tower and destroying everything of value before returning to base.

One major operation involving the 82nd Airborne Division was considered but never carried out. Early in the war, Gen. Schwarzkopf directed the division to come up with a plan for the seizure of H-2 and H-3 airfields, two major Scud launch sites.

Both targets were difficult to bomb. H-2 had five SAM launchers and 136 AA guns. H-3 had eight launchers and about 150 AA guns. The Navy had already lost two planes flying a low level mission at H-3, and that loss had forced CENTCOM to restrict its pilots to higher altitudes. This affected not only accuracy but bomb selection. The Rockeye cluster bomb was the ideal choice for taking out Scuds, but it could not be used because at high altitudes its fusing mechanism was unreliable. It tended to release the bomblets too high, releasing them over too wide an area for them to be effective. Guided bombs were not an option. Planes equipped to drop them were in short supply and were needed elsewhere. The chances of destroying Scud launchers by dropping unguided bombs at high altitude were so remote that planners quickly dismissed the idea.

The plan developed by the 82nd called for the envelopment of the airfields by all three brigades (two by parachute and one by helicopter). Division leaders were enthusiastic about the mission, but CENTCOM was concerned about the risk involved. Fortunately, enough planes were upgraded with smart bomb capability to make guided bombing of H-2 and H-3 possible, and planning for the paratroop mission was halted.

In mid-February, special operations teams began running into trouble. The Iraqis were out looking for roving bands of commandos, and were beginning to find them.

---

*After the fall of the Shah, two of Ross Perot's employees were jailed by revolutionary authorities. Perot hired the recently retired Simons to get them out of Iran. Simons refused to discuss the terms of the deal during the planning or execution of the operation. When, on the safe return of the employees, Perot told Simons he could name his price, Simons refused to accept any payment.

Frantic radio calls from teams fleeing Iraqi soldiers were becoming fairly common. In some cases, Air Force fighter-bombers were coming to the rescue in the nick of time. In early February, a pair of F-15Es saved a Delta Force team by scattering Gator mines between the team and the seven vehicles pursuing them. They then destroyed the vehicles as the team was extracted. On 12 February, nine armored vehicles were chased away from four running Delta commandos by Strike Eagles.

On the night of 13–14 February, another Delta Force team was compromised. A flight of two F-15Es responded to their calls for help just as three Iraqi helicopters were chasing the commandos toward a company of Iraqi troops. When one of the helicopters landed, possibly to unload troops, one of the Strike Eagles dropped a 2,000 lb. guided bomb. About ten seconds after the bomb was released, the helicopter took off. The Weapons System Operator, Capt. Daniel Bakke, kept the laser designator on the target as it lifted off. The fins on the bomb gently adjusted its trajectory until it slammed directly into the cockpit of the helicopter 800 feet above the ground. The other F-15E then swooped down to deliver six 500 lb. bombs on the spot where the helicopter had been, to kill any troops it may have dropped off. The other two helicopters escaped, but the way was clear for a Blackhawk helicopter to extract the Delta team.

The Green Berets played a key role in the Gulf War. The working unit of the Special Forces is the operational detachment, or "A-team." There are typically twelve men on an A-team. Each team is led by a captain. The team leader is assisted by a "team tech," a warrant officer whose specialty is special operations. A typical SF warrant will have about ten years of enlisted Special Forces experience before becoming a warrant officer. He is generally the most well-rounded member of the team, and is usually qualified to do any job within the team. The team sergeant is the senior NCO, usually a master sergeant (MSG) or a sergeant first class (SFC).

There are no privates on an A-team. The remaining nine men range in rank from sergeant to SFC, although on most teams the lowest ranking man is a staff sergeant (SSG). In practical terms, this means that the enlisted members of an A-team have from 5 to 20 years of experience. On each team there are two communications experts, two demolitions experts, two weapons experts, and two medics. The medics are the best in the Army, and can perform relatively delicate operations if necessary. Finally, there is an intelligence sergeant. Each team member is cross-trained in all areas. If, for instance, a demolitions man is killed, the remaining team members will know enough about explosives to get his assigned job done.

There are usually six A-teams in a Special Forces company. While regular army companies are commanded by captains, SF companies are commanded by a major. There are three companies in an SF battalion, commanded by a lieutenant colonel. Special Forces brigades are called "groups" There are three battalions in a group, which is commanded by a colonel.

The Green Berets are geared primarily to provide training and technical assistance to friendly developing nations' forces.* Toward that end Green Berets receive extensive language training. However, their high standard of training also makes them useful for a variety of other tasks, from reconnaissance, to sabotage, to sniping. They

---

*If ever there was a misleading term, it is "military advisor" as it applies to the Green Berets. One is given the impression of a director overseeing the action from afar. In fact, Green Berets often give their advice from the thickest part of the battle.

were among the first soldiers to find themselves behind Iraqi lines. As the Coalition began to lose aircraft, teams were helicoptered to crash sites to remove any sensitive documents, electronics equipment and black boxes that may have survived the crash and might otherwise have been captured by the Iraqis.*†

The day before the ground offensive, seven Special Forces teams were dropped by helicopter into southern Iraq to perform surveillance for the ground assault. CENTCOM already had an extensive collection of aerial and satellite photos of Iraqi positions, as well as JSTARS to track Iraqi movements. However, there was no substitute for having human eyes behind the lines.

Some of the surveillance teams were as small as three men, others as large as twelve. Nine missions had been called for, but one drop on the western flank had to be canceled because it conflicted with the operations of units in the area. Another team was spotted by Iraqi radar on the way to its designated location and had to return to its base. A third team reached its surveillance position but found that there was no natural concealment from the Iraqis, and the ground was too hard and rocky to dig an effective hiding position. The team reluctantly called for a helicopter extraction. The remaining six teams were spread out across the terrain which would be covered by the Coalition's left hook. Situated near main access routes, they were to report any Iraqi troop movements which might pose a threat to onrushing Coalition forces.

Two of the Special Forces teams were compromised, and hasty and dangerous extractions became necessary. One three-man team north of the Euphrates river was discovered by a curious eight-year-old girl. Had it been an Iraqi soldier, the three men would have dispatched him with their silenced Baretta pistols, dragged his body into the hole and continued their reconnaissance. But none of the Green Berets could shoot an eight-year-old girl. She ran to get her father and he ran off to warn some Iraqi soldiers nearby. The team was soon surrounded by an Iraqi infantry company. As a Blackhawk helicopter from Task Force 160 raced 150 miles over Iraqi territory in broad daylight to the rescue, F-16s pinned down the Iraqis. Nine Iraqis were able to get to within 50 meters of the hideout, and were shot dead by the recon team. Finally, the Blackhawk arrived. As two door gunners and two SF volunteers provided cover, the three men were pulled out. No one in the helicopter or on the recon team was killed or wounded.

Meanwhile, to the east, another team was fighting for its life. This team was also compromised by children they refused to shoot. This compromise also resulted in nearby Iraqi soldiers being alerted. Eight Green Berets, chest deep in a canal, fought for more than six hours against some 180 Iraqis until they were extracted. They were supported by F-16s from the 10th Tactical Fighter Squadron. The F-16s had been diverted from their original target 135 miles away. As they dodged intense anti-aircraft fire, they dropped cluster munitions on the Iraqis. Some of the bombs had to be dropped as close as 200 meters from the Green Berets' position. Finally, as the planes were running low on fuel, the Iraqis broke and ran. Army helicopters extracted the eight commandos and headed for home. No Americans were killed during the battle, but about 130 Iraqis were either killed or wounded.

---

*The pre-eminent Green Beret unit in the Gulf War was the 5th Special Forces Group of Vietnam War fame. The unit is presently stationed at Fort Campbell, Kentucky.

†During the war, 5th Group undertook several "direct action" missions aimed at Iraqi command and control. They cut fiber-optic cables and performed a variety of other sabotage missions.

American recon teams were not the only people operating behind Iraqi lines. The British Army's Special Air Service (SAS) was also active. There is one active SAS regiment (22 SAS) of about 700 men, and another two reserve SAS regiments (21 and 23 SAS) of similar strength. Soldiers volunteer for the SAS from their parent regiments, and undergo a four-month training and selection process, which only about 20% are able to complete. From that point, those selected undergo further training in more specialized military skills for the better part of two years before becoming fully qualified members of the regiment.

Unlike Gen. Schwarzkopf, Lt.Gen. Sir Peter de la Billiere, commander of all British forces in the Gulf, understood the possibilities of commando warfare, having once commanded the SAS. De la Billiere urged that the SAS be made an integral part of the war from the beginning of the air campaign. About two hundred SAS men took part in the Gulf War. Many of the SAS's missions involved raids behind enemy lines in which prisoners were brought back for interrogation, or equipment was brought back for examination. The British lost four dead (two of the dead were lost to hypothermia) and five captured. The SAS is shrouded in the same kind of secrecy as Delta Force. While SAS men received 17 gallantry medals for their actions, only the names of posthumous awardees were made public. No details of their exploits were officially released.

The clock was running on the Coalition. The Iraqi units on the Saddam Line were now combat nonentities, and the risks of additional delay were beginning to outweigh the benefits which might be gained by more bombing. Allied forces were at peak readiness. Further delay might result in Coalition ground units losing some of their fighting edge. Public support of the bombing was another consideration. The round-the-clock bombing had achieved most of its objectives. Soon, it would begin to look like overkill, and possibly arouse sympathy for the Iraqis. The *shamals* (Arabic for sandstorms) were looming large in the weather picture. Each year, the shamals begin in late February and reach a crescendo in March. Finally, *Ramadan*, the holiest month in the Islamic calendar would begin on 17 March. An attack during Ramadan was out of the question for obvious political reasons. Attacking after Ramadan would mean fighting in summer heat, condemning Coalition troops to operations in almost inhuman conditions. The Coalition had to force the issue.

On 15 February, Saddam offered to withdraw from Kuwait, but conditioned his withdrawal on all Coalition Forces leaving the region, and Israel leaving all occupied territories. The offer contained other conditions as well. All other U.N. resolutions beyond that which called for the withdrawal of Iraqi forces had to be waived, including the requirement that Iraq pay reparations for damage done to Kuwait. In conjunction with the so-called peace offer, an Iraqi delegation began negotiations with the Soviet Union. The Soviets felt that they could gain Iraqi withdrawal from Kuwait, but that more time would be required. The Bush administration believed that Saddam was stalling. President Bush set a deadline of noon (Eastern Standard Time) on 23 February for the withdrawal of Iraqi forces from all of Kuwait. If the Soviets could engineer a deal that got Iraqi forces out in accordance with the U.N. resolutions before then, the Iraqis would be allowed to withdraw in peace. If not, there would be a ground assault.

Saddam ignored Bush's ultimatum. While President Francois Mitterand of France was requesting that Saddam be given an additional 48 hours, Iraqi soldiers began blowing up oil wells in Kuwait. Mitterand dropped the request. It was clear that Saddam had no understanding of the offensive power arrayed against him. He had no concept of rapid, hard-hitting maneuver warfare, and believed that he could hold out against the Coalition as long as necessary. Evidence of that belief came in the gathering of refrigerated trucks. During the Iran–Iraq War, refrigerated trucks had played an important part in morale support. After battles in which the Iraqi Army had suffered murderous casualties, hundreds or thousands of dead soldiers would be kept on ice and released slowly, over a period of months. That way, the government could report moderate casualties over a long period, instead of reporting a military disaster. Apparently, Saddam believed that he could do the same against the Coalition, but when the ground attack came, the war would be over in days, not months.

Coalition preparatory activity was building to a crescendo. A total of 2,800 sorties were flown on 19 February. Saudi F-5s attacked and destroyed ammunition dumps, fuel depots, supply bases and six tanks. A-10s and helicopter gunships stalked Iraqi rear areas, shooting up tanks. Meanwhile, Allied guns and multiple rocket launchers pounded the trenches.

The B-52 force was extremely active on 23 February. During the war, Stratofortresses dropped almost 26,000 tons of bombs, about 30% of the total tonnage dropped. However, since the element of terror is greatest in soldiers who are experiencing a B-52 strike for the first time, no B-52 raids on the Saddam Line were scheduled until the night before the beginning of the ground offensive. Unfortunately, the destructive potential of B-52 carpet bombing raids would lead to the cancellation of raids on the Saddam Line.

During B-52 carpet bombing raids, 750 lb. unguided "dumb" bombs were generally used. A typical flight of three B-52s dropped one hundred fifty-three 750 lb. bombs, saturating a "bomb box" with over 57 tons of bombs, about 28 tons of explosives and another 29 tons of hot, jagged metal. When more punch was required, there was the half-ton Mk 83 or the one-ton Mk 84. A Mk 84 is capable of creating a hole 50 feet wide and 36 feet deep. It can kill exposed personnel at up to 400 meters.

In the weeks before G-Day, there had been a spirited debate regarding B-52 strikes between senior U.S. Marine unit commanders and the engineers who would be responsible for breaching the minefields. The engineers wanted no B-52 strikes on the Saddam Line because they feared that strikes on the trenches would result in many bombs landing in the obstacle belt. The bombs would blow live mines around and chew up the terrain. The unit commanders sympathized with the engineers, but with several Iraqi divisions in prepared positions, they believed that a high degree of Iraqi attrition would be required to keep Marine casualties down. They were prepared to overrule the engineers when the commanders of some of the units doing the preparatory work for the main assault also voiced concerns. These units would be working in close proximity to the Iraqi front lines. Some would be working in the minefields. A bombing strike would therefore not have to be off by very much to land on Marines, and carpet bombing was not a precision technique. This tipped the balance, and the raids were shifted northward, to the south of Kuwait City. There, there would be less chance of friendly fire incidents, but bombing would be less effective because there would be fewer Iraqis to bomb.

Air attacks carry the risk of fratricide when done in proximity to friendly troops. As if to drive home the point, there was a friendly fire incident when a HARM missile homed in on emissions from a Marine artillery-spotting radar, killing one Marine and wounding another.

While Allied forces in the west prepared to deliver the knockout blow, naval activity and gunfire from the Gulf reinforced Iraqi fears about a coastal assault. In the first week of February, about 8,000 Marines practiced amphibious landings on the coast of Oman. That same week, several gun emplacements on Faylakah Island were hit by British Jaguars. Two weeks later, the Iraqis on Faylakah were pounded for two days by Marine aircraft. A 15,000 lb. BLU-82 bomb was dropped on the island during early February. Then, on the night before the ground offensive, the USS *Missouri* shelled the island heavily.

As G-Day approached, a multinational armada of 31 ships conducted preparations for what looked like an amphibious assault. The battleships *Wisconsin* and *Missouri* hammered Iraqi shore defenses with their 16-inch guns, destroying radar installations, SAM sites and dug-in Iraqi coastal units. The guns were directed by pilotless drones equipped with TV cameras, and were capable of hitting a target the size of a tennis court from 25 miles. Their 2,700 lb. shells can penetrate over 20 feet of concrete. The two ships fired a total of 1,102 16-inch shells. This was equivalent to the dropping of almost six thousand 500 lb. bombs. The impact of four shells was equal to that of a bombing sortie from a carrier-based A-6E Intruder. Bomb Damage Assessments are available for 68 targets engaged by 16-inch guns. A total of 22 were completely destroyed, 7 were neutralized, 18 were heavily damaged and 21 sustained light or moderate damage.

Since January, Navy SEALs had conducted reconnaissance on Iraqi coastal defenses in Kuwait and its offshore islands. Some slipped into Kuwait City and provided laser target designation for Coalition aircraft. This allowed air strikes against targets in the city to go ahead when the weather went bad, and later, when smoke from burning oil wells obscured the city.

Three hours before the ground assault, a six-man SEAL team led by Lt. Tom Dietz created a diversionary assault on the Kuwaiti coast. The SEALS, supported by speedboats, landed along a 200 meter stretch of beach at Kuwait City. They placed explosives and laid large buoys, which the defenders assumed were lanes for incoming landing craft. When the explosions started and the speedboats began raking the shore with machine-gun fire, the Iraqis assumed that a major landing was imminent, and called for reinforcement.

After the war, there would be claims that as many as four Iraqi divisions were drawn to the coast, away from the site of the main assault. In fact, though the raid was conducted with a high degree of technical and tactical virtuosity, and it drew Iraqi attention toward the sea at a critical time, there was no significant Iraqi movement toward the coast. Perhaps this should have been expected. Unaware that five Coalition heavy divisions, three light divisions and two armored cavalry regiments had moved west, the Iraqis must have assumed the Allied force south of the Kuwait border to be massive. It was probably unrealistic to expect the Iraqis to pull significant armored forces away from a perceived threat of that magnitude to deal with a possible amphibious attack by a brigade or two of Marines.

Sea-launched operations continued after the start of the ground war, in order to keep the Iraqi units on the coast worried about amphibious landings and therefore pinned to their positions. In the early hours of 25 February, U.S. Marine CH-46 and CH-53 helicopters launched a raid on the Kuwaiti port of Ash Shuaybah. As soon as door gunners opened up with .50 caliber machine-gun fire, the Iraqis responded with a heavy volume of AAA fire. After ten minutes, and no losses, the raiders headed back to sea.

Shortly after the raiding force left, the Iraqis, apparently sensing an imminent amphibious assault, fired two Silkworm missiles at the USS *Missouri*. The first missile landed harmlessly in the water, possibly "spoofed" by Navy electronic countermeasures. The second was destroyed in flight by defensive missiles from HMS *Gloucester*. The U.S. Navy responded immediately. A carrier-based Intruder medium bomber dodged intense AA gun and missile fire to drop 12 cluster bombs, destroying both launch sites.

The next day's targets were Bubiyan and Faylakah islands. Bubiyan, a large island to the northeast of the Kuwaiti mainland was virtually undefended. Though strategically located, because the island was unsuitable for vehicular traffic, it was virtually indefensible. Its coast was marshland, and its interior was almost entirely sabkha. As a result, the Iraqis merely placed a few anti-aircraft batteries on the southern end of the island with the hope that they might make life a bit more difficult for pilots on their way to bomb targets near Basra. Faylakah, on the approach to Kuwait Bay, was almost completely flat, but its terrain was firm enough to defend, and contained the better part of an Iraqi brigade.

At about 4 a.m., three two-helicopter teams of Hueys, equipped with machine-guns and 2.75-inch rockets, hit Faylakah from the west at an altitude of 200 feet. As at Ash Shuaybah, the attack was met by AAA fire. After causing several secondary explosions, and losing no helicopters, the force headed out to sea.

Just before 5 a.m., another raiding force hit southern Bubiyan. CH-46 door gunners were met by AAA fire, again without loss. After ten minutes, the raiders left and Intruders took over, bombing the Iraqi batteries. Though few, if any, Iraqis were killed in the bombing, the Iraqi gunners abandoned their weapons and left the island.

On 2 March, after the cessation of Allied offensive operations, loudspeaker-equipped U.S. Marine helicopters approached Faylakah. The helicopters instructed the Iraqis on the island to move to a communications site and wait for the Marines, who would take possession of the island on the following morning.

At dawn on 3 March, the day the Armistice was to be signed, aerial reconnaissance confirmed that the Iraqis had abandoned their heavy weapons and gathered at the communications site. At 8:02, CH-46s landed Capt. Gregory Boyle's Company D, 1st Battalion, 4th Marine Regiment on Faylakah. After Company D had set up a defensive perimeter, Col. John Rhodes, commander of the 13th Marine Expeditionary Unit, arrived. Shortly thereafter, the commander of the Iraqi 440th Marine Brigade surrendered the island and its 1,413-man garrison, the last intact Iraqi unit in Kuwait, to Rhodes. By 3:30 that afternoon, the last of the Iraqi prisoners had been helicoptered off the island.

Part IV

How to Inflict a Disaster

"This war didn't take 100 hours to win. It took 15 years."

—Maj.Gen. Barry McCaffrey,
Commander, 24th Infantry Division

8

The Plans

No planning is done in the United States Armed Forces without carefully considering "METT-T." This stands for: Mission, Enemy, Terrain, Troops available, and Time. The first consideration is the mission. Before a military leader can do any planning, he has to know what he is being told to accomplish. Once he knows that, all further planning should be geared to achieving that end. Next, he has to consider his enemy. A knowledge of all aspects of the opposing force is required. The number of enemy soldiers, their morale, their level of training, the weapons with which they are equipped, their deployment, even their physical condition, are all taken into account. Weapons are an especially important consideration when determining an enemy's capabilities. All weapons have strengths and weaknesses. Military planners have to know their own equipment, and their enemy's. They must use tactics which allow them to exploit their own strengths and their enemy's weaknesses. The next consideration is terrain. War in a jungle, war in a city and war in a desert are three completely different enterprises. Next, the commander will have to know how many troops he has available for the mission. Finally, the commander has to know how much time he has to accomplish his mission. This will determine such things as how long he can soften up his enemy before he attacks.

Correct evaluation of the tactical situation, not genius, was responsible for the success of the ground campaign. The ground offensive was largely a response to the METT-T cards dealt Gen. Schwarzkopf and his staff.

The plan called for the I Marine Expeditionary Force and Joint Forces Commands North and East (made up of Arab forces) to drive into Kuwait, drawing the Iraqi High Command's attention, while the XVIII Airborne and VII corps destroyed the Iraqi Army from the flank and rear.

The XVIII Airborne Corps would be responsible for shooting ahead through the more thinly held areas in the far west and securing the left flank of the offensive. The French *Daguet* Division, with the attached 82nd Airborne Division, would set up a screen on the far left flank. The heliborne 101st Airborne Division (Air Assault) would land deep behind Iraqi lines, cutting off a key avenue of possible Iraqi retreat. The 24th

Infantry Division (Mechanized) would make the longest dash of the war, sweeping in a wide arc toward Basra, destroying Republican Guard motorized units on the way.[*]

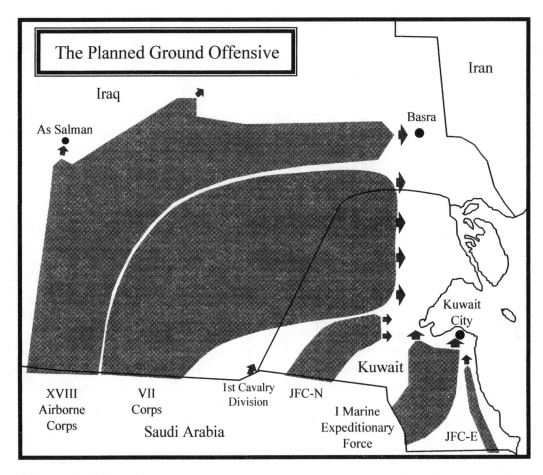

The VII Corps would do the heaviest fighting, as it took the inside route where Iraqi forces and Iraqi armor were thickest. VII Corps would ultimately account for over 60% of all Iraqi armored vehicles destroyed in the war. The 1st Infantry Division (Mechanized), in conjunction with the British 1st Armoured Division would establish the hinge on which the left hook would swing. The 2nd Armored Cavalry Regiment would then seek out the heaviest units of the Republican Guard and the regular armored formations that accompanied them. The 1st and 3rd Armored divisions and one other yet-to-be-determined heavy division would then move forward and destroy the Iraqi formations.[†]

Meanwhile, the 1st Cavalry Division, the theater reserve, would launch its diversionary attack up the Wadi al-Batin. The division's follow-on mission would depend on how the larger battle unfolded.

---

[*]The basic difference between U.S. armored and mechanized infantry divisions is that armored divisions usually have six armor battalions and four mechanized infantry battalions, while in mechanized infantry divisions it is the other way around.

[†]The 3rd Armored Division was not originally part of VII Corps. It was transferred from V Corps for the Gulf deployment.

The CIA insisted that the Iraqi terrain through which Schwarzkopf intended to launch his left hook was too soft for his vehicles. Neither Schwarzkopf nor his generals believed it. Six-man teams drawn from the A-teams of 5th Special Forces Group were secreted into Iraq by helicopter. After soil samples and terrain photos from the operation were analyzed in Riyadh, CENTCOM was satisfied. The offensive would continue as planned.

The Gulf War was fought in 1991, but it was won during the 1980s. In August, 1982, the Army adopted the AirLand Battle as its doctrine of offensive warfare. The AirLand Battle doctrine is a direct descendant of the German *Blitzkrieg* of World War II. The destruction of the Iraqi Army was very similar to the destruction of the French Army in 1940. The Germans achieved the swift defeat of the numerically superior French Army by striking at vulnerable points with massed armor, bypassing strongpoints, driving deep into rear areas, destroying artillery and logistical support and crippling command and control capabilities.

The Germans used overwhelming air superiority in conjunction with mobile forces. British and French aircraft were swept from the skies by superior German fighters. This allowed German reconnaissance aircraft to fly at will over France, relaying information about French and British troop movements. Dive bombers acted as airborne artillery, softening up positions, destroying artillery, smashing troop concentrations and preventing reinforcements from moving to the front. Anything which might have slowed the German advance was a target. Tanks then moved rapidly to encircle the defenders. Infantry followed to mop up.

The French Army was destroyed in six weeks with 180,000 dead, 200,000 wounded and 1,800,000 prisoners. The Belgians, Dutch and British lost another 100,000 men between them. The Germans suffered only 45,000 deaths in the fighting. Since the collapse of resistance in France in 1940, the Blitzkrieg has been the pattern after which several nations have designed their offensive doctrines.

The AirLand Battle involves offensive operations in depth. The doctrine is based on the idea that it is easier to paralyze an army than it is to destroy it in a slugging match. The goal of the AirLand Battle is to paralyze a numerically superior force using speed, maneuver and firepower that is both precise and massive. This phenomenon can best be described as "blitzgrinding." AirLand is spelled as it is to signify the marriage of air and ground power.

The AirLand Battle replaced the "Active Defense" doctrine. That doctrine was designed for the defense of western Europe. It had called for the containment of Soviet thrusts, attrition of the attacking forces, then counterattacks with reserves. However, it became apparent that NATO was not structured to implement an active defense. NATO forces, already badly outnumbered, could not have afforded the losses that the containment and attrition phases would have produced. The citizens of the democratic NATO nations were also unwilling to tolerate such a slaughter of their soldiers (as well as their civilians, since much of the fighting would have taken place in western Europe). In addition, overwhelming Warsaw Pact numerical superiority in troops, planes, tanks, and artillery would probably have stretched NATO defenders to the limit. Holding major NATO troop concentrations in reserve for counterattacks seemed unrealistic if every man would be needed on the front lines just to keep them from breaking. The Active Defense concept had to be abandoned.

The AirLand Battle doctrine developed largely in response to technological innovations. Advances in technology, particularly in the area of microcomputing, changed the nature of modern warfare. The computer chip was instrumental in the development of computerized aiming systems, which gave aircraft and tanks unprecedented accuracy. Targets could now be destroyed by accurate direct fire at previously unheard of ranges.

By 1991, the U.S. Armed Forces had perfected the AirLand Battle doctrine and had the people and equipment to make it work. Iraq provided the perfect terrain and enemy on which the doctrine could be effectively implemented. American manufacturers design weapons that are accurate at long ranges. While in hilly, heavily forested western Europe, unobstructed shots of even 500 meters are uncommon, in the desert, soldiers and pilots could maximize their range advantage. They could also spot targets more easily. The Iraqi Army would be pounded at every turn, day and night.

The Iraqi Army also occupied a front that was too long to be defended effectively at all points. There would be weak spots, and that meant that there would be opportunities for armored breakthroughs. "First, we're going to cut it [the Iraqi Army] off," said Gen. Colin Powell, "then we're going to kill it." Saddam compounded the problem by concentrating a large portion of his army in Kuwait. This offered the Coalition not just a weak spot on the Iraqi Army's flank, but a virtually undefended one. Von Moltke, the great German strategist once said that: "An error in the original concentration of armies can hardly be made good in the entire course of a campaign." Saddam had deployed his forces badly, and they would not be given a chance to recover.

The Gulf War was precipitated by a quick, successful Iraqi offensive operation, the conquest of Kuwait. However, at the time of the conflict, the Iraqi Army was essentially a defense-oriented organization. Of the 45 divisions deployed in the combat zone, only 12 (the armored and mechanized divisions) had serious offensive capabilities. Part of this stance may have been attributable to a belief in the inherent advantages of defensive warfare. Part of that belief may have been due to overconfidence bred by the Iranian failure to overcome Iraqi defenses during the Iran–Iraq War. But mostly, the Iraqi Army was defense-oriented because it had to be.

Even simple offensive maneuvers require a certain degree of sophistication. This means well-trained, experienced soldiers and plenty of unit-level practice. The Iraqi Army was deficient in terms of manpower quality, and equipped with hardware that could not stand up to the kind of wear and tear that comes with constant practice. A serious commitment to the offensive was not a realistic option. Defense, on the other hand, requires little or no unit maneuver, and far less sophistication. Even short service conscripts can do fairly well at it without much practice, provided that they are stubborn and the defenses are well set up and the tactics are sound.

A commitment to the defensive nevertheless has its down side. Whether it resulted from hubris or necessity, the Iraqi Army had the same defensive mentality as the French Army of 1940 and made all the same mistakes. The Saddam Line was dealt with in the same fashion as the Maginot Line had been.

The Maginot Line was the most formidable defensive barrier in the history of warfare. The line ran along the entire length of France's border with Germany and Luxembourg. Barbed wire and a series of anti-tank obstacles were backed up by block houses and pillboxes. Behind that, the main works featured a deep anti-tank ditch, behind which lurked fortresses of concrete and steel, 10 feet thick in some places. Armored gun turrets popped out of the ground to deliver cannon, anti-tank and machine-gun fire, as well as launched grenades. The fortresses incorporated fireproof ammunition storage facilities, and underground electric railways to carry men and ammunition to the gun turrets. Underground power stations provided heat and light. Air was circulated by a powerful poison gas-proof ventilation system. Each fort had enough food, water and supplies to last for three months in the event that the fort was cut off. The system was about 10 miles deep along the front.

The Germans just went around the Maginot Line, and when they did, one of the greatest military catastrophes in history ensued. This was one of the lessons which prompted Patton to label fixed fortifications: "monuments to the stupidity of man." Once . fixed positions are outflanked, the battle is just about over. Fixed fortifications can not be moved to meet unexpected threats. If they are outflanked, they have to be abandoned. By making the same mistakes the French made in 1940, the Iraqi Army guaranteed itself the same disastrous results.

The Saddam Line, which was not even close to finished when the bombing started, was no Maginot Line, but it lulled the Iraqi Army into a false sense of security for which it paid dearly. The Iraqis dug in and awaited the impending attack in a 2–5 mile deep defense system. The Iraqi Army dug an estimated 100,000 fighting positions of various types. As a result, Coalition warplanes could never be sure which positions were occupied and which were not. In addition, there were wooden tank dummies, as well as metal pipes protruding from shallow holes covered by camouflage nets. They all looked like real tanks from the air, and had to be engaged. The empty foxholes and dummy tanks resulted in a lot of wasted bombs and ammunition. The problem for the Iraqis was that the Coalition had the bombs and ammunition to waste.

The first obstacle that Allied forces would encounter would be berms several feet high. A tank attempting to drive directly over such a berm would expose its thin underbelly as it ascended, and the thin top of its turret as it descended, making it vulnerable to anti-tank fire. This sounds dangerous in theory, but if the defenders flee, as the Iraqis did, combat engineers can breach the berms with very little difficulty.

Next came several layers of razor or "concertina" wire. This usually has to be blown apart by explosives or cut. Tanks cannot drive directly over razor wire, because it can become entangled in the sprocket which drives the tank, immobilizing it. In theory, soldiers attempting to wade through it or jump over it would have to expose themselves to enemy fire to do it, and would find it slow going in any case. However, since the wire was not covered by Iraqi fire, breaching it would prove little more than a minor inconvenience.

Behind the wire were anti-tank ditches. These are simply ditches that are too wide for a tank to cross without falling in. In theory, each ditch would require a certain amount of engineer work and valuable time for Coalition tanks to cross, but most Iraqi tank ditches were narrow enough for Allied tanks to cross easily.

Many trenches had been filled with fuel, which the Iraqis intended to set ablaze when the attacking forces approached. Theoretically, these "fire trenches" would be too hot to even attempt to cross. Tanks would have to find another way around, unless, as was the case, the fire trenches had already burned themselves out by the time the tanks showed up.

Methodically laid throughout the system were at least a half-million anti-tank and anti-personnel mines. Most of the mines in the Iraqi inventory were Italian. The most common mines in the Iraqi arsenal were the Valmera-69 Bounding Anti-Personnel Mine, and the VS 1.6 and 2.2 anti-tank mines.

During World War II, most anti-personnel mines were lethal only to the soldier who stepped on it. The Valmera-69 jumps 18 inches into the air after it is stepped on (or is set off by trip wire), then explodes. The 1,200 pre-formed metal fragments it sprays can kill at 25 meters and wound at over 150. However, such mines are not a major problem to soldiers (like those of the Coalition) riding in armored vehicles.

The VS 1.6 and 2.2 are both made of plastic and cannot be detected easily. However, they can still be neutralized in a variety of ways. Anti-tank mines like these are mostly used to produce "mobility kills" by blowing off tracks, sprockets or road wheels. Crewmen will often be shaken up, but fatalities are relatively rare. In addition, anti-tank mines can destroy an APC or a truck, but the soldiers inside can be protected somewhat by the relatively simple expedient of lining the floor of the APC, or the bed of the truck, with sandbags. A mine may wreck the vehicle, but the sandbags will absorb much of the force, molten metal, or shrapnel that would otherwise have killed those riding in it.[*]

Pre-Ground War discussion of mines brought up images of the epic struggles between Rommel and Montgomery in the desert during the Second World War. Mine warfare played a key role in battles like El Alamein. However, there were crucial differences between the minefields in the Gulf and those at El Alamein. The Iraqi belts were thinner (500–1000 meters vs. 3–7 kilometers), less dense (2,000 mines per kilometer vs. 7,000) and less competently laid (Iraqi engineers vs. Afrika Korps engineers).

Of course, the composition of minefields is largely irrelevant if your opponent can simply go around them. When Rommel laid his famous mine belt, the British 8th Army had to go through it. The British could not go around the southern end of the minefields because they would have ended up in the Qattara Depression, a vast, impassable area of salt marsh and quicksand. On the northern edge of the mine belt was the Mediterranean Sea. The only option open to Montgomery's forces was to pick their way through the minefield with bayonets, yard by yard. Southern Kuwait was not a good place for a mine belt. The eastern end of the minebelt was anchored on the Persian Gulf, but the western end was wide open. Most Coalition units simply went around the mine belt.

Saddam's trump card was to be the Republican Guard heavy divisions backstopping his forces in Kuwait. These units were stationed largely on the northern borders of Kuwait, terrain on which they had trained and were familiar with. In theory, Coalition forces would be bled white as they slugged their way through Kuwait, or pushed up the Wadi al-Batin, destroying second- and third-rate Iraqi units. Then, having saved his best troops for last, Saddam would throw in the Republican Guard and turn the tide. Making use of prearranged artillery targets, fighting on terrain that they knew well, the Guard units were sure to achieve success, just as they had against Iran. So Saddam thought.

Instead, Guard learned an important lesson about taking shortcuts in training. What happened to the Guard was roughly equivalent to the experience of a student who steals the answers to a test, only to see a different test on the morning of the exam. Guard

---

[*]This was not done widely in the Gulf. Effective clearance of lanes through the minefields made this process, which weighs vehicles down, unnecessary.

units were formidable as long as they were fighting in carefully prepared defensive positions, waiting for a predictable enemy. When they realized that they were being cut off, they had to pull up stakes, move to the west and fight when they got there. The Guard simply did not know how to do it, and was torn to shreds.

In the final analysis, Iraq's defensive strategy played into the Coalition's hands. This surprised many pundits, who before the war had assumed that if anyone was going to be outsmarted, it would be the Allies. After all, they reasoned, the Iraqis had just finished fighting a decade-long war and surely had the edge in terms of combat experience. However, aside from a few bad experiences with Israel, the Iran–Iraq War was Iraq's only modern combat test, and the Iraqi Army apparently did not learn much from it. The Iraqi Army's almost complete inability to learn from experience would doom it in the Gulf War.

The war would show that the experience advantage really rested with the Coalition. Vietnam had been a losing enterprise, but when it ended, the United States found itself the world expert on the delivery of aerial ordnance and helicopter warfare. Grenada and Panama provided more combat experience. British and French forces have been deployed to combat several times since World War II. Egypt had seen three major wars. Lessons from every one of those conflicts have guided the military doctrine of these armies.

The painful or humiliating lessons were particularly helpful. On the third day of the ground war, a captured Republican Guard officer was riding in the back of an American armored personnel carrier when he noticed a picture of Erwin Rommel taped to the wall. "You admire your enemies?" he asked the young enlisted soldier guarding him. "Some of 'em," the soldier replied. "You can learn a lot from them sometimes. For instance, if you'd read more about Rommel you might not be a POW and your battalion probably wouldn't have been destroyed in five minutes."

Most of the Coalition troops in the Gulf had not personally participated in combat, but they had the benefit of the lessons that had been learned from previous conflicts. First hand experience can be useful, but a soldier can get the point without it. "I never personally harpooned a whale," remarked one U.S. Army officer, "but I understood Moby Dick just fine."

9

The Armor: Physics in Action

The result of the Gulf War's tank battles was basically a foregone conclusion. The battles came out the way they did essentially because the laws of physics and probability required them to. When two tanks face each other in combat, it is easy enough to figure out which one has the edge. In fact, there is a simple mathematical formula for it, expressed in percentages. Your chances of killing your opponent involve: (A) the chance of you hitting your opponent; (B) assuming that you do, the chance of your tank round penetrating your opponent's armor, and (C) assuming that it does penetrate, the chances of it doing catastrophic damage inside your opponent's tank. AxBxC will give you your chances of killing your opponents, and them their chances of killing you. In previous wars, the two percentages were usually reasonably close, so the tank that scored the first hit almost always won. Some tanks were better than others, but very seldom was one tank so much better than its opponent that it could afford to take the first hit. This war was different.

In a head-to-head engagement with an Abrams at 1,800 meters, a T-72 had roughly a 50% chance of hitting its target. If it did, there was a 0% chance that the round would penetrate the M-1A1's (or the British Challenger's) frontal armor. Since the Iraqi rounds could not penetrate, there was a 0% chance that they would do catastrophic damage inside the tank. Thus, a T-72 had a 0% chance of killing an Abrams or a Challenger from the front.

In a head-to-head engagement with a T-72 at 1,800 meters, an Abrams (or a Challenger) had roughly an 85% chance of hitting its target. If it did, there was a 99% chance that the round would penetrate the T-72's frontal armor. If it penetrated, there was about a 95% chance that it would do catastrophic damage inside the tank. Thus, each round had about an 80% chance of killing a T-72 from the front

There were instances where Iraqi tanks ambushed American tanks at point-blank range and penetrated thinner side armor, but about 80% of history's desert tank engagements were front-to-front, and that held true in this war. Thus, in most cases it would not have mattered whether the Iraqis scored the first hit or not. The qualitative gap between Coalition and Iraqi tanks was simply too great. When one tank has an 80%

chance of achieving a kill, and the other has a 0% chance, the outcome of the engagement is not in question. How such an overwhelming qualitative disparity can be accounted for is an important question.

Much of the accuracy of Coalition gunnery was due to ballistic computers. These computers take almost all of the guesswork out of tank gunnery. They make calculations and automatically adjust the gunnery system to compensate for the type of ammunition being fired, the cant (the degree to which the tank is tilting to the left or right) of a tank when the gun is fired, and the velocity of crosswinds. The computers even adjust for the degree of wear inside the gun barrel, and the degree of its warping, or "droop."

Over 60% of Iraq's tanks had no computers at all. On the ballistic computers the Iraqis had, corrections had to be calculated with charts and entered manually into the computer by the gunner. This system had two main disadvantages: it took time, and the corrections were only as good as the math of the poorly trained Iraqi in the gunner's seat. There was no computer compensation at all for things like crosswinds or the tank's own motion, basic features of Western ballistic computers.

The Iraqis had more basic gunnery problems. Iraqi tank guns generally did not point where they were aimed. Gun barrels tend to get bounced around significantly, and turrets rattle as tanks travel across country. Running the engine causes the turret to vibrate. Even when a tank is sitting around doing nothing, the long, heavy tank gun barrel is subject to the effects of gravity. All of these factors affect the way the gun sits in the turret, causing the barrel to get out of alignment with the sight. Eventually, the gunsights can be trained on the center of a target while the gun is actually pointed three feet to the left or right.*

For this reason, tank guns are periodically "boresighted" to ensure that the gun is aligned with the sight. A bull's-eye is put up 1,200 meters from the tank. The gunner points the gun barrel at what his sight tells him is the center of the target. A crewman places an optical device in the end of the gun barrel. The crosshairs in the optical device show the crewman where the gun is really pointing, usually not at the center of the target. He shouts instructions to the gunner who adjusts the gun's traverse and elevation with two small knobs until the gun is aligned with the sight. A few rounds are then put through the target for confirmation, and the tank is ready for action. While every Coalition tank was boresighted before ground fighting began, Iraqi tanks were not. Bombing and strafing make basic maintenance activities dangerous, and an activity like boresighting impossible.

The Coalition's tanks were equipped with laser rangefinders. A laser return gives the target's range in meters instantly, at the touch of a button, with great accuracy. Over half of Iraq's tanks still depended on the gunner's ability to estimate distance with the aid of a reticle in the gunsight. Obviously, with this method accuracy suffers. Iraq also found that buying laser rangefinders was one thing, but keeping them in working order was another. Laser rangefinders require care and maintenance. Maintenance is not a significant problem in the U.S. Army where there are skilled repairmen at battalion-level to fix the rangefinders. In the Iraqi Army, if a laser went down, it usually stayed down.

Laser rangefinders also need to be "zeroed," or aligned with the gun sight. The Iraqi Army's few lasers were apparently not properly zeroed. Unzeroed lasers don't point

---

*However, many Abrams crews found that their tank guns were still perfectly aligned after a 200 mile gallop across Iraq.

where they are aimed. For example, a gunner can aim his laser at a tank 1,000 meters away. If the laser misses the tank and hits a sand berm 400 meters further down the line, it will tell the gunner that his target is 1,400 meters away instead of 1,000. Or, the laser can miss and keep going, giving the gunner an "error" reading. If the gunner gets a bad reading he can try again, but while the gunner is playing around with the laser, an enemy gunner may be drawing a bead on his tank.

Iraqi tank gunnery was also hurt by the lack of durability in the tank fleet. The gun barrel on a T-72 wears out after firing about 100 rounds. On Western main battle tanks, gun barrels last about ten times as long. As a result, Iraqi tank crews could not fire their guns as often in training as their Coalition opponents. While Western crews can fire 1–200 rounds a year in training, the crews of Soviet- or Chinese-built tanks were generally limited to a dozen or so. Iraqi tank crewmen were therefore less skilled in basic gunnery. They were not able to deliver rounds as quickly or as accurately as Allied crews.

Advanced night vision technology would turn the battlefield into a graveyard for Iraqi tanks. Western tanks used thermal sensors to see at night. Thermal sensors pick up the heat given off by troops and equipment. Some are extremely sensitive. The night sight of an Abrams can pick up a man's footprints in the snow at long range from the minimal amount of heat that his boot has left behind. It can spot a soldier at 3,000 meters. The ground war was fought in rain, sandstorms, dust, haze and smoke. By using their superior thermal gunsights, Allied tank gunners could acquire targets through obscuration that blinded their opponents. Smoke, sand and dust are cooler than a tank, so thermal sights basically "ignore" the obscuration and pick up the much warmer tank behind it. In previous wars, tank commanders had to worry about such things as the direction of the wind when selecting targets. If there were two tanks to the front, and the wrong one was destroyed first, the smoke from the burning tank could blow across the other tank, hiding it. In this war, there would be no hiding from Allied tank guns.

Iraqi tanks had no comparable night sights. The Iraqi tanks that were equipped for night fighting had only the most primitive equipment that was of no use in dust, smoke, or haze. Most of Iraq's tanks depended on infra-red searchlights. These searchlights only have a range of about 800 meters, and have a tendency to give the vehicle's position away. Infra-red searchlights are also extremely fragile. To protect them from shrapnel damage during air or artillery strikes, crews must bolt steel covers on them when they are not fighting tanks. If enemy tanks show up before a crew has a chance to remove the cover, the searchlight will be useless. The speed of the Allied advance would catch many Iraqi tank crews with their searchlights covered.

Life would be much easier for tank gunners if they could rely on one type of ammunition, but what is effective in destroying some targets is not as effective against others. Tanks therefore need solid-shot penetrator rounds for other tanks, and explosive rounds for armored personnel carriers and bunkers. Understanding how these rounds work is an important step to understanding why the tank battles went the way they did.

APFSDS (Armor Piercing, Fin-Stabilized, Discarding Sabot) or "sabot" (pronounced "say-bo") rounds are fired by tanks at other tanks. The round consists of a super-dense metal penetrator (in most countries, made of tungsten) surrounded by "sabots" of a softer metal which discard as the round leaves the gun barrel. The Abrams has a 120mm main gun. This means that the inside of the gun barrel is 120mm, or about 4.8 inches across. The penetrator on an Abrams 120mm main gun round is actually about

40mm, or 1.6 inches in diameter. The sabots fill the bore of the gun so that the full power of the explosive charge can get behind the smaller penetrator, giving it maximum velocity. The solid penetrator looks like a metal arrow and is designed to smash through enemy armor at high velocity. This causes pieces of armor from the inside of the tank (known as spall) to detach and fly around the turret. Between the flying pieces of armor and the penetrator tearing through the turret, crewmen stand a good chance of being killed or wounded.

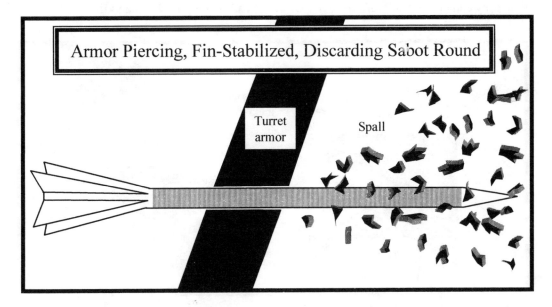

In American sabot rounds, tungsten had been replaced by depleted uranium, which is more effective than tungsten as a penetrator. In addition, though they do not contain any explosives, depleted uranium penetrators can cause fires in the vehicles they hit. During the penetration of armor, particles of uranium ignite, setting fire to flammable materials within the turret.

Shortly before the war, the U.S. Army introduced the 120mm M-829A1 Sabot round. It was about 25% longer than the M-829, which gave it more mass, so it hit with more momentum. It was the most lethal tank round in the world. However, U.S. tank crews were still somewhat worried, because the M-829A1 round was in short supply, and was rationed. On average, only about 10 were carried in the basic load of 40 rounds. Regular M-829s made up the bulk of the Army's sabot rounds, and there had been some concern that the round might not be able to penetrate Iraq's latest, up-armored T-72Ms. About a third of Iraq's T-72s were M models with 40% thicker frontal armor. The American crews need not have worried. Most tank crews never had to rely on the older rounds. About 88% of the sabot rounds carried on U.S. tanks were never fired. The crews that did use the older rounds found that they were powerful enough to destroy the most heavily armored T-72s.

Since Iraq's badly designed armored personnel carriers had fuel tanks or exposed ammunition in all the wrong places, sabot rounds worked surprisingly well against APCs during the war. However, as a general rule, sabot rounds are not used against APCs. An APC has a fraction of a tank's armor. Sabot rounds can tear through both sides of an APC without doing much damage or creating enough spall to injure its occupants.

Sabot rounds are no good for shooting at bunkers or buildings because they contain no explosive. Another reason sabot rounds are not used in bunker clearing operations is that in such situations, there will often be friendly soldiers to the front of the tank. Those troops can be injured or killed if a sabot round is fired. The pieces of softer metal that surround the penetrator in the barrel are referred to as "discarding sabots." However, the sabots, which weigh several pounds, don't just discard. They fly off the penetrator at extremely high velocities and bounce along the ground. If they hit a limb they can crush it or tear it off. If they hit a head or a torso, they can kill.[*]

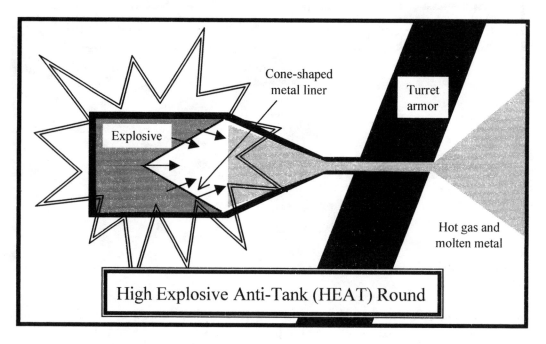

High Explosive Anti-Tank (HEAT) Round

HEAT (High Explosive Anti-Tank) rounds are explosive and do not have sabots, so they are useful against APCs and bunkers. They travel at relatively low speed and use a high explosive hollow (or shaped) charge warhead. The front of the charge is a hollow, metal-lined area with a cone-shaped partition between the hollow area and the explosives in the back of the shell. When the explosive charge detonates, the energy is focused inward by the shape of the explosive. The pressure and heat flow through the hollow section and focus on a very small area. Instead of distributing the energy of an Abrams' 120mm HEAT round along a circle 4.8 inches in diameter, the energy is focused on an area about the size of a dime. The heat and pressure within that area are roughly quintupled. The high pressure from the explosion pushes a jet of hot gas and molten metal into the crew compartment at about 27,000 feet per second. The temperature of the jet is about 3,000°F, and it frequently causes ammunition or fuel to explode, killing or wounding the vehicle's crew. The entire process takes a fraction of a second.

Even if the ammunition doesn't explode, the extreme heat and pressure produced by the round is devastating to anyone in the target vehicle, especially if the hatches are closed and the pressure has no outlet. A soldier standing in an open hatch of an armored vehicle that has been hit by a HEAT round will usually be jettisoned from the vehicle by the force beneath him.

---

[*]On American tank rounds, the sabots make up about a third of the round's launch weight.

HEAT rounds have disadvantages, though. They are generally not as effective on tanks as sabot rounds. Some main battle tanks have armor plates over sensitive areas of the tank. This is known as "spaced" armor. The armor plate is not designed to stop anti-tank rounds. It is designed to cause HEAT rounds to explode prematurely, causing much of the round's energy to be dissipated in the space between the plate and the tank. The energy will also focus on the thin armor plate, so that by the time the molten jet reaches the tank itself, it is not as tightly focused. While there will be enough remaining energy to penetrate an APC's thin armor, there often will not be enough to penetrate a tank, with 10–20 times the armor thickness.

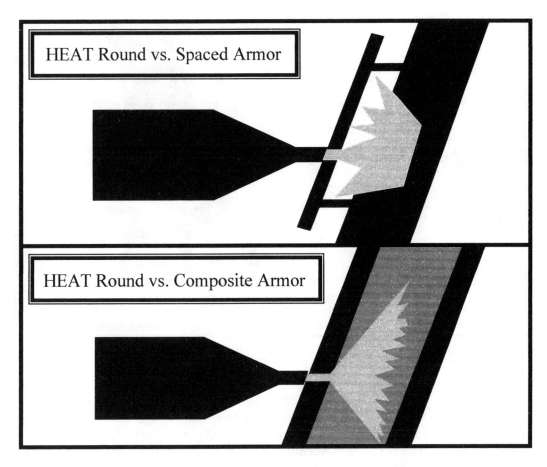

HEAT Round vs. Spaced Armor

HEAT Round vs. Composite Armor

HEAT rounds also do not work well against composite armor, a feature of newer Western tank models. Known also as "Chobham" armor, after the British foundry that invented it, composite armor is essentially an "armor sandwich" of hard layers on the outside and inside, with softer material in between. The softer material dissipates and absorbs most or all of the molten jet. Both the Abrams and the British Challenger used it. None of Iraq's tanks had effective composite armor.

The British use the HESH (High Explosive Squash Head) round in place of the HEAT. Unlike sabot and HEAT rounds, HESH rounds are not designed to penetrate armor. The head of a HESH round essentially "squashes" when the round hits an enemy tank. The plastic explosive inside then spreads out on the target in a glob, a fraction of a second before a fuse in the back of the shell detonates it. The explosion causes an intense stress wave to ripple through the target vehicle's armor. Like sabot rounds, HESH rounds cause pieces of the inside of the tank to fly around the turret at high speed, killing or wounding its occupants, but HESH rounds cause much larger chunks to break off.

HESH rounds cannot defeat as many inches of armor as sabot or HEAT rounds, however. Like HEAT rounds, HESH rounds can be defeated by spaced armor plates. The round explodes prematurely against the outer plate, and this prevents the stress wave from reaching the turret armor with enough intensity to cause the inner turret to scab. These disadvantages notwithstanding, the HESH was more than powerful enough to destroy the Iraqi tanks (which had no spaced armor) that faced the British.*

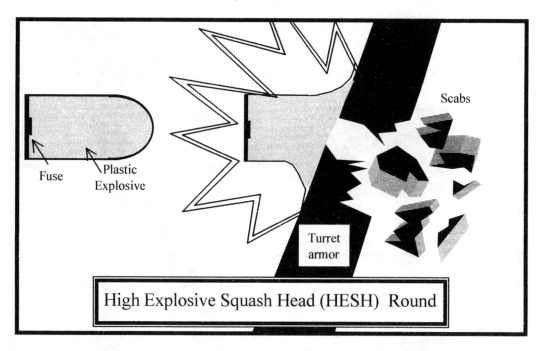

Fuse   Plastic Explosive

Scabs

Turret armor

High Explosive Squash Head (HESH) Round

The design of armored vehicles involves tradeoffs between room for the crew, protection for the crew, size and weight of the vehicle, and fuel efficiency. If you put more armor on a vehicle, you will have to design a larger, heavier vehicle or take room away from the crew. Give crewmen more room, and you will have to either make a larger vehicle (and a bigger target), or make it with thinner armor. If you want a large vehicle for its room or armor, you will need a bigger engine, and that will cost you fuel efficiency. If you want fuel efficiency, it will cost you armor and crewspace.

Citizens of democracies tend to insist that their tank designers put a premium on protection for their soldiers. If it takes a lot of money, or bigger engines burning more fuel, taxpayers may grumble a bit, but they will vote out an administration that is cavalier about soldiers' lives. This is not to say that money is no object. Elected officials with countries to run have budgets to worry about, so cost is a factor in design. Democracy does impose design requirements though, and the Abrams was a logical result.

The Abrams is the world's dominant tank. Nothing in the Iraqi Army's arsenal could penetrate its frontal armor. The Abrams is protected by composite armor while all of Iraq's tanks depended upon steel. The two hard layers are designed to stop sabot

---

*Most of the world's tanks rely upon HEAT rounds for explosive effect. British tanks are unique in their use of the HESH round.

rounds. The plastic and ceramics between the two layers are laid in a pattern designed to absorb and distribute the energy of HEAT rounds.

Composite armor saves both weight and room. The Abrams' composite armor is about 12 inches at its thickest point, but it gives the tank protection equivalent to about 16 inches of steel against sabot rounds and about 40 inches against HEAT rounds.

Shortly before the war, the Army introduced a new type of composite armor, consisting of thick outer and inner layers of super-hard depleted uranium surrounding the layers of plastic and ceramics.* This depleted uranium armor is encased in steel, so that even though the low levels of radiation it emits are within Nuclear Regulatory Commission standards, the crew is not exposed directly to the uranium. The new armor increases the tank's maximum steel-equivalent protection to 24 and 50 inches against sabot and HEAT rounds, respectively. A tank equipped with this armor was often referred to as an "Abrams D.U." or a "Heavy Package Abrams." Many of this type took part in Desert Storm.

The Abrams' main gun performance would surprise American gunners during the war. Before the war, most gunners had only fired training sabot rounds. A combat-issue sabot round will travel for about five miles, or until it hits something solid enough to stop it. None of the Army's leaders wanted to live with the very real possibility of sabot rounds piercing wooden targets at a gunnery range, smashing through berms, then flying off the range, hitting cars or buildings, so they had a training version of the combat round developed. That version has a less powerful propellant charge, and is modified so that its velocity drops off sharply after 1,500 meters (about 1,625 yards). The round will nose-dive into the ground after about 1½ miles if it doesn't hit anything. This allows gunners to practice engaging targets at the same ranges (800 to 1,500 meters) at which tank engagements have traditionally taken place, without putting civilians at risk. This caused many in the press to assume that the gun's maximum effective range was less than the T-72's. They would soon learn otherwise.

In the desert, firing actual combat rounds, Abrams gunners were surprised to find that they could regularly hit targets at 3,000 meters and beyond. The main gun's maximum effective range has been quoted at 4,000 meters (about 2.5 miles), but anything over 3,500 meters (about 2.2 miles) is a tricky shot.† Actually, the fault is not with the tank, but with the humans inside. The laser rangefinder will work perfectly at 4,000 meters. The thermal sight will pick up a tank at 4,000 meters or more. However, the sight only magnifies the target to ten times its normal size, and at that magnification, the human eye is not a perfect enough instrument to put the aiming dot exactly on the target, which appears very small at 4,000 meters. Still, a 3,500 meter maximum effective range was almost twice the effective range of Iraq's T-72 main guns when one takes into account bad Iraqi crewmanship and the shape the T-72s were in.

The Abrams' engine guzzles fuel not because it was badly designed or inefficient, but because it is essentially a helicopter engine mounted in a tank. Powerful engines consume a lot of fuel. The new engine was necessitated by the increased armor

---

*Depleted uranium is a by-product of the production of enriched uranium for nuclear power or weapons. One pound of enriched uranium leaves about five pounds of depleted (less radioactive) uranium.

†The term "maximum effective range" refers to the distance after which your chance of hitting an enemy tank drops below 50%.

protection. A tank that is designed to be impenetrable by any anti-tank warhead in the world is going to be heavy. If you make a heavier tank without upgrading the engine, the tank is going to be slower, less maneuverable, and will get stuck more often in bad terrain. The new engine solved the problem. The Abrams' turbine engine is the most powerful on any tank in the world, about twice as powerful as that of the T-72. This allows the Abrams to carry about 20 more tons of armor than the most heavily armored T-72s with no loss of speed or power.

These turbine engines suck in a tremendous volume of air. Before the war, there was a great deal of media attention on the possibility of air filters being clogged with sand. In recent years, some units had reported clogging problems, but these had more to do with lazy tank crews than with poor design. In the desert, with combat looming, there was no problem with laziness or inattention. The filters were cleaned often, and the Abrams fleet in the desert had an operational readiness rate of better than 90%.

The design of the Abrams makes it an excellent vehicle for sustained, high intensity operation. Fatigue is not as much of a factor in the Abrams as it is in some tanks. Ventilation systems ensure that fumes which might make crewmen drowsy or nauseous do not build up in the turret. The Abrams also has a roomy turret, which makes for good crew operating conditions. Crewmen have the elbow room necessary to perform combat tasks effectively.

Its roomy turret also offers the Abrams an advantage in terms of ammunition. Most tank turrets, even Western ones, are cramped to some degree. As a result, there are limitations as to how long rounds can be. Every pound of warhead at the front of a sabot round requires about two pounds of explosive at the back to blow it out of the gun barrel. One can load just so much explosive into the back of a shell before it becomes too long to store or load effectively in the turret. Cramped conditions also impose restrictions on how big crewmen can be, and thus, how heavy rounds can be. Smaller loaders are limited in terms of the weight of shell they can load efficiently. Larger caliber rounds can get very heavy. A 105mm round weighs about 40 lbs. A 120mm round weighs about 60 lbs. One can load just so much explosive into the back of a shell before it becomes too heavy for smaller crewmen to load effectively.

At a certain point, length or weight considerations make it necessary to separate the propellant charge from the projectile. Generally, shells 105mm or smaller will be one unit, while anything larger will be separated. Separating the warhead and the propellant charge makes loading the gun a two-step process, and this reduces a tank's rate of fire. However, the Abrams' roomy turret can accommodate longer rounds and larger crewmen, who can load heavier rounds efficiently. As a result, the Abrams can fire one-piece 120mm ammunition with its higher rate of fire.

In the minds of many Americans, tank warfare conjures up images of trapped crewmen burning to a crisp. American experience during World War II left a lasting impression. Badly designed tanks with weak guns, running on ultra-flammable gasoline (instead of much safer diesel), had very bad experiences against superior German models. In the intervening years, life has become much safer for American tank crewmen. Iraqi tankmen still had to worry.

Fire is still the tankman's most dangerous foe, but some armies deal with it better than others. In addition to providing their tanks with the best possible armor protection, Western nations fireproof tank turrets to the greatest degree possible. For example, the Abrams features sliding doors to seal off its ammunition storage compartment. It also has a blowout panel outside the ammunition storage compartment, so that if the ammunition does explode, the force of the blast will be directed outside the tank and away from the crew. There is also an armored bulkhead between the fuel tanks and the crew. In addition, Western tanks and APCs have effective fire suppression systems. When fire is present in the turret, automatic extinguishers are activated. The Abrams' system activates in two thousandths of a second, and extinguishes the fire in a quarter of a second.

Iraq's tanks were firetraps. When Allied rounds hit Iraqi tanks, secondary explosions were almost a foregone conclusion. Their fuel tanks and main gun ammunition were dangerously vulnerable. They also used hydraulic fluid that was mostly alcohol. Western armies have developed far less flammable varieties of hydraulic fluids.

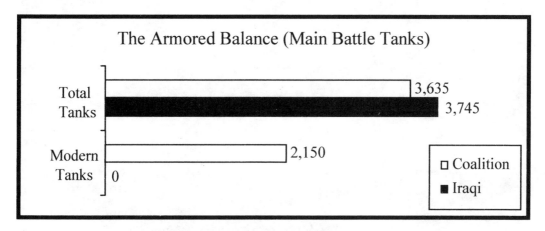

Pre-war comparisons of relative numerical tank strength gave rise to fears of a Kursk-like tank confrontation producing a similar level of carnage. However, the numbers were extremely misleading. The tank battle, when it came, was a rout. In this case, the decisive factor was quality, not quantity. Most tanks look pretty much the same, but there are crucial differences between the modern ones and the obsolete ones. The definition of the term "modern" changes, but at the time of the Gulf War, a tank had to have four features if it was to be considered modern. It had to have all of these features. Failure on any count constituted a fatal liability.

For starters, any tank that did not have high-tech composite armor was obsolete. While this may sound like an irresponsibly sweeping statement, it is true. The most modern conventionally armored tanks generally could offer only about 60% of the Abrams' or British Challengers' protection against sabot rounds and only about 30% against HEAT. A tank laboring under such a handicap can hardly be called modern. Another requirement was the ability to fire a main gun round capable of penetrating at least 500mm of conventional armor. This eliminated the T-72. It has a 125mm gun, but the gun only has a maximum penetration capability of 450mm. To be considered modern, a tank's main gun also had to have a maximum effective range of at least 3,000 meters. Tanks without that kind of reach could be picked off before they got close enough to bring their guns to bear on their opponents. Iraqi T-72 main guns had a claimed maximum effective range of 2,000 meters, but in reality the range was about 1,800 meters. Finally, the tank needed a computerized ballistic fire control system. If a tank did not have one, it could not hit targets quickly or consistently enough to survive an encounter with modern tanks.

The shortcomings of Iraqi tanks were fatal liabilities. Modern Coalition tanks (U.S. Army and Marine M-1A1s and British Challengers) destroyed slightly over 900 Iraqi tanks in combat (this does not include the destruction of abandoned or captured vehicles) by direct fire, losing two tanks knocked out by Iraqi main gun fire, a 450:1 ratio. As one of these tanks was later repaired, the kill ratio was actually 900:1. The pre-war analytical yardstick therefore should not have been total numbers of tanks in the combat zone (which fails to explain the lopsided nature of the tank engagements), but total numbers of *modern* tanks in the combat zone (which explains it perfectly).

A T-72. (Photo: Thomas Houlahan)

Iraq had about 1,350 T-72s. Most of those were in Republican Guard tank units. Unlike the Abrams, which can hit targets while it is rolling along at 30 miles per hour, the T-72 can only fire from a stationary position, or when it is moving forward very slowly. The T-72's rounds could not penetrate the Abrams' frontal armor at any range. The weight of the respective tanks gives us some idea of their armor protection. The T-72 weighs about 40 tons, while the M-1A1 weighs about 65 tons.

There had been some concern before the war about whether Coalition tank rounds would penetrate the T-72. After all, the T-72 boasted composite armor. Technically that was true. The armor was described officially as outer and inner layers of steel with "pelletized filler agent" in between. After the cease-fire, a battalion commander in the 1st Infantry Division ordered the turret armor of a captured T-72 cut open. The "pelletized filler agent" was then sent to a laboratory for analysis. The commander was informed by the laboratory that the filler agent was a simple silicate, similar to common sand. The T-72 was a mobile coffin.

While most tanks have four crewmen, the T-72 incorporated an automatic loader to replace the human loader. Autoloaders tend to be more trouble than they are worth, and they break down often in Third World armies due to poor maintenance procedures. If an autoloader breaks down during combat, crewmen do not just load rounds manually. The ammunition is in a carousel below the floor of the turret, so crewmen cannot get at it easily. The gunner has to turn a hand crank, slowly, until the automatic loader chambers the projectile, then the powder charge.

A T-72 after a hit by a sabot round. The round entered through the front slope, passed through the driver's head and entered the turret, where it caused a catastrophic explosion. There were no survivors. (Photo: U.S. Army)

Even when it does work, the autoloader does not do much for the T-72's rate of fire. It still has to load the projectile and the propellant charge separately, because single-unit rounds would be too long to fit in the carousel. So, loading remains a two-step process. That process is usually fairly quick when done by humans. Done by mechanical devices, it is slow. Also, in the event of a missed target, the gun is taken off the target so that the breech will be in the right position for the autoloader to chamber the round. It generally takes about 10 seconds before the gun is back on the target and ready to engage. Thus, even a tank with a functioning autoloader has a practical rate of fire of only five rounds per minute. In addition, the autoloader has a tendency to snag the gunner's sleeve and try to load his arm into the gun barrel.

The autoloader's carousel takes up almost half of the crew compartment. That makes the T-72 one of the most cramped tanks in the world. T-72 crewmen have a problem over and above the cramped conditions, however. Life on a tank crew is hard work. It involves banging things with sledgehammers and replacing heavy parts. Even when the work is divided among four crewmen, the job requires heavy manual labor. Divided among only three crewmen, each usually 5' 6" or smaller (because taller men have trouble working in the cramped turret), the job can be almost unbearable.

For all of its shortcomings, tank crews in the rest of the Iraqi Army would have eagerly traded in their tanks for T-72s. Regular Iraqi armored and mechanized units used a variety of different tank types. The tanks of these units did have one thing in common. They were no match for the tanks they would soon be facing in combat.

Iraq had about 700 T-62s. The T-62 is susceptible to transmission breakdowns, and "throws tracks" easily. A thrown track is a track that has fallen off the sprocket on which it travels. This usually happens when the tank hits an obstacle at the wrong angle. Inexperienced drivers (like those in the Iraqi Army) hit things at the wrong angle. When this happens, the tank is immobilized. A good crew can replace a thrown track in about an hour. Badly trained crews (like those in the Iraqi Army) may take several hours, and some will simply abandon the tank. In addition, while Western tanks have automatic transmissions, T-62 drivers often have to bang on the gear shifter with a small sledgehammer to change gears. T-62s are also cramped, and their armor is about 20% thinner than that of the T-72.

The T-62's fuel and ammunition are vulnerable, so if a round enters the crew compartment, there is a good chance that the ammunition and fuel will explode, killing the crew. In fact, the fuel tanks are shaped so that they partially surround the ammunition stored in the forward portion of the tank. When the fuel explodes, so does the ammunition. Even if there is no secondary explosion, a direct hit by a sabot round through the front left side of the tank will usually kill the driver, the gunner, and the commander, since they are seated directly behind one another.

In addition, while about 88% of the world's soldiers are right-handed, for some reason the T-62 was designed with the loader on the right side of the turret (loading left-handed). In addition, after each shot, the main gun automatically elevates so that it can be reloaded. During that time, the turret cannot be moved, so the gunner cannot track targets. These and other design defects slow the T-62's rate of fire to a maximum of four rounds per minute, about half the rate of fire of a modern Western tank. The T-62 also fires ammunition (115mm), that is not a standard type, causing some difficulties in supply. Worse, the penetrator of the T-62's sabot round, the BM-6, is not made of a high density metal like tungsten or depleted uranium, but steel.

The T-62 is equipped with an automatic shell casing ejection device. The shell casing is supposed to be ejected through a hole in the back of the turret. Unfortunately, in the bumping and jarring that is part of the normal operation of the tank, the mechanism and the hole tend to get out of alignment. Crewmen are sometimes injured when the hot 5 lb. brass casing bounces off the turret wall and ricochets around the turret.

Before the war, Iraq had about 1,725 Soviet-built T-55s, about a hundred of which were fitted with ineffective jerry-rigged armor upgrades. T-55 series models do not throw tracks as easily as T-62s or T-72s because of their relatively simple suspension system, but they are unsafe to fight in and lack durability. The T-55's 100mm smoothbore main gun was one of the weakest guns on any main battle tank in the world.

The turret design of the T-55 dates back to 1963, and the chassis to late 1946. Like the T-62, the T-55 was designed with the loader on the right side of the turret, loading left-handed and the driver, gunner, and commander sitting one behind the other on the left side of the tank. So, like the T-62, it has the same slow rate of fire, and a sabot hit on the left side of the front slope will kill three crewmen.

The T-55 had an effective operating life of about 750 hours. After 500 hours of use, the engine, transmission, etc., had to be completely replaced. In fact, due to poor Soviet workmanship, engines did not always last that long. Many engines were completely shot after only 100 operating hours. In some instances, Polish and Czech mechanics found more than a half-pound of metal shavings in engines after only 25 hours of operation due to badly finished parts. Replacing the engine bought the tank about 250 more operating hours. By the 750 hour mark, the tank's performance degraded to such an extent that the Soviet Army basically had to either scrap the tank, or sell it to Third World countries like Iraq. Those tanks that were in fairly good operating condition when they got to Iraq were not by the time the Iran–Iraq war ended. Some of the tanks on the Saddam Line in Kuwait had not been in running condition before the war. Since their main guns still worked, they were shipped from Iraq on transporters and towed to revetments to be used essentially as pillboxes.

There were also about 300 Chinese copies of the T-55, known as Type 59s. The Type 59 had a rifled 100mm gun in place of the smoothbore. Its rounds had a little more penetrating power, but the gun was less effective than the T-55's smoothbore gun in the long run because of faulty metallurgy. The gun had a tendency to become too hot too quickly, and the resulting barrel distortion adversely affected its accuracy. Intense engine vibration also made it hard for the gunner to aim the main gun. Another problem was the Type 59's lack of power turret traverse. That is done by hand crank. Type 59 turrets were also susceptible to jamming. Sometimes the turrets rotated on ball bearings that were not quite round. Sometimes the turrets did not fit the tank hulls as well as they should have. These types of problems are unheard of in Western armies, but are all too familiar to users of Soviet or Chinese equipment. Iraq also had about 100 Chinese Type 69Is. The Type 69I was essentially a Type 59 with a smoothbore 100mm gun instead of the rifled version. Weak main gun performance caused the Chinese to discontinue the model after only a few hundred copies were produced.

Iraq also had around 825 Chinese Type 69IIs. The Type 69II, an improvement on the Type 69I, has a decent ballistic computer, and its 100mm main gun is rifled. Like the Type 59 and Type 69I, it has a laser rangefinder. These improvements are not enough to cause it to be regarded as a modern tank, however. It has the same manufacture-related problems as the Type 59. Ironically, since it was under embargo at the time, the Iraqi Army got most of its Type 69IIs through Saudi Arabia when the two countries were close during the !ran–Iraq War.

Maintenance of its already inferior tank fleet was a problem for the Iraqi Army during the war. Allied air superiority made it impossible for Iraqi tank crews to perform routine maintenance. Working on a tank became very dangerous with the world's largest air armada cruising around looking for things to destroy, so most Iraqi tank crews found it was best to stay under cover and away from their tanks.

The armor disparity between the U.S. and Iraq extended to armored infantry vehicles. The U.S. Army had about 2,200 Bradley Fighting Vehicles in the desert.* Bradleys can keep pace with advancing tanks, so M-1A1s do not have to wait for their infantry support to catch up. They also offer protection from shrapnel and small arms fire, neutralizing the two biggest killers of infantrymen.

---

*All armored troop carriers are "armored personnel carriers" or APCs. Those which have thicker armor and carry small cannon are also referred to as "Infantry (or Cavalry) Fighting Vehicles."

Once Bradleys reach an objective, the infantry squad dismounts and fights, while the Bradley supports them with its 25mm rapid firing chain-gun. They are not designed to slug it out with enemy tanks, but on a fluid battlefield, a Bradley might find itself up against an enemy tank, so each Bradley has a TOW missile launcher with two missiles on the turret. The cavalry version carries eight more missiles inside the vehicle while the infantry version carries five.

On paper, the Bradley would have appeared no match for the BMP-1, Iraq's main infantry fighting vehicle, which had a much bigger gun and had received much better press. The Bradley had received considerable negative press attention during the early 1980s because it could be penetrated too easily by too many types of ordnance, and its undependable fire suppression system made ammunition explosions more likely in the event of a penetration.

However, with little fanfare, the Bradley had been completely redesigned. Two new versions had been introduced since the flawed first model. For increased safety, the A1 had a safer fuel system and a more effective fire suppression system. The Bradley A2 followed, with thicker armor, a larger engine, and better ammunition storage. The A2 even had an interior spall liner, so that in the event of a sabot round penetration, crewmen were far less likely to be killed or wounded by flying chunks of steel from their own vehicle. With all of the improvements, the A2 weighed about 33% more than the basic model, and was practically a different vehicle.

The improved Bradleys were so new that they had not been widely distributed by the time Iraq invaded Kuwait. The units initially sent to the Gulf were equipped mostly with the basic Bradley. Steps were then taken to get as many of the improved Bradleys to the theater as quickly as possible. Bradley A2s were even sent directly from production to the Gulf. By the time the ground campaign began, 48% of the fleet were A2 models, 33% were A1s and only 19% were the more vulnerable basic models.[*]

The Bradley is well-armed. A gunner can fire 25mm armor piercing or high explosive rounds one at a time. He can also fire them at a rate of 100 or 200 rounds per minute. During the war, rapid fire proved impractical, however. There had been worries about the supply of armor piercing 25mm ammunition for Bradley Fighting Vehicles. A depleted uranium 25mm round had been developed, but it was in extremely short supply when Iraq invaded Kuwait. The Army was forced to rely on the older tungsten penetrator rounds. Unfortunately, these were also in short supply. The Army calculated that it would need 3.75 million tungsten rounds for a war with Iraq, but a world-wide search for tungsten rounds produced only about 3 million for the forces in the Gulf. Unit commanders dealt with the shortfall by demanding and enforcing firing discipline.

The BMP, the most modern APC in the Iraqi inventory, was a 25-year-old design. The original Bradley had twice the armor protection of the BMP. The Bradley A2 model had four times as much. The BMP was also a fire trap. It had nothing resembling the Bradley's fire suppression system. It also had fuel tanks located in its rear doors. Although this fuel was always used first, there was no guarantee that the tanks would be empty when opposing warplanes or armor showed up.

The vast majority of Iraq's 1,650 BMPs were BMP-1s. Although the Iraqi Army had later model BMP-2s (including 50 captured from Kuwait) equipped with the

---

[*] "Murphy's Law" asserted itself here. Though only 19% of the Bradleys in the theater were basic models, the majority of the Bradleys hit by fire during the war were of this variety.

reasonably effective 20mm rapid-fire cannon, it did not have a significant number of them. The BMP-1 was badly underarmed. Its 73mm main gun fired a relatively weak round and was inaccurate, largely because of a maddeningly complicated aiming system. The main gun was also almost useless in high winds. The round it fired was fin-stabilized, but the BMP had no computer to compensate for the effect of wind on the fins, which was significant. The round's main propulsion was a relatively primitive rocket motor in its base. There was no certainty about exactly when the motor would kick in or how long it would burn, and these are crucial questions in determining the required trajectory. This meant that hitting anything past point-blank range was a problem. Like the T-72, it had an autoloader that occasionally tried to tear the gunner's arm off and shove it into the breech. Like the T-72, the gun elevated when the autoloader kicked in, disrupting the gunner's ability to evaluate the effects of his first round. The gun could fire a maximum of eight rounds per minute. For a 60 lb. 120mm round, this would be impressive. For a 73mm round weighing about 20 lbs., it is slow.

Rear view of a BMP-1. The holes are for fuel, which is pumped into the spare fuel tanks within the rear doors. (Photo: Thomas Houlahan)

The BMP-1 carried a Sagger anti-tank missile mounted on the turret. The Sagger was inaccurate and almost useless against Coalition tanks. It could not penetrate the frontal armor of the Abrams or the Challenger. By contrast, the TOW-2s fired by Bradleys were extremely accurate, and with 2¼ times the Sagger's penetrating power were capable of destroying any Iraqi tank.

In fact, the BMP-launched Sagger is almost useless against modern APCs. The Sagger is guided by joystick, and sharp movements and simple evasion procedures can reduce the possibility of a Sagger hit on an APC by as much as 70%. The missile operator's ability to track targets is affected not only by the stresses of combat, but by a design defect in the vehicle. There is an infra-red searchlight on the left side of the vehicle's front slope. To keep the main gun from knocking off the searchlight when it swivels, a feature in the turret ring causes the gun to be thrown to maximum elevation when it approaches the searchlight. That means that if a missile operator is guiding a missile toward a vehicle moving to his left, the gun (and his aiming sight) may be thrust toward the sky during the crucial final seconds before the Sagger reaches its intended target. It also leaves the gunner with a 15 degree blind spot. In practice, fewer than one missile per minute can be fired, since reloading takes almost a minute, and the vehicle commander cannot reload until the missile has reached its target. By contrast, the Bradley mounts two TOW missiles on the turret, so that if one misses, the other can be fired immediately.

Front view of a BMP-1. Note that the infra-red searchlight on the vehicle's front slope is directly in the path of the gun barrel. (Photo: Thomas Houlahan)

BMPs are extremely cramped. Comfort has never been a priority in Soviet design. Soviet designers produced armored vehicles that were small and low to the ground, with as low a profile as possible. The Soviets were able to achieve this only at the expense of crew comfort and armor protection.

BMPs are ill-suited to combat under desert conditions. The BMP is not air conditioned. Some of the effects of these problems were eliminated by leaving the BMP's seven hatches open when not actually involved in a battle. This gave troops some relief from the stifling heat inside the vehicle, and let them stand up and get their circulation back after long periods in an almost fetal position, but it left them exposed during surprise air or artillery strikes.

Still, the Republican Guard's BMPs were better than what the rest of the Iraqi Army was using. However weak and obsolete the BMP's 73mm smoothbore gun was, at least it had a gun. The rest of Iraq's roughly 4,600 APCs were equipped only with machine-guns.

10

Better People, Better Results

Perhaps Saddam's biggest mistake was in underestimating the United States Armed Forces. He was not alone. Many Americans had come to expect U.S. military operations to end badly. First, there was Vietnam. Then, there was the *Mayaguez* incident, when U.S. Marines were sent to attack an island where Cambodian communists were thought to be holding the ship's 51 crewmen. The Marines took heavy casualties and the crewmen were not there.

In the aftermath of the Vietnam War, the U.S. Armed Forces became hollow, especially the Army. By 1979, half of the Army's 14 active divisions were rated non-combat ready by the Army. In 1980, an attempt by heliborne commandos to rescue American hostages in Teheran resulted in disaster. Three years later, 241 Marines were killed in Beirut by a truck bomb, while another force of Marines, paratroops, and Navy SEALs was on its way to Grenada and more problems.

While the American military had brought many of its problems upon itself during and after the Vietnam War, bad press treatment did not help matters. Reporting in the period between Vietnam and the Gulf War was not particularly balanced. The American public was exposed to hundreds of news reports over the years portraying American soldiers as a gang who couldn't shoot straight, equipped with weapons that didn't work.

To a certain extent, this was to be expected. The draft ended in 1973, so the vast majority of the nation's younger reporters had never been in the military. They therefore had no experience with what they were reporting on. Much of what works in an army makes no sense to someone who has not been in one. For instance, why design tanks that guzzle gas? A tank officer knows that if the tank is more fuel efficient, it cannot carry as much armor, and the crew is not as safe. A reporter, especially one who was in journalism school when Saigon fell, just sees waste and more Army stupidity.

There was more wrong with America's press corps than just a lack of military experience, however. There was a significant anti-military bias in the press, and this showed in the early stages of the Gulf Crisis. As David Gergen pointed out in a post-war commentary:

[M]any reporters went beyond their appropriate and important role of asking tough and probing questions and basically approached the early days of this conflict from an anti-war perspective. They were still fighting the last war in Vietnam, always suspecting that the United States would eventually screw up, that its generals would lie and that its soldiers would die in droves.

The Armed Forces had quietly undergone a metamorphosis, however. With each military setback had come experience that was put to good use during Desert Storm. Better people and better equipment also had their impact. The Army of the 1970s had been replaced by a professional force that fielded high-tech equipment, and had troops with the intelligence and training to employ it effectively. During the late 1970s, American units had regularly finished last or near-last in NATO competitions. By the late 1980s, the Army regularly dominated the competitions that had been so humiliating a decade before. This was a completely new organization with better leaders and better soldiers.

Trust plays a vital role in war. In this respect, the forces of the Coalition held a decisive edge over Iraqi forces. Coalition officers could rely on their men to follow orders. Their men could rely upon the officers not to throw lives away unnecessarily. Trust is a function of leadership. Gen. Schwarzkopf probably cut to the essence of leadership as well as anyone:

> Leadership is getting people to willingly do that which they ordinarily wouldn't do. If I said that everyone coming through this door gets a $50 bill, I'd be overrun. That's not leadership. Leadership is asking someone to do something that may get him killed. By virtue of your rank, you have the right to ask them to die. But it takes a hell of a lot more than rank before they'll do that.

American servicemen were in capable hands. They knew that their leaders were not asking them to do anything they had not already done themselves. Almost all American commanders above battalion-level had seen combat in Vietnam, and many had been wounded, some quite severely.

In addition, in the U.S. Armed Forces, generals do not get to be generals without proving themselves in a number of different jobs. Promotions are based upon merit, and at each level of promotion, there is a significant amount of weeding out. During the 1980s, while 80% of all captains could anticipate promotion to major, only 70% of all majors made lieutenant colonel and only half of those made full colonel. Only a portion of those were selected to command brigades. The competition was really stiff as brigade commanders were evaluated for selection to brigadier general. The weeding continued as officers competed for additional stars and command of divisions and corps. Only a tiny handful (like Powell and Schwarzkopf) got four stars.

One important fact went largely unnoticed before the war. American senior officers had gotten a lot smarter since Vietnam. A pre-Gulf War study of almost 200 recently promoted brigadier generals showed that their average I.Q. was in the top 8% of the population, far higher than that of equivalent corporate leaders. Another study found that 80% of the Army's colonels and lieutenant colonels held at least a master's degree. By comparison, only about 20% of the corporate executives in similar positions held advanced degrees.

The military is a profession, and like any profession it has its own body of specialized knowledge which must be mastered. That body has expanded exponentially in recent years. Officers are therefore required to complete a significant amount of military education throughout their careers in order to maintain proficiency and keep abreast of the latest developments in military science. As the Gulf War would prove, modern war has become a highly technical enterprise, and amateurs fare badly at it.

It is said that once in a great while, wars will be won by generals, but most often they are won by sergeants and privates. The U.S. Army had better sergeants and privates than the Iraqis.

During the 1970s, many Army units had been gripped by indiscipline and drug problems. During the 1980s, discipline had returned. "I have fewer disciplinary problems commanding a third of a million men," said Lt.Gen. John Yeosock, commander of the U.S. 3rd Army in the Gulf, "than I did in 1973 commanding 1,000 men." During the 1970s, some 40% of the soldiers in the Army had to be dismissed for unsuitability or indiscipline before the end of their first enlistment. More than 12% of the soldiers stationed in Germany had been charged with serious crimes. Drug use had been common among soldiers in the late '60s and early '70s. The Army estimates that about 40% of its soldiers in Europe were engaged in recreational drug use during that period, and about 7% were addicted to hard drugs. Random drug testing had largely eliminated the drug problem. Alcoholism had also been a problem in the '60s and '70s, but in the years before the Gulf War, the Army had discouraged heavy drinking, and alcohol-related problems had declined sharply. Alcohol was not a problem at all in Saudi Arabia, because none was allowed.

Like their officers, American soldiers had gotten smarter since Vietnam. Some 80% of American soldiers in World War I had not graduated high school, and 37% of those who served in World War II were non-graduates. By 1980, the proportion of recruits without high school diplomas had shot back up to 50%. Even worse, 74% had mental aptitudes below the national average. During the 1980s the armed forces made a commitment to recruiting soldiers with the education levels demanded by sophisticated equipment. By 1990, 93% had high school diplomas. Those who did not get an equivalency diploma during their first tour were not allowed to re-enlist.

Attracting good people is important. So is keeping them. Western armies took great pains to maintain a more professional, less brutal environment than the Iraqi Army, so their soldiers tended to stay longer. At the time of the Gulf War, about half of all members of the U.S. Armed Forces were re-enlisting at the end of their first tour. This yielded practical advantages. While the Iraqi Army had to constantly train new conscripts in basic combat skills, Allied armies could concentrate on upgrading the skills of soldiers who were already trained. This was most noticeable in the area of heavy weapons crewmanship. When a tank or gun crew has been working together for a significant period of time, it will show in the crew's performance. Even if the members of a crew are new to each other, if they are at least familiar with the equipment they will perform to an acceptable standard. About half of the average Iraqi tank or gun crew was "green." The end result was that the average Allied crew could get off more shots per minute than their Iraqi opponents, and had a much higher probability of hitting what they were aiming at.

The U.S. Army spends a great deal of time and money training its soldiers. The Chinese have an ancient proverb to which the U.S. Army subscribes wholeheartedly:

"The more you sweat in peacetime, the less you bleed in war." American soldiers are among the most thoroughly trained in the world. Basic and advanced individual training lasts from four to six months in the United States, and regularly costs $50,000 and up. In technical fields, or those involving advanced weaponry, costs can run significantly higher. Graduation is not a foregone conclusion, either. Only about 75% of those who are accepted for enlistment ever make it to a line unit. The remainder are returned to civilian life. Training continues at unit-level.

Most Iraqi soldiers had received only the most rudimentary training. Iraqi soldiers received no basic training to speak of. Training was supposed to happen at unit-level, but aside from the "elite" units of the Iraqi Army, soldiers generally received little training in their units. Soldiers mobilized after Iraq's invasion of Kuwait received no training at all. They were picked up off the streets and rushed to the front with nothing more than a rifle and an army jacket to wear over their street clothes.

The U.S. Armed Forces have been able to produce training programs that are realistic in every detail except wounds and death. Soldiers, sailors and airmen train against competent opposing forces in realistic exercises. The "Opfor," or mock opposing forces at the Army's National Training Center at Fort Irwin, California, the Navy's "Top Gun" air combat program, and the Air Force's "Red Flag" exercises at Nellis Air Force Base in Nevada are well-versed in Soviet-style tactics.[*] The Opfor units at these programs are considered better than any of the units whose performance they were designed to copy. Training in these programs is conducted under conditions of fatigue, confusion, and stress.[†] Maneuvers are conducted at a high tempo. An element of risk is present. If death is not a possibility, careers are still on the line.

Training took on a new urgency in the aftermath of the Panama invasion. Before that, the U.S. Army had a peacetime mentality. No matter how much money is spent or how much attention is paid to training, no matter how high the quality of personnel, it is difficult to train people who do not believe that they will ever be sent anywhere to fight. Panama made believers out of most soldiers. It also had a sobering effect on senior officers. After Panama, the temptation to gloss over failure in training exercises, or to deal lightly with nonperforming units and their commanders, tended to be outweighed by the fear of the consequences of sending unprepared units into combat.

When military analysts discussed their concerns about the coming conflict, many of their fears centered on the emotional impact of combat on young American soldiers. Many lost sight of several important points, not the least of which was the fact that Iraqi soldiers were also afraid. In fact, they were terrified. Iraq's army had not taken the kind of care that the U.S. Armed Forces had in selecting the kinds of people who could hold up under the strain of combat. The Pentagon has long been keenly aware that it makes no sense to waste thousands of training dollars on people who will fold under pressure.

Analysts had also not considered the steps the U.S. Armed Forces had taken to limit the adverse impact of combat on the emotional state of its soldiers. The U.S. Army did not give much thought to the psychology of combat before the Second World War.

---

[*] The aerial programs are especially realistic. A Soviet MiG pilot defected to the West in 1989 and instructed the U.S. Air Force in detail on Soviet tactics. In many cases, American pilots knew what their Iraqi adversaries would do before they did it.

[†] In another concession to realism, the U.S. Armed Forces do much of their field training at night. The Iraqi Army's training took place almost entirely during daylight hours.

After World War II, the Army realized that this failure had cost it dearly. The noted military historian, Col. S.L.A. Marshall, found that during the war, while defending against enemy attack, only about 15% of U.S. soldiers fired their rifles, even when their positions were under intense assault and their own lives were at stake. That percentage rarely rose above 25%, even in units with the most savage combat reputations. The other 75%–85% were guided by the basic and understandable desire to avoid exposing themselves unnecessarily or killing any more than they had to. In defense, they did not run away, but they did not play an active part in the battle either. Statistics were similar on the offensive, where soldiers dutifully advanced, but only a minority fought aggressively. Thus, the Army's combat strength had been degraded by 75%–85% not by enemy fire, but by human nature.

Another Army historian, Col. Trevor Dupuy, found that in terms of combat capability, by mid-1944 100 Germans were the equal of about 125 Americans. Others had similar findings. The U.S. Army found that it had sustained psychological casualties at about ten times the rate sustained by the German Army. Desertion rates were also higher. Over 21,000 Americans, the equivalent of almost two divisions, deserted during the war.[*] The Army was eager to find the root of these disparities, since Germans were not inherently any stronger, braver, smarter or more motivated than Americans.

The Army found that the main problem was that the whole idea of combat runs counter to human nature and common sense. Most Americans are not born killers, and they are taught from their earliest days that killing is wrong. They also learn to avoid exposing themselves to potentially fatal dangers. In combat, they are told that they must kill, and they must knowingly enter life-threatening situations. This presents a significant contradiction, and in the absence of effective training, human instincts take over.

Another finding was that the strength of unit-level leadership, and the amount of confidence soldiers had in their weapons, had a major impact on the number of psychological casualties sustained by an army. Telling men that their chances of survival are better if they fight aggressively than if they hide is one thing. Whether or not they actually believe it depends on the quality of their training, leadership and equipment.

Although the major figures of the U.S. Army in World War II were West Point graduates, the majority of its junior officers, the men who actually led units into combat, were drawn from the 90-day Officer Candidate Schools. German junior officers received about a year of officer training. The German course was more selective of its applicants and more rigorous. The Germans also had a six-month noncommissioned officer training course, while the U.S. Army had no NCO training course at all. Soldiers were promoted to sergeant and left to sort things out for themselves. No matter what conditions they found themselves in, German soldiers at least had the comfort of knowing that their leaders were trained to a fairly high standard.

German soldiers also received far more thorough training than American soldiers. The United States had to expand its Army rapidly. Soldiers were whipped into adequate physical condition, taught a few basic combat skills and sent off to war. German soldiers learned a far wider variety of combat skills during their basic training.

---

[*]This was actually relatively good news. Though little is written about it in textbooks, during World War I, nearly 100,000 Americans left their units *during one offensive*. To stem the disintegration, Gen. Pershing's staff found it necessary to order large numbers of MPs to follow many units to the front to help guide "lost" soldiers back to their units.

They then moved on to further training in the more technical aspects of their specialties (communications, engineer, etc.). So, both German soldiers and leaders had more confidence in their abilities when they hit the battlefront. This translated into better performance and fewer psychological casualties.

German soldiers also had more confidence in their weapons, which were superior to almost everything American soldiers were equipped with. American leaders believed that massive quantities of inferior weapons would eventually overcome far smaller numbers of superior weapons.[*] In that particular war, they turned out to be right. However, that didn't do much for American tank crews who watched their shells bounce off German tanks while American tanks (which were notorious fire traps) went up in flames all around them after being hit by German anti-tank shells.[†]

The lessons of superior leadership, training and weaponry on the performance and mental state of the individual soldier were not lost on the U.S. Army's leaders, who took immediate action to correct the Army's shortcomings. When S.L.A. Marshall was sent to study the combat performance of the Army in Korea, he found that on average, about half of the infantrymen actively took part in combat. Under intense pressure, the percentage approached 100%. By Vietnam, almost every American soldier was actively fighting in every battle.

Most of what was learned about soldiers during World War II, Korea and Vietnam was still valid when the Army was deployed to Saudi Arabia. While warfare has changed, the essential role of the individual in combat has not. He must still work with others to perform military tasks in life-threatening situations.

---

[*]After a battle in Italy, an American officer asked a captured German: "If you people are such a God-damned master race, how come we just overran your position?" The German replied: "Because we ran out of ammunition before you ran out of Americans."

[†]In one instance, during the battles immediately following D-Day, one German tank destroyed 16 American Sherman tanks in one hour. Not all battles were this lopsided, but each German tank was worth several American tanks.

Part V

Tell It to the Marines

"Now we will attack into Kuwait, not to conquer, but to drive out the invaders and restore the country to its citizens."

—Lt. Gen. Walter Boomer,
Commander,
I Marine Expeditionary Force

11

Trampled Under Foot:
The 1st Marine Division

The easternmost Marine breach would be conducted by the 1st Marine Division, under the command of Maj.Gen. James M. Myatt. Myatt, holder of a master's degree in engineering electronics, had great confidence in the Coalition's technology. But he had also done two tours in Vietnam, where he had learned that even a great technological edge does not always guarantee success.* His division would be involved in minefield breaching and trench clearing, two endeavors which tend to minimize the advantages of technology and claim high casualty and mission failure rates. There was, therefore, some tension in the command post, but all were sure that the fighting qualities of the Marines would provide the margin of victory.

A major goal of the division's breach plan was to render the Iraqi defenses in southeastern Kuwait untenable. The division would smash through the Saddam Line and break into the Iraqi rear. This, Marine planners believed, would cause Iraqi units to the east to withdraw, to avoid being outflanked or trapped in southern Kuwait as the Marines advanced toward Kuwait City. Essentially, they believed that a successful 1st Marine Division breach would cause these units to leave on their own.

The Iraqi response would be puzzling. The eastern front line defenses would crumble, not for tactical reasons, but because the troops manning them were heartily sick of the war. Meanwhile, in the 1st Marine Division sector, the Iraqis would throw virtually every armored vehicle in the area into a desperate but surprisingly well-coordinated two-pronged assault at the site of the breach. The attempt to plug the breach would fail disastrously, defeated in the largest tank battle in Marine Corps history.

---

*Myatt was awarded the Silver Star for gallantry in that conflict.

There would be another surprise. Both Marine divisions would encounter far more Iraqi armor than had been expected. The Iraqi 6th Armored Division, originally stationed just outside the western edge of the Marines' zone of attack, had been broken up into units of battalion or company size and sent to reinforce other divisions. A T-62-equipped armored brigade from the division was scattered throughout southern Kuwait to bolster the Iraqi defenses.

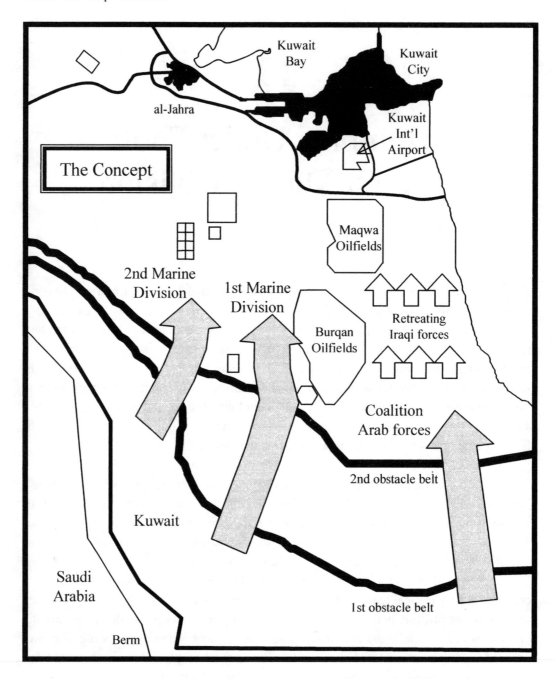

The breach was a complex affair. Two task forces, Grizzly and Taro, each consisting of two light infantry battalions with engineer reinforcement, would perform the first night minefield infiltration in the history of the U.S. Marine Corps. They would pick their way through the first obstacle belt and take up positions between the two belts. From these positions, they would guard the division's flanks. The main assault would be conducted by Col. Carlton Fulford's Task Force Ripper on the left, and Col. Richard Hodory's Task Force Papa Bear on the right. Ripper and Papa Bear each had a tank battalion and two mechanized infantry battalions. Both were heavily reinforced by engineers.

The main breach would be conducted by Task Force Ripper. It was vital to the division plan that Ripper get its combat units through the two minefields quickly. For this reason, the task force would receive the lion's share of the division's engineer equipment, and would establish four breach lanes to Papa Bear's two.

Iraqi armor posed a more serious threat to the 1st Marine Division than it did to most other Coalition divisions. The division had better tanks than the Iraqis, but while M-1A1s or Challengers were virtually immune to any weapon the Iraqis had, the division's M-60A1s had significant vulnerabilities. Marine M-60A1s had no laser rangefinders and no ballistic computers. They also had no thermal night vision capability.[*]

Unable to destroy tanks at previously unheard of ranges, or at night, the way an Abrams could, Marine tank crews would have to face the fact that Iraqi tanks stood a fair chance of getting close enough to their tanks to score hits. This was a real problem, because the M-60A1 had no depleted uranium or composite armor. It had less than half the armor protection of M-1A1s against sabot rounds, and less than one-fifth against HEAT rounds. And, though it had automatic internal fire extinguishers, the M-60A1 did not have fireproof ammunition storage compartments, so in the event that the armor was penetrated, secondary explosions were a distinct possibility.

Part of the lack of armor was made up by fitting blocks of "reactive armor" to the M-60A1s. Basically, a block of reactive armor is a steel box containing two steel plates with a layer of plastic explosive between them. These steel boxes are fixed to the more vulnerable parts of the tank. When a block is hit by an enemy shell or rocket, the jet penetrates the cover of the box and the top steel layer. When the jet comes into contact with the plastic explosive, an explosion results. The explosion counters some of the force of the incoming round. More important, the top steel layer and the cover plate from the steel box are driven forward into the path of the jet by the detonation of the plastic explosive. This deflects part of the jet itself. Reactive armor is capable of reducing the effectiveness of shaped-charge warheads by as much as 70%.

Reactive armor would not have protected Marine tank crews against sabot rounds. The only protection against sabot rounds was sound tactics. Marine units would have to destroy as many Iraqi tanks as they could before those tanks could get close enough to Marine tanks to fire sabot rounds effectively. If Iraqi threats could be spotted as they were developing, artillery barrages and helicopter gunship and ground attack aircraft strikes could thin out the attacking force before it got within main gun range of a

---

[*]The reactive armor on Marine tanks was designed to explode when hit by enemy shaped-charge rounds. It was believed that the explosions might knock out some of the more sophisticated gunnery instruments on the M-60A3, so the Marines stayed with the more basic M-60A1.

line of Marine tanks. At that point, hopefully, the superior training of Marine tank crews would enable them to destroy the remaining tanks with relatively light losses. Ultimately, the tactics worked better than expected. No M-60A1s would be hit by tank gun or anti-tank weapon fire during the war.

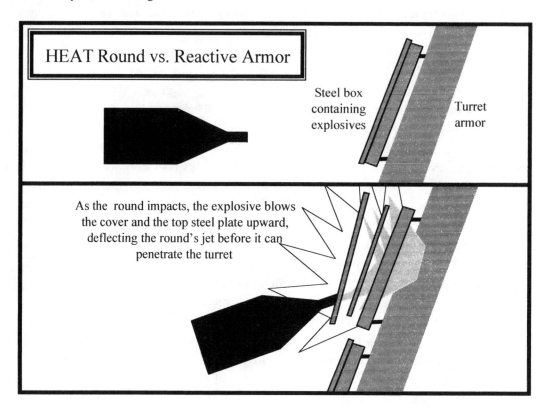

HEAT Round vs. Reactive Armor

Steel box containing explosives

Turret armor

As the round impacts, the explosive blows the cover and the top steel plate upward, deflecting the round's jet before it can penetrate the turret

Though M-60A1s may not have been as formidable as Abrams or Challenger main battle tanks, they represented a large proportion of the division's combat power. The threat of armored counterattack on the western end of their front prompted the division planning staff to assign the majority of the division's tanks to Ripper. However, the exact distribution of tanks became a bone of contention between the division staff and Papa Bear's planners. The loss of a tank company is a much more serious matter to a Marine unit than it is to an Army unit. In the Army, the loss of a tank company will usually be offset somewhat by the receipt of a company of TOW missile-firing Bradley Fighting Vehicles. In the Marines, the best a commander can reasonably expect in return for his tanks is an infantry company riding in Armored Amphibian Vehicles, or AAVs (popularly known as Amtracs), which have no anti-tank capability.

The commanders and staffs of Task Force Papa Bear understood that because Task Force Ripper's breach was the division's main effort and Ripper faced the greater armored threat, they would be giving Ripper one of their four tank companies. They also understood that Ripper would require first call on attack aircraft, helicopters and artillery. However, when division planners began to discuss taking away a second tank company to give Ripper more striking power, Col. Hodory's officers objected strenuously. This would have left Ripper with six companies of tanks and Papa Bear with two.

While they appreciated the threat faced by Ripper, and understood the need to get the task force into the Iraqi rear quickly and with as much combat power as possible, Papa Bear's staff officers argued that the threat in their sector was not insignificant. Intelligence had indicated that there would be more Iraqi armor on the division's left flank than its right, where the Iraqis had taken heavy losses in and around Khafji, but there were still plenty of Iraqi tanks on Papa Bear's side. They reasoned that if the aerial damage inflicted on these units turned out to be less than advertised, or the units were more warlike than expected, Papa Bear could have a problem beyond the ability of two tank companies to contain.* Things would be particularly dicey if the division's air and artillery assets were busy supporting Ripper while Papa Bear was being attacked.

Division planners countered that the success of Ripper would make an attack against Papa Bear almost unthinkable. No Iraqi commander in his right mind, they argued, would allow his unit to be trapped on the eastern side of the al-Burqan Oilfields when it was obvious that there was a Marine division driving for Kuwait City on the other side of the oilfields. They believed that any competent commander would have to recognize the clear danger of being cut off. He would therefore withdraw his forces to the north at high speed, not ensure their ultimate destruction by ignoring that threat and attacking Papa Bear.

In the end, plans for reassigning the second company were dropped, though division planners still felt that Papa Bear's concerns were unwarranted. Ripper's leaders felt that they could make do with five tank companies, and if events proved otherwise on the battlefield, another tank company would be transferred. There would be no arguments about it at that point.

The division actually began its assault on the Saddam Line a week before G-Day. Three reconnaissance teams from the 1st Marine Division spent the night of 18–19 February assessing the first obstacle belt. The teams, from the 1st Reconnaissance and 1st Combat Engineer battalions, consisted of six recon men, one Navy corpsman (medic) and one engineer each. Their mission was to determine the location and composition of the southernmost minebelt in the division's zone and to find paths through it for task forces Taro and Grizzly, the two units responsible for establishing blocking positions for the main breach on G-Day. The first night's activities were only partially successful. The teams brought back a good deal of information about the minefields and were able to establish a path for Taro, but could not find one for Grizzly.

The teams went back on 21 February, and discovered that the first obstacle belt was largely undefended. This is a fairly common tactic, so it did not strike Marine commanders as particularly unusual. Sometimes, while the enemy's artillery bombards vacant forward positions, defenders wait in force for the enemy's ground troops at a second line. Marine planners had no way of knowing that the entire Iraqi front was collapsing.

---

*Estimates of air-inflicted damage would indeed prove extravagant. Ground units would find that the infantry divisions along the line had lost only 25%–33% of their tanks to bombing. The two heavy divisions in the area probably lost about 10%.

143

The teams returned with a detailed survey of the first obstacle belt. Their reports were encouraging. The scouts had spotted few anti-tank ditches, and found that the minefields were not particularly deep. However, for all the detail of their reports, the teams still could not find a path for Task Force Grizzly. Without that path, the 1st Division's left flank might not be secure for the breaching.

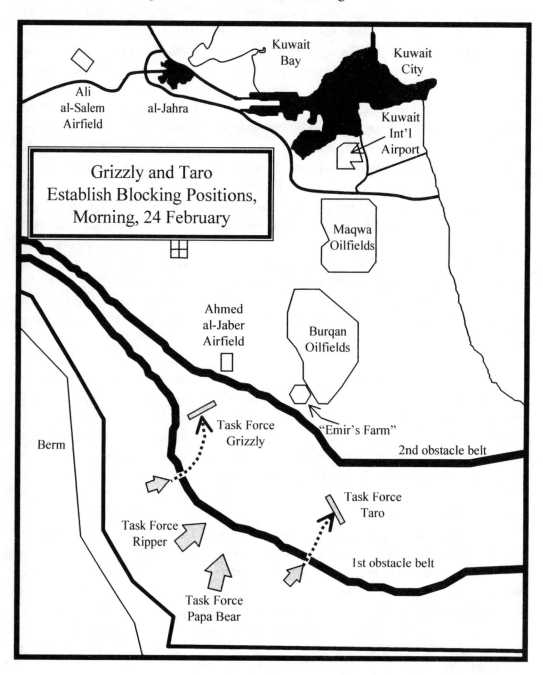

Grizzly's commander, Col. James Fulks, marched his task force to positions near the first minefield just after midnight on the 22nd. By dawn, the task force dug in with Lt.Col. Roger Mauer's 2nd Battalion, 7th Marines (2/7) on the left and Lt.Col. Timothy

Hannigan's 3/7 on the right. Fulks placed his small complement of vehicles in a slight depression behind the main force.

At 10:22 that morning, 2/7 was hit with a few Iraqi artillery rounds. The Iraqi guns were immediately destroyed by counterbattery fire, but Fulks suspected that his unit had been spotted. His suspicions were confirmed when a force of 10 T-62 tanks and a handful of APCs appeared in front of 2/7's positions. The arrival of 10 surrendering Iraqis and the appearance of eight more tanks prompted Fulks to order a move to less exposed positions. The move was covered by artillery strikes directed by forward observers from 2/7 and 3/7 against the Iraqi armor and a few known and suspected artillery positions. An F/A-18 strike was also called in on an Iraqi artillery battery. The move went smoothly, and though 3/7 received some artillery fire, there were no casualties.

As night fell, Fulks' recon teams went forward to find a path through the minefield. With the entire night ahead of them, things looked promising, but as soon as the teams began work, an Allied air strike went in against a nearby Iraqi unit. The strike was too close for comfort. Rather than risk a friendly fire incident, the teams pulled back. The air attack had come without prior coordination, and Fulks was furious. After several radio transmissions from Fulks, the air activity ceased. The scouts gave it one last try, but there were not enough hours of darkness left for the teams to do their job. The mission had to be canceled.

It was now the last day before the beginning of the ground war, and Task Force Grizzly still did not have its path. Col. Fulks was getting desperate. He ordered a daylight reconnaissance of the minefield. The recon teams moved out at 8:30 in the morning. As the teams approached the minefield, they called in artillery and air strikes on the Iraqi bunkers on the other side of the minefield to divert the Iraqis' attention from their activities. Marine artillery destroyed two bunkers and four artillery pieces, but the Iraqis spotted the recon teams and called in their own artillery on them. The artillery stopped after an air strike hit the bunkers containing the spotters, but the teams had been compromised and had to return to their lines.

Fulks now made plans for something he had not wanted to do —conduct a hasty breach of the minefield. Planning was well under way when, at 3 p.m., luck and alert scouts provided Task Force Grizzly with a major break. In 3/7's sector, a handful of Iraqis came across the minefield to give themselves up. They were observed by a three-man recon team which bounded across the minefield, retracing the Iraqis' steps. Once across, they shot and killed three Iraqis, took several prisoners and occupied a bunker that overlooked the path. Unfortunately, Fulks now received a presidential order by way of CENTCOM headquarters. No American units were to cross the obstacle belt until all diplomatic efforts had been exhausted. Fulks was told to recall his scouts.

Fulks radioed his objections to division headquarters. He understood that attempts were being made to get the Iraqis out of Kuwait peacefully. However, he felt that withdrawing and letting the Iraqis set up a defense on the other side of his only path through the minefield could have unpleasant consequences *when* (most Marines were now convinced that combat was unavoidable) the diplomatic efforts failed. After a detailed discussion of the situation, Maj.Gen. Myatt told Fulks not to do anything he couldn't reverse, but agreed to let Grizzly keep its positions.

If Fulks couldn't send more men across the minefield to reinforce his forward positions, he could still call in artillery strikes to keep the Iraqis under cover and away from them. Every Iraqi position Fulks' men could identify was shelled. Two Marine artillery batteries spent the afternoon firing 144 artillery projectiles into this sector.

At 5:40 p.m., 22 more Iraqis walked across the minefield to surrender, this time in 2/7's sector, revealing another path. Twenty minutes later, Fulks got the go-ahead from CENTCOM, and his men began clearing lanes across the minefield. An engineer team led by SSG Charles Restifo crawled through the minefield, prodding for mines as TOW gunners kept watch over the Iraqi positions on the other side through their thermal sights.* Though riflemen from Company K, 2/7 stood ready to deal with Iraqi attempts to disrupt the breach, there were no such attempts. By nine, the lanes had been cleared and marked with glowing "Chem-Lights." By 11 p.m., Task Force Grizzly's infantrymen were filtering through the minefield and heading for their assigned blocking position, pulling their heavy weapons behind them on handcarts which the unit had fabricated while in Saudi Arabia.

At dawn on the 24th, having secured positions between the minefields, Grizzly would create a vehicle-width path through the first minefield for the division's self-propelled artillery battalion, 5/11. From forward firing positions, 5/11 could reach deeper into Iraqi defensive positions and provide more effective cover for Ripper's breach. For this breach mission, Col. Fulks had requested and gotten an AAV specially equipped to carry three Mine Clearing Line Charges (MiCLiCs) internally, in a configuration known as a Mk-154 "Triple-Shot Line Charge." He had also secured a tank equipped with a mine plow, to ensure that any mines which had survived the explosion of the line charge could be pushed aside. As dawn broke, the AAV launched a 5-inch rocket over the minefield, carrying a string of 1,750 lbs. of C-4 plastic explosive behind it. After a massive explosion, the plow tank went in. Within minutes, 5/11 was moving toward its firing positions between the two minefields.

Col. John Admire's Task Force Taro had already begun moving through its obstacle belt at 10 p.m. on the 23rd. Aside from driving off two small groups of armored vehicles with artillery strikes at 6 and 6:30 the next morning, the task force would face no serious opposition during the breach.

Taro was supposed to be made up of the 2nd and 3rd Battalions of the 3rd Marine Regiment, but had received unexpected reinforcements before it moved out. Admire's 1st Battalion had been detached to create a task force of its own, Task Force X-Ray. Maj.Gen. Myatt planned to deliver X-Ray by helicopter to positions on the Iraqi side of the two minebelts on G-Day. Once there, it would guard the division's right flank as it began its drive northward. However, on the morning of the 23rd, it became apparent that the 3rd Marine Aircraft Wing (3rd MAW) could not support the insertion of an entire

---

*Restifo was awarded the Silver Star for his actions.

battalion. Too many of its helicopters would be needed for medivac and logistics missions. Myatt had no choice but to return two of 1/3's infantry companies to Task Force Taro. Task Force X-Ray was now down to one infantry company and a heavy weapons company equipped with TOW missile launchers mounted on Jeeps.

While Taro and Grizzly were establishing their blocking positions, the main breaching forces, Ripper and Papa Bear, occupied their jumping-off positions. Because of the chemical threat, these two task forces were in Mission Oriented Protective Posture (MOPP) 3, with the men wearing all of their chemical-protective gear and carrying their masks at the ready.

As Task Force Ripper approached its designated breach site a few hours later, there was a friendly fire incident. Task Force Grizzly had already moved between the obstacle belts to secure the division's left flank. Just after five in the morning, three T-72s and three BMPs wandered into Grizzly's path, and were engaged by TOW-equipped Humvees attached to 2/7. After a short exchange, the Iraqi armor retreated northward. Shortly afterward, the task force's combat trains began taking main gun fire from Task Force Ripper, to their right rear.

The vehicles hit by Ripper were mistaken for the small Iraqi force which Task Force Grizzly had just chased off. That force had previously been chased away from Ripper's breaching operation by Navy A-6E Intruders. The Intruders had reported the presence of the vehicles, and that information had been relayed to Lt.Col. Christopher Cortez's 1st Battalion, 5th Marine Regiment, which was then approaching the minefield. When the unit's tankmen (Company A, 1st Tank Battalion, attached to 1/5) saw vehicles to their left front on the other side of the minefield, they assumed that they were the Iraqi vehicles that the Intruders had reported.[*]

Seconds after 1/5's tanks opened fire, a red flare appeared over the targeted vehicles. Recognizing this as the prearranged signal for a unit to indicate that it was receiving friendly fire, the tank company commander ordered a cease-fire. One Marine had been killed in the incident, and three had been wounded. Grizzly's Mk-154 had been damaged and a truck had been destroyed. Grizzly had been fortunate. Because the task force had been engaged from maximum range, Ripper's tanks had fired more than two dozen main gun rounds at the convoy, but had only hit two vehicles. In addition, the remaining two line charges in the Mk-154 did not explode when the vehicle was hit.

At 6:18 a.m., at the point chosen for Task Force Ripper's Lane 1, one of 1/5's tanks approached the first minefield towing a trailer. From the trailer, a MiCLiC was launched into the minefield. The MiCLiC was designed to be the primary minefield

---

*In the Army, when battalions trade armor and infantry companies, they become "task forces." The Marines generally do not use that term for organizations smaller than regiment size. The official designation of a unit like this one would therefore be: "1st Battalion, 5th Marine Regiment(-)(rein)," to reflect the fact that the battalion had given up an organic unit and been reinforced with a unit from another battalion. In practice, Marines would refer to the unit as "1st Battalion, 5th Marines," or simply "1/5."

breaching tool of the U.S. Armed Forces. The MiCLiC launcher would halt 70 meters from the beginning of a minefield and launch its charge. The line charge, 100 meters long, would be brought to rest a safe distance from the launcher by a 62 meter long arrestor cable. For planning purposes, the Marines assumed that an 80 meter long path would be cleared, because the line charge would not land in a perfectly straight line, and the first eight meters or so of the line charge would detonate short of the minefield's forward edge. After the 80 meter lane was combed by plow-equipped tanks, another MiCLiC would be launched. The process of line charges followed by plow tanks would be repeated until the lane was cleared to the far side of the minefield. Mine rollers would then be used to "proof" the lane, exploding the few mines which might have been missed.

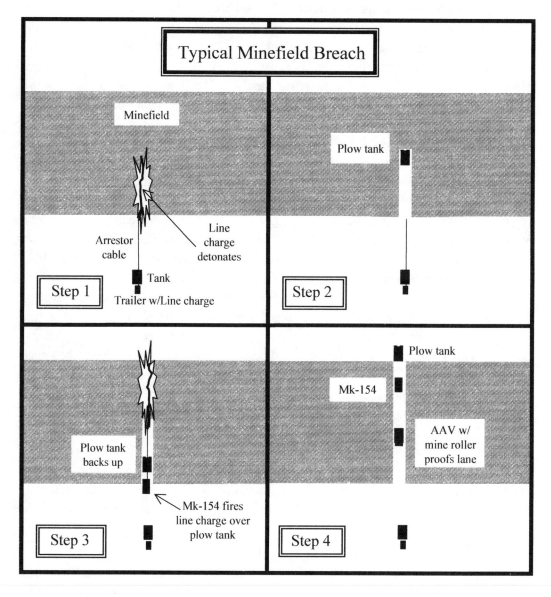

After the charge launched by 1/5's tank exploded, the tank held in place to provide cover as a tank equipped with a "Track-Width Mine Plow" (TWMP) moved into the lane. Mine plows physically shove remaining mines to either side of the vehicle. If there is a detonation, most of the blast is absorbed by the earth pile created by the plow, or by the plow itself. The TWMP is basically a set of two blades, one mounted in front of each fender of the tank. Each blade has six large teeth (tines) on its bottom edge. The teeth are designed to burrow beneath buried mines and scoop them up. Each blade clears a path 3 feet, 9 inches wide, and can remove mines buried up to a foot down. The blades were readily available (there were hundreds in the Gulf), easy to mount and effective. Usually, about 95% of the mines in the plow's path were pushed aside or detonated harmlessly.

Mine Plow. (Photo: Lt.Col. Mike Tucker)

In their preparations, Marine combat engineers found that a MiCLiC explosion would often leave as many as 25% of the mines in its path intact. This meant that instead of proofing lanes that were virtually mine-free, the plows operated in areas still thick with mines. As a result, instead of serving as an ancillary lane proofing tool, they became an essential component of the breaching operation.

When it reached the end of the trough created by the MiCLiC's detonation, the plow tank backed to the beginning of the lane to avoid the blast of the next MiCLiC and a Mk-154 fired one of its line charges over the plow tank and into the minefield.

This time, detonation was unsuccessful. The engineer who had launched the line charge dismounted his vehicle, climbed on the back of the plow tank, and was taken to a spot within running distance of the point where the arrestor cable ended and the C-4 explosive chain began. The engineer hand-emplaced a 1 lb. block of TNT with a 30-

second time fuse beneath the first block of C-4, then ran back to the protection of the plow tank. Incredibly, the TNT detonated, but failed to set off the line charge.

Lt. Wayne Sinclair, the engineer platoon leader responsible for clearing the lane, ordered the engineer (now back inside his AAV) to fire a second line charge directly onto the first. This was done, and a successful command detonation of the second line charge produced the explosion of both line charges. The third and last line charge in the trailer also worked perfectly, and got the engineers to the other side of the first minefield. Lane 1 had taken less than 15 minutes to clear. Lane 2, in which the engineers had also experienced one fuse failure, had been completed about a minute earlier. In each of the lanes, mine rollers were used to proof the lanes and set off any mines that the MiCLiCs and the plows missed.

"Roller Dude." (Photo: Lt. Wayne Sinclair)

The Marines would have far fewer problems with their mine rollers than the Army would with theirs. The Mine Clearing Roller System used by the Army consisted of two sets of five large, heavy rollers which, like mine plows, are fitted to the front of each track. The performance of that system was disappointing. The rollers were cumbersome, heavy (the entire system weighed about 20,000 lbs.) and hard to transport. In addition, since they were originally designed for the firmer soil conditions of Europe, they were unsuitable for the softer soil of the desert. Instead of rolling, they often merely skidded, pushing soil in front of them until they bogged down. Worse, they often failed to detonate mines, so troops passing through a "proofed" lane could never be sure that it was really free of mines.

The Marines created their own roller system. Dubbed "Roller Dude" by its creators, it was essentially a pipe filled with concrete, designed by engineers from

Company A, 3rd Combat Engineer Battalion and fabricated by the Naval Construction Regiment ("the Sea Bees"). Because the roller had a wide diameter and only weighed about 8,000 lbs., the Marine system worked well in soft soil. Also, unlike Army mine rollers which only clear a 3 foot, 9 inch wide path in front of each of the tank's tracks, the Marine system rolled the area across the entire width of a tank.

Another difference between the two roller systems was that the Marine rollers were towed behind AAVs, not pushed in front of tanks. At first glance, this would appear a dangerous or even ridiculous configuration, since the vehicle had the proofing device behind it instead of in front of it. However, the roller was really only needed to proof the area between the treads of the plow tanks. The AAV could travel safely in those tracks, because if there had been mines there, they would have been set off by the much heavier tank. Still, the Marine rollers occasionally failed to detonate mines and vehicles were crippled as a result. There also were not enough of these rollers available by G-Day, so the Marines were forced to rely upon Army rollers in some instances.

After the lanes were proofed, they were marked by combat engineers. While marking the lanes, the engineers looked for any obstacle or mine that had either somehow escaped destruction or fallen back into the lane. Anything which could not be moved was destroyed in place. By seven, the engineers were reloading their line charge launchers and waiting for the order to breach the second minefield

The minefield through which 1st Battalion, 7th Marines under Lt.Col. James Mattis would establish its lanes was about 100 meters thinner then 1/5's minefield. In both of 1/7's lanes, two successful line charge detonations would be enough to breach the minefield. There were complications, however. In Lane 4, the trailer-launched line charge failed to detonate, and could not be manually primed. A Triple-Shot system was brought forward. Though both would have to be primed manually, two line charges from the AAV were enough to clear a path to the far side of the minefield. In Lane 3, the MiCLiC launched and detonated perfectly, but failed to detonate at least one anti-tank mine. When an M-60 tank equipped with a mine roller attempted to proof the lane, it was crippled. The Marines started over, 25 meters to the left of the blocked lane. After firing and manually priming two line charges from a Triple-Shot system, the engineers reached the other side of the minefield.

About two hours after Task Force Ripper's friendly fire incident, the Iraqis had a friendly fire incident. At 7:55, Ripper was making good progress through the first obstacle belt when scores of Iraqi soldiers began to approach the Marines with their hands up. The Marines gathered prisoners until 8:40, when Iraqi artillery began landing on the surrendering Iraqis. Marine spotters identified an Iraqi observation post, which was then destroyed by a Cobra gunship. The artillery fire, now without direction, dropped off dramatically.

Division artillery had been able to cover the breach of the first minefield. However, with the exception of 5/11, which was deployed forward, the second minefield was at the outer edge of Marine artillery range, and the Iraqi artillery covering the minefield was beyond its range. Maj.Gen. Myatt considered it unwise to attempt a second breach without effective artillery support, so he halted his engineers short of the second minefield. Once his maneuver units had moved through the breach and were in position to provide security for the guns, the artillery was brought forward.

At noon, combat engineers began breaching the second minefield behind an intense barrage of airburst rounds from 3/11, Ripper's direct support artillery battalion. The shells exploded over the trenches on the other side of the minefield, killing several Iraqis and pinning the rest down.

The Iraqis chose to fight for the second minefield. As it approached the minefield, 1/7 took mortar and artillery fire, wounding two tank crewmen. It also took machine-gun fire from its right flank. The battalion's tanks silenced the machine-gun fire with heavy machine-gun fire of their own. They then silenced the mortars with HEAT rounds at long range.

Again, the minefield in 1/7's sector was relatively thin and again there were complications. Lane 4 was cleared with two line charges, both of which had to be manually primed. As in the first minefield, the breaching of Lane 3 began with the complete failure of a trailer-launched line charge. A Mk-154 launched one of its three line charges over the dud charge. Though the second charge had to be manually primed, both detonated. This left only 10 meters of minefield to clear. Unfortunately, both of the AAV's remaining line charges were complete failures. Capt. Craig Baker, commander of the company responsible for the breach, ordered a mine plow to clear the remainder of the minefield without benefit of a MiCLiC. No mines were set off in the process, and the lane was proofed and marked by 12:25.

In 1/5's sector, the engineers in Lane 1 had planned to conduct this breach in the same way that they had cleared the first minefield. Unfortunately, when the tank tried to fire its line charge, nothing happened. Earlier, when the tank turret had swiveled to engage Iraqi machine-gunners on the other side of the minefield, the MiCLiC's firing cable had become caught on the storage rack on the back of the turret and had been ripped out. A Mk-154 pulled behind the tank and fired one of its line charges into the minefield. It failed to detonate and had to be manually primed. The next two line charges worked perfectly and the lane was clear —only eight minutes after the first line charge had been launched. Again, things had gone smoothly in Lane 2, which had been cleared a minute earlier.

Explosive mine clearing techniques like the MiCLiC offer some advantages. The charges can be launched from the edge of the minefield, and from the relative safety of an armored vehicle, so combat engineers do not have to do as much work inside the minefield in an exposed position. The disadvantage was their undependability. The majority of the MiCLiCs fired by the two Marine divisions did not function properly. The fuses failed on some of them. On others, the arrestor cable snapped, its connection to the tank or AAV was severed, and the ability to command detonate was lost. During the war, only 49% of all MiCLiCs could be command detonated by operators inside their vehicles. More often than not they had to be primed manually.

Almost as soon as the assault lanes were open, Marines were besieged by hundreds of surrendering Iraqis. Soon, the breach lanes became clogged. Assault units tried to move north while streams of Iraqis were herded south. Improvisations had to be made to keep the lanes open. Combat elements were told to bypass the Iraqis and drive to the other side. EPW holding areas were hastily set up just south of the breach lanes. The Iraqis were hustled into these areas and guarded by support personnel. Progress was still slow, but at least traffic was flowing.

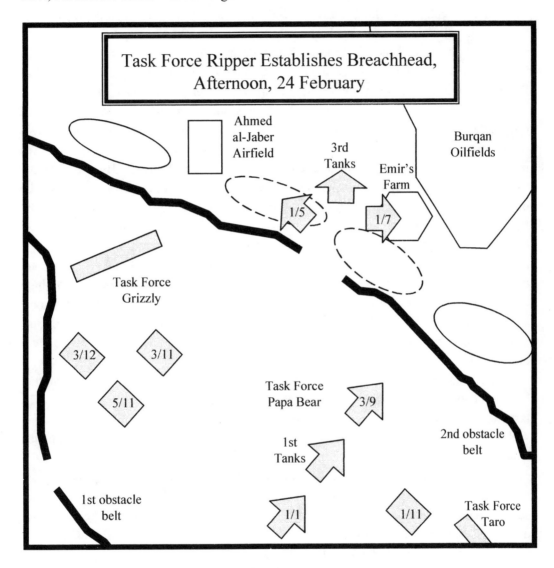

Task Force Ripper Establishes Breachhead, Afternoon, 24 February

After the breaching companies had made it through the minefield, Lt.Col. Alphonso Diggs' 3rd Tank Battalion rumbled through all four of Ripper's breach lanes and established a powerful presence on the other side of the minefield. The three battalions then pushed outward, expanding the breach area.

In the center, Cobras destroyed seven T-62s, while 3rd Tanks destroyed four more and took hundreds of prisoners. No one would have been surprised to see 120mm

Abrams rounds slice through Iraqi tanks with ease, but the sight of much less powerful 105mm rounds from M-60s doing likewise was a pleasant surprise to Marine gunners. In one case a 105mm round went in through the front of a T-62 and out through the engine in the rear. Some 60 Iraqi tanks and almost as many other armored vehicles would be destroyed by the 3rd Battalion's gunners during the course of the war.

On the right flank, 1/7's tanks pushed ahead 1½ miles past surrendering Iraqis and abandoned bunkers. The tanks halted shortly after destroying two Iraqi tanks in a brief engagement. Meanwhile, the rest of the battalion moved into position for its next mission, the attack on the "Emir's Farm."

On the left flank, 1/5's tanks were destroying four tanks. Lt.Col. Cortez's Marines also took 500 prisoners while dodging sporadic mortar fire. By 2:10, Task Force Ripper's fight was over and the lanes were clear. There were no Marine casualties.

At 2 p.m., while elements of Task Force Ripper were finishing off the last Iraqi resistance at the breach area, 1/7 reached its next target, a large tract of tamarind groves to the southwest of the al-Burqan Oilfields, known as the "Emir's Farm." The tract was made up of several rows of trees, each containing several bunkers. By the time the Marines neared the objective, the defenders' heavy weapons were a charred memory. The objective's main firepower, 56 towed 152mm artillery pieces, had been destroyed by Marine aircraft using cluster bombs in the last days before the ground offensive. Over 80% of Iraq's 3,000 artillery pieces were towed guns. This meant that Iraqi artillery was not very mobile, and could not move quickly to avoid air or artillery attack. It also meant that somewhere in the proximity of most Iraqi gun crews was a large pile of high explosive shells and propellant charges waiting to be set off by Allied cluster munitions, as they were at the Emir's Farm. Cobra attack helicopters also claimed a number of guns and a few multiple rocket launchers with Hellfire missiles in the hours before the assault units arrived.

During the breaching, the area had been heavily shelled by 3/11. Lt.Col. Mattis' battalion called in more artillery as it approached the Emir's Farm, but had to call off its last two planned missions. Iraqis were now coming out of the orchard to surrender in such numbers that the additional artillery strikes would have killed and wounded unarmed Iraqis. After giving the fleeing Iraqis time to get clear of the orchard, 1/7's mortarmen dropped a barrage of smoke rounds on the western side of the objective.

The Marines rolled up the bunkers from the flank. Hundreds of Iraqis either surrendered without a fight, or did so after offering only token resistance. Where the Iraqi defenders were more stout-hearted, the Marines hammered them with tank, heavy machine-gun and TOW missile fire. Occasionally, Cobra gunships from HMLA (Helicopter, Marine Light Attack)-369 were called in to unleash hails of 20mm rounds and waves of 2.75-inch rocket fire into a tree line. In less than two hours, Iraqi resistance collapsed. The fall of the Emir's Farm yielded 200 more prisoners and a huge cache of landmines that the Iraqis had not had time to emplace.

With the Emir's Farm secured, the task force headed for its next objective, Ahmed al-Jaber Airfield. The plan called for Task Force Shepherd to set up a screen to the north, keeping the Iraqis from attacking Ripper's right flank as it drove toward the airfield. With its flank secure, Ripper could position most of its tanks forward for the assault on Ahmed al-Jaber.

Task Force Shepherd had followed Ripper through the breach, and had not faced serious contact, since its path had already been wiped clean of Iraqi resistance by Task Force Ripper. By 1:30, most of Task Force Shepherd was through the second minefield. Shepherd immediately pushed north to deploy its screen, destroying 11 T-62s and taking a few hundred prisoners in the process.

By 4 p.m., Task Force Ripper had reached its attack positions, and at 4:30 it began rolling over Iraqi defenders around the airfield. Ahmed al-Jaber had originally been defended by the 56th Armored Brigade. Most of that brigade had been moved out of the airfield and deployed in a wide area to the west, in front of the 2nd Marine Division, to stiffen defenses between the front line defenses and al-Jahra. Only a handful of the brigade's T-55s remained, reinforced by a company of T-62s.

For the attack, the task force assumed a wedge formation, with the 3rd Tank Battalion on point, 1/5 to its left rear and 1/7 to its right rear. Both mechanized battalions placed their tank companies forward. The Iraqis were no match for Marine tanks and TOW launchers. The Marines methodically picked their way through the bunker complex surrounding the airfield, which had been thoroughly softened up by air and artillery attacks. Most Iraqis on the position surrendered, and most of the Iraqi tanks supporting the complex had been abandoned. Just after 5:30, the task force began to encounter sporadic resistance, resulting in several destroyed T-62s and T-55s and no Marine casualties. By six, the airfield was completely cut off and a few hundred prisoners were being sent to the rear. The task force assumed defensive positions, where it would wait until the following day, when it would be relieved by Task Force Grizzly, which would seize the airfield itself. Once Grizzly was in position, Ripper would set out for its ultimate objective, Kuwait International Airport.

Task Force Papa Bear was the last unit to begin breaching operations. Papa Bear began breaching just after 9 a.m., to the right of Task Force Ripper's lanes. Leading the task force would be 3rd Battalion, 9th Marines, under Lt.Col. Michael Smith, followed by Lt.Col. Michael Kephart's 1st Tank Battalion. Smith's infantrymen were supported by an attached company from 1st Tanks. In return, Kephart's battalion had received 3/9's Company I. By 9:40, 3/9 had established two lanes through the first minefield and had secured the other side.

With two lanes secure, 1st Tanks joined 3/9 on the other side of the first obstacle belt. As the rest of the task force made its way through the lanes and prepared for the next breaching, 1st Tanks directed Cobra and Harrier strikes on Iraqi tanks and bunkers behind the second minefield. These strikes resulted in the destruction of two tanks, two observation posts, a mortar position and a number of bunkers.

Meanwhile, scouts from 3/9 began probing the second obstacle belt, but had to pull back because of Iraqi machine-gun and mortar fire. As they did, forward air controllers called in more air strikes on the second line of Iraqi defenses. The strikes destroyed an additional two tanks, two mortar positions, one observation post and one bunker.

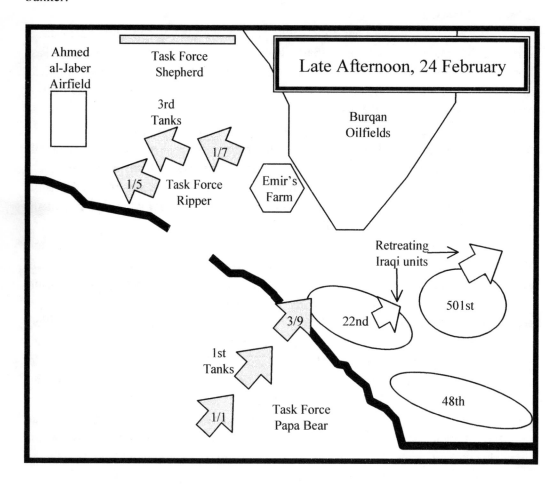

At about 8 a.m., when it had become apparent that Task Force Taro would not be seriously engaged, Maj.Gen. Myatt had ordered the task force's engineers to open two additional lanes through the first minefield. Myatt wanted to ease traffic congestion in the main breaching lanes so that he could get his artillery forward quickly to support Papa Bear's second breach. By one in the afternoon, Taro's engineers had established two additional lanes.

By 3 p.m., Task Force Papa Bear's direct support artillery, 1st Battalion, 11th Marines under Lt.Col. John Sollis, was set up between the two obstacle belts and was shelling Iraqi positions. At 3:20, the task force began breaching the second obstacle belt, but problems with line charges slowed the breaching effort. Then, during the proofing of Lane 1, a mine disabled a roller tank, blocking the lane. Engineers finished work on Lane 2 while the first breach team worked on a detour lane around the disabled tank.

At 4 p.m., the first assault company was pushing through Lane 2. As it did, it caught five Iraqi tanks fleeing their positions, destroying two. With the Iraqi armor gone, the Marines set about consolidating the second breach. As 3/9 moved forward and began clearing trenches, Iraqi mortar rounds wounded ten Marines. After a thorough pounding by artillery and gunships, the main Iraqi strongpoint fell, causing the collapse of the rest of the position and the surrender of hundreds more Iraqis.

While 3/9 was clearing the trenches, 1st Tanks pushed through Lane 2. At 4:15, led by Humvee-mounted TOW launchers, the tanks wheeled east and smashed through a line of dug-in tanks and infantry. The TOW launchers opened the attack, destroying six tanks. Cobras arrived, and destroyed another eight tanks before the Iraqi line broke and 650 more Iraqis gave themselves up. At this point, units in reserve positions, from the Iraqi 22nd and 501st brigades, began pulling back from their positions. Task Force Papa Bear would see these units again the next day.

At 5:00, 1st Battalion, 1st Marines, under Lt.Col. Michael Fallon, followed 1st Tanks through the breach and began pushing the Iraqis in the center northward. TOW missiles from Fallon's battalion accounted for three T-55s and three Type 63 APCs, while Cobras picked off four more Type 63s. By 6 p.m., Iraqi resistance to the north of the minefield had largely ceased and engineers had completed alternate Lane 1. Work on a third lane was stopped when a mine rake-equipped tank was crippled by a mine while proofing. As darkness fell, the task force halted and consolidated its positions while its engineers used armored bulldozers to create dirt-walled compounds to hold the vast numbers of EPWs taken during the day.

During the afternoon, there had been a lively exchange of artillery between Marine gunners and Iraqi artillery firing from the al-Burqan Oilfields. Both 3/11 and 1/11 sustained casualties during these exchanges. The counterbattery fight was a confused affair, and the confusion led to another friendly fire incident. Marines from 1st Battalion, 25th Marines, a reserve unit, were establishing an EPW collection point for some of the thousand or so prisoners 3/11 had taken, when four rounds of DPICM burst overhead. Two Iraqi prisoners were killed and 40 were wounded. One Marine and one corpsman were also wounded.

Iraqi opposition during the day had accomplished little, but it had been enough to force the cancellation of Task Force X-Ray's insertion. It had taken Papa Bear most of the afternoon to establish a breachhead large enough to accommodate the landing. This left only 40 minutes of daylight to establish a landing zone. A daylight landing was therefore impossible. Worse, when the helicopters arrived over the breach site later on, there were two landing zones (the other being in Task Force Ripper's zone, for the medivac of Marines and Iraqi EPWs wounded by artillery in the friendly fire incident), and the disoriented pilots could not distinguish between them. When the flight leader attempted to get guidance from division headquarters over the tactical radio net, he found it swamped with radio traffic from the maneuver units establishing the breachhead. He finally got through to Maj.Gen. Myatt, who decided that the ground task forces had the situation in the breach areas well in hand. He felt that to attempt to land Task Force X-Ray at this point would just expose the helicopters and their occupants to an unnecessary risk of strikes by shoulder-launched surface-to-air missiles. Myatt ordered the task force to return to base and attempt another landing the next morning.

The division began the second day of the ground war with a series of alarming indications of a possible Iraqi counterattack. Just after 1 a.m., captured Iraqi officers began telling Marine interrogators about attacks that would "come out of the flames." Captured maps indicated that a counterattack was imminent, but painted a confusing picture of its exact source and objectives.

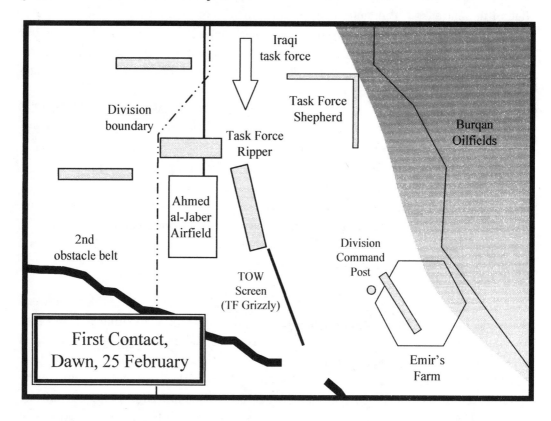

Myatt had originally planned to go around the oilfields, because scientists had told CENTCOM that the toxins produced by the burning oil wells made the area uninhabitable. Now he was being told that an enemy force was lying in wait in the thick black smoke of the oilfields. Myatt decided not to take any chances. He posted Task Force Shepherd as a screening force between task force Ripper and the oilfields. The screen line was bolstered by 36 TOW launchers from Task Force Grizzly, which Col. Fulks had sent through the breach to screen the east side of Ahmed al-Jaber Airfield.

At 5:15 a.m., Task Force Shepherd spotted an Iraqi armored column from the 3rd Armored Division moving due south, toward Ahmed al-Jaber Airfield. Shepherd's LAVs fired at the flank of the Iraqi column, knocking out five T-62s tanks and one truck with TOW missiles and 25mm chain-gun fire. At 6:20, the two dozen remaining Iraqi vehicles, mostly T-62s, ran into TOW gunners from Task Force Ripper's 3rd Tank Battalion and lost seven more T-62s before scattering.

The second contact was made by Task Force Papa Bear. Papa Bear would have its hands full this morning, beating off a spirited counterattack. Division planners had believed that there would be little or no chance of an attack on Papa Bear because Ripper's success would force units to the east of the al-Burqan Oilfields to withdraw northward. While their logic had been sound, the Iraqis nevertheless attacked Papa Bear in force. Whether the commanders of these units were unaware of the threat posed by Ripper's success, whether they were aware but felt that Iraqi units in the west could contain it, or whether they were launching what amounted to an armored *Banzai* charge remains unclear. Whatever their reason, Iraqi armored units to the east attacked Papa Bear in a desperate attempt to close the breach.

At 8 a.m., an Iraqi task force made up of armored vehicles and infantrymen from the 22nd and 501st Infantry brigades was headed west toward Papa Bear, shielded by a dense fog. These brigades had originally been part of the 8th Infantry Division, but had apparently been placed under the operational control of the 5th Mechanized Division.

Much of the 22nd Brigade had been overrun on the previous day, but small units from the brigade had made their way north with a handful of assigned tanks and had linked up with the 501st. The 501st, stationed behind the 22nd Brigade, had been able to fall back in reasonably good order when the units in front of it began to give way.

Guarding Papa Bear's right flank was 1st Tanks and a screen line of TOW launchers. At the northern end of 1st Tanks' line, stretched along a wide front, was Company D, 1st Tanks. Company C, 1st Tanks comprised the reserve. On the southern end of the line was the attached Company I, 3/9. In front of 1st Tanks' line was the TOW screen. However, due largely to events on the previous day, Papa Bear's dispositions left a small gap on the southern end of the perimeter.

Papa Bear had not originally intended to set up defenses in this area for the night of the 24th. The G-Day plan of operations had called for the task force to occupy these positions temporarily, then head west as soon as Task Force X-Ray had landed and assumed its flank guard responsibilities. However, just after six in the evening on G-Day, X-Ray's landing had been called off because of low visibility, sporadic artillery duels and general confusion in the landing area. Papa Bear would have to remain where it was.

Col. Hodory's staff and commanders immediately got to work setting up a perimeter for the night. They faced two significant problems in setting up their defenses. First, the task force had to set up an unusually large, and therefore relatively thinly defended, perimeter to accommodate a landing zone for Task Force X-Ray. This was especially hard on Maj. John Terrell's TOW company, which, screening at the edge of this large perimeter, was left with a great deal of ground to cover. Second, there was an extensive trench system north of the second minefield, but just south of I/3/9, on the task force's right flank. Since night was already falling, Lt.Col. Kephart feared that launching an immediate trench clearing operation would result in unnecessary casualties. He decided to deploy part of his attached infantry company facing south, toward the trenches. The infantrymen could keep an eye on the trenches during the night, then clear them next morning. There would be a kill zone between the Marines and the trenches, in case the Iraqis in the trenches tried to attack northward. By chance, a small group of Iraqi armored vehicles would slip through this gap on the morning of 25 February.

The Iraqi force moved westward, orienting itself on a packed-dirt access road that the Iraqis had built behind the trenches to the north of the second mine belt. At the head of the formation was a T-55, followed by three APCs. Once inside the perimeter, one APC became separated and headed due north, toward 1st Tanks' rear, while the other three vehicles ran directly into Task Force Papa Bear's headquarters, where Col. Hodory was holding a briefing.

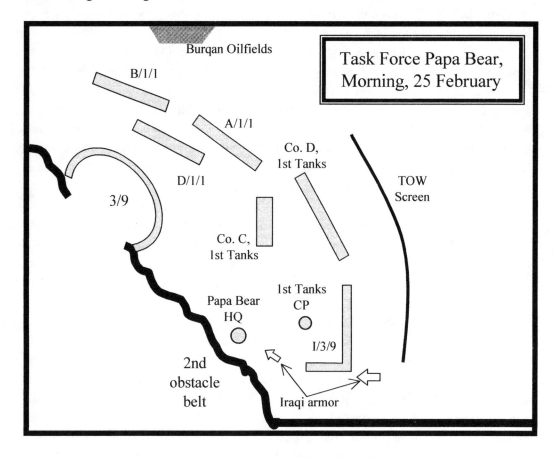

Burqan Oilfields

B/1/1

A/1/1

Co. D,
1st Tanks

D/1/1

TOW
Screen

3/9

Co. C,
1st Tanks

1st Tanks
CP

Papa Bear
HQ

I/3/9

2nd
obstacle
belt

Iraqi armor

Task Force Papa Bear,
Morning, 25 February

In the thick fog, Lt.Col. Smith, 3/9's commander, had been unable to find the command post in time for the morning briefing, at which Hodory would be assigning missions for the day's movement. Papa Bear was supposed to hook around the western edge of the al-Burqan Oilfields and take its place on Task Force Ripper's right flank for the next day's advance on Kuwait International Airport. For that advance, Hodory wanted his two infantry battalions leading and 1st Tanks trailing behind in the center, ready to maneuver against any Iraqi armor that popped up in the task force's path.

Maj. Robert Wagner, 1/1's operations officer (Lt.Col. Fallon had remained forward with his battalion), was told that 1/1, then at the top of the task force's perimeter, would move northward to secure Papa Bear's eastern flank for the day's movement. The battalion would seize a piece of high ground inside the al-Burqan Oilfields, dubbed "Gathering Center 4."[*] The gathering center, theoretically, would give Fallon a perch

_____

[*]In major oilfield complexes, oil is pumped from individual wells to central gathering centers.

from which he could see several miles in any direction.* On the western end of the perimeter, 3/9, which was providing security for Papa Bear's breach lanes, would form up and head north, driving along the western edge of the oilfields. Lt.Col. Kephart would be forming 1st Tanks and driving it westward to take its place behind the infantry battalions.

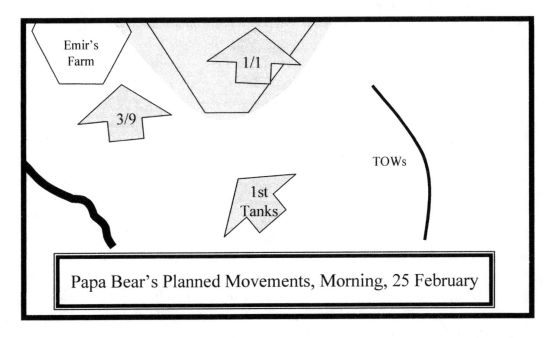

Papa Bear's Planned Movements, Morning, 25 February

By the time Lt.Col. Smith arrived, Wagner and Kephart had already returned to their battalions to brief company commanders. As Col. Hodory began briefing Smith, the T-55 and two APCs appeared out of the fog. The T-55 had its main gun pointed directly at the command post, but it was flying a white flag. In the tank was an Iraqi battalion commander who explained that he wanted to surrender, but the rest of his unit did not. The commander provided the Marines with a map showing the location of Iraqi units in southern Kuwait as well as his brigade's radio frequencies. He also told the Marines that an Iraqi counterattack was imminent. Translators immediately made contact with the Iraqi assault force, offering surrender terms, but the offers were ignored. To complicate matters, as Papa Bear's headquarters was trying to talk the Iraqis into surrendering, a report of an Iraqi chemical attack (ultimately a false alarm) came in over the radio.

The APC which had strayed toward 1st Tanks' rear did not surrender. As corporals Brian Zickefoose and Michael Kilpatrick, Lt.Col. Smith's driver and radio operator, waited for him to return from the briefing, they spotted the APC heading north.† Both grabbed AT-4 light anti-tank weapons, leapt out of the Humvee and opened fire. Meanwhile, a scout Humvee near 1st Tanks' command group on the other side of the Iraqi APC had spotted it, turned around, and launched a TOW missile at it. Hit in the left

---

*Fallon would ultimately find that the thick pall of oily smoke rendered Gathering Center 4 useless for observation purposes.

†Corporal Zickefoose was also a qualified sniper.

side by two light anti-tank rockets and the right by a TOW missile, the vehicle disappeared in a fireball.

As the radio appeals continued and the chemical report was being checked out, a few more Iraqi vehicles approached the perimeter. Lt.Col. Kephart and his commanders at 1st Tanks' mobile command post, located behind I/3/9, watched as seven Iraqi Type 63 APCs in an offset column appeared about a mile to the southwest. The Iraqis stopped, swiveled in unison to face the Marines, then opened up with their heavy machine-guns. Taken aback by the futility of the Iraqi tactics, the two tank crews assigned to provide security for the command group hesitated slightly before they began methodically picking off APCs. Each tank started at one end of the Iraqi line and worked toward the center, until all seven vehicles were in flames. Meanwhile, a Type 63 approached 1st Tanks' operations officer, Maj. John Hemleben, who made a quick radio call to a TOW-equipped scout Humvee. Though the missile malfunctioned, diving into the ground, the APC was destroyed by a nearby Company C tank.

It was now apparent that the rest of the Iraqi commander's battalion would be coming from the same direction as the APCs, and Papa Bear took steps to deal with it. I/3/9 would hold its positions while Company D, 1st Tanks reformed and reoriented to the east. Meanwhile, Capt. Phil Patch's Company C moved from its position as battalion reserve to Company D's right flank. Company C would then slash into the Iraqi flank. Meanwhile, 1/1's drive into the al-Burqan Oilfields would continue as planned. The 1st Tanks' TOW screen would move northward, to ensure that no Iraqis slipped behind 1/1 as it advanced into the oilfields. Shifting the TOW screen would also give 1st Tanks a clear field of fire as it engaged the Iraqis.

Fixed-wing aircraft support would be unavailable for the first 40 minutes of the attack. Though the fog was beginning to clear slightly, it was still thick enough to shield the Iraqis from air attack. Artillery support was also unavailable, because 1/11 was already moving toward its new positions to support the day's planned movement and was not set yet. Though 1st Battalion, 12th Marines was supposed to cover 1/11's missions during the movement, it could not fire. Because helicopters bearing Task Force X-Ray had been scheduled to fly between the battalion's guns and Papa Bear's positions, firing was forbidden. Though X-Ray's insertion had been postponed because of the fog, the fire restrictions had not been lifted, and 1/12's guns would remain silent during the counterattack.

When the Iraqi attack came, it was met by a stiff burst of Dragon missiles and LAW rockets from the dug-in and well-camouflaged I/3/9. Though neither weapon is ideal against tanks, both can penetrate a T-55. The Iraqis became flustered, and their momentum was lost. By the time the Iraqis regained their balance, Company C was deploying to attack them. At about 9:15, as Company C's gunners were taking aim, the fog lifted, suddenly and completely, leaving the Iraqis exposed. Within minutes, Marine gunners would claim 18 armored vehicles.

The defense was supported by a flight of Cobra attack helicopters from HMLA-367, which arrived shortly after Company C commenced its assault. The four Cobras, positioned to the south of the second minefield, firing to the northeast, held decisive advantages. They were beyond the effective range of Iraqi heavy machine-gunners but the Iraqi vehicles were well within range of their TOW missiles. Cobras picked off about a half-dozen Iraqi tanks.

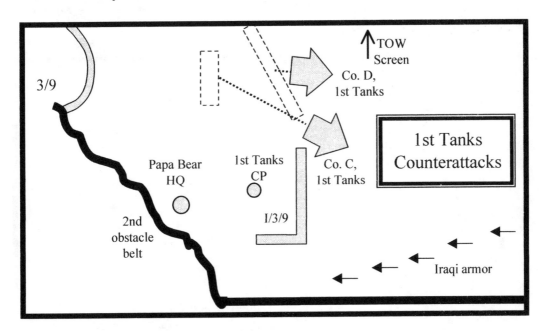

The lifting of the fog also allowed Marine fixed-wing aircraft to enter the fray. Up to that point, things had been going well for another Iraqi armored force to the east of the TOW screen. A flight of F/A-18s had been vectored to the scene shortly after the first skirmishes near the command posts. The pilots described their intended targets as: "twenty-four Soviet tanks with round turrets and no [aerial recognition] panels" to 1st Tanks' air officer, Capt. Cecil Turner. From the description, it sounded to Turner like the F/A-18s were probably looking at Iraqi armor, but he still felt there was a slight possibility the vehicles in question might be Marine tanks. Unlike M-1A1s, the M-60s the Marines were using also had rounded turrets. The fact that the pilots could see no aerial recognition panels was not conclusive either. Experience had shown that deployed panels often could not be spotted, even from fairly low altitude. Since the Iraqi armor was still too far away to inflict any damage on the Marines, Turner decided to play it safe and wave the planes away rather than risk a friendly fire incident.

The Iraqi force was from the 5th Mechanized Division's 26th Armored Brigade. It consisted mostly of T-55 tanks and was accompanied by APCs and a few dozen dismounted infantrymen. As the fog lifted, the concentration was spotted by an OV-10A (an observation version of the A-10) while it was still several thousand meters from 1st Tanks' positions.

A flight of Harriers soon arrived. This flight was certain of its target and was cleared to attack by Turner. Each Harrier brought four 500 lb. Mk-20 cluster bombs. The Mk-20 is a steel dispenser which breaks open in mid-air, scattering 247 M-118 2 lb. anti-tank fragmentation bomblets. When each M-118 explodes, it sends dense metal fragments through the air at speeds of up to 4,000 feet per second. The combination of speed and density is sufficient to penetrate six inches of steel. These fragments were capable of easily slicing through the top armor of the vehicles in the Iraqi force, and they did. About a half-dozen Iraqi armored vehicles stopped suddenly and burst into flames after Mk-20s burst over them. Most of the force's accompanying infantry was wiped out in these strikes.

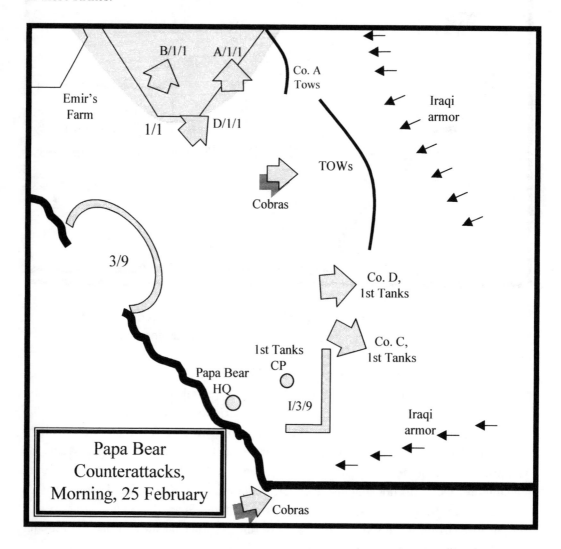

Once the bombs were dropped, another flight of Harriers arrived to strafe the Iraqis at low altitude. Before G-Day, there had been some question about whether 25mm rounds from the Harrier's high velocity rapid-fire cannon could penetrate tanks. Five Iraqi tank crews found that they could, when their tanks were destroyed by 25mm rounds.

Another flight of Cobras from HMLA-367 arrived next, firing Hellfire and TOW missiles. The Hellfires were fired first. Whereas TOW missiles are wire-guided, and limited by the length of their guide wires, Hellfires are laser-guided and have no such limitations. As a result, a Hellfire can destroy a target at 3¾ miles, roughly 1½ miles farther than the TOW-2. The gunships were aided somewhat in their mission by a bit of forward thinking by the staff of 1st Tanks.

The Marines have traditionally paid a great deal of attention to the use of air power in support of ground units. Over the years, effective air-ground coordination procedures had been developed and perfected. Still, during January and early February, as the offensive plan for the ground campaign was finalized, the battalion's planners became uneasy. They began to suspect that if the battalion became heavily engaged, calls for air support could easily overwhelm the one AO the battalion was assigned. A crash program was therefore instituted by Capt. Turner, to train four scouts and three company executive officers to coordinate directly with attack aircraft. Some of the controllers were equipped with laser designators and trained to guide munitions like the Hellfire to their targets. These designation teams, well in front of the screen line, made it possible for Cobras behind the screen to destroy six Iraqi tanks with Hellfires from maximum range.

Unfortunately, the conditions were less than optimal for the use of lasers. Due to dust and smoke, lasers were not performing properly. Because a stiff breeze was blowing almost due north, smoke from burning oil wells in the al-Burqan Oilfields never reached 1st Tanks' sector. However, there was enough smoke from burning Iraqi vehicles, as well as blowing dust and sand, to render the lasers' performance uneven. In addition, the ground was undulating, with large patches of high ground giving way to large troughs. As a result, a scout could bounce a laser off an oncoming vehicle at one moment and completely lose sight of it the next. For Cobra weapons operators, who could not use Hellfires without ground designation, the problems were maddening, and eventually caused them to lose patience and rely entirely on TOWs, which they could guide themselves.

By then, the Iraqi armored force was well within TOW range, and was annihilated by a wave of wire-guided missiles from both air and ground. Some two dozen armored vehicles were destroyed by TOWs, with kills divided about evenly between the Cobras and the TOW company.

The Iraqi force was now down to its last few armored vehicles, about a half-dozen APCs. The Cobras' ideal vantage point and sophisticated optics had allowed them to pick off the higher value targets (tanks) in the formation, and leave the APCs. No tank had gotten to within 3,000 meters of the Marine line, and now APCs were all the Iraqi force had left. These were finished off by Company D's main guns.

In the two thrusts, the Iraqis had lost over 50 tanks and 25 APCs to 1st Tanks and its supporting aircraft. More than 300 prisoners were taken. The vast majority of the prisoners came out of the trenches in the southern part of task force's sector, giving themselves up after the heavy fighting ended. Most of the Iraqis who had taken part in the counterattack had been killed. There were no Marine losses.

While 1st Tanks was picking off Iraqi armor, the three rifle companies of 1/1 under Lt.Col. Fallon's control (Company C had been assigned to Maj.Gen. Myatt's command post to provide security) moved out. Companies B and A drove into the oilfields. Capt. David Undeland's Company D, which had been attached to 1st Tanks the previous afternoon to help deal with prisoners, had returned to 1/1's control and would begin the attack in reserve.

Capt. James Trahan's Company B was the first to see action. Company B's 1st Platoon, mounted in AAVs and accompanied by a mixed section of Humvee-mounted heavy machine-guns and Humvee-mounted TOW launchers, had gone forward the previous day to inspect a pair of APCs that had been knocked out. The platoon had been told to stay where it was and establish a screen, where it was to guard against possible Iraqi attacks against the battalion's western flank. There, the infantry dug their vehicles in to hull depth behind them.

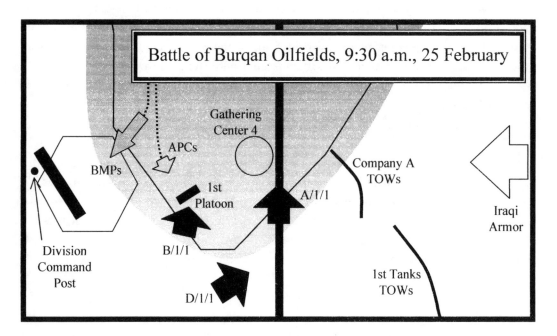

At 9:15 on the 25th, six Type 63 APCs ran into this screen line. The Marines greeted the Iraqis with TOWs and AT-4s. Company B rushed to join the fray, only to find on its arrival 15 minutes later that most of the Iraqis had been driven off, leaving behind three burning vehicles. After a sniper traveling with Trahan shot and killed three Iraqis attempting to man a knocked-out APC's mounted heavy machine-gun, 29 Iraqis surrendered.

As TOW missile and main gun fire was pounding the Iraqi armored force in 1st Tanks' sector to into extinction, Iraqis in another armored force had been feeling lucky. Just to the north of 1st Tanks' sector, an Iraqi force of about twenty armored vehicles was heading west. Though they could hear the punishment being inflicted on their comrades to the south, they had been spared up to that point. Because of a slight rise in the terrain running east to west along the force's southern flank, the Iraqis were shielded from 1st Tanks. Undoubtedly, officers within the force believed that they were about to sneak around the Marines' northern flank.

The Iraqis had no idea that they were being watched. Company A had moved into the al-Burqan Oilfields at 9:30, taking up positions just south of Gathering Center 4. Aware that there was Iraqi armor to the east, Company A's commander, Capt. Robert

Barrow, had posted his eight TOW launchers in a screen line on the company's right flank, facing east.* About 10 minutes after the company had begun moving, the Iraqi force was spotted. Barrow ordered the TOW crewmen to hold their fire until the Iraqis had closed to within 2,500 meters of the launchers. This was optimal range for the launchers, and roughly 1,700 meters beyond the maximum effective range of the Iraqis' tank guns. It was also 1,250 meters inside the TOWs' maximum effective range (3,750 meters). The Iraqis would be trapped. If the Iraqi force made a run for it once vehicles started exploding, Barrow's TOW section could pick off the would-be escapees before they made it to safety. If they charged, they would have to cover even more ground (1,700 meters) to bring their guns to bear on Barrow's TOW launchers, and would be wiped out before they got close.

As soon as the Iraqis reached the 2,500 meter limit, they were hit by a volley of eight TOW missiles. The Iraqis made no attempt either to break for their own lines or charge. Iraqi vehicles merely maneuvered eccentrically as missile after missile headed eastward, with some 80% hitting their targets. After about 20 minutes, there were no more targets to shoot at.

During the engagement, the TOW crews also spotted for the company's mortars and Mk-19 automatic grenade launchers. These weapons played havoc with the infantrymen of the Iraqi force, killing dozens of Iraqis.† In one instance, in the early moments of the barrage, a 60mm mortar round scored a direct hit on a truck from which infantrymen were beginning to dismount, blowing soldiers in several directions.

Just before eleven, Company A was ordered to continue northward along a paved road that ran from north to south through the al-Burqan Oilfields. The company drove slowly forward, with its TOW section in front. Barrow's TOW crews used their thermal sights to guide the rest of the company through the smoke, which grew progressively thicker as the Marines advanced deeper into the oilfields. After pushing through Gathering Center 4 without incident, Barrow's men began encountering Iraqis eager to surrender. Ultimately, the company collected about 50 prisoners. At about 12:45, after securing hills 114 (on the right side of the road) and 127 (on the left side), Company A was ordered to dig in.

Company B resumed its advance at the same time as Company A. Though Company B's advance to Gathering Center 13 was not contested by the Iraqis, it took the company until 2 p.m. to reach the top of the gathering center. The delay was caused primarily by the need to navigate through the maze of pipes surrounding Gathering Center 13.

---

*On 15 September 1950, Barrow's father, Capt. Robert Barrow (who would eventually become commandant of the Marine Corps), led A/1/1 during the landing at Inchon.

†The Mk-19 had originally been designed for the Navy during the Vietnam War, for use on its river patrol craft. During the late 1980s, the Army and Marine Corps decided that the weapon would be ideal for use in ground fighting. The Mk-19 fires grenades in one second bursts of 3–5 rounds. Its dual purpose grenades are lethal to unprotected troops within a 15 meter radius. They can also penetrate about two inches of armor, roughly five times the topside armor of Iraq's APCs. The Mk-19 can destroy pinpoint targets from about 1,500 meters, or bombard dug-in positions from about 2,300 meters.

The terrain opened up dramatically at the northern edge of the gathering center. There were far fewer pipes, and there was a road there, on which Company B immediately pushed northward in column formation. Trahan kept the main body of his company behind a slowly advancing screen of four TOW launchers. With sight lines badly obscured for everyone but TOW gunners with thermal sights, Trahan was unwilling to risk losing one of his AAVs to an unseen Iraqi anti-armor weapon.

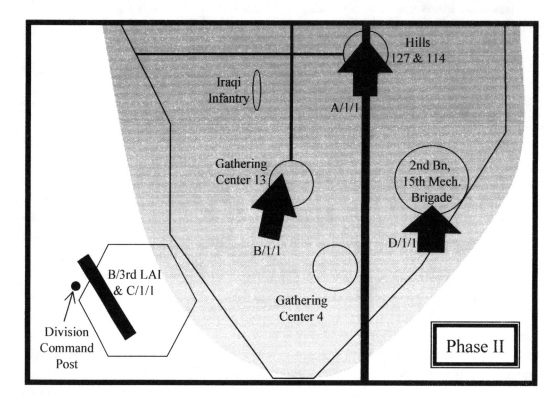

During its move, Company B's TOW screen picked off a few Iraqi vehicles darting between burning oilheads. In these engagements, TOW gunners had the benefit of experience from engagements the night before. From Company B's defensive positions, TOW launchers had engaged a few silhouettes in the distance. In two cases, TOW missiles had launched perfectly and flown their intended course for a while, then soared away from their intended targets. The TOW section leader concluded that because the two missiles had flown close to burning oil wells, the intense heat produced by the wells had melted the wires guiding the missiles. On this day, Iraqi vehicles were engaged only when they were clear of burning oil wells. The tactic worked, and there were no TOW failures.

The company's remaining four TOW launchers were spread out through the column, as were its four up-gunned AAVs, equipped with Mk-19 grenade launchers and .50 caliber machine-guns. This left no weak spots in the column, vulnerable to ambush from the flank. This proved a wise deployment.

Just short of the company's halt line, an intersection with an east–west road through the al-Burqan, the column was halted by a machine-gun emplacement to its front.

Trahan called for a mortar barrage. However, as the mortarmen were preparing to fire, two Iraqi Type 63s to the west of the road began to move. Their attention drawn by the APCs, the mortarmen and most of the heavy weapons crewmen in the column noticed that the APCs were part of a company-sized position of dug-in infantry. Along the line, Marine vehicles turned to engage the Iraqis. Both Type 63s were destroyed almost immediately, one by a TOW launched from the rear of the column, the other by a stream of .50 caliber rounds directed into its side.[*] Meanwhile, mortar rounds and Mk-19 grenades landed among the trenches, prompting the surrender of about a hundred Iraqis. Minutes later, the machine-gun bunker was silenced by heavy machine-gun fire. Shortly after the fall of the company position, two members of the machine-gun crew dragged their wounded comrade to the front of the Marine column and surrendered.

Shortly after moving out, the column reached its objective and tied into Company A's left flank, assuming defensive positions for the night. On the intersection was a well-prepared, but abandoned, defensive position. Its previous occupants had headed north on foot, leaving behind all of their heavy weapons and most of their small arms. Strewn across the position were "suitcase Saggers," portable Sagger anti-tank missiles designed to be employed by infantry. Though not particularly accurate, they would have made the position difficult to attack if had they been employed.

At about 10:15, Company D was moved to the battalion's right flank and ordered to head north, along the eastern edge of the al-Burqan. There, it would find the largest Iraqi concentration in 1/1's attack zone, the 2nd Battalion of the 5th Mechanized Division's 15th Mechanized Brigade, dug-in, facing south.

The company's progress slowed to a crawl. Most of the Iraqis on the position wanted to surrender. However, fanning across the position and gathering the prisoners was an operation that had to be undertaken with care, and one which took time. Aside from the usual concerns about snipers, there was concern that any one of the several tanks scattered across the position might spring into action against dismounted Marines. Each tank had to be approached with utmost caution. In addition, a few Iraqis still wanted to fight, and though the brief, violent encounters invariably ended up in the death or wounding of the resisting Iraqis, they interrupted prisoner collection.

Eventually, Company D rounded up the last of its 350 or so prisoners (including the 2nd Battalion's commander), and by 6 p.m. had joined the other two companies near hills 114 and 127. In the day's fighting, 1/1 destroyed 43 armored vehicles and took more than 500 prisoners at a cost of three wounded by an RPG round.

At 9:30 a.m., Iraqi shells had begun landing in the vicinity of Maj.Gen. Myatt's command post. Concerned about the exposure of the command post, Myatt had reinforced it with Company C, 1/1. He had also detailed Task Force Shepherd to provide reinforcements. Lt.Col. Myers had sent Capt. Eddie Ray with a platoon from his

---

[*]The Iraqi Army had about 600 Type 63s, which are about 20% smaller than BMPs and are designed to cram three more soldiers into them (14 soldiers to the BMP's 11). They are mechanically unreliable, and their short length renders them unable to cross ruts or ditches of any size. Coalition forces found several stuck in Iraqi anti-tank ditches.

Company B, 3rd LAI. As the first rounds landed, Capt. Ray ordered his men to remain where they were, climbed into his LAV-25 and drove off to investigate the situation.

As he arrived at the northern end of the screen line, a machine-gun nest behind a sand berm, manned by Marines from C/1/1, BMPs appeared to the east. The infantrymen engaged the BMPs with two LAWs. Though both rockets missed, they were enough to cause the BMPs to halt and dismount their infantrymen. Ray's gunner quickly destroyed two BMPs with 25mm fire. Suddenly, Ray noticed a yellow flash to his front right. Assuming that this was a Sagger missile, he ordered his driver to back up. As the vehicle sped rearward, the munition, which turned out to be a far less lethal 73mm rocket-propelled round from the BMP's main gun, fell short. Ray halted the vehicle as his gunner directed a stream of 25mm rounds into the offending Iraqi vehicle, causing a massive explosion which blew the BMP's crewmen from their hatches.

Ray radioed his platoon leader and told him to bring the detachment's other six LAVs to Ray's position. As the platoon moved northward, Ray probed southward to ensure that his position was not being flanked by the Iraqis. Satisfied that it was not, he returned to his previous position.

Just after ten, Ray's force was set, with three LAVs on each side of his vehicle and two Cobras from HMLA-369 overhead. Ray felt that he did not have enough combat power to effectively cover the ground he needed to cover defensively. He could not afford to let the Iraqis choose the site of the next engagement or risk being flanked by them. Ray decided to attack.

By chance, the attack preempted an Iraqi attack in progress. As the seven LAV's reached the top of a patch of high ground, they came upon a battalion of Iraqi BMPs headed straight for them. The Iraqis were still traveling in a column of two files. The Iraqi battalion commander, thinking that the Marines were still well over a kilometer to the west, was just bringing his battalion into attack formation.

Most of the BMPs could not even bring their guns to bear on the Marines. On the right side of the Marine line, the first two or three Iraqi vehicles were essentially defenseless targets. Due to a feature in the turret ring which causes the BMP's gun to be thrown to maximum elevation when it approaches the mounted infra-red searchlight (which is directly in the gun's path), gunners are unable to engage targets along a 15 degree arc to their left front. Marine LAV-25s were now riddling their vehicles with 25mm chain-gun fire from that arc. Other BMPs could not get clear shots because their own vehicles were in front of them. Raked by fire from LAV-25s and Cobras, BMPs and two T-55s exploded in quick succession until there were no more Iraqi vehicles left to shoot at.

Ultimately, almost 400 prisoners would be rounded up. At one point, a group of prisoners made a dash for their own lines. The Marines let them escape. Although it was allowable under the Geneva Conventions to fire on the Iraqis, Ray ordered his Marines to let them go.[*]

---

[*]For his actions during this battle, Ray received the Navy Cross, the Marine Corps' second highest award.

The confusion produced by the series of Iraqi attacks resulted in tense moments for some Marine artillery units as they moved to new positions. At 11:15, a battery from 1/11 had just moved through the second obstacle belt when a small Iraqi armored force approached it from the northeast. Quickly, the artillerymen readied their guns to fire directly at the oncoming armor. One of the Iraqi vehicles burst into flames as it was hit at short range by high explosive artillery shells. The rest of the Iraqi force withdrew. An hour later, another battery caught two Iraqi BM-21 multiple rocket launchers moving toward their firing positions. H Battery, 3rd Battalion, 14th Marines, a reserve unit from Richmond, Virginia, destroyed the Iraqi launchers with a few well-aimed 155mm howitzer direct fire shots. The Marines pulled Iraqi targeting data from the wreckage, and would find out later that the Iraqis had the coordinates of and were about to fire on the Emir's Farm, site of the division command post. Later that afternoon, a security patrol from 3/14 was sweeping a bunker complex when a Marine was mortally wounded by a booby-trap.

Task Force X-Ray, now under the control of Task Force Papa Bear, finally landed at 3 p.m., just inside the second minefield, near Papa Bear's right breach lanes. Col. Hodory moved X-Ray into the positions previously occupied by 1st Tanks. With X-Ray's Jeep-mounted TOW launchers now securing the division's right flank, Papa Bear was free to join the rest of the division in its drive toward Kuwait International Airport.

During the fighting, two Marine aircraft had been lost. An OV-10A had crashed after being hit by an Iraqi shoulder-launched anti-aircraft missile. Both the pilot, Maj. Joseph Small, and his observer, Capt. David Spellacy, were killed.[*] A Harrier piloted by Capt. Scott Walsh was hit while it was attacking targets well to the north of the battle. Walsh made for his own lines. Though he had no idea whether or not it was in Marine hands, Walsh headed for Ahmed al-Jaber Airfield to attempt a crash landing. His controls failed short of the airfield, however, and he was forced to eject. On landing, he crawled into a trench and waited until Marines from C/1/1 emerged from the smoke in a Humvee to pick him up.

Task Force Grizzly spent the morning and most of the afternoon of the 25th moving toward Ahmed al-Jaber Airfield. When the day began, the task force was still in its blocking position between the first and second minefields. Though the airfield was only a few miles to the northeast of Grizzly's positions, the second minefield blocked access by that route. Under normal circumstances, Col. Fulks could have simply ordered the minefield breached, but his task force had no mine clearing capability. His only Mk-154 had been destroyed on G-Day morning in a friendly fire incident. In addition, since the odds were slim that a plow tank could avoid being crippled while trying to clear a lane without the benefit of line charges, there had seemed no point in having the plow tank remain with Grizzly. It had therefore been recalled by Division Headquarters.

---

[*]Spellacy's body was recovered after the armistice by 1/1. In accordance with Lt.Gen. Boomer's instructions to recover all Marine dead, the battalion returned to conduct a search on foot.

The task force would have to travel eastward, pass through the lanes Ripper had established the day before, then travel back to the northwest. Trucks would take 3/7 and one of 2/7's companies to positions around the airfield, then return for 2/7's remaining companies. Meanwhile, recon teams from each of the two battalions would take up positions on the southern end of Ahmed al-Jaber and keep the complex, which included several buildings and many bunkers, under surveillance.

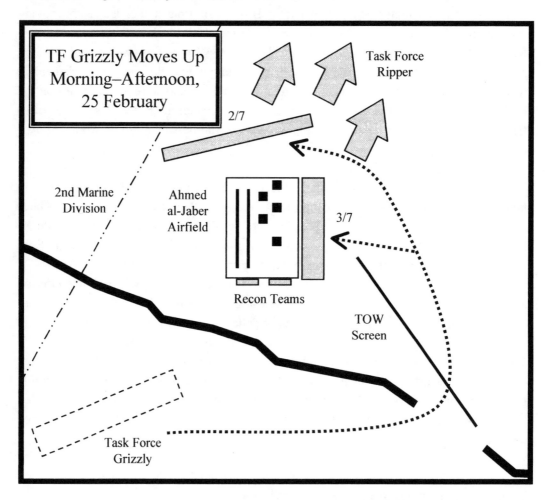

TF Grizzly Moves Up
Morning–Afternoon,
25 February

2/7

Task Force
Ripper

2nd Marine
Division

Ahmed
al-Jaber
Airfield

3/7

Recon Teams

TOW
Screen

Task Force
Grizzly

The first trucks bearing infantrymen from 3/7 approached the breach lanes late in the morning, shortly after Maj.Gen. Myatt's command post security force had beaten off the last of the Iraqi attacks against it. Col. Fulks received an erroneous report that some Iraqi tanks had slipped through and were headed for the breach lanes. Not wanting his truck-borne troops savaged by tanks as they emerged from the breach lanes, Fulks held his lead units south of the breach lanes until the situation was clarified.

By 3 p.m., the first wave of infantrymen had completed their journey, taken up positions around al-Jaber and relieved Task Force Ripper, but the delay at the breach lanes had ruined Fulks' original plan for storming the airfield. Fulks had intended for 2/7 and 3/7 to take the airfield in a coordinated attack, but there was now no way the trucks could return for the rest of 2/7 and get it into attack positions by nightfall. The assault would have to be made by 3/7. The forward company from 2/7 would deploy in a screen line between the departing Task Force Ripper and the 2nd Marine Division, to ensure that there was no Iraqi interference with the clearing operations. As the rest of 2/7 arrived, it would bolster that screen line.

By 4 p.m., 3/7 was ready to begin sweeping al-Jaber, which was now shrouded in thick, oily smoke that had drifted over the complex when the wind shifted. As the assault teams reached the fence surrounding the airfield, 18 Iraqi soldiers guarding the perimeter gave themselves up. Though they claimed that the airfield was abandoned, Fulks decided to make the attack slowly and carefully. This caution would pay off.

At 4:45, combat engineers blew gaps in the fence as the assault companies moved forward to their final jumping-off points. At 5:22, Grizzly's mortars began dropping rounds on suspected command centers and observation posts. Almost immediately, the assault companies were hit in their staging areas by Iraqi rocket and artillery fire. The barrage killed one Marine and wounded eleven.

Grizzly's Marines shook off the effects of the barrage and burst through the fence at 5:45. During the next four hours, the Marines pushed cautiously forward, from east to west, occasionally receiving light and inaccurate artillery fire. By 9 p.m., they had captured 32 more Iraqis and had surrounded the cluster of buildings on the airfield. During the planning before G-Day, Col. Fulks and his staff had debriefed a Marine reservist who had been a flight instructor at Ahmed al-Jaber, so Fulks' Marines were familiar with the layout of the buildings. However, even with this familiarity, clearing the buildings was an intricate and dangerous mission. Fulks requested permission to use tear gas to flush the Iraqis out of their hiding places within the buildings, but Lt.Gen. Boomer denied the request. The Iraqis had not employed chemical weapons and Boomer did not want to give them a pretext to use them. Faced with the possibility of room-to-room fighting in the dark, Fulks decided to suspend the attack for the night. He decided to wait for morning to attack rather than take unnecessary casualties.

Though the attack was suspended, the evening was eventful. Shortly after nightfall, patrolling Cobras identified a force of 22 Iraqi T-62s looking for someone to surrender to. After this was reported to Col. Fulks, Marines from TF Grizzly were sent forward to take the Iraqis' surrender.

The rest of the division also decided that it was necessary to suspend operations for the night. Maj.Gen. Myatt had planned on adequate levels of moonlight by which to move his forces at night, but the burning oil wells had turned the night pitch black. This presented a problem, since the night vision goggles used by the Coalition operated by intensifying starlight or moonlight. When the oily smoke blocked out the sky, the goggles became almost useless. Even in cases where there was a light source provided by a burning oil well, the goggles did not work. Lenses were covered with oil droplets almost as quickly as they could be wiped clean.

Ahmed al-Jaber was completely cleared on the following day. At first light, 3/7 resumed clearing buildings. Like the day before, the assault was slow and thorough. Every bunker and room was treated as if it were occupied by Iraqis until proven otherwise. By three in the afternoon, there were no rooms left to clear. Fulks' decision to avoid nighttime detailed clearing operations had turned out to be a wise one. The Iraqis had set tremendous numbers of booby-traps before they pulled out.

Day three of the ground offensive would bring the division to the brink of complete victory. Ripper would seal off the western approaches to Kuwait International Airport. Papa Bear would drive to blocking positions south of the airport. Shepherd would skirt the eastern edge of the airport on its way to its final objective, a highway system to the northeast. This would complete the isolation of the airport. At that point, Taro would arrive by truck convoy and take the airport itself. The Marine objectives were held by the remnants of the Iraqi 20th Mechanized Brigade, the last brigade of the 5th Mechanized Division still in existence.

Abandoned Type 63 APC. (Photo: Col. Richard Barry)

At around seven, on the division's right flank, Task Force Shepherd's LAVs destroyed 16 Type 63 APCs fully loaded with retreating Iraqi infantrymen. The vehicles, armed only with heavy machine-guns, were basically defenseless, and were so lightly armored that a hit of any consequence meant death for all of their occupants. After destroying the Type 63s, the task force stopped and waited for the rest of the division to catch up.

Just after 7 a.m., Ripper began its advance. The task force soon came upon scores of Iraqi vehicles, mostly T-62s from the 3rd Armored Division. Most were abandoned, or had been previously destroyed. Some were not, however, and contained crews waiting in ambush for a good flank or rear shot on Marine tanks as they passed by. Ahead of infantry units, TOW vehicles used their thermal sights to determine which tanks were manned. Those that were manned were immediately destroyed by TOW missiles. The 3rd Tank Battalion fired heavy machine-guns at suspect vehicles. Those that responded were destroyed by main gun fire.

Smoke from the burning oilfields made fixed-wing support of Ripper's advance impossible. Though the task force was not as close to the al-Burqan Oilfields as Papa Bear, smoke from the oil fires, blowing due west, was still thick enough over Ripper to shroud the task force and limit visibility to about 100 meters. Cobra support was available, but only because Lt.Col. Kurth, the commander of HMLA-369, used his specially equipped Huey to guide his Cobras to the lead task forces. Using the Huey's sophisticated night optics, Kurth flew northward alone from al-Jaber, through the dense oil smoke, until he had found Task Force Ripper. As the density of the smoke made it impossible for Kurth to find the lead units from high altitude, Kurth was forced to fly along the road from al-Jaber to Kuwait City at levels so low that he had to fly under power lines on several occasions.* Once he had located the ground forces, he turned back to al-Jaber to retrieve the rest of his squadron. By the time the Cobras arrived over Ripper, the task force was almost past the al-Burqan Oilfields. As a result, visibility had improved dramatically, and shots of 1,000 meters were possible.

Late in the morning, 1/7 ran into a large, apparently abandoned, quarry. Lead vehicles probed the quarry with heavy machine-gun fire. There was no response. A flight of gunships flew over the area, and could see no sign of enemy activity. The task force resumed its march. Shortly thereafter, lead units spotted a handful of Iraqi tanks to the north and drove them off. At the same time, 1/7's combat trains began taking fire from seemingly every part of the quarry. Showing a high degree of discipline and tactical ability, the Iraqis had waited until all of the Marine combat vehicles had passed by and engaged the supply trucks in the rear of the formation.

The Marines in the supply trains responded, directing streams of heavy machine-gun rounds and grenades from Mk-19s into the quarry. Lt.Col. Mattis sent an infantry company back to deal with the Iraqis. However, when the infantry arrived, they found that the mechanics had already broken the Iraqi attack without sustaining a single casualty. Ripper halted at 11:30 a.m. and prepared for the final push to the airport.

Papa Bear began moving along the western edge of the al-Burqan Oilfields at 8:00. During the drive, the task force encountered much the same problem as Ripper had with live tanks hiding among destroyed or abandoned tanks, and dealt with the problem in the same way, probing fire, then destruction when necessary.

As the rest of Papa Bear moved north, 1/1 was moving westward. The battalion had left Papa Bear's main body on the previous day to clear the al-Burqan Oilfields. Now it was near the top of the oilfields, feeling its way west along a set of power lines which would ultimately take it to a rendezvous with the rest of the task force. After the link-up, Papa Bear paused briefly to reform, then continued northward. At 1 p.m., the task force halted next to Ripper and awaited orders to begin the final push to the airport.

Though the two task forces had halted, they remained active. In Papa Bear's sector, 1/1 launched a probe against an Iraqi position to its front. The battalion took the surrender of the position's occupants and captured 10 tanks, 10 anti-tank guns and large

---

*For this action, Kurth received the Navy Cross.

quantities of ammunition. As Ripper waited, 1/7 was fired upon by Iraqi infantrymen in a cluster of buildings about 600 meters to its front. The Marines responded with artillery, mortars, and machine-guns until the small arms fire stopped. When the battalion went through the area later, they found several dead and dying Iraqis. The rest had fled.

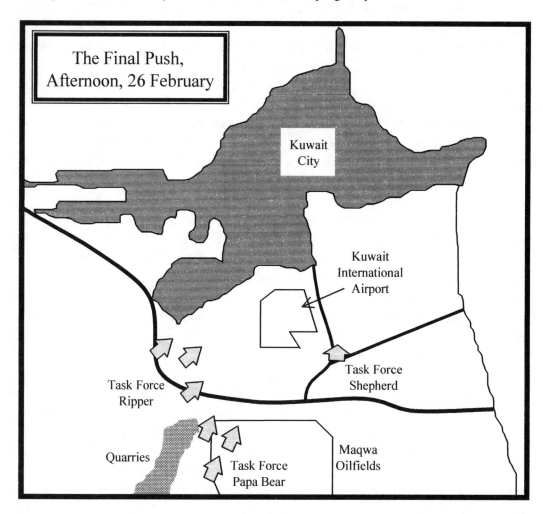

The Final Push,
Afternoon, 26 February

Kuwait City

Kuwait International Airport

Task Force Shepherd

Task Force Ripper

Quarries

Task Force Papa Bear

Maqwa Oilfields

The final push began in the early afternoon when Shepherd resumed its drive on the right flank. The task force drove northeast from its position inside the flaming Maqwa Oilfields. By four, its LAVs were driving along the airport's eastern edges. At five, having destroyed 6 tanks and 11 APCs on the way, Shepherd reached the outskirts of Kuwait City. While it waited for the rest of the division to catch up, the task force continued to reconnoiter the southern part of the city.

On the division's left flank, Ripper kicked off its assault at 3:30 p.m. Fifteen minutes later, after destroying a handful of Iraqi vehicles, 1/7, on Ripper's right flank, encountered a minefield behind three layers of double-strand concertina wire. Combat engineers prepared to breach the minefield while the task force exchanged fire with Iraqi armor and infantry on the other side, destroying eight APCs. When the engineers entered the minefield, two Iraqi tanks moved forward in an attempt to disrupt the breach, but were destroyed. By 4:30, several lanes had been opened, and assault units had crossed the minefield to establish footholds on the other side. Iraqi resistance collapsed, and the battalion continued northward.

A cause of concern to the commanders of task forces Ripper and Papa Bear had been the series of quarries which ran between the two task forces. They made tight flank coordination between Ripper and Papa Bear impossible. Concerns had deepened when Iraqis in one of the quarries attacked 1/7's supply trains. The problem was solved by the artillerymen of Lt.Col. Mark Adams' 3rd Battalion, 11th Marines. Adams' gunners secured the task forces' flanks by saturating the quarries with DPICM rounds. As the two task forces moved northward, an artillery barrage rolled northward between them, killing, wounding or terrifying into submission any Iraqis hiding in the quarries. There were no more surprises from any of the quarries. By nightfall, Ripper had taken its assigned objectives and sealed off the western side of the airport.

Papa Bear began its final assault between Ripper and Shepherd at 4:30. On Papa Bear's left wing was 3rd Battalion, 9th Marines. At 5:30, 3/9 ran into a minefield. The minefield was uncontested by the Iraqis and was quickly breached. By 6 p.m., the battalion was through the minefield and heading for an Iraqi defensive position south of the airport. The position was honeycombed with bunkers and fighting positions, and was backed by tanks and APCs. Had it been contested, the fighting could have been grim. However, most of the Iraqi defenders, having seen the handwriting on the wall, surrendered. The Marines crushed the few holdouts without breaking stride. The weather and the burning oil wells were more of an obstacle than the Iraqis. Driving through thick black smoke as well as a sandstorm, 3/9 found maneuver almost impossible. It took the battalion until almost midnight to establish a foothold inside the perimeter fence of the airport.

The right wing of Papa Bear's thrust, in which 1st Tanks followed 1/1, started its attack about a half-hour after the left wing. Unlike 3/9, 1/1 was engaged by Iraqi tanks and APCs all the way to the obstacle belt, but the Iraqi resistance was easily overcome, and by 10 p.m., 1/1 had captured a radio station inside the airport perimeter and had deployed along the airport perimeter road. Meanwhile, 1st Tanks took up positions along the perimeter road, securing the task force's right flank.

As 1/1 was deploying along the road, the task force's headquarters and its combat engineer detachment, commanded by Maj. Joseph Musca, were taking up positions for the night. Col. Hodory placed his headquarters a few hundred meters to the north of an elevated highway, while Musca set up his position due south of Col. Hodory's headquarters, a few hundred meters on the other side of the highway.

When Musca first selected his position, it was masked by smoke from burning oil wells. About an hour after pulling into the position, however, the wind shifted, blowing the smoke away from the engineers and leaving them silhouetted against the burning wells. They were soon spotted by a patrol of Iraqi BTR-60 wheeled APCs and 5-ton trucks on the elevated highway between the engineers and Papa Bear's headquarters. A stiff firefight erupted between the engineers and the Iraqis, who had dismounted and deployed along the highway, and were supported by machine-gun fire from the APCs.

The Iraqis were also supported by mortars, which began to walk shells toward the Marine positions. As Musca directed his troops from his AAV, his driver noticed mortar rounds creeping toward them, and was able to avoid being hit by pivoting the vehicle just before the barrage rolled past. The mortar rounds were followed by RPG rounds.

Concerned that tank rounds might overshoot the Iraqis and strike Papa Bear's headquarters, Musca told his attached tanks to hold their fire. The engineers could only reply with small arms and .50 caliber machine-gun fire from the AAVs. Before long, the Iraqis had found the range of the engineers, and were pouring fire into their position. An RPG round sliced through the rear end of a Mk-154. Fortunately, the projectile failed to set off its line charges.

The Marines continued to direct a torrent of fire from every assault rifle and heavy machine-gun they could bring to bear in the Iraqis' direction. However, this seemed to be having little effect on the Iraqis. Unable to suppress the Iraqi fire with small arms and heavy machine-gun fire, Musca determined that he would have to employ tank gun fire against the Iraqis.

Musca had his operations officer alert Marine artillery to be prepared to deliver a barrage on the highway if the main gun fire did not break the Iraqis. This was not an attractive option, as the rounds would be impacting on Col. Hodory's command post if they landed a few hundred meters long, or on Musca and the engineers if they landed a few hundred meters short. As if to impress upon him the seriousness of the situation, the AAV company commander, Capt. John Allison, was dragged to the shelter of Musca's vehicle with a bullet wound in his face. Musca alerted Hodory's headquarters that he would be authorizing his tank gunners to fire. In the next few minutes, main gun fire destroyed one BTR-60 and several 5-ton trucks. The surviving Iraqis piled into the remaining vehicles and fled. One Marine had been killed in the firefight.

Shortly after the engineers had chased off the Iraqis, Task Force Shepherd received an unexpected honor. Maj.Gen. Myatt told Lt.Col. Myers that Shepherd would clear the airport, not Taro as had been originally planned. Myatt wanted to capture the airport before the cease-fire, and Taro was still far to the south in the al-Burqan Oilfields. Since G-Day, Taro had remained in its blocking positions, guarding the supply route through the breach lanes. When the task force prepared to move north on the morning of the 26th, it could not find sufficient transport to do so. By 4 p.m., Col. Admire had rounded up the transport he needed and began his move. Iraqi resistance was not a problem. The vast majority of the Iraqis the task force came upon wanted only to surrender. However, the heavy black smoke and a sudden sandstorm made navigation impossible. At about 10 p.m., division headquarters ordered Task Force Taro to halt where it was and continue northward in the morning.

At 4:30 p.m. on 27 February, Task Force Shepherd began its assault on Kuwait International Airport. Company A pushed forward, destroying an APC and capturing three Iraqis. The drive ground to a halt, however, when several LAV-25s were immobilized. Naval gunfire had previously been called in on the airport. Though effective, it had produced a significant number of craters, at the bottom of which lay large, jagged pieces of shrapnel that shredded the LAVs' tires. Myers stopped the assault, giving the order to attack again at first light. By 6:45 the next morning, the flags of the United States and the Marine Corps flew from the flag poles in front of the terminal building. About an hour later, Lt.Col. Robert Blose's 2nd Battalion, 3rd Marines from Task Force Taro arrived and began clearing the remainder of the airport, capturing about 150 Iraqis in hiding. By nine, all was quiet in the 1st Marine Division's zone.

In the ground offensive, the division had destroyed or captured about 285 tanks and 170 APCs, as well as 7 ZSU 23-4 AA systems. The fighting had cost the division 3 killed in action and 46 wounded.

12

Slamming the Door:
The 2nd Marine Division
and the Tiger Brigade

O n G-Day, while the 1st Marine Division was breaching its minefield, Maj.Gen. William Keys' 2nd Marine Division was dealing with its own. Like Maj.Gen. Myatt, Keys was a decorated Vietnam veteran (Navy Cross, Silver Star) with a master's degree. Unlike Myatt, or any division commander in the history of the Corps, Keys had a major tank force at his disposal. With 20,500 men, including Marine Reserve tank and TOW anti-tank units, and the M-1A1s and Bradleys of the U.S. Army's Tiger Brigade, the 2nd Marine Division was the most powerful Marine division ever to take the field. The division would create a breach to the west of the 1st Marine Division.

The 2nd Marine Division had originally been tasked to follow the 1st Marine Division through a single breach. During the early stages of planning, a one-division breach seemed the most sensible option. Taking into account the minefields, the number of Iraqi artillery pieces expected to be firing on the breach area, and the number of tanks and anti-tank weapons expected to be covering the minefields, Marine planners felt that a 50% loss rate in breaching equipment was a reasonable expectation. In view of the expected high equipment loss rate, they did not believe that they had enough equipment for two breaches. A one-breach plan would allow the Marines to concentrate their breaching equipment on a single point. It would also allow them to concentrate their artillery. Ten battalions of artillery were thought to be enough to cover only one breach effectively.

Events in late January and early February had caused Marine planners to adjust their assessments of Iraqi capabilities downward. The battles in and around Khafji and a series of border artillery raids had raised doubts about the combat effectiveness of the Iraqi units that the Marines would be facing. Iraqi soldiers had displayed a lack of determination, Iraqi maneuver units had not shown any great degree of tactical competence and Iraqi artillery had been a non-factor. These lessons, and the arrival of additional quantities of breaching equipment, caused Marine planners to suspect that a two-division breaching operation might be feasible after all.

Though the single-breach plan had originally seemed the most sensible option, it was never an attractive one. Having a division breach two minefields while under enemy fire was a difficult enough proposition. Having to coordinate the passage of another division through it increased the mission's difficulty level exponentially. While a two-division breach would require the 2nd Marine Division to plan and execute a breach of its own, it removed entirely the myriad difficulties of coordinating its passage through the 1st Marine Division. It also allowed the Marines to employ twice as much combat power against the Saddam Line during the critical early stages of the ground offensive, and would force the Iraqi armored and mechanized reserves to remain spread over a wider front. Maj.Gen. Keys urged Lt.Gen. Boomer to allow the 2nd Division to establish its own breach. Three weeks before G-Day, Boomer agreed.

Final preparations for the breach began on the night of 17 February, when four reconnaissance teams from Lt.Col. Scott McKenzie's 2nd Reconnaissance Battalion entered Kuwait. Because of the need for stealth and the possibility that the Iraqis would have numerous anti-aircraft weapons in the area, helicopter insertion would be impossible. Each six-man team therefore began its journey in two Humvees, one with a .50 caliber machine-gun and the other with communications gear. When the teams reached the berm, they dug hull-deep pits for the vehicles on the friendly side of the berm, then covered them with camouflage netting. From then on, they would be on foot.

In the early hours of the 18th, the four teams pushed north on foot, while two more teams occupied their original positions. These teams would act as a radio relay station for the four forward teams. The need for stealth made the use of large antennae by the forward teams impossible. They had to rely on relatively short range high frequency radios, with communications relayed to the rear by the rearward teams. Two more teams, equipped with sophisticated optics, took up positions on the berm to provide overwatch for the forward teams. The teams were to spend the next four days monitoring Iraqi troop movements.

The 6th Marine Regiment was responsible for extracting any teams which were compromised. On the morning of the 20th, one of the teams was approached by a platoon of Iraqi dismounts supported by five APCs. After a Marine Harrier strike and an artillery barrage, LAV-25s from Company B, 2nd Light Armored Infantry Battalion, which had been attached to 6th Marines, completed the destruction of the Iraqi force, pouring 25mm chain-gun fire on it from 100 meters. The LAVs then picked up the team and fell back across the border. Later that day, a Marine artillery unit fired some experimental luminous marking rounds within 500 meters of another team's position. Fearing that the Iraqis might investigate, the team moved to a radio relay team position about two miles to the rear. That evening, the team moved back to within 1,000 meters of the minefield.

As night fell on the 20th, the teams made their way into the minefield. There were a few close calls. One team froze in place as a four-man Iraqi patrol walked past, unaware of the recon team only yards away. The leader of another team was moving toward the minefield when he heard muffled coughing beneath him. He was standing on top of an Iraqi bunker. Slowly, he moved away from the bunker and continued his mission. Over the next 24 hours, the teams took photographs and made detailed sketches of the obstacle belt. They also discovered a foot path through the minefield, and dug up several mines to determine what types the Iraqis had laid.

Making six cuts through the border berm would have given the Iraqis the exact location of the assault lanes, so Maj.Gen. Keys decided to make eighteen cuts and let the Iraqis guess which ones his Marines would come through. On 20 February, the division's engineers began work on nine cuts in front of the Tiger Brigade on the division's left flank. Though none of the breaching forces would emerge from any of these holes on G-Day, the Iraqis began to suspect that this would be the site of the main breaching operation. They believed that their suspicions were confirmed when the 2nd LAI began aggressive patrolling in that area.

Late on the morning of 21 February, two companies from 2nd LAI slipped into Kuwait. At 10:23, Company C, under Capt. Kenneth Amidon, crossed its line of departure. Company A, commanded by Capt. Dennis Greene, followed at 11:33. These were the two most practiced companies in the battalion and the only companies of regulars that Lt.Col. Holcomb had. Normally made up of four companies, A through D, the battalion's B and D companies were onboard ships as part of the 4th Marine Expeditionary Brigade. These companies would have given the 4th MEB reconnaissance and screening capability in the event that an amphibious landing had become necessary. The two lost companies had been replaced with two companies of reservists. Two more companies, also made up of reservists, brought the 2nd LAI's strength to six companies.

At 11:20, Company C began engaging dug-in Iraqis. Within 15 minutes, the company was under small arms, anti-tank and observed artillery fire. A Humvee carrying a two-man Low Altitude Air Defense (LAAD) team was hit by an artillery round. Though the blast blew the back of the vehicle into the air and threw the Marines out of it, neither was seriously injured. Fortunately for the vehicle's occupants, the round had a delay fuse, so it sliced through the bed of the vehicle, burrowed into the ground, then exploded. Had the round been properly fused (with an impact fuse), it would have exploded upon hitting the vehicle, killing the two occupants instantly. The two Marines were also fortunate because the windshields of the vehicle had been removed to avoid their reflections giving away Marine positions. Had the windshields been in, the two Marines would have been thrown against them with tremendous force, instead of being ejected through the empty frames.

This engagement revealed problems with both communications and fire support coordination. At 11:45, Holcomb decided to withdraw both companies until the bugs were worked out of the system. Within a few hours the problems had been solved, and at 2:05 in the afternoon, the two companies reentered Kuwait.

From the 21st to the 23rd, the battalion (minus companies B and D, which were screening for 6th Marines and the Tiger Brigade, respectively) monitored Iraqi troop movements and engaged enemy forces on 17 separate occasions.

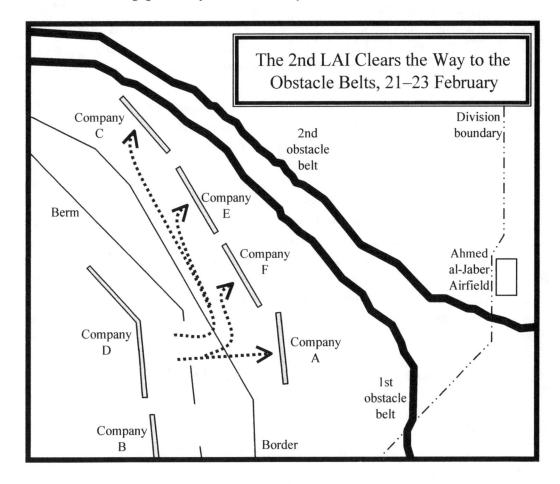

One of the most serious engagements involved an Iraqi counterattack of about 20 tanks against Company C at about 2:30 on the afternoon of the 23rd. The Marines' 25mm chain-guns were having no effect on the tanks, when a flight of Cobras arrived. Though they were met with intense anti-aircraft fire, the Cobras, guided by laser designation provided by Company C, destroyed several Iraqi tanks, stopping the counterattack.

During its three-day raid, 2nd LAI was heavily shelled by Iraqi artillery. The Marines wanted to be shelled. It allowed them to pinpoint the location of the guns so they could be destroyed by air strikes or counterbattery fire before the main breaching operation began. Thirty-three artillery missions were fired against Iraqi guns based on artillery-spotting radar intercepts resulting from 2nd LAI's actions.

In three days of operations under almost continuous mortar and artillery fire, 2nd LAI was responsible for the destruction by direct fire, or the direction of air and artillery strikes, of 12 tanks, 23 APCs, 30 wheeled vehicles and at least 10 artillery or mortar positions (the results of the 33 radar-based missions could not be definitively assessed). The battalion also netted 109 EPWs for Marine interrogators.

Although credit for it was originally given to fixed-wing aircraft, 2nd LAI was also responsible for setting the fire trenches alight, to burn themselves out before G-Day. Actually lighting the oil was trickier than expected. Attempts to ignite it with thermite grenades failed, because the grenades merely sank in what had become sand-filled black paste. Eventually, Holcomb's Marines discovered that firing 25mm High Explosive Incendiary (HEI) rounds from the LAV's chain-guns into the trenches would start the oil burning. Using this method (and calling in high explosive artillery rounds on one fire trench), they lit every fire trench in their sector.

The violence of the assault led the Iraqis to believe that they were facing far more than four companies of Marines. On G-Day, captured Iraqi officers would tell the Marines that they had believed that they had faced and held off the main Marine assault.

Maj.Gen. Keys' shell game had continued while the 2nd LAI was conducting its operations. On the 20th, as Iraqi units began shifting toward the nine cuts on the left flank from which 2nd LAI had emerged, three more cuts were made in the 8th Marines' sector, on the division's right flank, to further confuse the Iraqis. Two of these three lanes would actually be used on G-Day. Two days later, as the division's engineers began work on six more cuts (four real, two false) in the center, Col. Larry Schmidt, the 8th Marines' commander, sent the 3rd Battalion, 23rd Marines through the cuts in its sector to patrol the area to the 8th Marines' front. The battalion, commanded by Lt.Col. Ray Dawson, was a reserve unit headquartered in New Orleans and made up of companies from Tennessee, Alabama, Arkansas and Louisiana. After showing a high degree of readiness after being called up, the unit had been assigned an active role with the division and had been reinforced with about 70 active duty Marines from 8th Marines. On the 23rd, Dawson's battalion returned with 168 Iraqi prisoners.

At 4:30 a.m. on G-Day, the artillery preparation for the breach began. The night before, the division's artillery had taken up positions inside Kuwait. This put the Marine artillery in front of the maneuver units. This tactic may have been somewhat risky, but it allowed Marine gunners to extend their reach deeper into the Iraqi defenses. In only 11 minutes, 1,430 rounds, most carrying bomblets, were on their way to 40 Iraqi positions, mostly artillery batteries. To the tune of The Marines' Hymn, blared over psyops loudspeakers, the breach began at 5:30.

The breaching force consisted of three mechanized battalions, each of which would establish two breach lanes. Col. Lawrence Livingston's 6th Marine Regiment was responsible for the creation of the division's six breach lanes. Lt.Col. Thomas Jones' 1st Battalion, 6th Marines was responsible for breach lanes Red 1 and 2 on the left. The center lanes, Blue 3 and 4, were assigned to Lt.Col. Mitch Youngs' 2nd Battalion, 2nd Marines. Green 5 and 6, on the right flank, would be cleared by the 8th Marines' 1st Battalion, 8th Marines under Lt.Col. Bruce Gombar. Gombar's battalion had been attached to 6th Marines in the weeks before the beginning of the air war, and would return to its parent regiment on the second day of the ground war, after the breachhead had been established.

The infantry regiments were heavily supplemented by Marine tank units. The 8th Tank Battalion, U.S. Marine Corps Reserve, equipped with M-60s, was assigned to the 6th Marines. Company A was assigned to 2/2, while Company C was assigned to 1/6 and B and Headquarters companies joined 3/6, a motorized (truck-borne) unit. The 8th Marines received two Marine Reserve companies (B and C) from the 4th Tank Battalion. Like other Marine armored units, companies B and C were normally equipped with M-60A1s. When they were called to duty in the Gulf, the companies received transition training on the Abrams, then borrowed their M-1A1s from the Army when they got to the desert in late December. Company B was incorporated into 1/8 and would take part in the breach.

The actual engineering work on the six lanes would be done by Task Force Breach Alpha, two combat engineer companies (B Co., 2nd Combat Engineer Battalion and D Co., 4th Combat Engineer Battalion) with attached tanks and AAVs. Keeping Iraqis away from the breaching battalions was the responsibility of the 2nd LAI, which shielded the left flank, and the 3rd Battalion, 23rd Marines, which sealed off the right flank.

The breaching units were shelled heavily. Somehow, most of the artillery in the 2nd Marine Division's sector had escaped destruction during the air campaign. These guns, and the mortars behind the minefield, were able to deliver almost 500 rounds on Keys' men. Fortunately, the heavy, long range South African G-5 and Austrian GHN-45 155mm howitzers were with the Republican Guard or in the Wadi al-Batin, where they were too far from the breach lanes to do any good.

The poor weather made close air support difficult. Iraqi artillery often had to be pinpointed by artillery-spotting radar and destroyed by Marine counterbattery fire. Between 6 a.m. and 2 p.m., there were 42 instances of incoming artillery. Of the 42 targets, 24 were knocked out by Marine counterbattery fire, while air strikes were available for the remaining 18.

Just before 7 a.m., a Fox chemical reconnaissance vehicle indicated the presence of small amounts of mustard agent in Red 1.* Lt.Col. Jones' men donned masks and pressed onward, but progress in the lane slowed dramatically. Even so, by 7:30, both Red lanes through the first mine belt were cleared, and the task force was on its way to the second mine belt. Minutes later, 2/2 began passing through the two Blue lanes. By 7:45, the two task forces were ready to breach the second minefield, but they were beginning to receive stiffer opposition. Marine gunners efficiently suppressed Iraqi resistance. The Red and Blue lanes were complete by 8:45.

The Green lanes were a problem, though. The minefield here was deeper than it was in the Red and Blue lanes, and the mines were sown more densely. The engineer officer responsible for clearing the lanes would say later that the minefields in this sector must have been laid by a different and more dedicated Iraqi officer. These lanes also contained British bar mines, which had been captured from the Kuwaitis. Bar mines cannot be set off by explosive overpressure like the kind produced by MiCLiC. In

---

*This turned out to be a false alarm.

185

addition, they can be fitted with anti-disturbance fuses, designed to set the mine off if an attempt is made to move it. Many of the mines in this sector were fused in this fashion. As a result, they were exploding on contact with mine plows. Most of the division's engineer equipment losses occurred in the Green lanes.

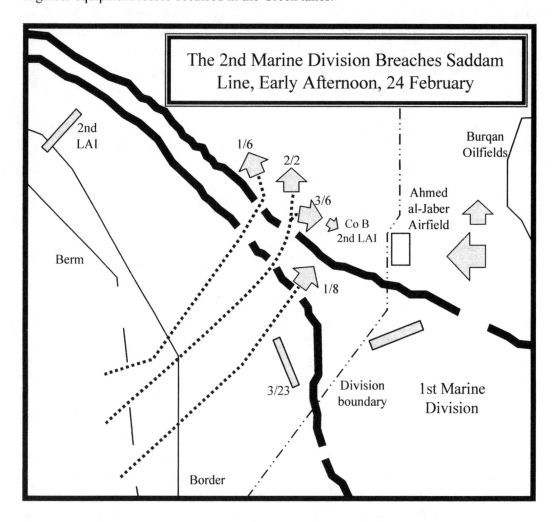

The 2nd Marine Division Breaches Saddam Line, Early Afternoon, 24 February

There were also power lines running across the minefield. The lines were not a surprise, since the recon teams had marked the lines on their sector sketches. However, since no one had ever attempted to fire MiCLiCs over power lines, no one could be sure whether or not they would be a problem, though Lt.Col. Gombar and his staff suspected that they would. They were.

In Green 5, the first line charge went off as expected. After the path was proofed by a plow tank, a second charge was launched. That charge became caught on the wires, however. Though it detonated, the explosion was too high to detonate any mines. Worse, the explosion also failed to cut the power lines. Fortunately, the rocket pulling the third charge sailed beneath the wires, and detonated on command. Unfortunately, the plow tank that followed was crippled by a mine. After the Mk-154 following the tank had backed out of the lane, another plow tank attempted to pass the immobilized tank, but it too struck a mine. A third plow tank was able to get within 20 meters of the end of the first minefield when it too was disabled by a mine. Though no Marines had been killed or seriously wounded, three plow tanks had been lost. Work on the lane had to be suspended while more engineering equipment was brought forward. Green 5 was not cleared until 9:30.

In Green 6, a plow tank led an engineer AAV to the point where it would fire its line charges. However, the crews of both the tank and the AAV failed to spot, and passed, the one foot stake marking the beginning of the minefield. The AAV hit a mine, which blew three of its road wheels off. Though the blast did not detonate the 5,250 lbs. of plastic explosive in the three line charges inside the AAV, the vehicle was crippled. The lane was now blocked. The plow tank was boxed-in by live mines on three sides and a wrecked AAV to its rear. Another breach was immediately attempted about 70 meters to the left of the blocked lane. Although both line charges failed to command detonate and had to be manually primed, the lane was ready for tank traffic by 7:36.

The 14 M-1A1s of Company B, 4th Tanks now readied themselves to cross the minefield. The company had been ordered to take up positions on the other side of the minefield to support the assault by one of 1/8's infantry companies on some Iraqi trenchworks. Unfortunately, five minutes after it was opened, the first tank through the lane struck a mine. In clearing lanes, mine plows push soil into berms along the length of the lane. The soil contains the unexploded mines which have been shoved aside. As the tank brushed against the soil, it set off a mine, which crippled the tank.

With another lane blocked, concern about the Green lanes was beginning to mount at division headquarters when individual initiative saved the day. While an alternate lane was being cleared, the commander of the boxed-in tank, Staff Sergeant B.M. Shaw, decided to take his chances with the minefield. Though the area to its front had not been prepared by line charges, Shaw's tank plowed ahead. Remarkably, the tank reached the far end of the first minebelt without detonating any mines. With another lane sorely needed, Shaw turned around and plowed a path back to the other side. For the moment, Shaw's paths were clear only for tracked vehicles. Seventeen minutes later, they were clear for all vehicles.

At 8:30, as soon as the lane was clear for tracked vehicles, Company A, 1/8 burst through and turned right to block a possible Iraqi counterattack. As it approached its blocking position, the company began taking fire from Iraqis in trenches and a three-story cinderblock building. The position, situated on a piece of high ground to the southwest of Ahmed al-Jaber Airfield, gave the Iraqis an excellent view of the Marines as they approached.

The 10 AAVs bearing the Marines headed straight for the Iraqi position, disgorging two platoons to clear the trenches, and another to clear the building. The 28 defenders in the trenches surrendered almost immediately. However, though Company A's 3rd Platoon was inside the building, the Iraqis there continued to resist. The Marines left the building as calls were made for heavier firepower. Air support was unavailable, and artillery had no impact on the building's defenders. Company A reentered the building and wiped its defenders out.

At 8:47, infantry reinforcements and combined anti-armor teams (CAATs) began pushing through the lanes. Each CAAT was made up of 16 Humvees, with eight mounting TOW launchers, four mounting Mk-19 automatic grenade launchers, and four mounting .50 caliber machine-guns. One CAAT drove to an Iraqi position north of the three-story building. As soon as they saw the Marines, the 67 Iraqis on that position, including the crews of three dug-in tanks, surrendered.

Meanwhile, the two other breaching battalions destroyed one infantry brigade and part of another. On the left flank, Iraqi resistance was shattered when 1/6 broke through the minefield, hooked left and rolled up much of the Iraqi 14th Infantry Division's 14th Brigade. The battalion then pushed into the 7th Infantry Division's sector, destroying part of the 19th Infantry Brigade and driving the rest of it away from the breach area. In the center, 2/2 and its attached tanks ran into defended trenches and bunkers supported by dug-in tanks and artillery immediately after leaving the second minefield. In a series of short, violent, small-unit engagements, the Marines overran the rest of the 14th Brigade.

Breaching on the second minefield in the Green lanes began at 11:00. Again, Green 5 claimed a plow tank. Due to a shortage of breaching assets, work on the lane had to be abandoned. All efforts had to be focused on Green 6, where there were also problems. Two line charges snapped their arrestor cables and flew free into the minefield, where they could be neither detonated from the vehicles nor reached for manual detonation. Two others had to be manually detonated. These problems notwithstanding, the lane was open for all traffic at 12:16.

The area to the front of the Green lanes had already been secured by Company B, 2nd LAI, under the command of Capt. Martin Wolf. Company B had pushed through the Blue lanes and hooked right while 1/8 was struggling with the two minefields. The company's LAVs destroyed a battery of 122mm guns and a heavy machine-gun position to the west of Ahmed al-Jaber Airfield. It also rounded up 610 prisoners, which it handed over to elements of Lt.Col. Arnold Fields' 3/6. Fields' motorized battalion had been assigned to follow 1/8 through the Green lanes. However, as it became apparent that the Green lanes were clogged, he had taken the part of his battalion that was not already in the lanes, and moved it through nearby Blue 4. The force then relieved Company B, 2nd LAI and continued clearing the area to the north of the Green lanes.

Once north of the second minefield, 1/8 assumed its attack formation, with the 13 remaining M-1A1s of Company B, 4th Tanks in the center, and the battalion's two remaining infantry companies, A and C, on the left and right flanks, respectively. The infantry companies were each reinforced by a CAAT.[*]

When the battalion attempted to expand the breachhead to the north, it ran into stiff opposition. At around four, Iraqis in trenches opened up on the battalion with small arms fire. This was soon followed by mortar fire, which wounded five Marines. Iraqi

---

[*]Before G-Day, Company B, 1/8 had been attached to 2nd Tanks (the division's armored reserve) to provide that battalion with infantry support.

resistance was broken by 45 minutes of punishment from 1/8. The Marines captured or destroyed 15 T-55s, 22 other vehicles, a BM-21 multiple rocket launcher and a ZSU 23-4 self-propelled AA gun. The battalion also took 480 prisoners.

Among the prisoners were two members of the Republican Guard. One of them, a captain, told a Kuwaiti interpreter that the battalion's position was targeted for an artillery strike which would occur in the next 30 minutes. The battalion, with its prisoners in tow, conducted an orderly withdrawal 1¼ miles to the south. Shortly after the battalion had vacated its positions, the artillery strike came in. Regimental headquarters was immediately notified, and the Iraqi guns were located and targeted for counterbattery fire. Within minutes, the artillery stopped.

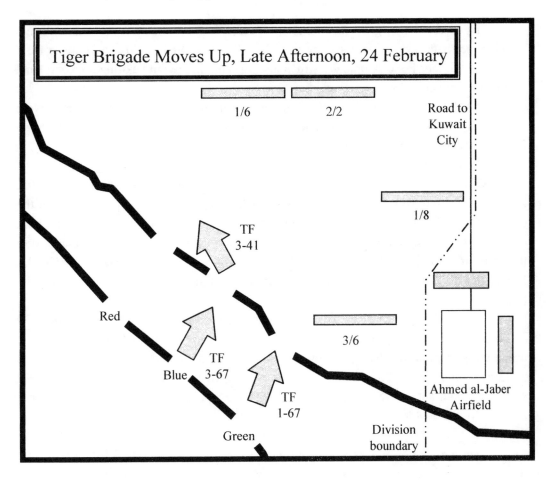

During the afternoon, the division expanded the breachhead and prepared to meet an Iraqi counterattack. The Tiger Brigade was told to move up to the breach area at 1:20. The brigade, under Col. John Sylvester, which was normally stationed in Fort Hood, Texas, had been attached to the 2nd Marine Division for added armored punch. Expecting heavy opposition in the Marine zone of attack, CENTCOM had replaced the brigade's M-1 tanks with the newer and more heavily armored M-1A1 model. Similarly, most of the unit's Bradleys were replaced by the more heavily armored and more survivable M-2A2 model.

The Tiger Brigade began moving through the obstacle belt at 3 p.m. Within 40 minutes, the balanced TF 3-41 had passed through the first obstacle belt.* The brigade's two armor-heavy task forces, 3-67 and 1-67 followed, using the Blue and Green lanes, respectively.

Shortly after the two armor-heavy task forces began moving, one of 3-67's tanks was crippled by a mine, blocking one of the Blue lanes. The tank hit the mine-laden spoil along the length of the lane and detonated one of the mines. Although the armor plate over the track absorbed most of the blast, the explosion did enough damage to the tank's running gear to put it out of action.† The battalion was forced to squeeze through the one remaining lane. By six, the brigade had emerged from the second obstacle belt and headed northward.

By dark, the brigade had taken its place on the division's left flank. While assuming its flank guard positions, the brigade suffered its first fatality. A Humvee from the 502nd Military Police Company struck an anti-tank mine while exiting a breach lane, killing one soldier and wounding another.

As the Tiger Brigade settled into its positions, company-sized patrols were mounted on the brigade's left flank. The patrols, run throughout the night, encountered no hostile Iraqis but netted 25 prisoners.

Meanwhile, 1/6 and 2/2 held their positions in the center. On the right flank, 1/8, after pulling back to avoid the Iraqi artillery strike, was well to the south of 1/6 and 2/2. At 5:30, Col. Livingston had ordered 1/8 to attack to the northeast and pull abreast of the other two battalions. Lt.Col. Gombar explained that his battalion was still consolidating after the recent hasty retreat, but would attack as soon as it was reorganized. Plans were ultimately developed to launch an attack at midnight, but just after eleven that night, Livingston decided to postpone the attack until first light. The battalion set in for the night.

The rest of 8th Marines would not be in position until dawn. Both 2/4 and 3/23 had been forced to halt, in order to allow the Tiger Brigade and units from the division's artillery regiment, 10th Marines, to move through the Green lanes. At about six the next morning, both units would head for the breach lanes. Meanwhile, 3/6 would stay where it was and would act as 1/8's reserve, rather than attempting to find its assigned reserve position (in the center, with 6th Marines) in the dark.

Marine air power was active during the consolidation. At 3:30 in the morning, Iraqi tanks and mortars began firing on 6th Marines. The Marines responded with air strikes. Using thermal sights, observers from 6th Marines spotted for ground attack planes, which destroyed the offending Iraqi units.

On the left flank, a flight of four Marine Cobra attack helicopters destroyed eight Iraqi tanks after tank crews from the Tiger Brigade reported thermal signatures heading

---

*The 3-41st Infantry Battalion had given an infantry company to each of the brigade's armor battalions, and had received an armor company from each in return. This resulted in a task force of two armored and two infantry companies

†The tank would be back in action the next day.

toward them from the north. The Cobras began taking surface-to-air missile fire from a self-propelled launcher. Marine artillery saturated the area, destroying the SAM launchers.

At about 6 a.m., as the men of 1/8 were preparing to mount the attack to the north that had been postponed the night before, Iraqi armor appeared along the horizon. As the tanks got closer, the Marines realized that they were T-72s. This was a surprise. All T-72s were supposed to be in Republican Guard units, none of which were even in Kuwait.

If the Marines were surprised by the T-72s, the T-72s were even more surprised when they stumbled into the Marines. The Iraqi task force was from the 8th Mechanized Brigade of the 3rd Armored Division. It had made its way south, guiding on the paved road running from Kuwait City to Ahmed al-Jaber Airfield, and was attempting to attack the 8th Marines' supply trains when it was spotted and engaged.[*]

Technically, the targets were just outside the division's zone of operations. The division boundary ran just east of the road. Roads are sometimes used as boundary markers, because unlike imaginary grid lines on a map, they can be seen. Unfortunately, for that same reason, roads are also useful for an enemy force which needs an orientation point. If the enemy is driving along a road that is being used as a boundary (or, as in this case, runs near a boundary), he will hit a seam, as he did here, and the defenders will usually find themselves with coordination problems. Fortunately, coordination for such an eventuality had taken place the night before, and 1/8 would be able to engage targets across the boundary. Task Force Shepherd, screening the 1st Marine Division's left flank, would be in communication with 1/8 throughout the engagement.

The Iraqis first became aware of the Marines when their tanks began exploding. The battle was decided in the first two minutes. TOW gunners from 1/8, attached TOW gunners from the Marine Corps Reserve's 24th Marines and Abrams gunners from the attached Company B, 4th Tanks picked off over 20 armored vehicles at long range. The remaining Iraqi armored vehicles attempted to make a run for it, but they did not know where to run to. The Iraqis knew they were being hurt badly, but they could not see the Marines, and had no idea where the TOWs and main gun rounds were coming from. Adding to the Iraqis' woes were several barrages from the artillery units which had moved through the Green lanes during the night and taken up positions behind 1/8. The Iraqi vehicles wandered around 1/8's front like targets at a shooting gallery until they were all destroyed. When the shooting stopped, 30 T-72s, 4 T-55s and 9 BMPs had been destroyed in what would come to be known as the "Reveille Counterattack."

The location of the 2nd Marine Division's breach had come as no surprise to the Iraqi High Command. Neither had the direction of the division's attack. Aware that the loss of al-Jahra, west of Kuwait City, and the critical road junction nearby, would leave most of their units in southern Kuwait cut off, the Iraqis had expected a Coalition thrust toward the town. A counterattack plan had therefore been designed to blunt that thrust.

---

[*]This road was also known as "Highway 71" because of its proximity to the 71 north–south grid line.

The plan was to have been implemented by the 3rd Armored Division, one of the most well-equipped divisions in the Iraqi Army. It was one of two regular divisions with BMPs and the only one with T-72s, though there were only two battalions of them. The T-72s, castoffs from Republican Guard units, were generally in poor mechanical shape. One of its armored brigades, the 12th, was equipped with two battalions of T-62s, a battalion of T-72s, and a battalion of BMPs. The other armored brigade, the 6th, was equipped with three battalions of T-62s and a battalion of BMPs. The mechanized brigade, the 8th, was equipped with one battalion of T-72s and three battalions of BMPs.

The counterattack plan called for the 8th Mechanized Brigade to assume blocking positions and absorb the blow of the Marine attack. Once the Marine advance had been halted, the other two brigades would mount attacks into the Marine flanks, the 12th attacking the western flank, and the 6th attacking the eastern. The plan would never come off.

The infantry divisions on the Saddam Line were overrun on G-Day, along with the 8th Brigade's intended blocking positions. Worse, these units had not informed anyone at 3rd Armored Division that they were being overrun. As a result, the 8th Brigade would have many vehicles destroyed before they could even deploy into combat formation. Iraqi units had developed the habit of moving in relatively tight column formations when they were traveling behind their own lines. Though visibility was a good deal better than it was farther to the east, smoky haze was still a problem for the Iraqis in the west. Moving in column formation minimized the chance of individual vehicles getting lost before they reached the front. It also made the units a smaller target, less likely to be spotted by air than if they were in a more spread out combat posture. This made sense tactically, except that the units involved thought they were well behind their own lines, but were in fact advancing into areas held by the Marines. The situation for the units of the 8th Brigade was made more complicated by the fact that their brigade commander had been well south of his unit on G-Day (possibly doing some personal reconnaissance) and had been captured. This left the brigade, deployed in blocking positions across Highway 71, leaderless. Several units would take the initiative, and would suffer for it. In addition to the Reveille Counterattack, the brigade would sustain heavy losses in attacks in the vicinity of the 1st Marine Division's command post.

The 6th Brigade was not much of a counterattack force by G-Day. It had begun the war with about 100 T-62s. In attacks on the OPs during the ill-fated Khafji offensive, and in fighting with 2nd LAI during its raids before G-Day, the brigade had lost about three dozen tanks. Air strikes had claimed another dozen or so. The roughly 50 remaining tanks waited in positions to the east of Highway 71. Many of these were lost on the 25th when they drove south into Task Force Ripper's positions north of Ahmed al-Jaber Airfield.

The 12th Brigade had not sustained any losses to ground action before G-Day, but had lost about a dozen tanks to air attack. One of its two T-62 battalions was sent to positions north of Ahmed al-Jaber Airfield. The other T-62 battalion and the T-72 battalion were scattered across and above two features south of al-Jahra, known as the "Ice Tray" and the "Ice Cube" because of their appearance on the map. The Ice Tray was a rectangular, hard-surfaced road grid. The Ice Cube was a walled-in area east of the Ice Tray and south of a large complex containing Kuwait's radio and television transmitters.

Any chance of a successful counterattack vanished when the 3rd Armored Division's commander abandoned his unit early on the second day of the ground offensive. This left his remaining two brigade commanders on their own. They followed the lead of their division commander and also headed north. The subordinate units of the now leaderless brigades were left to work things out for themselves. Some companies or platoons resisted and were destroyed. One tank company headed north to al-Jahra. Others abandoned their weapons and headed north on foot. Some smaller units would surrender as soon as the Marines showed up. One battalion would surrender its 22 remaining tanks to the 1st Marine Division's Task Force Grizzly without a fight.

After rounding up and disarming 76 fortunate Iraqi survivors of the Reveille Counterattack, 1/8 headed north. Companies A and C drove toward their assigned positions on 2/2's right flank while Company B, 4th Tanks received a much-needed resupply of fuel and ammunition. Shortly after moving out, the two companies began taking fire from a bunker complex. After a brief but intense firefight, during which the CAAT teams destroyed 3 tanks (a T-62 and two T-55s) with TOW missiles, the Marines overran the position, taking 91 prisoners.

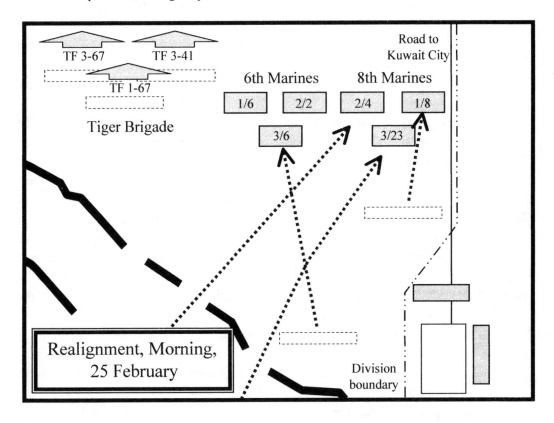

The Tiger Brigade's soldiers had discovered a bunker complex just over a mile north of its positions on the previous night. As daylight broke, TF 3-41 attacked the position. The task force's TOW gunners began methodically eliminating Iraqi bunkers and armored vehicles from long range. Bradleys moved forward and blanketed the position with 25mm fire. Dismounted infantry then cleared the bunkers. When an Iraqi force of four T-55s and 20–30 infantrymen attempted to attack the task force's right flank, it was spotted by a scout section from TF 1-67. The three Bradleys destroyed all four T-55s with TOW missiles and killed or drove off the infantrymen. By noon, it was all over. No Tiger Brigade soldiers were lost during the clearing, and 400 Iraqis from the

7th Infantry Division's 39th Brigade were taken prisoner. TF 3-41 also destroyed four T-55s, ten artillery pieces and several APCs. Meanwhile, on the brigade's left flank, TF 3-67 destroyed seven T-55s.

The division spent much of the morning realigning. After the Reveille Counterattack, 1/8 drove northward to take its position on the division's right flank. At eleven, the battalion was assigned back to the 8th Marines. By then, the regiment's two other battalions had passed through the Green lanes and were headed north. Lt.Col. Kevin Conry's mechanized 2/4 pulled up on 1/8's left flank. The motorized 3/23 was placed in reserve. Meanwhile, 3/6, which had been behind 1/8, moved to the northwest to take up positions as 6th Marines' reserve.

The division then turned to its main objective of the day, dubbed "Division Objective 1." The objective was a rise in the desert, a few miles across and sloping gently downward on all sides. It gave its occupants an excellent view of the surrounding terrain for several miles in every direction. The division needed to take this high ground to ensure that its operations in the area would not be interfered with. On the objective were trenches, bunkers and dug-in tanks. To the east of Objective 1 were the Ice Tray and the Ice Cube. Both areas contained extensive networks of bunkers and dug-in tanks. The three positions were occupied by elements of the Iraqi 3rd Armored, 1st Mechanized, and 7th Infantry divisions.

Originally, both the Ice Cube and the Ice Tray were to be taken by 8th Marines, on the division's right flank. Responsibility for Objective 1 was to be divided more or less equally by the Tiger Brigade and 6th Marines. However, at the last minute, Maj.Gen. Keys decided to shift the 6th Marines' zone of responsibility eastward, in order to give the Tiger Brigade more room to maneuver on the division's left flank. Under the revised plan, 8th Marines would still assault the Ice Cube, but the Ice Tray would be the responsibility of the 6th Marines. Though 6th Marines would still participate in the assault on the objective, the Tiger Brigade would claim the lion's share of Objective 1.

At 1:15, after securing the bunker complex, the Tiger Brigade turned to its part of Objective 1. Two objectives, code-named "Ohio" (to the west) and "Utah" (to the east), were attacked by task forces 3-67 and 3-41, respectively. The two positions were defended by the understrength 116th Brigade of the 7th Infantry Division.

All suspected enemy positions were taken under tank fire from long range. Several enemy tanks were destroyed from just under two miles. By the time the brigade reached the objectives, most Iraqis, including the 116th Brigade's commander, wanted only to surrender. Clearing the two objectives took only 90 minutes. Some 500 Iraqis were captured on Utah and Ohio. For the next two hours, the brigade consolidated and reorganized. There was no major contact for the rest of the day, though patrols along the brigade's left flank would net a few dozen prisoners that night.

As 6th Marines waited to launch its assault, lead units were hit by Iraqi artillery, which was quickly crushed. Throughout the morning, the division came under scattered artillery fire. These Iraqi batteries were quickly dealt with by Marine artillery. After it was picked up on Marine counterbattery radar, an Iraqi artillery battalion was vaporized by 10th Marines. The rounds of four battalions of artillery landed on the Iraqis simultaneously, essentially producing a single earth-shattering explosion.[*]

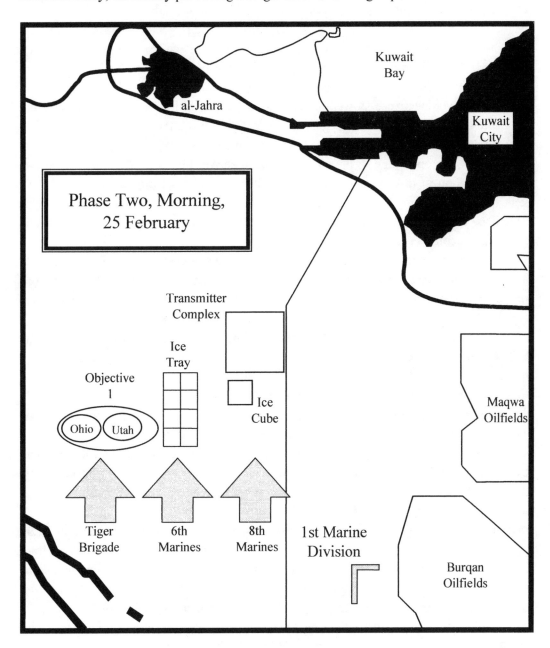

Just before 2 p.m., the assault units reached 6th Marines' share of Objective 1 in bad weather and intense smog from burning oil wells. For most of the afternoon,

---

[*]In a "time on target" (TOT) artillery attack (like this one), all of the guns of a unit are fired so that all of the rounds will land at the same time, maximizing shock value and offering the enemy no warning.

visibility would be less than 100 meters. The Marines advanced through Iraqi artillery fire, periodic tank engagements and small arms fire. However, most Iraqis on the position surrendered with very little prompting, and by nightfall, the eastern portion of Objective 1 was almost completely in Marine hands.

There were numerous aluminum buildings on the Ice Tray, and the position was heavily entrenched. Before the attack, the Ice Tray was the target of several air strikes. As soon as the airspace over the target was clear, a TOT artillery strike from 10th Marines impacted. Still, the Iraqis stood their ground, and the buildings and bunkers had to be cleared individually. It would take until 4:30 the next morning to clear the Ice Tray.

The Marines were slowed mostly by lack of visibility. Not only were Marines unable to use their night vision goggles because of the smoke, they could not even rely on conventional illumination techniques. Illumination rounds, essentially bright flares, are usually timed to open high in the air and descend slowly by parachute. This was not an effective option in this instance, because the heavy blanket of oily smoke would have kept most of the light from reaching the ground. The Marines improvised, fusing the rounds so that they would land on the ground, burning brightly beneath the smoke and acting as beacons.

Concerns about Iraqi infantry anti-tank weapons also slowed pace of the assault. These weapons were not a problem for Tiger Brigade with its M-1A1s. They were also not a problem for 8th Marines. Both of that task force's attached tank companies were equipped with M-1A1s. For the two companies of M-60A1s attached to 6th Marines, they were a serious concern due to a lack of reactive armor. Originally, only one breach had been planned, and that breach was expected to be heavily contested. As a result, most of the Marines' available stocks of the expensive reactive armor had been allotted to the M-60A1s of the 1st Marine Division. The remainder, allotted to 2nd Marine Division, only amounted to enough to cover the most sensitive areas of 6th Marines' attached tanks. This forced 6th Marines' tank company commanders to adjust their tactics.

The tank company commanders would have preferred to deal with the problem by attacking suspected targets from extended range with main gun fire. Unfortunately, due to the heavy smoke, tank commanders could barely see each other. Spotting targets at long range was impossible. The second option was to have tank commanders direct machine-gun fire at general areas where they suspected Iraqis might be hiding, and rely heavily on the infantry accompanying them to spot and deal with any clusters of Iraqi infantry which might pop up elsewhere. Unfortunately, the infantry had fallen behind as several AAVs had thrown tracks because of the choppy terrain. This brought the tank company commanders to their third option, putting their tanks on line and moving the companies slowly forward, with each tank saturating the terrain in front of it with machine-gun bullets. The tactic worked. Numerous Iraqi infantrymen were killed. The rest were terrorized to such an extent that they did not come out of their holes and trenches to surrender until the tanks were well past them.

At three, 8th Marines began pushing north. Resistance on the way to the Ice Cube was light. There were no disruptions, except for several APCs which were destroyed on sight, and a small minefield in 1/8's sector, which was easily breached. Like the Ice Tray, the Ice Cube and the transmitter complex had been hit by several preparatory air strikes, which destroyed five tanks and twelve other vehicles. Resistance in and around the Ice Cube was fairly stiff, with 2/4 and 1/8 destroying small groups of armored vehicles and storming infantry positions for much of the night. Much of the contact occurred along the seam between the two battalions. As the two battalions were members of the same regiment, coordinating assaults on these Iraqi positions was a fairly simple matter.

Dealing with pockets of resistance between the Ice Cube and the Ice Tray proved a bit more complicated. These Iraqis were situated on a boundary between regiments, so the battalions responsible for dealing with them, 2/4 (on 8th Marines' left flank) and 2/2 (on 6th Marines' right flank), were not on the same radio frequency, and were being supported by different artillery units. The complexities were worked through, however, and these Iraqi pockets were overcome with little difficulty.

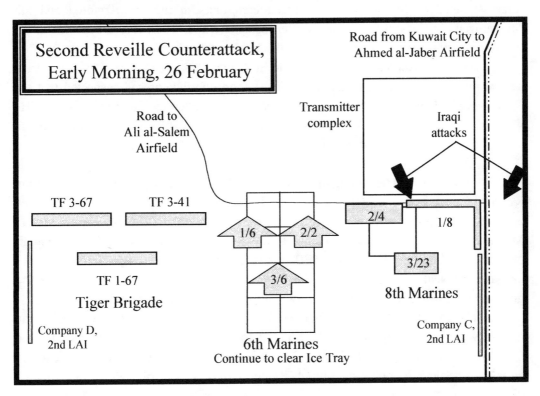

Like the night before, the night of 25–26 February was not quiet. At 2:30 in the morning, 2nd LAI destroyed four tanks. Throughout the night, lead units would monitor the movements of, and occasionally come into contact with, enemy units to the division's front. The most significant contact occurred at a road junction in 1/8's sector, just north of the Ice Cube. At 2:30, the position was hit by a two-pronged attack of dismounted infantry backed by APCs. One came from the northeast and hit the road junction. The other came from the northwest and hit near the boundary between 1/8 and 2/4.

The lineup for these engagements would be the same as it was for the Reveille Counterattack. The battalion position was anchored in the center by Company B, 4th

Tanks, stationed at the intersection itself. Company B was flanked on the right and left by Companies A and C of 1/8. Company A was deployed along Highway 71, facing east. Company C was deployed along the road which ran across the top of the Ice Cube, then hooked north to Ali al-Salem Airfield. Company C's left flank was tied into 2/4. Each flank company still had its attached CAAT teams.

The battle began when Company A was hit by a sudden artillery barrage, causing three casualties. The 10th Marines ensured that there was not a second barrage by locating and destroying the Iraqi guns. Their counterbattery mission complete, the Marine gunners turned their attention to the Iraqi APCs and foot soldiers.

Marine tanks and TOW gunners were already working on the attackers. Unlike the first Reveille Counterattack, which lasted only a few minutes, this attack took an hour and a half to beat off. Some Iraqi armored vehicles even made it to within 75 meters of their objective before being destroyed. The result was the same, however. The attacking force, an amalgam of survivors from shattered units in the 3rd Armored and 5th Mechanized divisions, was driven off after losing 9 T-55s, 14 BMPs, 4 Type 63s and 4 trucks without inflicting any casualties on the Marine defenders.

As quiet returned to the battlefield at 4 a.m., 1/8 called for an artillery strike several miles to its front. The battalion fire support coordinator had suspected that the Iraqis would attempt to regroup before retreating to an alternate defensive position. He was right. The artillery strike caused several secondary explosions. Several shattered survivors were rounded up at first light.

By now, it was becoming obvious that the Iraqis were attempting to escape from Kuwait City while they still had a chance. This meant that if the Marines hurried, they could catch the Iraqis while they were at their most vulnerable. The day before, the 5th Marine Expeditionary Brigade had come ashore just south of the Saudi–Kuwaiti border. Now, to speed the attack, the 5th MEB was directed to move through the breach lanes and take responsibility for protecting the 1st and 2nd Marine divisions' supply routes and guarding their prisoners. This freed the two divisions to press the attack.

The 2nd Division's main objective for the day would be al-Jahra. Through it ran the highway that was the last slender link between the Iraqi forces in Kuwait City and Iraq. On the division's left flank, the Tiger Brigade was assigned Objective 2. It would clear Ali al-Salem Airfield and Mutlah Ridge, a large stretch of high ground running diagonally from the north of al-Jahra to the southwest of Ali al-Salem. It would also cut the highways out of al-Jahra. In the center, 6th Marines would take Objective 3, a series of quarries south of the highways. Meanwhile, 8th Marines would take Objective 4, a wooded area at As Sulaybiyah, north of the transmitter complex, capture the Iraqi barracks there, and protect the division's right flank against a possible Iraqi counterattack from Kuwait City.

At noon, the Tiger Brigade began heading north toward its objective. Up to this point, the brigade's pace had been slowed by concerns for its, and the division's, flank. CENTCOM intelligence had warned the Marines that there was an Iraqi armored division (the 6th) and an independent armored brigade (the 80th) just off the 2nd Marine Division's left flank. From these positions, both units would have been in an ideal position to strike the division in the flank as it advanced northward. For this reason, Lt.Col. Cesare Cardi's Abrams-equipped 2nd Tank Battalion was kept back to guard the division command post and act as an emergency reserve. Also, as long as there was a threat of flank attack, the Tiger Brigade could not be sent deep without exposing its own fuel trains and the left flank of 6th Marines.

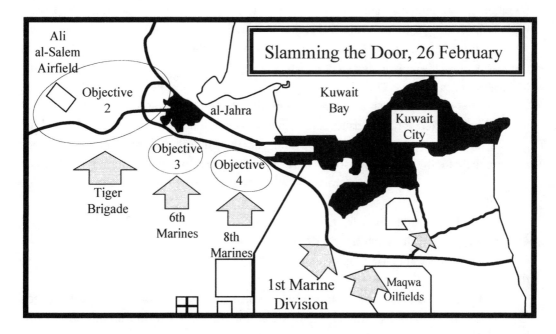

Unknown to CENTCOM, and therefore to the Marines, both Iraqi armored units were no longer on the Marines' flank. The 6th Armored Division had been broken up. About two-thirds of the division had been sent to the northwest and absorbed into the 17th Armored Division. An armored brigade had been sent eastward in battalions and companies to bolster the defenses there. Many of these units had already been destroyed. Those which had not been destroyed were directly in front of the Marines. The 80th Armored Brigade had been gone for over a month. It had been sent westward and combined with two other independent brigades to form the 52nd Armored Division, which would ultimately be overrun by the British 1st Armoured Division.

By late afternoon on the 25th, 2nd Marine Division planners had begun to discount the possibility of an Iraqi attack on the left flank. They had no absolutely reliable intelligence about Iraqi dispositions outside the division's sector, but reasoned that if there had been Iraqi forces intent on launching a counterattack, they would have done so already. They therefore concluded that there probably were no Iraqi forces off the flank, and if there were, they would not be very hostile. Col. Ronald Richard, the division's operations officer, suggested to Maj.Gen Keys that the Tiger Brigade could be sent ahead of the rest of the division safely. In the unlikely event that there was an Iraqi attack, he argued, Marine aircraft and 2nd Tanks, which would remain in reserve, could handle it. Keys agreed, and the Tiger Brigade was ordered to head for its final objectives at top speed.

On the Tiger Brigade's left flank was Lt.Col. Douglas Tystad's TF 3-67. On the right flank was Lt.Col. Michael Johnson's TF 1-67. Stretched across the rear of these two tank-heavy task forces was TF 3-41, under Lt.Col. Walter Wojdakowski. Because the brigade would be traveling well ahead of 6th Marines, there would be an open right flank. Lt.Col. Wojdakowski would minimize the risk of flank attack by posting the M-113-mounted TOW launchers (known as "I[Improved]-Tows") of his anti-tank company on his task force's right flank. From there, they would destroy over 40 Iraqi tanks and a few APCs in 6th Marines' zone. Because TF 3-41 was well ahead of 6th Marines throughout the attack, the TOW launchers could fire across the boundary without fear of hitting Marine vehicles.

TF 3-67 would push through a gap in Mutlah Ridge. The approach to the gap was guarded by a mixed force of armor and infantry. The defenders were entrenched on high ground on the western side of the gap and had the benefit of a thin minefield. Once through the gap, the task force would skirt the eastern edge of Ali al-Salem Airfield, then head eastward to Objective Colorado, a police station and a highway cloverleaf to the north of al-Jahra.

TF 3-41 would drive from its reserve positions, around TF 3-67's left flank. It would hook around the western end of Mutlah Ridge, then sweep Ali al-Salem Airfield. On the right flank, TF 1-67 would seize a highway cloverleaf leading out of al-Jahra to the west.

TF 1-67 was the first of the brigade's task forces to make significant contact. Like TF 3-67, TF 1-67 had traded one of its armor companies for an infantry company. Two of the task force's three remaining tank companies were then given an infantry platoon from this company in return for a tank platoon, and became teams of two tank platoons and one infantry platoon. D Company, 3-41st Infantry, having given up two of its three infantry platoons and gotten two tank platoons in return, also became a tank-heavy team. To avoid confusion between Team D/1-67 and Team D/3-41, the latter had been designated "Team F."

The only battalion commander in the Tiger Brigade with Bradley-mounted scouts, Lt.Col. Johnson used his scout platoon to find and fix enemy armor. The scouts came upon a battalion-sized unit of tanks and APCs on their right flank. The task force's Team A, with Team D behind it, closed quickly, and destroyed two dozen T-55s and a dozen APCs in a 20-minute battle. Meanwhile, Team F had knocked out five T-55s on the task force's left flank. The destruction of the five tanks resulted in the immediate surrender of the entrenched infantry battalion the tanks were supporting.

The task force continued to overrun small, scattered groups of Iraqi armor on the way to its assigned cloverleaf. Most of these vehicles were engaged in the rear as they tried to escape toward al-Jahra. At about 3:30 in the afternoon, the task force arrived at the cloverleaf. At the same time, an Iraqi convoy of six tanks, a dozen APCs, and about 40 trucks was also approaching the cloverleaf. The convoy, raked end to end with tank main gun and heavy machine-gun rounds, was destroyed in a few minutes.

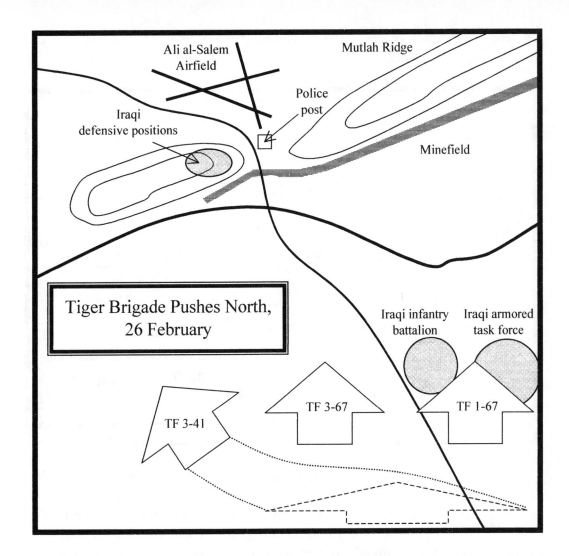

Tiger Brigade Pushes North,
26 February

To the west, following an artillery barrage on the police post on the north side of the gap in the Mutlah Ridge, Capt. Thomas Fluker's D Company, 3-67th Armor destroyed the Iraqi armor defending the approach. Stripped of their armor, the other defenders chose to surrender. As the Iraqis began walking toward the Americans with their hands up or waving white flags, Tystad's tanks and Bradleys headed for the minefield. As they did, and the task force's supply vehicles came within sight of the surrendering Iraqis, some Iraqis ran back to their crew-served weapons and opened fire. Though the uprising complicated prisoner roundup, it was quickly snuffed out with no surrendering Iraqis killed in the crossfire and no Americans killed or wounded.

The minefield had been hastily thrown together and was clearly marked by concertina wire. The mines were sparse and had not been buried. B Company was able to breach the minefield quickly with a mine plow as the rest of the task force provided fire support. Once the breach was forced, the rest of TF 3-67 pushed through. As it emerged from the breach, D Company began taking Iraqi artillery fire, which was being directed by spotters in the airfield's control tower. Two TOW missiles from Team C destroyed the tower, killing the spotters. With the artillery fire at an end, the task force headed for

Objective Colorado. Soonafter, TF 3-41, attacking from west to east, overran a bunker complex, then Ali al-Salem.

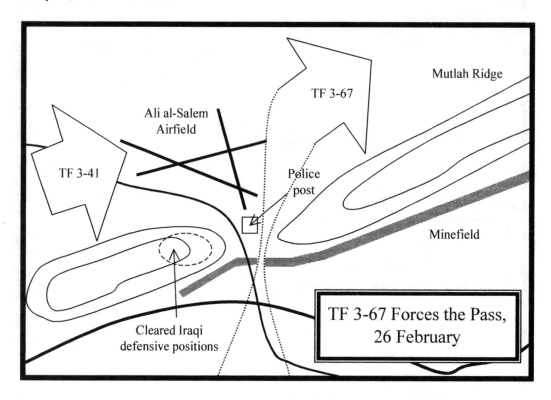

TF 3-67 Forces the Pass, 26 February

By the end of the first day of the ground war, Iraqi soldiers had been desperately trying to get out of Kuwait City in whatever had an engine. Since the retreating columns were full of armed Iraqi soldiers, they were still fair game for Coalition air power. On the night of 25 February, a JSTARS transmitted photographs of an escaping Iraqi column of some 2,000 vehicles to CENTCOM headquarters. Those present realized instantly that this was not a single unit, but virtually the entire Kuwait City garrison. While anxious to engage the fleeing column, Gen. Schwarzkopf instructed the Air Force to wait until the column was clear of the city. He knew that even though the units were a disorganized rabble, if significant numbers of Iraqis were trapped in Kuwait City and forced to fight, civilian casualties and collateral damage might be considerable. There was also some concern that Kuwaiti hostages might be in the column.

As CENTCOM was monitoring the situation, there was a massive explosion in Dhahran. Due to a Patriot software failure, a Scud had made it through without being engaged. On descent, the warhead had fallen from the rocket and hit a warehouse which had been converted into a military barracks. Twenty-seven soldiers died in the blast, twelve of them members of the 14th Reserve Quartermaster Detachment, based in Greensburg, Pennsylvania.

News of the Scud strike spread quickly, and angered Coalition airmen. Once the column was outside Kuwait City, Coalition pilots got an opportunity to exact a measure of vengeance. "Everyone in southern Kuwait knew something big was going down," said one pilot later, "and they didn't want to miss the party." While descriptions of the event tend to portray the air strike as a feeding frenzy resulting in slaughter, it was neither a frenzy nor a slaughter. The Iraqis in the column would benefit from a relatively humane Coalition air attack plan, and from the fact that most of the air-dropped ordnance would miss its targets.

The plan called for A-6E Intruders to drop Gator scatterable mines, creating a hasty minefield across the highway.* This would bar the column's progress, since the lanes of the highway were the only gap in a roughly 25 mile long Iraqi minefield running west to east and ending on the coast. Marine Harriers would be next, dropping cluster bombs at the head and rear of the Iraqi column, knocking out vehicles and effectively trapping any escape for the remaining vehicles. This would be followed by a long pause as Allied pilots waited for the Iraqis to run away from their vehicles and into the desert. CENTCOM was not interested in killing Iraqi foot soldiers, only in destroying their weapons. Once the Iraqis were clear of the highway, bombing and strafing would begin in earnest.

The attack went according to sequence and most Iraqis did abandon their vehicles, but virtually none of the ordnance landed where it was supposed to. The Gator drops landed well off course, and the highway remained unobstructed. Most of the cluster bombs also missed, and the strafing did little damage. When the men of TF 3-67 arrived at the scene, they would find that only about 40 Iraqis had been killed in the air attacks and that traffic was still moving, albeit slowly. They remedied that quickly.

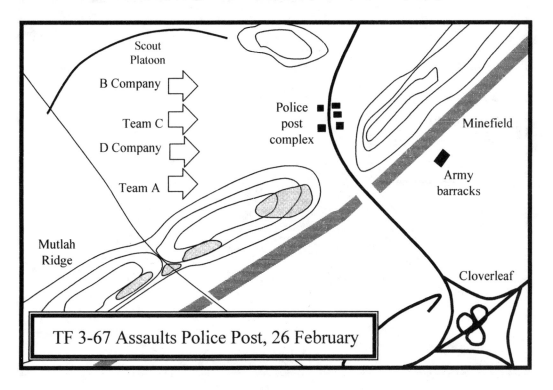

TF 3-67 Assaults Police Post, 26 February

---

*The Gator system works like a cluster bomb. Each Gator unit contains 72 magnetic anti-tank mines and 22 anti-personnel mines.

On reaching Objective Colorado, the tanks of B and D companies opened fire on the police station, a five-building complex straddling the highway. Capt. Mike Kershaw's infantry-heavy Team C, made up of two platoons of infantrymen from his own C Company, 3-41st Infantry and a tank platoon from A Company, 3-67th Armor, then assaulted the complex. Fighting in the complex was room-to-room, and bunker clearing operations became necessary in the hills to the north. The fighting lasted from 4:30 to 8:30, and ended with the death or capture of 40 Iraqis. Some 50 had already been killed by tank fire.

While Team C was closing on its objective, B Company, under Capt. Bart Howard, moved to cut the highway to the north of the police post, destroying three T-55s and a 122mm self-propelled artillery piece. When the artillery piece was hit, it exploded, blowing its shells and powder charges into the air. The ordnance landed on the vehicles around it, two fuel tankers and several cars. This caused secondary explosions and created a barrier of burning vehicles, blocking the highway.

By 6:30, D Company was breaching the minefield between it and the highway cloverleaf, the company's ultimate objective. After driving off an Iraqi probe while in support of Team C, a platoon of engineers was sent southward to assist D Company in the breach. Once through the minefield, D Company seized the cloverleaf, destroying several armored vehicles. By midnight, the cloverleaf was secure.

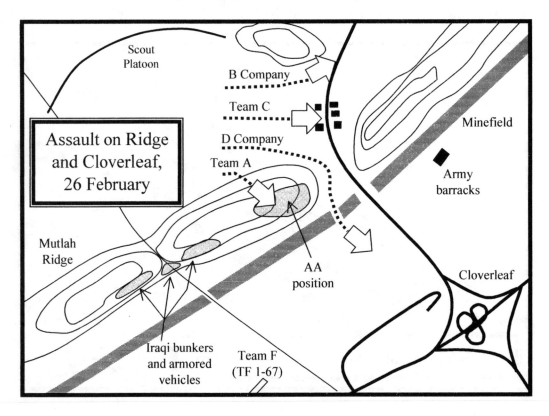

The seizing of the cloverleaf was far more complex than it appeared. To prepare the way for D Company's assault, the armor-heavy Team A, made up of two platoons of tanks from A Company, 3-67th Armor and an infantry platoon from C Company, 3-41st Infantry, had overrun an Iraqi position on the southern side of the ridge line. The position, an anti-aircraft battery supplemented by infantry, was posted on the western side of the gap through which the highway to Basra ran. Since the position covered the southern approach to the gap, its occupants would have been in a position to fire into the rear of D Company when it passed through the gap from the north, or while it was breaching the minefield.

Team A's mission was facilitated by TF 1-67. Because TF 3-67 had needed to breach a minefield and push through a gap in the ridge to get into its final attack axis, it arrived in the vicinity of al-Jahra about an hour after TF 1-67. On arrival, TF 1-67 had posted Capt. Matt Brand's Team F in defensive positions oriented to the northwest. As the tanks arrived in their positions, crewmen spotted bunkers and dug-in armored vehicles along the ridge line. Team F opened fire with main gun and TOW missiles. In short order, eight T-55s and four APCs were burning. The bunkers were then taken under fire, and the heavy machine-gun fire that had been coming from them ended almost immediately.

Also in Team F's field of fire was a gap in the ridge line through which a paved road ran. The road led directly into Team A's zone, and might have facilitated an Iraqi attack into Team A's rear as it cleared its objective. Team F suppressed the Iraqis in the gap by destroying everything it could spot with long range main gun fire. With the pass suppressed and its eastern approaches under Team F's guns, Team A could attack the AA position without worrying about its rear.

In the fighting on Objective Colorado, TF 3-67 suffered one fatality. As the command group stopped in positions west of the police post, it came under heavy machine-gun fire from a nearby junkyard. The fire lasted only a matter of minutes, but the first burst had hit the battalion's Master Gunner, SFC Harold Witzke.[*] One of the bullets severed an artery, and though medics arrived immediately and began life-saving measures, Witzke was beyond help.

While the Tiger Brigade was fighting its way toward Objective 2, 6th Marines began clearing Iraqi units out of a series of quarries and dumps south of al-Jahra, encountering little resistance. So many Iraqis were giving up that they had to be herded through the lead battalions, 1/6 and 2/2, and rounded up by 3/6. Most of the tanks in this sector had been destroyed earlier by the I-Tows of TF 3-41, but occasionally, the lead units ran across dug-in tanks and self-propelled artillery pieces. These were quickly destroyed either by direct fire or by helicopter gunships, a section of which was assigned to each of the lead battalions. By evening the fight was over, and the regiment's attached Kuwaiti liaison officers had made contact with the Kuwaiti resistance and were making arrangements for the final capture of al-Jahra itself. The Marines decided that since the resistance knew the town better than they did, it was better suited to clearing the final pockets of Iraqis. The resistance then took the town.

---

[*]The Master Gunner is the NCO on the battalion staff responsible for unit tank gunnery training.

On the division's right flank, 8th Marines had a shorter distance to travel than 6th Marines, but its zone was more heavily fortified. On 8th Marines' left flank, after overrunning a company-sized infantry position, 2/4 reached its assigned objective, a large agricultural area surrounded by a high cinderblock wall and honeycombed with bunkers and fighting positions. After several air and artillery strikes, Lt.Col. Conry's Battalion conducted a mechanized assault into the area, with infantry dismounting to begin the arduous process of building and bunker clearing. About a dozen armored vehicles on the position were destroyed or captured fairly quickly. However, the complex was so thick with bunkers that it would take the Marines two days to fully clear it.

On the regiment's right flank, after destroying nine tanks along the way, 1/8 found an agricultural area of its own. Near the battalion's objective, two hills which overlooked the road out of Kuwait City, was an Iraqi stronghold in an area which would become known as "The Dairy Farm." Preceded by a thorough artillery pounding of the position, Lt.Col. Gombar's battalion overran the Dairy Farm. By 6:00 that evening, 1/8 had seized the two hills and set up anti-tank ambushes along the road. The clearing of the captured areas in detail was postponed until morning.

After Objective Colorado was cleared, TF 3-67 settled into defensive positions for the night. Just before nightfall, D Company reported that there appeared to be Iraqi soldiers in a nearby mosque. The mosque was part of a hostel the Kuwaiti government maintained for pilgrims on their way to Mecca. Because it was a religious site, Capt. Fluker was told that if he received fire from the mosque, he could fire back. Otherwise, he was to take no action, other than to put a platoon in place to keep an eye on the mosque until morning, when it could be checked out. The night passed without incident, and in the morning, a small contingent of D Company soldiers made their way carefully across the mosque's parking lot. A Gator strike had landed off-line and left the parking lot strewn with anti-tank and anti-personnel mines. In the mosque they found Iraqi doctors were treating wounded Iraqi soldiers and Kuwaiti civilians. Battalion medics were immediately sent with medical supplies, to assist the Iraqi doctors.

TF 1-67 was also set in defensive positions. During the night, there were several instances of Iraqis attempting to infiltrate the task force's positions. These attempts invariably ended in the death or capture of the would-be infiltrators. At 10 p.m., scouts reported a column of headlights approaching the task force. The scouts attempted to halt the column, a convoy of seven civilian vehicles, but the vehicles sped past the checkpoint and into the middle of the task force's perimeter. Maj. Roy Bierwirth, the task force's operations officer, ordered Team D to stop the convoy with a warning burst of machine-gun fire, and if that did not work, with main gun fire. A burst of coaxial machine-gun fire in front of the lead vehicle brought the convoy to an abrupt halt. The occupants of the vehicles, a group of reporters from the BBC, CNN and the major U.S. networks, looked to their front and saw an Abrams with its main gun pointed at them. The reporters had been attempting to slip into Kuwait City. They would spend the night under guard in the task force's supply trains.

At first light on the 28th, in 8th Marines' sector, 3/23 and a tank platoon from Company C, 4th Tanks swept the Dairy Farm, broadcasting recorded encouragement to surrender over loudspeakers as infantrymen cleared the bunkers. Vehicles were blown up in place by combat engineers. One of the demolitions caused a massive secondary explosion in an Iraqi tank that killed one Marine tank crewman and wounded another. At the northern end of the complex, the Marines were greeted with sniper and RPG fire. In return, the Marines shot up an Iraqi ammunition truck and killed several Iraqi soldiers.

This was the last engagement of the 2nd Marine Division's war. Between the pre-ground war patrolling operations and the ground war itself, the division (including the Tiger Brigade) had destroyed or captured some 325 Iraqi tanks and 170 APCs.

Daylight gave soldiers and Marines a chance to inspect the logjam of Iraqi vehicles on the Basra highway. In the column was every conceivable type of stolen civilian vehicle, from school buses to police cars. Of the roughly 1,900 vehicles on the highway and the nearby coastal road, fewer than 50 were armored vehicles. There were several dead Iraqi soldiers scattered on the highway, prompting many American soldiers to feel a sense of pity. That sense lasted until they examined the vehicles. Virtually all of them were stuffed with loot. "These people were unbelievable," said one astonished soldier. "They were literally running for their lives, but they stopped to loot." "This was an army that came to Kuwait for one reason, to loot and pillage," said a disgusted Marine Brig.Gen. Paul Van Riper. Perhaps Iraqi avarice had been a good thing. CENTCOM had feared that thousands of hostages would be taken, to be used as human shields against Coalition air attack. Apparently, the Iraqis had decided that hostages would have taken space in vehicles that could better be used to carry loot.

The afternoon of the 28th saw a noteworthy humanitarian mission in TF 3-67's sector. An Iraqi soldier had tripped an Iraqi mine and was lying inside a minefield, badly wounded. Maj. Robert Williams, 3-67th Armor's executive officer, volunteered to retrieve the Iraqi. Williams donned an extra Kevlar vest and made his way into the minefield, only to find that the Iraqi had landed with his foot under another trip wire. After nudging the Iraqi's foot from under the wire, Williams carried him out of the minefield. For this act, Williams received the Soldiers' Medal.[*]

The Marines had probably caused more concern among Iraqi soldiers than any other unit in the Gulf War. Iraqi soldiers referred to Marines as "Angels of Death" and believed that they would kill every Iraqi they found. Many Iraqis had actually been told that in order to join the Marine Corps, one had to kill a close family member as a condition of enlistment. While the Iraqis found these wild stories to be untrue, they also found that their fear of Marines had been justified. The Marines had easily brushed aside every Iraqi unit which offered resistance. The two Marine divisions and the Tiger Brigade destroyed six Iraqi divisions and three armored brigades, killed over 1,500 Iraqi soldiers

---

[*]Had the incident occurred a few hours earlier, Williams probably would have received a Silver Star. However, because the cease-fire was in effect at the time, it was technically an act of heroism in peacetime.

and captured over 20,000. The Marines would leave Kuwait almost immediately, and this would make a systematic count of destroyed or captured armored vehicles impossible. However, detailed study of all Marine actions, to include Khafji, the pre-ground war raids and the ground offensive, established an estimate of about 610 tanks and 485 APCs destroyed in combat or captured and later destroyed.

The overall commander of the Marine Expeditionary Force, Lt.Gen. Walter Boomer, a Vietnam veteran with two Silver Stars for gallantry in action, had shown great confidence in his men and had seen it justified. Some planners had believed that Marine casualties could run in the thousands, but the two divisions sustained losses of 5 killed and 48 wounded. "We expected it to be hard," said one Marine. "[But] on a combat scale of 1 to 10 it was a 1."

Part VI

The Arab Solution

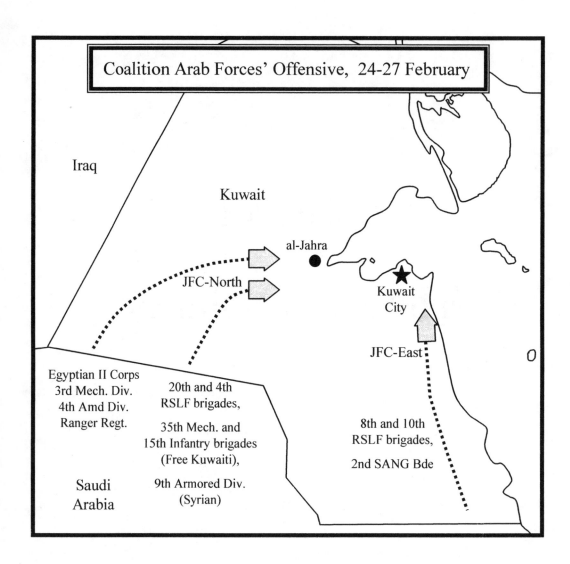

Coalition Arab Forces' Offensive, 24-27 February

Iraq

Kuwait

al-Jahra

JFC-North

Kuwait
City

JFC-East

Egyptian II Corps
3rd Mech. Div.
4th Amd Div.
Ranger Regt.

20th and 4th
RSLF brigades,

35th Mech. and
15th Infantry brigades
(Free Kuwaiti),

9th Armored Div.
(Syrian)

8th and 10th
RSLF brigades,

2nd SANG Bde

Saudi
Arabia

13

Coalition Arab Forces

The Arab forces of the Coalition, under the command of Lt.Gen. Prince Khaled bin Sultan, were divided into two separate commands. Joint Forces Command East (JFC-E), commanded by Saudi Maj.Gen. Sultan 'Adi al-Mutairi, would head directly up the coast for Kuwait City. The much larger Joint Forces Command North (JFC-N) was commanded by another Saudi officer, Maj.Gen. Sulaiman al-Wuhayyib. JFC-N's two-pronged assault would begin in western Kuwait, then sweep toward the coast in a wide arc.

Lt.Gen. Khaled was extremely concerned about Iraqi landmines in JFC-E's sector. The Coalition did not have enough mine clearing equipment to fully equip all of its breaching units. The Egyptians in JFC-N, operating in a sector where mines were expected to be especially heavy, had been given eight American mine rakes and sixteen MiCLiCs, but the rest of Joint Forces Command had to fend for itself. Though the Saudis were able to buy some old but fairly effective equipment from Turkey and Egypt, much of their mine clearing would have to be done by hand.

JFC-E was mostly Saudi, made up of the 8th and 10th Mechanized brigades of the RSLF and the 2nd SANG Brigade with contingents from Oman, Qatar and the United Arab Emirates. The task force began its assault into Kuwait at 4 a.m. on 24 February, with combat engineers from the 2nd SANG Brigade breaching the border berm. The SANG engineers were then joined by RSLF engineers in cutting six lanes through the mine belt. Mine clearing operations were aided immeasurably by the fact that the Iraqis had not buried the mines. In short order, three Saudi heavy trucks were full of disarmed mines and the task force was on its way.

The Saudis moved swiftly through the first line of defenses. The positions on the border had been abandoned. AVLBs (Armored Vehicle Launched Bridges) stood ready to bridge anti-tank ditches. The AVLB is a modified M-60 that extends a 60 foot folding bridge from it. However, none of the trenches were wide enough to stop Allied tanks or APCs, only Iraqi vehicles. In addition, the absence of Iraqi artillery on the breaching forces allowed the Saudis to bring in unarmored bulldozers to fill the ditches.

No defended bunker complexes were encountered, and JFC-E pushed up the coast, slowly rolling over abandoned defenses as it went. The Saudis did not see an Iraqi soldier until they were 13 miles into Kuwait. The way north was littered with scores of abandoned T-55 tanks and fighting positions.

The Saudis' main problem was the thoroughness with which the Iraqis had destroyed the six-lane coastal highway. The three northbound lanes were completely destroyed. The three southbound lanes were cut by ditches at roughly 100 meter intervals over the first three kilometers the Saudis advanced. Over the next seven kilometers, cuts were made halfway across the three lanes, again at 100 meter intervals. Farther north, there were bomb and shell craters in the highway, and wrecked Iraqi vehicles to be pushed aside. These difficulties notwithstanding, Saudi engineers were able to open two lanes (one for northbound traffic, one for southbound) by nightfall.

Occasionally, scattered artillery fire brought the Saudi column to a halt. In these instances, Green Beret sniper teams moved to the head of the column and dealt with Iraqi forward artillery spotters. With their forward observers eliminated, Iraqi artillery stopped firing, and the column could move again.

When the Saudis finally caught up with Iraqi units, their soldiers surrendered in droves. Movement up the coast slowed to a crawl south of Kuwait City as roads became choked by hordes of Iraqi prisoners. Movement then stopped altogether as night fell. The Arab contingents had limited night vision equipment, so except for a very few instances during the war, they did not fight at night. Among Coalition formations only British and U.S. Army units, which had state-of-the-art night vision equipment, were able to conduct extensive night operations.

The 4th Armored and 20th Mechanized brigades of the RSLF formed the spearhead of the eastern prong of the Joint Forces Command-North offensive. Because information about Iraqi defenses in this area was sketchy, Saudi units began patrolling into Kuwait four days before G-Day, as the Marines had done in their sector. Accompanied by tanks and U.S. Army Special Forces advisors, Saudi engineers located the beginning of the Iraqi minefield about eight miles inside Kuwait. Working through an Iraqi artillery barrage, an engineer platoon managed to clear and mark a 30 meter wide by 150 meter deep lane through the minefield. The engineers also brought back a videotape of the area. On the following day, another team cleared another path, bringing back 600 mines. The lack of Iraqi opposition to the Saudi patrols caused Lt.Gen. Khaled to suspect that the coming assault might be a good deal easier than he had anticipated.

Although the division's combat engineers contributed to the mine clearing effort on 23–24 February, the Syrian 9th Armored Division was destined to play a supporting role in the JFC-N offensive. Once the line was breached, it would follow behind the rest of the task force, providing artillery support and acting as a reserve. Coalition planners had decided not to use the Syrians in heavy combat for two main reasons. Since the Syrians were using T-62 tanks, which the Iraqi Army also used, friendly fire was a concern. The T-62 was also obsolete.

Following the Saudis on the right wing would be two Free Kuwaiti brigades. The Free Kuwaiti Army consisted of more than five brigades. Ironically, it was almost twice as large in exile as it had been in its homeland. The majority of the soldiers in the Free Kuwaiti Army were civilian refugees who had volunteered for duty after the fall of Kuwait. These volunteers were long on eagerness, but short on training and experience. It fell upon the Green Berets of the 5th Special Forces Group to mold the Kuwaitis into an effective fighting force. Each 12-man Special Forces team undertook the training of a brigade of soldiers. Their success was limited. Only the 15th Infantry and 35th Mechanized brigades were ready by G-Day.

Although much of the Kuwaiti Army's equipment had been lost in the Iraqi invasion, a good deal of it had been replaced. Many of the tanks that had been lost were replaced with Yugoslav-built M-84s. M-84 tanks are basically T-72s, upgraded with laser rangefinders and ballistic computers. Here was another irony. Not only did the Coalition have the best equipment on the battlefield, it also had the best Soviet-style equipment on the battlefield.

An hour after clearing the barrier, the Saudis and Kuwaitis were ordered to halt. This was a cause of tremendous frustration for the men of the 35th Mechanized Brigade, under Col. Salam al-Masoud. The brigade had distinguished itself during the Iraqi invasion of Kuwait in fighting near al-Jahra, when it had stood its ground until impending encirclement by Iraqi armor forced what was left of it to withdraw southward into Saudi Arabia. Now, six months later, the brigade was on its way home, and its soldiers were getting impatient. However, Saudi commanders had no choice but to suspend the assault. The Egyptian attack on their left had to overcome a formidable set of obstacles. Until the Egyptians broke through, any further advance by the Saudis would have exposed their flank.

An Egyptian armored corps made up the left wing of the JFC-N assault. Egypt provided the Coalition with the nearly 34,000 men of the II Egyptian Corps. The corps consisted of one mechanized division, one armored division and a Ranger regiment. The Egyptian government, like the other Coalition Arab governments, felt it would be inappropriate for its soldiers to attack positions within Iraq, so II Corps was tasked to drive into western Kuwait.

The corps' commander, Maj.Gen. Salah Halabi, would be fighting in his fifth war. In 1962, as a junior officer, he had fought in Yemen. He had fought the Israelis in the Six Day War (1967), in the War of Attrition along the Suez Canal (1970) and in the Yom Kippur War (1973). Most of the corps' senior officers had missed the war in Yemen, but had seen action in the wars against Israel.

Like the United States Army, the Egyptian Army had undergone a metamorphosis. The Egyptian Army has always been the strongest Arab army in the Middle East, but its reputation had taken a severe beating as a result of its collapse during the Six Day War against Israel in 1967.

In the war's aftermath, the Egyptian Army, which had been very similar to the modern Iraqi Army in structure, undertook radical reforms. Before the 1967 war, officers had been selected based almost solely on political reliability. After the debacle, ability became the primary consideration. In addition, more attention was paid to both officer and troop training. The reforms paid dividends in the 1973 war with Israel. Although Israel eventually prevailed, Egyptian units fought well, inflicted heavy casualties and came close to winning the war. Egyptian units were resolute and the officer corps performed well. In the final analysis, Israel's victory stemmed more from its superior Western equipment, tactics and training than any failure of Egyptian military character.

When Egypt made peace with Israel, her relations with the United States improved dramatically, and Egypt began receiving shipments of American weaponry to replace her inferior Soviet equipment. As the Abrams replaced the M-60A3 in the U.S. Army's tank inventory, many of the M-60A3s went to Egypt. The same was true of the

M-113 APC, which was then being replaced by the Bradley Fighting Vehicle. The Egyptians added extra armor to the M-113s, which almost doubled their protection.*

Training and tactics also improved. Infantry and armor officer training courses in the United States now included visiting Egyptian officers. "Bright Star" joint exercises involving Egyptians and U.S. Rapid Deployment Force units were held in the Egyptian desert. By the time of the Gulf War, CENTCOM had every reason to be confident about the quality of the Egyptian contingent.

Handling liaison between the Egyptians and the Americans was Maj. Bernard Dunn. Dunn, an infantry officer, had been a member of the forward (stationed in Germany) brigade of the 1st Infantry Division. Before being assigned to the brigade, he had served on the VII Corps staff. Lt.Gen. Franks, remembering that Dunn spoke Arabic and had a secondary specialty as a Middle East Foreign Area Officer, sent him to work with the Egyptians.

The first thing that struck Dunn about the Egyptians was how little the Iraqi Army seemed to concern them. Back at King Khalid Military City, news of Scud launches had sent CENTCOM officers running to don their chemical-protective gear and make their way to shelters. At the Egyptian headquarters, Scud launch reports would not cause officers to leave their sleeping bags. The Egyptians, having used Scuds themselves, knew what they could and could not do. They also had a keen sense of what the Iraqis would or would not do.

One of Dunn's first tasks was the coordination of the boundary between the Egyptians and VII Corps. Since the Egyptians and the 1st Cavalry Division would be coming together in the vicinity of the Wadi al-Batin, the VII Corps' staff was worried that the Iraqis might attack southward, through the Wadi, and penetrate a seam between the Egyptians and the Americans. This concern was heightened by frequent JSTARS reports of massive Iraqi movements north of the border.

The Egyptians were not worried. On II Corps' left flank was a small contingent of Egyptian Rangers at a border post. The Rangers were dug-in, and equipped with assault rifles, RPG-7s and mortars. This tiny force could not have withstood a major Iraqi assault, but since Maj.Gen. Salah's staff was certain that there would be no such assault, it felt that the Rangers would be enough.†

VII Corps' staff was not as comfortable, and wanted heavy units in the area, just in case an Iraqi attack did develop. Dunn helped produce a workable arrangement. There was an asphalt road that had been built on a hard-packed berm. The road ran from al-Ru'Qua, a small village near the point where the Saudi, Iraqi and Kuwaiti borders come together, to Hafir al-Batin, a town some 50 miles to the southwest. The 1st Cavalry Division would post a brigade in defensive positions several kilometers deep on the western side of the road. On the eastern side of the road, the Egyptians would bolster their screening forces slightly, and run mounted patrols in the area.

One thing the Egyptians were concerned about was their lack of information about the Iraqi positions in Kuwait that they would be attacking on G-Day. Dunn was able to secure several truckloads of maps, onto which Third Army had depicted front line Iraqi positions based on high altitude photographs.

---

*The Saudis also used the M-113. Their M-113s did not have the extra armor, but they were still far safer than what their adversaries were riding in.

†The staff was right. The movements north of the border were later found to be herds of sheep.

Happy as they were to have the maps, the Egyptians wanted more detailed information about their attack zone. To help provide this information, Lt.Gen. Franks ordered the British 1st Armoured Division to send an artillery reconnaissance unit equipped with a 1960s vintage drone. The drone, launched from the back of a truck, worked by flying a pre-set course, then dropping a film canister as it returned. The film would then be developed in a van and analyzed.

Unfortunately, when Dunn and the Egyptians got the photographs from the van, they found that they were extensively scratched from sand in the equipment. The drone had also been slightly mis-programmed, so it had missed part of its intended coverage area. Still, the photos provided some useful information, but the Egyptians needed better. They wanted an American Remotely Piloted Vehicle to overfly the Iraqi positions.

Dunn arranged for VII Corps to launch a Pioneer RPV from a small airfield in VII Corps sector on 22 February, two days before G-Day. This time, the flight track was perfect, and the RPV produced a videotape of the Iraqi front line positions for Dunn to take back to Maj.Gen. Salah.

The videotape was revealing. It showed the layout of the trenches, and that they were extremely shallow. Perhaps the trenches had not been properly dug. Perhaps they had, but had not been maintained, and had filled up with sand. Either way, the state of the trenches provided powerful evidence that the units manning them lacked discipline.

Maj.Gen. Salah knew a good deal about the makeup of the obstacle belt, thanks to the activities of Egyptian Rangers. Rangers had provided vital information about the nature of the Iraqi defenses. The Egyptians already knew that the company-sized strongpoints running along the southern edge of the Iraqi defenses were surrounded by minefields. The crucial question was whether or not there were minefields running between the strongpoints. Probes by the Rangers three days before G-Day proved that there were. Rangers were able to capture a few Iraqi engineers engaged in routine maintenance on the minefields. The engineers provided information about the layout not only of the minefields running between the strongpoints, but the two main minefields as well. The knowledge that there would be three minefields to breach instead of two allowed combat engineers to adjust their tactics. They would station mine clearing equipment forward from the outset of their assault, rather than bringing it forward as assault units approached the main minefields.

The Rangers then filtered through the southern minefield to gather intelligence about the fire trenches. Again, they were able to capture an Iraqi engineer doing routine maintenance on the system. The Iraqi provided the Egyptians with details about the layout of the fire trenches. Each trench was about 1,000 meters long, made up of ten 100 meter sections. Three barrels of thickened fuel had been placed in each section. The sections had then been filled with oil. The barrels of thickened fuel (also known as *phougas*) would be exploded electrically, to start the crude oil burning. The barrels would be set off by wires running back to the main Iraqi trenches. The entire fuel distribution system was underground. From a central valve in a bunker, a network of pipes ran to another set of pipes, which ran behind each of the trenches. From these pipes, underground fill tubes would bring more fuel to the trenches.

The Egyptian Army was the only Coalition army that had first hand experience with fire obstacles. Before the 1973 Yom Kippur War, Israel had built a series of bunkers along the Suez Canal. Underground oil storage tanks were built beneath the bunkers. Pipes leading from the tanks to points below the water line were designed to spray the canal with oil if the Egyptians tried to land. The oil could then be ignited from inside the bunkers, creating a wall of fire between the Egyptians and the shore. For good measure, the Israeli Army ran a well-publicized test on the system to intimidate the Egyptians. The Egyptians responded by sending commandos across the canal to sabotage the pipes shortly before the main attack went in. When the Egyptian Army crossed the canal on 6 October 1973, the Israeli system failed.*

As the commander of the first Egyptian assault company across the Suez Canal in 1973, Maj.Gen. Salah had been a beneficiary of those sabotage operations, so he knew the value of good commando work. He would use his Rangers in a similar way. Armed with detailed knowledge of how the Iraqi fire trenches worked, the Rangers sabotaged them the night before G-Day. They created what would be an almost four mile wide fire-free zone by cutting the wires to the phougas barrels over that stretch of the system.

As dawn broke on 24 February, the Egyptian corps was set in its attack positions, waiting to launch its assault at dawn of the 25th. Just before 10 a.m. on the 24th, Maj. Dunn was monitoring his radio at the Egyptian command post when he heard Lt.Gen. Franks ask each of his division commanders whether or not they could have their units ready to attack at three that afternoon instead of at dawn on the 25th. The Marine and XVIII Corps attacks were going so well that VII Corps' attack was being moved forward by about fourteen hours. It occurred to Dunn that if VII Corps' attack was being moved up, the Egyptians would soon be receiving similar orders. Dunn immediately informed Maj.Gen. Salah, who began making arrangements to push his attack forward.

These preparations were well under way when JCF-N's commander, Maj.Gen. Sulaiman, arrived by helicopter at 1 p.m. to meet with Salah. As Sulaiman flew back to his headquarters, Salah told his staff that permission to launch the main Egyptian assault immediately had been denied, and ordered them to prepare plans for a two-battalion raid. After the war, many would portray Egyptian activity on G-Day as an attack that bogged down. Description of this activity as a raid was taken by many to be a post hoc rationalization of an attack that failed. However, several American officers were present when the raid was planned and ordered. Salah told his assembled staff that the raid would have three purposes.

First, it would force Iraqi artillerymen to show themselves. Most Iraqi batteries in the Egyptian sector had not been located before G-Day. The RPV flights had provided vital information about Iraqi front line positions, but there had not been time to run flights over the Iraqi rear, where the artillery was.

Second, it would force the Iraqis to light their fire trenches. Following the Gulf War, the U.S. Air Force would claim to have neutralized most of the fire trenches by destroying the feeding apparatus with pinpoint strikes, then touching the fire trenches off with napalm strikes. In fact, Air Force claims to the contrary, there was no effective way to attack the feeding apparatus by air. As to the filled trenches themselves, none were set off by napalm strikes. In every instance where a fire trench was set off prematurely during the Gulf War, it was set off by ground action.

Third, there was Iraqi armor to the north of the main defense line. A raid would force the tanks to react in some way. Then, at least Salah would know the location and strength of Iraqi armored forces to his north.

At exactly 3 p.m., Egyptian artillery commenced a 20-minute preparatory barrage. Though much of the Egyptian Army's armor consisted of American models,

---

*Some pipes were dummies. Others were already clogged with sand.

most of its artillery was of Soviet design. While there were a few American self-propelled 155mm pieces at corps-level, towed 122mm guns made up the bulk of Egypt's artillery. Though light, 122mm guns can maintain a high rate of fire if their crews are well-trained and there is no serious counterbattery threat.

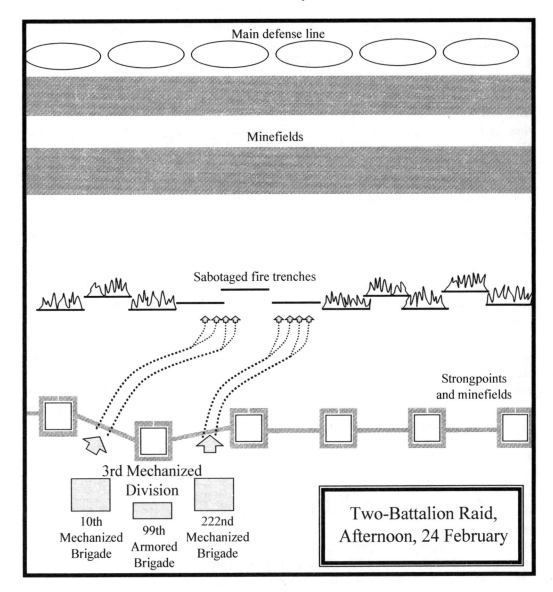

BM-21 multiple rocket launchers were also used in this bombardment. Katyushas are not particularly accurate, but since they could fire forty 122mm rockets within a few seconds and could saturate a relatively large area quickly, they were a useful terror weapon against the Iraqis. The Egyptians suffered one casualty during the barrage. An Egyptian artilleryman was wounded by shrapnel when a rocket went out of control, headed back toward the battery that fired it, and exploded.

As soon as the barrage ended, Maj.Gen. Yahed Alwan's 3rd Mechanized Division moved forward. Two armored battalions from the division's 99th Armored Brigade drove through gaps cut in the berm by engineers on the previous day. The four lead tanks in each battalion were equipped with mine rakes and MiCLiCs. Each of the breaches of the first minefield was made between Iraqi strongpoints, far enough from each so that they could not bring effective fire on the breach force.

Virtually the moment the two battalions breached the first minefield, the Iraqis lit the fire trenches. This worked to the Egyptians' advantage. The Iraqis' view of the western breaching force was obstructed by a wall of flames. Had the Egyptians attempted to breach directly to the south of the sabotaged fire trenches, both Egyptian units would have been under observed Iraqi artillery fire from the time they left their staging areas.

There would be no Iraqi counterbattery fire during the two days of the Egyptian breaching operation, but Iraqi artillery was still a problem. As this sector had not been a priority target during the air war, few guns had been destroyed by air. Most Iraqi guns in this area had also survived the preparatory barrage, and shelled Egyptian engineers as they picked their way through the minefields. Here, the Egyptians were victims of Coalition success. In an attempt to make the Iraqis think that this was part of a massive assault on the Saddam Line, U.S. Army signalmen filled the air with fake radio traffic as the Egyptians moved toward the Iraqi defenses. The Iraqis believed the ruse, and brought some 200 guns to bear on the Egyptian breaching effort.

Egyptian gunners were able to destroy Iraqi batteries throughout the day, but there was no question of wiping most of the Iraqi artillery complement away with one savage barrage as had been done in some other sectors. While CENTCOM had loaned the Egyptians Q-36 and Q-37 artillery-spotting radars, there were so many Iraqi guns that it took most of the day to locate a significant number of them, even with the benefit of radar. In addition, the Egyptians had not been given MLRS launchers, so it took a significant artillery effort to destroy each battery once it was located.

Fortunately, most Iraqi artillery fire was not guided by spotters. Most Iraqi gunners contented themselves with firing on pre-registered targets. In the instances where artillery was guided by spotters, shells landed in front of the Egyptians then behind them, as Iraqi gunners attempted to find their range. Then, just as Iraqi gunners reloaded for the payoff, they and their guns were destroyed by Egyptian counterbattery fire. The Egyptians were also fortunate in that several Iraqi batteries were abandoned. After A-10s had destroyed individual guns with Maverick missiles in the days before G-Day, the crews of the remaining guns had gathered their belongings and headed for Iraq.

Shortly after the breach was established, the 10th and 222nd Mechanized brigades joined the breaching battalions north of the first minefield. Maj.Gen. Salah had intended to send the two brigades through the first minefield on the next day. However, the lack of strong Iraqi resistance to the raid indicated to Salah that he could probably get the entire 3rd Mechanized Division through the breaches established by the two assault battalions then and there instead of waiting until the following morning.

As soon as both mechanized brigades were north of the strongpoint line, the Egyptians began to run into problems. By the time the two brigades passed through the minefield, night had fallen. Now, they had to make their way to the spot where the fire trenches had been sabotaged, and had to do so in the dark. The brigades became intermingled on the way, and had to halt for several hours while the situation was sorted out. Until it was sorted out, there was no room north of the minefield for the 99th Armored Brigade's remaining two battalions.

By dawn on the 25th, the 10th and 222nd brigades were almost untangled. However, the two kilometer space between the strongpoint line and the fire trenches was still congested. The two brigades offered Iraqi artillerymen an excellent target, especially since the fire trenches had burned themselves out, and Iraqi observers all along the main defense line had an unobstructed view of the Egyptians. The six to eight foot deep trenches had burned until the oil that filled them had burned away. The piping system that would have kept oil flowing into the trenches had not been hooked up properly by the Iraqis. Fortunately, though the two brigades received extensive artillery fire, the Iraqis could not concentrate their fire on these units.

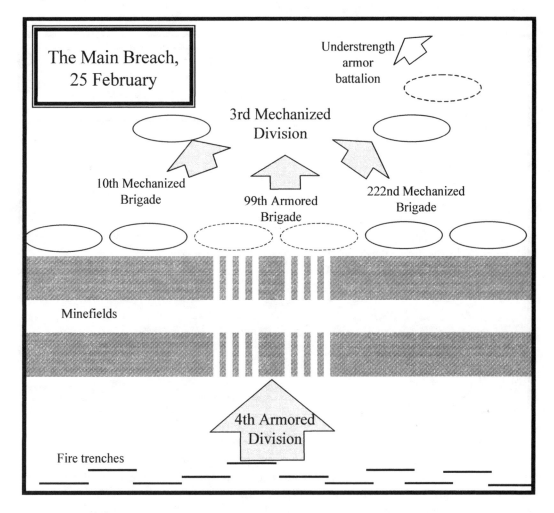

Meanwhile, the 99th Armored Brigade's two breaching battalions were at work in the main minefields. Despite heavy shelling, the battalions were able to push eight lanes through the two minefields by early afternoon.

After the lanes through the minefields were complete, the 10th and 222nd brigades plowed into the Iraqi trench lines. The Iraqis appeared ready to mount a defense, but at about 1:30, when the Egyptians came within small arms range, white flags appeared. Soon, the Egyptians had netted over 1,500 EPWs. The Egyptian corps spent most of the 25th collecting the remnants of the Iraqi 20th Infantry Division. In one case, after an attached Green Beret sniper shot an artillery spotter out of an observation tower, an entire battalion of 336 Iraqis surrendered.

The Egyptians found very few dead Iraqis. The Iraqi units in this sector had been hit hard by desertions. Most of the Iraqis who stayed either surrendered as soon as they saw Egyptians, or fired a few shots into the air before surrendering. Few Iraqi soldiers seemed interested in killing Egyptians. That Iraqi soldiers were more concerned with appearing to mount a defense than actually mounting one perhaps explains a curious discovery by an American liaison officer. Near an 85mm D-44 anti-tank gun, he found almost 100 shell casings. Though not a particularly lethal piece, a D-44 is capable of knocking out an M-60. A D-44 gunner trying to score hits could not possibly fire nearly a hundred rounds without scoring a single hit.

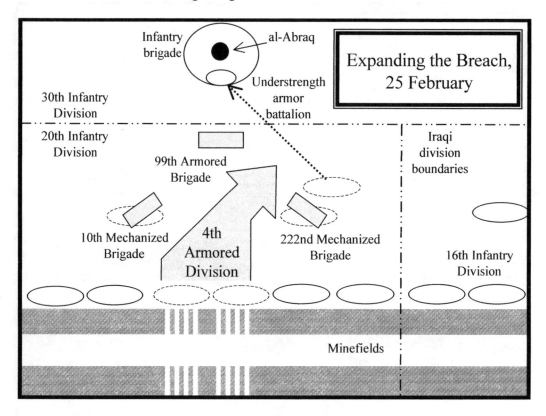

Almost all of the Iraqi units facing JFC-N were fighting without direction. Most senior officers and Ba'ath Party members had left their units. Some claimed to have important meetings to attend, then either left orders for the next few days or phoned their orders back from Baghdad. Others just left. For the units these officers commanded, this made effective resistance much more difficult, but it made surrendering much easier. These prisoners indicated that they never wanted to be in Kuwait in the first place, did not want to fight fellow Arabs, and were certainly not willing to die to keep Kuwait.

Some of the strongpoints on the southern edge of the obstacle belt had been defended vigorously. Iraqi infantrymen had engaged their attackers with RPG rounds and heavy volumes of small arms fire, but to no avail. The line of outposts was outflanked early in the battle, and the defenders found themselves fighting determined Egyptian assault teams attacking from their rear. About half of the outposts had fallen on 24 February. All had fallen by the next afternoon.

Once through the trenchlines, the division widened the breachhead in preparation for the passage of the 4th Armored Division through it. The 10th and 222nd Mechanized brigades drove to the northwest and northeast, respectively, knocked out the 20th

Division's two reserve infantry battalions, and established blocking positions. The 99th Armored Brigade, having absorbed the two breaching battalions back into its main body, established a blocking position on the northern edge of the breachhead. The only Iraqi armor in the vicinity, the 20th Division's armor battalion, which consisted of fewer than 20 T-55 tanks, made no attempt to interfere with the 222nd Brigade. Instead, it dropped back to a point due south of the village of al-Abraq, and hastily assumed defensive positions. After the 3rd Mechanized Division was set in its blocking positions, the 4th Armored Division passed through the minefields, hooked right, and headed for Ali al-Salem Airfield, its ultimate objective.

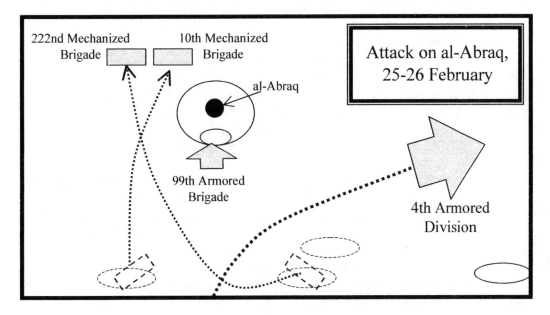

The village of al-Abraq, which contained an Iraqi corps headquarters, was the 3rd Mechanized Division's next objective. It was defended by a brigade of the 30th Infantry Division. That division had been posted behind the 20th and 16th Infantry divisions, with one of its two brigades behind each division. The southern approach to the village was guarded by the tanks which by then were all that was left of the 20th Infantry Division.

Once the 4th Armored Division had passed between the 99th Armored and 222nd Mechanized brigades, the 3rd Mechanized Division's three brigades took up their positions for the attack on al-Abraq. The attack was conducted in the deliberate, step-by-step style which characterized Egyptian operations throughout the war. The two mechanized brigades left their blocking positions and headed northward. The 10th Brigade established a blocking position to the northwest of al-Abraq. The 222nd Brigade swung around behind the 10th, and took up blocking positions of its own to the west of its sister brigade. Shortly after nightfall, when al-Abraq was sealed off by the two mechanized brigades, the 99th Armored Brigade attacked, wiping out the tank force to the south of the village. Al-Abraq itself would be cleared next morning.

By the time the Egyptians arrived at the village, there was little left to capture. Almost nothing was left of the twenty-odd mud brick and cinderblock buildings which used to be al-Abraq. Bombing and shelling had reduced the town to a few shapeless heaps of charred rubble. There were bunkers, some of them well-designed and well-built, and they were manned. However, when a brigade of Egyptian tanks showed up at around 10 a.m., the town's thousand or so defenders calculated the odds, then gave up. There was almost no resistance.

Meanwhile, the 4th Armored Division was traveling over almost 40 miles of difficult ground to reach Ali al-Salem Airfield. The Egyptians experienced no combat on the way and saw very few tanks. They were slowed, however, by their lack of self-propelled artillery. Forced to travel at a pace which would allow its towed artillery to keep up, the division did not arrive in the vicinity of the airfield until after dark. Coordinaton was immediately begun with the U.S. Marines to facilitate the division's occupation of the airfield at first light.

Ali al-Salem was in shambles. Its hardened aircraft shelters had been destroyed. The runways had been chewed up by British JP 233 missions, and there were unexploded submunitions strewn across the airfield. Still, the Egyptians were happy to take possession of it from the Tiger Brigade, because it signified the end of Egypt's participation in a victorious war. The Egyptian Army had suffered 11 dead and 84 wounded, with most of the casualties resulting from artillery fire received during the breach. It had also established itself as the world's pre-eminent Arab army.

The media beat Coalition forces into Kuwait City. CBS newsman Bob McKeown and his camera crew entered the city to find it free of Iraqis. The Iraqi 11th Infantry Division, the last force to occupy the city, had already surrendered to the Kuwaiti resistance during the previous night. Although the Marines had been poised on the outskirts of the city for several hours, they did not enter the city. The honor of retaking the capital had been reserved for Arab forces.

The Arab forces were also waiting, organizing for the triumphal entry into the city. Feeling that the final occupation of Kuwait City would be a sensitive political issue, Lt.Gen. Khaled ordered the commanders of JFC-N and JFC-E to form task forces made up of troops from all of the Arab nations which had taken part in operations Desert Shield and Desert Storm.

At about 9 a.m., Joint Forces Command units began entering the City. From the south came JFC-E. The Saudis, Bahrainis, Omanis, Qataris, Kuwaitis, troops from the United Arab Emirates and a few *Mujahideen* volunteers from Afghanistan entered to the cheers of thousands of Kuwaitis. From the west came the Saudis, Kuwaitis, Egyptians and Syrians of JFC-N. At around noon, the two forces met in the center of the city. For the Coalition Arab contingent, the war was over.

Part VII

Left Hook:
The XVIII Airborne Corps

"It is an approved maxim in war, never to do what the enemy wishes you to do, for this reason alone, that he desires it."

—Napoleon

14

Pardon My French:
The Daguet Division

On the western end of the battlefield, the French Daguet (Brocket) Division, reinforced by the 2nd Brigade of the 82nd Airborne Division, launched an attack toward Objective White, 105 miles inside Iraq.* The objective, near the town of As Salman, contained an airfield and stood astride a paved road which Coalition planners needed to push supplies to the units which would soon be executing the sweeping left hook toward Basra. By capturing Objective White, the Franco-American task force would secure this crucial route and establish a screen for the main Allied assault to the east.

Though the Daguet Division's mission was relatively simple, getting in a position to execute it had been relatively complicated. The division's first challenge was to integrate a brigade from a non-francophone division (the 82nd Airborne) into its assault. An exchange of bilingual liaison officers solved the problem.

A much more serious complication arose when the division found that it needed heavy armor. The deployment of main battle tanks outside Europe had not been seriously considered in France during the years before the crisis. Now that they were needed overseas, French law threatened to block the deployment.

All of France's heavy armor was assigned to the II and III corps in Germany and Lille, respectively. Though the officers and NCOs in these corps were professionals, these units were made up mostly of draftees, and were concerned with the defense of France and Western Europe. French law precludes draftees from being deployed overseas without the authorization of the Chamber of Deputies. While a vote in the Chamber probably would have been successful, President Mitterand was unwilling to risk a rebuff, so originally, no II or III Corps units were sent to Saudi Arabia.

The corps-sized *Force d'Action Rapide* (FAR) was made up almost entirely of volunteer, professional soldiers. It was prepared to do battle in Europe if necessary, but

---

*A brocket is a two-year-old deer of a variety found in Europe and Asia.

its main mission was to defend French overseas interests. Since its mission demanded that the FAR be readily deployable, it was small and short on heavy equipment.*

The FAR's 6th Light Armored Division and units from the 4th Air Mobile and 9th Marine divisions were among the first non-American units to arrive in Saudi Arabia.† The division's heaviest armor was its six-wheeled AMX-10RC reconnaissance vehicles. The AMX-10RC is really more a wheeled light tank than a reconnaissance vehicle, since it has a 105mm cannon, a laser rangefinder, computerized fire control, night vision systems and chemical warfare protection. It is a sound vehicle, but at 16 tons (Iraqi tanks ran 35–45 tons) it is too light for assaults on enemy tank formations. Its armor is extremely thin, about one-quarter of the thickness of France's AMX-30B2 main battle tank. For the Gulf War, the company that produced the AMX-10RC supplied add-on armor which was immediately shipped to the Gulf. This increased survivability somewhat, but it did not make the AMX-10RC a main battle tank. The French government decided that heavy tanks had to be sent.

AMX-10RC. (Photo: ECPA France)

The 10th Armored Division's 4th Dragoon Regiment, under the command of Lt.Col. Michel Bourret, was chosen to go to the Gulf with its 40 AMX-30B2 main battle tanks.‡ However, before it could deploy, the regiment had to be transformed from a draftee unit to a volunteer professional formation in order to comply with French law. Analysts worried about whether a recently formed unit could be readied for combat in time, but the mostly draftee unit was reborn as a volunteer professional unit with little difficulty.

---

*The combat units of the French Army now fall under the *Commandement de la Force d'Action Terrestre* (Ground Forces Command). The FAR and the two heavy corps no longer exist. The French Army is phasing out the draft, which will end in 2002. All units will be manned by professional soldiers.

†Unlike the U.S. Marines, which serve under the Department of the Navy, French Marines are part of the French Army.

‡In France, the term "regiment" refers to a battalion-sized unit.

The French Army had 25 armored regiments in the two heavy corps. Twenty-three were composed of three squadrons of draftees, with a few professional soldiers in each squadron.* Two (the 4th Dragoons and the 501st Tank Regiment) contained two squadrons of draftees and one professional squadron each. The 501st sent its regular squadron to the 4th Dragoons in return for one of its draftee squadrons. Now the 4th Dragoons was two-thirds volunteer, and not a single tank crew had been broken up.

The remaining professional squadron was created by reassigning scattered enlistees from the other regiments to the 4th Dragoons. Great care was taken to ensure that, wherever possible, the four crewmen of each tank at least knew each other. For example, four enlistees might be drawn from a draftee squadron of eighty men. These four men, who obviously knew each other from their previous squadron, would form a crew.

The re-formed regiment received extensive training before it left France. By the time the ground war began, the new 4th Dragoons had trained together for about four months, more than enough time for trained professionals familiar with the equipment they would be using. The Dragoons were as combat-ready as any other Allied unit.

The AMX-30B2 used by the 4th Dragoons was a relatively steady performer which suffered from the reputation of its predecessor. Mechanically, the original AMX-30 had been somewhat unreliable and was not a popular vehicle. French designers solved the mechanical problems, however, and introduced the AMX-30B2. Any questions about the effectiveness of the design changes were answered in the Gulf. French tanks were combat-ready over 90% of the time during the crisis. The B2's gunnery system was also a great improvement, with newer technologies like laser rangefinders and fire control computers. Thermal sights were also specially fitted for this operation.

AMX-30B2s of the 4th Dragoon Regiment. (Photo: ECPA France)

The Daguet Division's role in the war was determined largely by political considerations. France had withdrawn from NATO in 1966. Because VII Corps consisted mostly of Europe-based American units, there was concern in the French defense

---

*In France and Britain, all tank companies are referred to as squadrons. In American armored formations, that designation usually refers to a battalion-sized element of tanks and armored fighting vehicles in a cavalry unit.

establishment that if French units served under VII Corps, it might appear that France was slipping back into NATO. Having the division serve with XVIII Airborne Corps was clearly more attractive, as this implied no future obligations. It would be an ad hoc arrangement under which the division would be joining forces with part of the U.S. Rapid Deployment Force for one limited mission.

Another consideration was technical. With all of its improvements, the AMX-30B2 still had less than half the armor protection of the best Coalition main battle tanks, so facing even light anti-tank weapons could have been a problem. It was also relatively slow by modern standards. In addition, its main gun was unable to penetrate the frontal armor of the up-armored T-72M. However, the B2 could operate effectively in an area where Iraqi anti-tank weapons were relatively scarce, and thinly armored T-55s were the most dangerous threat. The French division was therefore sent to the left wing of the Coalition offensive to provide flank security.

Like the French, the 82nd Airborne Division was dangerously vulnerable in a number of areas. No one doubted the fighting spirit of the paratroops, but there was no ignoring the fact that the division is not designed for heavy offensive combat like that which was expected in other areas of Iraq and Kuwait. The division's Sheridan light tanks had been upgraded with thermal gun sights taken from M-60A3s before the start of the ground war. However, at 16 tons, they were still light tanks and were not designed to slug it out with main battle tanks. A hit by a main gun round from the worst of Iraq's tanks meant a sure kill against a Sheridan. Their thin aluminum armor could even be penetrated by heavy machine-gun bullets. The 58 Sheridans of the division's 3-73rd Armor Battalion were the 82nd Airborne's only armored vehicles. The paratroops had no protection against incoming shells or chemical rounds. Assigning division units to support the French flank guard mission would allow them to take an active role in the ground offensive while minimizing the risks to them.

While the French were more comfortable under XVIII Airborne command than under VII Corps command, there was still some concern in the French government about the idea of French troops serving under the command of another nation's generals. Sensitive to this concern, Lt.Gen. Gary Luck, the XVIII Airborne Corps' commander, placed the 2nd Brigade of the 82nd Airborne under French command. Thus, French soldiers would be commanded by an American general, but American soldiers would also be commanded by a French general.

A complication came up when the original Daguet Division commander, Maj.Gen Jean-Charles Mouscardes, had to be replaced when he became seriously ill in the first week of February. Lt.Gen. Michel Roquejeoffre, commander of all French forces in the Gulf, entrusted the operation to Brig.Gen. Bernard Janvier.[*] The change of command went smoothly.

The first combat occurred at 1:30 in the morning on 18 February, as artillery batteries from the 82nd, XVIII Corps and the Daguet Division launched an artillery barrage on several points along the border. The barrage succeeded in neutralizing Iraqi

---

[*]During the ground war, Roquejeoffre would become the highest ranking general of modern times to take prisoners personally. After spotting a group of Iraqis from his helicopter, he landed and took them prisoner.

air defenses and creating several passage points for two U.S. Army attack helicopter battalions, which crossed into Iraq at 2:00. While Army and Air Force aircraft jammed Iraqi communications, 11 Apaches from Lt.Col. William Tucker's 1st (Attack) Battalion of the 82nd Aviation Regiment and 12 Apaches from Lt.Col. Randy Tieszen's 5th Squadron, 6th (Air) Cavalry Regiment headed for objectives Rochambeau and White. Each flight was followed by three Blackhawks, prepared to pick up any downed Apache crewmen. They would not be needed.

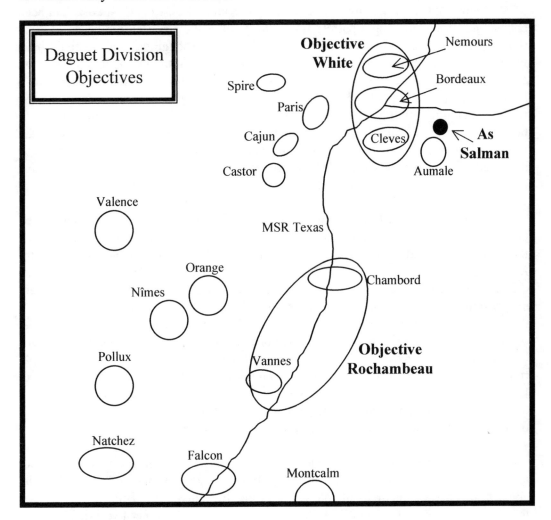

To maximize shock effect, the two attacks went in simultaneously. As 1-82nd Aviation hit Rochambeau, shooting up bunkers, destroying armored vehicles and killing 18 Iraqis, 5-6th Cavalry was destroying hangars, bunkers, anti-aircraft positions and supply stocks on Objective White. The objectives were also attacked by four A-10s. The Iraqis were virtually defenseless. Afraid to use their radars, and with minimal moonlight to work by, Iraqi anti-aircraft gunners were blind. A few hundred rounds from 23mm AA guns and a few wild surface-to-air missile shots yielded no results.

The 82nd's planners decided that a daylight follow-up raid should be mounted. At dawn on the 20th, another massive air defense suppression barrage cleared a different set of passage points for the same two battalions to strike the same two targets, with similar results. The most notable success of the second mission occurred when A

Company, 1-82nd destroyed a company of APCs, then picked apart a cluster of bunkers and gun pits.

For the next three days, French helicopters were active in the Daguet Division's zone of attack. Col. Jean-Luc Hotier's 1st and Col. Hubert de Larocque-Latour's 3rd Helicopter regiments flew numerous reconnaissance missions, looking for any Iraqi units entering the area in the final days before the ground attack. None were spotted.

The 82nd Airborne Division's 2nd Brigade, under Col. Ronald Rokosz, had been conducting dismounted night patrols since shortly after the air offensive began. At that time, there had been Iraqis manning a few border posts. Though the brigade could have wiped the Iraqi posts out with relative ease, it was limited in the means it could employ against the Iraqis. Since CENTCOM did not want the Iraqis to know that there was a major force that far west, the brigade's reconnaissance/counter-reconnaissance mission was conducted by small patrols sent out nightly from each of the three battalions. After nearly a month of these patrols, which featured several small skirmishes, the reconnaissance effort had been stepped up, and harassing artillery barrages had been delivered on known or suspected Iraqi positions near the border. On 21 February, most Iraqis along the border left their positions and headed north.

The ground attack began on 23 February. On the left flank, the French seized Objective Natchez, a steep escarpment that dominated the entire frontier across which the task force would attack on the next morning. The Foreign Legion's 2nd Infantry Regiment sent a few dug-in Iraqis fleeing and secured the objective at 8 p.m. In the center, the 2nd Brigade seized Objective Falcon, which overlooked the planned main supply route for the operation. Meanwhile, French Marines took Objective Montcalm on the right. On all three objectives, the Iraqis had abandoned their equipment and defensible terrain, making what should have been a prolonged, bitter and costly fight for the Americans and French a cake walk. Whether the Iraqis on the escarpment had simply run away, or had fallen back to rejoin the main body by design has not been established. However, the net result was that the Iraqis had vacated the most promising site for a defense. The lack of resistance along the escarpment made Brig.Gen. Janvier and his officers extremely optimistic about the prospects of the main assault.

Though it had not been singled out for aerial punishment the way many Iraqi units to the east had, the Iraqi 45th Infantry Division had nevertheless lost much of its combat power when hundreds of soldiers from the division's 840th Brigade surrendered to the 101st Airborne Division in the week before G-Day. The other two brigades were arrayed along the paved road the Allies had designated "MSR (Main Supply Route) Texas." The east side of the road was defended by the 841st Brigade, and the west by the 842nd.

There were about two dozen Iraqi tanks supporting the infantry. At the southern end of Objective Rochambeau there was a company of T-55 tanks. At the top of the position, in the vicinity of Objective Chambord, was a reinforced T-55 company, a few APCs and eighteen towed artillery pieces (nine 152mm and nine 122mm). Chambord was a patch of high ground which offered Iraqi spotters good sightlines to direct the fire of the 152mm and 122mm batteries.

Attacking these defenses would be Group East. The 2nd Brigade of the 82nd would push from Objective Falcon, just inside the Iraqi border, to Rochambeau, about 40 miles inside Iraq, along MSR Texas. Screening the paratroops' left flank would be the Reconnaissance Squadron of the 1st Hussar Regiment, 11th Parachute Division. The squadron had 12 eleven-ton ERC-90 armored cars equipped with 90mm main guns and 12 Milan anti-tank missile launchers carried in VAB armored personnel carriers.

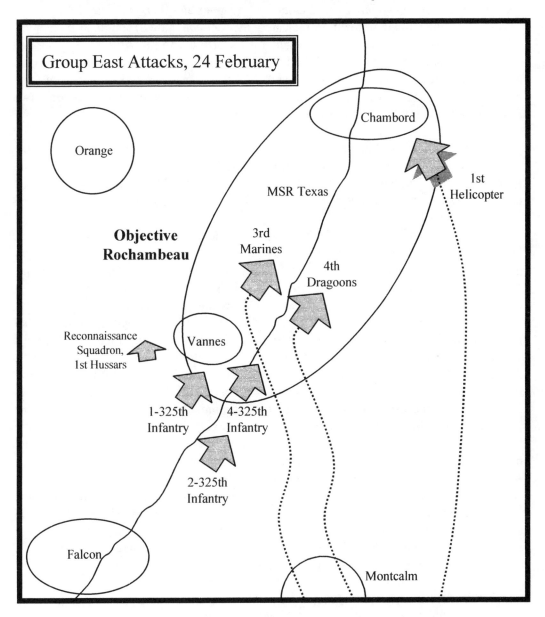

Col. Bernard Thorette's 3rd Marine Regiment and the 4th Dragoons would push northward from Objective Montcalm, then slash into Rochambeau from the side. The two regiments would end up in front of the 2nd Brigade, with 3rd Marines on the left side of MSR Texas and 4th Dragoons on the right. They would then push up the road, with the Americans in a supporting role.

On G-Day, 3rd Marines was the first to make contact with the Iraqis when it ran into a strongpoint at about 8:30 a.m. After a short mortar barrage, the Marines secured the position, capturing seven infantrymen, one of them wounded. The regiment got another indication of the lack of Iraqi fighting spirit when, after disarming the Iraqis, they found ten more assault rifles, three machine-guns and four RPG-7 anti-tank launchers. It was immediately apparent that the seven Iraqis were the remainder of a well-equipped platoon which had abandoned its weapons and fled.

After the strongpoint had been cleared, the regiment halted, and its lead elements spent the next two hours looking for targets for the artillery to hit. At 9:00, they spotted an infantry position in the center of Rochambeau and called in an artillery strike. About an hour later, they spotted eight T-55s and called in a massive strike of conventional artillery and MLRS rockets, destroying two of them. As soon as the smoke cleared, two A-10s began working over the position for a half-hour.

Meanwhile, the 2nd Brigade of the 82nd was driving into Rochambeau. In the early contacts, the paratroops faced Iraqi opposition. This opposition caused no American casualties, but would result in the death of some 150 Iraqis. The two lead units, the 1st and 4th battalions of the 325th Infantry Regiment, dealt with the opposition in different ways.

When his 1st Battalion, 325th Infantry Regiment made its major contact, Lt.Col. David Abrahamson halted the battalion and called in a "battalion one," in which every gun in the artillery battalion supporting 1-325th Infantry fired one round at the Iraqis. After the last of the 48 rounds impacted, he waited for the Iraqis to surrender. When there was no surrender, A-10s were called in. The Warthogs broke the Iraqis.

Lt.Col. John Vines' 4-325th Infantry had six distinct contacts with substantial forces of dug-in Iraqis, and dealt with them in a systematic fashion. First, loudspeakers warned the Iraqis that they would be fired upon if they did not surrender in 30 seconds. Then, exactly 30 seconds later, Sheridans began firing 152mm HEAT rounds into bunkers from point-blank range. A-10 strikes were called in when they were available. In most instances, these measures were enough to prompt the Iraqis to surrender. In the instances where they were not, infantry, which had been moving into positions on the Iraqis' flanks during the Sheridan cannonade or A-10 runs, began rolling up the Iraqi positions from the side. At that point, surrender was the Iraqis' only sensible alternative.

Neither battalion allowed EPW gathering to slow its advance. A company that captured a position would stop and round up prisoners while the rest of the battalion forged ahead. Then, after turning its prisoners over to follow-on units, it would catch up and take the place of another company, which by then would be rounding up prisoners of its own. This rotation system worked as well as any system could have under the strain of what became a torrent of surrendering Iraqis.

At 11:40, Brig.Gen. Janvier ordered an artillery and air preparation on Rochambeau for the attack of the two French regiments. Shells began to fall just before noon. For the first time, Iraqi gunners near Chambord answered back. Janvier's artillery responded with counterbattery fire, which included MLRS rockets.

While the artillery concentrated on the Iraqi guns, two more A-10s showed up and destroyed five bunkers. When the A-10s were finished, Gazelle attack helicopters from 3rd Helicopter Regiment used HOT wire-guided missiles to destroy one Brazilian-made armored car, 5 armored personnel carriers and 16 bunkers.

At 12:15, the artillery lifted and the Dragoons moved forward, but were almost immediately halted by a minefield. Foreign Legion combat engineers were brought forward to clear several paths, and soon the Dragoons were on their way again. However, no sooner were the tanks through the minefields than they were stopped in their tracks at 1 p.m. by hundreds of surrendering Iraqis. Though the desertion of many officers before G-Day made organized Iraqi resistance impossible, most soldiers would not have fought effectively had the officers stayed. The French were facing recently recalled, war-weary veterans of the Iran–Iraq War. Many had been wounded during that war. Many had lost close relatives. Most had no fight left in them. The Dragoons, without organic infantry, were forced to request an infantry company from 3rd Marines to help round up the prisoners. The request was granted.

Meanwhile, 3rd Marines was in action against several Iraqi bunker complexes. The Marines used AMX-10RC main gun fire and Milan missiles to pick off bunkers and 20mm cannon fire to pin the Iraqis down while VAB armored personnel carriers full of Marines maneuvered toward the Iraqi positions. Once they were within small arms range of the Iraqis, the VABs discharged their passengers, who cleared the positions in short order. The Marines also destroyed three T-55s with Milan anti-tank missiles.[*]

Janvier used air power effectively throughout the day. As the Dragoons were emerging from the minefield, 1st Helicopter Regiment was hunting north of Chambord. The Gazelles found a few targets between objectives Rochambeau and White, destroying three trucks, a strongpoint and an artillery piece at around 3:30. Thirty minutes later, 3rd Helicopter, screening the left flank of Group West, destroyed six bunkers, two APCs, three BRDM armored scout cars and four trucks, along with the artillery pieces they were towing. At 5 p.m., A-10 strikes prompted the immediate surrender of about 150 more Iraqis.

On the ground, the 4th Dragoons and 3rd Marines cleared about half of Rochambeau by nightfall. Artillery and tank fire destroyed a few T-55s in the 4th Dragoons' sector early in the attack. The regiment spent the rest of the afternoon desperately trying to take control of hordes of prisoners. At around 5 p.m., it came upon a command post and captured several senior officers of the 45th Infantry Division. Just after seven, 3rd Marines scuttled three abandoned T-55s and an MTLB in its sector. The tanks had escaped destruction by artillery or 3rd Marines, but were later abandoned by their crews during the fighting.

At 5:30, although there was still about an hour of daylight left, Brig.Gen. Janvier decided to concentrate on securing the terrain the division had taken and delay clearing the rest of Rochambeau until the next morning. There were still Iraqis holding out on Chambord, calling in mortar and artillery fire on the French. Janvier felt that the capture of the position would require a certain amount of maneuver as well as a firefight. He did not want any accidents or ambushes in the twilight. In addition, the division was being choked by Iraqi prisoners. By late afternoon, the French and Americans had taken at least 2,000 prisoners on Rochambeau before they lost count. There were also hundreds of Iraqis south of Chambord who were not resisting, but had not been rounded up yet. Though he was prodded by XVIII Corps staff to seize the objective immediately, Janvier declined. This proved wise. At 6 p.m., a major sandstorm closed in.

---

[*]In each infantry regiment, there were 36 troop-carrying VABs. Of these, 30 mounted 12.7mm heavy machine-guns and 6 (two in each company) were equipped with 20mm rapid fire cannon and Milan missile launchers. In addition, the 3rd Marines and the 2nd Foreign Legion Infantry each had a squadron of 12 AMX-10RCs. They also had three anti-tank platoons, each with 8 Milan launchers carried in VABs. The 4th Dragoons had no anti-tank launchers.

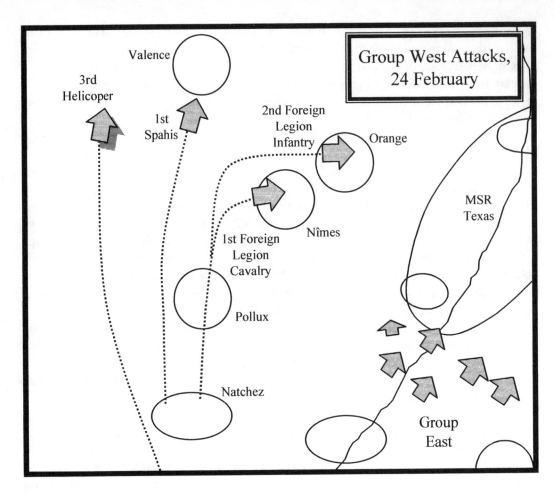

While the 4th Dragoons and 3rd Marines were pushing toward Rochambeau in the east, Group West pushed into Iraq. On Group West's left wing was the 1st Spahi Regiment, commanded by Col. Michel Barro.* On the right flank was Col. Hubert Ivanoff's 1st Foreign Legion Cavalry Regiment, followed by the 2nd Foreign Legion Infantry Regiment. Group West had two missions: protect the flank of Group East, and be prepared to use the east–west dirt trails that ran across the front to drive into the side of the Iraqi defenses on Rochambeau if the Dragoons and Marines ran into unexpectedly stiff resistance. Unaware that their opponents were equipped with satellite navigation devices, the Iraqis had discounted the possibility of major formations moving across unmarked wastes. The western thrust therefore faced almost no opposition. The Iraqis along MSR Texas did not even know they were being outflanked. There was a low ridge which dissected the battlefield between groups East and West. The Iraqis on Rochambeau had no idea what was happening on the other side of that ridge.

The Spahis and 1st Foreign Legion Cavalry were each equipped with 36 AMX-10RCs. Because these two cavalry units were equipped with three times as many AMX-10RCs as the infantry units, they had half as many anti-tank missile launchers (12

---

*During the 1800s, France maintained several regiments of Spahis. These were native Algerian and Moroccan cavalry units. Though Algeria and Morocco are no longer French colonies, the unit designation was retained as a matter of tradition.

vehicle-mounted HOT launchers as opposed to 24 non-vehicle-mounted Milan Launchers). The troops of Col. Yves Derville's 2nd Foreign Legion Infantry (like those of 3rd Marines) were carried in VABs. The VAB is designed to be light and fast. Its armor is about half as thick as that of the basic Bradley, but it is faster.

The 1st Legion Cavalry reached its first objective, Pollux, just before seven. The Legionnaires found it abandoned. The French had expected the objective, which included a run-down village, to be occupied by the Iraqis. The village had been well-stocked with supplies of food and water, and there were enough weapons there to mount a defense if the Iraqis had wanted to, but the Iraqis did not. After crossing Pollux, the 1st Legion Cavalry took Objective Nîmes to the northeast.

The Spahis, who had bypassed Pollux to the west, continued northward toward Objective Valence, which French planners believed to be a piece of commanding terrain. As such, resistance at Valence was expected to be fairly stiff. In fact, Valence was only a slight rise in terrain, with little military value. It was therefore not contested by the Iraqis.

Due to the need for surprise, large scale pre-ground war aerial reconnaissance had been impossible. Much of the intelligence about the terrain in the Daguet Division's zone had come from the French "SPOT" satellite. The satellite was designed to provide geographic information about Europe and North Africa. It could be used to photograph areas in the Middle East, but only at very sharp angles. As a result, variations in terrain tended to be exaggerated significantly.

Pre-ground war helicopter reconnaissance had not corrected the misconceptions. Though the 3rd Helicopter Regiment flew reconnaissance missions on the Daguet Division's left flank before G-Day, the missions were not authorized until a few days before the start of the ground war. At that point, the division had two options. It could direct 3rd Helicopter to do a thorough zone reconnaissance or one with more limited objectives. While a thorough zone reconnaissance would have provided a more accurate picture of the terrain, and a more complete picture of Iraqi dispositions in the attack zone, it might have enabled the Iraqis to deduce the division's attack axis. Discreet flights near the division's boundaries could spot Iraqi reinforcements without giving away the division's intentions. Since division planners' major concern at that point was not the nature of the terrain, but whether Iraqi units would move into the attack zone at the last moment, the latter option was chosen. As a result, Valence had not been the target of any pre-ground war reconnaissance missions.

With no Iraqis to fight, the Spahis pushed through Valence after only a short pause, moving on to Objective Castor, about 50 miles to the northeast, which it secured just after two in the afternoon. The regiment halted at Castor for the day.

The 2nd Foreign Legion Infantry had entered Iraq behind 1st Legion Cavalry. After clearing Pollux behind the cavalrymen at about 8 a.m., the regiment continued north, until it became clear that the Spahis would not need support. The regiment then hooked right to secure Objective Orange. The Legionnaires took Orange, capturing or driving off the few Iraqis who were there. By 1:30 in the afternoon, the two objectives on the low ridge that ran between groups East and West (Nîmes and Orange) were completely cleared. This gave the Foreign Legion control of that ridge line.

Group East experienced a quiet but busy night, processing prisoners and resupplying for the next day's operation. The quiet was broken at about 5:30 a.m. on the 25th, when two Iraqi guns south of Chambord opened up on French positions, prompting an immediate and massive counterbarrage of shells and MLRS rockets. This unexpected bit of Iraqi resistance delayed the start of the French advance by only a few minutes.

Shortly after six, 4th Dragoons secured the source of the earlier Iraqi artillery barrage. The two 122mm guns had been abandoned by their crews as soon as the counterbarrage had ended. The Dragoons then spotted and destroyed two BRDMs. At 7:45, the Marines found the 152mm guns, also abandoned. Nearby were ZSU 23-4 AA guns, which had been placed around the 152mm guns to protect them from air attack. These guns were also abandoned and looked like they had never been fired.

At ten, 3rd Marines was temporarily halted when it ran into an arms depot containing almost 1,000 assault rifles and scores of light machine-guns and RPGs. The Marines were torn between the need to root out whatever Iraqis might be hiding in the depot's many bunkers and the need to keep driving. Col. Thorette decided to keep moving and clear the depot later. Shortly after the Marines began moving, they spotted a lone T-55 and destroyed it. The destruction of the tank sparked another mass surrender, which halted the regiment again.

At eleven, after a short, intense pounding by Warthogs, followed by 15 minutes of heavy artillery, 4th Dragoons overran the last line of defense in front of Chambord. In under an hour, the Dragoons claimed eight T-55s, an American-made M-48A5 and a BRDM in addition to the seven T-55s which had previously been destroyed.* Shortly afterward, 3rd Marines destroyed a lone T-55 in its sector, the last serviceable Iraqi tank on Rochambeau.

After the last tank was destroyed, there was little trouble from the Iraqis on Chambord. However, the Dragoons ran into another delay just before two, when a minefield on Chambord caused a temporary halt. After Legion engineers breached the minefield, the Dragoons surprised and destroyed eight Iraqi supply trucks and an MTLB armored personnel carrier. By mid-afternoon, Chambord was clear. While 3rd Marines continued northward to take part in the assault on Objective White, 4th Dragoons moved toward its assigned position on high ground overlooking As Salman, where it would destroy two more T-55s. While the 1st and 4th battalions finished rounding up prisoners on Rochambeau, Lt.Col. Matthew Belford's 2-325th Infantry Battalion would follow the Marines and Dragoons, then help seal off As Salman by cutting MSR Virginia to the east of the town.

In the west, the Spahis overran Objective Cajun without resistance from the Iraqis, then took Objective Paris at 9:25. The Spahis expected that the Iraqis occupying Paris would fight for it, as they were the flank guard for the airfield, the town, and the nearby crossroads. They found only more abandoned weapons and ammunition.

Objective White had been divided into three parts by French planners. The northern third, containing As Salman Airfield, had been designated Objective Nemours. The center, which contained a radio station, the junction between MSRs Texas and Virginia and the ruins of a cinderblock gas station (a possible strongpoint) was dubbed Objective Bordeaux. Objective Cleves made up the lower third. Bordeaux and Nemours

---

*The M-48 was the U.S. Armed Forces' main battle tank during the Vietnam War. Later versions, like this one, weighed about 53 tons and mounted a 105mm main gun. The United States sold hundreds to Iran before the revolution. M-48s made up a significant proportion of the few hundred tanks that the Iraqi Army captured during the war with Iran.

would be attacked from the west. The Spahis would take Bordeaux. The 1st Legion Cavalry, which had followed the Spahis through Paris, would take Nemours. The 2nd Legion Infantry would follow, and clear the position in detail. Both objectives would be hit by the 3rd Helicopter Regiment before the ground assault. From the south, 3rd Marines would take Cleves.

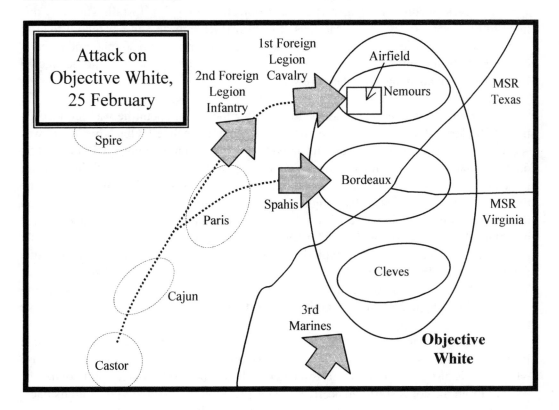

From 1 to 2 p.m., while the Legion closed in, the airfield was subjected to an intense attack by 3rd Helicopter. The attack destroyed one tank, killed several Iraqis and started a fire in the fuel dump. At 4 p.m., while still fighting the fire in the fuel dump, the Iraqis were hit by a rolling artillery barrage. As the Legionnaires closed to within 2,500 meters of the objective, they could see the shells and bomblets impacting on the runway. Within minutes, the airfield's ammunition dump exploded.

As the final shells were falling, Legion combat engineers moved forward and blew a gaping hole in the perimeter fence using a Mine Clearing Line Charge. Legion assault units poured through the gap. The dazed Iraqis offered little resistance, but unexploded bomblets strewn across the airfield slowed movement dramatically. Parts of Objective White were so saturated with unexploded bomblets that MiCLiCs had to be used to clear paths through them. These hazards notwithstanding, by nightfall the Legionnaires had secured Nemours after destroying several Iraqi artillery pieces with HOT missiles and capturing the airfield's remaining T-55.

The Spahis took Bordeaux at two. Col. Jean Novacq's 11th Marine Artillery Regiment, supplemented by six American guns, provided the Spahis with effective artillery support. This was one of the more delicate artillery missions of the war. There were numerous bunkers on Bordeaux, some close to the road junction. The Spahis wanted them destroyed, but CENTCOM wanted the roads to run supplies on, and did not want them damaged by stray artillery rounds. The precision bombardment provided by the artillerymen took out most of the bunkers without doing any damage to the roads. Then, bursting through a smokescreen laid by 11th Marine Artillery, the Spahis overran Bordeaux, moving carefully to avoid setting off bomblets from previous bombings of the gas station and artillery missions against the bunkers on the objective.

Cleves, secured at 5:30, was the last objective on White to fall. This was due more to the earlier delay of 3rd Marines at central Rochambeau and Chambord than to Iraqi resistance on Cleves, which was virtually non-existent. As on so many other parts of the battlefront, anti-aircraft guns which could have been turned on the advancing French had been abandoned by their crews.

Brig.Gen. Janvier again decided to halt for the night. Again he was prodded by the XVIII Corps staff to continue the attack, but again he declined. Objective White was secure for all intents and purposes, and Janvier saw no reason to expose As Salman's 5–6,000 civilians or his own men to the dangers of nighttime house-to-house fighting. As it turned out, the town had been abandoned, but Janvier had no way of knowing that at the time. Janvier also believed that night operations would mean soldiers stepping on unexploded bomblets. He was concerned that since cluster bombing had left unexploded bomblets all over As Salman Airfield, previous bombings of the town itself had probably produced a similar yield of unexploded submunitions there. Indeed, when his units entered the town the next day, they would find it littered with unexploded submunitions. The French were content to spend the night broadcasting surrender appeals and dropping leaflets. Throughout the night, Iraqis drifted toward the French perimeter to give themselves up.

Brig.Gen. Janvier's cautious approach ultimately proved correct, but at the time it caused some consternation at XVIII Airborne Corps Headquarters. As is often the case when there is disagreement between competent officers, both sides made valid points.

From the corps staff perspective, the Daguet Division needed to pick up its pace. The division may have been meeting its original schedule, but things had changed. The 101st Airborne and 24th Infantry Division attacks had been launched earlier than planned. At the time, there was concern that until the left flank was secure, an Iraqi force to the north of As Salman could drive to the southeast, into the 101st Airborne Division's sector, and disrupt the operation of the helicopter base that division had set up. Such a force could also disrupt the flow of 24th ID's supplies.

Janvier, on the other hand, was not particularly worried about a southeasterly Iraqi thrust. Nothing he had seen in his zone indicated that the Iraqis in the area wanted to do anything but escape. He therefore saw no pressing need to clear As Salman immediately. Even with the delay, the French would capture all of their assigned objectives two days before the end of the war. Had Janvier opted to take As Salman at night, he would have gained about 12 hours, and his men would have been left with virtually no one to fight for 56 hours instead of 44.

Other reasons for Janvier's caution were technical. American and British heavy units did attack all night, but they could afford to. Their tanks were essentially impenetrable, and were equipped with the best night vision devices available, so they did not have to worry about anti-armor ambushes and friendly fire incidents the way the French did. It should be noted, however, that even with those armor and night vision advantages, every American heavy division that fought night battles had friendly fire incidents. One, the 1st Armored Division, lost four tanks to ambushes.

In addition, Janvier had to consider the vulnerability of the truck-borne 2nd Brigade of the 82nd Airborne Division. While truck convoys of the 101st Airborne would drive through the night, they were not driving through areas thick with unexploded submunitions. It is highly likely that night operations would have resulted in unnecessary casualties to the paratroops.

It should also be pointed out that Janvier was not the only Coalition leader who was cautious at night. The U.S. Marines, whose fighting spirit was never questioned, faced many of the same equipment limitations as the French. Like the French, they chose to suspend offensive operations at night.

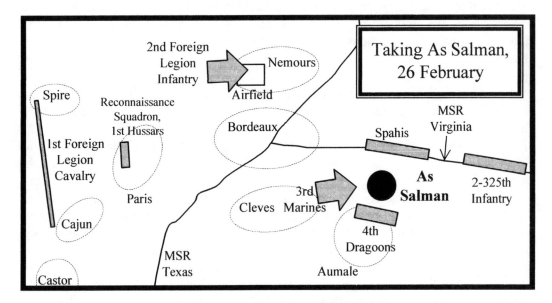

On 26 February, the Daguet Division tightened its grip on the territory it had captured. At daybreak, the 1st and 3rd Helicopter regiments fanned out to the west and north of As Salman, to screen the rest of the division from possible Iraqi counterattack. The 1st Legion Cavalry moved to the west, where it would set up a north–south screen line running from Objective Spire to Objective Cajun. The 1st Hussars' Reconnaissance Squadron took up reserve positions behind the Legionnaires, on Objective Paris. Meanwhile, the 2nd Legion Infantry picked its way through the airfield, removing Iraqi weapons and documents as it went. The Spahis headed east from Objective Bordeaux to seal off As Salman from the north. At 9:30, paratroops from 2-325th Infantry linked up with the 101st Airborne along MSR Virginia.

The job of clearing As Salman itself fell to the 3rd Marines and an attached company of French commandos. Progress through the town was slow. The Iraqi units in the town had left too hastily to set many booby-traps, but they had set a few, and the Marines had to be careful. As elsewhere, a far more significant problem was the tremendous number of unexploded cluster munitions lying around.

Once inside the town, the force split up, with about half of the force heading toward a castle on the northeast outskirts of the town. Marines and commandos made their way to the castle, which they found abandoned. Shortly after they began searching the inside of the castle, it was rocked by a pair of explosions. The cause of the explosions remains unclear, but they claimed the lives of two commandos and left 25 commandos and Marines wounded.

The other half of the task force cleared the town itself, splitting into two groups, each tasked with clearing one of the only two streets of any consequence in the town. The sweeps turned up a handful of troops who had been left behind when their unit had retreated northward. These troops surrendered without much prompting.

At 4:15 in the afternoon, there was a large explosion on As Salman Airfield. Two officers and five enlisted men from the XVIII Airborne Corps' 27th Engineer Battalion were killed. The engineers had been attached to the French to help dispose of explosive ordnance on the airfield. After having disturbed several unexploded cluster munitions which did not explode, a group of engineers became overconfident. They believed that instead of destroying each submunition in place, one at a time, they could save time by picking them up and consolidating them, then destroying them in larger piles. One of the submunitions exploded, setting off one of the piles and causing the fatalities.

On the 27th, having achieved all of their objectives, the French and Americans continued to round up Iraqis and destroy the tons of ammunition and equipment the Iraqis had left behind.

At about 2:30 in the afternoon, the 3rd Helicopter Regiment's helicopters hit an Iraqi company at As Shabaka, northwest of As Salman. After Gazelles destroyed the town's anti-aircraft defenses, two ZSU 23-4s, and a radio relay station, scouts landed and rounded up 84 prisoners. The 1st Legion Cavalry also saw action. The Legionnaires had positioned themselves to east of As Shabaka in case an armored assault on the town became necessary. Due to the ease with which the Iraqis in As Shabaka were rounded up, the Legionnaires had to content themselves with the capture of an Iraqi observation post and its 15-man garrison at four. The regiment did get one consolation prize when one of the prisoners mentioned a major electronic warfare station less than a mile away. The Legionnaires promptly drove off and wrecked that site after carrying off boxes of documents detailing Iraqi electronic warfare procedures and capabilities.

With this action, the Daguet Division's war was over. All that remained now was to get the division's massive collection of prisoners back to Saudi Arabia and wait for other Allied units to settle matters to the east.

15

Screaming Eagles: The 101st

The 101st Airborne (Air Assault) Division, with its 32 heavy Chinook and 122 Blackhawk helicopters, gave the Coalition its swiftest deep strike capability. This capability would be tested to the limit during the ground war as the division struck deep into the Iraqi rear.

The 101st would have two missions during the ground war. The first was the establishment of FOB (Forward Operating Base) Cobra, 70 miles inside Iraq. Cobra would serve as a supply depot behind enemy lines. The forward base, once established, would provide helicopters with the fuel and ammunition they would need to strike deep in support of XVIII Airborne Corps' drive across Iraq. Within 20 minutes of landing, each helicopter could be refueled, rearmed, and ready to rejoin the battle.

The second mission was the landing of a brigade in the Euphrates Valley, blocking Highway 8, which ran between Baghdad and Basra. This would block the Republican Guard's most direct path to Baghdad.

Preparation for the assault began on 14 February, when the division conducted aerial reconnaissance of the ground between itself and what would become FOB Cobra. Special attention was paid to the planned route of the ground convoy, which would reinforce and resupply the airhead on G-Day, code named "MSR Newmarket." The reconnaissance turned up two bunker complexes.

On 17 February, Apache attack helicopters from the 101st attacked one of the bunker complexes, just inside Iraqi lines. After a rocket attack, ten surviving Iraqis surrendered to the team of pathfinders that accompanied the Apaches. On the same day, another attack helicopter team hit the other complex. Thirty more Iraqis from the 45th Infantry Division surrendered to the infantry company attached to the Apache team.

The second complex was an intelligence bonanza. Documents captured in the raid revealed the command structure of the 45th Infantry Division, as well as the location of most of the division's remaining bunker complexes. Interrogation of captured officers provided information about almost every Iraqi air defense weapon between Tactical Assembly Area (TAA) Campbell (named for the 101st's home post of Fort Campbell, Kentucky), the 101st's jumping-off point, and Objective Cobra. The division could now deal with these weapons before they became a threat to its low flying, heavily laden transport helicopters on G-Day.

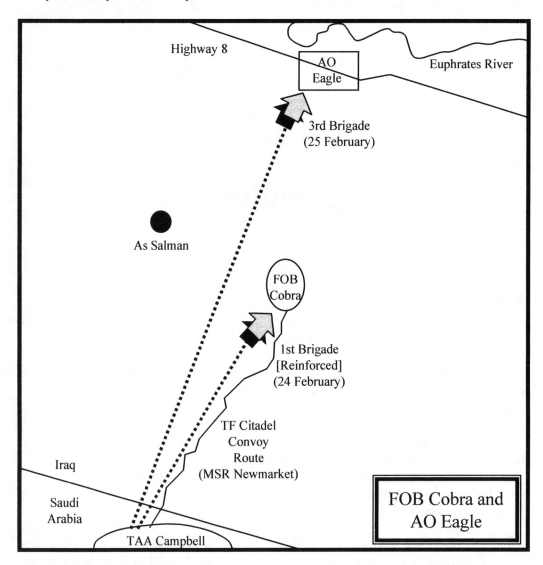

At 8:10 a.m. on 20 February, Cobra attack helicopters and A-10s hit another complex along MSR Newmarket. After 13 bunkers had been destroyed, Iraqis began to surrender. Two companies from Lt.Col. Henry Kinnison's 1-187th Infantry Battalion helicoptered into the objective and began rounding up prisoners. The operation, led by Lt.Col. Kinnison personally, netted 421 Iraqi prisoners. The 101st sent helicopters back the next day to round up 13 stragglers and pick up captured equipment.

The commander of the 101st, Maj.Gen. James H.B. Peay, was more impressed by what Kinnison's men didn't find than what they did. Not only were there no chemical munitions on the objective, there were no chemical protective suits and fewer than a dozen masks. This Iraqi unit was not prepared for large scale chemical operations. As a result of this revelation, Peay's soldiers would not be wearing their hot, bulky chemical-protective suits on G-Day. They would carry them in small bags below their rucksacks. Their masks would be carried at their sides.

However happy their leaders had been about the results of the raid, the raiders found one aspect of the operation disquieting. Before landing on the position, ground attack planes and helicopter gunships had blasted the Iraqis for about three hours. Most had expected to find only dead and wounded Iraqis in the positions that had been targeted. Instead, they found no dead Iraqis, and only five of the prisoners had been wounded. This caused a great deal of concern about the effectiveness of the air campaign. The occupants of these sound but hardly impregnable positions had emerged virtually unscathed from a violent air attack. Many of Kinnison's men wondered how many other Iraqis whom CENTCOM had assumed had been killed would still be alive and waiting for the assault.

The night before G-Day, four six-man long range reconnaissance patrols (LRRPs), were helicoptered into enemy territory. Each team member was equipped with an M-16 rifle, a silenced pistol, two or three LAWs and Claymore anti-personnel mines.[*] Three of the teams were placed around what would become FOB Cobra. The other team was sent farther north. At 7:00 a.m. on G-Day, three more LRRP teams were inserted between TAA Campbell and Objective Cobra with beacons to guide the main force.

On G-Day morning, the first wave, or "lift," of helicopters was scheduled to take off from TAA Campbell at 5:27. This would have given the pilots just enough light so that they would not have to risk flying in night vision goggles. However, the takeoff was delayed for two hours due to fog so thick that one of the division's scout helicopters crashed. Both crewmen survived the crash and were brought back to American lines by another scout helicopter.

The first lift of 67 Blackhawk, 30 Chinook, and 10 UH-1B "Huey" transport helicopters was led by a flight, or "chalk," of four Blackhawks. In the lead Blackhawk was Lt.Col. John Broderick, commander of the 426th Support and Transportation Battalion, which was responsible for setting up the airbase. At 8:08 Broderick's chalk touched down after dodging hills for 41 minutes at 215 mph, 15–20 feet off the ground.

Unfortunately, the group had landed in the wrong place. Using the hand-held digital satellite position locating device, an officer found that they were about 1¼ miles north of their intended landing zone.[†] The helicopter pilots had already spotted small groups of Iraqis, and artillery was now falling to the north of the chalk. The soldiers clambered back aboard the Blackhawks, which took off so hurriedly that an officer and an NCO in the second Blackhawk almost fell 30 feet to the ground. At 8:15, they were in the right place. Broderick's team and the 60 infantrymen responsible for providing security for it calmly set about their tasks. The only people noticeably excited were the NBC camera crew and the *Newsweek* photographer riding in the third Blackhawk.

Broderick hopped back into his Blackhawk and began the search for firm ground for his six fuel points. The technique he used was low-tech but effective. As Broderick saw what might be a suitable site, he ordered the pilot to hover low, and watched to see

---

[*]The Claymore weighs only 3.2 lbs. and blows out 700 steel shards in a 60 degree arc. Anyone within 80 meters who is not lying flat on the ground will probably be killed. The shards can wound as far as 250 meters.

[†]At a cost of about $5,000 apiece, these devices were one of the great bargains of the war. They allowed Coalition forces to navigate across the wastes of Iraq without fear of becoming lost, and they allowed the Army to place its vital forces and equipment with precision that would otherwise have been impossible.

how much sand the rotor wash kicked up. When he was satisfied with the firmness of a given piece of ground, he dropped a team of scouts off. His original plan had called for four fuel points within the perimeter, and two Forward Area Arming and Refueling Points (FAARPs) just outside the perimeter to the northeast, one for Apache attack helicopters and one for Cobras. Iraqi artillery prevented the placement of the FAARPs on the first try, however. Broderick landed, waited for the artillery to be dealt with, then established FAARP sites on the second attempt.

While Broderick was selecting sites, helicopters were already landing. Immediately behind the first chalk came the Chinooks. Scouts on motorcycles streamed down the back ramp of one of them and raced around the perimeter marking the spots where each unit was to set up. More Chinooks followed, carrying Col. Tom Hill's task force. Hill's 1st Brigade (the 1st, 2nd and 3rd battalions of the 327th Infantry Regiment, commanded by Lt.Col. Frank Hancock, Lt.Col. Charles Thomas and Lt.Col. Gary Bridges), made up the heart of the task force. The brigade was supplemented by the 2nd Brigade's 1-502nd Infantry Battalion, under Lt.Col. James Donald, and a few 105mm artillery pieces. In short order, the Screaming Eagles had secured a perimeter five miles deep and three miles wide. With the base now secure, the three LRRP teams which had landed at Cobra the previous night boarded helicopters and returned to Saudi Arabia.

An unexpected problem soon developed just outside the perimeter. Scattered small arms fire was directed at the scouts from a battalion of the 45th Infantry Division that Army intelligence had missed. Two Apaches attacked the complex, followed by Cobras and A-10s. Once the airspace above the complex was clear, 105mm guns inside Cobra dropped shells on the Iraqis. Just as the gunners began to run out of shells, an Iraqi major walked out of the desert and offered his surrender. Lt.Col. Hancock told him that if his men did not also surrender, he would call in more air strikes on them. Soon, 340 members of the battalion were shuffling toward the perimeter with their hands up.

Units in the perimeter tried to decide what to do with the EPWs. The Chinooks had plenty of room for prisoners but no time to load and unload them. The airflow had been tightly programmed to begin with. Now, because of the earlier weather delay, it was already two hours behind. Inside the perimeter, troops were scrambling to get FOB Cobra set up, and few men could be spared for guard duty. Luckily, the Iraqis were docile enough to be held in an improvised compound by a handful of MPs.

Helicopters continued to ferry in equipment. Some Chinooks carried two command and control Humvees slung beneath them. An unfortunate incident occurred when a Chinook ran into difficulty and was forced to cut loose its slung load. Two of the four vehicles that were to make up the 1st Brigade's Tactical Operations Center, or TOC, crashed to earth, destroying their radio equipment.

Just before 11:00 a.m., fuel deliveries began. Ten Chinooks dropped off huge 10,000 gallon fuel bags. During the planning and preparation phase, the 426th's leaders had found that it was possible to deliver these huge bags by connecting two cargo nets with the metal "D-rings" used in mountain climbing, as long as the bags were filled to no more than one-fifth of their capacity. Each pumping station was built around one of these "10K bags." Other Chinooks dropped bundles of five full 500 gallon bags near each 10K bag. After the fuel from the 500 gallon bags was pumped into the 10K bags, it was pumped through filters to helicopters at the end of flexible hoses. The 10K bags were kept filled by continually emptying 500 gallon bags into them.

The stations were ready to pump by 11:30, but soon ran into problems. Planners had envisioned having the 10k bags filled and 500 gallon bags in reserve by the time the first helicopters showed up. Instead, weather had delayed the original takeoff, and there had been difficulties in siting the two FAARPs. All the while, Apaches were hunting for Iraqi armor and using up fuel. The Apache burns 2½ gallons of fuel per minute, and can only operate for about 2 hours and 40 minutes before it needs to refuel. As soon as the first pumping rigs were set up, near-empty attack helicopters were already lined up waiting for fuel. To make matters worse, a company of Iraqi T-55s from the 45th Infantry Division trying to escape the French Daguet Division, was headed directly for Cobra. The helicopter gunships from the 101st's Aviation Brigade were the base's only cover, and had to be refueled to meet the threat. Several of the pumping stations almost ran dry, but they made it until the end of the day. The Iraqi tanks did not. The company was wiped out by gunships.

Late that night, 1st Brigade's vehicles and several fuel tankers arrived at Cobra. Task Force Citadel had begun to convoy at the same time that Lt.Col. Broderick's Blackhawk was taking off that morning. The residents of Cobra were thrilled to see the 700-vehicle convoy, especially its fuel trucks. At that point the 10K bags were almost dry. Originally, the Chinooks supplying Cobra had intended to make five flights each. The first delivery was mostly vital equipment. The next four trips would place some 250,000 gallons of fuel on the ground. Unfortunately, the two-hour delay at the beginning meant two fewer hours of daylight, and one flight bearing some 60,000 gallons had to be canceled due to darkness. Citadel's fuel trucks kept Cobra pumping through the night. At first light, the Chinooks resumed fuel deliveries. The toughest part of the mission had passed. By 11:30 a.m. on the 25th, the stations had been operational for 24 hours, and had pumped 370,000 gallons of fuel.

All was now ready for Col. Robert Clark's 3rd Brigade to leap into the Euphrates Valley. The brigade was made up of three battalions of the 187th Infantry Regiment and its support elements. The regiment is known as the "*Rakkasans*," a Japanese term meaning "falling umbrellas from the sky." The term originated when the unit was an independent parachute regiment on occupation duty in Japan after World War II. The unit later served with distinction in the Korean War, making two combat parachute assaults. In view of its distinguished combat record, the unit was not disbanded when the Army reduced its size after the war. Eventually, it was incorporated into the 101st Airborne Division. During the Vietnam War, it figured prominently in the fighting for "Hamburger Hill." Like the rest of the division, the unit abandoned the parachute in favor of heliborne operations in 1975.

The brigade would be hauled in by 66 Blackhawks and 30 Chinooks. The plan called for the helicopters to start their first run at 11:30 on the night of the 25th. They would fly directly to their assigned landing zones from their bases in Saudi Arabia, drop off their soldiers and refuel at Cobra on the way back.

Events were having an impact on 3rd Brigade's plans, however. First, the success of XVIII Airborne Corps operations had allowed the second phase of the 101st's mission to be pushed up five hours, to 6:30 p.m. on the 25th. This would allow the brigade to go in earlier while still having the advantage of darkness. However, the weather soon robbed the brigade of that advantage. The weather forecast for the evening was worse than expected. The brigade would have to either launch early in the afternoon, before the storms came in, or wait until the next day. Col. Clark decided to take his chances on a daylight launch.

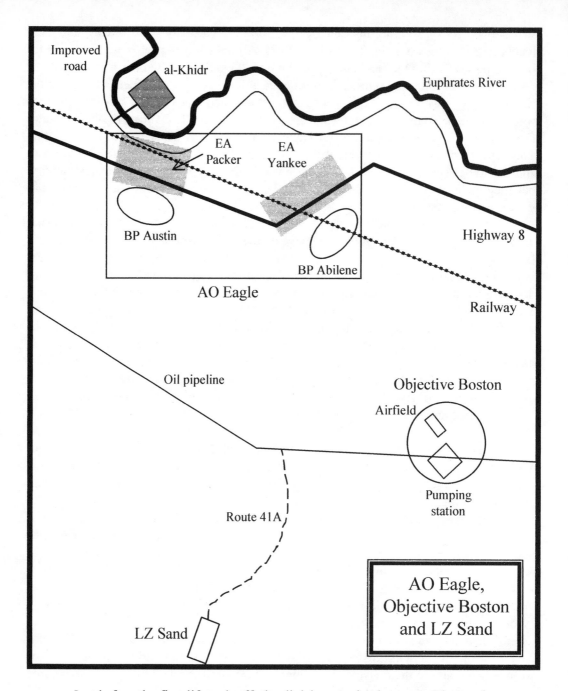

Just before the first lift took off, the division received a scare. The northernmost of the four-man LRRP teams inserted the night before G-Day had been compromised. The only one of the four original teams still in Iraq, it had been spotted by Iraqi civilians and was calling for immediate extraction. Two Blackhawks (for extraction) and two Apaches (for firepower) had been on alert for such an eventuality. The four helicopters now raced to the rescue. They whisked the LRRP team away, just as several trucks full of Iraqi soldiers were within a half-mile of the position and closing fast.

Lt.Col. Tom Greco's Task Force Rakkasan was the first to land in the Euphrates River Valley, just after noon. In the task force, Greco had two companies from his own 3-187th Infantry Battalion, one infantry and one anti-tank company. Both were mounted on Humvees. Greco had also been given the anti-tank companies of the brigade's other two battalions. The 48 TOW missile-equipped Humvees provided the task force's main combat power. The rest of the task force was made up of twelve 105mm artillery pieces and engineers equipped with four vehicles and heavy demolition material.

Because it had most of the brigade's heavy equipment, TF Rakkasan would have to be delivered by Chinooks. Unfortunately, the Chinooks did not have the fuel capacity to fly the 155 miles from TAA Campbell to Highway 8 then fly another 85 miles back to Cobra safely. As a result, Greco's task force would have to land at LZ (Landing Zone) Sand, about 25 miles to the south of the highway. It would then drive along a dirt road dubbed "Route 41A" (after the Kentucky state highway that runs past Fort Campbell) to the brigade's main positions to the north, AO (Area of Operations) Eagle.

On G-Day, Greco's Scout Platoon, under the command of Lt. Jerry Biller, had been dropped off at LZ Sand. Biller's task was to mark the landing zone for Greco's task force, ensure that it was free of Iraqi units and check the trafficability of the ground route to AO Eagle. Aerial photographs never tell the whole story, and this was no exception. The original landing zone, which had looked so inviting during the planning of the operation, was found to be a sea of mud. Several of the scouts' motorcycles became mired. With trafficability almost impossible, the scouts were forced to spend much of the night of the 24th ranging across wind-swept mudfields in near-freezing temperatures looking for a more suitable site. They finally found one, six miles to the west of the original landing zone. Biller and his men spent the remaining hours before TF Rakkasan's arrival marking the new LZ Sand.

Task Force Rakkasan began arriving on LZ Sand at 12:16 in the afternoon. TOW Humvees of D Company, 1-187th Infantry were among the first vehicles to land. As the rest of the force arrived behind them, a platoon from D Company headed north, reconnoitering Route 41A. In the process, the platoon captured 12 Iraqis and two vehicles, one of which was a tank and pump unit which would be put to use refueling the task force's vehicles as they headed north.

The force at AO Eagle would be dropped off in two lifts. The plan called for the first wave to establish an airhead on the south side of the Euphrates, near the town of al-Khidr. The Blackhawks would return to Saudi Arabia and take off again at about 2:30 on the morning of the 26th, bringing the remainder of the brigade's combat soldiers and the rest of its supplies.

Lt.Col. Kinnison's 1-187th Infantry would secure a pumping station and an airstrip on the southeastern edge of AO Eagle, while Lt.Col. Andrew Berdy's 2-187th Infantry would occupy Battle Position Abilene astride Highway 8 and set up an ambush zone, Engagement Area (EA) Yankee. To the west of Abilene, the remaining two companies of 3-187th Infantry, accompanied by four TOW Humvees, would occupy BP Austin, with an ambush zone dubbed EA Packer. This would effectively cut Highway 8. This force would be led by Greco's executive officer, Maj. Jerry Bolzak.

The airstrip and pumping station had not been an objective during the early stages of the planning for the brigade's assault. However, the brigade's operations officer, Maj. Peter Kinney, had pushed hard for its inclusion. With the brigade deep in enemy territory, possession of an airfield might be invaluable. Possession of the objective would also be valuable as a seal on another possible Iraqi escape route. With the Euphrates River running above Highway 8, there was no way that Iraqi forces heading for Baghdad could swerve northward to avoid the brigade's blocking positions on the highway. Their only option would be to pick their way along the oil pipeline to the south. Since the pipeline ran through the pumping station, a force positioned there would be in an ideal position to cut short any attempts to escape along that route. Col. Clark eventually agreed to include the objective, which was designated Objective Boston, in honor of Kinney's home city.

After a 1-hour, 15-minute flight from TAA Campbell, the first wave of Blackhawks landed at AO Eagle at 4:45 in the afternoon. Surprise was total and opposition was light. At Objective Boston, the Rakkasans found only a few soldiers who could not flee the area quickly enough. Lt.Col. Kinnison's men secured the pumping station and airfield in a matter of minutes.

To the north, the 2nd Battalion, after landing in thick mud, chased a platoon of Iraqis out of its area and set up its ambush zone. Lt.Col. Berdy's men then blew up both sides of a Highway 8 overpass, causing it to drop on the railroad tracks below, closing the highway and the railway with one blow. That night, there was a firefight in EA Yankee, resulting in several Iraqi dead and wounded, with the wounded being captured and removed to the battalion's aid station. About 40 civilian vehicles which had been commandeered by NCOs from the Republican Guard's al-Fao Division were also destroyed. The vehicles were filled with looted goods from Kuwait. Captured Iraqis said that their officers had left their units as soon as the ground war began, and that they had been heading for home as well.

As 3-187th Infantry's Blackhawks touched down, their wheels sank as Bolzak's men jumped into mud over a foot deep. Within minutes, infantrymen were slogging toward their main ambush site, a piece of terrain which paralleled and overlooked the highway. Roughly 50 meters south of the highway, possession of this high ground would give the Americans command of Highway 8. The high ground also overlooked an irrigation ditch about a hundred meters to the south, which also paralleled the highway. Since Bolzak intended to have his men take cover in this ditch, this high ground had to be taken.

Just after moving out, the infantrymen closest to the objective noticed that a platoon of Iraqi infantrymen had dismounted their trucks and were heading toward the high ground. Seconds later, the Iraqis spotted the Americans, and a dash for the key terrain ensued. PFC Charles Woody II opened fire on the Iraqis with his SAW (Squad Automatic Weapon), pinning them down while the task force's mortarmen occupied the terrain. Moments later, the Iraqis were driven off by 60mm mortar rounds.

Consolidating the position was relatively simple after that. One old man and sixteen women and children were rounded up on the position, along with their goats. Keeping the civilians and the goats out of the line of fire became an additional responsibility for MSG Donald Occhi, the task force's acting sergeant-major.

There were no American casualties and about two dozen Iraqis were killed or wounded on AO Eagle. About 40 prisoners were taken. The EPWs had not eaten in two days or been issued water in three. Food and water stocks had been maintained in the officers' bunkers. What little food there was consisted mostly of dried fruits such as figs and dates. The prisoners were given MREs (Meals, Ready to Eat). "They were so hungry they could have eaten as many as we'd given them," said one captain.

If the soldiers were hungry, the civilians were starving. The Rakkasans saw very few civilians at first. Most had been told that when the Americans came they would rape women, steal possessions and kill everyone they found. When the Bedouin found that this was untrue, they came to the brigade's perimeter and asked for food. Some soldiers gave them what they could, and let them pick over the Iraqi supply trucks they had machine-gunned, but organized food distribution was out of the question. The brigade had barely enough food for its own soldiers.

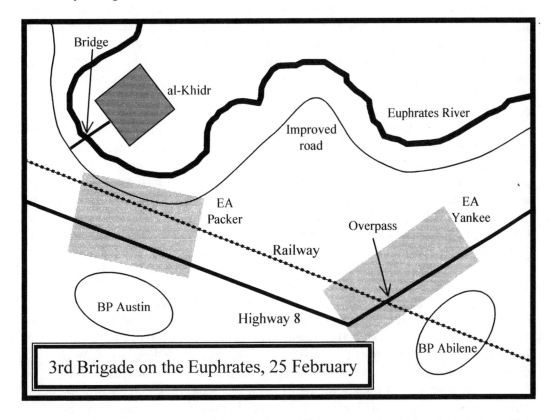

3rd Brigade on the Euphrates, 25 February

As the Rakkasans settled into their positions, a massive shamal, closed in. The landing of the second wave was put off until the sandstorm passed, but the troops in the valley were never in serious danger. The possibility that bad weather might interrupt the second wave had been taken into consideration. The first wave contained enough troops, weapons and ammunition to hold off an Iraqi counterattack for several days if necessary. Each soldier's rucksack contained 80–100 lbs. of gear. Most of that was ammunition. Sleeping bags or tents would have taken up too much room, so they were left behind.

Though prepared for possible counterattack, the troops spent a tense night on AO Eagle. Many of the brigade's units were unable to talk to each other for much of the night because of the shamal. Backpack-mounted radios were useless, as their smaller batteries would not allow them to put out a powerful enough signal to cut through the blowing sand. Vehicle mounted radios, powered by vehicle batteries, offered some, but not much, relief.

The shamal also seriously delayed the arrival at AO Eagle of Task Force Rakkasan. TF Rakkasan had already been having problems pushing its heavy weapons over Route 41A, which had become a quagmire. The shamal complicated matters. It also grounded the brigade's helicopter gunships. At a time when JSTARS was reporting some 200 radar blips moving from the west toward the perimeter (a false alarm), the infantrymen at Eagle were being told that they would be on their own for the night.

At Objective Boston, 1-187th Infantry was in a fairly safe position, far from main thoroughfares, but the soldiers posted along Highway 8 felt less secure. Of the 850 men Lt.Col. Berdy was supposed to have on BP Abilene, he had 150. The men on BP Austin found themselves unable to dig in effectively due to the muddy conditions. They also had no overhead cover. This was a source of concern to Lt.Col. Greco, still heading north along Route 41A. Greco was worried about the possibility that the Iraqis might attempt to move artillery units within range of BP Austin. He also had no way of knowing whether or not there were artillery spotters in al-Khidr. Greco sought permission from brigade headquarters to move at least one of the two companies on BP Austin from their exposed positions across the bridge over the Euphrates and into the town of al-Khidr if they received indirect fire.

Col. Clark denied the request. Artillery units do not function as independent entities. They support maneuver units. Since all of Clark's intelligence indicated that there were no Iraqi maneuver units in the immediate area, he felt that it was extremely unlikely that there would be any significant artillery threat. Even if there were artillery units in the area, nothing about the Iraqi artillery's performance thus far had made Clark fear that the Iraqis would be able to put effective artillery fire on AO Eagle. If they could, Clark reasoned, there was no point in moving troops to al-Khidr. The town's flimsy buildings would not have offered much protection. Of far more concern to Clark was a brigade of the Republican Guard's Baghdad Division. There was a possibility that the Iraqi brigade might attempt to disrupt the 187th's mission by attacking eastward down Highway 8. The false JSTARS reading heightened these concerns. If there was an attack, and 3-187th Infantry was not along the highway in sufficient force, the Iraqis might end up driving through BP Austin and into the flank of Lt.Col. Berdy's then understrength 2-187th Infantry on BP Abilene. Finally, Clark wanted to avoid unnecessarily endangering civilians by bringing combat into populated areas.

The night passed quietly though, and on the 26th, Task Force Rakkasan began arriving at AO Eagle in small groups over several hours. By early afternoon, all of TF Rakkasan had reached AO Eagle. No sooner were the forces consolidated than the brigade was presented with a problem. A Cobra had been hit by small arms fire and had gone down just outside al-Khidr. Now at AO Eagle, Lt.Col. Greco pointed out that he always kept one platoon on 15-minute alert, and that if he could get a helicopter, he could ferry this rapid response team into the town to secure the area. Using the only helicopter available, a command Huey, the platoon moved to the crash site and surrounded the downed helicopter until a Chinook arrived to take the Cobra and its crew back to FOB Cobra.

The weather cleared and the residents of Eagle were joined that night by the second lift of Blackhawks, bearing the rest of the brigade's men and equipment. The door was now essentially closed on one of the Guard's most important escape routes. The force on AO Eagle had enough men and anti-tank weapons to hold their positions against Republican Guard armor. An encounter with the Republican Guard was unlikely, however. The 24th Infantry Division was already on its way to cut Highway 8 to the east of the Rakkasans. For the Iraqi forces trapped by the longest airborne insertion in military history, the end was not far off.

16

The Big Sweep: The 24th Infantry Division and 3rd ACR

Maj.Gen. Barry McCaffrey's 24th Infantry Division (Mechanized) was the XVIII Airborne Corps' only heavy unit.[*] It would hit Highway 8 to the east of the 101st Airborne Division, drive eastward, and destroy whatever Iraqi units were between the division and Basra. The division's mission would require it to move farther than any other Coalition unit, 230 miles, and speed would be of the essence.

McCaffrey had a reputation for taking the initiative. During the initial buildup in August, he had sent his 2nd Brigade to the port at Savannah fully loaded with fuel and ammunition before he had even received orders to do so. With only one paratroop brigade in Saudi Arabia, McCaffrey had simply assumed that heavy armor would be needed, orders would come eventually, and that there was therefore no point in waiting.

Col. Ted Reid's 197th Mechanized Infantry Brigade from Fort Benning, Georgia had been added to the 24th ID during the Desert Shield deployment. The 24th ID had only two brigades of regulars. The 48th Georgia National Guard Brigade was supposed to join the division as its third brigade in the event of hostilities. However, that brigade was deemed not ready for combat operations, and the 197th, a regular unit, got the call. One of the lesser-known units in the war, the 197th would be referred to erroneously as "a school brigade from Fort Benning" by a national news magazine.[†]

On G-Day, the division's main body would enter Iraq with three brigades abreast. The 197th would be on the left flank. Col. Paul Kern's 2nd Brigade would be on the right flank. In the center, slightly behind the other two brigades, would be Col. John LeMoyne's 1st Brigade. Shortly after entering Iraq, 1st Brigade would fall behind 2nd Brigade, and the division would head northward in two prongs.

---

[*]A veteran of the Vietnam War, McCaffrey had been awarded two Distinguished Service Crosses, two Silver Stars and three Purple Hearts.

[†]The brigade's solid performance led to its permanent incorporation into the division as its third brigade after the war.

Actually, part of the division was already in Iraq on G-Day. The 2nd Squadron of the 4th Cavalry Regiment (2-4th Cavalry), commanded by Lt.Col. Tom Leney, was reconnoitering in front of the division's 1st and 2nd brigades. Lt.Col. Bill Chamberlain's Task Force 1-18 was patrolling the area to the front of its parent 197th Brigade.

In the U.S. Army, a squadron is a battalion-sized unit of cavalry, and generally consists of 5–600 men. A divisional cavalry squadron usually has four troops (cavalry companies), two ground and two air (helicopters). Lt.Col. Leney's squadron, however, had only one organic ground troop with 19 Bradleys. The other ground troop was supposed to be provided by the 48th Georgia National Guard Brigade upon mobilization. Instead, it was provided by the 197th, which, as an independent brigade, had its own ground troop with 12 M-1A1s and 9 M-113-mounted TOW launchers.* The squadron was bulked up significantly for the war. With the attachment of a tank company from the 24th ID's 2nd Brigade, additional engineer, intelligence, chemical warfare, anti-tank and artillery assets, Leney's command was around 1,000 men strong.

In the days before the ground war, the 2-4th Cavalry used laser-guided Copperhead artillery rounds to destroy Iraqi border observation posts and chased several Iraqi patrols away from American lines. On the 23rd, the squadron drove almost 40 miles into Iraq, doing a thorough reconnaissance of the area that 1st and 2nd brigades would be covering on the following day. Upon completion of the reconnaissance, the squadron returned to positions six miles north of the Saudi border.

Though not a cavalry unit, for most of the ground war TF 1-18 would be the 197th Brigade's lead unit. Since the 197th Brigade had given its cavalry troop to 2-4th Cavalry, the task force would also perform cavalry duties for the brigade. The 1-18th Infantry Battalion normally had four infantry companies riding in M-113A2 armored personnel carriers. It also had an anti-tank company equipped with I-TOWs. Before the ground war, the battalion received a company of tanks from the brigade's 2-69th Armor Battalion. A company of combat engineers was also assigned to TF 1-18.

Both commanders had expected to refuel and give their men a few hours rest before resuming operations on 25 February. However, the success of the Marine assault, combined with alarming reports from Kuwait City, prompted Gen. Schwarzkopf to push the kickoff time ahead by almost a full day. The units hurriedly refueled and were joined by the division's main body on the 24th.

The main body's crossing into Iraq proceeded according to plan through the morning and early afternoon. The 2-4th Cavalry, traveling 4–6 hours ahead of the 1st and 2nd brigades during the drive into Iraq on G-Day, provided a screen for the brigades. Leney's scouts also provided guideposts for the brigade to follow. Traveling across largely featureless terrain, the brigades were able to guide on the tall poles with hanging chem-lights emplaced by the cavalrymen. Behind the brigades, engineers set up high metal poles with suspended blinking amber lights to mark three lanes at the border, to guide each brigade's logistics units after nightfall. In mid-afternoon, movement slowed dramatically as a blinding sandstorm closed in. Vehicles had to move slowly to avoid losing contact with vehicles to their front and rear. The division nevertheless progressed well ahead of schedule, due to lack of Iraqi opposition.

In fact, the division was moving so fast that it was pulling away from the 3rd Armored Cavalry Regiment, which was guarding its right flank. At around 1:00 a.m.,

---

*Ground troops belonging to independent brigades have tanks. Those belonging to divisional cavalry squadrons do not.

Lt.Col. Ray Barrett, commander of the 2nd Brigade's TF 3-15, the division's right flank unit, received a radio call from Lt.Col. Edward O'Shaughnessy, commander of the 3rd ACR's 2nd Squadron, the unit on Barrett's flank. O'Shaughnessy asked him to slow down. Barrett told him that slowing down was out of the question. He would have to maintain his speed in order to get into position to attack his first objective on schedule. If an Iraqi unit was lucky enough to find his flank, he would leave a unit behind to engage it while O'Shaughnessy's squadron came up from the south. No such contact occurred.*

The division's first two objectives, Brown and Gray, were situated on the two ends of a major Iraqi supply road that ran from As Salman in the west to al-Busayyah in the east. As Salman was a French objective on 24th ID's left flank and al-Busayyah was a 1st Armored Division objective on the division's right flank. Maj.Gen. McCaffrey did not want the Iraqis using the road to launch counterattacks across his rear against either of the objectives. He would forestall that possibility by shutting down the road from both ends before the Daguet and 1st Armored divisions attacked those towns.

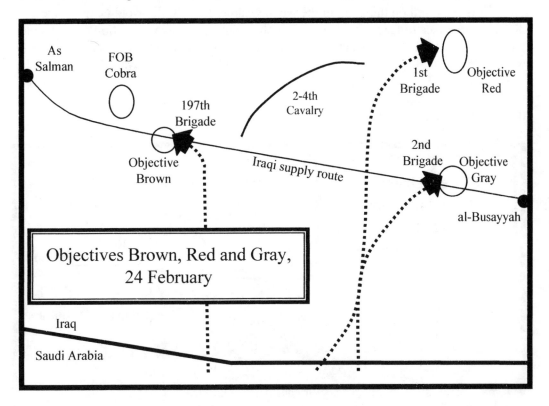

Objectives Brown, Red and Gray,
24 February

At 3:00 a.m. on the 25th, the 197th reached Objective Brown, an Iraqi logistics complex. After an air strike overshot its target to the north, Task Force 1-18 swept its portion of the objective, collecting 49 prisoners and 20 maintenance and electronics vehicles. To TF 1-18's left rear was Lt.Col. Eric Olson's 2-18th Infantry Battalion, which had received a company of tanks from the 2-69th Armor Battalion in return for one of its four infantry companies before G-Day. In its part of the objective, TF 2-18

---

*The 3-15th Infantry Battalion had given 1-64th Armor, one of 2nd Brigade's two tank battalions, an infantry company in return for a company of tanks.

netted three officers and eight men from an early warning air defense unit. By 6:16 a.m., the objective was secure.

While the 197th was sweeping across its first objective, the 2nd Brigade was trying to negotiate a steep escarpment. It took the brigade slightly over three hours to negotiate the escarpment. By 4 p.m., the brigade had taken Objective Gray, an Iraqi electronic intelligence station. After sustaining an intense artillery barrage, its dazed occupants staggered toward their attackers with their hands up. Almost 300 prisoners were rounded up. This surprised the Americans, since a station of this size is usually garrisoned by no more than a few dozen troops. They soon realized that most of their prisoners were soldiers heading northward from units which were disintegrating.

As 2nd Brigade was attacking Objective Gray, 1st Brigade, which had been trailing it, went around the brigade's left flank and took Objective Red, a piece of high ground to the north that commanded the approaches to the Euphrates River Valley. There were no Iraqi soldiers on the position, only startled Bedouin. The Americans secured the position by 9:30 p.m. and moved on.

As night fell on the 25th, in the worst weather the 24th ID would experience, the division came face to face with its toughest challenge, a massive collection of wadis and swamps. Stretching across much of the division's line of attack, this natural obstacle would come to be known as the "Great Dismal Bog." The 2-4th Cavalry had to pick its way through the bog and create a screen line so that when the brigade turned east, its left flank would be secure. After temporarily stranding several vehicles, the scouts took up their flank guard positions.

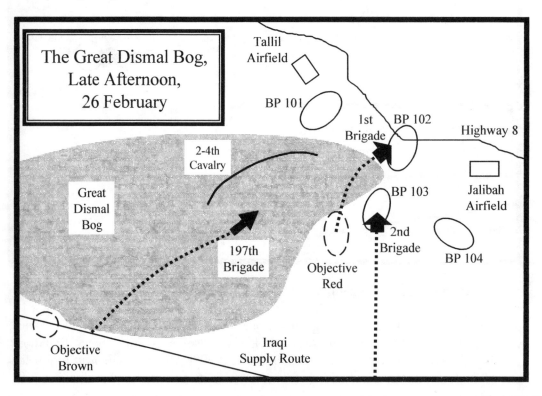

To the west, the 197th was also having problems. After securing Objective Brown, the brigade split. Task Force 1-18 pushed east to clear the Iraqi supply route. Task forces 2-18 and 2-69 continued their drive to the north. Around 11 p.m., TF 1-18

ran into a wadi just to the north of the supply road. The wadi was not on the task force's maps, and was roughly 200 feet deep with extremely steep sides. This was only the beginning. The climbs and drops in the Great Dismal Bog would be many and steep, and the narrow tracks through it long and winding. After the war, Lt.Col. Chamberlain would find that while the straight-line distance his unit had covered was 230 miles, vehicle odometers would show that the task force had actually covered about 350 miles.

After a short delay, the Scout Platoon, under Lt. Larry Aikman, Jr., was able to find a safe path down the near side of the wadi, and another up the far side. Chamberlain moved most of his unit down the path, leaving behind his executive officer, Maj. Dan Bourgoine, to coordinate the movement of the wheeled vehicles that followed. With Bourgoine was a company of APCs to provide security for the wheeled vehicles and pull out any which became stuck.

At 2 a.m., after determining that the terrain in front of them was impassable, Col. Reid decided to send his other two task forces to the east, to follow TF 1-18 through the wadi. TF 1-18's rear detachment would provide guides to the other task forces. Chamberlain, ordered to halt and wait for the rest of the brigade, posted security as his men got their first real sleep in two days.

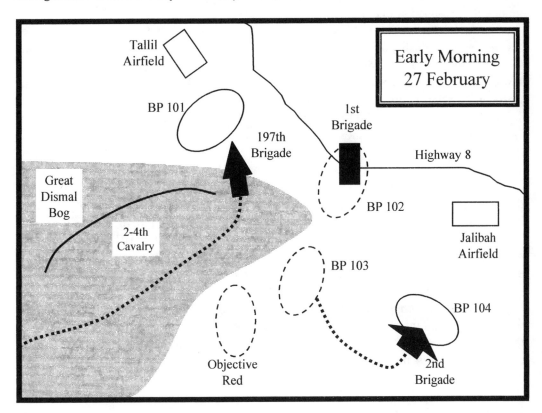

The 1st Brigade also spent several hours picking its way through the Great Dismal Bog. At about 3 p.m. on the 26th, the brigade reached Battle Position 102 on Highway 8. BP 102 was a major logistics site defended by roughly half of a special forces brigade from the Republican Guard. The Guardsmen had been joined by infantry, a few dug-in T-55s and a few towed anti-tank guns from the 47th and 49th divisions.

The attack on BP 102 began with a half-hour artillery bombardment. As Lt.Col. John Craddock, commander of TF 4-64, led his two tank and two infantry companies across the objective, a round from a 73mm SPG-9 recoilless anti-tank weapon exploded on the front of his turret as another hit the armor over his rear fuel tanks. Craddock's Abrams barely slowed down.* Iraqi resistance was spirited but pointless. TF 4-64 destroyed 20 guns as well as 175 trucks, and took over 300 prisoners.

Meanwhile, Lt.Col David Jensen's TF 3-7 and Lt.Col. Charles Ware's TF 2-7 were also facing determined resistance. Each had received a tank company from 4-64th Armor in return for an infantry company, and the tanks of both task forces were instrumental in smashing Iraqi resistance. The two task forces were able to slice through the Iraqi positions and into the Iraqi rear, laying waste a large column of trucks carrying artillery ammunition as night fell. By 7 p.m., 1st Brigade controlled Highway 8.

The brigade overcame stiff resistance from the commandos, who were dug-in and reinforced by air defense and support troops. During the fight, the brigade also had to contend with hundreds of rounds of artillery from about six Iraqi artillery battalions in the area. The heaviest Iraqi shelling lasted from 2 p.m., when the brigade was approaching BP 102, to about 5 p.m. Each time an Iraqi battery, or even gun, fired, it was spotted by Q-36 radars.† A battalion-sized counterbattery barrage followed.‡ As gun losses in the Iraqi battalions mounted, shelling dropped off sharply, and just before midnight, it stopped altogether.

At 1:10 a.m., Col. LeMoyne reported that his brigade controlled BP 102. He then set up hasty ambush positions across the highway to intercept Iraqi convoys fleeing toward Baghdad. Throughout the night, about 40 vehicles, mostly military trucks, with a few civilian cars and one tank on a transporter, would be destroyed here. Meanwhile, the prisoner roundup continued. Ultimately, the brigade's bag of prisoners would exceed 1,200. The next day, after the brigade moved eastward, the 82nd Airborne Division's 3rd Brigade would round up another 400 prisoners.

In the west, task forces 2-18 and 2-69 had linked up with TF 1-18 at about 8 a.m. on the morning of the 26th. The 197th had moved out shortly thereafter, with TF 1-18 in the lead. Throughout the day, it had slowly worked its way through the bog, through heavy rain, a sandstorm, 50 mph winds and sand dunes over 100 feet high.

At about 2:30 a.m. on the 27th, as it neared Battle Position 101, TF 1-18's scout platoon rounded a berm and found itself in the midst of a substantial Iraqi force. In the ensuing firefight, fought at ranges as close as ten feet, six Iraqis were killed and two scouts were wounded. With the berm behind them, Aikman's platoon was unable to fall back. It could only continue to fight while the two lead companies of the task force, one tank and one infantry, sprinted forward over the approximately two miles between themselves and the scouts. Within a few minutes, the tanks and APCs had arrived and extracted the scouts under intense Iraqi fire.

------

*For his actions during this fight, Craddock would receive the Silver Star.

†The Q-36 is an older system than the Q-37. It is smaller than the Q-37, which is roughly the size of a tractor-trailer rig. Because of its immense size, the Q-37 does not travel particularly well over rough terrain. The Q-36, though not as sophisticated as the Q-37, is nevertheless effective. Leaders will therefore rely on the Q-36 when faced with terrain like that encountered by the 24th ID.

‡When a single gun fires, it is usually ranging for a larger group of guns. Spotters adjust the fire based upon where the round lands. So, when a battalion fires a counterbattery strike against a single gun it will generally claim at least a battery.

The engagement continued. As there were no Iraqi vehicles to fire their main guns at, American tank crews had to content themselves with raking Iraqi positions with coaxial and heavy machine-gun fire. The infantry company joined in with its Mk-19 automatic grenade launchers. Maj.Gen. McCaffrey had obtained large numbers of these potent weapons for his division. Lt.Col. Chamberlain had received 54, and had assigned 13 to each of his four infantry companies, to be mounted on M-113s, keeping one for his command group and another in reserve for whatever needs might arise. Throughout the night, the Iraqis would be pelted with roughly 2,000 grenades. As the grenades were lobbed over hills and into trenches and gun pits, Iraqi soldiers found it difficult to hide from them. Of the 381 Iraqis wounded by TF 1-18 during the war, well over half were wounded by fragments from Mk-19-launched grenades.

The Iraqis responded with flat trajectory fire from over 50 anti-aircraft guns. For 30 minutes, thousands of anti-aircraft rounds flew harmlessly over the task force's armored vehicles. Hours later, when the area was secured, Chamberlain would discover that the Iraqis had dug their guns in so deep that they could not depress their guns enough to get a straight shot at his vehicles.

As the rounds streaked overhead, Capt. Eric Grassman, the commander of Chamberlain's attached tank company, reported that his tanks were down to their last 30 minutes of fuel. This was a significant problem. There were no auxiliary power systems on the tanks, so when the engine was shut off, night vision was lost. At their present rate of fuel consumption, in a half-hour the task force's tank complement would become virtually useless, not only immobile, but blind.

Lt.Col. Chamberlain examined his options. He had been told that he was facing eight Iraqi battalions. Knowing that his tanks were unavailable for sustained combat, and that at close range, even an assault rifle can penetrate an M-113A2, he decided that his task force was in no position to clear out the Iraqi defenders by overrunning them. Artillery was unavailable, because the self-propelled guns were still working their way through the Great Dismal Bog. There was also no question at that point of bringing TF 2-18 forward to deal with the Iraqis. Though there were elements of Lt.Col. Olson's task force to TF 1-18's left rear, most of TF 2-18 was still back in the Great Dismal Bog. Chamberlain realized that he would have to live with the fact that there were Iraqis in front of his unit until the tactical situation improved enough for him to do something about them. He also realized that unless steps were taken immediately to preserve the Abrams' fuel, the Iraqis would outlast his tanks.

Chamberlain ordered Grassman to shut down three-fourths of his tanks immediately, leaving only one tank at a time running in each platoon. Far better, he reasoned, to have 25% of his tanks keeping an eye on the Iraqis for the next two hours than to have all of his tanks observe the Iraqis for a half-hour, then go blind until daybreak. He also ordered his units to observe and report enemy movements, but not fire on the Iraqis unless they fired first.

Meanwhile, the lead elements of TF 2-18 were up against roughly 300 dismounted Republican Guardsmen. A barrage of 155mm DPICM was called in on the Iraqis. Bomblets cascaded onto the position, killing and wounding Guardsmen and destroying trucks. A second strike followed, and the Iraqi position became a lake of exploding mud. When the explosions stopped, forty-nine enemy soldiers lay dead, with another seven wounded. Fifteen trucks were burning. Fifty-six Guardsmen surrendered. The remainder fled into the desert.

Back in TF 1-18's sector, the fighting had subsided. Lt.Col. Chamberlain was beginning to feel much better about his situation. Though he was unsure why, the Iraqis did not seem to be preparing any major attacks. There were also no reports of Iraqi armor. Still, he felt he needed a clearer picture of what was in front of him. Aikman and his scouts were sent forward again.

The scouts reached Highway 8 without meeting any opposition, but shortly after crossing the highway, they were surrounded by dismounted Iraqis who opened fire. Chamberlain ordered the scouts to break out and return to the main body. This they did, without loss, though they were engaged in a running firefight with the Iraqis all the way back to the main body.* The breakout was aided by soldiers in 1st Brigade's combat trains. Seeing the firefight, they oriented their few machine-guns to the northwest and opened fire on the Iraqis.

While Aikman and his men were fighting their way back to their lines, Lt.Col. Ricardo Sanchez's TF 2-69 made contact with TF 1-18. TF 2-69 would have to be conducted through TF 1-18's lines. A tricky enough operation under perfect conditions, when attempted at night without prior rehearsal, a forward passage of lines can easily result in chaos. Fortunately, the Iraqis made no attempt to interfere with this delicate operation, which went smoothly. By dawn, TF 2-69 had completed the passage and was consolidating its positions.

As the sun rose, TF 1-18's tanks were still waiting for their fuel, so Lt.Col. Chamberlain ordered his four infantry companies to clear the Iraqi positions to the front. They encountered no Iraqi resistance, and soon found an explanation for the Iraqis' lack of aggressiveness during the previous hours. Dismounted troops came upon a wounded brigadier general surrounded by dead and wounded members of his staff. During the machine-gun saturation of Iraqi positions by the tanks and APCs sent to extract Aikman's scouts during the battle's first minutes, a burst of 7.62mm co-axial fire had found the brigade command post, killed several staff officers and left the unit leaderless.

As the infantrymen were rounding up prisoners, an Iraqi anti-tank company of 6 officers and 103 men walked forward and surrendered to Chamberlain's anti-tank company. This had been another bit of good fortune. The Iraqis had been equipped with AT-5 "Spandrel" anti-tank missiles. The AT-5 has a reasonably good night sight, a range of 3,500 meters, and can easily destroy an M-113. These had been posted only 1,000 meters off TF 1-18's left flank. Task Force 2-69 had been even closer, coming within 500 meters as it passed through Chamberlain's task force. The commander of the company had not fired because he mistakenly believed that these units were Iraqi. At first light he realized his mistake, but saw the full extent of the American forces in front of him and surrendered immediately.

At 2:30 a.m. on the 27th, as TF 1-18 was approaching BP 101, the 3rd Armored Cavalry Regiment was approaching a small airfield complex northeast of al-Busayyah. The attack on the complex would take about a half-hour and would result in a friendly fire incident.

Part of the complex straddled the boundary between XVIII Airborne and VII corps. When planning the attack on the airfield, 3rd ACR had requested permission for some of its units to cross the boundary but permission had been denied by 1st Armored Division, the VII Corps' northernmost unit. To have granted the request would have

---

*For his actions during these engagements, Aikman would receive the Silver Star.

required the 1st AD to do a certain amount of coordinating to keep 3rd ACR from accidentally taking its supply vehicles under fire. At that point, the division was approaching the Republican Guard. Most members of the division staff felt that once contact was made, the 1st AD would be fighting more or less continuously for almost 24 hours. Under the circumstances, it made little sense in their view to divert staff officers, or even staff attention, to coordinate an attack on an area that the 1st AD staff knew (because the division had passed the area hours earlier) contained few, if any, Iraqis.

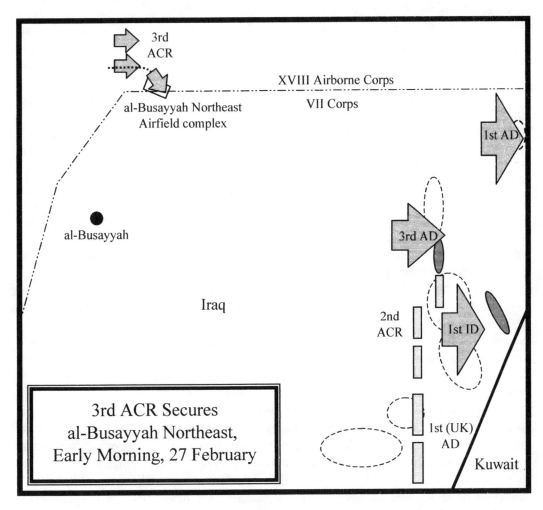

3rd ACR

XVIII Airborne Corps

VII Corps

al-Busayyah Northeast Airfield complex

1st AD

3rd AD

al-Busayyah

Iraq

2nd ACR

1st ID

3rd ACR Secures
al-Busayyah Northeast,
Early Morning, 27 February

1st (UK) AD

Kuwait

At 9 p.m. on 26 February, the regiment began moving slowly eastward toward al-Busayyah Airfield, with 2nd (north) and 1st (south) squadrons on line and 3rd Squadron following 1st Squadron.

An hour later, Col. Douglas Starr, commander of the 3rd ACR, was informed that a second request to cross the boundary had been denied by 1st AD. Based upon this denial, Starr canceled all artillery missions near the 50 Northing east–west grid line, the corps boundary. There would be a 10-minute artillery barrage on the airfield only, commencing at 1 a.m. on the 27th.

Starr and his staff ultimately accepted 1st AD's assessment of the situation, especially after the pilot of a reconnaissance helicopter reported at 1:15, five minutes after the end of the barrage, that he had detected no Iraqis on the airfield. With virtually no possibility of serious resistance, Starr and his staff viewed the coming mission as essentially a training mission under combat conditions. The attack was therefore structured more to optimize training value than to apply combat power efficiently. Instead of having 1st Squadron turn to the south and take the objective, the squadron would stop and allow Lt.Col. John Daly's 3rd Squadron to pass through to take it. This maneuver would almost certainly not have been attempted if strong Iraqi resistance had been expected. If attempted in the face of determined enemy resistance it would have resulted in confusion and loss of momentum, and left both squadrons vulnerable to counterattack while the passage was being conducted. Col. Starr would say later that one reason for the passage of lines was to give Lt.Col. Daly the experience of leading a regimental attack, because up to that point, 3rd Squadron had performed reserve functions.

None of this was clear to Starr's squadron commanders though, and there would be problems as a result. The operations plan had been unclear. It had described enemy resistance as "stiffening," with mines, fighting positions and local counterattacks a possibility. Squadron commanders were also advised that battalion-sized Iraqi units were located "at the airfield." However, the intelligence had pertained to the regiment's mission as a whole, which involved the capture of this airfield, then another well to the northeast. "Stiffening" resistance actually referred to a belief that as the regiment advanced toward the second airfield, Iraqi resistance would get progressively tougher, mines and fighting positions would be more common and local counterattacks would be more likely. The battalion-sized units were expected at the second airfield, not the one 3rd Squadron was preparing to attack.

The regiment had also been told repeatedly by 1st AD that there would be American logistics and support personnel on or near the airfield. This information, and the fact that the boundary change had been denied, had not been passed on to the squadrons. At 1:18 a.m., three minutes after the scout helicopter crew reported that it could see no Iraqis on the airfield, the 3rd ACR's Tactical Operations Center (TOC) advised 1st Squadron to fire eastward only if fired upon, and 3rd Squadron not to fire across 50 Northing. The reasons for the order were not given.

As there had been communications problems between 3rd ACR and the squadrons, there were communications problems between 3rd Squadron and its subordinate units. The attack plan called for the squadron to continue eastward about 800 meters after passing through 1st Squadron before turning to make its attack. The original plan called for the squadron to pivot, then attack due south. When the squadron's direction of attack was changed from due south to southeast, only M Company (the squadron's tank company) and K Troop got the word.[*] As a result, I and L troops drove due south, while M Company and K Troop headed to the southeast.

The al-Busayyah Northeast complex consisted of the airfield itself and a fenced-in area about two kilometers to the southwest, which contained the control tower and a helicopter pad. There was a hard-packed dirt road running from the airfield to the tower-helipad compound. Another road ran through the compound from the northwest to the southeast. This road had been a source of concern to 3rd ACR planners, and had been a

---

[*]Armored cavalry regiments have three ground squadrons and one air squadron. Unlike divisional cavalry squadrons, which have two ground and two air troops, ground squadrons in ACRs have four ground troops and no helicopter assets. All helicopters are assigned to the air squadron. In addition, ACR ground squadrons have tanks, while divisional cavalry squadrons do not.

major reason they had requested permission to cross the corps boundary. They saw a possibility that Iraqi units might drive along the road to reinforce the complex. The staff of 1st AD had discounted this possibility, because the division had already cleared the area south of the complex.

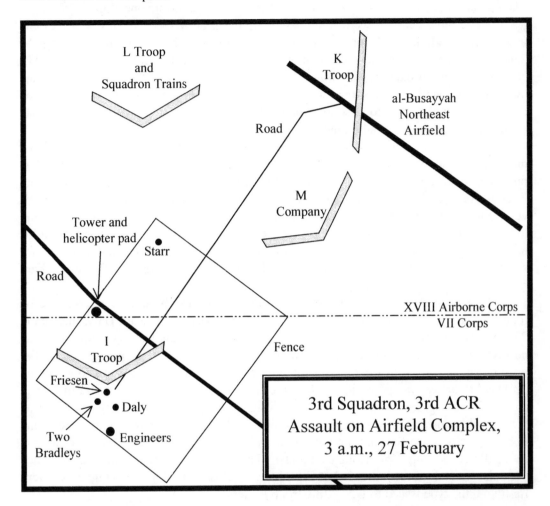

L Troop
and
Squadron Trains

K
Troop

al-Busayyah
Northeast
Airfield

Road

M
Company

Tower and
helicopter pad

Starr

Road

XVIII Airborne Corps
VII Corps

I
Troop

Fence

Friesen

Daly

Two
Bradleys

Engineers

3rd Squadron, 3rd ACR
Assault on Airfield Complex,
3 a.m., 27 February

At about 2:30, I Troop, which had been told to expect Iraqi resistance, arrived at the tower-helipad compound. Capt. Bo Friesen, I Troop's commander, was given permission by Lt.Col. Daly to breach the fence. The troop passed through the breach, crossed the helicopter pad and fanned out into a wedge formation. Though they did not realize it at the time, the men of I Troop were in VII Corps' zone shortly after they passed through the fence.

A few minutes before three, Friesen reported two human thermal signatures moving around what appeared to be buildings. Daly relayed this information to Starr, and added that he had spotted an M-548 (a tracked cargo carrier). Starr's gunner looked at the target area through his thermal sight and told Starr that he saw a Humvee and an M-548. Both were American-made vehicles, but Daly thought that the vehicles had been bought from the United States by Iraq when the two countries were on friendly terms. Starr told Daly to develop the situation, try to get the dismounts to surrender, and secure the M-548 for later destruction. Starr also ordered Daly twice to confirm that the target was Iraqi before firing.

Friesen ordered two of his Bradleys to positions roughly 250 meters from the suspected Iraqi position. He then requested permission from Daly to fire warning shots. A few seconds after the warning shots were fired, Friesen's driver and gunner reported return fire.* Friesen ordered the two Bradleys and his gunner to open fire on the target. The fusillade of 25mm rounds hit two of the three vehicles, setting one alight.

The three vehicles were American: a Humvee, an M-548 full of explosives and now on fire, and an excavator, in which a sleeping soldier had been hit in the legs by 25mm fire. The vehicles were from an engineer unit of the 1st Armored Division. The cargo carrier had broken down while following the division, and the three vehicles and their five occupants were waiting for a recovery vehicle. With no idea who was firing on them, the engineers tried to raise their parent battalion on the radio, but the 1st AD had by then advanced beyond radio range.

Lt.Col. Daly arrived with a psyops team, which broadcast a taped surrender message in Arabic. There was almost another friendly fire incident at that point. Daly pulled up to the left front of Friesen's vehicle without attempting to coordinate with Friesen. As a result, one of Friesen's tank gunners was preparing to open fire on Daly's vehicle when the gunner's platoon sergeant realized what the target was and ordered him to hold his fire. Actually, Daly could not have reached Friesen if he had tried. With his hands full controlling his own troop, Friesen felt that Daly's constant requests for situation reports had been adding to the confusion, so he had turned off the auxiliary radio which had been tuned to Daly's frequency.

By now, the engineers were moving away from the burning cargo vehicle on foot. Friesen's executive officer, who was monitoring Daly's net, heard Daly, then about 200 meters from the engineers, order I Troop to stop the Iraqis from escaping. Hearing no response from I Troop, the gunner of Daly's Bradley asked for permission to fire warning shots in front of the group. Daly denied the first request, but granted a second. As Daly's gunner was preparing to pull the trigger, Lt. Kevin Wessels, the officer in charge of the engineers, shot a green star cluster in hopes that the Americans firing on them would realize their mistake and cease firing. The star cluster was spotted, resulting in a temporary cease-fire, but not until after Daly's gunner had fired a burst of 7.62mm co-axial fire, killing Cpl. Douglas Fielder. The cease-fire became permanent when Wessels walked toward the 3rd ACR Humvee closest to him, waving a red lens flashlight, the type issued to U.S. Army troop leaders.

VII Corps later pressed for, and got, a Government Accounting Office investigation. This action might not have bothered VII Corps and 1st Armored Division leaders as much if the suspect vehicles had been combat vehicles, but this was not the case here. Neither the vehicle commanders nor their gunners could tell with absolute certainty by their thermal sight pictures exactly what kind of vehicles were in front of them, but at 200–450 meters, they could tell that they were not tanks or infantry fighting vehicles. In addition, whatever doubt there might have been about whether or not the dismounts were a threat should have been removed when they began walking away from their vehicles (one of them burning) on foot.

The GAO investigation found that Col. Starr's failure to communicate vital information to his subordinates contributed to the friendly fire incident. It also found that Daly's failure to communicate vital information to his subordinates was another

---

*There was no fire directed at Friesen's Bradley during the engagement.

contributing factor. In addition, it found that both Daly and Friesen had disobeyed Starr's orders by not determining that the suspect figures were Iraqi before they opened fire.

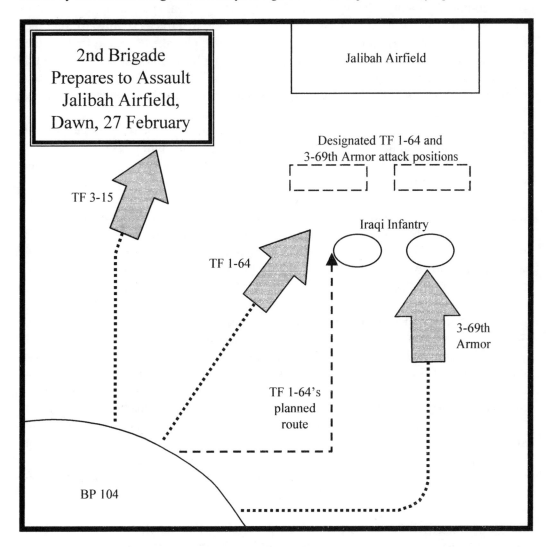

A few hours after al-Busayyah Northeast was secured, 2nd Brigade, 24th ID stormed Jalibah Airfield. While 1st Brigade had been clearing BP 102, 2nd Brigade had occupied BP 103, a position southwest of Jalibah Airfield. Just after midnight on 27 February, the brigade had seized BP 104, several miles closer to the airfield. The two brigades then waited until dawn, when 2nd Brigade would launch its attack.

The attack plan was simple. Lt.Col. Randy Gordon's TF 1-64 and Lt.Col. Terry Stanger's 3-69th Armor Battalion (minus one company which had been assigned to 2-4th Cavalry) would take positions south of the airfield. Once the Iraqis were convinced that they were being attacked from the south, Lt.Col. Barrett's TF 3-15 would overrun the airfield from west to east. Keeping Iraqi units to the north away from the airfield would be 1st Brigade's responsibility. There had been reports (erroneous, as it turned out) of a Republican Guard tank battalion to the north of the airfield.

Though the plan was simple, bringing it off proved to be difficult. As Barrett's task force began moving toward its attack position, his M-1A1s were down to their last quarter-tank of fuel, and there was nothing to refuel with. In the early hours of the 26th, the tanks had refueled for the third time since G-Day, and had left the task force's 11 fuel trucks completely empty. Having outrun the support battalion, and unable to reach it by radio, Barrett had instructed Lt. Clark Barnes to take the fuel trucks southward, find fuel, then return to the unit. Barrett had no idea how long it would take Barnes to find the fuel, or exactly where the task force would be when he came back. Barnes was therefore told that he would probably just have to head north until he hit Highway 8, then head eastward until he found the task force. Barnes and the fuel trucks rejoined the unit just before it reached its positions overlooking Jalibah Airfield.

Barrett would attack with all four of his companies on line. Since the only possible Iraqi armored threat was in the north, and most of the buildings on Jalibah were on the southern half of the airfield, Barrett put most of his tanks on his northern flank and his infantry on the southern flank.

To the east, as the brigade's other two maneuver units moved toward their positions, there were unexpected difficulties which resulted in a friendly fire incident. Lt.Col. Stanger's battalion had experienced no problems in maneuvering toward its position on the right flank. It had, however, run into Iraqi infantry positions well before it was supposed to. As a result, 3-69th Armor's tanks were engaged in a firefight before they had even reached their assigned positions for the attack on the airfield.

TF 1-64, on the other hand, had experienced difficulties in navigating toward its assigned position. These difficulties had cost precious time. In an attempt to gain back some of that time, the task force took a short-cut, heading northeast instead of due east, then due north as had been planned. As it neared its assigned position, the task force was therefore not on 3-69th Armor's left flank, but northwest of it. TF 1-64 had also cut behind an Iraqi infantry position, which was then under fire from 3-69th Armor. To Stanger's gunners, Bradleys from TF 1-64's right flank unit, an attached company from 3-15th Infantry, appeared to be Iraqi APCs supporting the infantrymen they were firing at. At 3,500 meters, it was difficult to distinguish one type of APC from another, but since they had no reason to expect American units to be in that area, the tanks engaged the vehicles. Three Bradleys were hit by main gun rounds. Two crewmen, Spec. Andy Alaniz and PFC John Hutto, were killed and eight others were wounded.

At exactly 5:00 in the morning, a devastating five-battalion, 45-minute rocket and artillery barrage rolled onto Jalibah Airfield and its defenders. The barrage destroyed eight tanks. Believing that they were under air attack, the Iraqis turned their anti-aircraft guns toward the sky and began firing. Just before six, the Iraqis were engaged from the south. As soon as TF 1-64 and 3-69th Armor had the Iraqis' attention, TF 3-15 struck.

The Iraqi battalion was clearly unprepared. The two dozen Iraqi T-55s and 13 other armored vehicles offered what resistance they could, but were soon overwhelmed. When the 2nd Brigade's gunners were finished with the Iraqi armor, they destroyed ten MiG jet fighters and six helicopters.

By 10:00, it was all over. In addition to the tanks and aircraft they had destroyed, the brigade had taken 80 anti-aircraft guns and over 600 prisoners. Over a hundred Iraqis had not been so lucky. Most had been killed by the artillery barrage. Some had sought shelter in bunkers, and had been killed when high explosive rounds from the tanks tore the bunkers apart. After the fighting was over, the brigade's engineer detachment located a supply of fuel-air bombs stockpiled by the Iraqis. Scouts found the airfield commander hiding in his bunker.

By noon, the 2nd Brigade had finished up at Jalibah Airfield, regrouped, and headed east at full speed. The brigade became the southern prong of the division's attack toward Basra. To the north, 1st Brigade had already begun moving down Highway 8, destroying small units of the al-Fao Division as it found them.

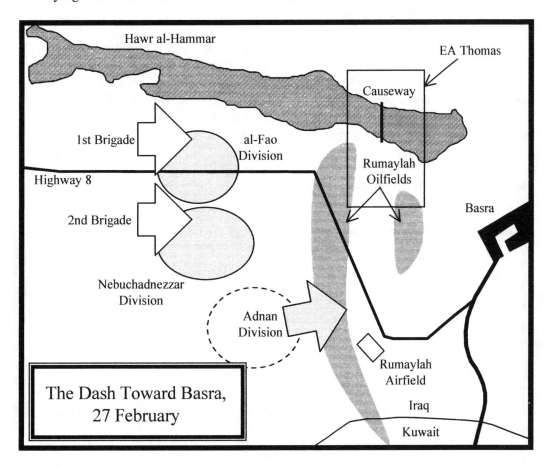

The attack zone ran through one of the world's largest military storage facilities. Built during the war with Iran, the site measured about 50 miles from north to south, and over 60 miles from east to west. The thousand or so underground bunkers in the complex contained ammunition stockpiles for about four full divisions. Dug-in and well-concealed, the facility had escaped the air war largely unscathed.

Helicopter gunships ranged ahead of the division on its eastward dash. Whenever an Iraqi column was spotted, the lead vehicle was destroyed. If other vehicles in the column attempted to go around the wrecked vehicle, they too were hit. Then, after the occupants of the convoy were given sufficient time to escape on foot, the vehicles were destroyed by the gunships.

One convoy of 30 trucks was destroyed by self-propelled artillery racing behind the tanks. The 24th ID's artillery traveled right behind the lead units. This gave the division instant artillery support and the ability to reach farther ahead of the tanks. Nothing was allowed to slow the division's advance. Massive barrages kept the Iraqis in front of the division constantly off balance. Any time an Iraqi force attempted to set up a defense in front of one of the brigades, or fire artillery at it, the Iraqi opposition was usually destroyed by artillery before the armor reached it.

No Iraqi vehicles were safe. Some were able to save themselves from gunships or artillery by hiding under bridges and overpasses. This merely delayed the inevitable, as these vehicles were destroyed as soon as the division's armor reached them. Between artillery, gunships and armor, the two brigades would destroy hundreds of trucks as they attempted to flee toward Baghdad.

The 197th Brigade was assigned the capture of Tallil Airfield, 40 miles to the northwest of Jalibah Airfield. Col. Reid sent TF 2-69, now a force of two armor and two infantry companies after the addition of one of TF 1-18's infantry companies, to take the airfield. Tallil was not originally on the 24th ID's target list. However, the division had already begun to encounter large logistics sites, and Maj.Gen. McCaffrey suspected that there might also be a major supply depot on the airfield. He reasoned that with all of those supplies lying around, there had to be a significant complement of combat troops to defend them. McCaffrey had to be sure the airfield was clear. He wanted to put his own fuel depot on BP 102, and did not want any Iraqis in the area to menace it. McCaffrey asked for and received permission to attack the airfield.

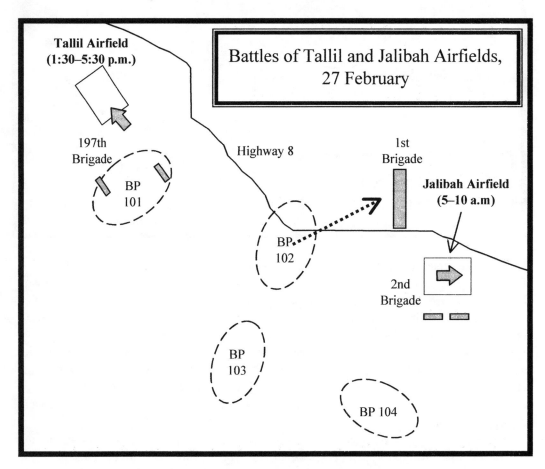

On the morning of the 27th, scouts from TF 2-69 approached Tallil on a reconnaissance mission. Before they were driven back by artillery fire from within the airfield, they discovered that the Iraqis had erected a 20 foot high berm around most of the airfield. Having no engineer equipment with which to breach the berm, Lt.Col. Sanchez decided to attack the airfield directly through the gates. This was a somewhat risky maneuver. It would give the attackers the advantage of a high speed attack route, but high speed avenues of approach are usually covered by heavy weapons.

The attack on Tallil kicked off at 1:30 in the afternoon, with 28 close air support sorties and a short but intense artillery preparation. TF 2-69 burst through the front gate and rolled down the runways. Incredibly, the Iraqis had neglected to cover the gate, concentrating instead on the possibility of an assault over the berm. In a desperate attempt to reorient their weapons, some Iraqis shot each other. By 5:30, the airfield was secure. In all, Sanchez's tanks destroyed six MiGs, three helicopters, a cargo plane, four ZSU 23-4 AAA pieces and two T-55 tanks without loss. No prisoners were taken. The survivors of the attack fled, and Sanchez's task force, ordered to rejoin the brigade for the move to Basra, did not have time to chase them.

Lt.Col. Sanchez's men also did not have time to destroy what they had captured on Tallil. That job would fall to the 82nd Airborne Division's 3rd Brigade, which was on its way to take possession of the airfield. When the brigade arrived, it would destroy 19 fighter aircraft, 10 armored vehicles, 490 air defense weapons and 341 trucks. In addition to its function as a military airfield, Tallil had been a major weapons storage site. The brigade also destroyed 124 artillery pieces and mortar tubes, 4,986 anti-tank weapons, 200,500 small arms, 165 ammunition bunkers and 45 ammunition storage buildings.

Tallil turned out to be the 197th Brigade's final action. After refueling, task forces 2-18 and 2-69 moved to rejoin the division's main body, which was by then outside Basra. Maj.Gen. McCaffrey had ordered that TF 1-18 be left behind with a battery of self-propelled artillery pieces to guard the division's rear. An intelligence report, which turned out to be erroneous, claimed that the Baghdad Division of the Republican Guard was moving in force toward the 24th ID's rear.

The 5th (Baghdad) Motorized Division was used to protect Baghdad and Saddam Hussein. The 5th Motorized was the largest of the Republican Guard units, with four brigades instead of three. The division had four brigades because in theory, if other Guard units got into dire straits, it could be split, with two brigades going to reinforce the hard-pressed Guard units and two staying in the city to protect Saddam Hussein. In practice, with almost all the bridges in the Baghdad area knocked out, and a brigade from the 101st Airborne Division blocking Highway 8, the Baghdad Division could not move anywhere in force.

While TF 1-18 waited for an attack that never came, it continued to clear BP 101. By war's end, the task force would round up over 1,500 prisoners. On BP 101 and Tallil Airfield, the Iraqis had lost the better part of a brigade. "School brigade my ass," remarked one of the brigade's officers.

Also on the 27th, Lt.Gen. Luck ordered the 101st to occupy Objective Tim (al-Busayyah Airfield). Shortly after 9 a.m., 2nd Brigade landed a battalion of infantry and a battalion of artillery. Soon, 500 infantrymen, 60 anti-tank Humvees and 18 105mm artillery pieces were set in their positions. Within four hours, enough fuel and ammunition had been delivered to provide temporary support for four helicopter battalions. Objective Tim was now renamed Forward Operating Base (FOB) Viper.

Viper was to be the launch point for helicopter raids on an area just north of Basra dubbed "Engagement Area Thomas." Within EA Thomas was the two-lane causeway that ran across the Hawr al-Hammar (a large, shallow lake). In four hours of continuous raids beginning at 2:30 p.m., 64 Apaches destroyed 14 APCs, 8 multiple rocket launchers, 56 trucks, 4 anti-aircraft guns, 2 SA-6 anti-aircraft missile systems and

4 helicopters on the ground. To Maj.Gen. Peay's disappointment, after the first series of raids, few worthwhile targets, and no tanks, showed themselves on EA Thomas. That night, he suspended further attacks on EA Thomas. The benefits of the attacks were now outweighed by the risks to his pilots, who were too tired to continue flying safely.

By the evening of the 27th, the 24th ID had bottled up most of what was left of Iraq's KTO army inside the "Basra Pocket." The Hammurabi Republican Guard Division had fallen back to the outskirts of Basra in the face of VII Corps' assault. There, it set up a defensive arc running from the west of Basra to As Safwan, directly to the south of the city and just north of the Kuwaiti border. The Hammurabi Division was joined by a large portion of the Adnan Division, which was retreating to Basra while the 24th ID was overrunning two other Republican Guard motorized divisions (the al-Fao and Nebuchadnezzar divisions).

Portions of several regular army units were also in the pocket. A major retreat had begun on the morning of the 26th, when the Revolutionary Command Council had announced that Iraqi forces would be leaving Kuwait. At that time, retreat orders went out to armored and mechanized units there. The announcement had come too late to save the units in southern Kuwait then being ground up by the 1st and 2nd Marine divisions, but some of the units stationed in the north, close to major roads, had been able to escape in reasonably good order. About a third of the 51st Mechanized Division's armored vehicles and half of its artillery survived to take their place in the southern portion of the Hammurabi perimeter. Meanwhile, a significant portion of the 58th Armored Brigade (stationed northeast of al-Jahra) and many of the roughly 100 tanks belonging to the four infantry divisions (19th, 22nd, 34th and 46th) defending the northern coast of Kuwait had escaped into Iraq. Most of the vehicles from these units were then in Basra itself. By the time the 24th ID arrived, there were some 525 tanks and 250 other armored vehicles between the northern border of Kuwait and the western approaches to Basra. There were also the equivalent of about nine artillery battalions.

Maj.Gen. McCaffrey decided he would pour all the artillery he had under his control (more than nine battalions) on the Iraqis outside Basra before going in for the kill. From 6 p.m. on the 27th to 5 a.m. on the 28th, 54 MLRS launchers, 132 155mm and 48 8-inch pieces kept up a steady drumbeat of artillery. Occasionally, Iraqi artillery attempted to fire back, only to be pinpointed by artillery-spotting radar and silenced. By 1 a.m., Iraqi artillery had stopped firing altogether. From 4–5 a.m., the division's artillery launched a particularly violent barrage in preparation for the assault that promised to destroy the Hammurabi Division.

Then, with the Victory Division poised for the final assault, word of the cease-fire came. The cease-fire would not take effect until 8 a.m., but no further advances into Iraqi-held territory would be allowed, not even Apache strikes. McCaffrey's soldiers would have to settle for one last barrage from the division's artillery. The barrage focused primarily on artillery units, to devastating effect. Even the armored, self-propelled artillery pieces could not escape destruction. Although they were better protected than towed guns, they were thinly armored and unable to stand up to American cluster munitions. The barrage destroyed or forced the abandonment of most of the Hammurabi Division's artillery. Also abandoned were dozens of tanks and APCs.

Not all fighting ended with the cease-fire, however. Late in the afternoon of the 27th, an F-16 piloted by Capt. William Andrews had been shot down to the southwest of

Basra, apparently by a shoulder-launched missile. Andrews ejected into Iraqi-held territory, reporting on his survival radio that he was being fired upon by Iraqi infantry during his descent. During his parachute landing, he sustained a broken leg. Two Apaches and a Blackhawk from the 2-229th Attack Battalion attempted a rescue. Both Apaches were hit but were able to return to their base, but the Blackhawk was shot down, with five killed and three injured and taken prisoner. Rescue attempts were abandoned, and Andrews was also taken prisoner. At 9:45 a.m. on the 28th, 3rd ACR was ordered to drive 12 miles east and secure Ar Rumaylah Airfield, the site of the Blackhawk crash.

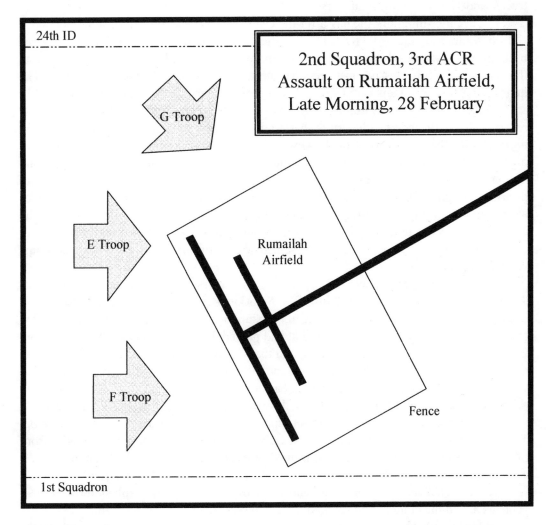

24th ID

2nd Squadron, 3rd ACR
Assault on Rumailah Airfield,
Late Morning, 28 February

G Troop

E Troop

Rumailah
Airfield

F Troop

Fence

1st Squadron

The capture of the airfield was assigned to Lt.Col. O'Shaughnessy's 2nd Squadron. At 10:47, O'Shaughnessy's squadron reached the airfield and began its assault. In the center, E Troop followed a mine plow-equipped tank through the chain link fence that surrounded the airfield, while G and F troops hit the airfield to the north and south. The heaviest fighting occurred on the airfield itself, where dug-in tanks, self-propelled ZSU 23-4 AA guns, heavy machine-guns and infantry with RPGs opened up on E Troop. While M-1A1s eliminated the tanks, Bradleys swept the airfield with chain-gun and coaxial fire. Meanwhile, G and F troops destroyed a few twin 14.5mm AA guns, and wiped out scattered groups of infantry along with a few RPG teams. After about 20 minutes, the battle was over. The squadron had destroyed five T-55s and five ZSU 23-4s, killed dozens of Iraqis and captured 165 prisoners as well as over 200 tons of aircraft munitions. One soldier was killed, however, when a piece of unexploded ordnance he had picked up exploded.

The 24th ID was busy after the cease-fire. Division engineers had to destroy large numbers of Iraqi vehicles and tremendous amounts of equipment and supplies that had been captured or bypassed in the dash to Basra. On the day after the cease-fire, they destroyed 34 tanks, 41 APCs, 43 artillery pieces, 27 anti-tank guns, 319 AA guns, 224 trucks, and 150 ammunition bunkers.

Just after midnight the day after the cease-fire, a busload of Iraqi soldiers opened fire on soldiers of the 24th ID's TF 2-7 after being challenged. The Americans fired back, disabling the bus, killing seven Iraqis and wounding six. Fifteen minutes later, both the 1st and 2nd brigades began to receive mortar fire from the outskirts of Basra. The division's artillerymen answered with another massive barrage. Resistance ceased.

At 2:30 a.m. on Saturday, two days after the cease-fire, scouts from TF 2-7 reported to 1st Brigade headquarters that a concentration of Iraqi vehicles was heading north toward the causeway. Col. LeMoyne began to suspect that a major Iraqi move might be afoot. He radioed division headquarters, requesting priority of helicopter and artillery assets, since 1st Brigade was guarding the approaches to the causeway. After priority was granted, LeMoyne briefed Maj.Gen. McCaffrey on his intended plan of attack in the event of an Iraqi breakout attempt. The plan was approved, and the commanders of the units involved were given their missions and instructed not to fire unless they were fired upon. All that remained was to find out whether or not the Iraqis were trying to break out.

As dawn approached, a flight of helicopters accompanied by Col. Burt Tackaberry, commander of the 24th ID's Aviation Brigade, flew to the causeway to determine what the Iraqis were up to. Col. Tackaberry, flying within visual range of the causeway, discovered that the column that had passed TF 2-7 was an assortment of about 200 trucks with a few armored vehicles, and that it had slipped over the causeway across the Hawr al-Hammar. Since they were outside the division's protective zone, these vehicles could not be engaged. However, Tackaberry could also see that another column of about 500 trucks and 100 armored vehicles was headed north, toward the causeway.

Tackaberry sent a loudspeaker-equipped helicopter to order the column to stop. The order was ignored. He then ordered a Cobra to fire 20mm chain-gun rounds in front of the column. As the column continued northward, ignoring the 20mm rounds, Tackaberry ordered the Cobra to launch a TOW in front of the column. After this gesture was ignored, Tackaberry ordered the lead vehicles destroyed. The explosion of the lead vehicles halted the column and sparked a mass exodus from the trapped vehicles.

Meanwhile, in 1st Brigade's southern sector, a group of Iraqi anti-tank teams fired RPG rounds at TF 2-7's scouts. As soon as three Bradleys approached the anti-tank teams, the Iraqis immediately surrendered. As the scouts were rounding up the prisoners, the Bradleys were engaged by Sagger guided anti-tank missiles from BMPs and main gun fire from T-72s. Lt.Col. Ware asked for permission to return fire. LeMoyne granted permission and ordered his other units to implement the brigade attack plan.

The assault began with a 20-minute artillery barrage by four artillery battalions and one MLRS battalion. To throw a roadblock in front of the Iraqis, Lt.Col. John Floris, commander of the 1-41st FA Battalion, requested and received permission to fire

FASCAM (Field Artillery SCAtterable Mines) rounds. These rounds work the same way as DPICM rounds, only they scatter mines, creating instant minefields. The mines are relatively small, but they can blow tracks or wheels off of vehicles, and can kill dismounted personnel. FASCAM is ideal for isolating parts of the battlefield by keeping out unwelcome visitors, and it is especially useful for slowing down retreating forces. However, before the mission could be fired, DPICM rounds and MLRS rockets turned the abandoned Iraqi vehicles on the approach to the causeway into a barricade of wreckage, and made the FASCAM mission unnecessary.

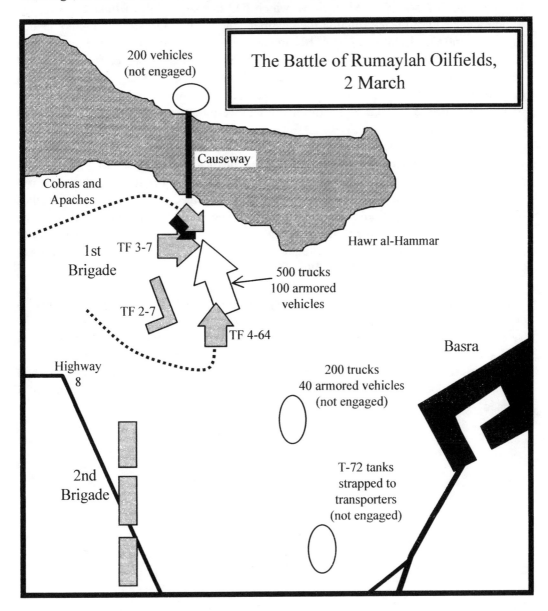

The Battle of Rumaylah Oilfields, 2 March

200 vehicles (not engaged)

Causeway

Cobras and Apaches

1st Brigade

TF 3-7

Hawr al-Hammar

500 trucks 100 armored vehicles

TF 2-7

TF 4-64

Basra

Highway 8

200 trucks 40 armored vehicles (not engaged)

2nd Brigade

T-72 tanks strapped to transporters (not engaged)

With the road blocked, a company of Apaches from Lt.Col. Tom Stewart's 1-24th Attack Battalion arrived to take their turn. After waiting for Iraqis to run away from their vehicles, the gunships let loose with 107 Hellfire missiles. All but five found their targets. After the Apaches were finished, TF 4-64 swept the highway, destroying everything that was not already burning. When the battle was over, 31 tanks (24 T-72s, 7 T-55s), 49 APCs (43 BMPs, 5 MTLBs, a French-built AMX-10 infantry fighting vehicle), 15 BRDMs, 9 BM-21 multiple rocket launchers, 34 artillery pieces, a ZSU 23-4, 417 wheeled vehicles (377 trucks, 40 jeeps) and 6 FROG missile launchers were on fire. The 24th ID lost one soldier wounded, one Bradley damaged, and an Abrams destroyed when an Iraqi ammunition truck exploded as it drove by it, causing a fire that could not be controlled.

Neither of the remaining two concentrations were engaged. A group of about 40 armored and 200 soft-skinned vehicles which had been traveling behind the wrecked column decided not to risk running the gauntlet. The column turned around and headed back to Basra. Col. LeMoyne had A-10s and artillery to call upon, and could have wiped the remaining Iraqi vehicles out with a few radio commands. However, since they had not crossed the cease-fire line, LeMoyne let the Iraqis go. Directly in front of 2nd Brigade was an armored brigade on tank transporters. The Americans kept an eye on the Iraqis, but as they displayed no hostile intent and were not trying to escape, Col. Kern's men held their fire.

After the prisoners were rounded up, Col. LeMoyne released most of them and sent them back to Basra. Only Iraqis in need of medical treatment and comrades who refused to leave them were detained. LeMoyne suspected that the Iraqis had made a run for the causeway because they had not been aware that the 24th ID had the approaches blocked. He wanted any Iraqis who did not already know that his brigade was there to be made aware of it. Undoubtedly, the bedraggled Iraqis shuffling back into Basra would recount their harrowing experience to their comrades in the city. This, LeMoyne hoped, would be enough to discourage any future breakout attempts. It was.

During the war, the 24th Infantry Division (including the 197th Brigade) destroyed 363 tanks and APCs, 207 AA guns, 314 mortars and artillery pieces, 1,278 trucks, 19 FROG missile launchers, 22 multiple rocket launchers and 25 fighters and helicopters. It also captured 1,300 bunkers containing over 100,000 tons of ammunition, and took over 5,500 prisoners. The division had lost eight dead, including two who had died in a helicopter crash and two who died as a result of the premature explosion of a grenade. Another thirty-six were wounded.

Part VIII

VII Corps: Heavy Metal

"The Army's armored and mechanized forces can play no offensive role against the vast defensive strength of the Iraqi army."

—Edward Luttwak
(December 1990)

<u>VII Corps Final Statistics</u>

VII Corps drove more than 160 miles and destroyed or captured (and later destroyed) 1,749 tanks, 1,672 other armored vehicles, 285 artillery pieces, 105 air defense systems and 1,229 trucks. The corps lost 47 killed and 192 wounded.

17

The Breach: The 1st Infantry Division Buries the Iraqis

The key unit in the VII Corps breaching operation was the U.S. 1st Infantry Division (Mechanized) under Maj.Gen. Thomas Rhame.* The division was also known as "The Big Red One," a reference to the unit's shoulder patch, a large, red "1" on an olive green shield. Before the war, the division consisted of two brigades stationed at Fort Riley, Kansas and one in Germany, designated 1st Infantry Division (Forward). However, the Army was scaling back, and as a result, the forward brigade was in the process of deactivation. Its senior officers, their staffs, and many of its troops deployed to the Gulf without their armor to help run the ports of Dammam and Jubail during the Desert Shield deployment, then returned to Europe to finish the unit's deactivation process. To round out the division for combat, the Army added the 2nd Armored Division's forward brigade in November.†

While the 2nd Armored Division (Forward) was considered part of that division, it had a separate command structure and functioned much like an independent unit. The 2nd AD (Forward) was stationed in Garlstedt, Germany, and was under the overall command of one of the division's two brigadier generals. Serving under him was his staff and the brigade commander, a colonel.

Forward brigades were designed to deploy in a European crisis in one of two ways. If only the forward brigade was needed, it would be commanded by the brigadier general in overall command. If the deployment of the entire division was required, the forward brigade would take matters in hand until the rest of the division arrived. Then, the brigade would be absorbed back into the parent division. The brigadier general would become an assistant division commander, and the colonel would command the brigade. The staff would stay with the brigade.

---

*Though it is referred to as the 1st Infantry Division for the sake of lineage, the Big Red One was really an armored division, with six armored battalions and three infantry battalions.

†The 2nd AD's forward brigade was stationed in Germany, while the division's other two brigades were based at Ft. Hood, Texas.

Integrating the unit into a different division turned out to be surprisingly easy. The 2nd AD (Forward) became the 3rd Brigade of the 1st ID instead of the 2nd AD. During the train-up before G-Day, the brigade was treated as though it had always been part of the division. There was one complication, however. The commander of the brigade was medically non-deployable and had to be replaced. Col. V. Paul Baerman had been a popular commander, but he was an insulin-dependent diabetic. Because proper refrigeration of insulin would have been difficult if not impossible in the Gulf, he had to be left behind. Col. David Weisman, Secretary of the General Staff at Headquarters, U.S. Army, Europe was named to replace Baerman.

The successful incorporation of 2nd AD (Forward) into the division solved one problem. Maj.Gen. Rhame then turned to his other major problem, replacing the two stateside brigades' basic M-1s with M-1A1s. The attempt to deal with this problem would only be partially successful.

Col. Lon Maggart's 1st Brigade was the first to arrive in Saudi Arabia. Shortly after its arrival, the brigade received its M-1A1s, drawn from warehoused reserve stocks in Germany. Next to arrive was Col. Tony Moreno's 2nd Brigade. Unfortunately, the ships carrying Moreno's tanks broke down in Cyprus, so the brigade headed westward with its M-1s to take its positions and prepare for the ground war. If the M-1A1s arrived in time, they would be brought to the brigade.

Ultimately, the M-1A1s did arrive —five days before the start of the ground war. Maj.Gen. Rhame allowed Col. Moreno to decide whether or not to accept the tanks. In making the decision, Moreno faced a dilemma. If he accepted the M-1A1s, he would have better tanks. On the other hand, five days would be barely enough time just to swap out 120 tanks. Radio and encryption gear would have to be moved from the M-1s to the M-1A1s. In some cases, communications technicians would have to be brought in. Moreno, like any experienced armor officer, knew that just because a set of communications gear worked in one tank did not necessarily mean it would work in another. In addition, the lasers would have to be zeroed, and the tank guns would have to be boresighted. All of this would be taking place at a time when Moreno wanted his men to focus on their missions in what promised to be a complex and dangerous breaching operation.

Moreno's M-1s may not have been as good as M-1A1s, but they were better than anything the Iraqis had. Their composite armor would stand up to anything the Iraqis could hit them with. They had plenty of depleted uranium sabot rounds (including stocks of an experimental round with added penetrating power) for their 105mm guns. This would allow their guns to pierce the frontal armor of all but the heaviest Iraqi tanks, and there would be none of those in the breach area. These considerations, and the fact that his men were comfortable with their tanks, prompted Moreno to go to war with what he had.

Tanks were not the only new items the division received. Before the two brigades had even left Fort Riley, Rhame had seen to it that all of their old Humvees were replaced, as were their radios. In addition, five hundred Magellan Global Positioning System receivers were procured and distributed.

The success or failure of 1st ID's breach would go a long way in deciding the success or failure of the Coalition ground assault. Central to the breaching operation was the issue of getting through the minefields division planners expected to encounter. Thus, during January, effective mine clearing techniques were worked out. The task forces with mine clearing responsibilities discovered almost immediately that there were serious problems with the initial mine clearing plan. The plan called for each task force to send two teams of three M-1A1s with Track-Width Mine Plows (TWMPs) into the minefields. Each team would plow in an echelon formation, creating two tank-width paths through the minefields.

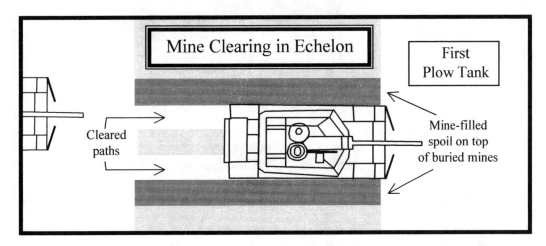

In theory, the plan made sense. The first tank would clear two track-width paths through the minefield. Of course, the mines between the two plows would be missed. Mine plows, like Army mine rollers, only clear a 3 foot, 9 inch wide path, wide enough for each of the tank's tracks. Although a heavy chain slung between the two blades will set off any mines that are activated by above-ground tilt rods, it does not clear pressure activated mines between the blades.

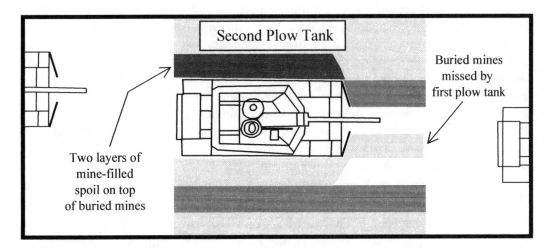

These mines would be shoved aside by the second tank. Since it was traveling to the rear and slightly to the left of the first tank, the second tank's right plow would be perfectly positioned to take care of these mines. The second tank's left plow would burrow under the mine-filled spoil produced by the first plow tank (and the mines buried under the spoil) and push it farther to the left. The result would be a cleared lane exactly as wide as a tank.

The third tank, following to the second tank's left rear, would to shove the pile even farther to the left. This would provide the tanks that followed with a bit of extra width for the passage.

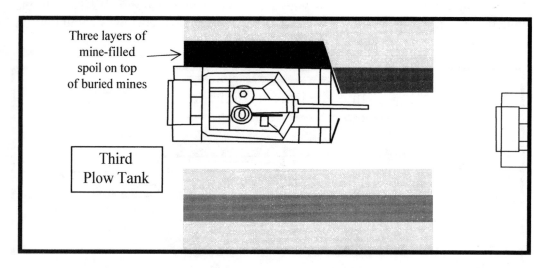

Three layers of mine-filled spoil on top of buried mines

Third Plow Tank

However, tests conducted in January showed that in burrowing into the spoil, the right side of the second tank's left plow tended to dig in, causing the left side to rise a few inches. This was just enough cause the plow to miss a few buried mines. These mines posed a danger to the third plow tank. In addition, while the third tank's right plow was essentially not necessary, as it passed down the middle of the cleared lane, its left plow was confronted by a massive spoil berm. This berm contained the dirt and mines plowed by the other two tanks, and there were mines buried under the berm. The size and weight of the spoil the plow was trying to push made the plow less effective at clearing buried mines. This created the possibility that after plowing the spoil, the track behind the plow could be blown apart by a buried mine, crippling the tank and blocking the lane.

Another problem with using plows on spoil was that while most of the spoil was pushed away from the tank, occasionally the churning of the mine-filled spoil caused one or two mines to spill to the inside, between the blades. This created a hazard that had to be cleared before vehicles could begin moving through the lane.

In the end, units with breaching responsibilities lost confidence in techniques that involved plowing spoil. The three-tank formation was abandoned. Instead, each team would send two plow tanks into the minefields, creating two separate track-width lanes. The third plow tank would stand by as a reserve.

Because the 5 foot, 3 inch wide area between the tank plows would not be free of pressure-activated mines, the paths had to be widened to full tank-width to make them suitable for narrower vehicles whose tracks or wheels would not fit neatly into the Abrams' tracks. For this, combat engineers would use Full-Width Mine Rakes (FWMRs).

The mine rake is a wedge-shaped frame with a series of steel tines that burrow into the ground. In the Gulf it was mounted on the front of a Combat Engineer Vehicle, an M-60 tank modified for engineer work. The main advantage of the mine rake is that it clears a path for the full width of an Abrams, with about a foot to spare on either side. Mine rakes also stand up exceptionally well to mine explosions. Mine plows and rollers are solid and absorb much of a mine's blast. A mine plow will therefore usually be put out of action by a single anti-tank mine detonation. Mine rakes allow most of the energy of the blast to pass through the tines, so they can survive multiple blasts. At only two tons, mine rakes are light, easily transportable, and easy to mount.

Full-Width Mine Rake. (Photo: Lt.Col. Mike Tucker)

The down side of using the mine rake is that it is an exceptionally slow process. Since commanders often cannot afford to have their tanks and Bradleys backed up waiting for the mine rake to finish clearing a lane, it is usually employed only after the vital armor assets have been pushed forward. Mine rakes also have a tendency to let smaller anti-personnel mines slip through their tines.

The mine rake is one of the great American ingenuity stories of the war. Though the concept had been studied, at the time of Saddam's invasion of Kuwait, there was no effective full-width mine clearing apparatus in existence. In November 1990, the Army's Countermine Systems Directorate at Ft. Belvoir, Virginia was tasked with producing the equipment. Using computer-aided design and stress assessment programs to develop the structure of the rake, engineers quickly made and field-tested two prototypes. Production was begun in early December. In January and early February 1991, 59 mine rakes were delivered to the Gulf (35 to the Army, 16 to Marines, 8 to the Egyptians).

While the breaching task forces and their attached combat engineers were working out effective mine clearing techniques, other division units were engaged in tactical operations. Great pains were taken to keep Iraqi patrols away from the logistics bases which were then being set up to support the coming VII Corps ground offensive. On 28 January, before the division's main body had arrived, Lt.Col. Robert Wilson's 1-

4th Cavalry, the division's cavalry squadron, set up a screen across the division's 30 mile sector. Because of the length of the screen line, the ground troops had to rely extensively on attack helicopters. The division's 1-1st Aviation Battalion, under the command of Lt.Col. Ralph Hayles, was attached to 1-4th Cavalry, joining the squadron's own two air troops.

Almost as soon as the screen was set, both of Wilson's ground troops were reporting significant Iraqi flare activity (the flares being used to guide dismounted patrols). At 6:30 a.m., five days after the squadron took up its positions, 1-4th Cav had its first prisoners, four Iraqis carrying a white flag. The Iraqis had thrown away their rifles, and had walked seven miles to the south, carrying only a few hand grenades. A day later, north of the border berm, Cobra gunships inflicted the squadron's first battle damage, claiming an Iraqi bulldozer, a radar tower and two buildings.

On 3 February, reinforcements arrived, in the form of 2nd Brigade's Task Force 3-37 and the 1-5th Field Artillery Battalion (1st Brigade's direct support battalion). The squadron and the other two units now formed an ad hoc unit under the command of the division's Assistant Division Commander for Maneuver, Brig.Gen. William Carter III. At 6 a.m. on the 4th, TF 3-37 assumed responsibility for the eastern half of the screen line, allowing 1-4th Cavalry to cover 15 miles of front instead of 30.

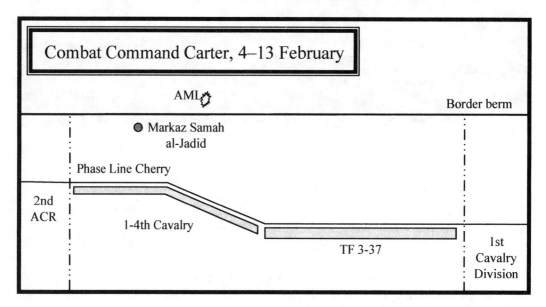

As soon as it was set in its positions, Combat Command Carter, as the unit was called, received instructions from VII Corps headquarters to pull back to Phase Line Cherry, a line running between two and three thousand meters from the border, and not engage Iraqi troops or vehicles inside Iraq. Lt.Gen. Franks was concerned about alerting the Iraqis to the presence of a major force in the area.

The Iraqis seemed to suspect something, and were patrolling the area. Only one vehicle, a French-built AML armored car, was spotted (and destroyed with a TOW missile launched by a C Troop Cobra), but Lt.Col. Wilson felt that the Iraqi presence might be significant. The Iraqis were continuing their flare activity, and ground surveillance radars were picking up extensive Iraqi vehicle movement in the area just south of the border. The movement seemed to be centered on the abandoned town of Markaz Samah al-Jadid, on the Saudi side of the border. At 8:41 a.m. on 5 February,

Bradleys dropped three Long Range Surveillance Detachments just south of the border, and at 7 a.m. on the 6th, Lt.Col. Wilson led a raid on the town.

The raid was conducted by two OH-58 scout helicopters and two Cobra gunships. Two Bradleys were close by, on alert to evacuate prisoners or recover pilots if their helicopters were shot down. Wilson ordered the gunships to open fire on the town with 20mm cannon to prompt an Iraqi reaction. The only reaction was the immediate surrender of an Iraqi soldier stationed in the town's largest building. The raiders found no other soldiers, but did discover communications gear and a radio log.

While the raid disrupted Iraqi intelligence efforts in the area to some extent, Lt.Col. Wilson found that the division commander was not pleased. Maj.Gen. Rhame ordered Wilson not to lead any more raids personally, and reminded him that in using Bradleys, he had brought them forward of Phase Line Cherry, behind which the corps commander had ordered Combat Command Carter on 4 February.

The restrictive guidelines still allowed for a good deal of activity, and 1-4th Cavalry remained active. On the evening of the 8th, new antennae were reported atop a building in Markaz Samah al-Jadid. An Apache raid just before eleven that night destroyed part of the communications site. The following morning, Lt.Col. Wilson received permission for a follow-up raid. Cobras from D Troop used TOW missiles to destroy the rest of the site.

The cat-and-mouse game continued, however. By evening, the Iraqis in the town had posted more antennae. That night, Apaches struck again. This time, they destroyed all of the antennae and most of the building with Hellfire missiles.

On the 13th, the division's main body arrived, and late that night, Combat Command Carter was replaced by Task Force Iron, which was made up of the 3rd Brigade's TF 1-41 and 1-4th Cavalry. The squadron had one last mission to conduct with TF 3-37, however.

On 15 February, the division would be sending Task Force Iron north of the berm and into Iraq. Markaz Samah al-Jadid was between 1-4th Cavalry and the berm it would be breaching, so the town had to be cleared beforehand. D Company, 2-16th Infantry Battalion (part of TF 3-37) was assigned to the squadron for the operation. The company would conduct an assault to clear the town. A Troop, 1-4th Cavalry would support the assault with mortar fire.

At 12:50 on the afternoon of the 14th, as A Troop's mortars were still preparing to fire, D Company attacked. D Company's commander soon lost control of the attack. In addition to pelting the town with 25mm chain-gun, coaxial machine-gun, M-16 and SAW (Squad Automatic Weapon) fire, the infantrymen threw hand grenades into every structure in which Iraqis might be lurking. Unfortunately, many of the buildings were thinly walled, and some were aluminum. Bullets and shrapnel tore through these structures and caused minor wounds to three Americans before order was restored.

The next day, Task Force Iron slipped into Iraq on a counter-reconnaissance mission. Just before noon, as scouts from B Troop, 1-4th Cavalry approached the berm, they took fire from a dirt-walled fort just north of the berm. Three TOWs destroyed the fort and a nearby truck. At noon, with Iraqi resistance silenced, engineers began punching 20 four meter wide holes in the border berm, which the Saudis had built before the war to prevent smuggling. While the engineers worked on the berm, division artillery dropped barrages on known and suspected Iraqi positions up to 10 miles inside Iraq. When the barrage lifted, the task force moved forward. Though there were a few firefights with Iraqis in bunkers, resistance was light. By three, the task force had established a 19 mile wide screen, three miles inside Iraq. By nightfall, the task force had advanced another three miles.*

The task force spent the 16th conducting extensive dismounted patrolling. For most of the day, there was no contact between the Iraqis and the Americans, although TF 1-41 spotted but did not engage some Iraqi dismounts far to the north, and as evening fell, there was flare activity in 1-4th Cavalry's sector.

Just before midnight, however, C Company, 1-41st Infantry identified three armored vehicles coming toward it from three miles away. The Americans believed that the vehicles were probably a tank and two APCs. Maj.Gen. Rhame ordered Apaches into the area to find and destroy the Iraqi vehicles, as well as others which had been reported beyond direct fire range of Task Force Iron's forward units. Two Apaches soon reported that they had spotted two armored vehicles, one large and one small, with soldiers on the ground moving gear. The Apache battalion commander, Lt.Col. Hayles, piloted the lead helicopter.

Hayles radioed TF 1-41's commander, Lt.Col. James Hillman, to determine if there were any of his vehicles in the area. Hillman said that there were not. Hayles was now almost sure that the vehicles were Iraqi. Unfortunately, Hayles had misread his position locator. The grid square Hayles had asked Hillman about was indeed clear of American forces, but it was actually 1¼ miles north and almost 4 miles west of the grid square Hayles was actually looking at. On that grid square were two APCs from 1-41st Infantry.

From the air, the two vehicles seemed to fit the description of the vehicles spotted earlier by C Company. A Bradley (the larger vehicle) and an M-113 (the smaller one) were in stationary positions. The M-113 was equipped with a ground surveillance radar. When these radars were turned on, they had a tendency to cause a warning signal to go off in the Apache as if it was being locked on by the radar dish of a ZSU 23-4 anti-aircraft gun. To avoid such false alarms, ground surveillance radars were turned off when Apaches were in the area. The crew of the M-113 had turned off its radar and was gathering its equipment.

Hayles fired two Hellfire anti-tank missiles, destroying the Bradley first, then the M-113. The missiles killed Spec. Jeffrey Middleton and Pvt. Robert Talley and wounded seven other crewmen.

Hayles was relieved four days later. Maj.Gen. Rhame had issued guidelines prohibiting any of his battalion or brigade commanders from becoming personally engaged in firefights unless there was an absolute need to do so. He had clarified the guidelines for his leaders after learning that Lt.Col. Wilson had gone to Markaz Samah al-Jadid with his cavalrymen. If a commander had to defend himself unexpectedly, or the tactical situation made his participation in a firefight imperative (if his unit was so hard-pressed that everyone was needed in the fight), that was one thing. However, as far as Rhame (and most of the Army's senior leaders) was concerned, these men were trained and paid to control large units and manage large battles. A commander personally attacking Iraqis could do neither effectively. To Rhame, Hayles' claim that he was his battalion's most qualified pilot did not, even if true, constitute a tactical imperative.

Aside from two Soviet-built BRDM armored scout cars engaged with TOW missiles by B Troop, 1-4th Cavalry, there was no further contact on the 17th. That

---

*Over the next few days, while Task Force Iron was inside Iraq, the engineers would widen the cuts to 100 meters and add four more.

afternoon, VII Corps headquarters ordered the division to pull Task Force Iron out of Iraq. In addition to its counter-intelligence mission, the task force's original intent had been to gain ground, to put distance between Iraqi artillery and the division's front line, and destroy whatever artillery it could. However, CENTCOM planners were beginning to worry that Task Force Iron's activities might tip off the Iraqis to VII Corps' intentions, so the force was ordered south of the berm.

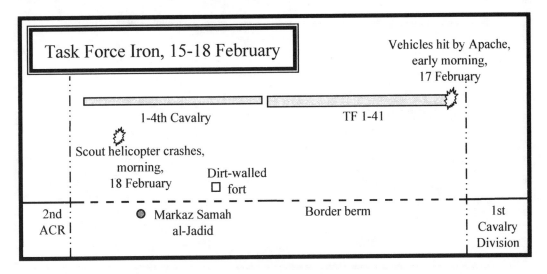

The rearward move on 18 February went relatively smoothly. Though engine failure resulted in the crash and complete destruction of a scout helicopter in 1-4th Cavalry's zone, both occupants escaped unharmed. There was also sporadic Iraqi artillery and mortar fire across the front, which wounded several soldiers in TF 1-41. Despite these problems, Task Force Iron was south of the berm before noon.

The division spent the next week rehearsing. On G-Day, the 1st ID would be responsible for breaching the obstacle and mine barrier, and securing the breach. The British 1st Armoured Division would follow. After the 1st ID had cleared the breach area and driven a bulge into Iraq, the British armor would pass through the division and deal with Iraqi armored forces in the vicinity. The British would then drive eastward, rolling up armored units backstopping the Saddam Line and cutting off the retreat of Iraqi units on the line. With the threat at the hinge neutralized, the western Allied thrusts could continue without fear of an Iraqi flank attack.

The maneuver, called a "passage of lines," is one of the most complicated and dangerous maneuvers in warfare. There are a number of coordination-related risks involved. For instance, if an enemy counterattack takes place during the passage, and it is unclear which force is to deal with it, units can end up shooting at each other, or worse, holding their fire while an enemy force slips between them. The fact that the two units came from different countries was another problem. The maneuver would require intricate preparation and coordination.

On 4 February, the 1st ID and the 1st (UK) Armoured Division had held a seminar to review and refine coordinations for the passage. The 1st ID had constructed a five kilometer by five kilometer training area which replicated Iraqi defenses. The training area had been used by the division to test breaching systems and tactics over the previous month. Now, it was the site of a walk-through of the coming passage of lines involving officers of the two divisions, followed by full dress rehearsals with the entire 1st (UK) Armoured Division, in daylight, then at night.

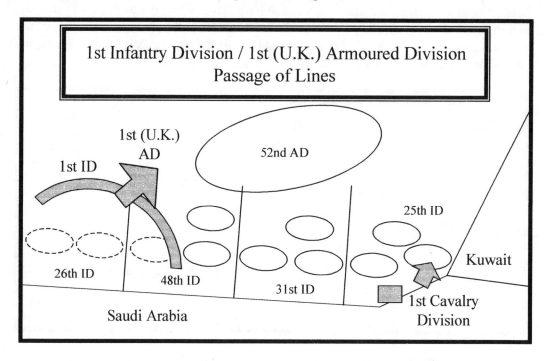

Working with the British turned out to be an intelligence bonanza for the Americans. Having been forced to develop their own intelligence over the previous weeks, the 1st ID's officers now found that the U.S. Air Force had detailed aerial photographs of the Iraqi positions. For reasons that are still unclear, the photos had been given to the British, but not the Americans. Fortunately, British officers turned over the Air Force's photograph collection to the 1st ID.

The photographs were primarily useful in confirming what the division staff already knew, as were later flights of videotape-equipped drones. The division's breach area had been thoroughly reconnoitered, and Maj.Gen. Rhame and his brigade commanders had detailed information to use in planning their breaching operation. They knew the exact location of a significant portion of the Iraqi fighting positions within the roughly 35 square mile area. They knew where they would find Iraqi anti-tank weapons and machine-guns and where they would not. They also knew which areas were heavily mined and which were not. When the commander of the 110th Infantry Brigade of the Iraqi 26th Infantry Division was captured by the 1st Brigade on G-Day, he would find that the American graphics of the Iraqi positions were more detailed and more accurate than his own. From this information, division planners were able to determine the most favorable points at which to open breach lanes. By contrast, their opponents had no intelligence, and had not even heard from their higher headquarters in over a week.

Part of the Iraqis' blindness in the 1st Division sector was the result of the Iraqi Air Force's inability to fly over American positions. Part of it was the result of a concerted effort ordered by Maj.Gen. Rhame to sweep the area to the division's front, the 11 mile "security zone" between the Americans and the main Iraqi defenses, clear of enemy observation posts and patrols. The effort began when 1-4th Cavalry established a screen line in front of the division. It continued with the incursion by Task Force Iron on

15–18 February. Though the mission had ended with the friendly fire destruction of a Bradley and an M-113, it had succeeded in pushing Iraqi observers several miles away from 1st ID's lines. Supplementing this effort was a series of heavy artillery raids on suspected Iraqi positions in the security zone. The raids began on 16 February and continued until G-Day. On G-Day, Rhame denied the Iraqis the ability to put observed artillery fire on his men during their approach to the main breach area by clearing the security zone between the division and the main Iraqi defense line in the morning and eliminating whatever observation posts remained in it.

At 5:30 a.m. on 24 February, with 1st Brigade on the left and 2nd Brigade on the right with 3rd Brigade directly behind it, the division began moving through the gaps cut in the border berm by Task Force Iron. The security zone was secure by 9:15. The next phase was the conduct of the main breach.

The two brigades were perfectly organized for the breach. The 1st Brigade's 2-34th Armor, under Lt.Col. Greg Fontenot, had given two of its tank companies to Lt.Col. Sidney "Skip" Baker's 5-16th Infantry in return for two of Baker's Bradley companies. Likewise, in 2nd Brigade, Lt.Col. David Gross had given two of 3-37th Armor's tank companies to Lt.Col. Daniel Fake's 2-16th Infantry and had received two Bradley companies in return. This gave all four of the battalion task forces assigned to breach the forward defenses plenty of firepower, and enough infantry for clearing bunkers and trenches. These four task forces would begin the assault by plunging into the Iraqi trenchworks, then turning and rolling down the trenchlines, widening the two breaches.

With the flanks of the two breaches secure, the two tank-pure battalions, 1st Brigade's 1-34th Armor, under Lt.Col. Pat Ritter, and 2nd Brigade's 4-37th Armor, under Lt.Col. David Marlin, would push through the breaches, destroy Iraqi units beyond the obstacle belt and block any possible armored counterattack. With tank-pure battalions, Ritter and Marlin had maximum mobility and maximum firepower to exploit the attack and deal with counterattacks. The 1-4th Cavalry Squadron would also push through the breach, helping 1-34th Armor clear the 1st Brigade's sector in depth.

At around ten, the division began making contact with the main trenchlines. Task forces 2-34 and 5-16 reached Phase Line Plum, where they were supposed to stop. However, the phase line ran below the crest of a low ridge, and left the two task forces with no view of the Iraqi positions to their front. Both Fontenot and Baker decided to edge their armor over the ridge line to get a better view of the defenses and confirm or adjust artillery targets for the preparatory barrage to come. As they did, they found themselves within 1,200 meters of fully manned Iraqi positions. Having gotten a good view of the positions, but not wanting to start the main engagement prematurely, both commanders pulled their forces back.

As the Americans were getting a good look at the Iraqis, the Iraqis had been taking a good look at American armor. Now set back along Phase Line Plum, the Abrams and Bradley crews of the two task forces began to see unarmed Iraqis stumble over the top of the ridge with their hands up. Larger groups followed until there were over 300 prisoners being processed and sent to the rear.

The incident gave the 1st Brigade one last piece of vital information, an insight into the emotional makeup of the units on the other side. These Iraqis had decided that stopping the Americans was not a priority. Faced with a choice between surrendering and being temporarily deprived of their freedom, or fighting and being permanently deprived of their lives, more than 300 had chosen the former. Those who remained, while more dedicated than their surrendering colleagues, were not fanatics. No attempt had been made to shoot those who had surrendered, or even to try to stop them. Indeed, most of those who survived the coming preparatory barrage would reconsider, and give up when the Americans arrived at their positions.

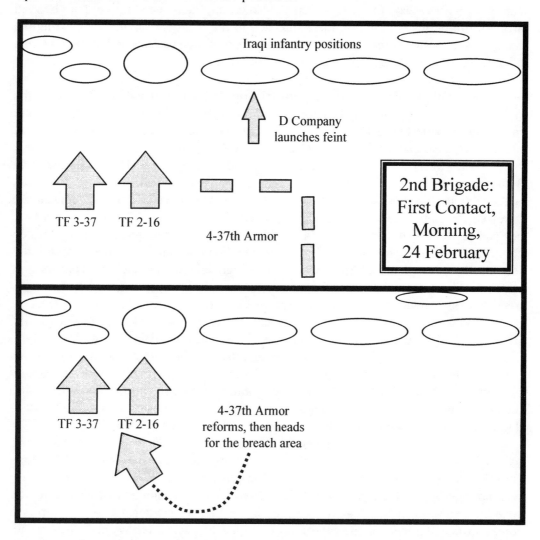

On the tip of the 1st ID's right flank, 4-37th Armor's task was to create a diversion as 2nd Brigade's two breaching battalions edged toward the main breach site. At around ten, the battalion's D Company, commanded by Capt. Thomas Wock, drove toward the Iraqi trenches and blew up a few bunkers with main gun fire. This prompted a mass surrender. The company then called in artillery on ten dug-in armored vehicles behind the trenchline while collecting the prisoners. D Company was able to round up nearly 700 prisoners before it was ordered to rejoin the battalion and move to the breach area. To the west of the area hit during the feint, some 250 Iraqis would surrender to TF 2-16 while it was waiting for the barrage to begin.

The Iraqis in front of the 1st Cavalry Division had shown a high degree of spirit and aggressiveness during the fight in the Wadi al-Batin on 20 February. This had raised concern that units to the east and west of the breach site might be just as aggressive, and that one of them might attempt to enter the 1st ID's zone to interfere with the breach. As

TF 2-34 was laying a smokescreen on the division's western flank, 4-37th Armor would be responsible for laying a smokescreen along the eastern flank. This would leave Iraqi units outside the breach zone blind to the developments in 1st ID's area of operations.

In the last days before G-Day, the wind had been a concern to the men of 1st ID. For a week, it had been moderately windy. The wind had also blown from north to south. The least experienced private recognized these as the perfect conditions for an Iraqi chemical strike. The point was further driven home during the artillery barrages before G-Day. As American guns fired, their propellant charges emitted gases which wafted southward, triggering chemical agent warning alarms. These numerous false alarms had intensified the pre-combat jitters experienced by Rhame's men.

The wind had changed direction on G-Day, though, and was now blowing into the faces of the Iraqis. As an added bonus, the winds were still moderate, so the clouds of smoke created by Marlin's smoke generators were staying thick as they were carried northward along the 1st ID's boundary. The Iraqis to the east of 4-37th Armor would have no idea what was going on to the west of them until it was too late for them to do anything about it.

The main action would be kicked off by a massive artillery barrage. The average U.S. Army division has one brigade of artillery support to call upon, but since the division's movement into Iraq was expected to be the most heavily contested, 1st ID's organic artillery had been heavily augmented. For the breaching operation, the Army had added the 42nd, 75th and 142nd Field Artillery brigades. To that, the British added the 1st (UK) Armoured Division's artillery brigade. Thus, for the breaching operation, 1st ID would have some five times the artillery support of the average Army division. This artillery was put to good use. From 20–23 February, 13 battalions of artillery fired 9,208 rounds of conventional artillery and 1,606 MLRS rockets at the Iraqis.

A two-hour preparatory barrage of 48,000 rounds had been planned for the kickoff of the VII Corps attack, but this had to be modified. Another reason (beside the need to remove Iraqi forward observers) 1st ID had attacked across the security zone that morning was to allow VII Corps' artillery to move as far forward as possible. This would allow it to engage Iraqi targets in depth. However, the planned start time of the attack was moved up about 14 hours, and although there was plenty of ammunition in stock, not enough had reached the new forward positions to fire a two-hour barrage. There was only enough ammunition at the guns for a 30-minute barrage. Still, the half-hour preparatory barrage was devastating. At 2:30 p.m., 60 MLRS launchers and 260 guns hit the Iraqi positions with 414 MLRS rockets and 6,136 conventional artillery rounds.

About 45% of the American shells carried bomblets. In addition to killing Iraqis when they went off, the bomblets limited the mobility of Iraqi defenders when they did not. Unexploded bomblets made moving around risky for Iraqi soldiers. By virtually restricting them to their individual positions, they also created an unforeseen misery for the defenders. American troops would find that many had been forced to urinate and defecate in their fighting positions and live with the smell rather than risk having their feet or legs blown off trying to do it outside.

Unfortunately, while bomblets were effective in softening Iraqi resistance, they also caused some problems for the Americans. Though Rhame's soldiers had been thoroughly briefed on the dangers of unexploded submunitions in the weeks before G-Day, the sheer number of duds in the breach area made them a problem. The unexploded bomblets slowed dismounted movement and blew tires on fuel and supply trucks.

During the war, there were claims that about 20% of all bomblets failed to detonate properly. The General Accounting Office (GAO) later claimed that the dud rate on howitzer-delivered bomblets was about 2%, and on MLRS-delivered bomblets it was about 5%. Most of 1st ID's combat leaders strongly disagree with the GAO estimate. Even accepting the lower GAO figures, there were at least 75,000 unexploded bomblets in 1st ID's 12 by 24 mile sector, since there were about 1.8 million bomblets delivered on it in the four days before the ground units hit the Iraqi line.

Because of the dud problem, wherever possible, the use of DPICM rounds was restricted to weapons that had to be neutralized, located on ground that did not necessarily have to be cleared by dismounted troops. Artillery positions were therefore ideal candidates to receive DPICM barrages. Having already lost 17 guns during the air offensive, the commander of the Iraqi 48th Infantry Division's artillery now saw every one of his 83 remaining guns destroyed within minutes.

Bad doctrine and lack of training in Iraq's artillery corps was costing Iraqi gunners their lives. Since Iraqi artillerymen were not as well-trained as their Coalition counterparts, Iraqi guns had to be bunched close together for better command and control. This made Iraqi batteries excellent targets, especially for cluster munitions.

Most of the rest of the shells fired that morning, especially those used on the Iraqi trenches and other areas where dismounted American soldiers would be operating, were standard high explosive shells. High explosive rounds turned out to be enough to destroy Iraqi bunkers. The Iraqi bunkers were so poorly constructed that delayed action fuses, which allow artillery rounds to burrow into the ground before exploding, were also not necessary. High explosive shells with impact fuses were more than enough to cause dugouts to cave in on their occupants or kill or incapacitate them with concussion.

Just building dugouts able to withstand hits from 155mm shells for one Iraqi battalion would have required 3,500–4,000 tons of engineering material. Even if the material had been available, every man in each infantry battalion would have needed to work all day, every day, for about three months just to build a sufficient number of bunkers for the battalion's own protection. Allied air power made that impossible.

Many Iraqi defenders survived the barrage, and continued to man trenches and bunkers, waiting as Rhame's tanks edged toward them. Some Iraqis tried to resist, but it was pointless. In many cases, they could not even see their attackers, since the earlier artillery barrage had contained enough smoke rounds to blind the defenders. Smoke generators were also used to help obscure the tanks and Bradleys. Abrams gunners, whose thermal sights allowed them to see through the smoke, opened up on the trenchline with a volley of HEAT rounds. A handful of Iraqi tanks showed themselves, but were destroyed by tank rounds or TOW missiles fired from Bradleys.

Just after 3 p.m., the task forces moved forward and began cutting lanes through the minefield. Plow tanks led the way into the minefield as artillery and tank fire suppressed the Iraqis in the trenches to the north. The Abrams' heavy armor made them the ideal vehicles to venture into territory which the division's leaders had believed would be stoutly defended. In the 2nd Brigade sector, tanks with mine rollers followed the mine plows to proof the lanes. The 1st Brigade had found the rollers too slow and cumbersome, and had decided not to use them. After a track-width path was cleared, the rest of the tanks followed, with Bradleys close behind.

Once through the minefields, which turned out to be much less heavily mined than those the two Marine divisions had encountered, Rhame's four breaching battalions headed for the Iraqi trenchlines. Unlike Iraqi units elsewhere, these Iraqis would receive no broadcast appeals for surrender. Rhame considered such appeals an unnecessary delay. He was aware of how important it was to establish his breach quickly so the British could get into position to deal with Iraqi armor. He was also not about to give the Iraqis time to call in artillery or chemical weapons strikes on his men.

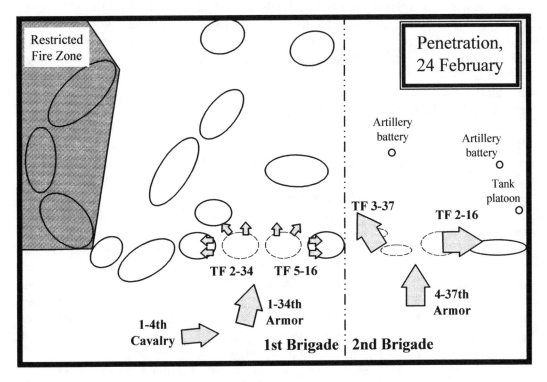

Bradleys provided cover as plow tanks rolled toward the trenches. Sometimes, the Iraqi occupants jumped out to surrender just before the tanks reached them. Others offered token resistance before giving themselves up. Iraqis who surrendered were taken to the rear. Incredibly, many Iraqis continued to fire at the Americans from their bunkers. Those who chose to stay in their positions and fight were killed were they stood. Many were killed by tank or Bradley fire. Some were killed when Vulcan anti-aircraft guns were turned on them. Many were simply buried alive. Within a half-hour, all 16 breach lanes were open.

In Army trench clearing doctrine, armored vehicles provide cover while infantrymen attack bunkers with grenades and small arms, killing their occupants or forcing them to surrender. However, the division's senior officers were unwilling to risk the loss of life which would have occurred if their soldiers had been forced to leave their armored vehicles. So, the tanks merely filled in the trenches, burying the holdouts alive. Typically, a plow tank drove along a trench pushing the earthen berm in front of the trench back into it, much like a snowplow. Meanwhile, another tank did the same on the rear of the trench. Armored bulldozers, known as Armored Combat Earthmovers (ACEs) were also used to fill in trenches.

Rhame's main purpose in using this tactic was to ensure the safety of his infantrymen to the greatest degree possible. His secondary aim was to pressure the Iraqis inside the bunkers into surrendering. The tactic achieved both ends. No Americans were killed by Iraqi fire during the breaching operation. The tactic also saved Iraqi lives. Many Iraqis who otherwise would have been killed in their bunkers by grenades or cannon fire saw their comrades buried alive and decided to surrender. "People somehow have the idea that burying guys alive is nastier than blowing them up with hand grenades or sticking them in the gut with bayonets, but it's not," Col. Maggart would say later. Rhame also had no regrets. He stressed that he did not come to the Gulf to fight fair, he came to win. "I optimized my technology, I optimized the quality of my soldiers, and I sent fewer young men home in body bags," he said. "I came to put maximum destruction on this son of a bitch [Saddam] with as few American casualties as possible." Schwarzkopf echoed Rhame's sentiments. "You don't pursue a battle worried about the casualties you inflict upon the enemy," Schwarzkopf explained. "The war was not our choosing. They had ample opportunity to avoid the war."

Lt.Gen. Franks was more concerned with the tactic's legality than its fairness. He had one of his staff officers call the corps' Judge Advocate General to find out if any rules of war had been violated. The answer was no. The tactic had already been ruled allowable by the United Nations, and since Rhame's soldiers had been taking fire from the trenches, their actions had been proper.[*]

Lt.Col. Fontenot found that Mine Clearing Line Charges also came in handy for trench clearing. During training exercises, the 1st ID had experienced the same problems with the MiCLiC that the Marines had experienced, and 1st Brigade's leaders had decided that the system was too undependable to use as the division's primary mine clearing tool. However, Fontenot had brought his MiCLiCs along, just in case. In one instance, his task force was taking fire from a trench protected by a hastily laid Iraqi minefield. A MiCLiC was launched. Seconds later, the chain of explosives, draped across the minefield and the trench beyond, exploded. Fontenot's men rushed through the cleared path to attack the trench, but found all of its occupants dead.

Events beyond Fontenot's or the division's control resulted in some irritation for TF 2-34. Days earlier, Iraqi artillery formations had been identified just outside 1st ID's breach zone. Because the artillery was in a position to fire on the 3rd Armored Division, the commander of that unit's Aviation Brigade had offered to destroy it with an Apache strike. CENTCOM had refused permission to hit the target, opting for a B-52 strike instead. The B-52 strike had been called off, however, and the Iraqi guns dropped shells (without effect) sporadically on Fontenot's men until they were destroyed by counterbattery fire.

Another problem was the 3rd Armored Division to the west. As 1st ID was clearing trenches, the 3rd AD was moving northward. The 3rd AD's cavalry squadron was posted on its right flank to keep Iraqi units in 1st ID's zone from moving westward into 3rd AD's fuel and supply trains. Unfortunately, three of the Iraqi positions in TF 2-34's sector could not be engaged without the risk that rounds might overshoot the targets and land among 3rd AD's cavalrymen. As they moved westward, Fontenot's men would have to endure periodic sniping (again, without effect) by the 6–12 Iraqis on the three positions within the restricted fire zone.[†]

---

[*]Before G-Day, while planning the attack, Fontenot and Baker had checked with the division Judge Advocate General. They had also been told that the tactic was legal.

[†]These Iraqis would stop firing and go into hiding as the scope of the 26th Division's defeat became apparent. They would eventually surrender to a supply unit.

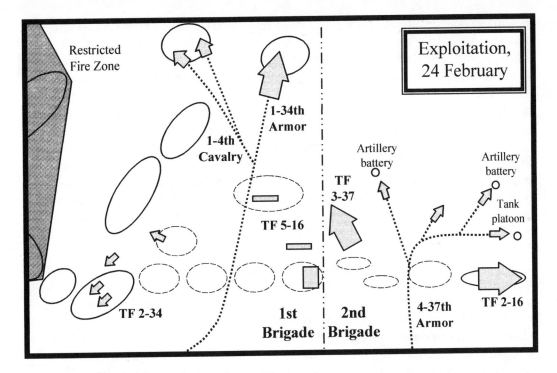

Once the two breaches were established, the exploitation forces raced through and fanned out to deepen the breachhead.

In the 1st Brigade sector, 1-34th Armor destroyed a battery of AA guns, an artillery battery and a tank company. It also captured the commander of the 110th Brigade and his entire staff. The 1-4th Cavalry drove northward, destroying three anti-tank guns, two tanks, an armored car and several trucks, killing several Iraqis and capturing over a hundred.

In the 2nd Brigade sector, 4-37th Armor had begun the morning on the brigade's right flank, and had remained there until its D Company had completed its diversionary attack. The battalion then pulled out, drove west, hooked northward and pushed through the breach lanes created by the brigade's task forces 3-37 and 2-16.

Once through the lanes, 4-37th Armor destroyed scattered artillery positions and several trucks, as well as numerous bunkers and machine-gun nests. Marlin's tanks found no significant reserve formations. Prisoner interrogations would later reveal that air and artillery strikes had been far more devastating in this sector than the Americans had imagined. One battalion commander in TF 2-16th's sector claimed to have lost 250 men killed by air or artillery before G-Day, roughly half of his command. This was an unusually high number of fatalities, but death, wounds and desertions had left most of the units in the sector at about half-strength. Whatever troops could have been used as reserves behind the trenchlines had to be moved forward as replacements to stiffen the line immediately prior to G-Day.

The four breaching task forces had been expected to sustain heavy casualties in clearing the trenches, but the day's losses had been exceptionally light. TF 2-34 had overrun three Iraqi infantry companies and a mortar platoon without sustaining a single fatality. TF 5-16 had rolled up two Iraqi companies, killing about two dozen Iraqis and capturing 160 at a cost of one soldier killed by an unexploded bomblet. There had been no casualties in the 2nd Brigade sector. TF 3-37 rolled over two infantry companies, capturing about 150 Iraqis before it reached the boundary with 1st Brigade, its limit of advance. TF 2-16's area was far more heavily manned, but resistance was not much stiffer. Approximately 950 of the 434th Brigade's shakier troops had already surrendered to D Company, 4-37th Armor during the feint, or to TF 2-16 before the bombardment. The more stout-hearted had remained in their trenches, but the artillery barrage had broken most of their spirits as well. By day's end, another 4–500 would surrender.

As darkness fell on Sunday, the corps commander was trying to decide whether to continue the attack through the night or wait until daylight. The corps had faced little opposition, but was running into problems. A sandstorm had reduced visibility to fewer than 1,000 meters and had cost the corps its air support. In addition, units were running into tactical problems. Lt.Gen. Franks consulted with his division commanders before making a final decision. All recommended suspending offensive operations until morning.

While the 1st ID had made tremendous progress in its breaching operations, it was only half finished. Maj.Gen. Rhame was concerned that continuing operations at night would result in unnecessary casualties to his men. Vulnerability to counterattack and fratricide were major concerns. The second phase of the breach clearing would require a three-brigade assault. The three brigades would be executing a fairly complicated maneuver. The 3rd Brigade would have to be brought up between the other two, then the three brigades would launch an attack from a very compressed area at night. Any Iraqi counterattack (a possibility that could not yet be completely dismissed) would catch the division in a relatively disorganized and vulnerable state. Tactical reverses would be a possibility. Deaths by friendly fire would be a virtual certainty. Even if there were no counterattack, navigating through minefields at night is inherently hazardous, as is clearing trenches and bunkers, even for the most practiced units.

Col. Holder of the 2nd Armored Cavalry Regiment, which was providing a screen in front of the corps, was concerned that his unit was getting too far ahead of the rest of the corps. He worried about the possibility of running into the Republican Guard without proper support from the heavy divisions. He was also concerned that advancing at night would guarantee that small Iraqi units would accidentally be bypassed and that these units might pop up later to ambush fuel and supply trucks.

Maj.Gen. Funk of the 3rd Armored Division was also worried about his supply lines. "In that rapid a movement, I don't want to lose my fuel," Funk said. Gen. Schwarzkopf had promised that he would position six million gallons of fuel for the corps, at the town of al-Busayyah, about 70 miles inside Iraq, as soon as the 1st Armored Division took it. However, corps planners felt that they could not take fuel deliveries for granted. The corps therefore brought as much of its own fuel with it as possible.[*] The fuel trucks had to be protected. "The concern was they could muster up some kind of counterattack, come right into the division rear and we wouldn't know it," said Funk later. "A tank platoon could just wreak havoc," he added.

Fuel was already a problem for the 1st AD, even without an Iraqi counterattack. The 1st Armored Division had met no resistance, but some of its units had exhausted 70% of their fuel. At the time of Schwarzkopf's order to VII Corps to move its attack forward, 1st AD was still 20 miles from its jumping-off point. Thus, Maj.Gen. Griffith's tanks had burned some 70 gallons of fuel apiece by the time they crossed the border.

---

[*]Fuel self-sufficiency turned out to be a good idea. Fuel was never delivered to al-Busayyah.

In view of the vulnerable positions of all of his subordinate units, Franks decided to suspend operations for the night. Franks told the Third Army commander, Lt.Gen. Yeosock, that in his judgment, continuing the attack through the night was not worth the risk. Yeosock agreed.

The next morning, when Schwarzkopf found that VII Corps had suspended the attack, he exploded. Schwarzkopf felt that the Republican Guard was not girding itself for a major engagement with VII Corps, it was "bugging out." Therefore, he reasoned that VII Corps needed to assume an exploitation and pursuit posture to destroy the Guard before it escaped, not move deliberately and prepare painstakingly. Schwarzkopf wanted Lt.Gen. Yeosock to explain to Lt.Gen. Franks, his direct subordinate, that if VII Corps did not move more rapidly and attack more aggressively, the Guard might slip away.

In Washington, Gen. Powell was also unhappy. Powell did not like second-guessing his battlefield commanders, but VII Corps' pace appeared slack to him, especially when compared with that of the 24th Infantry Division, which was slashing through Iraqi territory with record-shattering speed. Powell called Schwarzkopf. "It's hard to justify VII Corps in Washington when you see what the 24th is doing," said Powell. "What are the 1st and 3rd Armored divisions doing?" he asked. The heavy punch of VII Corps lay with these two divisions.[*] Powell was sure that the Iraqis knew VII Corps was coming, and that all of this waiting was giving the Iraqis a chance to prepare rear guard positions to buy time for the rest of the Republican Guard to escape. Powell believed that if the full power of VII Corps was immediately brought to bear upon the Iraqis, it would spell doom for Saddam's army. If not, then much of the Republican Guard might slip away.[†]

Things looked much different from Franks' vantage point. Though much of the Iraqi Army seemed to be disintegrating or retreating, the units in VII Corps' zone looked like they were getting ready for a fight. Just because Iraq's front line units had quit did not mean that the Republican Guard would do the same. Franks' intelligence could not detect any rearward movement of the Republican Guard's armored Medina or mechanized Tawakalna divisions, or the regular 10th and 12th Armored divisions. As far as Franks could see, they were preparing to fight. He would ultimately be proven correct. The units in front of VII Corps were getting ready to mount a defense.

The Tawakalna and 12th Armored divisions had been deployed at the top of the Wadi al-Batin, in expectation of a Coalition attack up the Wadi. An attacking force driving up the Wadi (which ran along the Iraqi side of the border with Kuwait) would smash directly into the 12th Armored Division as it emerged from the Wadi. Then, theoretically, it could be attacked on the flanks by the Republican Guard's Tawakalna Division, the 10th Armored Division, or both. If more power was needed, the 10th Armored Brigade of the Republican Guard's Medina Division was nearby, stationed just outside Kuwait's northern border, due north of the 10th Armored Division.

---

[*] Though the 1st ID also packed a heavy punch (as it would later prove), at that time it was not included in the plan for the attack on the Republican Guard.

[†] Schwarzkopf did not tell Powell that VII Corps had been ready to attack at 1 p.m., but Franks had been denied permission to do so. VII Corps had been told to launch its attack at three, but Franks, concerned that he might run out of daylight, wanted to go at one. He was told by Lt.Gen. Yeosock that Schwarzkopf wanted the attack coordinated with the Egyptian attack to the east, and that the Egyptians could not be ready until three. The corps had thus lost two crucial hours of daylight.

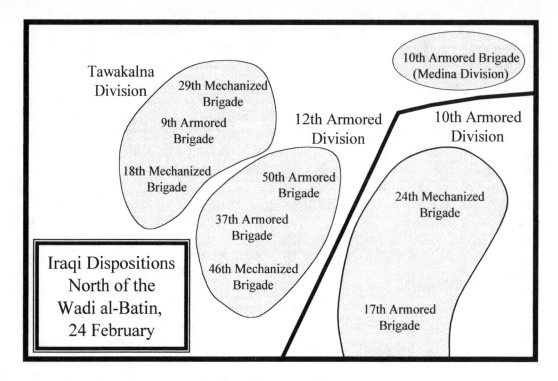

Iraqi Dispositions
North of the
Wadi al-Batin,
24 February

The Iraqis now knew that an attack was coming from the west, and they reacted accordingly. The Tawakalna and 12th Armored divisions redeployed along a line running north to south. The 10th Armored Division would be unable to deploy into the new defense line. At that point, two Egyptian divisions were conducting breaching operations south of the 10th Armored Division. This force of Egyptians would ultimately turn east and head for the coast, but the Iraqis did not know that. The Iraqis also could not afford to ignore the possibility that the 1st Cavalry Division, then in action on the southern end of the Wadi al-Batin, might succeed in fighting its way through the Wadi. Having an American heavy division emerge from the Wadi and drive uncontested into the rear of the new defensive line would effectively end Iraqi hopes of gaining even a stalemate. Though more than half of the division's 24th Mechanized Brigade was sent into Iraq to bolster reserve positions behind the Tawakalna Line, these threats were enough to keep most of the 10th Armored Division (and the vast majority of its tanks) in Kuwait. Most of this loss was made up by rushing about half of the Medina division (the entire 10th Armored Brigade and half of the 14th Mechanized Brigade) to bolster the line.

The Tawakalna's 29th Mechanized Brigade was posted on the new line's northern flank along a roughly 10 kilometer (6¼ mile) front and heavily reinforced by units from the Medina Division, stationed above the northwest corner of Kuwait. The total force on the position amounted to about 50 tanks and 110 APCs, the equivalent of a reinforced brigade.

Below these positions was a roughly 5 kilometer sector containing about 20 tanks and 30 APCs. This force, equivalent to a reinforced battalion, was a composite with contributions from several different units, some as small as a platoon. This would result in a complete lack of coordinated action in the battle to come. Though this sector was the most thinly garrisoned in terms of armor, it was not an easy mark. It was extensively dug-in, covered with bunkers and trenches. It also could not be attacked recklessly without inviting flank attack because there were massive numbers of armored vehicles to the south, in the central sector.

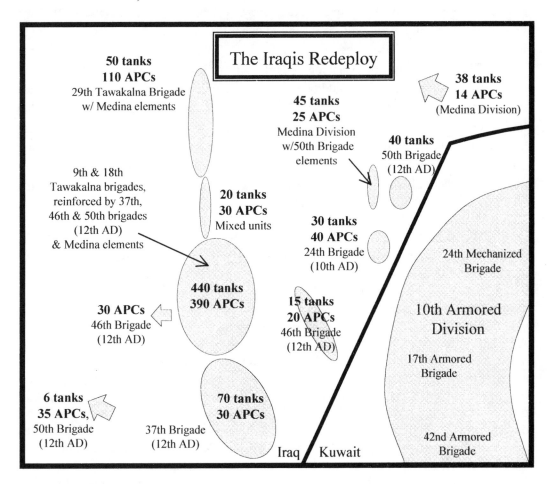

The Iraqis piled units in the center. There, the Tawakalna's 9th Armored and 18th Mechanized brigades were joined by most of the 12th Armored Division's 46th Mechanized Brigade. The Medina Division and the 12th AD's 37th and 50th Armored brigades combined to provide the equivalent of an additional brigade of tanks. All told, the Iraqis packed the some 440 tanks and 390 APCs in a sector measuring about 10 kilometers north to south and 7 kilometers east to west.

Captured documents would show that senior Iraqi officers had always considered an attack from the west a distinct possibility. However, they were relatively certain that a force attacking from that direction would be no larger than one division. In their view, to move a larger force that far west would be impossible from a logistical standpoint. In addition, unaware of Coalition satellite navigation capabilities, they believed that even if a larger force could be moved west, attempting to move it tactically across unmarked wastes would result only in units getting lost and running into each other. The Iraqis were therefore preparing to defend against a division-sized attack from the west, but were unsure of where it would fall. Packing units in the center, the Iraqis thought, would leave these units in a position to defend in place or shift to the north or south, depending on where the Coalition blow ultimately fell.

The 12th Armored Division moved most of its 37th Armored Brigade to the southern end of the Tawakalna line. These defenses slanted to the southeast, so that the brigade would be in a position to react in the event that the 1st Cavalry Division fought its way out of the Wadi al-Batin.

The Tawakalna Line was competently set up. Running behind the line was an oiled, packed-dirt road, which could be used to move units where they were needed once the Coalition ground forces hit the line. The Iraqis also maintained a reserve behind the line of about 130 tanks and 85 APCs. To provide a trip wire for the main defense line, a battalion of APCs from the division's 50th Armored Brigade moved to take up screening positions several miles to the west of the Tawakalna positions. Another battalion from the 12th AD's 46th Mechanized Brigade would venture westward from the central sector with the same intent.

Whatever the intent of the defenders, the battle would be fought on VII Corps' terms. Lt.Gen. Franks would hit the Tawakalna line along its entire length. Some accounts after the war made it appear that Franks was hesitant because he was some way intimidated by the Republican Guard. However, no one who came in contact with him during the war ever sensed any doubt on Franks' part that his corps would defeat the Guard soundly. Franks' concerns were entirely tactical. Though it had been a target of Allied air power from the earliest stages of the war, the Republican Guard was still very much intact. The Guard had been bombed heavily, but the bombing had been done mostly from higher altitudes, so accuracy suffered. As they were well behind the front lines, during the air campaign, Guard units largely escaped the precision bombing that the units to the south were subject to. They had also been able to avoid annihilation by digging in and spreading out. Most Guard battalions would fight the coming battle with 36–38 of their assigned 44 tanks and 28–30 of their 36 assigned BMPs, losing only a handful of vehicles to air attack and a few more to maintenance problems. The Republican Guard may not have been a juggernaught, but it was strong enough to inflict large numbers of casualties if it was engaged carelessly.

What Schwarzkopf and Powell were demanding called for nothing less than the temporary suspension of American armored doctrine. That doctrine stresses the need to attack in a unified fashion with maximum mass at the critical point, not "shooting from the hip" with units spread out and attacking at different times. "I want to hit them [the Republican Guard] with a fist," Franks had repeatedly emphasized before G-Day, "not with five outstretched fingers."

"If Franks hadn't halted on the first day, we would have run into the Republican Guard hungry, exhausted and out of gas," one key commander would say after the war. Neither Powell nor Schwarzkopf had ever been responsible for anything like what was being asked of Franks. Neither had ever had to move a unit that large tactically. Schwarzkopf had commanded the 24th Infantry Division, but his next command had been of an administrative cadre, not a maneuver corps. Powell had never commanded a division, and while he had commanded a maneuver corps, that command had only lasted five months before he was promoted and recalled to Washington.

Franks was certain that his corps would defeat the Guard, but he knew that once he attacked, a certain amount of disorganization would be inevitable, regardless of how lopsided the victory was. If his forces were tightly organized when they met the Guard, there would be some disorganization, some friendly fire casualties and some loss of momentum. If his units attacked haphazardly, there would be chaos, dozens of friendly fire incidents and his attack might well be halted by confusion.

In addition, while it was the world's premier tank, the Abrams also burned fuel at a higher rate than any other tank in the world. Franks understood that neither "can-do" thinking nor browbeating his subordinate leaders would change the fact that his tanks could go just so far before they had to stop and refuel.

Finally, if Franks pushed the 1st and 3rd Armored divisions forward without giving the British 1st Armoured Division time to get through the barrier and attack Iraqi armor behind it, that Iraqi armor would be in a position to drive westward and slice into the 3rd AD's right flank or into its fuel and supply trains. Franks was not the only one worried about flank attacks. Though Schwarzkopf would later be portrayed as a supremely confident commander who never had any doubt about the battle's outcome, he refused to release the 1st Cavalry Division to Franks because he felt he needed it in case the Iraqis counterattacked against the Egyptians. This raises questions about how certain Schwarzkopf was *at the time* that the Iraqis were "bugging out."

During his tirade, Schwarzkopf told Yeosock that "if Franks can't handle the job, I'll get someone who can," and threatened to replace Franks with his deputy at CENTCOM, Lt.Gen. Calvin Waller. Because Yeosock, who had extensive experience with large armored forces, felt that what Schwarzkopf was asking was unrealistic, he did not relay the threat to Franks. When he spoke to him at dawn on the 25th, he told Franks that the corps was doing fine, but that Schwarzkopf had voiced concerns about the pace of the attack. Since Franks was planning to pick up the pace anyway, he did not give Schwarzkopf's concerns much thought.

Franks told his division commanders that he intended to drive the corps hard for the next 24 to 36 hours to overcome Iraqi resistance and prevent the withdrawal of major Republican Guard concentrations. Next morning, before first light, VII Corps was moving again. Though it would require extraordinary leadership from Franks and his commanders, the 2nd ACR and the 1st and 3rd Armored divisions would strike the Tawakalna Division of the Republican Guard almost simultaneously, with the 1st Infantry Division only a few hours behind.

On the 24th, the 1st ID had destroyed the Iraqi 26th Infantry Division's 434th and 110th brigades and taken 2,500 prisoners. On the 25th, it would overrun another brigade and take about 1,500 more EPWs. Just after dawn, the 3rd Brigade moved up between the other two brigades, and all three drove outward to widen the breach.

In 1st Brigade's sector, 1-34th Armor and 1-4th Cavalry pushed out to Phase Line New Jersey, the division's limit of advance, against light resistance. Meanwhile, the other two task forces rounded up what was left of the 26th Infantry Division's border units. In a three-pronged attack, TF 2-34 captured the 20 remaining defenders of a company-sized position. TF 5-16's job would be slightly more intricate. On G-Day, the unit had cleared the trenchlines eastward to the brigade's boundary with 2nd Brigade. Having reached its eastward limit of advance on the previous day, the task force had moved back to the west and begun planning and coordinating for the next day's task, the capture of a ridge line. As the task force's two attacking companies approached the objective, they would be exposing themselves to top and flank shots from the Iraqi defenders. The tanks of B Company, 2-34th Armor, would suppress Iraqi opposition on the position and guide the companies to their assault lanes (and blind the Iraqis to a degree) by generating smoke. The M-113-mounted TOW launchers of E Company (5-16th Infantry's anti-tank company) were positioned to the northeast of B/2-34th Armor. E Company would cover the units clearing the position as the attack progressed. E Company would also watch for Iraqi tanks. Lt.Col. Baker felt that there was a chance that his attack might flush out a few previously unseen Iraqi tanks. Baker wanted to keep any tanks attempting to escape to the north from reaching the rear of 1-4th Cavalry.

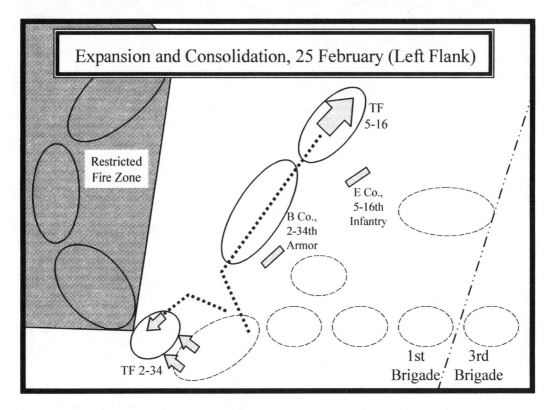

Expansion and Consolidation, 25 February (Left Flank)

Restricted Fire Zone

TF 5-16

E Co., 5-16th Infantry

B Co., 2-34th Armor

TF 2-34

1st Brigade

3rd Brigade

After receiving two HEAT rounds and a blanket of .50 caliber machine-gun fire from B/2-34, the Iraqis on the ridge chose not to contest the assault companies' approach. Once on the objective, the attacking companies had to clear it slowly and carefully to avoid fratricide, since they would be advancing directly into the rear of 1-4th Cavalry. During the attack, TF 5-16 and 1-4th Cav would be in constant radio contact. All went according to plan, and by 9 a.m., the attackers had finished clearing the position. In the assault, TF 5-16 killed at least six Iraqis, captured several more and destroyed several bunkers. No tanks were found.

The heaviest contact was made by 2nd Brigade's TF 2-16 and 4-37th Armor. TF 2-16 rolled due east along the trenchlines, mostly against the 807th Brigade of the 48th

Infantry Division, until it reached the division's boundary with the 1st Cavalry Division. TF 3-37 had attacked westward the previous day, and could not drive any farther without crossing into 1st Brigade's sector. It therefore spent the second day of the ground war following TF 2-16 eastward. The 4-37th continued to attack to the northeast, widening the bulge in preparation for the passage of the British 1st Armoured Division.

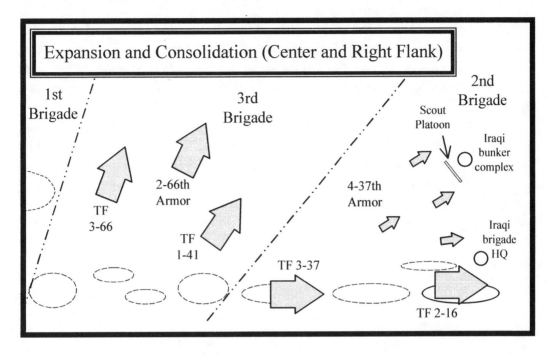

The defenders facing TF 2-16 were more willing to fight than the Iraqis the task force had faced on the previous day. These troops faced an attack that was not preceded by a heavy bombardment as had been delivered on the Iraqis the day before. Fighting spirit notwithstanding, the defenders never stood a chance. The 807th Brigade had been attacked by air for 39 straight days. Bombing, strafing and desertion had left it at about 50% strength. Its artillery support had been wiped out to the last gun by American artillery fire the day before. Now, TF 2-16 was plowing into its side. The fighting largely followed the previous day's pattern. The roughly 800 Iraqis who surrendered were herded to the rear. Those who did not were pounded by direct fire or churned under by mine plows and bulldozers.

The 4-37th came across two large complexes. To the north, the scout platoon ran into a large network of trenches, containing about 200 infantrymen. After TOW missile shots and A-10 strikes destroyed the Iraqis' transport vehicles, the A-10s went to work on the Iraqis in their trenches. After a few passes, the defenders were subjected to a barrage of mortar rounds fused to explode 2–3 feet over the trenches, spraying shrapnel into them. After the barrage, those Iraqis who were still physically able walked out of their trenches with their hands up.

On the southern flank, near the boundary with TF 2-16, the battalion came upon what was later determined to be a brigade headquarters. The position contained several cement buildings and was surrounded by trenches. Ground elements called in air strikes by two A-10s and two Apaches, which destroyed the soft-skinned vehicles near the headquarters. Next, mortar fire was directed onto the headquarters. A company of M-1A1s also opened up with main gun fire. This punishment prompted about 140 Iraqis, led by a brigadier general, to surrender to TF 2-16.

In the center of the division's attack zone, the few Iraqi tanks and APCs that were encountered were quickly destroyed by 3rd Brigade. Prisoners taken by all three brigades would report that about half of the armor that had been supporting the line units in 1st ID's sector had been destroyed by the Air Force. Most of the remainder had fled northward on G-Day.

By 11 a.m., 1st ID was ready to pass the British through its lines. Again, casualties had been light. Just before dawn, a soldier from TF 2-34 had been wounded by an anti-personnel mine. An engineer attached to TF 5-16 was wounded when he disturbed the ground near an unexploded bomblet. In the most serious incident, a mechanic on an M-88 armored recovery vehicle picked up an unexploded submunition, which exploded. He and another mechanic were killed, and another was wounded, losing an eye.*

---

*The two soldiers who died had their flak vests open (though the soldier holding the submunition would not have been saved by the vest anyway). The closed vest saved the other soldier.

18

The British Are Coming

Great Britain supplied one armored division for the ground campaign. In the British Army, when division-sized formations are necessary for a combat deployment, they are created by bringing together units suited to the requirements of the mission at hand. In this instance, the infantry-heavy 4th Armoured Brigade (57 Challenger tanks and 90 Warrior armored fighting vehicles) and the tank-heavy 7th Armoured Brigade (117 Challengers, 45 Warriors) came together to form the 1st Armoured Division. For artillery support, the division had 12 MLRS launchers and 76 self-propelled howitzers.

The division was commanded by Maj.Gen. Rupert Smith. Maj.Gen. Smith was an ideal choice to command the division. Though his regimental affiliation was with the Parachute Regiment, he was an expert on armor and armor tactics, having directed the Higher Command Staff Course and lectured on Soviet armor tactics.[*]

The division's mission was to pass through the breachhead created by the 1st Infantry Division. Once clear, it would roll eastward, slashing through armored units backstopping the Saddam Line, eliminating them as a threat to VII Corps' right flank and cutting off Iraqi front line units in the trenches.

Maj.Gen. Smith understood that the better his forces maintained their momentum, the more Iraqi units they would catch off guard or keep from escaping. If momentum was to be maintained, it was vital that fuel and ammunition reach his combat units in a timely fashion. Toward that end, he created the Route Development Battle Group, under the command of Col. Alwin Hutchinson. The RDBG, made up mostly of the 32nd Armoured Engineer Regiment, would follow the two brigades, building a road along which wheeled support vehicles could follow the attacking tanks and APCs.

The key weapon in the British offensive would be the Challenger main battle tank. At 68 tons, the Challenger is the heaviest main battle tank in the world. Like the

---

[*]Maj.Gen. Smith was a holder of the Queen's Gallantry Medal, which he earned by rescuing a subordinate officer after a car bomb explosion in 1978.

Abrams, the Challenger was designed with crew safety in mind. It too features composite armor. Though the Challenger was already regarded as one of the best protected tanks in the world, the Challengers of the 1st Armoured Division had been upgraded before the ground offensive. With reactive armor added to the front glacis plates and extra composite armor mounted on the sides of the hull, these Challengers were actually better protected than M-1A1s. It is also fairly durable. In the 100 hours of the ground war, the 1st Armoured Division moved 180 miles with few mechanical breakdowns.

Unlike the M-1A1, where the loader just shoves a round into the gun, on Challengers, the projectile and the charge that blows it out of the gun barrel are two separate items. The Challenger's charges are stored beneath the turret. Normally, this arrangement would leave a tank vulnerable to mines. A mine explosion which penetrated the tank's belly armor could set the charges alight, causing a catastrophic explosion. On the Challenger, however, the charges are stored in armored containers. Inside each container is a fire-suppressant fluid, to prevent explosions in the event that the container is penetrated.

Before the war, technical problems had limited the main gun's accuracy. However, by the time of the Gulf War, the bugs had been ironed out. A new depleted uranium projectile with more penetrating power had also been developed. Though about a dozen of these rounds were issued to each tank, few would ultimately be fired, since the British would encounter nothing larger than T-55 tanks.

The Warrior is the British Army's infantry fighting vehicle. It is similar in appearance to the Bradley and is almost identical in terms of automotive performance. It carries a Rarden cannon, which fires 30mm rounds in three-round bursts, instead of a 25mm chain-gun. Because British armor leaders believe that there is little or no excuse for infantry fighting vehicles to be taking on tanks, the Warrior has no anti-tank missile launcher, though each vehicle carries several shoulder-launched, short range 94mm Light Anti-Tank Weapons.

7th Brigade

The British began their passage at 2 p.m. on the 25th. The operation had originally been scheduled to take place that night, but the success of the ground war and the need to catch retreating Iraqi units necessitated an early passage. The first brigade to attack would be the armor-heavy 7th Brigade, under Brigadier Patrick Cordingley.

The 7th Brigade had three maneuver units: the Queen's Royal Irish Hussars (QRIH), the Royal Scots Dragoon Guards (Scots DG), both tank units, and the 1st Battalion, the Staffordshire Regiment, an armored infantry unit.[*] The units had been reorganized extensively for the assault. The 1st Staffordshire had detached one of its three armored infantry companies to the Scots DG in return for one of its four squadrons of Challengers. The Staffords also took a Challenger squadron from the QRIH, which went into the offensive with its remaining three tank squadrons and no infantry.

---

[*]Most British regiments started out with several battalions. However, as the British Empire shrank, battalions were disbanded until most regiments had only one, so in practice, the term now usually refers to a battalion.

The brigade completed its passage of lines at 3:15 p.m., took up its position on the division's left wing, and began driving eastward with the QRIH under Lt.Col. Arthur Denaro in the lead, the Staffordshire Battle Group commanded by Lt.Col. Charles Rogers to its left rear and the Scots DG Battle Group under Lt.Col. John Sharples to its right rear.* The brigade's first objective was Copper North, which was believed to contain a communications complex. The attack against the complex would be the responsibility of the Scots DG Battle Group.

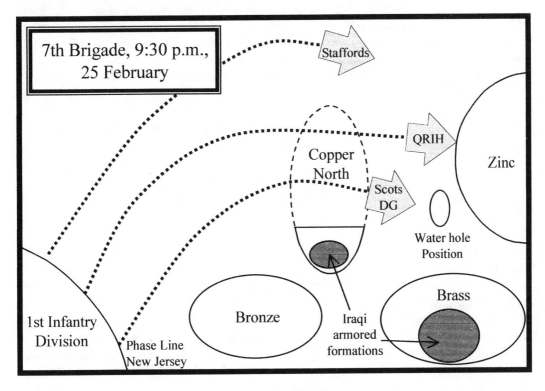

At 7:30, the communications complex was sighted. The attack plan was straightforward. The Challengers of D Squadron would drive into the position, followed by the Warrior-mounted infantry of the attached A Company, The Staffordshire Regiment, which would clear the trenches and bunkers.

Most of the light available to the attackers would be provided by the 8-ton Scorpion tracked reconnaissance vehicles of the Scots DG's Reconnaissance Troop, which used the vehicles' 76mm guns to fire parachute illumination flares. The rest of the light on the battlefield would come from burning Iraqi vehicles. Brigadier Cordingley denied Lt.Col. Sharples' request for artillery illumination. Because Iraqi artillery strength and counterbattery capabilities in this area were unclear, Cordingley felt that it would be unwise for his guns to give their positions away just to provide illumination rounds on a relatively small position.

The Warriors rolled onto the position and released the infantrymen. Due to uncertainty about enemy dispositions and the darkness of the battlefield, clearing individual bunkers by going into them was deemed too risky. Bunkers and trenches were

---

*The term "battle group" is equivalent to the American "task force," a battalion-sized unit made up of companies from different battalions.

cleared by tank and 30mm cannon fire from a distance, or white phosphorous and high-explosive grenades from closer in. After about an hour and a half of trench and bunker clearing with sporadic firefights, the position had been taken.

Meanwhile, the battle group's other two tank squadrons, A and C, had skirted around the northern edge of the communications complex and probed slowly eastward. Roughly four miles to the northeast of the complex, both squadrons encountered substantial Iraqi positions. At 11:14, A Squadron came upon an Iraqi position to the front, a network of trenches, bunkers and berms supported by a few dug-in T-55s and APCs. The position was quickly overwhelmed. About 10 minutes later, as C Squadron crested a hill, it encountered a line of several T-55s and APCs coming toward it. All 14 of the squadron's tanks fired at once, wiping out the Iraqi armored force.

In the Scots DG's battles, ten Iraqi tanks and nine APCs had been destroyed. Between 50 and 100 Iraqis had been killed, at a cost of five British wounded. About 150 prisoners had been taken.

The Scots DG moved toward its next target, a water hole between objectives Copper and Zinc. The position was occupied by dug-in infantry, tanks and APCs. As the battle group approached the trenches, six tanks left their revetments and were destroyed. A few minutes later there was a report that there might be a hospital on the objective. Lt.Col. Sharples received permission from Brigadier Cordingley to delay the attack until first light, so that he could check out the report before assaulting.

While the Scots DG Battle Group was fighting near Copper North, the QRIH was approaching Objective Zinc. The battle group had been running into small groups of Iraqi infantrymen since about 4:30 in the afternoon, and had destroyed two tanks before reaching the eastern edge of Zinc at about 9 p.m. Lt.Col. Denaro instructed each of his squadrons to edge three tanks forward to gain as much information as possible about the objective while the brigade's artillery moved into position for a fire mission.

Cordingley would bring every gun he could to bear on Zinc. He had been provided with virtually no information about Iraqi dispositions on the objective. Though Zinc actually contained about 55 operational armored vehicles (about 35 tanks and 20 APCs), Cordingley believed that the objective might contain as many as a hundred tanks. He therefore wanted to assault it with as much force as he could muster.

Cordingley had planned to attack the objective with all three of his battle groups, but with the Scots DG Battle Group held up at the water hole until daybreak, only two were immediately available. As a result, he was inclined to delay the attack until shortly after daybreak. However, when he asked Maj.Gen. Smith what he thought of the idea, Smith indicated that he would be "disappointed" if the attack were delayed until morning. At 11:30, Cordingley, divining the division commander's intent through his understatement, gave orders for a two-battle group assault on Zinc. QRIH would attack first, through the southern half of the objective. The 1st Staffordshire Battle Group, well behind QRIH, would hit the northern portion a few hours later.

Thirty minutes past midnight, Lt.Col. Denaro pulled his tanks back in preparation for the artillery strike. At one, two batteries of MLRS launchers and 48 guns opened up on Zinc for about 20 minutes. After the barrage, the QRIH attacked Zinc from west to east.

The QRIH advanced cautiously until about 3:30, when over thirty thermal signatures appeared on B Squadron's gunsights. Though both tanks and artillery were ready to fire, the hot spots were not engaged, since it was not clear whether they were enemy or friendly. By 4:15, the QRIH gunners were sure they were Iraqi. D Squadron engaged the Iraqis at long range. As soon as the first rounds impacted, destroying three tanks, the Iraqis withdrew toward Objective Platinum at top speed, outrunning an artillery barrage called in by D Squadron's commander.

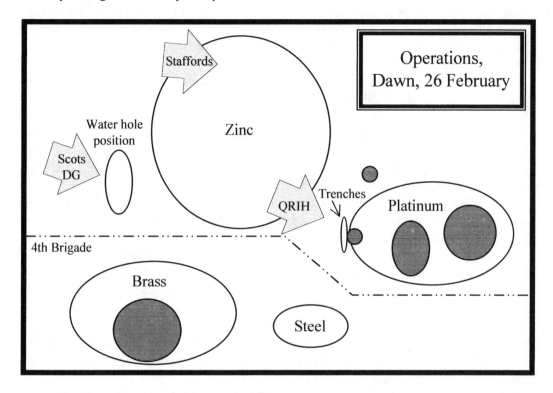

At about 5:30, the Staffordshire BG, which had bypassed Copper North, began its drive across Zinc. The Staffords found only abandoned positions and vehicles which had been destroyed during the air campaign or by the earlier artillery bombardment. In QRIH's sector, there was no resistance, but there was still a delay. B Squadron's medics were swamped by Iraqis wounded in the artillery barrage. As the casualties were treated, the squadron found and destroyed five abandoned armored vehicles.

Meanwhile, the Scots DG Battle Group began its assault on the water hole after it was determined that this was not a hospital, but a headquarters and logistics site. By now, the one-sided nature of the battle had become apparent, so Brigadier Cordingley had directed his men to avoid slaughtering Iraqi troops if possible. He ordered that where tactically possible, warning shots or small artillery barrages should be used to persuade Iraqis to surrender. All tanks, artillery pieces and AA guns, however, were to be treated as hostile and destroyed on sight.

As Lt.Col. Sharples' Challengers trained their guns on every vehicle or building they could see, an American psychological operations vehicle was brought forward to broadcast a call to surrender in Arabic over loudspeakers. The Warriors then rolled on to the main Iraqi positions. Not a shot was fired by the Iraqis, who began to surrender. By dawn, the British had rounded up 500 EPWs.

In the QRIH's sector, daylight revealed not only the wreckage of Iraqi vehicles destroyed the night before, but a large network of berms and trenches that intelligence had overlooked, just a short distance ahead. From 7:30–7:40, the QRIH destroyed nine T-55s, three BMPs, and an MTLB armored personnel carrier. Some of the vehicles were trying to escape. Others were moving toward the squadron.

Another position was spotted to the northwest of the QRIH's next objective, Platinum. The position dominated the ground across which Lt.Col. Denaro intended to attack. It was manned by dug-in infantry and tanks. As the position was within the 1st Staffordshire Battle Group's zone of advance, Brigadier Cordingley ordered the battle group to take it.

Lt.Col. Rogers sent the Challengers of C Squadron, QRIH, which had been attached to the 1st Staffordshire Battle Group before G-Day, followed by the Staffords' B Company to clear the strongpoint. The attack kicked off at 9:20, and began with C Squadron destroying abandoned trucks dug-in along a berm. The tankmen soon noticed a number of T-55s and MTLBs dug-in along the same line and began destroying them. After the Challengers had destroyed every vehicle along the length of the berm, they bypassed Iraqi infantry positions and rolled to the far end of the objective.

Following behind the Challengers, B Company's Warriors moved forward and debussed infantry to clear the Iraqi trenches in detail. Many of the Iraqi positions were so well-concealed that the Staffords did not spot them until they were on top of them or even past them. Fortunately, many of the positions were unoccupied, or occupied by Iraqis who decided to surrender rather than take advantage of an opportunity to spring an ambush. By about eleven, the 1st Staffordshire Battle Group had eliminated the last resistance and was on its way to its portion of Objective Platinum.

The positions between the British and Objective Platinum marked the beginning of the heart of the 52nd Armored Division's defenses. The division was made up of two independent armored brigades (the 52nd and 80th) and a recently formed mechanized brigade (the 11th). The 52nd Brigade, in the division's western sector, had been rendered combat-ineffective by Coalition air power before G-Day. In an attempt to bolster it, the 80th Brigade had been ordered to give the 52nd its only mechanized infantry battalion. To the south of the 52nd Brigade, the 48th Infantry Division had lost 18 of its 25 tanks to air attacks. The 80th had been ordered to give one of its three armored battalions to the 48th Division. The 48th also received a battalion of APCs from the 11th Brigade. The 80th and 11th Brigades then essentially merged, to form a force of three tank and three mechanized battalions. Though nearly fifty armored vehicles in the northern portion of the force's dispositions would be destroyed by the U.S. Army's 2nd Armored Cavalry Regiment's 1st Squadron, most of it was in 7th Brigade's sector.

Objective Platinum contained almost a thousand troops, about 40 tanks and 20 APCs (including the roughly 20 tanks and 10 APCs which had escaped there from Zinc). It had been divided by brigade planners into two sub-objectives, Platinum 1 (the western half) and Platinum 2 (the eastern half).

The attack on Platinum 1 would be preceded by a 90-minute artillery barrage. Brigadier Cordingley had concluded that the Iraqis his men were facing were largely a broken force, and that massive artillery barrages were unnecessary. For this reason, and because he felt that he might need MLRS rockets if the brigade ran into the Republican Guard, Cordingley relied solely on tube artillery for the barrage. Next, while the QRIH (and the Staffords' C Company, borrowed for the assault) cleared Platinum 1, the 1st Staffordshire Battle Group would move to the north of Platinum. After a barrage on Platinum 2, it would drive to the southeast, slashing through the objective.

Just after noon, QRIH launched its attack. While B Squadron laid a base of fire, the rest of the battle group launched a two-pronged attack to clear Platinum 1. A Squadron and the attached company of Staffords pushed southward on the northern flank, while D Squadron swung down toward the bottom of the objective, then drove eastward. The only resistance came from a pair of T-55s which opened fire on D Squadron. Both were quickly destroyed. TOW missiles, launched by Lynx helicopters, claimed an additional three MTLBs and four T-55s.

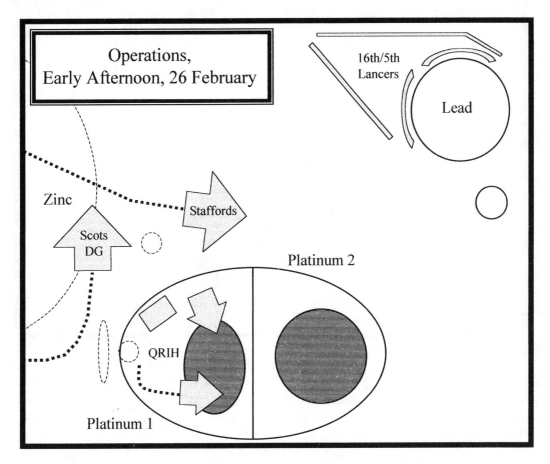

Slightly after 12:30, Lt.Col. Denaro radioed Brigadier Cordingley and told him that an English-speaking Iraqi had said that the Iraqis on the position wanted to surrender and that their commander had ordered them to do so. Denaro suggested that if this were the case, the Staffords might not need artillery preparation for their assault on Platinum 2. Cordingley had a feeling that the Iraqi was telling the truth, but felt that he could not take chances. He decided that there would be a short preparatory barrage on Platinum 2, after which the Iraqis could surrender to his advancing ground troops.

By 12:45, the QRIH had secured Platinum 1, had taken about 150 prisoners and was laying a base of fire to support the Staffords' attack on Platinum 2. By now, well-concealed Iraqi infantrymen in a screen line were jumping up and surrendering between the Challengers and the tanks they were shooting at. Firing over or around the surrendering Iraqis, the Challengers destroyed several Iraqi armored vehicles.

On Platinum 2, the Staffords' reconnaissance platoon and the attached mobile Milan anti-tank missile launcher section came upon a group of dug-in T-55s, APCs and some trucks. Firing 13 Milan missiles from behind the Iraqis, the section scored 12 hits, destroying 11 vehicles and a command bunker.*

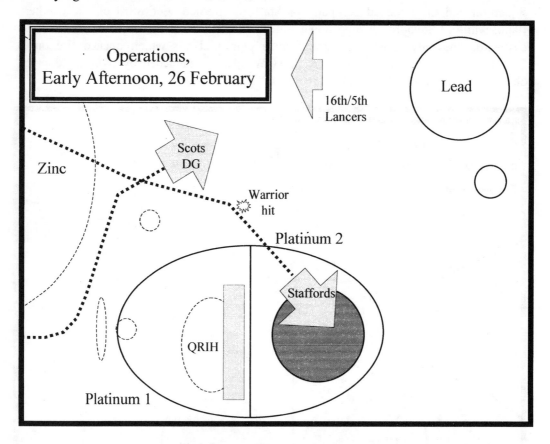

Operations,
Early Afternoon, 26 February

16th/5th
Lancers

Lead

Scots
DG

Zinc

Warrior
hit

Platinum 2

Staffords

QRIH

Platinum 1

After the Milan launchers had taken a large bite out of the defenses on Platinum 2, the Staffords' assault went in with the attached tank squadrons from the QRIH and the Scots DG leading and the Staffords' B Company trailing in the center. There was almost no Iraqi fire. Iraqi fighting spirit was now broken to an extent which would astound the British. One staff officer noticed that there was a large group of Iraqis in the center of the position walking around with their hands in their pockets. Each time a Challenger would fire a round over their heads to destroy a T-55 in the distance, they would run to a different (and safer) location and begin walking around with their hands in their pockets again. By just after five, the Iraqi armor on Platinum 2 lay in ruins. The battle group paused briefly to collect its 800 prisoners before moving northeast, to Objective Lead.

The prisoners, which included a brigadier general and two full colonels, were seemingly all old men or teenagers. As some of them were interrogated, the brigade's officers were surprised to learn that a handful of the prisoners were from the 17th Armored Division, which had been stationed 40–50 miles to the east. Having been cobbled together from three independent brigades, the 52nd Armored Division had no assigned division-level support troops. These were provided by assigning various support units from other divisions to the 52nd. These Iraqis were from an attached medical unit.

_____

*The Milan is an exceptionally potent weapon. During this engagement, an Iraqi tank commander was blown from his hatch and 40 feet into the air.

During the fighting for Platinum 2, a Challenger accidentally hit a 1st Staffordshire Battle Group command vehicle (a Warrior) with a HESH round. The incident occurred slightly after two. The Scots DG Battle Group was heading north to take its place for the assault on Objective Lead. The battle group's path brought it close to the rear elements of the 1st Staffordshire Battle Group. In a blinding sandstorm, a Challenger from the Scots DG Battle Group engaged what its commander thought was an Iraqi tank. Fortunately, because the HESH round struck a block of add-on composite armor on the side of the Warrior, no one inside the vehicle was killed or wounded, although an officer outside the Warrior received fragmentation wounds which later resulted in the amputation of his leg.

While the QRIH and the 1st Staffordshire Battle Group were securing Platinum, part of the 7th Brigade was already fighting at Objective Lead. Intelligence had estimated that between Lead and a command post just south of the main position, the brigade would be dealing with a battalion of dug-in mechanized infantry supported by a company of tanks. However, while the number of armored vehicles was accurate, there would turn out to be roughly a full brigade of soldiers on the two positions.

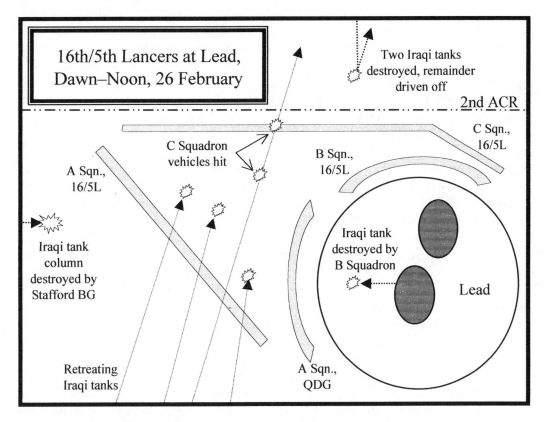

Lt.Col. Phillip Scott's 16th/5th Lancers and the attached A Squadron, The Queen's Dragoon Guards had reached Objective Lead on the previous night. The Lancers' mission was to screen the objective from the west and bring it under fire at dawn on the 26th. This would keep Iraqi units there from interfering with the attack on Platinum, to the southwest. The screen was thin due to the amount of ground the regiment had to cover. The northern and western edges of Lead had to be screened, and this was done by 16th/5th Lancers' B Squadron and A Squadron, The Queen's Dragoon Guards. To keep Iraqis from driving southward into the rear of these squadrons, C Squadron set up a screen line along 1st Armoured Division's northern boundary, which it shared with the 2nd Armored Cavalry Regiment. A diagonal screen line was set up by A Squadron, 16th/5th Lancers to keep Iraqi tanks fleeing Objective Platinum from venturing into the rear of C-16th/5th Lancers and A-Queen's DG.

As day broke, the Lancers probed the position, called in artillery strikes and directed an air raid on it by two A-10s. The air raid, lasting from 7:20 to 7:40, destroyed 10 Iraqi tanks and APCs. A short while later, a tank was destroyed by a 4,090 meter flank shot by a B Squadron Striker with a Swingfire anti-tank missile as it approached A-Queen's DG.* Meanwhile, an Iraqi column of about six tanks moving southward from 2nd ACR's sector was driven off after losing two T-55s to C Squadron Swingfires.

By late morning, Iraqi tanks fleeing 7th Brigade's attacks on and around Platinum began making contact with A-16th/5th's screen line. Using 30mm cannon, the squadron's Scimitars destroyed one tank and disabled another, while one of its Strikers scored a kill with a Swingfire.† There were losses, however. Aided by a sandstorm which limited visibility to around 100 meters, an Iraqi Type 59 tank retreating northward slipped past A Squadron and caught two unarmed armored recovery vehicles in the open and gave chase. One broke down, but before it could be destroyed by the Iraqi tank, the second vehicle's crew used the swirling sandstorm to their advantage, and swung around to evacuate the other crew. During the evacuation, two crewmen from the second vehicle were killed by heavy machine-gun fire from the tank. The same tank then later hit a Scimitar on the C Squadron screen line. Luckily, the sabot round tore through that vehicle's thin armor so easily that it did not produce enough spall inside the vehicle to kill or wound any of the three crewmembers. The Iraqi tank's crew was also more concerned with continuing its escape than with finishing off the crewmen.

At around the same time, a column of about six T-55s moving from west to east was spotted by A Squadron. As the squadron deployed its Strikers, however, the tank column was wiped out by tanks attached to the Staffordshire BG, which at the time was moving toward its jumping-off positions for the assault on Platinum 2.

Just after noon, Lt.Col. Scott began to reappraise the tactical situation. There was no need for 16th/5th Lancers to remain where it was. The Iraqis on Lead had sustained heavy losses as a result of the combination of the air and artillery attacks, and their morale had been shattered. There was no longer any danger of them interfering with the attack on Platinum. In addition, with visibility severely limited by the sandstorm, there was a risk that Scott's vehicles might be mistakenly engaged as the Scots DG approached Lead. He requested permission to withdraw. Permission was granted.

At 3:15, the Scots DG arrived at Lead, and found that most Iraqis on the objective were ready to give up. By nightfall, the battle group had succeeded in mopping up the few pockets of remaining Iraqi resistance and had taken some 800 prisoners.

Having spent the afternoon fighting on Platinum, then rounding up prisoners, the Staffords did not reach the command post south of Lead until 5:30. Thus, the sun was already setting when the a company of the battle group's Warriors approached the trench lines in front of the objective. Though it was immediately apparent that the trench

---

*The Striker is similar to the Scorpion in that it also weighs eight tons and is tracked, but it has no turret, no gun, and fires the Swingfire anti-tank missile.

†A Scimitar is essentially a Scorpion with a 30mm Rarden cannon instead of a 76mm.

network and the garrison were much more substantial than the Staffords had been led to expect, it appeared as if this would be another routine Iraqi prisoner roundup. As soon as the first warning shots were fired, large groups of Iraqis began to surrender.

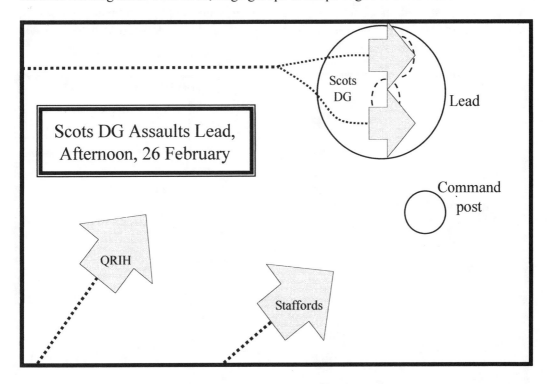

Scots DG Assaults Lead, Afternoon, 26 February

Events soon took a violent turn, however. As several Warrior squads dismounted to round up the surrendering Iraqis, a group of Iraqis launched a counterattack from the cluster of buildings that made up the command post. An RPG round cut through one infantryman's chest, killing him. The RPG then hit a Warrior, setting it afire and wounding another squad member. After two hours of close combat, Iraqi resistance was broken, with the Iraqis suffering heavy casualties and losing another 524 prisoners.

At daybreak on the 27th, 7th Brigade was on its way toward Objective Varsity, inside Kuwait. The objective was believed to be occupied by an Iraqi brigade. A Squadron, The Queen's Dragoon Guards would provide the brigade's cavalry screen for the remainder of the war. The 16th/5th Lancers would be responsible for guarding the division's support units during the advance.

At 8 a.m., the Scots DG halted at the north–south grid line 74 Easting and called in an artillery strike on 16 T-55s and a few hundred infantrymen in defensive positions. This was the last intact unit of the 12th Armored Division's 37th Armored Brigade, which had been overrun by the 1st Infantry Division the night before. As the three battle groups moved forward, they would find hundreds of Iraqis who had decided that enough was enough, and were waving white rags.

By ten, the brigade had crossed into Kuwait. Up to this point, the brigade's advance had been almost picture perfect. However, almost as soon as the brigade entered Kuwait, things began to go wrong.

Just after eleven, a QRIH headquarters vehicle broke down, and was left behind with several other APCs and a field ambulance with a section of medics. Almost immediately, the vehicles began taking small arms fire. There was confusion as to whether the fire was friendly or enemy until an officer from D Squadron reported seeing green (Iraqi) tracer fire coming from a position to the vehicles' rear.* Just before 11:30, A Squadron's second in command headed toward the Iraqi position at high speed, causing the Iraqis to flee. The thirteen Iraqis were then chased down, disarmed, and sent west to join the other prisoners.

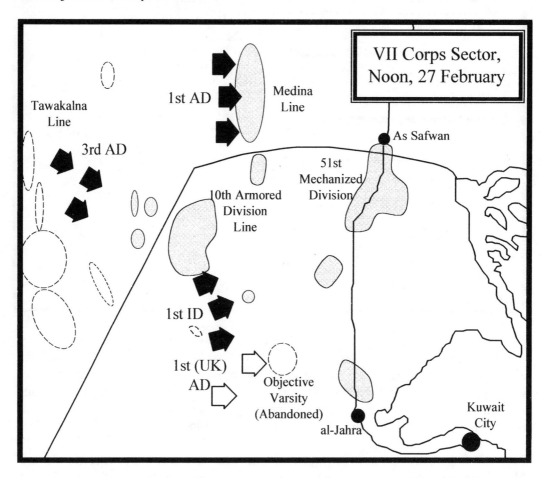

At almost the same moment that these vehicles came under fire, the QRIH Reconnaissance Troop was destroying the weapons of some prisoners it had just taken when it came under tank fire. In the first volley, a sabot round sliced through the front right corner of a Scorpion and lodged in the gearbox. A command vehicle was also hit. That volley was followed by intense machine-gun fire. The vehicle crews dismounted their vehicles and headed for the cover of a nearby berm. The tanks then switched from sabot to HEAT rounds, all the while directing a torrent of machine-gun bullets at the dismounted crewmen. The British were sure that the tanks were American, but the fire coming at them was so intense that they could not reach their radios to report it. Finally,

---

*Regular ground soldiers are not equipped with rifle-mounted night vision scopes, so in a night fight, every fourth or fifth bullet fired by a soldier will be a "tracer" round. Tracer rounds leave a trail as they streak toward the enemy, allowing the infantryman to adjust his fire. NATO standard tracers are red, Warsaw Pact standard tracers were green.

after about 10 minutes, a white flag was fashioned and raised. The tank fire, which was coming from the 1st Infantry Division, stopped. The British had sustained two wounded and lost a Scorpion, which had been damaged beyond repair.

By one in the afternoon, Objective Varsity was secure. The brigade's soldiers found the objective virtually abandoned, littered with discarded rifles and cartridge belts. There were only a few dozen Iraqis, all of whom were happy to surrender.

Although there were no Iraqi units to impede the brigade's progress, it halted at Varsity until the next morning for fear of becoming entangled in more friendly fire incidents with American armor. It was here that Lt.Col. Sharples' Challenger recorded the longest confirmed kill of the war, a T-55 destroyed at about 3.2 miles.

At 6:00 a.m. the next morning, the 7th Brigade headed for Objective Cobalt (a point north of al-Jahra), to cut the Basra Road. There, it would take up defensive positions, tie in with the U.S. 1st Infantry Division to the north, and the Tiger Brigade, attached to the 2nd Marine Division, to the south. The brigade traversed rough ground at top speed to reach Cobalt at 7:30, 30 minutes before the cease-fire went into effect.

4th Brigade

On 25 February, the infantry-heavy 4th Brigade, under Brigadier Christopher Hammerbeck, began its advance at 7:30, about four hours after 7th Brigade. The 14th/20th King's Hussars, under the command of Lt.Col. Michael Vickery, was the brigade's armored battalion.[*][†] The 1st Royal Scots, under Lt.Col. Iain Johnstone, and the 3rd Battalion, Royal Regiment of Fusiliers (3rd RRF), commanded by Lt.Col. Andrew Larpent, were the brigade's armored infantry battalions.[‡] Once the brigade cleared the breach, it assumed its place on the division's southern flank and headed east. The brigade's first opponents would be from the 52nd Armored Brigade of the 52nd Armored Division.

The 52nd Armored Brigade had begun the war with a serious shortage of tanks, with 79 of the 108 it was supposed to have. Worse, it was positioned at what would be the pivot point of the VII Corps' attack, so it was given special attention during the bombing campaign. At 10 a.m. on 17 January, only hours after Baghdad was first struck, the brigade received a visit from an A-10. The air attacks continued throughout the day, killing 15 soldiers and destroying 13 tank transporters and fuel trucks.

The brigade had only moved into its positions five days before the bombing began. On rocky ground, with only hand shovels and one backhoe to work with, the brigade was totally unprepared for the bombing. One battalion had dug its tanks in to an average depth of one meter. The other two tank battalions, its mechanized battalion, and all of the unit's soft-skinned vehicles were fully exposed. Almost daily visits from

---

[*]The 14th/20th's unusual numerical designation is the result of a merger with another unit. During an earlier defense cutback, the Army could not bring itself to disband either the 14th or the 20th regiments, both units with distinguished histories, so it merged the two regiments.

[†]The regiment had only 43 of its full complement of 57 tanks during the war. One of its squadrons remained in Germany.

[‡]A carryover from an earlier era, the term "fusilier" refers to a soldier with a light flintlock musket. The term has been retained by some British Army units as a matter of tradition.

ground attack aircraft ravaged the unit's tanks. Division headquarters sent a replacement force of 20 MTLBs and a T-55 from the 80th Brigade, but within a day, three of the MTLBs were wrecked. Thirty-five Iraqis were killed and another forty-five wounded in the air raids, which continued up to G-Day. Another 550 had deserted. The vast majority of the unit's armored vehicles were a memory. What remained of the brigade's armor, 27 tanks and 24 APCs, was in no position to threaten VII Corps' flank, back up Iraqi front line positions, or even defend itself.

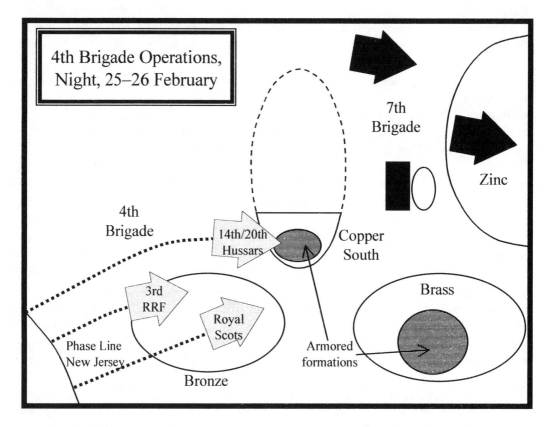

At about 10 p.m., the 4th Brigade made its first contact when 14th/20th Hussars destroyed an Iraqi communications site. To the south, the 1st Royal Scots surprised and overran an artillery position. Almost immediately after these engagements, the regiment came upon a system of berms and bunkers occupied by about two companies of mechanized infantry, Objective Bronze.

At 10:30 p.m., after a massive barrage of both conventional and MLRS artillery, the attack on Bronze began. Warriors of the 1st Royal Scots and an attached squadron of tanks from the Life Guards cut through the southern part of the position. The Warriors opened up on the Iraqis with 30mm cannon, while the Life Guards' 14 Challengers added HESH rounds and heavy machine-gun fire. Lt.Col. Johnstone's intelligence officer, who spoke Arabic, was able to hastily construct a map of the Iraqi defenses from the first prisoner interrogations. Armed with this information, the Royal Scots were able to clear the rest of their sector much more quickly. By 2:30 a.m., the fight was over. The Royal Scots quickly reformed and moved out with more than a hundred prisoners in tow.

To the north of Bronze, the Challengers of the 14th/20th Hussars destroyed a handful of armored vehicles and took a number of Iraqis prisoner. While the 1st Royal

Scots continued to clear their portion of Bronze, the 14th/20th Hussars headed for the brigade's next objective, Copper South.

The Hussars had been told to expect a few guns and infantrymen. Instead, as they approached the objective just before midnight, they spotted more than 30 Iraqi armored vehicles, artillery pieces and supply trucks, as well as scores of infantrymen.

Challengers opened the battle by surprising and destroying several tanks in their revetments. Some of the Iraqi tanks had been abandoned. Others were immobilized when their crews removed the tank batteries for use in providing light and heat for the bunkers. Some were inoperative due to mechanical failure and could not have moved if the batteries had been left in. After the initial shock wore off, the Iraqis attempted to fight back, and although the Hussars would suffer no casualties in the fighting that ensued, it would take 5½ hours to clear Copper South.

By 10:00 on the morning of the 26th, the entire 4th Brigade was deployed on line above Objective Brass with the 1st Royal Scots in the west, 14th/20th Hussars in the center, and the 3rd RRF in the east. The brigade had hooked to the north of the position in the hours before dawn, and would now attack the Iraqi defenders from the rear.

Brass contained a battalion of tanks and a battalion of APCs which had been assigned to the 48th Infantry Division by the 52nd Armored Division's 80th Armored and 11th Mechanized brigades, respectively. The western portion of the objective (Brass 1) contained about 10 armored vehicles and about 200 infantrymen. There were about 40 live armored vehicles and a few artillery pieces in the center of the position (Brass 2). The eastern portion (Brass 3) was the most lightly garrisoned and held just a few artillery pieces. All of the Iraqi equipment was dug-in. The battle groups would attack one at a time, so that all of the brigade's available artillery could be concentrated in support of each attack. Each battle group would attack as soon as the last shells were falling, while the Iraqis were still huddled in their shelters.

At 10:30, the 1st Royal Scots went in. The opening salvo from the Life Guards' Challengers left four T-55s in flames. The Challengers then destroyed several APCs in their fighting positions. Moments later, Warriors plowed into the position, releasing a company of Royal Scots infantrymen who went to work clearing the trenches. Next, 14th/20th Hussars overran the Iraqi center, destroying 21 tanks and 16 APCs.[*] By 1 p.m., Brass 1 and 2 had fallen. The last trenches on Brass fell to the 3rd RRF at three.[†]

During the fighting, several Iraqi tank crews fired on British armored vehicles (without effect), but Iraqi resistance on Brass was not coordinated. Units were on their own. Command and control, which had never been very effective, was now non-existent. In many instances, Iraqi officers had simply run away, leaving their men to their own devices. Those men were in no position to offer organized resistance when the British arrived.

After securing Brass 2, the 14th/20th Hussars was tasked with holding the brigade's southern flank while the other two battle groups prepared for a night assault on Objective Tungsten, an Iraqi artillery site defending the Wadi al-Batin. Brigadier Hammerbeck reorganized his brigade extensively for that assault. The 14th/20th Hussars

---

[*]An additional 17 tanks and 7 APCs on the position had previously been destroyed by air attacks.

[†]After the fighting, in an astounding medical feat, British surgeons were able to save the life of an Iraqi who had been shot 16 times.

lost its three squadrons of tanks, one to the 1st Royal Scots Battle Group and two to the 3rd RRF. In return, it received a company of Warrior-borne infantry from each of those battle groups.

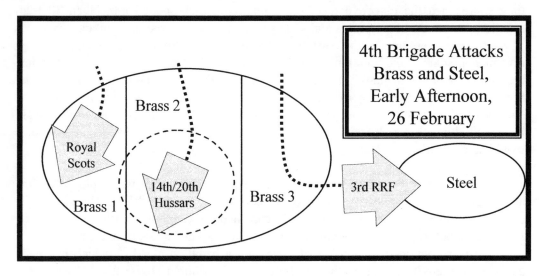

The added infantry came in handy. In addition to its flank guard duties, 14th/20th Hussars now had to deal with vast numbers of Iraqi prisoners. Lt.Col. Vickery would say later that at this point, his men had begun to count prisoners in acres rather than in numbers. The decomposition of the Saddam Line had sent hundreds of terrified Iraqis fleeing into the brigade's path. The 14th/20th already had, among its bag of prisoners, two division commanders, several brigade commanders, a number of battalion commanders, and even a Ba'ath Party commissar who had been in charge of one of the "execution squads" responsible for catching and shooting Iraqi deserters.

The British Army had found during World War II that when units are outflanked in the desert, their only rational choice is surrender. With no food and no water, there can be no question of prolonged sieges. One of the more memorable images of Britain's World War II experience in the desert was the sight of tens of thousands of Italian and German prisoners of war tramping across the desert. These vast hordes became a major logistical problem as the undermanned British force struggled to secure, feed and move the Axis POWs. The rate of surrenders soon outraced the 8th Army's ability to process the POWs, and the Desert Army began to choke on its prisoners. At one point, 30,000 British soldiers had taken 130,000 prisoners.

This time, the Army had planned ahead. Attached to the division were the King's Own Scottish Borderers, the 1st Coldstream Guards and the Royal Highland Fusiliers. These three battalions were assigned to the handling of Iraqi prisoners. However, even with some 25% of Britain's combat troops in the Gulf dedicated to prisoner handling, the division was ultimately swamped by prisoners.

Almost immediately after securing Brass 3, the 3rd RRF, with an attached company of Grenadier Guards and Challengers from 14th/20th Hussars, attacked Objective Steel. On the way, the battle group passed dozens of Iraqi artillery pieces, the vast majority of which were pointed to the south, in the wrong direction. After another heavy bombardment, the ground assault went in. With the competitive phase of the war long since over, most Iraqis chose to surrender. The few positions that held out were dealt with quickly by either main gun or 30mm cannon fire. Prisoner roundup, by now a practiced skill for the Fusiliers, was going smoothly, especially since the sandstorm had broken and visibility had cleared dramatically.

Suddenly one Warrior exploded, then another. Soldiers looked frantically for an Iraqi tank they might have missed. Seeing none, many stopped in their tracks, suspecting that the vehicles had been the victims of mines. When the division and brigade Air Liaison Officers (ALOs) realized that a report of the location of a strike by an A-10 coincided with the location of the stricken Warriors, it was apparent that the British had suffered a friendly fire incident.

Nine soldiers were killed and eleven wounded in the air strike. Some of the casualties were actually a safe distance away from the APCs during the A-10 strike, but were killed or injured trying to pull wounded comrades from the burning vehicles. Six of the dead were Fusiliers and three were members of the Queen's Own Highlanders assigned to the battle group for the attack.

The seeds of this tragedy were sown in mid-February. Iraqi ground forces had to be softened up in preparation for the ground war. This was best done by low level air attacks, and Iraqi SAM capability had been degraded to the point where low level attack runs seemed possible. Altitude restrictions were dropped. Within 24 hours, two A-10s had been shot down and another had been badly damaged. Chastened, the Air Force reimposed the altitude restrictions. As a result, the A-10 which fired the missiles at the Warriors did so from a relatively high altitude, which, though safer for flying, made target identification far more difficult.

The accident only held up the assault for a few moments. By 4 p.m., the objective was in British hands, and the 4th Brigade was headed for Objective Tungsten. The most difficult part of this assault was negotiating the terrain between objectives Steel and Tungsten. The terrain got increasingly rough as the brigade approached its target. The tanks also had to maneuver around a pipeline to the west of Tungsten. By 11:30 p.m., after a seven-hour drive, 4th Brigade was forming for its final assault.

The assault was preceded by a massive rocket and artillery barrage, in which the British were joined by the 142nd Arkansas National Guard Field Artillery Brigade. The 3rd RRF and the 1st Royal Scots advanced mostly to surrendering Iraqis and only sporadic gunfire. Though they had seen some indication that the barrage had been effective from secondary explosions on the objective, the advancing troops had no way of knowing that 59 of 76 Iraqi guns on Tungsten had been destroyed and that 90% of the enemy gunners had been killed or wounded. The British were surprised to find a number of South African-made G-5 155mm artillery pieces, which the Iraqis had hidden for use against an Allied attack through the Wadi al-Batin which never came.

An Iraqi observation post was the last holdout on Tungsten. The Royal Scots began by calling in artillery on the position. After the barrage lifted, Warriors and a platoon of dismounted infantry pelted the Iraqis thoroughly with a hail of 30mm cannon and small arms fire, periodically calling by loudspeaker on the Iraqis to surrender. Finally, several of the Royal Scots' bullets found the position's commanding officer, killing him and enabling his men to surrender. Two tanks and two MTLBs were also captured, and were destroyed.

Tungsten was the brigade's last battle of the war. There would be one more engagement, as Challengers from 14th/20th Hussars mistakenly engaged two Spartan air defense vehicles. In one of the vehicles, the hit did not produce a catastrophic explosion, and two crewmen were able to escape from the vehicle and rescue the third crewman, who had only been slightly burned. In the other, a massive explosion resulted, and it was obvious to onlookers that no one inside the vehicle could have survived. Fortunately, shortly before the strike, all three of the crewmen had walked away from the vehicle to relieve themselves after a long drive.[*]

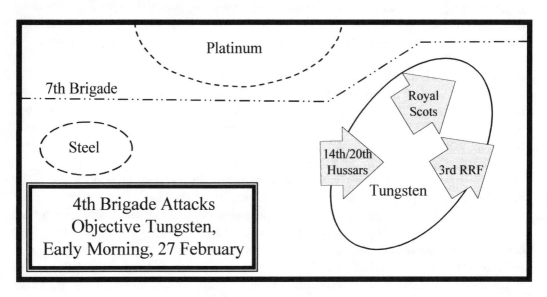

During the ground war, the 1st Armoured Division captured over 8,000 Iraqi soldiers and destroyed some 120 tanks, 90 APCs, 50 wheeled vehicles, 30 artillery pieces and 5 anti-aircraft guns. At its position along the Basra Highway, the division gathered roughly 160 abandoned armored vehicles, most of them from what used to be the 1st Mechanized Brigade of the 1st Mechanized Division and the independent 58th Armored Brigade before those units' soldiers abandoned their vehicles and headed northward. There were also about 20 tanks from the nearby 2nd Infantry Division, which had been guarding the coast against amphibious assault. The British also found a variety of armored vehicles, including a handful of T-72s and BMPs, from the tiny groups of armor which had escaped the U.S. Marine zone before the fall of al-Jahra. The majority of the vehicles captured along the highway were sent back to Britain for analysis, use in exercises, or as unit trophies. In the days following the cease-fire, British soldiers retraced their path, destroying about 65 tanks, 35 APCs, 60 wheeled vehicles, 160 artillery pieces and 150 AA guns abandoned by the Iraqis. In all, the 1st Armoured Division had removed about 240 tanks and 195 APCs from Iraqi service. In the process, the division lost 12 dead and 27 wounded in combat (3 killed and 11 wounded by Iraqi fire).

---

[*]The Spartan is a member of the same family of vehicles as the Scorpion, Scimitar and Striker. Like the Striker, it has no turret.

19

The Battle of 73 Easting

The tip of the VII Corps' spear was Col. L.D. Holder's 2nd Armored Cavalry Regiment. The 2nd ACR's mission was to find and engage the Republican Guard, then pull aside to let VII Corps' heavy divisions make the kill. It was fitting that Holder would lead the charge into Iraq. As a member of the Department of Tactics at Fort Leavenworth, he had written the final draft of Field Manual 100–5, the AirLand Battle doctrine. Later, as the director of Fort Leavenworth's School of Advanced Military Studies, he had helped revise it. Now, he would be on the leading edge of its application.

Though its mission dictated that it not become decisively engaged, the regiment had the combat power to take care of itself if it did. With 125 M-1A1s and 115 Bradleys, the 2nd ACR had about as much armor as a reinforced armored brigade. In addition to its own battalion of self-propelled 155mm howitzers, the regiment had been given Col. Gary Bourne's 210th Field Artillery Brigade by VII Corps. The brigade consisted of two battalions of self-propelled 155mm howitzers and an MLRS battery (nine launchers), about enough artillery to support an entire division. VII Corps also added the 82nd Engineer Battalion to the regiment's own engineer company —again, enough for a division. Incorporating the additional artillery and engineer units into the regiment proved no problem, as the units had trained together regularly in Germany.

The regiment's own Cobra attack helicopters were supplemented by a battalion of 18 Apache attack helicopters from the 1st Armored Division. Counting intelligence, psyops, logistics and special purpose troops (like a smoke generating company), the 2nd ACR would go into Iraq with about 9,000 soldiers.

The 2nd ACR slipped into Iraq on 23 February. At 1:30 p.m., every gun and launcher in the regiment opened up on the northern side of the border berm to deal with any Iraqi artillery spotters who might be lurking there. While the shells and rockets were still falling, engineers moved forward and began cutting 43 lanes through the berm.

Through the smoke and dust from the final rounds of the barrage, the regiment's air scouts edged north of the berm to provide cover as the engineers completed their tasks. Just after two, ground squadrons began passing through the lanes. Lt.Col. Michael Kobbe's 2nd Squadron (on the left) and Lt.Col. Scott Marcy's 3rd Squadron (on the right) advanced about six miles into Iraq without finding any Iraqis. At 3:30, Holder halted his lead units, which prepared to deal with any Iraqi units attempting to disrupt VII Corps' breach. No such disruption was encountered. The 1st Squadron, under Lt.Col. Tony Isaacs, as the regiment's reserve, stayed at the border.

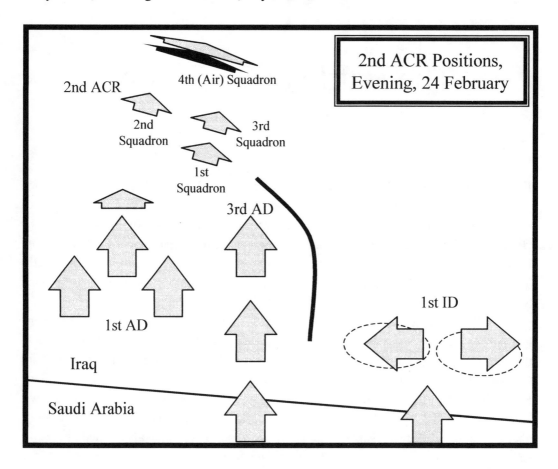

At 9:10 a.m. on the 24th, the regiment faced its first resistance, in the form of Iraqi artillery. The Iraqi guns were radar-located and silenced by counterbattery fire after firing only a few rounds. Two hours later, the regiment's helicopters engaged a group of dug-in armored vehicles several miles in front of the ground units, prompting the surrender of scores of Iraqis. The Iraqis were disarmed by air cavalrymen, given food and water, and told to wait for the ground units. At about 12:45, an OV-10A engaged a group of 12 tanks, destroying one and damaging 2–4 more.

Holder's attack plan called for his air squadron to fly 10–12 miles ahead of the main body, whenever the weather allowed the helicopters to fly. It would locate Iraqi formations, report their locations to the Air Force liaison officer attached to the regiment and engage them until Air Force planes showed up. When Holder's artillery was close enough, it too would hit the targets. Anything that was left after that would be finished off by the ground squadrons.

The ground squadrons made rapid progress on the 24th, advancing over 25 miles against light Iraqi resistance. Throughout the day, L Troop, 3rd Squadron, became involved in nine minor firefights while traveling on the regiment's right flank, destroying a T-55, a BMP and a PT-76 light tank.

Most of the day's ground engagements involved 2nd Squadron, however. In the early afternoon, an Iraqi infantry platoon surrendered after F Troop opened fire on it. At around 4:30, A-10s and F-16s pounced on an Iraqi infantry battalion on Objective Merrell, 2nd Squadron's main objective of the day, about 40 miles inside Iraq. Just after dusk, Apache attack helicopters from Lt.Col. Jon Ward's 2-1st Aviation Battalion struck a cluster of headquarters buildings. The air strikes destroyed a command post, several bunkers, an armored personnel carrier and six trucks.

When the squadron arrived, Merrell's occupants were eager to surrender, and did so in such numbers that they overwhelmed the squadron's EPW holding capabilities. By midnight, F Troop alone had collected about 240 EPWs. Among the squadron's prisoners was the 26th Infantry Division's Assistant Division Commander for Artillery, a lieutenant colonel, who provided a good deal of information about Iraqi defenses. There was some resistance. Just before midnight, E Troop wiped out a platoon of Iraqi infantry that had been firing small arms at it.

Iraqi opposition picked up slightly on the 25th. At around 8 a.m., 2nd Squadron's F and G troops overran a reinforced company of dug-in infantry a few miles past Objective Merrell, inflicting heavy casualties without loss. At about 12:30, the squadron rounded up about 200 more prisoners. At about two in the afternoon, G Troop destroyed a reconnaissance company and captured six APCs.

Iraq's leadership was aware that there was a significant Allied force in the west, heading toward Kuwait. Headquarters ordered General Ayad Futayih al-Rawi, commander of the Republican Guard, to dig in and intercept the American armored thrust. Al-Rawi promptly took over the *Jihad* Corps (made up of the 10th and 12th Armored divisions) and began forming two defensive lines, both running from north to south. The first was made up primarily of the Tawakalna and 12th Armored divisions. The line behind it was made up of the Medina and 10th Armored divisions.

Col. Mohammed Ashad was responsible for providing a screen for the first defense line. His 50th Armored Brigade (of the 12th Armored Division) had never been at full strength. It had begun the war with only 98 of the 108 tanks it was supposed to have. The brigade had remained largely intact despite weeks of Coalition bombing, due to Mohammed's firm discipline. He had been able to keep most of his men alive, and most of his tanks serviceable, by demanding and enforcing near perfection in the construction and camouflage of the unit's fighting positions. Mohammed had 90 of his tanks and most of his MTLB armored personnel carriers serviceable on G-Day.

The Iraqi High Command had considered the possibility of a breakthrough in the west. Two weeks before G-Day, Mohammed had been ordered to prepare alternate positions to block a Coalition flanking maneuver, if it came. Unable to work safely in daylight, his combat engineers had worked on the positions every night since then. On the night of 24 February, he was ordered to occupy the positions.

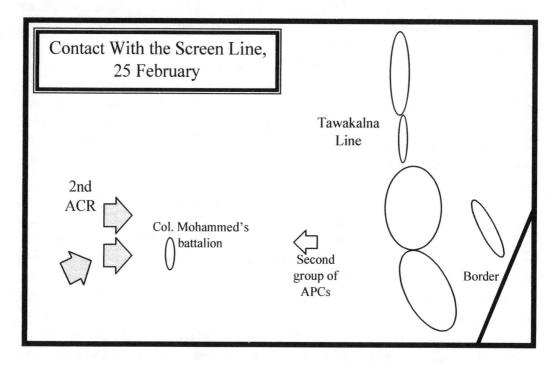

Mohammed had two problems. First, the positions were not finished yet. Second, it would take 6–8 hours of hard road march for the 50th Brigade to reach the positions. Shortly after Mohammed left with his mechanized battalion, accompanied by a handful of tanks, he was handed an even bigger problem by his superiors. Without his knowledge, his three tank battalions were siphoned off and absorbed into the main defensive line. Though he did not know it, Col. Mohammed was on his own.

Just before sunrise on the 25th, Mohammed's force arrived at its assigned location. It was welcomed by Coalition aircraft, which destroyed several MTLBs as they were pulling into their revetments. Now, bone-tired from a six-hour ride in cramped vehicles, partially in shock from the air attack, Mohammed's men had to grab shovels and try to complete as much of their defense network as possible before American armor arrived.

Around 2:30 p.m., 3rd Squadron ran into Mohammed's positions. The Iraqis were taken completely by surprise. Many of the 24 thinly armored MTLBs to the front of Capt. Dan Miller's I Troop were not even manned. Their crews were still digging in. As the Bradleys approached, many Iraqis looked up at them, then went back to digging. Captured Iraqis would say later that they thought the Bradleys were Iraqi vehicles until one of the MTLBs exploded after being hit by a TOW missile. The MTLBs that were manned were armed only with light machine-guns, and were no match for Bradleys. When the M-1A1s came up, the odds shifted even more dramatically in favor of the Americans. MTLBs were intended for use with tanks, the idea being that since they did not offer their troops much protection or firepower, the tanks would. In practice, the Iraqi Army often deployed them with virtually no tank support and they were annihilated, as they were here. Dismounted Iraqis attempted to fire RPGs without success as MTLBs exploded around them. After 13 MTLBs had been destroyed, Iraqi resistance fizzled. I Troop collected almost 200 prisoners.

Meanwhile, to the south of I Troop, Capt. Ashley Haszard's K Troop destroyed five Type 59s and ten MTLBs, then rounded up nearly 200 prisoners, including Col. Mohammed and his executive officer. To K Troop's south, Capt. Douglas Moore's L Troop destroyed a tank and an APC, capturing another. L Troop's men were delighted to find that the APC was full of maps and plans.

At about 4 p.m., as his units finished rounding up their prisoners, Holder ordered his units into a horseshoe-shaped defensive perimeter. The regiment had advanced some 80 miles since G-Day, and the halt would give the rest of VII Corps a chance to catch up. It would also give 2nd ACR a chance to deal with the overwhelming numbers of Iraqi prisoners it had on its hands. That night, Chinook heavy cargo helicopters began ferrying prisoners to the rear. The flights would continue until the end of the war.

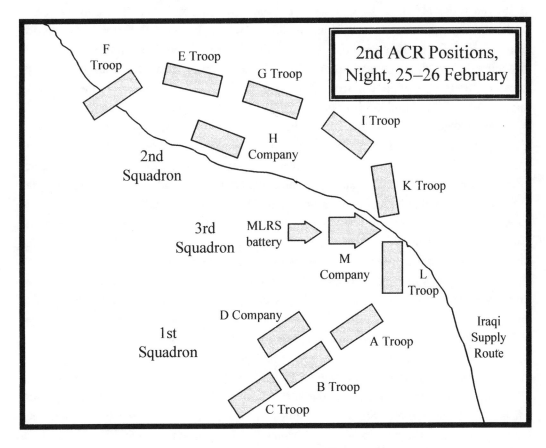

Since the 2nd ACR was now deployed astride an Iraqi supply route, its soldiers expected contact with the Iraqis that night. They were right. Throughout the night and into the morning, Iraqi units probed the defenses along 3rd Squadron's front. Unfortunately, due to the pressing need to evacuate EPWs, the squadron had not had an adequate opportunity to develop and coordinate a precise defensive scheme during daylight hours. It had also cost valuable time which could have been used to coordinate night movement and engagement scenarios. As a result, there would be problems.

The first contact occurred at about 11 p.m. An MTLB and about a dozen dismounts were spotted by I Troop scouts, who called in artillery fire on the Iraqi force. Bomblets destroyed the vehicle and killed several of the dismounts.

At around midnight, the first of three planned MLRS strikes against the main positions on the Tawakalna defense line was fired. As the MLRS battery's target was near the system's maximum range, the battery was forced to move outside the regimental defenses to fire its missions. Following a moving screen provided by the tanks of M Company, under Capt. Benjamin Valenzuela, the launchers advanced to their firing positions, let loose a salvo of 20 rockets, then returned to the regimental perimeter while M Company's tanks provided cover.

The first two missions came off flawlessly, and without interference by the Iraqis. However, just after 2 a.m., a third mission was in progress when a reconnaissance force of 11 armored vehicles appeared in the distance. A salvo of 14 tank rounds destroyed four MTLBs and a tank, and sent the remaining six MTLBs fleeing eastward. Valenzuela's company then held its positions while the MLRS battery, its mission aborted, returned to the perimeter. K Troop then drove off another force of six MTLBs accompanied by dismounted infantry. Meanwhile, I Troop destroyed four APCs in its sector. Things quieted down from 3:00 until 5:14, when the squadron destroyed 12 probing MTLBs and took 65 prisoners.

Unfortunately, as daylight approached, it was discovered that two of the APCs destroyed earlier by I Troop were American. Two K Troop M-113 APCs which had strayed into I Troop's sector had been destroyed by M-1A1s. Both drivers, Cpl. James McCoy of K Troop and PFC Aaron Howard of C Company, 82nd Engineer Battalion had been killed instantly. Two engineers, sergeants Dodge Powell and William Strehlow, had been killed by machine-gun fire from an Abrams as they crawled away from one of the burning APCs. That vehicle, with a pile of explosives two feet deep in the back, erupted in a mushroom-shaped fireball. During the incident five others were wounded.

The APCs and their crews had been guarding prisoners near K Troop's screen line. When the fighting began, K Troop's commander ordered the two APCs and a ground surveillance radar-equipped APC to move to safer positions in the rear. The three APCs had become disoriented, and ended up in I Troop's sector.

To make matters worse, the crews had deployed the trim vanes on the front of their vehicles. Trim vanes are designed to be deployed during river fording operations. They flip forward from the front of the hull to give the box-shaped M-113 more of a boat shape. Crews sometimes deploy trim vanes during ground operations when they need extra space to pile their equipment. Unfortunately, they cause the easily identifiable, box-shaped M-113 to look very much like a BMP or an MTLB through a thermal sight. Such was the case here.

K Troop had a Bradley destroyed during the night's fighting when another K Troop Bradley engaged it with 25mm fire. No crewmen were killed or wounded.

At daybreak on the 26th, the 2nd ACR resumed its advance with the three ground squadrons on line. Shortly after moving out, the regiment found itself in a sandstorm, which worked to the 2nd ACR's advantage, even though it grounded the regiment's helicopters. The Iraqis in front of the 2nd ACR had been told to expect an American attack after the sandstorm had passed, not while it was in full force. Thus, the Guardsmen would be caught totally unprepared, and in many cases, not even in their tanks.

In the south, clusters of Iraqi armored vehicles were steamrolled by 1st Squadron. Most were dug in, facing south. These were the northernmost elements of the Iraqi 52nd Armored Division, which the British 1st Armoured Division was destroying to the south of 2nd ACR. By noon, Lt.Col. Isaacs' squadron would destroy 23 T-55s, 23 APCs, 10 trucks and 6 artillery pieces. Though Iraqi opposition presented no particular problem on this day, the squadron would face its share of challenges.

As the 2nd ACR's southernmost squadron, the 1st Squadron was responsible for maintaining contact with the British 1st Armoured Division. Coordination would be difficult. Because the British and American radios were not compatible, the two units had to communicate on a radio carried by an American liaison officer attached to the 1st Armoured Division. This presented problems when immediate identification of a group of vehicles was required, especially if the units involved were beyond the range of the liaison officer's FM radio.

Just after his unit moved out that morning, Isaacs discovered that he had a more dangerous problem. Capt. David Edwards, the commander of C Troop, reported about a dozen vehicles to his front. Though he was sure they were British, they had to be checked out. Lt.Col. Isaacs was shocked to find that there was a five kilometer overlap in the unit boundaries. The vehicles were British (from the 16th/5th Lancers), engaging T-55s in an area that was in both the 2nd ACR's zone and the British zone.

An overlap between units is almost as dangerous as a gap. While a gap invites enemy attacks into it, an overlap invites friendly fire incidents within it. When a unit is operating within its assigned boundaries, it will often assume that any other vehicles within those boundaries are hostile. When two units have the same assigned sector, and make the same assumption about each other's vehicles, the result is a battle between two friendly units. In this case, the units and leaders involved were alert to the possible presence of friendly units, so fratricide was avoided. By 8:15, the boundary was adjusted.

Meanwhile, 2nd Squadron in the north and 3rd Squadron in the center spent the morning and early afternoon rolling over the forward security elements of the main Republican Guard armored force. Shortly after I Troop moved out, it came upon an Iraqi warning post made up of an MTLB and a BTR-50.* Crewmen inside the vehicles were making a desperate attempt to alert their comrades to the presence of the 2nd ACR by launching flares. The attempt failed. No Iraqi units were close enough to see the flares.[†]

---

*MTLBs and BTR-50s are similar, tracked APCs armed only with light machine guns. The BTR-50 is slightly larger and holds 22 soldiers, nine more than the MTLB.

[†]Aside from command vehicles and some reconnaissance vehicles, Iraqi APCs were not equipped with radios. These probably were not radio-equipped.

Both vehicles and their occupants were dispatched by main gun rounds from two M-1A1s. A few miles north, 2nd Squadron's E and G troops destroyed six MTLBs on reconnaissance. At about 2:30, I Troop came upon two more Iraqi advanced warning posts. On one, two APCs and ten infantrymen with communications equipment were hit with a hasty but accurate mortar barrage. The survivors were then rounded up. On the other, a single MTLB was destroyed by 25mm chain-gun fire.

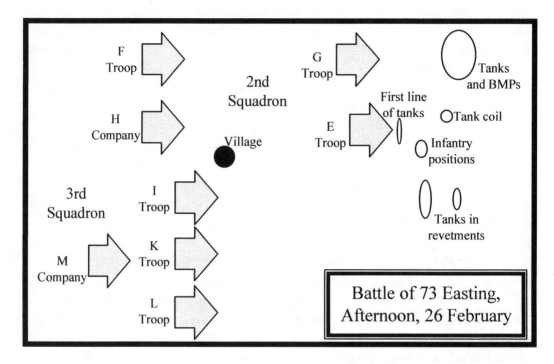

In the early afternoon the sandstorm broke, allowing ground attack planes and helicopter gunships to go back to work. Working over an area 2–6 miles in front of the lead ground elements, they destroyed several tanks, APCs and artillery pieces.

At 3:30 p.m., the regiment was heading east toward the Republican Guard, still with three squadrons on line. The major contact would take place along the seam between the 2nd and 3rd squadrons. The 2nd Squadron moved in a box formation with G Troop to the north, followed by F Troop, and E Troop to the south, followed by H Company, a pure tank unit. The 3rd Squadron was deployed with I Troop to the north, K Troop in the center, L Troop in the south and the tank-pure M Company in reserve.

Shortly after resuming its eastward movement, Capt. H.R. McMaster's E Troop began receiving airburst artillery fire. A few minutes later, at about 3:45 p.m., the first shots in what would become known as the Battle of 73 Easting were fired. At north–south grid line 68 Easting, E Troop took fire from Republican Guard infantry in a village that had been used as a storage point for ammunition, fuel, food and water. Nine M-1A1s answered with main gun fire, demolishing several buildings in the village. Within seconds the Iraqi fire ceased, and E Troop pushed eastward.

Since he was expecting contact with Iraqi armor, McMaster had placed his nine tanks forward in a wedge and his twelve Bradleys a few hundred meters behind. Joining

E Troop for the engagement was the squadron's operations officer, Maj. Douglas Macgregor. Macgregor placed his tank and Bradley behind McMaster's tanks. Uncertain what was ahead and wanting the best (and earliest) view of any Iraqi positions the unit might come upon, McMaster placed his tank at the tip of the wedge.

At 4:07 p.m., McMaster's tank crested a rise in the terrain at 70 Easting. Eight Iraqi tanks were parked on the eastern side of the slope. This tactic shielded the Iraqi tanks from the view of the oncoming Americans. It also should have allowed them good, close range shots at American tanks as they crested the rise. However, the Iraqis had heard the earlier engagement in the village. Expecting the American attack to come from that direction, they had their guns pointed to their southwest, toward the village.

McMaster's plan was for him to fire first on contact and have his tanks orient on the explosion produced by his tank round. For that reason, he had a high explosive anti-tank (HEAT) round in his main gun breech. When his gunner fired at the Iraqi tank nearest him, the Iraqi vehicle exploded in a fireball. The pressure produced by the HEAT round caused the Iraqi tank commander, on fire from head to foot, to be shot out of his hatch like a cork from a champagne bottle. As the rest of the troop's tanks crested the rise, they too opened fire. Some of the Iraqi tanks were able to get shots off before being destroyed, but all missed. In a matter of seconds, all eight Iraqi tanks were in flames.

Col. Holder had moved his unit cautiously throughout the day. That morning, VII Corps had ordered 2nd ACR to move to 60 Easting. Once there, it would halt and wait for the 1st Infantry Division to pass through the regiment at around 5 p.m. On reaching 60 Easting, Holder had reported that his unit had found a line of Iraqi outposts, which was clearly the security line for the main body. About an hour later, he had received word from Lt.Gen. Franks that the 1st ID would not be ready to pass through the 2nd ACR for several hours. Franks therefore ordered him to proceed to 70 Easting, make contact with the Iraqi defense line, but not become decisively engaged. Holder's regiment undertook this delicate mission in intermittent sandstorms which periodically grounded its helicopters and reduced visibility to less than 100 meters. Dogged by sandstorms and certain that he would run into the Tawakalna's main body at any time, Holder had continued to move the regiment forward in short bounds, about a kilometer per bound, and had ordered the regiment to consolidate along the 70 Easting line.

McMaster was now at 70 Easting. However, he could see Iraqi positions ahead, and he was certain that there had to be a good deal of Iraqi armor behind those positions. Wanting to destroy the Iraqis while they were still off balance, he pressed the attack.

E Troop drove through an infantry position next, destroying BMPs and cutting down scores of infantrymen. In many cases, Iraqi infantrymen played dead, lying on their RPG launchers, hoping to get a rear shot at the tanks as they passed by. Some were spotted by tank gunners and machine-gunned at close range. Some were not spotted. As McMaster's wave of tanks passed by, these Iraqis shouldered their RPG launchers and took aim. Because of the sandstorm and the smoke from burning vehicles, the Iraqis never saw what killed them —Bradleys trailing behind the tanks.

As E Troop crested another rise, it spotted a coil of 18 T-72s on a small plateau near the 73 Easting line. The tanks parked there had just started their engines and were attempting to deploy toward their positions, which were now being overrun by McMaster's tanks. The Americans surged toward the plateau, firing on the move and scoring several hits.

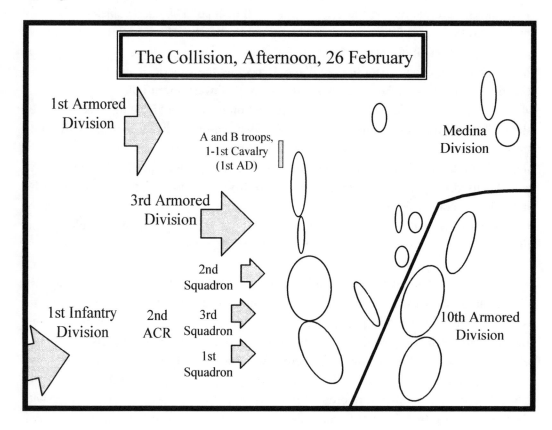

After finishing off the remaining few tanks in the coil at close range, E Troop advanced to the 74 Easting line, about 2½ miles east of the regiment's limit of advance where it halted and consolidated. The troop had destroyed 26 tanks, 16 APCs and 3 trucks in 23 minutes.

While the troop's mortar section began lobbing shells into an Iraqi trenchline a kilometer to the east, McMaster sent his scout platoon to link up with G Troop's scouts to the northwest. On the way, it spotted a coil of 13 Iraqi tanks on the boundary between the two troops. Whether the tanks had been missed in the chaos of the earlier battle or because of confusion over which troop the targets had been the responsibility of is unclear, but they were operational. They were not operational for long. From 900 meters, the scouts opened up with 25mm armor piercing rounds and TOW missiles, destroying 12 of the tanks. On the way back from the link-up with G Troop's scouts, the scouts destroyed the one tank they had overlooked earlier.

While E Troop was killing Iraqi tanks and infantrymen, the 2-1st Aviation Battalion was destroying Iraqi artillery. At 4:30, two Apaches attacked two artillery batteries with Hellfire missiles, destroying six guns. On the way back to base, they strafed a convoy with 30mm cannon fire, destroying several APCs and wheeled vehicles.

At about 4:45, I Troop began its battle. At that point, there was a 7 kilometer (roughly 4½ mile) gap between E and I troops. Not knowing how deep McMaster had penetrated, 3rd Squadron's commander, Lt.Col. Marcy, had ordered Capt. Miller to halt, in accordance with the regiment's instructions to advance to the 70 Easting line. In addition, the 2nd and 3rd squadrons had different standing operating procedures when it came to occupying a phase line. When Col. Holder ordered his squadrons to advance to 70 Easting, 2nd Squadron had physically occupied that line. The 3rd Squadron had halted at a line which allowed the squadron's tanks to control the 70 Easting line by main gun fire. Thus, 3rd Squadron had halted 3,000 meters short of 70 Easting, along the 67 Easting line.

As soon as the tactical picture became clearer, and he was permitted to do so, Miller advanced his troop eastward. I Troop's battle began with small arms fire from Iraqi infantrymen in the village McMaster's tanks had suppressed. Having gone to ground as a result of E Troop's volley of HEAT rounds, the Iraqis had since regained their equilibrium and began firing at Miller's troop from the southern portion of the village. I Troop unleashed a hail of heavy machine-gun bullets and HEAT rounds. Again, Iraqi fire ceased.

I Troop rolled past the village toward the main Iraqi positions. Miller's gunners looked for the heavy machine-guns on top of the T-72 turrets, aimed three feet down and pulled the trigger. Sabot rounds smashed through berms and into turret rings of the Iraqi tanks.[*] Gunners soon found that such precision aiming was unnecessary. "We had been told that you had to hit them in the turret ring with sabot," one gunner said later, "but anything you shot them with, anywhere you hit them, they blew up." There were few return shots, and in a matter of seconds the position was strewn with burning Iraqi armored vehicles.

As I Troop was collecting prisoners, seven T-72s and a few APCs 3,000 meters to the east came out of their fighting positions and attempted to close with I Troop's tanks. The attackers were engaged at long range and wiped out almost immediately. The closest T-72 was destroyed at 2,000 meters. During the counterattack, one Bradley was accidentally hit by a sabot round fired by a misoriented K Troop tank, wounding five crewmen, two seriously. In the two battles, I Troop had destroyed 24 T-72s, 4 T-55s, 4 BMPs, 4 MTLBs and a ZSU 23-4. After gathering the prisoners and evacuating its wounded, the troop withdrew to the 70 Easting line, where part of the 1st Infantry Division would pass through 3rd Squadron later that night.

Something was wrong. E and I troops had made contact with the positions of the Tawakalna Division's 18th Mechanized Brigade and had left 50 T-72s in flames. This was more T-72s than the brigade was supposed to have, and almost everyone in the 2nd

---

[*]The turret ring, where the turret meets the hull, is one of the weakest points of a tank's structure.

ACR was sure that there would be many more Iraqi tanks nearby. The events of the next few hours would prove them right. The Iraqis had moved most of the Tawakalna Division's 9th Armored Brigade into the sector.

Just before dark, the Iraqis launched a counterattack against E Troop with 17 T-72s, about a dozen BMPs and over a hundred dismounted infantrymen. The tanks and BMPs were picked off before they could close to within range of their main guns. Stripped of their armor, Iraqi infantrymen nevertheless pressed the attack. They never got close to the Americans. While machine-gun and 25mm fire held them at a distance, high explosive airburst mortar rounds exploded over the Iraqis, exacting a terrible toll.

With the counterattack broken, a few trucks full of Iraqis attempted to escape, but were destroyed by TOW missiles. After an hour and a half of punishment, unable to attack or retreat, the Iraqis had only one option. When a Kuwaiti interpreter broadcast surrender instructions over a loudspeaker, several dozen Iraqis came forward with their hands up. Later that night, McMaster's scouts would destroy two BMPs attempting to probe the perimeter, bringing E Troop's kill total in its part of the Battle of 73 Easting to 56 tanks, 30 APCs and 10 trucks with no losses.

Capt. Joseph Sartiano's G Troop had been destroying small groups of scattered armored vehicles since 3 p.m., and had accounted for three tanks and several APCs by the time it began engaging Iraqi armor on 73 Easting at 4:45. In the next 15 minutes, an additional 13 tanks and 13 APCs were destroyed. At 5:00, Iraqi shells began bursting over the Bradleys. The barrage was followed almost immediately by a rush of Tawakalna dismounted infantry. The Iraqis ran forward, shooting from the hip as they were mowed down by machine-gun and 25mm fire from the Bradleys.

At 5:40, a Bradley was hit by an Iraqi main gun round. The vehicle had been "skylined," or silhouetted against the sky.[*] The Iraqi round hit the vehicle's TOW missile launcher, causing the missiles to explode. The explosion caved in the left side of the turret, killing the Bradley's gunner, Sgt. Nels Moller, and wounded two other crewmen. Five minutes later, an Iraqi armored force to the northeast began forming for an assault on G Troop's left flank. At 6:00, the force of seven tanks and eighteen BMPs was sighted by the troop's scouts. An immediate suppression artillery strike was called in as M-1A1s began to engage the T-72s at long range. A minute later, bomblets were landing on the Iraqis, causing the tanks and APCs to halt.[†] When they did, they became better targets for main gun fire from M-1A1s and TOW missiles from Bradleys.

G Troop's artillery support had prevented part of the troop from being overrun. It disrupted Iraqi armor as it massed, and slowed down the T-72s, so that they could be destroyed by TOWs at long range before their main guns could be brought to bear on the Bradleys. The artillery also caused heavy casualties among the Tawakalna infantrymen.

_____

[*]Armored vehicle crews are trained to spend as little time as possible at the very top of high ground, as this offers enemy gunners a clear target.

[†]Each artillery submunition contained 88 bomblets which exploded on top of tanks and armored vehicles, where the armor is thinnest.

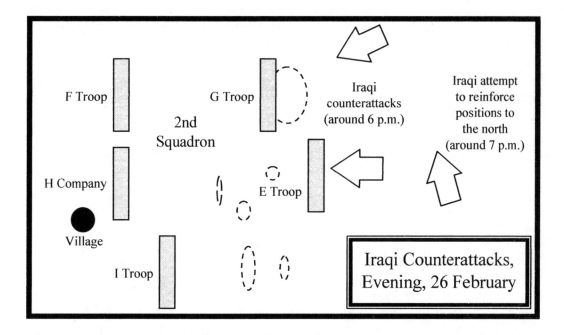

F Troop

G Troop

2nd
Squadron

Iraqi
counterattacks
(around 6 p.m.)

Iraqi attempt
to reinforce
positions to
the north
(around 7 p.m.)

H Company

E Troop

Village

I Troop

**Iraqi Counterattacks,
Evening, 26 February**

The 2nd Squadron's artillery was the squadron's only heavy support. A close air support mission which had been on the way to support G Troop had been diverted to another sector at the last minute. The artillerymen worked to the brink of physical exhaustion. The squadron's howitzers would fire over 2,000 rounds in support of its troops, 720 rounds of which were used in support of the hard-pressed G Troop. The guns fired for so long without a break that carbon began to build up in the gun barrels, causing flames to shoot out of the howitzers with each round fired, some as long as 20 feet.

G Troop's own mortarmen were also extremely active, firing 368 rounds during the day, including 240 rounds in two hours during the most intense fighting. Sartiano had kept his two 4.2-inch (107mm) mortars right behind his lead vehicles. Positioning them so far forward allowed them to engage Iraqi targets much deeper than they would otherwise have been able to.

Sartiano had given his mortarmen another crucial edge by providing them with far more ammunition than they were supposed to have. Instead of the 120 rounds of mortar ammunition a troop usually carries with it, G Troop had carried 370 rounds. Each of the troop commanders had been assigned one extra Bradley. Sartiano had moved all of his command and control equipment from his modified M-113 (known as an M-577) to his extra Bradley. That Bradley became his new Tactical Operations Center, and the M-577 had become an extra ammunition carrier. The extra ammunition came in handy. At the time it was pulled out of the line to refuel and rearm, G Troop had two mortar rounds remaining.

After the first Iraqi attack was beaten off, an Iraqi armored force of 10 T-55s and 10 MTLBs was spotted heading northward. The unit was attempting to reinforce the Iraqi positions to the north of 2nd ACR. Those units were being mauled by the 3rd Armored Division. The attempted reinforcement failed, as the unit was destroyed when it came within range of G Troop's TOW launchers.

As the battle wound to a close, the squadron's artillerymen scored a major success. E Troop's artillery officer, Lt. Dan Davis, suspected that there was Iraqi armor on the reverse slope of a ridge to the east. At 10:40 p.m., he called for an artillery strike. Soon, 228 DPICM rounds, 92 high explosive rounds and 12 MLRS rockets were on the way. This fire mission destroyed 3 tanks, 4 BMPs, 2 SA-9 anti-aircraft missile launchers, 35 trucks, 5 fuel tankers and 27 ammunition vehicles.

While the other two squadrons were fighting the Battle of 73 Easting to the north, 1st Squadron had monitored the area to its front, picking off about two dozen tanks and taking over a hundred prisoners. The squadron's main job was to ensure that no Iraqi armor slipped past it or interfered with the 1st ID's 3rd Brigade, which was maneuvering toward it to conduct a forward passage of lines to overrun the southern end of the Tawakalna Line. Once that passage was complete a few hours later, the 2nd ACR would assume a reserve role for the rest of the war.

The next morning would bring one last unexpected bit of fighting. Just after eight, the support squadron accidentally became engaged when 10 Iraqi MTLBs which had entered the zone after the regiment's heavy armor had passed, stumbled into its rear. The commander of the support group maneuvered his military police and an attached M-1A1 platoon toward the wayward Iraqis. After the tanks had destroyed several of the APCs, Cobra gunships from Q Troop showed up to finish off the rest of the Iraqi force.

In its part of the ground war, the 2nd ACR had not only located and engaged the Tawakalna Division but had taken a large chunk out of it. Fighting largely without air support because of bad weather, the regiment had destroyed 161 tanks, 180 APCs, 81 trucks, 12 artillery pieces and 6 AA systems and captured over 4,500 Iraqis. It had lost only 6 dead and 17 wounded, as well as three Bradleys and two M-113s.

20

The Battle of Norfolk

O nce the VII Corps' breaching operation was complete, the 1st Infantry Division had prepared to settle into a reserve role. During the planning of the VII Corps' assault, casualty projections for the division's breaching operation had run from 10% to 45%. Planners could not ignore the possibility that the 1st ID might be severely weakened at the end of it. Lt.Gen. Franks therefore planned to have the 1st Cavalry Division join the 1st and 3rd Armored divisions as they moved against the Republican Guard. The 1st ID would follow behind as the corps' reserve.

Fate had other plans for the division. As VII Corps turned toward the Republican Guard, Gen. Schwarzkopf refused to release the 1st Cavalry Division for the attack. Since the 1st ID had lost none of its considerable combat power during the breaching operation, the division was ordered to join in the attack on the Republican Guard's Tawakalna Division. Within hours, the 1st ID would be engaged in one of the largest battles of the war, and the largest night tank battle fought by the United States since World War II.

The southern end of the defense line established by the Tawakalna Mechanized and 12th Armored divisions was dubbed "Objective Norfolk." The northern portion of Norfolk was manned by the Tawakalna Division's 18th Mechanized Brigade. The southern sector was occupied by the 12th Armored Division's 37th Armored Brigade. Norfolk had been heavily reinforced when most of the Tawakalna Division's 9th Armored Brigade joined the 18th Mechanized in the northern sector, though all but about two companies of this force would be destroyed by 2nd ACR before the 1st ID arrived.

The attack on Objective Norfolk would be conducted by 1st and 3rd brigades, with 2nd Brigade in reserve. The 2nd Brigade was the only U.S. brigade in the theater still equipped with the basic model M-1 tank. Though the basic M-1 was still one of the best tanks in the world, Col. Moreno's tanks were not as well-protected as the other two brigades' M-1A1s. The M-1A1 was about 25% better protected than the M-1 against sabot rounds and about 33% better protected against HEAT rounds. M-1s also had

105mm guns instead of the more powerful 120mm guns carried by M-1A1s. The tanks were also an average of seven years old, and there was some question about how many tanks the brigade would lose to breakdowns as it advanced into Iraq. Finally, the brigade was at two-thirds strength. TF 2-16 was responsible for providing security in the breach lanes and could not be spared for the attack.

Just getting the brigade in position to act as a reserve was a remarkable feat. On G-Day, because the brigade would be facing mostly bunkers and dug-in infantry, about two-thirds of each M-1's load of 55 main gun rounds had been High Explosive Anti-Tank rounds instead of sabot rounds. Now, contact with the Republican Guard T-72s was a very real possibility for the 2nd Brigade. This meant that Moreno's tank crews not only had to refuel, they had to unload most of their HEAT rounds and replace them with sabot rounds, a time-consuming process. Once the brigade was rearmed and refueled, it would then have to weave its way though the 1st ID's support units to get to its position behind the other two brigades. These difficulties would ultimately be overcome, and 2nd Brigade would be in its assigned position by the time the attack took place.

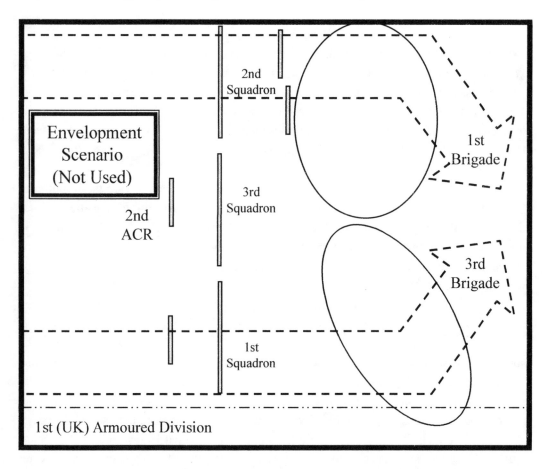

The division would be conducting its second passage of lines in two days. On the second day of the ground war, the British 1st Armoured Division had passed through the lines of the Big Red One to attack Iraqi armor behind the Saddam Line. Now, 1st ID would have to pass through the lines of 2nd ACR. However, unlike the earlier passage, this had been neither pre-planned nor rehearsed. Maj. John Burdan, operations officer for the 1-4th Cavalry Squadron, was sent ahead to coordinate the 1st ID's passage through the 2nd ACR with Lt.Col. Stephen Robinette, the regiment's deputy commander. At the time the two officers were making plans for the passage, about 4:30 in the afternoon, the center of the regiment's sector was the scene of intense fighting, as captains McMaster and Miller plunged their troops into the Iraqi defenses. The northern and southern flanks, on the other hand, were relatively quiet. Burdan and Robinette therefore recommended sending the 1st ID's 1st Brigade through 2nd ACR's 2nd Squadron in the north and its 3rd Brigade through 1st Squadron in the south. This would have allowed the two brigades to execute a pincer movement on the Iraqi defenders while 3rd Squadron, in the center of the 2nd ACR's line, continued to pour direct fire into them.

Col. Holder did not like the idea, because he felt that there might be friendly fire incidents when 1st and 3rd brigades curled back into 3rd Squadron's line of fire. Maj.Gen. Rhame agreed that the movement probably was unnecessarily risky, and decided to pass his brigades through the 2nd ACR's 3rd (center) and 1st (southern) squadrons and have them drive directly eastward, steamrolling Iraqi units in their path. This decision was fortuitous. Minutes after the pincer idea was vetoed, 2nd ACR's northernmost troop under Capt. Sartiano became embroiled in intense combat which would last until about nine. Once the nature of the passage had been agreed upon by Rhame and Holder, Burdan and Robinette worked out the details and radioed the passage plan back to the 1st ID. A few hours later, Brig.Gen. Carter arrived with the 1st ID's tactical command post to make further coordinations.

At dusk on the 25th, the 1st and 3rd brigades had been notified that they would be moving to take part in the climactic battle. During that night, brigade and battalion commanders scrambled to develop operations orders for their subordinates from three-week-old diagrams of Iraqi dispositions. Intelligence for the attack would be nowhere near as thorough as it had been for the breach. On G-Day, the brigade's leaders had been armed with detailed templates of Iraqi defenses. At Norfolk, once the brigades were past the 2nd ACR, the eyes of the men in the lead tanks and Bradleys would be the leaders' primary source of information.

The brigades moved from the breach area on the morning of the 26th. By noon, they had traveled just over 50 miles to the northeast and had reached Phase Line Harz, where they were to refuel.

On the way, the 1st Brigade rounded up some 200 Iraqis who had been disarmed and sent to the rear by the 2nd ACR. At PL Harz, they were greeted by another 220 Iraqis who had also been sent back by Col. Holder's cavalrymen. By 2 p.m., after the prisoners had been processed, the tanks had been refueled and the men had been fed, 1-34th Armor and TF 2-34 were headed east.

Just getting into position for the passage involved quick judgment calls and intricate coordination. When the division had moved out on the morning of the 26th, Col. Maggart had all but decided that his brigade would fight the Iraqis that night with the two balanced task forces in the lead, and the armor-pure battalion trailing. Maggart felt that since he would be attacking armor supported by dug-in infantry with significant numbers of anti-armor weapons, two mixed forces of tanks (to deal with the armor) and Bradleys (to dismount their infantry to clear dug-in positions) were his best bet. In addition, the units would have to coordinate on the fly, and the commanders of task forces 2-34 and 5-16, Lt.Col. Fontenot and Lt.Col. Baker, had been in the brigade and worked together for some time. Lt.Col. Ritter had been a relative newcomer.

Unfortunately, at 4:30 p.m., Baker informed Col. Maggart that delays in refueling would make it difficult for him to take his place on the right flank in time for the passage. During the two days of the breaching operation, TF 5-16 had used much more fuel than the brigade's other two battalions. Though 1-34th Armor had more high-consumption M-1A1s, Ritter's tanks had done little maneuvering. They had burst through the breach lanes on G-Day, assumed defensive positions and waited. Defending in place consumed relatively little fuel. TF 2-34 had the same trench clearing mission TF 5-16 had, but had no I-TOW anti-tank company. With 13 more vehicles burning fuel, and no extra fuel tankers, TF 5-16 found itself short on fuel by the afternoon of the 25th. Baker had sent his fuel trucks back to the bulk refueling point in Saudi Arabia. Half of them had been stopped short of the breach lanes on the way back, however, forced to wait until the British 1st Armoured Division had completed its passage. As a result, TF 5-16 was in the middle of refueling when 1st Brigade had received orders to move out. The task force had been driving to catch up to the two forward units and had missed the refueling pause at PL Harz. The task force stopped later to refuel, but because it had 13 more vehicles to refuel, and again, no extra tankers to refuel them, it took about an hour longer to refuel TF 5-16 than it did to refuel the other units.

Maggart decided that an adjustment in his plan of attack was safer than gambling and trying to rush TF 5-16 into position. For the assault, Ritter's tank-pure 1-34th Armor would take its place on the right flank. Having no infantry, Ritter was instructed to push across the objective, but not to attempt to clear dug-in positions in detail as TF 2-34 would do. That would be done by TF 5-16, which would be trailing behind.

The leading units of the 1st Brigade worked out the details of the passage with the 2nd ACR by radio as they approached. At about 10 p.m., TF 2-34 and 1-34th Armor began picking their way through 2nd ACR's rear. To ensure that there were no friendly fire incidents, the men of 2nd ACR were ordered to put glowing chem-lights on the rear of their vehicles, where they would be visible to the 1st ID troops but not to any Iraqis who might be out to their front. The cavalrymen were further ordered to stay inside their vehicles until the division had passed through. The precautions worked, and there were no friendly fire incidents during the passage, but progress was slow. The slowness of movements through these rear areas was a blessing, however, as it gave TF 5-16 and the brigade's artillery a chance to catch up. By 11:30 p.m., the passage was complete.

The 1st ID would reap the benefits of coalition air supremacy. Though the Iraqi units the division would be attacking had only lost a handful of vehicles to air attacks, they had been forced to spread out. As a result, while American battalions would be attacking positions defended by forces larger than their own, they would continually enjoy significant local superiority.

The 1st Brigade drove into the northern portion of Norfolk. Though the brigade had artillery to call upon, it could not use it because VII Corps helicopter gunships headed toward targets inside Iraq had been forced to divert southward by the battle in the 3rd Armored Division's zone. Their air lane now ran over Objective Norfolk. The brigade could not use artillery without interfering with the Apaches' attack.

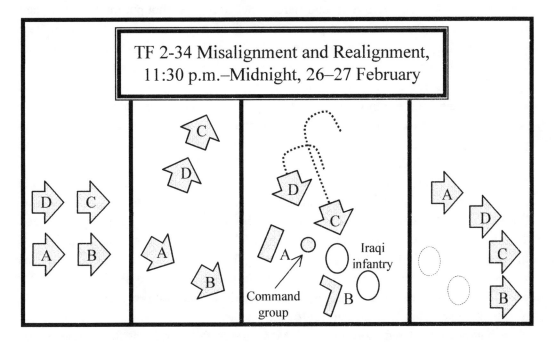

TF 2-34 Misalignment and Realignment, 11:30 p.m.–Midnight, 26–27 February

TF 2-34 passed through 2nd ACR in a box formation at around 11:30 p.m. Lt.Col. Fontenot had formed all of his companies into mixed teams of tanks and Bradleys. Two of the teams were made up of two tank platoons and one Bradley platoon. The other two were made up of two Bradley platoons and one tank platoon. At this point, the two tank-heavy teams led, and the two infantry-heavy teams followed. In the north, Team C was followed by Team D. In the South, Team B led, Team A followed. As they emerged from the passage of lines, however, two of the teams lost their way.

As soon as the task force was forward of the 2nd ACR's lines, the teams deployed into their combat formations. In order to give themselves more room to maneuver, teams C and D shifted northward. Unfortunately, after the move was complete, the teams were facing northeast (instead of east, as they believed), and a gap had developed between the two teams and the other two teams in the south. Even worse, on the southern flank, Team B was now in contact with Iraqi infantry.

Shortly after Team B reported contact, the two northern teams realized their mistake and steps were being taken to correct the situation. To help guide the stray teams back to the rest of the task force, Team B's commander, Capt. Juan Toro, ordered a flare launched. Both northern teams saw the flare, but so did the Iraqis, who intensified their fire on Team B. Because of the mix-up, Toro's team had been forced to set up hasty defensive positions and spread out to cover the gap to his north. His team was fighting Iraqis all along that line, including the northern part, where his men were taking fire from dug-in infantry in the gap. While Team B killed dozens of Tawakalna infantrymen and destroyed at least one BMP, Toro moved up and down the line to monitor the situation. Meanwhile, teams C and D, now reoriented, maneuvered back toward the main body.

The flare had given the lost teams a general idea of where the rest of the task force was, but they were still having trouble pinpointing it. A flare launched by Lt.Col. Fontenot helped guide them. A second flare launched by Fontenot put the teams on their final approach to their designated positions, but it also attracted the attention of Iraqi infantry. A truck and an APC opened fire on Fontenot's command group with machine-guns, but were destroyed by Team B before they could inflict any casualties.

The lost teams' odyssey was not over yet, however. Shortly after Team C passed Fontenot's command group on its way to link up with Team B, it ran into roughly a company of dug-in Republican Guardsmen equipped with RPGs. The Iraqis had gone to ground earlier, when 2nd ACR had attacked the positions in front of them. As the infantrymen were directly between his team and Team B, Team C's commander, Capt. Robert Burns, told Fontenot that to avoid endangering Team B, his vehicles would attempt to run the Iraqis over without firing. Fontenot had a better solution. He told Burns to have his men use coaxial machine-gun fire to deal with the Iraqis and told Capt. Toro to keep the men of Team B inside their vehicles. The tactic worked, and Team C linked up with Team B shortly thereafter. During the delay, there had been no American casualties, but Fontenot's men had been put on notice that the defenders of Norfolk would be more steadfast than those they had faced during the two previous days.

By midnight, TF 2-34 had regrouped and was headed eastward. The task force immediately encountered more infantry. Many Iraqis, believing that they could not be seen at night, made themselves easy targets for American gunners by running between bunkers or at American vehicles. When the Iraqis learned that they could be seen, they hunkered down and fought from their holes. Burns dismounted his attached infantry, which swept the area. Those Iraqis who wanted to surrender were taken prisoner. Those who did not were killed in their fighting positions.

The 1-34th's battle began with a fratricide. Some of Lt.Col. Ritter's tank crews were getting jittery. They were aware that there was a good deal of fighting going on in TF 2-34's zone, but they had not hit the main Iraqi line yet, and expected to do so at any moment. The battalion advanced with B Company in the north, C Company in the center, A Company in the south and D Company in reserve. The battalion's scouts, well to the front of the rest of the battalion, were nearing Iraqi infantry positions.

At 12:18, SFC Johnny Cameron, the platoon sergeant of B Company's northernmost platoon reported a hot spot to his front. Since he had been told by his company commander, Capt. John Tibbetts, that there were no American forces to his front, Cameron reported that the hot spot might be a ZSU 23-4. Tibbetts replied that if he was sure it was a ZSU 23-4 he could fire. On the last word of Tibbetts' transmission, Cameron's wing man fired a sabot round at the hot spot. Seconds later the battalion's Scout Platoon reported that it was taking friendly fire. A cease-fire order immediately followed on the battalion radio net. The sabot round had hit a Scout Platoon Bradley in the rear. There were no fatalities among the five crewmen, who received burns and arm and leg wounds.*

The Scout Platoon leader, Lt. Glen Burnham, moved to evacuate the stricken Bradley's crew. When Burnham's vehicle was within 200 meters of the Bradley, Burnham noticed three tracer rounds coming at his vehicle from long range. One of the rounds penetrated the left side of the turret, cutting a cable and disabling the 25mm gun. The round and the spall it produced, wounded Burnham and killed his gunner, Sgt. David Douthit. The burst had come from a misoriented Bradley inside TF 2-34's zone.

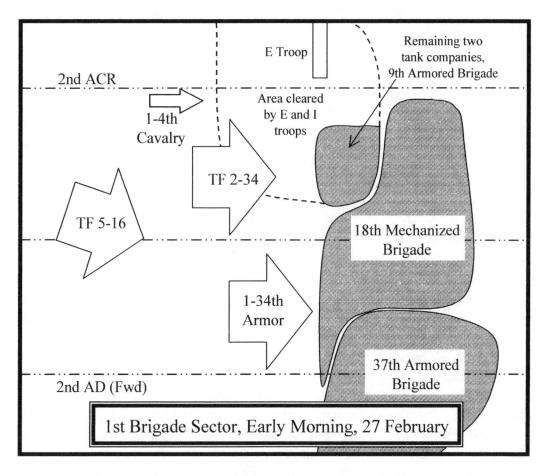

After arrangements were made to evacuate the wounded from the two Bradleys, 1-34th Armor moved on. As Lt.Col. Ritter traveled behind C Company on the point of the battalion wedge, his B Company commander reported engaging T-72s and BMPs on the left flank, while on the right, his A Company commander was reporting Type 59s. At first, Ritter thought one of his commanders didn't know his nomenclature, since armored units seldom have two different types of tanks assigned to them. While he was trying to find out which one was wrong, C Company began reporting T-72s on its left and Type

---

*A hole, possibly from an RPG strike, was later found on the front slope of the Bradley, on the right side. During the evacuation of the wounded, the scouts took sporadic small arms fire from the east. The round was probably fired at this time and mistaken for a secondary explosion.

59s on its right. Ritter now realized that his battalion was driving into the seam between what he would later find out was the Tawakalna's 18th Mechanized and the 37th Armored Brigade of the 12th Armored Division.

Because the Guard units had arrived recently, almost all of the T-72s the two battalions encountered occupied inadequate fighting positions. As the tanks had not been dug in deep enough, 1st Brigade tanks were able to spot them easily from 2,500 meters and engage them while still well beyond the range of Iraqi tank guns.

As Ritter's tanks came within range of the Iraqi tanks, a few Iraqi tank rounds passed harmlessly overhead. The Iraqi tanks were not equipped to find the range of American tanks at night. The best they could do was try to approximate it by the muzzle flashes of the American guns as they fired. Unfortunately for the Iraqis, the Abrams' computerized gunnery system allowed the American tanks to fire as they moved toward the Iraqi lines, so in most cases the Iraqis were firing at targets that were no longer there.

Ritter's instructions from Col. Maggart had been to destroy tanks, APCs and as many anti-armor weapons as possible and let TF 5-16 clear the zone in detail. This the battalion did, with relative ease. A few tanks had been dug in properly, had not been spotted, and surprised some of Ritter's tanks. Most of these tanks were from the 37th Armored Brigade. Spotting Type 59s was sometimes difficult. Type 59s have no engine-driven power turret traverse. Gunners turned their turrets by hand crank as they scanned the horizon. In the eight hours since the sun had set, the tanks had cooled, and with their engines off they stayed cool, and were harder for the American thermal monitors to pick up. One was destroyed by a platoon leader's tank just as it was preparing to destroy Ritter's tank with a flank shot.

Some of the BMPs were also well-camouflaged. These vehicles launched numerous Sagger anti-tank missiles at the Americans, though without effect. In the confusion of battle, most of these launches went unnoticed by the Americans. When officers from the battalion revisited the site in daylight several days after the attack, they would be surprised to find the battlefield crisscrossed with Sagger guide wires.

The fact that Ritter had no attached infantry was both an advantage and a disadvantage. When Iraqi infantrymen attempted to crawl between M-1A1s looking for vulnerabilities, 1-34th Armor's gunners could be quick on their co-axial 7.62mm machine-gun triggers, knowing that there were no friendly infantrymen to the front or sides. However, when the Iraqis' spirit was ultimately broken and they began trying to give themselves up in large numbers, there was no one on the ground to take their surrender. The best the battalion could do was pass them by and have TF 5-16 round them up later. By 3:15 a.m., 1-34th Armor had overrun its portion of Norfolk, cleared the bunkers to the east, and halted along Phase Line Milford, the division's limit of advance, roughly six miles past Norfolk.

TF 2-34's battle began in earnest at about 1:30. At first, Lt.Col. Fontenot had ordered some vehicles bypassed. Since they were not giving off heat signatures, he believed that they had already been destroyed by the Air Force. Eventually, one of his scouts noticed Iraqis making a dash for some of the vehicles from nearby bunkers.

Fontenot immediately realized that some vehicles were cold not because they had been destroyed, but because his unit had achieved surprise and caught their crews away from their tanks. From that point on, every vehicle that was in any way suspicious was engaged, whether it gave off a thermal signature or not. Within an hour, TF 2-34 destroyed 35 armored vehicles and 10 trucks, killed several dozen infantrymen and captured nearly a hundred.

That hour produced an intelligence update. The task force's leaders had been told that they would be attacking two battalions from the 17th Armored Division. They believed that they would be facing a mechanized battalion equipped with wheeled BTR-60 APCs, and an armored battalion behind it, equipped with T-55 tanks. Though it is often difficult to distinguish between different types of tracked vehicles using thermal sights at long range, it was easy enough for Fontenot's men to see immediately that they were not fighting wheeled APCs. Most just assumed that intelligence had been mistaken and that the 17th Division had been equipped with BMPs. Abrams gunners opened up with HEAT rounds, causing massive explosions on impact. However, many Bradley gunners spent minutes firing 25mm armor piercing ammunition, which should have destroyed a BMP, with no effect. Only after these targets had been destroyed by M-1A1s, and the battalion had moved forward, did it become clear that these were not BMPs but T-72 main battle tanks. Captured Republican Guardsmen confirmed the now widely held suspicion that the battalion was fighting not one mechanized and one armored battalion from the 17th Armored Division, but almost two battalions of tanks from the Tawakalna Division. The realization that they were facing T-72s prompted a switch by tank gunners to more effective sabot rounds, though later examination of their victims would show that HEAT rounds had destroyed every T-72 they had hit.

TF 2-34's attack was conducted methodically. When a group of targets was spotted and confirmed, the task force would stop on line 1,500 meters from it, within easy main gun range of the Abrams and close enough to distinguish friend from foe, but near the maximum effective range of the T-72. Commanders then worked out which units would fire at which vehicles and made one last check to see that none of the targets was friendly. At that point, the targets were engaged and destroyed.

After 3:30, fighting was more sporadic. Over the next hour, the task force destroyed a few abandoned vehicles as well as a handful of tanks attempting to escape. It also ripped through a logistics base. Fontenot's men rounded up fleeing drivers and mechanics, then began machine-gunning trucks. This proved to be ill-advised, as the trucks, which were fully loaded with ammunition, blew up and showered the task force with burning and exploding debris. Fontenot asked Col. Maggart for permission to bypass the rest of the site so that TF 5-16 could destroy the stocks more systematically when it came through. Permission was granted.

By 6:30, TF 2-34 had reached Milford after destroying two more tanks and four more APCs. Both 1-34th Armor and TF 2-34 began refueling for the coming day's operations. Since 1-34th Armor's scouts had been hit, the only additional losses were two 3rd Brigade Bradleys which had strayed into 1st Brigade's zone and had been destroyed when Lt.Col. Ritter's gunners mistook them for Iraqi armor.

Against 1st Brigade, the Iraqis had gotten off fewer than two dozen tank gun rounds with nothing to show for it. Ritter's battalion had destroyed some 40 tanks and 50 APCs, as well as several trucks, guns and bunkers. Fontenot's task force destroyed about 50 tanks, 10 APCs and 20 trucks. Continuing to engage pockets of Iraqi resistance until 9 a.m., TF 5-16 destroyed two tanks, 18 APCs, 11 armored scout cars, 11 trucks and the supply base that had been bypassed by TF 2-34. Hundreds of Iraqis had been captured.

To the south, 1st ID's 3rd Brigade (2nd AD [Forward]) attacked the 12th Armored Division's 37th Armored Brigade. Like all other Coalition brigades, 3rd Brigade had done some reshuffling of its units before G-Day. Lt.Col. Taylor Jones' 3-66th Armor had given two of its tank companies to Lt.Col. Hillman's 1-41st Infantry, and Hillman had given Jones two Bradley companies. These two balanced task forces would make up the northern and southern wings of the brigade. Lt.Col. John Brown's 2-66th Armor, which had remained tank-pure, would make up the center.

Unlike 1st Brigade, this would be 3rd Brigade's first serious combat of the war. TF 1-41 had gotten a taste of combat before G-Day as part of Task Force Iron, but most of Col. Weisman's men still had pre-combat jitters, and this would eventually cause problems. Like 1st Brigade, 3rd Brigade would have to coordinate with the 2nd ACR as best it could. At 9:18 p.m., as the brigade neared the 2nd ACR, the commander of a company in 3-66th Armor made an entry into his tape-recorded diary. "[W]e're supposed to have a coordinated night attack with no graphics, no rehearsal, no talk-through," he said. "If this thing goes off without us killing each other, I'd be extremely surprised."

Where 1st Brigade had attacked its position with two battalions up front, and the other trailing behind, 3rd Brigade would attack with each of the three battalions attacking in its own lane. Maj.Gen. Rhame wanted a clean sweep of Objective Norfolk, and had issued relatively tight bypass criteria. Forces were, if possible, to be deployed in such a way that no Iraqi force larger than a platoon would be bypassed. Rhame wanted no significant Iraqi units popping up in his fuel trains. Col. Weisman felt that deploying his three battalions on line, minimizing space between units and between vehicles, was the most certain way to comply with the bypass criteria. Col. Maggart had reasoned that between the two battalions up front, and the one sweeping up behind them, his brigade would meet this requirement in the end. In any case, because one of his task forces had experienced delays in refueling, he could not have brought his entire brigade on line without delaying the start of his attack.

The brigade would pass through the 1st Squadron, 2nd ACR. Just after midnight, the maneuver elements would pass through six lanes. The lanes ended at 71 Easting. The 1st Squadron, lined up along 70 Easting, had monitored the three kilometers to its front before the passage and had destroyed every Iraqi vehicle that had shown any indication of being manned. Thus, as they approached the passage lanes, the brigade's lead elements were told that any operational tanks west of 73 Easting would probably be abandoned.

Once the brigade's maneuver units reached 71 Easting, they would deploy into attack formation. The deployment would involve a fair degree of maneuver, due chiefly to the fact that the passage lanes did not line up well with the brigade's attack zones. In the north, some of TF 3-66's units would have to make relatively sharp turns to the north to align themselves for the attack. The task force's northernmost passage lane was right on its southern boundary. Its other passage lane, 500 meters to the south, was actually outside its attack zone. The two southern companies would therefore be out of sector the moment they emerged from the passage. In the center, 2-66th Armor's problem, though not as bad, was bad enough. The battalion's southernmost passage lane was on its southern boundary. Its other lane, one kilometer to the north, was three kilometers from its northern boundary. The situation was least problematic in the south, where one passage lane was in the center of TF 1-41's attack zone, and the other, the only perfectly placed passage point in the brigade's zone, was one kilometer to the south.

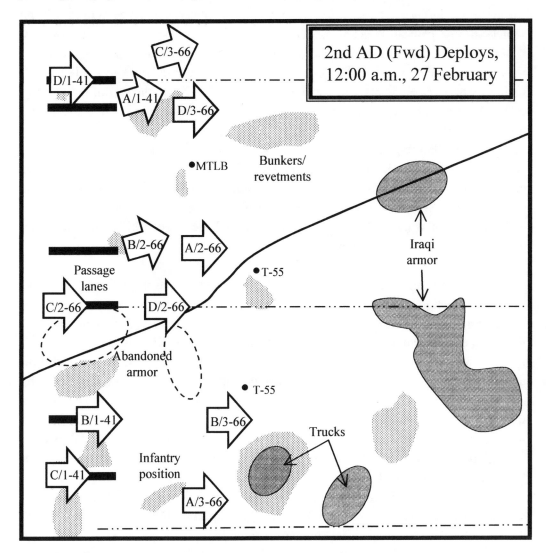

Contact with the Iraqis was made even before the brigade was completely clear of the passage lanes. About two kilometers after it emerged from its passage lane, Capt. William Hedges' B Company, 3-66th Armor opened fire on a group of Iraqi armored vehicles about 3,000 meters to the northeast, spread across a two kilometer by two kilometer area. Firing as it drove eastward, the company destroyed 16 T-55s and 9 MTLBs. There was no Iraqi return fire. The vehicles were probably all abandoned. To the south, Capt. Garry Bishop's A/3-66 drove through an infantry position on its way to its assigned attack lane, then destroyed 20 trucks on two positions as it drove eastward through a bunker complex. About 15 minutes later, 2-66th Armor's lead company, Capt. Brad Dick's A Company, emerged from its passage lane and engaged a small cluster of Iraqi armored vehicles about 3,000 meters to the northeast, destroying two T-55s, an MTLB and a ZSU 23-4.

At around 12:30 a.m., the Bradleys of B Company, 1-41st Infantry were hit by friendly fire. During the passage, B Company's commander, Capt. Lee Wilson, lost his vehicle to mechanical breakdown. This forced him to move to another Bradley. Unfortunately, the second vehicle had no Global Positioning System. Wilson was forced to navigate by guesswork, without even the benefit of terrain features to guide him. He set out for his company's place in the task force attack formation, the rear of B Company, 3-66th Armor. When he found himself in the rear of A/3-66, Wilson realized that he had drifted too far to the south.

After reporting this over the task force radio net, Wilson and Capt. Hedges arranged to rendezvous behind Hedges' tanks. Wilson then moved out to effect the link-up. Nearby, SFC Jim Sedgwick, 3rd Platoon's platoon sergeant, noticed that Wilson was traveling alone. Sedgwick placed his vehicle to Wilson's right rear, to act as a wing man. Sedgwick's own wing man went along as well, and the three vehicles headed to the northeast in an echelon formation.

Moments later, to the north, Iraqi riflemen began firing in the center of 2-66th Armor's formation. They had remained hidden as 2-66th Armor's lead companies had rolled past. As the battalion's unarmored supply vehicles in the center of the battalion formation came within range, several Iraqi infantrymen opened fire with assault rifles.

The battalion's command sergeant-major, CSM Vincent Conway, had been traveling with the 2-66th's supply trains when he began to notice green tracer fire to his rear. Conway knew that since American tracer bullets are red and Soviet-made tracers were green, this could only mean that there were Iraqi foot soldiers behind him. Conway set out with his driver, Specialist James Delargy and Sergeant John Rowler, a photographer who was accompanying the battalion, and began hunting for Iraqis on foot. Within minutes, the team had wiped out an RPG team with rifle fire.

Suddenly, a T-55 which had been bypassed by A/2-66th Armor began swiveling its turret. The sergeant-major climbed aboard the Iraqi tank. Dropping a grenade down the hatch, he heard the Iraqis inside the tank scrambling as he dropped a second grenade. He then turned to jump off of the tank, but the explosion of the first grenade caused a catastrophic explosion of the tank's ammunition, which blew him off of the tank before he had a chance to make his leap. Shaken but uninjured, he and the other two members of his team headed back to their vehicles. On the way, the team destroyed a machine-gun emplacement by dropping two grenades inside it while the Iraqi machine-gunners were trying to reload. The blast killed most of the bunker's occupants, but four armed survivors were killed as they came out of the bunker.*

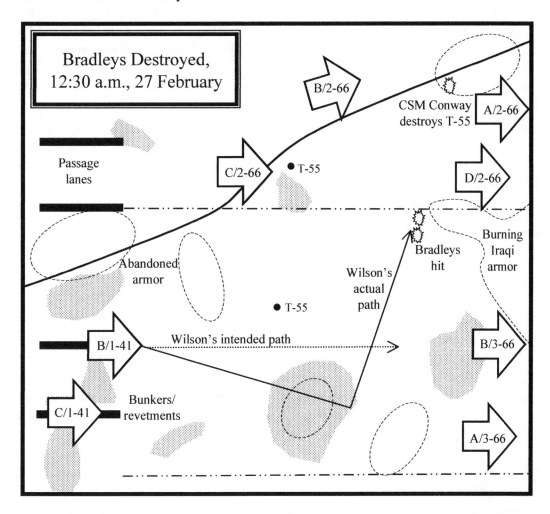

Bradleys Destroyed, 12:30 a.m., 27 February

By now, Capt. Wilson had overshot the rendezvous point he had arranged with Capt. Hedges, and the three Bradleys had continued northward, where they were spotted by gunners in C Company, 2-66th Armor, the rear tank company in that battalion's formation. As far as the tank gunners of C Company knew, the brigade's vehicles were all moving from west to east, yet they were seeing vehicles in front of them (Wilson's), moving to the northeast. Worse, about 500 meters beyond Wilson's Bradleys were three burning T-55s. The tanks, on the northern tip of the position that B/3-66 had recently wiped out, were pointed in roughly the same direction as the Bradleys. In addition, there was Iraqi rifle fire in front of C Company, causing the gunners to assume (correctly) that there were Iraqis between themselves and the battalion's lead elements, and that perhaps some of the Iraqi tanks that had been bypassed were manned after all.

At the center of the company wedge, C Company's 1st Platoon leader reported to his company commander, Capt. Robert Manning, that he saw a T-55 moving in front of

*For his actions, CSM Conway was awarded the Silver Star.

him. Manning, who was not in a position to see the vehicle, asked the platoon leader if he was sure that the vehicle was Iraqi. After the platoon leader told him he was, Manning authorized him to fire. A few seconds later, a sabot round was on its way toward Wilson's Bradley. The platoon leader had used the "Tank Commander's Override," the control that allows tank commander to fire the main gun, to fire from his station. The round struck the ground short of its target, skipped once, then tumbled across the front of the Bradley.

Both Wilson and his driver saw the sabot round. The driver thought it was a burning road wheel. Wilson thought it was an RPG. The driver slammed on the brakes. Wilson, not wanting to become a stationary target, ordered his driver to move out. However, before the vehicle could resume movement, it was hit in the left side. Wilson was blown out of the turret, hitting his head on landing with sufficient force to split his plastic CVC helmet down the middle. Some of the soldiers inside the vehicle were wounded. After the first round had missed, the platoon leader's gunner had fired. This time, the round had hit the target.

SFC Sedgwick could see that there were tank rounds coming at the Bradleys. As he informed the crew of his vehicle that they were taking incoming fire from the left, he ordered his driver to pull to the right of Wilson's Bradley. This would shield the vehicle from incoming rounds as its crewmen provided cover for the crew of the stricken Bradley and evacuated its wounded. As Sedgwick's Bradley neared its destination, it was hit on the back of the turret by an RPG from the right front, throwing metal fragments into Sedgwick's face and eye. The impact did not immobilize the Bradley, which pulled alongside Wilson's vehicle and released its infantrymen. SFC Sedgwick, though wounded, was able to form his men and the uninjured men of Wilson's Bradley into a defensive perimeter.*

Meanwhile, SFC Sedgwick's wing man had been hit. The hit knocked out that vehicle's engine but caused no deaths, although three men were injured by the round's concussion or while exiting the vehicle. The round was fired by 3rd Platoon, on C/2-66 Armor's right flank. The gunners for the two tanks on the southern side of 3rd Platoon's formation (and therefore the southernmost vehicles in C Company) had seen vehicles moving to their front. When 1st Platoon fired, the commanders of both tanks took it as confirmation that the vehicles were enemy, and authorized their gunners to fire. Both fired sabot rounds.

At the time, B/1-41st Infantry's 2nd and 3rd platoons, each traveling in column with their platoon leaders at the front, were attempting to rejoin Capt. Wilson. About 200 meters to the south of the stricken vehicles, the Bradley belonging to SFC Sedgwick's platoon leader, 2LT John Bircher, pivoted just before the second 3rd Platoon C/2-66th Armor sabot round arrived, causing it to glance off the side of the vehicle. Bircher had

---

*One of the wounded, Specialist Anthony Kidd, would die three days later from his wounds. The sabot round sheared both of his feet off at the lower shin. The nature of his wounds led to initial reports that they had been caused by mines. This was relayed to and reported by the press. When the mistake was corrected by the Army after the war, some in the media would attack the original report of mine-inflicted wounds as an attempted cover-up.

seen the round fired at Sedgwick's wing man and had turned his vehicle toward the source of the fire. Shortly after his close call, Bircher looked behind him to see a burning 2nd Platoon Bradley.

The Bradley had just been hit by a 120mm HEAT round from the same Abrams that had just narrowly missed Bircher. The gunner believed that he had hit his first target (Bircher's Bradley) with the sabot round, but there had been no explosion. For his next target, he wanted an explosion that would confirm a hit, so he called to his loader for a HEAT round.

The burning Bradley was commanded by 2LT Mickey Williams, 2nd Platoon's leader. When Capt. Wilson had changed vehicles, he had taken Williams' Bradley. Williams had moved to this Bradley and had been blown out of the hatch by the explosion of the HEAT round, breaking a leg when he landed outside the vehicle. Though two men were killed instantly and another was mortally wounded, most of the occupants of the vehicle were fortunate for three reasons.

Had the HEAT round impacted squarely on the vehicle, it might well have killed everyone inside. Instead, the round glanced off the driver's cupola and hit the front left side of the turret at an angle. The explosion occurred directly in front of the gunner's station. The shock of the explosion caused chunks of the inside of the turret to dislodge, resulting in extensive wounds, including a mortal head wound, to the vehicle's gunner, Sgt. David Crumby. Because of the angle the round hit the vehicle at, its jet of molten metal shot past Crumby, and hit PFC David Kramer, who was sitting behind the turret, on the left side of the vehicle, killing him instantly. The jet also killed Spec. Manuel Davila, who was sitting next to Kramer.

The round's impact was not as lethal as it could have been, but it did cause a serious fire inside the Bradley. The fire would almost certainly have claimed the lives of the rest of the men in the crew compartment had it not been for the efforts of the Bradley's driver, PFC Kevin Pollock. Though knocked groggy by the explosion above his hatch, and on fire, Pollock stayed at his post long enough to lower the ramp, allowing his comrades to escape from the vehicle before escaping himself.

Finally, 2LT Bircher's vehicle arrived shortly after Williams' Bradley was hit. Bircher and his crewmen, disregarding the danger to themselves posed by the fire and the periodic ammunition explosions which resulted from it, were able to pull several badly wounded or unconscious men from the burning vehicle.

There was a line of Iraqi armor running from northwest to southeast in TF 3-66's sector. At each end of the line was a mechanized infantry position. The two positions had slightly less than a battalion of BMPs between them. Each position was reinforced by two T-62s. Strung between the two positions were 12 T-72s.

In the north, Capt. Craig Bell's C Company, 3-66th Armor emerged from its passage lane four kilometers (2½ miles) from its northern boundary. This presented Bell with a difficult choice. He could make a 90 degree turn and head due north to assume his attack lane, or approach it from a shallower angle. A 90 degree turn would limit the possibility that his company would accidentally bypass Iraqi armor in the northwest corner of the attack zone, but it would expose his tanks to Iraqi flank shots. Concern about flank shots from the east prompted Bell to take a shallower angle. The company did bypass a mechanized infantry position of 12 BMPs, 2 T-62s and an MTLB off its left flank, but the situation was not as dangerous as it appeared. The position was overlooked because it had been abandoned. Virtually the entire position had been within main gun range of 1st Squadron, 2nd ACR, and many of the vehicles had been destroyed that afternoon. The Iraqi vehicles were therefore cold enough not to be seen on the tanks' thermal monitors. Had the position been occupied, either movement or warm vehicles would have been spotted by C Company. In any event, D Company, 1-41st Infantry, following C/3-66, initially headed almost due north when it came out of the passage lane. Because the infantry company had a tank company (C/3-66) east of it, its commander, Capt. Hans Meinhardt, had no worries about exposing its flank. Had there been live Iraqi vehicles on the position, Meinhardt's Bradleys would have destroyed them with TOW missiles.

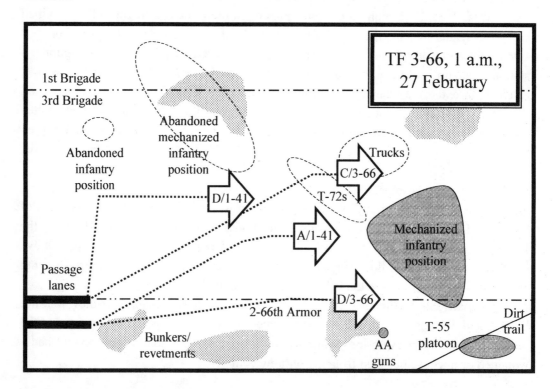

As C Company approached its attack lane, it spotted and destroyed 11 of the 12 T-72s between the two mechanized infantry positions. Behind the tank line was a group of 15 trucks, which was also destroyed. Shortly after it began driving eastward, the company destroyed seven BMPs in a position behind the tank line.

The seven BMPs were on the northern tip of the southern mechanized infantry position. At about 12:45, D/3-66 spotted that position about 1,900 meters to the front. Capt. Tim Ryan, commander of the company, knew that since Iraqi tanks were blind at night, he could get close enough to enemy tanks to positively identify them as Iraqi without exposing his men to unnecessary risk. By one, the company had closed to 1,300 meters (almost point-blank range for an Abrams), and had confirmed that the targets were Iraqi. As Ryan prepared to give a company fire command, he noticed through his sight that several Iraqis were sitting on top of their tanks, totally unaware of his company's presence. As he gave the command, two Iraqi T-62s, seven BMPs and two trucks exploded. A second volley destroyed two more BMPs and two MTLBs.

Though their armor had been wiped out, the infantrymen on the position refused to surrender. Two ground-mounted Sagger anti-tank missiles were fired at D Company, but both missed their targets by a wide margin. For a moment, the Iraqis received some help from their anti-aircraft machine-guns to the south. Firing on a flat trajectory, a few 57mm AA guns opened up on D Company. Within moments, however, the three Scout Platoon Bradleys which had been attached to the company pinpointed the source of the fire and destroyed the guns with 25mm chain-gun fire.

Still, the Iraqis resisted. While two of his platoons drove through the position and pushed eastward, destroying a platoon of three T-55s attempting to mount a counterattack from the southeast, Ryan detached a platoon and the company's attached engineers to clear the position in detail. As the scout Bradleys provided cover, occasionally riddling bunkers with 25mm fire, tanks with mine plows pushed dirt into Iraqi trenches until the firing ceased and the Iraqis surrendered.

As C and D companies moved on, the mechanized A/1-41, which had been in the center of the task force, trailing slightly behind the two tank companies, drove through the wrecked mechanized infantry position and came on line with C and D companies.

After destroying two T-55s and a few pockets of infantrymen, D/3-66 encountered a sizable logistics complex at around two. D Company halted on line and began destroying trucks and machine-gunning Iraqi dismounts. The nature of this engagement was extremely one-sided. The Iraqis were sustaining such a drubbing that one of Ryan's platoon leaders suggested that they should hold their fire, because his gunners were massacring potential EPWs. Ryan asked if the Iraqis were armed. The platoon leader said that they were. Slightly irritated, Ryan explained that EPWs were Iraqis who had been disarmed and were lying face down on the ground with their hands tied behind them. Potential EPWs were Iraqis who were apparently unarmed and had their hands in the air. As far as Ryan was concerned, Iraqis running around with weapons could conceivably kill Americans, so they should be considered hostile. The fact that for tactical reasons they had not been able to kill any Americans up to that point did not make them potential EPWs. The shooting continued until the Iraqis on the position finally stopped firing and surrendered. The task force then pushed eastward, overrunning a battalion-sized artillery position before halting at 3:30.

In the center, 2-66th Armor made steady progress in the two hours after it emerged from its passage lanes, overrunning pockets of infantry and armored vehicles. Just after two, the battalion encountered the worst terrain in the brigade's sector, an extensive, dug-in infantry position. Between two and three, 16 of 2-66th Armor's 58 tanks, including Lt.Col. Brown's, would fall into anti-tank ditches or through the roofs of bunkers. Fortunately, the obstacles were not covered by anti-tank weapons, and the Americans had time to extricate themselves. The fighting was intense, and remained so right up to the point that the battalion was ordered to withdraw at three.

In the south, after the brief engagement following its emergence from the passage lanes, Task Force 1-41 had pushed on through a major Iraqi artillery position, where it encountered Iraqis eager to surrender. After 1:30, the task force encountered mostly empty terrain. Just after three, B Company, 3-66th Armor and A Company, 3-66th Armor, the two tank companies on the forward edge of TF 1-41, experienced a friendly fire incident.

Believing that Capt. Wilson's Bradleys had been destroyed by Iraqi tanks, Lt.Col. Hillman had told Capt. Hedges to send one of B Company's three platoons back to deal with the tanks. Hedges had formed his two remaining platoons into a wedge, with his tank in the center, at the point, and continued to push eastward.

As Hedges' tank topped a ridge, his driver turned the tank to the left to avoid a bit of rough terrain. Within seconds, a sabot round sliced through the left side of the vehicle and ripped through the breech of the main gun before passing out the other side of the tank. The strike wounded Hedges in the groin and left leg with spall, and killed his gunner, SSG Tony Applegate.* Hedges ordered the tank evacuated. As he climbed onto the tank's back deck, a second round crashed through the turret ring and exited the right rear of the turret, knocking him to the ground.

The fire came from A Company, 2-66th Armor. The company was meeting desperate resistance from Iraqi infantry in front of it at the time. Iraqi infantrymen occasionally even popped up within the company's formation. Capt. Dick watched as his loader killed Iraqis within 25 meters of his tank.

When Hedges' tank appeared on the horizon, the leader of A Company's right flank platoon and his wing man assumed that it was Iraqi. Believing that they were oriented due east, they had no reason to assume otherwise. Any vehicle from one of the flank task forces would have to be badly lost to drift into A Company's zone. The vehicle would have to cross its task force boundary, then drive across another 2-66th Armor company just to get in front of Dick's gunners. However, the lay of the land and the Iraqi defenses had drawn the company off course. A Company was not oriented to the east, but to the southeast. As a result, the gunners were unknowingly firing into TF1-41's sector.

Generally, a company commander can determine his direction of travel by watching the readings on his GPS monitor change as his tank moves. However, Capt. Dick's tank, like the rest of his company, was stopped by the bunker complex. As a result, the GPS could tell him nothing more than his present location. The presence of Iraqi infantry also made it impossible for Capt. Dick to leave the vehicle to take a compass reading to check his company's orientation.

---

*Applegate had been wounded by shrapnel eight days earlier during the Task Force Iron mission, but had refused to be evacuated.

It had been a stroke of luck that the driver of Hedges' tank had turned the vehicle to the left. This put heavier armor between the crew and the sabot rounds. Had the driver been pointed due east, the rounds would have entered the tank at a much more thinly armored point, on the left side of the tank, toward the rear.

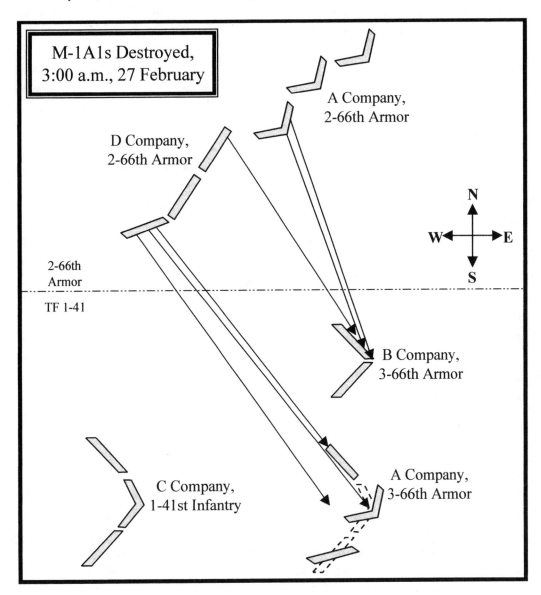

M-1A1s Destroyed,
3:00 a.m., 27 February

A Company,
2-66th Armor

D Company,
2-66th Armor

2-66th
Armor

TF 1-41

N

W ← → E

S

B Company,
3-66th Armor

A Company,
3-66th Armor

C Company,
1-41st Infantry

The turn had been fortunate for another reason. The first shot, fired by the platoon leader's wing man, had missed, but it drew the attention of Capt. Dick, traveling behind the platoon that fired the rounds. The second round, fired seconds later, hit. Dick looked through his thermal sight at the site of the hit. Because of the angle of the tank, he could see enough of its profile to identify it as an Abrams. He immediately began radioing cease-fire orders. The wing man immediately stopped, but in the excitement, the order was not heard by the platoon leader until another round (which also hit) had been fired. The damage had been kept to a minimum, however. Had Dick not been able to identify the Abrams, it is certain that more than three rounds would have been fired. It is likely that A Company would have engaged other tanks from B Company as they reached the high ground.

Seconds after the second hit on Hedges' tank, as the loader was preparing to jump off of the back deck (the driver had already exited the vehicle), the tank was hit again. The final strike caused an internal fire which burned for almost two hours before an ammunition explosion destroyed the tank.

When Hedges' tank was hit, the commander of the tank to his left rear had turned his vehicle to the north, placing its heaviest armor between the crew and the incoming rounds he was sure would hit his tank at any moment. Seconds after the tank turned, a sabot round penetrated the front slope of the tank and hit an electrical circuit box behind the driver's head, wounding him. This round, and the last round fired at Hedges' tank were fired by D Company, 2-66th Armor's right flank company, which was also misoriented to the southeast.

Moments after firing on B Company ceased, Capt. Bishop's A Company was hit. Aware that Hedges' company was being fired on, Bishop had ordered his northernmost (3rd) platoon to orient to the northeast, in the direction of Hedges' tank. Seconds after the platoon turned, its northernmost tank was hit in left side by an American sabot round fired by D/2-66. Though no one in the tank was killed, the round, which passed across the floor of the turret before exiting the vehicle, wounded the gunner in the legs with spall. The gunner, loader and driver evacuated the vehicle, while the tank commander, 3rd Platoon's platoon sergeant, grabbed individual weapons for the crew's defense. Another round then sliced through the left side of the vehicle and passed through the turret, throwing him against the side of the tank, breaking his jaw and knocking out several teeth. The round then hit the platoon leader's tank in the left side. The impact ruptured a fuel cell, but damage was limited because the round had spent much of its kinetic energy slicing through the platoon sergeant's tank.

Unaware that the fire was American, Bishop thought he had driven into an infantry anti-armor ambush. To escape what he believed was an Iraqi kill sack, he ordered his company to turn 90 degrees and gather at a rally point 500 meters to the south. This would take A Company out of the range of the RPGs Bishop believed were being fired at his company. In the front of the company, as one of 1st Platoon's tanks began to turn southward, it was hit in the left side, towards the rear. Two seconds later, as the tank continued to turn, it was hit in the rear by another sabot round from the same direction. The first round penetrated the turret, wounding three crewmen. The second round knocked out the engine.

Bishop, about 400 meters directly behind that tank, could now see that his company was taking friendly fire, and tried to report it as two sabot rounds were directed at his tank. Fortunately, Bishop's tank was in a low point in the terrain at the time, and was about a meter lower than the stricken tanks. This proved crucial, as both rounds sailed about 18 inches over his tank.

After about 30 seconds, a cease-fire order on the brigade command net brought the firing from 2-66th Armor to a halt. Bishop moved eastward to evacuate the wounded from Hedges' tank and the wrecked 1st Platoon tank while his 3rd Platoon leader evacuated his wounded. A Company then reformed at the rally point while Capt. Mike Sanders' C Company, 1-41st Infantry secured the terrain vacated by Bishop's company.

At that point, Lt.Col. Brown radioed Col. Weisman, reporting that Iraqi infantrymen were too thick to continue to engage without more fratricides. He requested that he be allowed to pull back and reengage the Iraqis at dawn. Lt.Col. Hillman, who had overheard Brown's request on the brigade command net, told Weisman that for his battalion, pulling back would be out of the question, as he now had medics on the ground treating several wounded men from the friendly fire incident.[*] He was also concerned that a pullback by 2-66th Armor would leave TF 1-41's left flank unprotected. Brown ultimately pulled back most of his battalion, but left his right flank company shielding TF 1-41's flank. Weisman ordered TF 3-66 to pull back as well. Most of the brigade fell back to reform and refuel.

At 5:45, TF 3-66 sustained its friendly fire fatality. D Company, 1-41st Infantry's mission had been to clear the task force's rear in detail and be prepared to deal with any stubborn infantry positions passed off to it by the lead tank companies. No defended positions had been passed to the company, however, so for most of the attack, D Company swept up behind the lead units. On the task force's northern flank, a section of two Bradleys was rounding up prisoners. Since they had no Global Positioning Systems, they had no way of knowing that they had gone too far north and were about a half-mile inside 1st Brigade's sector. The 1-34th Armor Battalion had driven through the area, but, being an all tank formation, had not cleared it in detail. TF 5-16 was on its way to perform that task, but had not arrived yet. As a result, there were pockets of armed Iraqis in the area.

As D Company's infantrymen were gathering surrendering Iraqis, they began taking fire from behind the Iraqis. Iraqis in defensive positions were firing small arms and several RPGs at the Americans, who returned fire. Some of the return fire overshot the Iraqi defenders and landed among tanks from 1-34th Armor. Ritter's tankmen assumed that they were being fired on by Iraqis. Two tanks opened fire. One Bradley was hit by a HEAT round and completely destroyed. There were no fatalities, as the crewmen were all outside the vehicle rounding up prisoners. Seeing that dismounts were under fire, SSG Joseph Moreira, the commander of the second Bradley, moved his vehicle forward to shield them. That vehicle's driver, PFC James Murray, Jr., was killed when the Bradley was hit in the front slope by the first of three sabot rounds.[†‡]

Meanwhile, Bradleys from 1-34th Armor's Scout Platoon opened fire on the dismounted infantrymen with 25mm HEI rounds. The infantrymen, led by SSG Mark

---

[*]Lt.Col. Hillman moved his Bradley forward to see to the evacuation of the crews of the stricken vehicles, an action for which he would receive the Bronze Star with V device. Hedges, who refused to leave until his wounded were evacuated, was awarded the Silver Star.

[†]Though it had been hit by three sabot rounds and needed a new engine, the vehicle was still repairable. However, it was later scuttled with C-4 explosive by overzealous combat engineers.

[‡]Murray and Moreira were each awarded the Bronze Star with V Device.

Sandercock, immediately herded their prisoners into bunkers and out of the line of fire.[*] Several dismounts were wounded by shrapnel during the engagement. Shortly thereafter, tanks from 1-34th Armor closed on the area, realized that the targets were American, and firing ceased.

In its part of the Battle of Norfolk, the 2nd AD (Forward) had four M-1A1s destroyed and another damaged. Five Bradleys had been destroyed. All losses had been from friendly fire. Six Americans had been killed and another thirty had been wounded. The brigade had destroyed 36 tanks, including 11 Republican Guard T-72s, as well as 11 MTLBs and 16 BMPs (in addition to the nearly two dozen armored vehicles destroyed by 1st Squadron, 2nd ACR). It had killed or taken prisoner over 450 Iraqis. The next day, the brigade would drive through a large concentration of supply units, capturing and destroying some 600 trucks.

---

[*]SSG Sandercock was awarded the Bronze Star with V Device.

21

Take a Little off the Top:
The 1st Armored Division
Hits the Tawakalna Line

Before deploying to the Gulf, Maj.Gen. Ronald H. Griffith's 1st Armored Division had been extensively reshuffled to maximize its combat power. When the reorganization was finished, the new and improved 1st Armored Division would have more total combat power than the one which had been stationed in Germany.

Before the war, Col. Dan Zanini's 1st Brigade had two tank battalions and one mechanized infantry battalion. Unfortunately, the infantry battalion was still equipped with outdated M-113A2 APCs, not Bradley Fighting Vehicles. The most widely used APC in the world, the M-113 is extremely maneuverable and mechanically reliable, but it is under-armed, with only one heavy machine-gun. Its box shape is not particularly good for deflecting projectiles, and its aluminum armor burns ferociously if the vehicle catches fire. During the Vietnam War, many soldiers felt it was safer to ride on top of an M-113 than inside it. The M-113A2 also does not have the speed to keep up with M-1A1s. The mechanized infantry battalion and one of Zanini's armor battalions were left in Germany. His other battalion, 1-37th Armor, was absorbed into the division's 3rd Brigade. The 1-37th, the only battalion in the division that had M-1A1s with depleted uranium armor, was just too well-equipped to leave behind. It had also just completed an intensive program of gunnery training in preparation for the Canadian Army Tank Gunnery Competition, so it was also too well-prepared to leave behind.

To replace the 1st Brigade, a brigade of the 3rd Infantry Division (Mechanized) was attached to the 1st AD. The 3rd ID's 3rd Brigade, under Col. James Riley, consisted of two Bradley-equipped mechanized infantry battalions (1-7th and 4-7th Infantry) and an armor battalion (4-66th Armor). Riley's brigade became the 1st Brigade of the 1st

Armored Division, though the brigade's troops would continue to wear the 3rd ID shoulder patch.

Col. Montgomery Meigs' 2nd Brigade was the most powerful maneuver brigade in the U.S. Army, with three tank battalions and one infantry battalion.[*] Its infantry battalion (2-6th Infantry) was Bradley-equipped, but had only received its Bradleys a short time before. Since the battalion's soldiers had not had adequate time to familiarize themselves with the vehicles, and had not been through a gunnery qualification, 2-6th Infantry was replaced by the 3rd Brigade's 6-6th Infantry Battalion.

Col. John Schneeberger's 3rd Brigade had consisted of two mechanized infantry battalions and an armored battalion before the war. Its mechanized infantry battalions were equipped with Bradleys, so they would not have to be left behind. The brigade's 6-6th Infantry Battalion was reassigned to the 2nd Brigade but had been replaced by 1-37th Armor. In the process, the brigade had lost a battalion of Bradleys, but gained a battalion of M-1A1s, a tremendous net gain in combat power.

Just before the division was scheduled to deploy to Saudi Arabia, there was an unexpected bit of shuffling when Schneeberger had to be relieved for health reasons.[†] Generally, replacing a brigade commander weeks before deployment to a combat zone would be a major problem, but Griffith's Assistant Division Commander for Maneuver, Brig.Gen. John Hendrix, pointed out that Col. Zanini, who had been shuffled out of the deployment with his brigade, would be an ideal replacement. Griffith agreed. Zanini had already served as a brigade commander under Griffith, and would not need any adjustment period. In addition, 1-37th Armor, which was now part of the 3rd Brigade, had been part of Zanini's 1st Brigade before the reorganization.

At the time the division deployed, there were still worries that the Iraqis might launch a preemptive attack west of the Wadi al-Batin. To forestall this possibility, the division would be sent to assume a blocking position. Col. Zanini and a small command group were sent ahead of the main body. As units arrived, battalion by battalion, Zanini set them in defensive positions, established defensive and counterattack plans and prepared for any attacks the Iraqis might launch before the rest of the division arrived. Task Force Zanini was backed up by four battalions of XVIII Airborne Corps Apache attack helicopters.

With the beginning of the air war, any hopes the Iraqis might have had of a successful strike against Task Force Zanini vanished. With its defensive worries behind it, the division turned its attention to preparing for the upcoming offensive. While the

---

[*]Captain Montgomery Meigs (an ancestor) had been the engineer officer in charge of overseeing the construction of the U.S. Capitol Building when the Civil War broke out. After performing with distinction in a number of other assignments, he became Quartermaster General of the Union Army. In that capacity, it was he who made the decision to bury Union soldiers on the grounds of an estate abandoned by Robert E. Lee at the war's outset. That project eventually became Arlington National Cemetery.

[†]This is still a matter of controversy. Schneeberger holds that he was subject to fainting spells due to a head injury he sustained while he was stationed at the National Training Center. However, many Army officers believe that Schneeberger suffered a crisis of confidence.

mixing and matching of units had created a more powerful division, it was a division in which many units and leaders were working with each other for the first time. Training in the desert would be the key to making the division a cohesive unit. As soon as the rest of the division had joined Task Force Zanini, training began, and was conducted vigorously right up to G-Day. By the time it entered Iraq, Griffith's division would be functioning as smoothly as if its units had been together all along.

At 6:30 a.m. on G-Day, using armored bulldozers, division engineers began punching 250 eight meter wide holes in the berm. By mid-afternoon, 1st AD had entered Iraq in a wedge formation, with the 1st Brigade on point, and 2nd and 3rd brigades to its left and right rear.

The division faced no opposition on the first day. Its main worry was friendly fire. There would be scouts operating to the division's front, and Griffith did not want them mistaken for Iraqis. To ensure that there were no mistakes, Griffith's scout vehicles attached special infra-red lights to their antennae, giving them a unique signature. The problem of accidental air attacks was addressed by posting blinking strobe lights on the lead vehicles. The strobe lights were fitted with shields, so that the lights would be visible to Coalition aircraft but not Iraqi ground forces.

The first combat would come around noon on the 25th. Just prior to entering Iraq, the division had received aerial photographs of a company-sized concentration of Iraqi infantry from the 26th Infantry Division supported by armor about 30 miles southeast of the village of al-Busayyah. Not wanting his division to become bogged down in a fight before it reached al-Busayyah, Griffith realigned it according to a prearranged plan. The 3rd Brigade would deal with the Iraqi position while the rest of the division shifted to the west to avoid it.

The brigade had an abundance of information about the Iraqi positions. Aerial photographs had pinpointed almost every revetment and piece of military equipment on the objective. Those photos had then been disseminated to every platoon leader in the brigade, and the attack plan had been worked out in detail.

Brigade planners divided the Iraqi defenses into three objectives. Most of the infantry was on the southernmost position, Objective Club. Behind Club, on Objective Shield, were a handful of artillery, anti-tank and anti-aircraft pieces. Information about the defenses on Objective Hand, the northernmost position, was sketchy. Planners knew that it contained a small group of cinderblock buildings, and believed it to be a division headquarters. Just before G-Day, tanks had been spotted in the area, and there was a chance they were on Objective Hand. Zanini decided to send his heaviest tanks, those of Lt.Col. Ed Dyer's TF 1-37, ahead to seize the objective.

The vast majority of the Iraqi trenches, revetments and weapons on the objectives were oriented facing southwest. Zanini therefore planned to swerve around Club and Shield to the east, then roll up the Iraqi defenders from the flank.

The brigade was forced to attack the position without rocket support, since the MLRS battalion was on the division's left side and could not shift in time to support the attack. Conventional artillery proved to be enough, however. During the attack, 3-1st Field Artillery Battalion would fire 756 DPICM rounds in four fire missions to devastating effect.

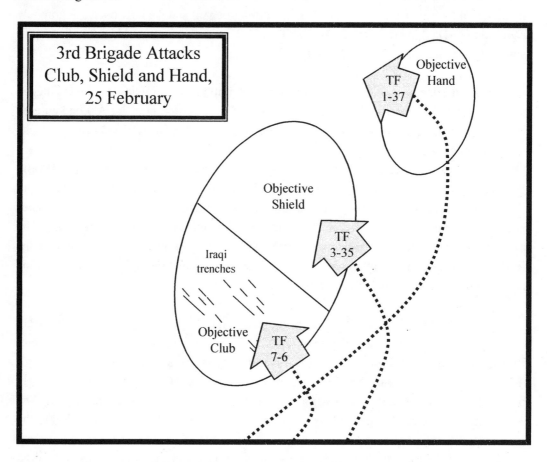

3rd Brigade Attacks Club, Shield and Hand, 25 February

Objective Hand

TF 1-37

Objective Shield

Iraqi trenches

TF 3-35

Objective Club

TF 7-6

The attack went like clockwork, beginning at 1:23 p.m. with a 668-round artillery barrage. At 1:31, when the artillery was finished, tanks from Lt.Col. Ward Critz's TF 7-6 surprised and destroyed an Iraqi Type 59 and two BRDM armored scout vehicles on Objective Club.* Fifteen minutes later, TF 7-6 began rolling across the Iraqi trenchlines on Objective Club from the side. Lt.Col. Ed Kane's TF 3-35 began its drive across Objective Shield 12 minutes later. Meanwhile, TF 1-37 dealt with Iraqi opposition on Objective Hand, finding no tanks, only eight towed ZPU-4 four-barreled, 14.5mm AA machine-guns. After sweeping Hand, Dyer's tanks hooked around the rear of Shield.

Iraqis were interrogated almost as soon as they were captured. They were able to furnish information about changes in the Iraqi defenses since the aerial photos had been taken. This information was then passed over the radio to the units clearing the objectives. By 4:30 in the afternoon, the three objectives had been cleared. The brigade had destroyed one tank, eight other armored vehicles, three artillery pieces and 34 trucks.

---

*The 7-6th Infantry Battalion had given a company of infantry to 1-37th Armor and a company to 3-35th Armor, receiving a company of tanks from each of those battalions.

Zanini had incorporated all three of his task forces into the assault. A veteran of two tours in Vietnam, he knew that a little combat experience would go a long way in preparing his men for the Republican Guard. Now, as his units rearmed and refueled, Zanini called his staff and battalion commanders together to review the battle and analyze what had worked and what had not, in preparation for the upcoming fight with the Republican Guard.

In addition to providing information about the tactical disposition of Iraqi forces on Objectives Club, Shield and Hand, the interrogations provided crucial information about how much the Iraqis knew about what the Americans were doing. Of particular concern was whether the defenders had warned the defenders of al-Busayyah of the division's presence. As Maj.Gen. Griffith and Lt.Col. Keith Alexander, the division's intelligence officer, looked on, the prisoners told their interrogators that they had not had any communications with the Iraqis in al-Busayyah for a week. Griffith still had the element of surprise.

The interrogations also revealed how completely the Iraqis had been fooled, and how poor a job Baghdad had done keeping its units in the field informed. The Iraqis were surprised at how far west the Americans were. However, an even bigger shock to captured officers, who had access to enough intelligence to distinguish one American unit from another, was that they had been hit by a Europe-based heavy unit. Though the deployment of the divisions from Europe had been widely reported in the Western media, this information had not reached these officers, who now knew that the Iraqi Army was facing a far larger and far more well-equipped foe than they had ever imagined.

While 3rd Brigade was taking Club, Shield and Hand, there was action on and around Objective Bear, to the northwest. Lt.Col. William Reese's 1st Squadron, 1st Cavalry Regiment had the most contact with the Iraqis on Bear. The 1-1st Cavalry was made up of two air cavalry troops (reconnaissance and Cobra attack helicopters) and two ground cavalry troops (in Bradleys). The unit had been placed under the operational control of 1st Brigade, to be directed by Col. Riley. The squadron, traveling ahead of the brigade, faced a battalion of dug-in Iraqis supported by several armored vehicles. After a short artillery barrage, 1-1st Cavalry attacked. Within 10 minutes, the squadron destroyed a Type 59 tank, two APCs, and took 299 prisoners. Driving northward, over the next three miles it destroyed two Type 59s, eight APCs, four artillery pieces, several trucks and rounded up nearly a hundred more Iraqis. By 2:28, the objective was secure.

That was when the squadron's problems began. Not expecting stiff resistance from the low grade units near the border, the unit's soldiers had expected to take prisoners. However, with almost 400, there were now more Iraqis than Americans with the squadron's two ground troops. At first, individual Bradleys were detached to watch over large groups of prisoners, then catch up to the rest of the unit after the prisoners were handed over to follow-on units. When the unit's prisoner total eventually reached almost 900, that strategy became impossible. Rather than fritter away the division's ground cavalry on guard duty, the unit chose to disarm the Iraqis, pile the weapons on trucks, and start the Iraqis walking southward on their own.

The 1st Brigade also saw action at Objective Bear. TF 1-7, at the tip of the brigade wedge, destroyed three armored vehicles and took 70 prisoners. The brigade had been forced to shift its axis of advance to the northwest, but had made the adjustment with ease. Knowing that the brigade would be on the leading edge of the division, and would be responsible for fixing enemy units, Riley had drilled the unit constantly before G-Day. The brigade had conducted rehearsals on 1/100, then 1/10 scale before moving on to full scale rehearsals, then full scale rehearsals at night. By the time they were called upon to perform their mission in combat, the brigade's soldiers found that it was largely a conditioned reflex.

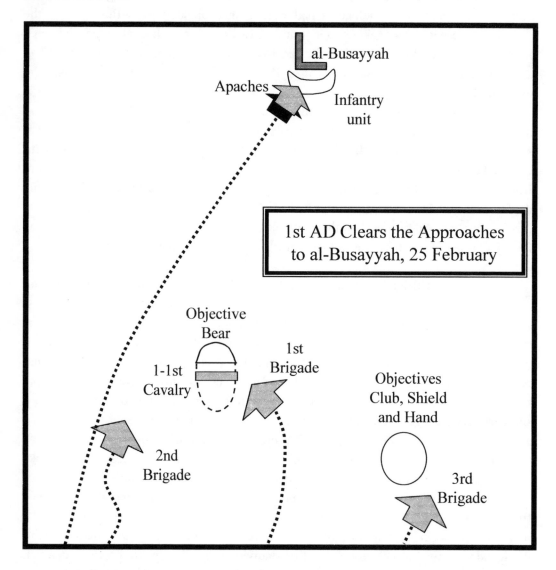

Meanwhile, Apaches from Col. Dan Petrosky's Aviation Brigade ranged far ahead of the main body. After herding about 100 surrendering Iraqis toward 1st AD's lead elements, Apaches and Air Force ground attack planes struck an infantry unit guarding a logistics site near al-Busayyah, about 75 miles inside Iraq. Several trucks and artillery pieces were destroyed in the attack.

Between 10 p.m. and 2 a.m. on the night of the 25th, 2nd Brigade took up positions short of al-Busayyah. The brigade had not been engaged that day. Having assigned it the capture of al-Busayyah, the day's main objective, Maj.Gen. Griffith had kept the brigade away from the earlier engagements to ensure that it would get to the town as quickly as possible.

The town, a one-road, L-shaped collection of about 35 small stone buildings, was defended by a company-sized unit of tanks and APCs as well as two companies of commandos. Griffith did not want to involve his men in house-to-house fighting at night, so he asked for permission from Lt.Gen. Franks to soften up al-Busayyah that night, then attack next morning. Permission was granted, with the understanding that Griffith would not let operations in the town cause undue delay to his advance.

That night, Apaches made one strike against the town, but a second mission had to be scrubbed due to high winds and poor visibility. The division then unleashed a savage artillery barrage. By 6:15 next morning, a total of 346 MLRS rockets and 1,441 artillery shells had fallen on al-Busayyah.

At 6:30 a.m., the attacking forces, aligned two brigades abreast, closed in quickly on the town, before the Iraqis could recover from the last barrage. On the right flank, 1st Brigade met little resistance. The only contact with the Iraqis occurred on the brigade's left flank, when TF 4-66's tanks were met by a few terrified Iraqis looking for someone to surrender to. The tank crews directed the Iraqis to the infantry behind them. After shooting up a few bunkers east of the town, the brigade passed al-Busayyah and refueled on the other side.

On the 2nd Brigade's right flank, TF 6-6, under Lt.Col. Mike McGee, had instructions not to go into the town. McGee's task force poured fire into al-Busayyah while bypassing the town to the east. Meanwhile, Lt.Col. Steve Whitcomb's TF 2-70, to the left of TF 6-6, swept the western outskirts of the town.* As TF 6-6's lead tanks approached the town, a T-55 attempted to draw a bead on an Abrams, but was destroyed before it could get a shot off, as were three other T-55s, a *Cascaval* (a Brazilian-made wheeled light tank with a 90mm gun) and a few APCs. A BTR-60 attempted to flee but was hardly under way when it was destroyed by a main gun round. Two Iraqi infantry anti-tank teams were wiped out by machine-gun fire from the tanks. By 9:00, resistance around the town had ceased with the destruction of another T-55, and the Americans were preparing to take the town itself.

Remembering Lt.Gen. Franks' instructions not to let the fighting for al-Busayyah slow his advance, Maj.Gen. Griffith knew he would have to continue his advance soon. However, he did not want two largely intact Iraqi commando companies in his rear, directly in the path of his supply trains. Griffith elected to send the bulk of his division forward and leave TF 6-6 and some engineers behind to clear the town.

For the attack, Lt.Col. McGee positioned a firing line to the east of the town, running from north to south. On the northern end was Team C, made up of two tank

---

*The 6-6th Infantry Battalion had given a company of infantry to 2-70th Armor and a company to 4-70th Armor, receiving a company of tanks from each of those battalions.

platoons. In the center were the three Bradley platoons of C Company, 6-6th Infantry. In the south was Team G, a mixed team of two tank platoons and a Bradley platoon. McGee's assault team, consisting of a platoon of Bradleys, two armored bulldozers and a Combat Engineer Vehicle (CEV) took up positions on the southern end of town and waited for the order to attack.* McGee positioned Team B, two tank platoons and a Bradley platoon, to the northwest of the town. Any Iraqis who might attempt to sneak out of the town would have to head to the west, northwest or north. From its position, Team B would be in an ideal position to intercept would-be escapees on any of these axes. The team would also be out of the rest of the task force's line of fire. The firing line would be oriented to the west. The assault team would be firing to the north.

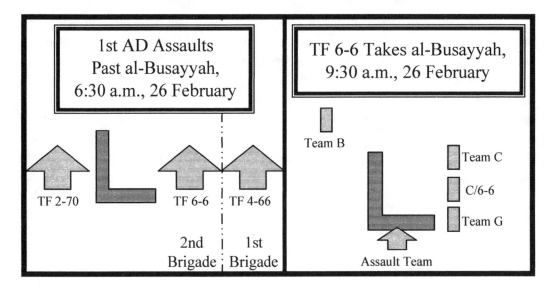

As the task force approached al-Busayyah, it began taking small arms fire. A Bradley fired 60 rounds of 25mm ammunition into a building, destroying it and killing an Iraqi machine-gun team. A T-55 and a Cascaval were spotted by American gunners and were destroyed instantly. Some Iraqi soldiers came to the edge of the town with their hands up feigning surrender in an attempt to draw the Bradleys within anti-tank projectile range. When dismounted infantrymen moved forward to take their surrender, the Iraqis fell back into the town and opened fire.

McGee pulled his units back and called for a 10-minute artillery barrage. Artillerymen fired high explosive shells, fused to penetrate the bunkers and buildings before detonating. Iraqi machine-gunners who only minutes earlier had been jeering defiantly and making obscene gestures at the Americans from rooftops, now disappeared in dust and smoke as their buildings collapsed beneath them.

When the barrage lifted, the firing line poured a hail of main gun, 25mm chain-gun and machine-gun fire into al-Busayyah, then lifted their fire while the assault team

---

*The CEV was a modified M-60 tank equipped with a bulldozer blade and a demolition gun. The gun fired the 65 lb. 165mm HEP (High Explosive Plastique) round which contained about 50 lbs. of Composition A-3 plastic explosive.

entered the town. The battle was short and one-sided. The CEV's gun was extremely useful against the fortified buildings the Iraqis were firing from, firing 20 rounds and destroying 19 fighting positions. All but about two dozen Iraqis died in their positions. Thirteen came out of the town and surrendered before the final assault began and a few more were pulled from the rubble.* After taking the town, the task force bypassed a corps-level Iraqi supply dump beyond the town before moving out to catch up to the rest of the division. The supply dump would be destroyed on 1 March by engineers.

While 1st AD's ground units were fighting at al-Busayyah, its Aviation Brigade was involved in high drama 40 miles to the north. The Aviation Brigade received word that two of the Special Forces surveillance teams which had been inserted before G-day had been spotted by the Iraqis. Lt.Gen. Franks ordered the brigade to extract the two teams immediately. Due to the urgency of the mission, the two Blackhawks assigned the task had no time to refuel before taking off. As a result, they only had enough fuel for 15 minutes of searching if they wanted to make it back to base. Once they reached the Green Berets' location, they would have to find them quickly, in the face of bad weather and poor visibility.

Just before noon, the two helicopters took off and headed for the two teams. When they arrived at the location of the first team about 30 minutes later, they could not find it. After a few passes, the mission commander, CW(Chief Warrant Officer)2 Robert Caprara decided to go for the other team nine miles away and hope to find the first team on the way back. The Blackhawks found the second team immediately, picked them up and headed back to the first pickup point.

On this attempt, the helicopters received visual assistance from the first team's leader, who had jumped out of his spider hole and was waving a 3 by 5 foot American flag. Caprara set his helicopter down and began loading the Green Berets as his wing man, Capt. William Young, hovered overhead keeping an eye out for Iraqis. Almost immediately, Young spotted a force of about two dozen Iraqi APCs accompanied by dismounted troops less than a mile away from the pickup point and heading straight for it. The Special Forces team destroyed what gear it could not load immediately and jumped aboard the helicopter. As the Blackhawk took off, it was locked on by Iraqi ground radar. Using violent evasive maneuvers, the pilot broke the radar lock and headed for home. At about 1:30, the two Blackhawks and their passengers were safely on the ground.

By 2:30, the division (minus TF 6-6, which was finishing up at al-Busayyah) had pivoted, and was headed due east, with 2nd Brigade in the north, 1st Brigade in the center and 3rd Brigade in the south. The 1-1st Cavalry, still ahead of the three brigades, was looking for more Iraqi units to fix and destroy. At 2:45, air scouts spotted a battalion of dug-in T-72s near 1st AD's southern boundary and within minutes, a section of the squadron's Cobra gunships went to work, firing 2.75-inch rockets and Tow 2 wire-guided

---

*The next day, six Iraqis would come out of hiding to surrender to an engineer unit destroying dud bomblets.

missiles. Though the TOW 2 (2¼ miles) has a shorter range than a Hellfire (3¾ miles), it has roughly the same destructive power, and was powerful enough to destroy any Iraqi tank. The Cobras also called in an MLRS strike to keep the tanks pinned down while eight A-10s and two Jaguars streaked toward the position.

Still waiting for the ground attack planes, one of the Cobras lost a compressor and was forced to make an emergency landing within 1,500 meters of the Iraqi positions. The Cobras laid suppressive fire while a platoon of Bradleys from B Troop, 1-1st Cavalry was redirected to the crash site to pick up the downed crewmen. The Bradleys and a flight of two A-10s arrived almost simultaneously a few minutes later. As the scouts and crewmen transferred classified items and secret equipment to the Bradley, Warthogs hit the Iraqis with Maverick missiles and 30mm cannon fire. After the crew was safely extracted, the Cobras broke off and headed for home, replaced by Jaguars and more A-10s. In all, the Iraqis lost about a dozen armored vehicles to the Cobras, A-10s and Jaguars. The Iraqis on the position were then left with a few hours respite before 3rd Brigade arrived.

The brigade moved toward the Tawakalna positions in a wedge formation, with the two mechanized and two tank companies of TF 7-6 in the lead, preparing to fix the Iraqis, and the two armor-heavy task forces to its left (TF 3-35) and right (TF 1-37) rear. The 3-1st Field Artillery Battalion was traveling behind TF 7-6, ready to blow a hole through the middle of the Iraqi line. Unfortunately, the pilots of the A-10s that had attacked earlier had misreported the location of the Iraqi lines. At around 8 p.m. that evening, when 3-1st FA fired two missions on grid coordinates based on those reports, its bomblets landed in the open desert, about 1¼ miles short of the Iraqi defensive line.

At 8:30, TF 7-6 opened up on the Iraqis, pinning them down while TF 1-37 moved in for the kill. At the outset of the attack, the Iraqis thought that they were being hit by another air attack. Many defenders were cut down by machine-gun fire from M-1A1s and Bradleys as they tried to make their way back from their bomb shelters to their vehicles. Meanwhile, an artillery strike by 3-1st FA destroyed four tanks on the southern end of the first Iraqi defense line with DPICM rounds.

At 9:25, a wave of tanks from TF 1-37 swept toward the first Iraqi defense line, made up mostly of T-72s. The Iraqis who had made it back to their vehicles tried to fight, but were no match for Lt.Col. Dyer's tanks. The M-1A1s fired on the move, destroying most of the vehicles in the first line in only a few minutes. This left so many Iraqi armored vehicles burning so fiercely that American gunners were starting to have trouble using their thermal sights. As a result, when Dyer's tanks rolled toward the second line, mostly BMPs reinforced by a few T-72s, they passed by a few live T-72s, offering them flank and rear shots at point-blank range. During the battle, four of the battalion's tanks would be knocked out, two by main gun rounds from T-72s, one by an RPG round, and another by a Sagger missile launched from a BMP.

Though their sighting and range advantages were now largely gone, the American tanks retained a tremendous armor protection advantage. Of the sixteen crewmen in these tanks, six were wounded and none killed. Four of the wounded would return to duty the next day. One of the tanks was hit in the ammunition compartment. There was a massive explosion as many of the main gun rounds blew up, but the tank's blowout panel channeled the explosion away from the crew.[*]

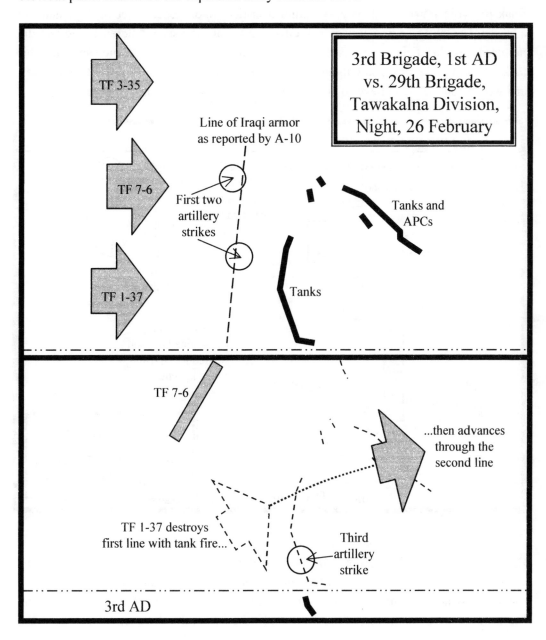

At 9:40, just as Dyer's tanks began moving toward the second defense line, Apaches appeared on the brigade's right flank and began firing Hellfire missiles at the Iraqis. The Apaches were from the 3rd Armored Division. They were in the process of supporting that division's 2nd Brigade, which was engaging Iraqi positions to the south.

---

[*]Three of the four tanks were eventually repaired. The tank hit in the ammunition compartment was gutted by fire.

In doing so, they had strayed a few hundred meters north of the division boundary. Col. Zanini was not happy to see the Apaches. The Apaches forced Zanini to pull back his lightly protected Humvee-mounted scouts from their position on the division's southern flank to avoid fratricide. This cost Zanini a critical intelligence asset on the flank. In addition, Lt.Col. Dyer was already maneuvering toward the second defense line and did not need Apaches firing over his tanks. In fact, since this occurred at the same time his tanks began to take hits, some thought that the tanks were being hit by Hellfire missiles, and would continue to believe so until a subsequent investigation proved otherwise.

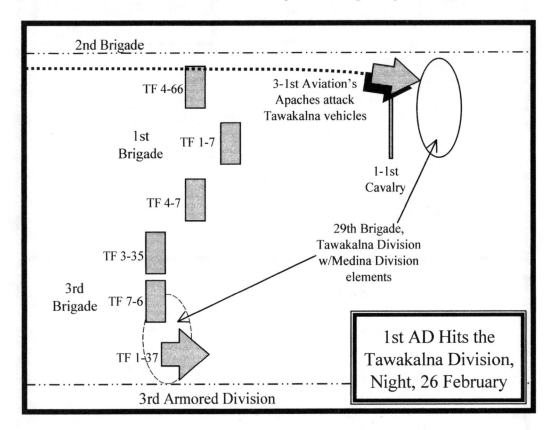

2nd Brigade

TF 4-66

3-1st Aviation's
Apaches attack
Tawakalna vehicles

1st
Brigade   TF 1-7

1-1st
Cavalry

TF 4-7

29th Brigade,
Tawakalna Division
w/Medina Division
elements

TF 3-35

3rd
Brigade   TF 7-6

TF 1-37

1st AD Hits the
Tawakalna Division,
Night, 26 February

3rd Armored Division

By 10 p.m., the last Iraqi armor on the position had been destroyed. The 3rd Brigade had amputated the northern flank of the Tawakalna Line. Behind it were the wrecks of 26 tanks, 46 APCs, 8 artillery pieces and 32 trucks.* Zanini's men would spend the next few hours rounding up over 400 prisoners, rearming, refueling, and forming up for the move to rejoin the rest of the division, by then several miles ahead.

At around 10:00 p.m., while the 3rd Brigade's battle was ending, Bradleys from 1-1st Cavalry, 30 miles in front of the division, were pinned down by T-72s and BMPs. Maj.Gen. Griffith ordered Apaches from 3-1st Aviation Battalion to the area. In a series of attacks, the Apaches destroyed 38 T-72s, 14 BMPs and some 70 trucks.

---

*Although most of the destroyed vehicles found in this zone were destroyed by 3rd Brigade, about a dozen had been destroyed in the earlier Cobra/A-10/Jaguar raid.

As in the 2nd ACR and the 1st Infantry Division to the south, unit leaders in the 1st AD were wondering who they were fighting. The 29th Mechanized Brigade of the Tawakalna Division was authorized 45 tanks, but probably began the war with 41 or 42.* If the Air Force's damage estimates were to be believed, only about 25 should have been operational. Yet, between air and ground attacks, the division had just destroyed over 60 T-72s. There would be more confusion the next day, when the 1st AD would find only about half of the Medina Division. In fact, the 29th Brigade had been reinforced. About half of the Medina Division had moved to reinforce the Tawakalna Line. Some tanks from the Medina Division's 10th Armored Brigade had been in the 29th Mechanized Brigade's sector.

Just after 1 a.m., after B Troop had destroyed several BMPs, 1-1st Cavalry was ordered to stop where it was so that heavier units could take over the fighting. As it consolidated to let the 1st Brigade through, five DPICM rounds fell on B Troop and the squadron Tactical Operations Center (TOC). Lt.Col. Reese radioed a check-fire order over the 1st Brigade command net. Hearing the order, the brigade's operations officer, Lt.Col. Roy Adams, quickly put a check-fire order on the division net. The artillery stopped. However, 23 cavalrymen, all from the TOC, had been wounded by the submunitions. The cavalrymen assumed that since bomblets were involved, this was friendly fire.

The cavalrymen were right. The 75th Field Artillery Brigade, a unit from Fort Sill, Oklahoma, had been assigned to VII Corps. The unit had taken part in the massive preparatory bombardment in support of 1st ID's breaching operation. Having been released from its breach support responsibilities, it had raced to join the 1st AD, and had arrived just in time to take part in the artillery bombardment which would precede the passage of 1st Brigade through 1-1st Cavalry. The unit's first few rounds landed short of the Iraqi positions, and on 1-1st Cavalry.

Having been reminded of the vulnerability of his scouts by the events of the past few hours, Maj.Gen. Griffith pulled his ground scouts back for the remainder of the war. In its role as the tip of the division spear, 1-1st Cavalry had destroyed 35 tanks, 30 APCs, 134 trucks, 14 artillery pieces, 16 AA guns and had taken 894 prisoners.

The division then resumed its slow, deliberate advance, which it would sustain until morning. Between sporadic engagements with individual tanks, probably stragglers from the 10th Armored Brigade, or small bands of infantrymen, individual crewmen grabbed what sleep they could. Tomorrow would bring another, larger battle, at Medina Ridge.

---

*The brigade's tank battalion was authorized 44 tanks. The brigade commander also had a tank.

22

Three Baseball Bats and a Whip: The 3rd Armored Division

Centering the VII Corps attack would be Maj.Gen. Paul Funk's 3rd Armored Division. By far the least publicized division in the Gulf War, the 3rd AD's mission was among the most difficult. Sandwiched between 1st Armored Division on the left and 1st Infantry Division on the right, Funk's division would have little room for maneuver from G-Day until the end of the war.

Funk was fortunate in that he had experienced far less turmoil in his division than the other VII Corps division commanders had, so his units would not have to spend as much time getting to know each other. Of the ten maneuver battalions he had led in Germany, nine were deployed to the Gulf. When attempts were made to leave his 1st Brigade in Germany and replace it with another, Funk had fought the move, and had won. Ultimately, he was ordered to leave one of his battalions behind for security and community support duty and was given the 4-34th Armor Battalion from the 8th Infantry Division to replace it, but basically, the 3rd Armored Division came as it was.[*]

Funk prepared his division meticulously for its mission. In addition to detailed briefings, he had conducted two mounted rehearsals, HUMMEX I and II. In these exercises, leaders down to company-level were mounted on Humvees and run through the phases of the attack plan. They practiced operations at combat interval and speed until they were working smoothly within the framework of the division plan. The three brigades also developed and practiced several contingency maneuvers that might be

---

[*]The 4-34th Armor Battalion had been in the process of deactivation, and was at two-thirds manpower strength. This shortfall was made up by absorbing four platoons from the 1-68th Armor Battalion, which was also deactivating. The 4-34th thus went to war with two of its own platoons and one from 1-68th Armor in each of its four companies.

required by tactical situations during the fighting. Once the tactical maneuvers were mastered, logistics operations, such as refueling in tactical situations, were practiced. Finally, the 75 mile journey to the division's final jumping-off point for the ground war was used as a training exercise and combat rehearsal. The division's cavalry unit got a particularly thorough workout finding paths for the rest of the division to follow.

While the division's ground units were preparing, so were its air units. All U.S. divisions planned to rely heavily on their attack helicopters during the ground war to add punch to their assault. Funk, a qualified attack helicopter pilot himself, decided to take the idea a step farther. His aviation brigade, under Col. Mike Burke, would be totally integrated into the attack plan. He would use it like a fourth maneuver brigade. While other divisions would use their Apaches for periodic strikes, Burke's brigade would be consistently involved in the battle. Whenever the division's ground units were bludgeoning an Iraqi unit, Burke's pilots would see that it was whipped in the rear.

As the division rolled into Iraq, all of Burke's aviation support would roll right behind it. Everything his helicopters needed —fuel, tools and spare parts —would be with the ground convoy. Every two hours, his helicopters would land at a homing beacon carried with the convoy, refuel, perform maintenance, then get back in the fight.

Burke decided to have all of his Apache pilots monitor the division radio net. He felt this was only common sense, since his area of responsibility included the entire division front. If any ground unit ran into trouble, it would have to report it on the division frequency. When it did, Burke's pilots would be listening, and could respond immediately, instead of waiting for orders to be passed from net to net.

By G-Day, the particulars of the offensive had all been worked out, in the air, on the ground, in the combat units and in the support units. All that remained was for the division to receive the order to attack.

The first day of the ground offensive was relatively uneventful as the 3rd AD crossed the border at three, and advanced 19 miles into Iraq. Events on the flanks forced the division to make some adjustments, however.

Because there were 75 miles between 1st Armored Division and its first major objective, the town of al-Busayyah, Lt.Gen. Franks did not want 1st AD, on 3rd AD's left flank, using valuable time shifting from a traveling to a combat formation. He therefore gave the division room to cross the border in wedge formation. This extra room had to come at 3rd AD's expense, and the division, squeezed into a narrower front, was forced to cross the border in a column of brigades.

The need to steer clear of the violent trench battle that was expected in the 1st Infantry Division's attack zone, on 3rd AD's right flank, further narrowed the division's front. Concerns about possible friendly fire incidents had prompted Lt.Gen. Franks to place a five kilometer gap between the 3rd AD and the 1st ID.

As the day wore on, a lengthwise gap also developed between the 3rd AD and the 1st ID, as expected. While the 3rd AD was advancing with relative ease, the 1st ID was picking its way through Iraqi trenches and unexploded bomblets. As a result, the gap between the two divisions widened with every yard 3rd AD advanced. Securing that gap was Col. Burke's responsibility. Burke sent his gunships east with instructions to destroy anything that moved toward the division. In the event of a major flank attack, any Iraqi forces that got past his gunships would run into the Bradleys of Lt.Col. Terry Tucker's 4th Squadron, 7th Cavalry Regiment 1–3 miles east of the main body's right flank. In the unlikely event that the Iraqis could launch an attack that Burke's pilots and Tucker's cavalrymen couldn't stop, Funk would still have 2–4 hours warning, and could turn units to meet the threat.

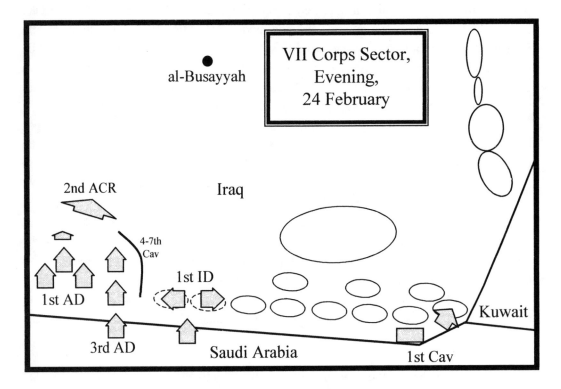

There was only one significant contact with Iraqis in the gap, however. Tucker's squadron discovered an entrenched Iraqi unit just off the right flank at 5:15 p.m., and opened fire with 25mm chain-gun and TOW missile fire. The underfed and poorly equipped Iraqis were no match for the Bradleys. Within a few minutes of opening fire, Tucker's scouts began taking prisoners. By seven, 20 Iraqis had surrendered. Throughout the night and into the next morning 4-7th Cav kept the Iraqis pinned down while the rest of the division refueled. That night, another 39 Iraqis walked over to the scouts' perimeter and gave themselves up. At dawn, the squadron took possession of the Iraqi trenches and rounded up the remaining 52 Iraqis on the position.

Maj.Gen. Funk was known throughout the armor community for his unflappability. His calm nature came in handy during the Gulf War, because he was asked to deal with levels of uncertainty that might have moved less even-tempered men to fits. All Funk could be absolutely certain of was that he would ultimately be fighting Iraqis. His division's mission was largely contingent on whether or not Lt.Gen. Franks could come up with a third division for his attack on the Republican Guard.

Franks would try to get Gen. Schwarzkopf to release the 1st Cavalry Division for the attack. If Franks could not get 1st Cav, 1st ID might still be available if it came through the breach in reasonably good shape. Actually, a relatively unscathed 1st ID might be preferable to 1st Cav, since it was closer to the rest of the corps and had three brigades, while 1st Cav had only two. Either way, 3rd AD would hit the main Iraqi defenses in the center, with 1st AD to the north and the third division to the south, passing through 2nd ACR.

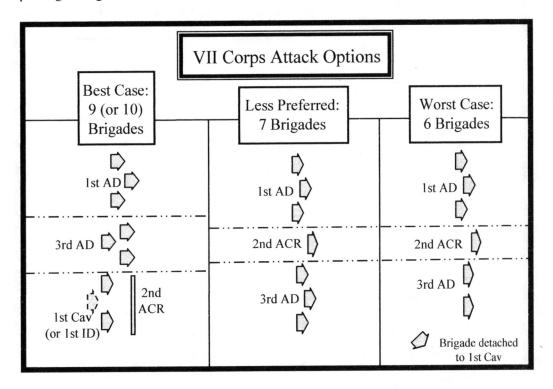

If neither 1st Cav nor 1st ID was available, 1st AD would still strike in the north, but 3rd AD would make a sharp turn and hit the Iraqi defenses in the south, while 2nd ACR abandoned its screening mission and hit the Iraqis in the center. If, in addition, 1st Cavalry needed to fight in support of the Egyptians, 3rd AD would still hit the Iraqis in the south, but would have to send one of its brigades to 1st Cavalry, which had only two.

On 25 February, 3rd AD advanced another 35 miles before stopping to allow its fuel and supplies to catch up. During the day, the division realigned on the move. The 2nd Brigade took its place on the point of the division wedge, with 3rd and 1st brigades to the left and right rear.

The division also received more combat power. The 42nd Field Artillery Brigade had been assigned to provide artillery support for the 1st Infantry Division's breach, but now that the breach had been established, the brigade was needed by 3rd AD. With the link-up, the division would have over twice its normal artillery complement.

Though the link-up was achieved in a timely manner, the operation started off badly. Several wheeled vehicles were disabled as the brigade picked its way through the unexploded bomblets that littered the breach area. Once clear of the breach, the brigade, traveling in column formation, was supposed to be met by a platoon from 4-7th Cavalry and shepherded to the division. However, due to a mix-up, the cavalry platoon was not at the link-up point at 11 a.m. when the artillery arrived.

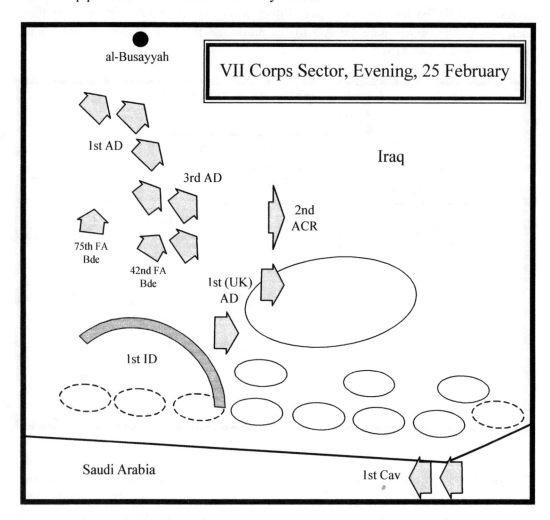

By that time, the division was already so far ahead of the 42nd Brigade that it could not be reached by radio. The 3rd AD would soon be fighting with the Republican Guard. There was no time to arrange for another escort to be sent back to lead the brigade forward. Lt.Col. Henry Stratman, commander of the 2-29th Field Artillery Battalion, at the head of the column, suggested that the brigade could make its way to the division without an escort. Col. Morrie Boyd, the brigade commander, reasoning that there would be few, if any, Iraqi units between the brigade and the division, and realizing the importance of speed, agreed. Stratman calculated that a 30 degree azimuth would bring the brigade to the 3rd AD in a few hours. At noon, the brigade moved out, with 2-29th FA in the lead and Lt.Col. Ron Faircloth's 3-20th FA Battalion behind. Though every howitzer's mounted .50 caliber machine-gun was manned throughout the movement, no Iraqis were encountered, and at three, the link-up was effected.

At 9 p.m. on the 25th, the VII Corps' plan for the attack on the Republican Guard was finalized, as was the 3rd AD's place in it. By then, it had become apparent that although the 1st Cavalry Division had been released for VII Corps use, in all likelihood it could never reach the corps' main body in time to take part in the attack on the Tawakalna Line. The 1st Infantry Division would be available for the attack. It had finished clearing the breach area and had suffered only a handful of casualties. It would now hit the southern end of the Tawakalna Line. This meant that 3rd AD would pass to the north of 2nd ACR, and take its place in the center of the VII Corps attack.

That night, Brig.Gen. Paul Blackwell, the 3rd AD's Assistant Division Commander for Maneuver, was sent to meet Lt.Col. Robinette, the deputy commander of the 2nd ACR, to prepare for the movement of 3rd AD around 2nd ACR. At that point the division was about eight miles from the 2nd ACR. Robinette had halted, set up an operations center, and made satellite contact with VII Corps Headquarters. He had learned that a few hours before, VII Corps had changed the boundaries between the 3rd Armored Division and the 2nd ACR. This was extremely short notice, but Robinette and Blackwell worked out the details of the boundary shift and disseminated the new boundaries to their maneuver units. At dawn, the movement took place without incident.

On 26 February, 4-7th Cavalry continued its screening mission on the division's right flank, with Capt. Gerald Davie's A Troop at the head of the squadron, just ahead of the division's main body, and B Troop behind it. A Troop drove through the morning and much of the afternoon without making significant contact. In the vicinity of the Republican Guard, Lt.Col. Tucker would, under normal circumstances, have pulled the Bradleys back in favor of helicopters, which can provide a better view of the battlefield. However, the sandstorm had grounded his air scouts, and left the Bradleys of A and B troops as the division's only available scout assets.

Throughout the afternoon, the width of A Troop's zone became progressively smaller, shrinking from five kilometers to one kilometer, from just over three miles to just over a half-mile. As the division neared what was expected to be a strong defense line of armored or mechanized Republican Guard forces, 1st Brigade moved up, taking its place to the right of 2nd Brigade. To avoid blocking the 1st Brigade's southernmost battalion, 4-7th Cav tightened its front.

Just after four, A Troop ran into elements of the Tawakalna Division. This was the beginning of what would come to be known as the "Battle of Phase Line Bullet." The Tawakalna positions had been competently sited in rolling terrain, and were extremely well-camouflaged. The Guardsmen were also well-disciplined. When Davie's scouts opened fire on suspected Iraqi positions, there was no return fire. This led Davie to believe that perhaps his troop's thermal sights had just picked up heat reflecting off some pieces of metal. Immediately after he reported this to the squadron commander, his 3rd Platoon reported that it was exchanging fire with dismounted Iraqis. Even after receiving the probing fire, the Guardsmen had held their fire until the Bradleys were about 100 meters inside their position before opening fire. The Iraqis were supported by a few BMPs, which were quickly destroyed by 25mm chain-gun fire from the Bradleys. As A

Troop pressed the attack, the cavalrymen ran into several more BMPs, accompanied by tanks and more infantry. At 4:20, on the north edge of the screen line, a Bradley was hit by a tank gun round. Its gunner, Staff Sergeant Kenneth Gentry, was mortally wounded, and the vehicle commander, Sergeant First Class Raymond Egan, was wounded badly.

Three other Bradleys raced to the stricken vehicle's aid under heavy tank, mortar and machine-gun fire. The three Bradleys placed themselves between that vehicle and the Iraqis, acting as shields. In one of the Bradleys was the squadron's command sergeant-major, Ronald Sneed. Having served for nearly five years in Vietnam, and having been wounded several times during that conflict, Sneed would not have been blamed if he had chosen to perform the normal combat role of a sergeant-major, to coordinate the activities of the squadron's support elements. However, before the battle he had told Lt.Col. Tucker that he wished to position himself forward. Tucker had no objections. After the war, Tucker would say that all of the credit for his unit's success belonged to Sneed. Of the 39 Purple Hearts awarded to the 3rd Armored Division, 14 would be earned by the men of A/4-7 in this fight. As far as Tucker was concerned, the successful performance of the unit under such adversity was a function of the level of training which CSM Sneed had demanded from its men before the ground war, and of the example he set for them during it.

The three Bradleys' gunners engaged Iraqi infantrymen as close as 75 meters from the stricken Bradley while dismounted scouts attempted to evacuate the wounded. Lt.Col. Tucker soon arrived to assess the situation. During the training prior to the start of the ground war, Tucker had come to the conclusion that as the division's chief scout, he needed to travel near the lead elements of his squadron and see things for himself. During the war, he would pass virtually no second-hand information over the command net. In Tucker's view, if an event was important enough to report to the division commander, it was important enough for him to see and evaluate with his own eyes before reporting it.

As Tucker's Bradley pulled up near the evacuation site, his gunner killed an Iraqi RPG team which had been trying to sneak up on his scouts. There were now well-armed and determined Tawakalna infantrymen in the vicinity of the Bradleys. Many were carrying RPGs. Some were carrying suitcases containing far more lethal Sagger wire-guided anti-tank missiles.

The battle became a confused brawl. A sandstorm was raging and visibility was no more than 300 meters. As they evacuated the wounded, the scouts were fired on by an Iraqi Type 59 200 meters to their front. Unexpectedly, a tank round fired from 1st Brigade's TF 4-34 to their rear whizzed over their heads and destroyed the Type 59. The scouts found this especially gratifying, as they assumed that the Iraqi tank had been responsible for the destruction of the Bradley. In fact, the Bradley had been hit by an American sabot round.

In order to ensure that 4-7th Cavalry was not in TF 4-34's way, the squadron had been ordered to move to the south of the 11 Northing east–west grid line. However, four Bradleys and a medic vehicle on A Troop's left flank had yet to clear 11 Northing when the fighting broke out. These vehicles, which included SSG Gentry's Bradley, were therefore still in TF 4-34's zone.

On the right flank, a Bradley destroyed a T-72 with a TOW missile while almost simultaneously, heavy machine-gun bullets ripped into another Bradley, wounding its commander. Another Bradley was disabled when a stream of armor-piercing 30mm rounds from the chain-gun of a BMP-2 sliced into its engine and transmission. Although no one inside the vehicle had been wounded, the Bradley was stranded. As another Bradley moved forward to evacuate the crewmen, the crippled vehicle was hit again, this time in the front slope by an Iraqi anti-tank missile. All four crewmen, though now wounded, managed to scramble aboard the rescue vehicle. However, seconds later, that vehicle was hit by an Iraqi sabot round which sliced through the front left side of the turret, smashed through the gun breech, then exited the right rear of the turret. Seconds after that, another Iraqi sabot round passed through the turret along the same axis. Luckily, no one inside the vehicle was killed.*

In the center, another Bradley took a hit from an American main gun round. The vehicle's gunner, Sgt. Edwin Kutz, was killed and two of its crewmen were wounded. At this time, no one in A Troop was aware that they were taking friendly fire. However, Tucker had received a report from his other ground troop that there was tank fire coming from its rear. Tucker immediately called Lt.Col. Michael Burton, TF 4-34's commander. Within a few minutes, firing from the rear ceased.

A/4-7 destroyed one additional tank, a T-72, before the sandstorm began to break, and a flight of Apaches from Lt.Col. William Stevens' 2-227th Attack Battalion were able to fly to the troop's aid. The Apaches spent the next hour hovering over Tucker's Bradleys to deter the Iraqis from launching a counterattack while the squadron handed the battle over to the heavy armor.

In this encounter, two scouts had been killed and another twelve had been wounded. Four Bradleys had been destroyed, two by friendly fire. The Iraqis had also suffered heavily, losing 6 tanks and 18 BMPs. Casualties could have been much worse. In addition to his troops' level of training, Tucker attributes the low casualty and fatality rate to the design of the Bradley and his medical support.

The 4-7th Cavalry was equipped with the basic model Bradley Cavalry Vehicle. Though Tucker's vehicles did not have the thicker armor, better fuel and ammunition storage, interior spall liners and upgraded fire suppression systems of later models, none of the hits on his Bradleys caused a catastrophic secondary explosion. The Halon fire suppression systems, which had been suspect on the basic Bradley, worked perfectly.

However well the fire suppression systems worked, there were still soldiers wounded by bullets and spall, and the prompt medical attention they received saved some of their lives. Neither Maj.Gen. Funk nor Lt.Col. Tucker had been naïve about the risks that the men of 4-7th Cavalry would be exposed to. Both had expected that the unit would sustain a significant number of casualties. Before G-Day, Funk had offered Tucker a second platoon of medics and Tucker had eagerly accepted. Six of the medics were

---

*Many blamed this strike on TF 4-34. However, the rounds were Iraqi. They were fired from positions to the vehicle's front left side, where there were no American forces. There was also nowhere near the level of damage that would have been inflicted by two American depleted uranium sabot strikes, and there was no residual radiation.

women, but whatever qualms Tucker might have had about exposing women to what promised to be violent combat were outweighed by the acute need he felt for additional medical support.

That extra support proved critical during the battle. Tucker's medics treated his wounded in exposed positions during the height of the battle. As Tucker arrived at a wrecked Bradley, he found Sgt. Patsy Hinton already working on a wounded soldier as Bradleys and BMPs were exchanging fire and Iraqi artillery was landing around her unarmored Humvee ambulance. Tucker credited the immediate care provided by his medics for saving at least one life. "Had SFC Egan not been taken care of immediately, I'm almost certain that he would have died, either from shock or loss of blood," he said.

Another noteworthy aspect of the medical support Tucker received was prompt helicopter evacuation of his casualties to field hospitals in the rear. When the casualties were first reported, medivac pilots were hesitant to fly in extremely bad weather to the squadron aid station, which was located not far from an ongoing firefight. After raising their concerns they were overruled by Col. Burke, who ordered them forward. Within minutes, helicopters were loading Tucker's wounded for transport to the rear.

While 4-7th Cavalry was fighting its battle, the division's main body was coming up behind it. In the south, Col. William Nash's 1st Brigade spotted a major system of trenches and bunkers supported by several dug-in tanks and APCs. Most of the fighting in the complex would be done by the infantry-heavy TF 3-5 on the point of the brigade's wedge. The 3-5th Cavalry Battalion, a mechanized infantry formation under Lt.Col. John Brown, had given one of its four Bradley companies to 4-34th Armor in return for one of its armor companies. After spotting the bunker complex, TF 3-5 halted and began trading fire with the Iraqi defenders. By 6:15, the task force had destroyed a Type 59, two T-72s and 3 APCs. TF 3-5 would spend the rest of the night and early morning hours calling air and artillery strikes on, and pouring direct fire into, Iraqi infantry positions.

There were two armor-heavy task forces to TF 3-5's rear, TF 4-34 to the south and Lt.Col. John Kalb's TF 4-32 to the north. Kalb had given one of his four tank companies from the 4-32nd Armor Battalion to 5-5th Cavalry (another mechanized infantry battalion) in return for a Bradley company.* Col. Nash wanted his most powerful task forces available to maneuver against Iraqi armor formations.

In the north, TF 4-32 sent scouts forward. At 7:20 p.m., the scouts spotted Iraqi infantry about a mile ahead of the battalion's main body. When three Bradleys, one commanded by Lt. James Barker, another by his platoon sergeant, SFC Dennis DeMasters and the third by Staff Sergeant Christopher Stephens, went in for a closer look, the platoon sergeant's Bradley was spotted by a T-72, which was carrying dismounted infantry on it. While DeMasters' Bradley took evasive action, Barker's Bradley opened up with 25mm fire, prompting the dismounts to jump off the tank and sprint for the protection of a series of dunes about 600 meters to the northeast. Stephens

---

*5-5th Cavalry was normally a part of 1st Brigade. However, before the ground war, it was placed under division control, and was used for screening missions until the morning of the 27th, when it was placed under the control of 3rd Brigade.

fired a TOW missile at the T-72, but the missile's guide wire tangled, causing it to dive harmlessly into the ground. Stephens' gunner quickly launched a second TOW from point-blank range, destroying the tank's suspension system. Barker's Bradley then finished off the immobilized T-72 with a TOW missile, blowing the turret off the tank.

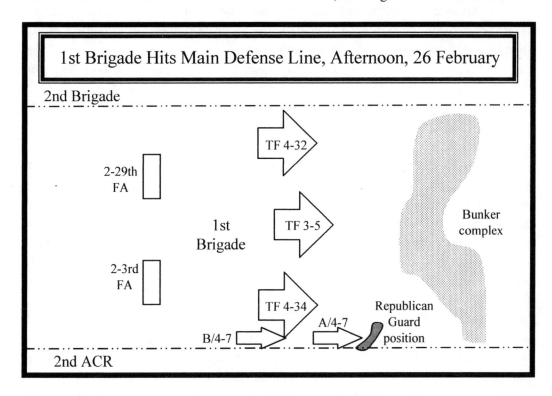

At the same time, flashes appeared on Stephens' Bradley. Attempts to contact Stephens by radio were unsuccessful. A fourth scout, to the rear, observed crewmen exiting the Bradley. It was now plain that the Bradley had been crippled. Lt.Col. Kalb, not wanting to abandon the vehicle, told Barker that medics and reinforcements were on the way and ordered him to stay where he was. Kalb ordered his operations officer, Maj. David Estes, to move to the scouts' position with his tank, a platoon of tanks from C Company and two armored ambulances. As the tank platoon set up a protective wall to the north of the wrecked Bradley, and Estes positioned his tank between the Bradley and the destroyed T-72 (which was due east of the Bradley), medics arrived at the vehicle and found Stephens dead, PFC Adrian Stokes mortally wounded and two other crewmen with less serious wounds. The vehicle's rear had been laced with 25mm armor piercing rounds from a Bradley.

At that point, the Iraqi infantrymen in the dunes began moving toward the stricken Bradley. Several were carrying RPGs. Estes opened up on the Iraqis with his .50 caliber machine-gun and made a quick radio call to the task force's mortarmen. An illumination round appeared over the Iraqis, followed by a flurry of high explosive mortar rounds, which killed several of the Iraqis and caused the rest to flee.* As soon as the

---

*Maj. Estes would receive the Bronze Star with V device for leading the rescue force.

casualties had been evacuated, the rescue force and the remainder of the Scout Platoon returned to the task force perimeter. The Bradley was towed to the rear by an Abrams.

At about eight, D Company, on the northern flank of TF 4-32, spotted Iraqi infantrymen advancing toward it. Because of concerns about friendly fire incidents, heavy weapons could not be used. There was some uncertainty at that point as to exactly where the southern flank of 2nd Brigade was. D Company therefore called for mortar illumination, then scattered the infantry with a torrent of coaxial machine-gun fire.

This would be the night's last major direct fire engagement between the Iraqis and 1st Brigade. Though TF 4-34 would destroy a Type 59 chased into its zone by TF 3-5, the expected Iraqi armored response never materialized. Perhaps chastened by the intensity of the battering being visited on the infantrymen to their front, the Iraqi armored units to the rear held their positions.

Col. Nash's ground units held their positions, but the Iraqis in his zone would be allowed no respite. From his command post, located only 400 meters in front of his artillery battalions, Nash would personally orchestrate the brigade's artillery fires, and apply them liberally. Throughout the night, the brigade's direct support battalion, Lt.Col. Richard Treharne's 2-3rd Field Artillery Battalion, and the reinforcing 2-29th Field Artillery Battalion, combined to hit the Iraqis with over 1,400 rounds, mostly DPICM.[*] At 8:20, the Iraqis were hit with a barrage of 154 DPICM rounds. The bomblets were followed by a second barrage of high explosive and white phosphorous (referred to as "Willie Pete," or "Wilson Pickett" by U.S. troops) rounds. White phosphorous rounds generate some shrapnel, but they mostly throw chunks of lethal white phosphorous. White phosphorous ignites as soon as it is exposed to air. The fire cannot be smothered or put out. Unless it is scraped off or dug out of the flesh, it will burn at about 540°F until it is spent, usually in about one minute. Its fumes can also cause significant lung damage, so these rounds can be effective if they land near the opening of a bunker. WP shells are also excellent for causing fuel or ammunition explosions.

The sandstorm had passed, and air attack assets were available again. Attack helicopters and A-10s were used extensively, often attacking targets marked for them by 25mm fire from Bradleys. Whenever the aircraft left, the artillery barrages resumed.

As it approached the Iraqi defensive line, Col. Robert Higgins' 2nd Brigade was traveling on line with, and to the north of, 1st Brigade. However, because the Iraqi defenses in 2nd Brigade's zone began about 1¼ miles farther west than those in 1st Brigade's zone, 2nd Brigade would hit them earlier than its sister brigade. The brigade would therefore encounter resistance at a time when 1st Brigade was still making good progress. This would create the appearance that perhaps the brigade was not pushing hard enough until the nature of the Iraqi defenses became clear later on.

The 2nd Brigade advanced toward the Iraqi line in a shallow wedge formation, with Lt.Col. Beaufort Hallman's TF 4-8 in the lead, Lt.Col. Robert Fulcher's TF 4-18 to

---

[*]The brigade also used two guided "Copperhead" 155mm artillery shells on a pair of bunkers, the only two such rounds fired by the division during the war.

the north and Lt.Col. Timothy Lupfer's 3-8th Cavalry to the south. An armor battalion, 4-8th Cavalry had given one of its four tank companies to 4-18th Infantry in return for one of its Bradley companies. Lupfer's unit, an armor battalion, had remained tank-pure.

The 2nd Brigade began running into Iraqis at about 4:15 in the afternoon, when TF 4-8's scouts surprised and wiped out an advanced guard position slightly over a mile in front of the Iraqis' main defense line. On the position were a BRDM armored scout car, a ZSU 23-4 self-propelled AA gun and a squad of infantrymen. Within minutes, airburst artillery and mortar rounds began exploding over and among the scouts, without effect.

TF 4-8 drove forward, and by 4:35 had destroyed a BRDM and an APC on another advanced position. C Company, 4-8th Cavalry, at the tip of TF 4-8's wedge, opened fire on the Iraqis from about 1,500 meters. The first volley caused about a hundred infantrymen to come out of their holes. About thirty ran towards the Americans to surrender. The rest either dragged wounded comrades back to the main positions or manned crew-served weapons.

At 5:22, TF 4-8 reached the main Iraqi defense line. As C Company drove into the Iraqi defenses, artillery began impacting among the formation, and RPG rounds were coming from all sides. Some found their marks, but did no damage to the heavily armored M-1A1s. The crews of the tanks they hit were usually not even aware that they had been hit. Nevertheless, Hallman decided to pull back C Company slightly. To the north, airburst artillery was also exploding on B Company, with little more than some shredded personal gear stowed outside the tanks to show for the Iraqi artillerymen's efforts. One tank commander was wounded by fragments when an RPG round glanced off a machine-gun mount and exploded against a sponson box on his tank.

Both TF 4-8 and 4-18 called for artillery support, and within minutes, 205 rounds of DPICM were on the way. After halting for 10 minutes to watch their artillery devastate unprotected Iraqi infantry, the ground units began engaging targets again. In quick succession, TF 4-18 claimed a tank and four trucks, 3-8th Cavalry picked off a tank and TF 4-8 destroyed a BMP.

Iraqi infantrymen in TF 4-18's zone were particularly feisty. At one point, a section of Vulcans was pressed into service to snuff out an attempt by Iraqi infantry to exploit a small gap within the task force. The Vulcans' 20mm HEITSD (high explosive, incendiary, tracer, self-destructing) ammunition, designed for use against aircraft, was extremely effective. It tore apart the Iraqis it hit and exploded over the rest, spraying them with hot metal fragments. Two mortar barrages hit Iraqi infantrymen regrouping in a trench while six DPICM rounds caught another group of infantrymen in the open.

Meanwhile, Lt.Col. Hallman sent his scouts forward again, and within five minutes they spotted four BMPs in the distance. The brigade halted and established a hasty defense as Iraqi mortar rounds were directed on TF 4-8 and part of TF 4-18 on the left flank.

The 3-8th Cavalry had been taking sporadic 60mm mortar fire, but had not faced serious Iraqi resistance. As a result, Lt.Col. Lupfer asked Col. Higgins if he wanted 3-8th Cavalry to press forward. Higgins instead ordered Lupfer to move his unit back 1,000 meters. Lupfer complied, and began refueling his tanks despite the occasional falling 60mm rounds.

At that point, the Americans experienced an embarrassing moment. Lt.Col. Tom Davis, commander of the 4-82nd FA Battalion, noticed that his attached MLRS battery had gotten too close to the fighting. The MLRS cannot engage targets closer than five miles, and the company was only 3½ miles from the Iraqi defenses. The company was ordered to move back. As the launchers turned to leave, some Humvees belonging to support units headed westward, their drivers thinking that the Americans were being forced to retreat by an Iraqi counterattack. As the Humvees were rounded up, the launchers established themselves on their new firing positions. They soon had a target. Artillery-spotting radar picked up a battery of French-built GCT 155mm self-propelled artillery pieces. A salvo of 12 MLRS rockets instantly silenced the guns.

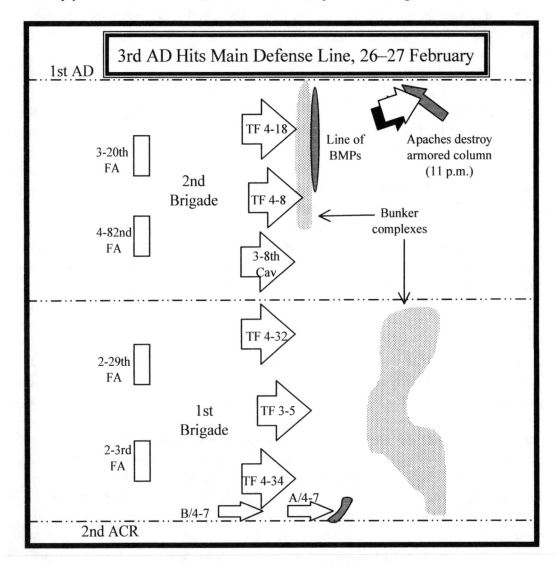

At 7 p.m., the brigade had been in defensive positions for an hour, and Maj.Gen. Funk was becoming concerned about the unit's lack of progress. Brig.Gen. Blackwell ordered Col. Higgins to pick up his pace. Higgins explained that the Iraqi defenses had turned out to be more solid than expected, and now the brigade's intelligence officers were being warned of an armored ambush by three captured Iraqi officers. Blackwell, convinced that 2nd Brigade was up against an Iraqi screening force, agreed to send scout and attack helicopters to check out the report, but told Higgins to conduct an attack at 10 p.m., ambush or no ambush.

The next three hours were used to refuel Higgins' nearly empty M-1A1s and soften up the Iraqis with artillery. By 7:45, the mortars which had been harassing task forces 4-8 and 4-18 had been pinpointed. A barrage of 48 high explosive shells destroyed the mortars and set off their ammunition supply. At about 8:48, Apaches from the 2-227th Attack Battalion spotted the concentration of Iraqi armor the prisoners had warned of, a line of BMPs behind the bunkers and trenches. Apaches and A-10s swarmed over the Iraqi reserve positions, destroying 2 T-72s, 14 BMPs and 11 artillery pieces. Maj.Gen. Funk, now aware of the nature of the defenses in the 2nd Brigade's zone, allowed Col. Higgins to develop the situation as he saw fit.

At ten, Higgins edged his brigade forward. By the time the brigade began its advance, some two dozen vehicles had already been destroyed by the air and artillery strikes. The strikes had also caused large numbers of secondary explosions as ammunition inside the bunkers cooked off. As the brigade pushed ahead, artillery impacted among the tanks sporadically and without effect. The few Iraqi tanks and armored vehicles which presented themselves were quickly destroyed.

During the fighting, navigation was problematic. Because of the positions of the satellites at this time of day, GPS systems were not functioning properly, and were not being used. As a result, drift became a problem as vehicle commanders who thought they were heading east were, in fact, heading to the southeast. The problem first became apparent when part of TF 4-8 ended up in front of 3-8th Cavalry's scouts, which were positioned on the battalion's northern flank. Lt.Col. Lupfer reported the situation to Lt.Col. Hallman and halted his battalion while TF 4-8 reoriented. He also ordered his unit commanders to get an accurate compass bearing. This involved vehicle commanders either getting out of and away from their vehicles or standing on top of them so that proximity to the vehicles did not throw off their compasses. Lack of Iraqi resistance in 3-8th Cavalry's zone made possible what would otherwise have been an extremely dangerous activity.

Just after ten, Maj.Gen. Funk was told by VII Corps headquarters that JSTARS had spotted a column of Iraqi armor to his front, heading northwest. At eleven, a flight of Apaches spotted the column as it was approaching the boundary between the 1st and 3rd Armored divisions. In three minutes, the Apaches destroyed 8 T-72s and 19 BMPs.

For the next four hours, the brigade's tanks used heavy machine-gun and HEAT rounds to clear bunkers. The brigade continued to make good use of its artillery, dropping hundreds of DPICM rounds on the bunkers ahead of the slowly advancing American armor. The brigade suffered its only fatality of the night at 11:17, however, when a DPICM round burst over the fire support officer's vehicle, short of its target, and killed Sgt. Young Dillon.

A half-hour after the friendly fire incident, 3-8th Cav spotted a column of about 20 trucks carrying Iraqi infantry about 1,700 meters to its front. The battalion opened fire, destroying most of the vehicles and killing or wounding many of the infantrymen. The trucks which were not destroyed were quickly abandoned. EPW interrogations would later reveal that the Iraqis did not know what had hit them. Unaware of 3-8th Cav's presence, when their trucks began exploding, they assumed that they were being attacked from the air. Those who could continued north on foot.

During the engagement there were more orientation problems. Though it produced no casualties, heavy machine-gun fire from TF 4-8 landed among Lupfer's tanks. Again, navigation difficulties had left TF 4-8 slightly misoriented. Another radio call to Lt.Col. Hallman straightened out the situation.

At 1:30 a.m., an Iraqi force hit TF 4-18. Though the Iraqis lost several BMPs to TOW missiles in the opening minutes of the battle, dismounted infantry continued to attack, inflicting no damage and suffering heavy casualties. At 2:15, the Iraqis, badly stung, withdrew to the west.

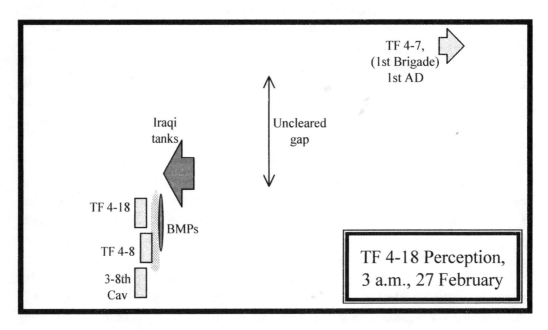

At three, TF 4-18 reported what appeared to be a large Iraqi tank force to its north, headed west into what was believed to be an uncleared gap between the 1st and 3rd Armored divisions. Such a force could either have driven into the rear of the 1st Armored Division, the combat units of which were now well to the east, or passed to the north of TF 4-18, then turned south into the 3rd AD's trains. With only 14 tanks in his task force, Lt.Col. Fulcher decided to ask for reinforcements. Fulcher asked Col. Higgins for a tank company from 3-8th Cavalry on the brigade's now quiet southern flank. Higgins granted the request.

There was neither a large armored counterattack nor an uncleared gap, however. Though 11 live Iraqi T-72s would be hit by the D/3-8th Cavalry tanks by daybreak, the majority of the tanks in the area had already been destroyed. A few had been destroyed earlier (between 6 and 7 p.m.) by TF 4-18. A few more had been destroyed just before nine by 3rd AD's Apaches. Some of the T-72s were in 1st AD's zone, and had been overrun by 1st AD at around 9:30.*

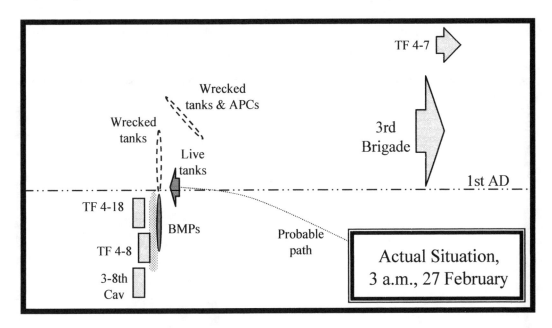

The confusion had two major causes. First, after a wrecked tank has had five or six hours to burn itself out, it becomes essentially a warm skeleton, and looks a lot like a live tank when viewed through thermal sights at a distance. Second, the boundary between the 1st and 3rd Armored divisions remained unclear throughout the night. Some of the tanks that had been spotted by TF 4-18 were in 1st AD's zone.

Somehow, TF 4-18's operations staff had the mistaken belief that the units on the 1st AD's right flank (and its left flank) were the 1-1st Cavalry Squadron, and behind it, 1st Brigade, 1st AD. This probably stemmed from confusion over which of 1st AD's two 3rd Brigades was on the flank. The 1st AD had two 3rd Brigades, its own, and 3rd Brigade, 3rd Infantry Division, now acting as the division's 1st Brigade. TF 4-18's signal officer had been monitoring the transmissions of the 1-1st Cavalry, 1st Brigade, and TF 4-7 (1st Brigade's southernmost unit) command nets, following the units' progress. The transmissions indicated that these units were now well to the west, and had traveled a path almost four miles north of the 3rd AD, leaving a substantial uncleared gap between the two divisions.†

In fact, the 1-1st Cavalry and the 1st Brigade had been in the *center* of the 1st AD, not on the right flank. So, while these units had indeed traveled a path almost four miles north of the 3rd AD, there had been no uncleared gap. The 1st AD's *actual* right

---

*It is conceivable that some of these vehicles were hit three times, by Cobras, A-10s and Jaguars on the afternoon of the 26th, 1st AD's TF 1-37 at 9:30 that night and 3-8th Cavalry in the hours before dawn on the 27th.

†By that time, 1-1st Cavalry had pulled behind 1st Brigade.

flank unit, its 3rd Brigade, had driven through the zone between TF 4-7 and TF 4-18, destroying about two battalions of Iraqi armor, including many of those which TF 4-18 had spotted. Though a company of T-72s entered the area after the zone had been cleared, and would be destroyed by D/3-8th Cavalry, the majority of the tanks TF 4-18's observers were looking at were wrecks. Because TF 4-18's operations staff had been unaware of 3rd Brigade's presence on their left flank, they had no way of knowing that.

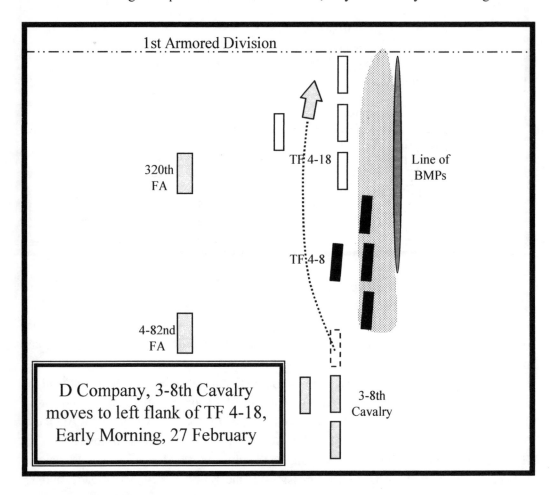

1st Armored Division

320th FA

TF 4-18

Line of BMPs

TF 4-8

4-82nd FA

D Company, 3-8th Cavalry moves to left flank of TF 4-18, Early Morning, 27 February

3-8th Cavalry

Lt.Col. Lupfer, unsure of the exact whereabouts of the 1st Brigade's TF 4-32 on his southern flank, decided to keep his reserve company where it was in case a gap developed there. He chose to pull his northernmost unit, Capt. Joseph McDaniel's D Company, out of the line and send it north. This would put some room between 3-8th Cavalry and TF 4-8, and reduce the risk of further cross-boundary shooting. He then placed his tank, that of his operations officer and the six Bradleys of his scout platoon in the space vacated by D Company.

McDaniel's company headed north through the area just cleared by TF 4-8. In a complex maneuver, Lt.Col. Fulcher's reserve team of one tank and two Bradley platoons pulled back to create a path for the tanks, which were met and led to their place on the left flank of TF 4-18 by Fulcher's scouts. By 4:30, D Company was set. In addition to the tanks it destroyed, D Company engaged large numbers of Iraqi infantrymen, who had made their way northward, looking for a weak spot in the American line.

The Iraqis now seemed confused and despondent. Everywhere they probed, they had found American armor. Soon after the arrival of McDaniel's company, the Iraqis' fighting spirit collapsed, and the attacks petered out. With that, the brigade halted just short of a rise in the terrain and waited for daybreak.

In its fight, the 2nd Brigade had destroyed 37 tanks, 39 APCs, 2 BRDMs, 22 trucks, 2 anti-aircraft guns and one artillery piece. Some 260 fortunate Iraqis passed into captivity. Over 600 of their less fortunate comrades had been killed.

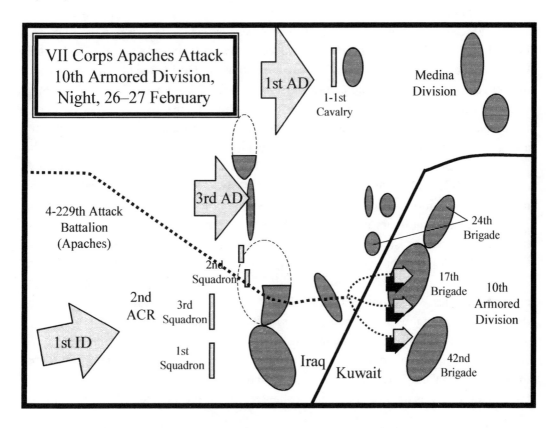

VII Corps was blessed with lavish helicopter gunship support, and it made the most of it. While the 3rd AD was in action at Phase Line Bullet, VII Corps Apaches went to work deep in the rear areas of the Iraqi 10th Armored Division. Lt.Gen. Franks ordered Col. Johnnie Hitt, commander of the 11th Aviation Brigade, to hit the division inside Kuwait before it could launch a counterattack. Hitt gave the mission to the 18 Apaches of Lt.Col. Roger McCauley's 4-229th Attack Battalion.

With three companies on line, the 4-229th swept slowly eastward. A (in the north) and B (in the center) companies began destroying armored vehicles from the 10th Armored Division's 17th Armored Brigade at around 9:45. At around 10:15, C Company, which had flown to the south of the 17th Brigade, made contact with the 10th Armored Division's 42nd Brigade and destroyed every armored vehicle it could find.

Unfortunately, the battalion's attack zone ended at the 20 degree north–south grid line. When the Air Tasking Order had been written up a day earlier, the Air Force had assumed that at this point targets behind that line would still be well beyond the range of VII Corps' aviation units, and even farther beyond its ground units. The Air Force therefore assumed that F-111F "tank plinking" strikes could be programmed for that area without interfering with corps operations. Since then, however, VII Corps had smashed through Iraqi defenses more violently and more quickly than anyone but Lt.Gen. Franks and his commanders had expected. VII Corps was closing in on the Kuwaiti border, and Franks' attack aviation wanted desperately to get at Iraqi armor east of the 20 degree grid line, but was unable to because single F-111F sorties were coming in every 20 minutes and could not be called off.

McCauley's men had to content themselves with a second strike on the same area just before 1 a.m. on the 27th. This time it was only a two-company strike, and targets were more scarce, but there was still fairly good hunting. During the attack, the Apaches used a recently developed submunition version of the 2.75-inch rocket to devastating effect. Known as "Hydra-70s" (2.75 inches is roughly 70mm), these rockets fly over a target and drop eight shaped-charge munitions designed to punch through the thin top armor of the armored vehicles below. Though the victory was not as complete as his pilots had hoped for, McCauley's battalion had helped break the Iraqis' backs. In the two attacks, the 4-229th had destroyed 53 tanks, 19 BMPs, 16 MTLBs, an air traffic control tower, an ammunition carrier and a bunker.[*] About 40 Iraqi infantrymen had been killed.

About seven hours later, the 3rd AD's Apaches began inflicting punishment on the 10th Armored Division. To the 24 Apaches already under the division's control, VII Corps added the 18 Apaches of the 2-6th Cavalry Squadron. For the next 10 hours, Apaches would attack Iraqi positions inside Kuwait without let up, picking off Iraqi armored vehicles. When one of Col. Burke's battalions was attacking, the other was on the ground rearming, refueling, and waiting for its turn to torment the Iraqis.

As a result of the Apache attacks, the 10th Armored Division disintegrated. Its soldiers were now abandoning their vehicles, and deserting en masse. Once considered the finest unit in Iraq's regular armored force and perhaps the equal of any Republican Guard unit, the division's fighting spirit collapsed. When the 1st and 3rd brigades arrived at these positions, the 10th Armored Division would be a memory.

The ground units began the advance toward their objectives inside Kuwait at sunrise. Intelligence about the dispositions of the Tawakalna Division had been sketchy. Intelligence about Iraqi unit dispositions between the 3rd AD and Objective Minden, the division's final objective, was nonexistent. To help provide the ground units with some degree of advanced warning about Iraqi defenses, Maj.Gen. Funk directed Lt.Col. Tucker to send his two air cavalry troops forward. While they would remain technically under Tucker's control, they would report directly to the commanders of the 1st and 3rd

---

[*]During the war, the 11th Aviation Brigade destroyed a total of 90 tanks, 86 APCs, 69 trucks, 8 artillery pieces and 11 AA guns.

brigades. For the remainder of the war, these helicopters would be a vital intelligence asset for the two maneuver brigades, spotting many targets for them and destroying several armored vehicles themselves.

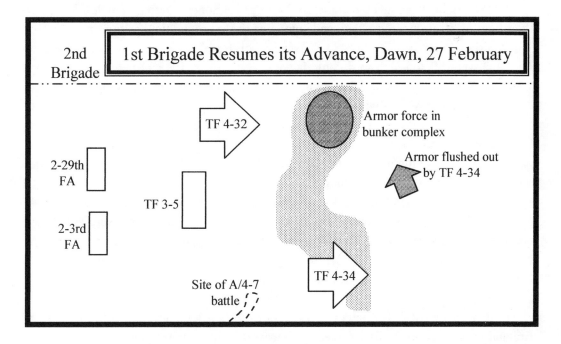

The first contact came in the south, where 1st Brigade was preparing to resume its advance. Col. Nash had begun the battle the day before believing that there were Iraqi armored formations in the area. Throughout the night he had expected to encounter them, but had not. He was still certain that there was Iraqi armor nearby, and he suspected that the Iraqis were lying in wait on the reverse slopes of one of the folds in the terrain to his front. Surprising attacking forces as they crested a hill was a favorite Iraqi tactic.

Surprising Iraqis in defensive positions with massive artillery barrages was a favorite Nash tactic. He ordered Lt.Col. Stratman to have 2-29th FA mark the forward limit of the brigade's advance with illumination rounds. Three minutes later, three illumination rounds burst simultaneously, marking the brigade's forward line. At 6:20, once each task force commander confirmed that all of his forces were behind that line, Nash ordered massive artillery strikes on two suspected Iraqi positions, one of which turned out to be an Iraqi occupied bunker complex in TF 4-32's zone.

The brigade then began moving eastward by task force bounds. At about 6:30, TF 4-34, on the brigade's southern flank, moved about 3,000 meters to the east. The tanks "reconned by fire," probing for Iraqis in the terrain in front of them by lacing the area with coaxial machine-gun fire as they rolled forward. By seven, the probing fire had produced what Lt.Col. Burton described as "EPWs coming out of the woodwork."

At around seven, TF 4-32, on the northern flank, bounded forward. Almost immediately, C Company, at the tip of the task force wedge, crested a ridge and saw the extent of the bunker complex. It was about 2½ miles deep, and was defended by about 400 infantrymen supported by 9 tanks and about 30 APCs, with numerous wheeled support vehicles nearby. Bradleys from Team B on the southern flank opened the battle by picking off tanks with TOW missiles.* The two pure tank companies to the north then joined in with main gun fire. DPICM barrages were called in until A-10s arrived.

The Iraqis were taken completely by surprise. Some armored vehicles drove into their fighting positions, some fled, and some just drove around the position in confusion. A few airburst mortar rounds went off over Lt.Col. Kalb's task force, but they were too light and went off too high to do any damage. By 7:30, A-10s and helicopter gunships were pounding the position. After about 15 minutes, the Iraqis in the complex began to come out of their positions with their hands up.

Meanwhile, about two dozen armored vehicles were identified by Team B. The Iraqi vehicles had been flushed out by TF 4-34 and had fled to the northwest, into the path of TF 4-32. Within minutes, the Iraqi force was being hit by artillery, TOW missiles and main gun fire. By 8:00, the battle was over.

In the morning's fighting, the brigade had killed almost 200 Iraqis and taken 345 prisoners. As they assessed the damage they had done, the Americans were struck and confused by the variety of different armor types which had been on the position. The situation was clarified when prisoner interrogations revealed that this force was actually a hodgepodge of tanks and APCs from three different Iraqi divisions.

The arrival of A-10s had given the two artillery battalions an opportunity to cease fire and move forward three kilometers. Once set in their new positions, they fired on Iraqi forces in depth throughout the 1st Brigade's zone. At 9:30, 2-3rd FA and 2-29th FA battalions massed fire on the last resisting enclave in the bunker complex. As the bomblet explosions from the first DPICM strike died down, Iraqi soldiers began leaving their bunkers waving white flags. Unfortunately, by that time a second volley of DPICM had already been fired. The Americans could only watch helplessly as a second wave of bomblets tore through the surrendering Iraqis.

The next obstacle confronting the brigade was an Iraqi defense line on the southern portion of Objective Dorset, the last Iraqi position between the division and the Kuwaiti border. There were about 50 tanks and 50 APCs along the western edge of Dorset, spread across a line ten miles long and about three miles deep. About half of the armored vehicles were in 1st Brigade's zone. From 1:45 to 3:00, TF 3-5 destroyed at least a dozen T-62 and T-72 tanks as well as several BMPs. TF 4-34, to the south and slightly behind TF 3-5, overran a bunker system reinforced by two T-72s and two BMPs. For the first time, the Americans were seeing large numbers of abandoned vehicles and fighting positions.

About three miles farther east was another deep series of trenches and revetments. The position contained hundreds of infantrymen. Because the brigade's supply trains would be passing through the area, these infantrymen would have to be rooted out and rounded up. The job would be made somewhat easier by the fact that by

_____

*B Company had given one of its tank platoons to the attached D Company, 5-5th Cavalry Battalion (then in reserve) in return for one of that company's Bradley platoons.

the time the brigade's lead elements showed up, many Iraqis were eager to surrender. While task forces 3-5 and 4-34 had been picking their way through the first defense line, Col. Nash had subjected the defenders of the second line to about 40 minutes of punishment from the 2-3rd FA and 2-29th FA battalions. During the barrage, the two battalions had dropped some 300 DPICM and 100 high explosive rounds on the Iraqis.

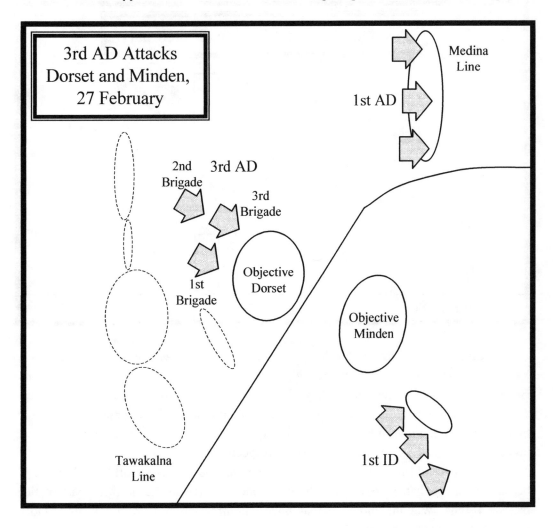

As on the previous position, there were large numbers of abandoned vehicles, but fighting would be required and clearing the position would take 6½ hours. The battle began at about five, when TF 3-5 overran a bunker complex, destroying six T-62s. From 7–9:30, the two task forces would destroy a dozen more tanks and two dozen APCs, taking about 300 prisoners.

About three hours after 1st Brigade began its advance that morning, Col. Leroy Goff's 3rd Brigade had begun passing through the lines of 2nd Brigade to take its place on 1st Brigade's left flank for the division's final push. Lt.Col. Dan Merritt's 2-67th Armor and Lt.Col. Timothy Reischl's 4-67th Armor had each received a Bradley company from Lt.Col. Harold Neely's 5-18th Infantry in return for one of their tank companies. This had left task forces 2-67 and 4-67 with three tank companies and one infantry company each and TF 5-18 with two companies of each type. The three Bradley companies and one tank company of Lt.Col. Mike Deegan's TF 5-5 had also been placed under Goff's command for the final drive.

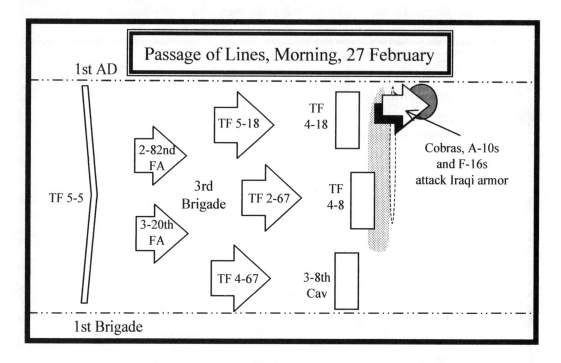

Passage of Lines, Morning, 27 February

Col. Goff had planned for the brigade to conduct the passage in a box formation. His heaviest units would be up front, with TF 2-67 on the left and TF 4-67 on the right. Behind them would come the artillery. The 3-20th Field Artillery Battalion had been attached to the brigade for the final push, joining its normal artillery support, the 2-82nd Field Artillery, doubling the brigade's artillery firepower. Behind the artillery would be task forces 5-18 and 5-5 on the left and right, respectively.

However, during the coordination of the passage between Goff and Higgins, it became apparent that there was a substantial enemy force in the northern part of the brigade's zone. Wanting more combat power up front to deal with this unit, Goff realigned his brigade into a wedge formation, with TF 5-18 moving up on the left flank and TF 2-67 pushing forward to take the point. Goff decided to deploy TF 5-5 in a line across the brigade rear, to gather up Iraqi prisoners and destroy abandoned equipment. TF 5-5 only had one tank company while TF 5-18 had two. In addition, TF 5-5 had only been added to the brigade the night before, and had not been with the unit during the pre-offensive planning or rehearsals.

While Goff was shifting his units, the Iraqi armored force was attacked by air. The division's Cobra gunships knocked out 6 T-72s and 4 BMPs while Air Force A-10s and F-16s claimed 2 T-72s, 5 BMPs and a fuel truck.

During the air attack, Col. Goff discovered in a radio conversation that TF 2-67 was traveling with loaded main guns. He ordered the unit to remove the rounds from the breeches before proceeding. Lt.Col. Merritt had reasoned that since he would be passing directly into a firefight his tanks should be ready, but Goff pointed out that traveling with loaded guns was unnecessarily dangerous to friendly units to the front, especially since it only takes a few seconds to load a main gun.

At 10:53, TF 2-67 emerged from the passage. After advancing past vehicles destroyed during the night, scouts claimed the unit's first kill, a BMP-2, destroyed by a TOW missile. TF 5-18 then pushed forward, destroying several armored vehicles the earlier air attacks had missed and taking about 150 prisoners. The brigade then continued to its first major target, the northern portion of Objective Dorset.

Most of the day's ground action would be in the TF 2-67 and TF 4-67 zones. The first serious contact occurred at about three in the afternoon, when TF 2-67 came upon a large bunker complex which stretched across its zone and into TF 4-67's zone. This was part of the Iraqi defensive line running along the western edge of Dorset. TF 2-67's portion of the complex contained several tanks and APCs. Within minutes, most of the Iraqi armored vehicles had been destroyed by TOW missile and main gun fire. As 1st Brigade was finishing up its portion of the line on Dorset South, Lt.Col. Merritt halted his battalion and called in a massive artillery strike. Over 200 DPICM rounds, six from each gun in two artillery battalions, completely wiped out the Iraqi infantry on the position. Unfortunately, during the bombardment a soldier in the brigade logistics task force picked up an unexploded submunition, which went off, killing him instantly. It was the brigade's only fatality of the war.

After about 40 minutes, TF 2-67 had cleared its part of the bunker complex, and the brigade was on the move again. Almost immediately, TF 4-67's scouts ran into the southern portion of the complex, which contained a much larger Iraqi armored force. In a 15-minute battle, Lt.Col. Reischl's task force destroyed a dug-in force of about 35 tanks and APCs and numerous trucks, using TOW missiles and main gun fire from extended ranges. Reischl's men faced only small arms and scattered and inaccurate artillery fire in return. They would not have a tank round fired at them all day.

Minutes after the end of the engagement, at 4:07, one of Reischl's company commanders reported numerous tanks in the distance moving diagonally across his front. The tanks appeared to be an Iraqi armor company in retreat. Reischl directed the company commander to close in and get a positive identification on the vehicles before firing. A switch from the thermal sight to the daylight sight, which offered a sharper picture, showed the tanks to be American. The right flank company of TF 2-67 had strayed in front of Reischl's battalion and had narrowly missed becoming the victim of what would have been the worst friendly fire incident of the war. From that point on, TF 4-67's gunners would switch to daylight sights to confirm targets prior to every engagement.

Shortly after the brigade began moving again, TF 4-67's combat trains came under assault by a small Iraqi infantry force attacking from the south. Reischl ordered D Company to deal with the threat. The company commander detached a force of five tanks led by Lt. Tom Skinner, the company executive officer, to peel back to the rear of the formation and eliminate the Iraqi attackers. Skinner, accompanied by the four tanks of Lt. David Raymond's 3rd Platoon, found two Iraqi BMPs and a truck mounted with a machine-gun firing at the battalion's supply vehicles. The force made short work of the Iraqis, destroying the two BMPs with main gun fire and, after giving its occupants every opportunity to surrender, machine-gunning the truck. The vehicles were engaged at about 700 meters, point-blank range. In one case, two depleted uranium sabot rounds hit a BMP simultaneously, vaporizing the vehicle and blowing its turret about forty feet into the air.

At 4:43, 3rd Brigade entered Kuwait. The 3rd AD's preferred method of engagement had been to close with the Iraqis only after massive damage had been inflicted by air attacks (if available and practical), artillery, TOW missiles and long range tank gun fire. Then, if necessary, Bradleys would pelt the position with 25mm chain-gun fire, followed (again, if necessary) by an assault using dismounted troops.

This plan had been developed with the expectation of spirited Iraqi resistance. The 3rd Brigade was running across large numbers of abandoned vehicles, however. Col. Goff suspected that the Iraqi units to the division's front were collapsing. Helicopters operating in front of 3rd Brigade confirmed that suspicion. After this was reported to Maj.Gen. Funk, he revised his attack plan. His new guidelines called for his ground units to deal with pockets of Iraqi resistance. There would be no stopping for Apaches or artillery to work over positions, since it was no longer necessary and would only slow the division's advance. He left decisions about how to deal with Iraqi resistance to his brigade commanders.

Goff chose to adopt an exploitation posture. Only those vehicles which posed a threat would be engaged. Abandoned vehicles would be bypassed. He did not want to lose time engaging abandoned vehicles. He also did not want to waste sabot rounds which might be needed if the brigade ran into more stubborn Iraqi armored units later on. He had no way of knowing that there were no such units left in Kuwait.

Before G-Day, Iraqi heavy units had been spread throughout Kuwait. On the western border, in anticipation of a possible attack up the Wadi al-Batin, was the 10th Armored Division. In the east, there had been two heavy divisions (the 3rd Armored and 5th Mechanized) and another two armored brigades (the independent 56th, and the 30th, detached from the 6th Armored Division) between the U.S. Marines and their objectives of Kuwait City and al-Jahra. Another division-sized formation (the 1st Mechanized Division's 1st Mechanized and 34th Armored brigades and the independent 58th Armored Brigade) surrounded al-Jahra. Guarding the interior of the country were the two remaining brigades of the 6th Armored Division, as well as the 17th Armored and 51st Mechanized divisions. The Iraqi plan called for the heavy units in Kuwait to inflict losses on Coalition forces advancing from the south, to soften them up for Republican Guard units, which were then fortifying positions to the north of the Kuwait–Iraq border.

By the end of 24 February, it was clear to the Iraqi Army's leadership that the western border would have to be reinforced. The Allies, as expected, were attacking up the Wadi al-Batin (the 1st Cavalry Division). However, the Egyptians were attacking to the east of the Wadi. They had not penetrated the front line yet, but the possibility that they could thrust northward into the 10th Armored Division's flank (or rear, if the division needed to move west to combat a force emerging from the Wadi) was a threat that could not be ignored. In addition, there was another force (VII Corps), believed by the Iraqis to be of division size, coming from the west. The Tawakalna Division, about half of the Medina Division and the 12th Armored Division had been sent to meet it.

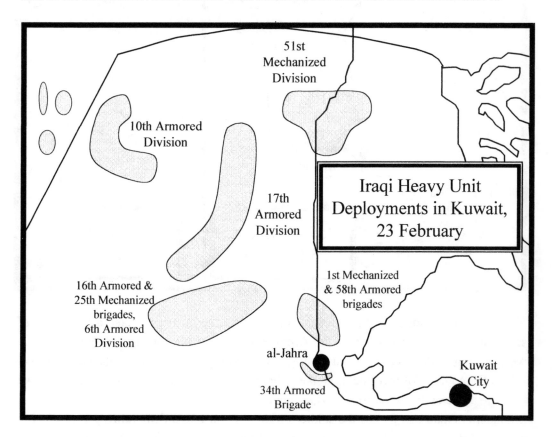

On the 25th, the 6th Armored Division's remaining two brigades, the 16th Armored (minus a tank battalion that had been sent to reinforce positions in the Wadi al-Batin) and the 25th Mechanized, were absorbed by the 17th Armored Division. That division then moved to the west. Most of the division took up positions directly behind the 10th Armored Division, which had reoriented to the west. A mechanized infantry-heavy force of roughly three battalions took up positions in the gap between the 10th Armored and Medina divisions. Meanwhile, the 51st Mechanized Division spread out to the north and south.

For the newly arrived units, the events of the 26th had been disheartening. To the west, VII Corps smashed through the Tawakalna Line. Before the fighting was even finished, Apaches were tormenting the occupants of the 10th Armored Division Line. To make matters worse, six battalions from the 17th Division, having only recently arrived in their positions, were ordered northward to join the Medina Division. The Medina Division had sent roughly half of its armored vehicles forward to bolster the Tawakalna

Line. Not one of these vehicles had survived the battle, and now the 1st Armored Division was heading for what was left of the Medina Division.

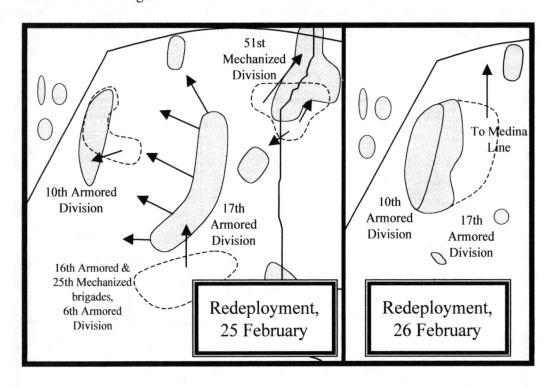

To the residents of the Medina Line, these battalions represented a faint hope of salvation. To the residents of the 10th Armored Division Line, they represented units that were leaving. Though it is unclear whether the departure of these units played a decisive role in the collapse of that line, it is likely that it was a significant factor. Maneuvers like this are inherently hazardous. What appears to be a clever redeployment on a headquarters map can feel to the soldier on the ground like a demoralizing rout. With a massive Allied force rolling toward them, and their own units in the rear leaving, there seemed little reason for the occupants of the 10th Armored Division Line to stand and fight.

From 5:00 to 5:30 p.m., TF 4-67 would roll through an Iraqi tank battalion, then a tank company. In each case, Lt.Col. Reischl moved his tanks to within 2,500 meters of the Iraqi vehicles, then used concentrated tank fire to destroy all live vehicles before his armor swept through the position. On the second position, one volley from the lead tank company was enough to cause the entire Iraqi company to stand up and surrender. The Iraqis were quickly disarmed and handed over to MPs, and Reischl's tanks were on their way again.

Though Lt.Col. Merritt had ordered his men to bypass abandoned vehicles, he found that firing did not lessen. During the afternoon, his men were having trouble distinguishing between live and abandoned tanks. Some were hot because their engines were running and they were manned, and some were hot only because of the sun. The determinations were especially difficult because the gunners were making them at long range, having been instructed to engage from extended distances to take advantage of the Abrams' superior main gun. Merritt finally concluded that limiting the aggressiveness of his gunners, or making them get close enough to tell which vehicles were and were not occupied before firing, exposed them to more risk than potential sabot shortages did, so he did not push the issue. As night fell, the temperature dropped, making identification easier, and sabot usage dropped off sharply.

Merritt did place one restriction on his men. Realizing that having tanks shooting in all directions was a recipe for fratricide, he ordered his men not to engage any targets outside their front fenders. That way, if a tank round missed its intended target, there would be little chance of it hitting another American vehicle. Iraqi tanks were visible at long ranges, and there was no way that any Iraqi tank could hit an Abrams at those ranges, so there was no need for hasty shots taken at bad angles. Any targets at difficult angles would be passed off by radio and engaged by a tank with a better shot.

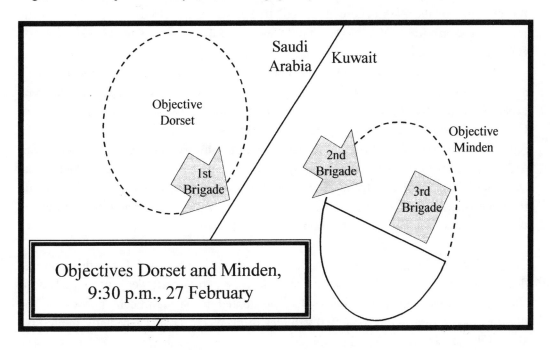

By seven, 3rd Brigade had secured Objective Minden North. As TF 2-67 approached the eastern edge of the objective, a small group of Iraqi armored vehicles to the task force's front gave its position away by careless use of infra-red searchlights in an attempt to spot American tanks. While not visible to the naked eye or on thermal sights, they shone like beacons to night vision goggles, and allowed the Americans to spot the vehicles. The unit's scouts reported the Iraqi locations while A and D companies closed in on the position. Unfortunately, one scout Bradley was immobilized when it threw a track while retreating into the task force's main body. Merritt ordered the crew to get inside the vehicle, close the hatches, and turn on its tail lights so that the battalion's tanks could distinguish it from the Iraqi vehicles. A few seconds later, three Iraqi tanks, two BMPs and a tank recovery vehicle erupted in fireballs. TF 2-67 had now destroyed 32 tanks, 12 APCs, 4 BRDMs, 14 trucks, one ZSU 23-4 AA gun and one artillery piece. It had also taken 124 prisoners.

In setting up its positions for the night, TF 4-67 discovered a prowling tank and BMP within its perimeter. Both were quickly destroyed. The capture of 13 bedraggled Iraqis turned out to be the task force's last act of the war. Reischl's men had destroyed 51 Iraqi tanks and BMPs, but they could easily have destroyed three times as many. His soldiers and his attached engineer company would spend the next few days after the cease-fire retracing their steps, destroying well over 100 abandoned armored vehicles which they had bypassed earlier. During those days they also added 12 more prisoners to their wartime total of 90.

It had taken 1st Brigade until 9:30 p.m. to clear Objective Dorset South, and its three task forces had not entered Kuwait until after ten. After overrunning scores of abandoned armored vehicles, the brigade reported its portion of Minden secure at 1:15 on the morning of the 28th. There it halted, tied in with 3rd Brigade, and awaited the impending cease-fire. Since G-Day, the brigade had destroyed 93 tanks, 129 APCs, 3 BRDMs and 29 trucks.

The maneuver units would have to wait almost five hours for the brigade's supply trains. The wheeled vehicles carrying the brigade's supplies and fuel had been separated from the main body by rough terrain and a berm on the eastern end of Objective Dorset. Though the brigade had effectively cleared its zone, handfuls of retreating Iraqi armored vehicles were still drifting northward into the 1st Brigade's rear. Col. Nash, concerned that his trains might become easy targets for these vehicles, had sent back a tank company from TF 4-32 and a Bradley company from TF 3-5 to find them and shepherd them back to the brigade's main body. The mission was completed without incident, and by 6 a.m. the trains were on Minden.

The 3rd Armored Division's war was over. It had traveled 125 miles, and had destroyed 195 tanks, 203 APCs, 45 artillery pieces, 8 anti-aircraft weapons and 241 soft-skinned vehicles. Attack helicopters had accounted for a significant portion of the division's kills, destroying some 250 vehicles of all types. This is especially impressive since 3rd AD had been ordered to assign one of its Apache battalions to XVIII Airborne Corps during Desert Shield, and had gone through most of the war with only one battalion of Apaches.[*] The division also captured 2,552 Iraqis. It had accomplished all of this with the loss of only 8 killed and 31 wounded. After the cease-fire, 3rd AD soldiers would destroy 171 tanks, 98 APCs, 22 artillery pieces, 12 AA guns and 174 trucks which the division had bypassed earlier.

More impressive than the division's battle damage statistics is the fact that they were limited only by its mission. Maj.Gen. Funk could easily have had all three of his

---

[*]The other battalion, Lt.Col. Anthony Jones' 3-227th Attack, had been instrumental in providing cover for the helicopters ferrying long range reconnaissance teams into Iraq in the days before G-Day.

maneuver brigades actively involved in destroying Iraqi units throughout the offensive had his zone of operations not been so restricted.

In previous wars, commanders had to hold back a substantial part of their ground forces in case it became necessary to react quickly to an enemy counterattack, or an offensive opportunity presented itself. Usually, that meant one of an armored division's three brigades had to be kept in reserve, where it was consuming fuel but not inflicting damage on the enemy. Because of the unprecedented exploitation of his aviation assets, Funk had no such need. His gunships had the speed to react to any threat or opportunity instantly. If they were attacking in one zone and the enemy counterattacked, or broke, somewhere else, the gunships could have simply broken off the engagement and moved to destroy the threat or exploit the opportunity. The 3rd Brigade was kept in reserve before the Battle of Phase Line Bullet only because there was no room within the division's boundaries for three brigades to attack on line. Had Lt.Gen. Franks needed to widen the 3rd AD's zone to include part of 1st AD's, or part of 1st ID's zones, he could have done so, and the 3rd AD would have inflicted 25%–33% more damage than it did with little or no loss of momentum.

23

The Battle of Medina Ridge

Before G-Day, the Medina Division had been deployed with three brigades on a line running from east to west on the Iraqi side of the northern border of Kuwait. When the Republican Guard's leaders realized that the main Coalition attack was coming from the west, they recognized that this formation would be useless, and that extensive realignment would be necessary.

Like the Tawakalna Line, the new Medina Line would run from north to south, and would be set up to the west of an improved dirt road, so that its defenders had something to orient on. However, this line would have fewer units to man it and would have to be set up much more hastily.

The Medina Division was by then at less than half strength. The division had sent just over half of its tanks and BMPs to bolster the Tawakalna Line. What remained of the division swung to the north, and would make up the northern half of the Medina Line when the 1st AD hit it.

The Iraqi High Command knew that if the line was to serve any useful purpose, the Medina Division's remnants would have to be extensively reinforced. The Republican Guard's Hammurabi Division would not be available for that purpose. The Coalition flanking maneuver was also a threat to Basra, and the Hammurabi Division had to be sent to the northeast to set up a defense in front of the city. The 10th Armored Division was highly regarded, and could have moved units north from its positions inside Kuwait's western border, but it had its own line to hold. The division, which had lost most of a brigade in the Tawakalna Line, was facing the likelihood that Allied divisions would soon be barreling across the border into it.

There really was only one option. Large concentrations of armor from the 17th Armored Division were now in reserve positions behind the 10th Armored Division. Traveling up an improved dirt road behind the 10th Armored Division, five battalions of tanks and one battalion of APCs were able to take up positions in the Medina Line by the time 1st AD arrived on the 27th. Because of the rushed nature of its establishment, the units on the Medina Line would be dangerously exposed and not particularly well-organized when the Americans arrived.

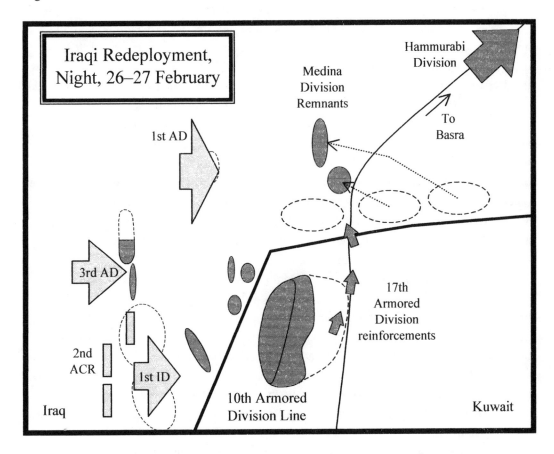

The Medina Division's 2nd Armored Brigade (in the north) traveled the farthest to its new positions, and had little time to dig in. It also had no pre-dug positions to take advantage of. When Maj.Gen. Griffith's men showed up, they would catch the 2nd Brigade almost completely above ground.

What was left (about half) of the Medina Division's 14th Brigade (posted in the center) had lost valuable time uprooting and moving, but had had sufficient time to dig respectable fighting positions. This force was joined by four tank battalions from the 17th Armored Division. The tanks and APCs reached the positions during the night of the 26th and the early hours of the 27th, and were hastily emplaced as soon as they arrived. Behind the central defenses was the logistics complex which had been set up to supply the original east–west Medina defense line. This complex was full of artillery shells and other ammunition, and was honeycombed with bunkers, some of which were occupied by anti-armor teams.

A tank battalion and a mechanized battalion from the 17th Armored Division made up the defenses on the southern end of the line. Although the southern zone was extensively dug-in because part of it had been previously occupied by the 10th Armored

Brigade of the Medina Division, these were the most sparsely defended positions in the line.

Daybreak on the 27th found the 1st AD's maneuver units pushing through the rear areas of the units they had destroyed the night before. There were many abandoned and wrecked vehicles, mostly trucks. Unfortunately, the area was also littered with unexploded artillery submunitions from the previous night's bombardment. This slowed the division down. The armored units were forced to wait for their fuel and supply trucks, which were slowed to a crawl by their need to avoid the submunitions.

At about 8 a.m., the division halted. A few minutes later, Lt.Gen. Franks arrived at division headquarters in a Blackhawk helicopter. To his chagrin, he was informed by Maj.Gen. Griffith that 1st AD was down to its last two hours of fuel. The corps had used over seven million gallons of fuel since G-Day. The 1st AD had used more fuel than any other VII Corps division and its supply was dangerously low. On the outer edge of the VII Corps' wheel, the division had traveled farther than any other VII Corps unit. It had also needed to refuel the 75th Field Artillery Brigade, which had arrived on the night of the 26th with nearly empty fuel tanks.

The 2nd Brigade (now at full strength after TF 6-6 had caught up and refueled) was faced with a particularly bad fuel situation. It had more tanks than either of the other brigades, so it burned fuel at a higher rate. In addition, the brigade was on the outer edge of the division wheel, and had traveled farther than the other two brigades. Because the brigade was so tank-heavy, Griffith had placed it on the division's left flank, which he knew would be uncertain. If XVIII Airborne Corps' 24th Infantry Division, on 1st AD's left flank, fell behind (as it ultimately did), the flank would be open, so Griffith wanted his heaviest brigade there. By the morning of the 27th, 2nd Brigade's fuel supply was almost exhausted.

Lt.Gen. Franks had a decision to make. He could keep 1st AD where it was, and pass the 1st Cavalry Division around it to continue the attack, but this would take time, and would give the Iraqis a half-day's respite, something Franks wanted to avoid at all costs. Franks' second option, the one he decided upon, was to tell Maj.Gen. Griffith to resume the attack, order more fuel from corps stocks, and hope it arrived before 1st AD's tanks ran out of fuel.

Fortunately, fuel was already on the way. The 3rd AD, aware of 1st AD's fuel problems, had sent 20 tankers with about 40,000 gallons. The tankers arrived soon after Franks left, and allowed the 1st AD to continue its attack. More fuel would arrive throughout the day. In an amazing logistical feat, the division's helicopters guided 46 tankers carrying 90,000 gallons of fuel from corps reserve stocks to 1st AD.

Almost immediately after the division resumed its advance, the 2nd Brigade's northernmost task force, TF 4-70, under Lt.Col. William Feyk, spotted three Iraqi tanks, an M-113-mounted TOW launcher captured from the Kuwaiti Army and about 200 infantrymen from the Adnan Division in dug-in positions. Technically, the Guardsmen were just slightly outside TF 4-70's northern boundary. Since Feyk's battalion was VII

Corps' northernmost unit, that meant that the Iraqis were also outside the corps' boundary. The textbook method of dealing with the Iraqi force would have been to report it to XVIII Airborne Corps and let it take the position. Unfortunately, the 3rd Armored Cavalry Regiment, the XVIII Corps' flank unit assigned to maintain contact with Feyk's unit, could be neither located nor contacted. Feyk would find out later that at this time, 3rd ACR was roughly 40 miles behind the 1st AD. Faced with a choice between firing across a corps boundary and leaving Iraqi troops and armor in a position to attack his supply trains as he passed, Feyk chose the former.

As soon as Feyk's tanks came within sight of the Iraqis, several tried to surrender but were gunned down from behind by a group of Guardsmen riding in a truck. The truck and its occupants were promptly machine-gunned to pieces by an Abrams. The four armored vehicles were destroyed at long range. As the M-1A1s approached the Iraqi fighting positions, they were met by small arms fire and 40–50 RPG-7 rounds. Substandard Iraqi troop training was again in evidence. Only four or five RPGs actually hit their targets, and none of them exploded because they had not been properly armed before they were fired.[*] After dropping a few mortar rounds on the objective and machine-gunning a few of the more stubborn defenders, Feyk's troops rounded up a few Guardsmen. Those who retreated deeper into XVIII Corps' sector were not pursued.

Task Force 6-6, following behind TF 4-70, was responsible for screening the division's northern flank. Lt.Col. McGee's task force found a variety of vehicles along the boundary. Of the almost two dozen vehicles were five T-55s and four Type 63s belonging to the 47th Infantry Division and six BMPs, an AMX-10 infantry fighting vehicle and an M-113 armored ambulance belonging to the Adnan Division. The armored vehicles had been hidden in folds in the terrain and had been missed by TF 4-70. Though most of the armored vehicles were destroyed by TF 6-6 while trying to escape, the troops accompanying them turned and fought when confronted by McGee's unit. As with TF 4-70's fight, TF 6-6's encounters were over quickly and were one-sided. Another similarity was the poor training of the Iraqis. Though there were very few unarmed RPG launches in these skirmishes, all RPG rounds missed their targets, and most missed by wide margins. During the morning, TF 6-6 also destroyed several ammunition trucks. Unaware that the units they were taking the ammunition to had already been destroyed, the drivers had blundered straight into the guns of McGee's task force.

Meanwhile, at the southern end of the division wedge, the 3rd Brigade ran into a cluster of T-55s. The ten T-55s were destroyed in one minute, after which the division took a short pause to refuel for the larger battle ahead.

At about ten, while the 2nd Brigade's artillery units were still working their way through the bomblet fields which they had earlier created, Iraqi mortar and artillery shells began impacting a few hundred yards behind the brigade. The brigade Fire Support Officer (FSO) called for counterbattery fire. Unfortunately, the guns were in XVIII

---

[*]This is similar to throwing a grenade without pulling the pin.

Airborne Corps' sector, and the division's MLRS rockets could not be launched until it could be confirmed that 3rd ACR was not in the target area. There had already been a friendly fire incident between the two units earlier that morning, when a ground cavalry squadron of the 3rd ACR had fired on 1st AD engineers as they attempted to recover a disabled vehicle. One engineer had been killed and another had been wounded. After a flurry of radio traffic between the two corps, and about 30 minutes, a fire mission was authorized and 42 MLRS rockets destroyed the Iraqi guns.

Almost immediately after silencing the guns in the XVIII Airborne Corps' sector, a Q-37 radar located more guns firing, this time from inside the VII Corps' boundary. A fire mission was instantly authorized, and 18 more rockets were launched with the same result.

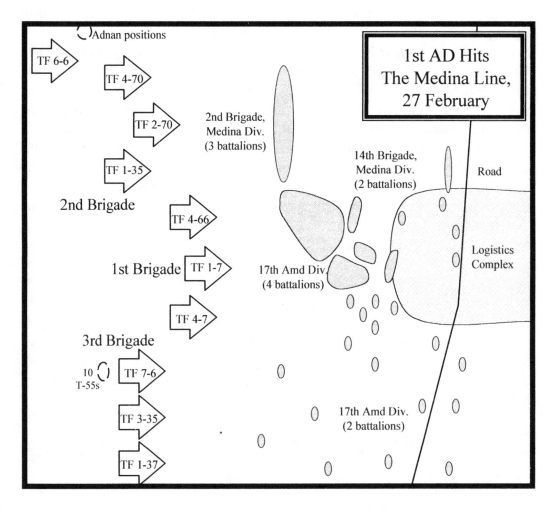

Just after eleven, the division continued its advance. At the point of the 15 mile wide division wedge, also advancing in a wedge formation, was the 1st Brigade. Lt.Col. Stephen Smith's infantry-heavy TF 1-7 was at the point, with Lt.Col. Thomas Goedkoop's armor-heavy TF 4-66 to its left rear and TF 4-7, another infantry-heavy task force under Lt.Col. Edward P. Egan to its right rear. In its final preparatory fire, division artillery punched in the coordinates of seven Iraqi artillery sites previously identified by aerial scouting. Eighty-four rockets ensured the destruction of any artillery still occupying those sites. Just before noon, Goedkoop's task force made contact with the main defense line and began destroying Iraqi armor.[*]

Col. Meigs now brought 2nd Brigade forward for the kill. The brigade rolled forward in a wedge of three armor-heavy task forces, with TF 4-70 in the north, Lt.Col. Steve Whitcomb's TF 2-70 in the center and Lt.Col. Jerry Wiedewitsch's TF 1-35 in the south. Just after noon, Whitcomb's tanks began engaging Iraqi armor as the other two task forces pulled up on line.

There were scores of T-72s and BMPs on the ridge. Surprised by the number of Iraqi tanks to his front, Meigs called for air support to thin out the Iraqi force. Apaches from Lt.Col. Bill Hatch's 3-1st Aviation Battalion arrived above 2nd Brigade's tanks and opened fire with Hellfire missiles.

If configured for anti-tank action, the Apache can carry 16 TOW or Hellfire missiles. The Apache's weapons, including the 30mm gun, were electronically linked to a monocle fitted to the helmet of the weapons operator. Basically, all the WO had to do was look at a target, fire the weapon, and the target was destroyed.

Just minutes after the Apaches began picking off Medina tanks, Iraqi artillery began landing behind the firing line. This would spark the beginning of 1¾ hours of sustained counterbattery activity by division artillerymen. Iraqi batteries would be pinpointed by Q-37 radar immediately after they opened up, and silenced by counterbattery fire. By 2 p.m., when Iraqi artillery activity ceased completely, the division's artillery had fired 288 MLRS rockets and 480 8-inch rounds. It had destroyed roughly four battalions of artillery.

Apaches were active throughout the counterbattery battle. In two instances, Q-37 radars picked up Iraqi batteries in areas that were off limits to artillery because of Apache activity. In both cases, the artillerymen merely gave the coordinates to the Apaches, who destroyed at least 15 guns.

After the Iraqi shells began striking behind them, 2nd Brigade's tank gunners opened up on the Iraqi tanks from a range of 2,000 meters, leaving a dozen tanks in flames. The Iraqis could not even see their attackers through the fog. The best they could do was to use the muzzle flashes from the Abrams' guns as aiming points. Had they been able to see the M-1A1s it would not have mattered. The Americans were beyond the effective range of the Iraqi tank guns. In many cases, Iraqi rounds fell several hundred meters short of their intended targets.

In just over 30 minutes, the 2nd Brigade and the Apaches destroyed 54 T-72s, 6 T-55s, 28 BMPs, 5 MTLBs, an AMX-10 and 5 SAM launchers without loss. This engagement was unusual in that there were more Iraqi dead than prisoners. Fewer than 60 prisoners were taken, while over 300 Iraqis were killed.

---

[*]The 4-66th Armor Battalion had sent an armor company to 1-7th Infantry and had received an infantry company in return. The 4-7th Infantry Battalion had sent one of its infantry companies to 2nd Brigade's 1-35th Armor Battalion in return for an armor company.

Units behind the Iraqi tank line were mauled by Apaches, A-10s and F-16s as well as MLRS and conventional artillery for an additional two hours. The pounding left the Iraqi rear strewn with burning or abandoned vehicles.

While 2nd Brigade and TF 4-66 were working over the heavy concentrations of Iraqi armor on Medina Ridge, the other two battalions of 1st Brigade engaged more widely spread, but still significant, concentrations. During the day, TF 1-7 would destroy 25 tanks (8 T-72s, 16 T-55s and a T-62), 25 BMPs and 14 other APCs. TF 4-7 would destroy 10 tanks (8 T-55s and 2 T-62s), 13 BMPs, 5 other APCs and 2 BRDMs.

Like the units fighting on Medina Ridge, both TF 1-7 and TF 4-7 would be harassed by Iraqi artillery. At around 1 p.m., Lt.Col. Smith noticed Iraqi shells landing to the rear of TF 1-7. Smith then saw shells land directly in front of his firing line. He immediately realized that his unit was being "bracketed," and that the artillery was being directed by spotters. He also understood that in accordance with standard artillery practice, the next salvo would split the difference and land directly on top of his vehicles. Smith ordered his units to stop what they were doing and pull back 100 meters immediately, then called his artillery. As expected, as soon as his vehicles reached their new positions, their previous position exploded under the weight of an Iraqi barrage. While the brigade's artillery support, the 2-41st Field Artillery Battalion, located the Iraqi guns by radar and prepared to launch a counterbarrage, Smith ordered his men to lay fire on every piece of terrain on which a spotter might be located. Though they would never know whether or not they had killed the spotter or spotters, the question became moot when the offending Iraqi artillery unit perished at the hands of 2-41st FA Battalion.

At around the same time, a few shells fell well behind TF 4-7's forward line of Bradleys, impacting near the unit's supply trains. Lt.Col. Egan ordered the task force's soft-skinned vehicles to fall back, and there were no casualties. For approximately 30 minutes, other small groups of shells landed progressively closer to his Bradleys. The artillery was not as competently directed as that falling on TF 1-7. Nevertheless, Egan was starting to worry. Eventually, the shells would fall on his armor. He was tempted to pull his tanks and Bradleys forward and let the shells land behind them, but there was a bunker complex ahead. To move forward would mean risking an anti-armor ambush to escape the danger of a light artillery barrage. Moments after Egan resigned himself to take his chances with the shells, the artillery stopped. The 2-41st FA Battalion had added the Iraqi battery to its battle damage totals.

At around three, 3rd Brigade began driving through eight large logistics sites and destroying Iraqi armor that was trying to defend them. Participants would later refer to the battle as a "continuous Table 8," referring to the Army's tank gunnery qualification exercise. American tanks moved at a constant pace of 6–8 mph, destroying Iraqi armored vehicles as they popped up.

Col. Zanini did not use artillery during the brigade's advance. By now, he knew that the Abrams' superiority made large preparatory barrages unnecessary. As long as Iraqi tanks were not allowed to get flank and rear shots, the Americans had nothing to fear from them. Artillery would only have slowed the attack, as forward units would have to stop during the barrages. Zanini also wanted to avoid problems with unexploded bomblets. His decision would be proven correct. Ultimately, the brigade would take 503 prisoners and destroy 41 T-55s, 35 APCs (mostly MTLBs), 8 artillery pieces and 43 trucks with no losses.

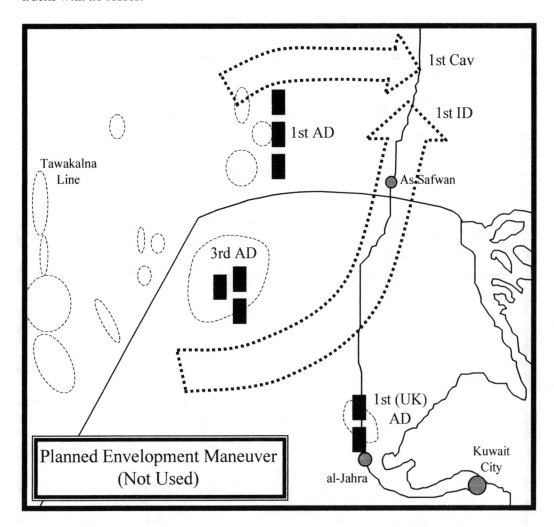

At 4 p.m., the division began realigning for the final push. Lt.Gen. Franks intended to bring the 1st Cavalry Division around 1st AD's northern flank and into the fight. If all went according to plan, Brig.Gen. Tilelli's division would link up with the 1st Infantry Division north of As Safwan. With the link-up, any Iraqi forces in VII Corps' sector that had not been overrun would be trapped.

In order to make room for the 1st Cav, Maj.Gen. Griffith decided to push 1st Brigade farther east. The brigade would clear the large bunker complex in front of it, and capture a road beyond. This move would accomplish two things. First, it would make room for 2nd Brigade to pull to the south, creating a space on the northern flank for 1st Cav to pass through. Col. Stanley Cherrie, the corps' operations officer, had requested (at Lt.Gen. Franks' behest) that the corps' boundary with XVIII Airborne Corps be shifted

10 kilometers to the north. This would have given the 1st Cav the room it needed to pass around 1st AD, but the request had been denied, necessitating the southward shift of 2nd Brigade. Second, by securing the road, the division would keep any Iraqi units from wandering northward and interfering with 1st Cav's move.

Col. Riley decided that he could also use the move to realign his brigade for the next day's fight. At that point, the brigade was on line, with TF 4-66 in the north, TF 1-7 in the center and TF 4-7 in the south. Riley wanted the brigade in a wedge, with his armor-heavy task force on the point, and his two infantry-heavy task forces to its left and right rear. To bring about that configuration, TF 4-7 would attack due east, stopping just short of the road, while TF 1-7 stayed where it was. Meanwhile, TF 4-66 would attack eastward, then hook in front of TF 1-7, securing the road and stopping to the left and front of 4-7th Infantry. At that point, TF 1-7 would simply pull up on TF 4-66's left rear. The road would be secure and the brigade would be properly aligned for the next day's attack.

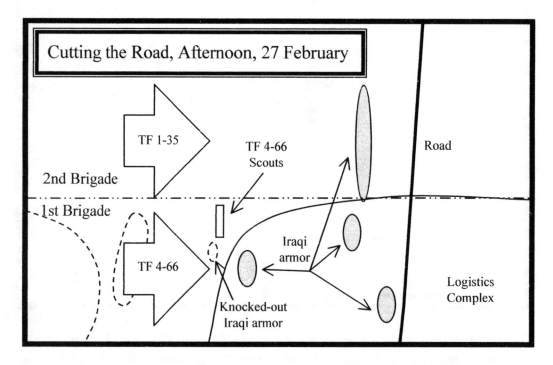

Cutting the Road, Afternoon, 27 February

TF 1-35

TF 4-66 Scouts

Road

2nd Brigade

1st Brigade

TF 4-66

Iraqi armor

Knocked-out Iraqi armor

Logistics Complex

Accompanying TF 4-66 in the capture of the road would be 2nd Brigade's TF 1-35. Lt.Col. Wiedewitsch's task force would advance on the northern flank of TF 4-66. While TF 1-35's zone of attack was not honeycombed with mounds and bunkers the way TF 4-66's was, navigation would still be difficult. While the terrain could have been worse, it was still rough.

Shortly after moving out, the battalion encountered a group of Iraqi tanks in a north–south line to the west of the road. The tanks, which were supported by infantry, had been assigned the task of keeping the road open. The Iraqis began trading main gun fire with the M-1A1s.

Meanwhile, the six Bradleys of TF 4-66's Scout Platoon stopped about 200 meters short of the main Iraqi bunker complex and began exchanging fire with Iraqi infantry in the complex. An RPG struck the Bradley on the northern end of the scouts' line, immobilizing it and forcing its crewmen to bail out. The platoon sergeant, SFC Frederick Wiggins, whose Bradley was posted near the southern end of the line, immediately edged his vehicle ahead of the other Bradleys and began laying suppressing fire on the Iraqis to cover the crewmen of the stricken Bradley as they made their way to the safety of other vehicles.

When he was sure the crewmen of the knocked-out Bradley were safe, Wiggins ordered his driver, Spec. Clarence Cash, to back the vehicle up. As soon as the Bradley began moving, it was hit in the front slope by an RPG. Almost simultaneously, an American sabot round pierced the right rear of the vehicle, passed through the drivers compartment, and exited through the left front slope of the Bradley. A TF 4-66 Abrams to the scouts' right rear had mistaken the second Bradley for an Iraqi vehicle. The Bradleys had just passed a platoon of knocked-out Iraqi tanks to their south. From the point of view of the gunner who fired the shot, the Bradleys looked like part of an Iraqi tank line. Cash was dead.[*] Wiggins had received wounds which would later result in the amputation of his leg.

At that point, on TF 1-35's southern flank, heavy Iraqi small arms fire was forcing the exposed tank commanders of Capt. David Erickson's B Company back into their hatches, compromising their ability to see and deal with the Iraqis to their front. Erickson pulled his company back roughly 200 meters. This would greatly reduce the Iraqi infantrymen's chances of hitting one of Erickson's tank commanders, and give him a better perspective on what his company was facing.

However rational Erickson's actions were, all TF 4-66's scouts could see was a large number of TF 1-35's tanks retreating at top speed. From Lt.Col. Goedkoop's vantage point, it looked like TF 1-35 was disengaging and falling back. He radioed Col. Riley, and told him that he could still complete his mission, but that TF 1-35 was pulling back, and that this was jeopardizing his left flank. Riley radioed Griffith, told him that he had Bradleys burning, crewmen wounded, and that he recommended that TF 1-35 remain in place. TF 1-35's operations officer, Maj. Michael Tucker, replied that the task force was already in place, since it had not gone anywhere.

It was becoming increasingly apparent to Griffith that the attack had bogged down in confusion. Liaison between the two attacking task forces had broken down, ammunition bunkers were exploding, Republican Guardsmen were still in the complex waiting in ambush, and nightfall was approaching. Whatever benefit might come from bringing the 1st Cavalry Division into the offensive was rapidly being offset by the risk of fratricide, which seemed to be growing by the minute. Griffith told Riley to halt TF 4-66 where it was. He then radioed Lt.Gen. Franks, explained the situation, and suggested

---

[*]His death has been attributed to friendly fire, but it is possible that Cash had already been killed by the RPG blast by the time the sabot round struck.

that the 1st Cavalry Division's passage be postponed. The corps commander agreed, and plans to push the 1st Cav around the division were shelved until the following morning. The delay, and the sudden end of the war, would ultimately frustrate the plan to use 1st Cav in an enveloping maneuver.

As soon as the situation was sorted out, the two battalions resumed their attack toward the road. TF 1-35 destroyed the tanks guarding the road, routed the infantry accompanying them, and halted on the east side of the road. Meanwhile, having taken Iraqi fire and casualties, TF 4-66 was no longer concerned with encouraging Iraqis to surrender. Lt.Col. Goedkoop's battalion drove into the complex, shooting it up with ruthless efficiency, killing many Iraqis with tank gun, 25mm and machine-gun fire. By nightfall, the task force had crushed Iraqi opposition in its zone and joined TF 1-35 on the east side of the road. Though 2nd Brigade's battle received the most media attention after the war, TF 4-66 had actually destroyed almost as much Iraqi armor during its battles as the entire 2nd Brigade. Goedkoop's task force destroyed 66 T-55s, 12 BMPs, 11 BRDMs, 3 ZSU 23-4s and a PT-76 light tank.

The division spent the night refueling and consolidating its positions. There were hundreds of bunkers to clear and a significant number of abandoned vehicles to destroy. It would take until dawn to finish the job.

The pause gave the division's soldiers a chance to examine enemy positions and equipment. They were shocked at the unpreparedness of their adversaries. The Iraqis had clearly received no advanced warning of the American attack. The Tawakalna Line had been overwhelmed, but at least the handling of its defense had been basically competent. Here, there had not even been a screen line, and no scouts had been sent forward. Thirteen BRDM armored scout cars had been available, but for some reason they were placed a few hundred meters *behind* the main defense line.

The consequences of this tactical blunder could still have been avoided if there had at least been a reasonable degree of communication between Iraqi units. TF 4-70 had overrun a unit of the Adnan division some four hours before the Medina Line had been hit. Though Adnan artillery activity followed, indicating that a report of the action had been made to Adnan headquarters, apparently, no report had been made to the Medina Division. Around the same time, to the south, 10 T-55s were destroyed by 3rd Brigade. Again, apparently, no report was made. Thus, as a wave of American tanks was preparing to slaughter it, the Medina Division's 2nd Brigade was eating lunch. One T-72 was destroyed as its crewmen boiled a chicken behind the tank. Others were milling around outside their tanks smoking cigarettes when the fighting started. Such total surprise on the third day of a major ground offensive is almost unheard of.

The remains of the Iraqi tanks produced more surprises. What had appeared to be extra armor on the sides of the T-72s turned out to be only rubber, installed to cut down on dust and reduce the tank's heat signature somewhat. There were more bizarre revelations, however. As a company commander examined the wreckage of one of his victims, he noticed that several of the ball bearings on which the turret rotated were lying on the ground. "They weren't even round," he recalled. "They were kind of round, but they weren't nearly as round as they should've been." Analysis of eighteen captured sabot rounds would later reveal that nine had been shipped from the factory without tungsten penetrators inside.

More curiosities awaited. Troops found bunkers full of food and water. While the rest of the army had been existing on meager rations of the poorest quality, the Republican Guard had been receiving regular supplies of fresh food. While front line units had gone without water, the Guard had enough to boil chickens. The Americans also found considerable quantities of ammunition (much it from supposedly neutral Jordan). The bunkers themselves were fairly well put together, though they were considerably less formidable than advertised. They were dug-in and reinforced with concrete and steel, but they were not the huge 1,200-man bomb-proof fortresses with chemical filtration systems the American public had been warned of.

At 5:30 next morning, six artillery battalions delivered a 45-minute barrage of 186 MLRS rockets and over 4,000 shells. Apaches from 3-1st Aviation then moved in. Finding mostly burning vehicles, the Apaches nevertheless found eight tanks, ten APCs and several trucks to destroy. The three brigades then advanced about 12 miles through the Medina Line's reserve positions and supply trains before the division was forced to stop at 8:00 by the cease-fire. In this final drive, the division destroyed 41 tanks, 60 APCs, 15 artillery pieces, 244 trucks and 11 air defense systems. Another 281 Iraqi prisoners were rounded up. Meanwhile, two ATACMS missiles destroyed four FROG rocket launchers.

Fighting with the 1st Armored Division had cost the Iraqi army 352 tanks, 306 APCs, 504 trucks, 64 artillery pieces, 32 air defense weapons and 6,686 prisoners. The fighting had cost the division two dead and fifty-two wounded, as well as four M-1A1s and two Bradleys. The division would continue to inflict damage in the days following the cease-fire, scuttling 100 tanks, 191 APCs, 877 trucks, 92 artillery pieces and 104 AA systems it had bypassed earlier. Combat engineers also destroyed tons of ammunition in the complexes the division had overrun.

24

The Final Blows

Just before dawn on the morning of the 27th, the 1st Infantry Division was preparing to make a dash for the highway that linked Kuwait City and Basra. However, there were a few pockets of Iraqi resistance on Objective Norfolk to be overcome before the division went on its way.

During the fighting at Objective Norfolk, the 1-4th Cavalry Squadron had provided a screen line to the north. As the fighting wound down for the 1st and 3rd brigades, it flared up in 1-4th Cavalry's sector.

At about four in the morning, the two Bradleys and one M-113 of Lt.Col. Wilson's command group were inspecting the screen line. As the group approached A Troop's line, Maj. Burdan, the squadron's operations officer, riding in the lead Bradley, spotted a T-72 and a T-55 behind Capt. Kenneth Pope's A Troop. Both were dug-in and surrounded by dozens of bunkers, from which a number of Iraqi infantrymen were emerging. To improve the command group's odds, Burdan called for assistance from B Troop, which had just reported destroying a T-55 on the eastern end of its screen line. B Troop sent an Abrams, which quickly destroyed the T-72 while Burdan's Bradley used 25mm armor-piercing rounds to destroy the T-55. Meanwhile, Lt.Col. Wilson's Bradley (behind Burdan's) sprayed the Iraqi infantrymen with 25mm and coaxial machine-gun fire, killing several and causing many more to return to their bunkers.

As the command group pulled back, B Troop's commander, Capt. Mike Bills, sent two Bradleys and two M-1A1s to deal with the Iraqi infantry and five more T-72s which had been spotted. However, before the force moved out, B Troop was hit by artillery fire. There were no casualties, but suspecting the presence of chemical agents, B Troop donned full chemical-protective gear, including masks. The tanks and Bradleys engaged the T-72s, destroying three with 120mm main gun fire and two with TOW missiles. Shortly after the last of the T-72s were disposed of, tests showed that no chemicals were present, and the "all clear" was given.

At 6:15, the squadron began a sweep of a large logistics base to the southeast of the screen line. To the south of 1-4th Cavalry, 2nd Brigade would be passing through 1st Brigade. Clearing this area would ensure that there was no interference with the passage of lines. Over the next two hours, the squadron's ground troops and Cobras would destroy 11 armored vehicles, several artillery pieces and a number of trucks.

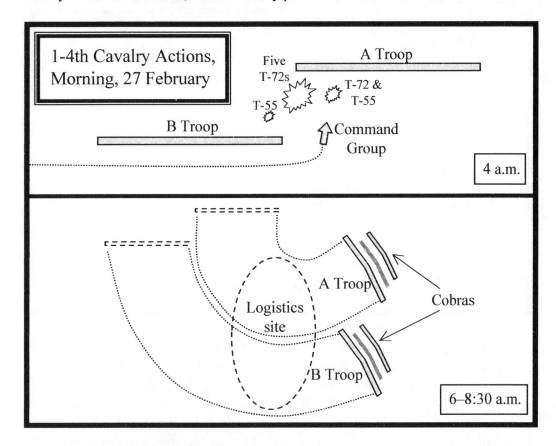

During the sweep, the command group returned to the site of its earlier fight. There, it found a dug-in T-72 which had been overlooked earlier. When the tank's commander, standing in his hatch, spotted the command group, only 150 meters away, he sunk inside his tank, obviously preparing to engage. Maj. Burdan's gunner immediately lunched a TOW missile, but the missile malfunctioned, diving into the ground 50 meters in front of the Bradley. Seeing this, Wilson's gunner launched a TOW missile, which destroyed the tank.

The 2nd Brigade replaced 1st Brigade on the division's left flank at around seven. Rhame's plan called for the 2nd and 3rd brigades to push eastward for another 20 kilometers. At that point, 1st Brigade would pass between the other two brigades, then make a wide turn to the northeast. When it had driven 10 kilometers ahead of them, it would stop, and 2nd and 3rd brigades would take up positions to its left and right rear. The 1st Brigade would then lead the division wedge to Objective Denver, on the highway from Kuwait City to Basra.

Before moving out, 3rd Brigade finished off the Iraqi armor it had failed to destroy during the night. The brigade's accurate long range main gun fire, and the fact that it was now daylight and the Iraqis could see what they were up against, was enough to cause 937 Iraqis, to give themselves up.

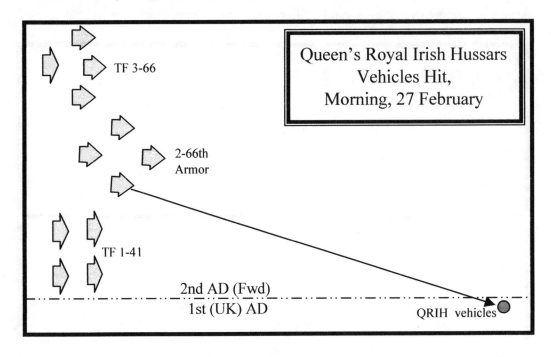

At about nine, the brigade was moving in a wedge, with 2-66th Armor at the point and the two balanced task forces on the flanks. At around 11:30, D Company, on 2-66th Armor's right flank, spotted vehicles to its front right at long range. After several attempts to hail it on 2-66th's and TF 1-41's frequencies produced no response, the company opened fire with sabot rounds and machine-gun fire, then HEAT rounds. Eventually, a white flag was raised. As Americans moved forward to round up prisoners, they found to their horror that the vehicles belonged to the Queen's Royal Irish Hussars, and that two British soldiers had been seriously wounded. The shots were fired by the company that had fired on Capt. Bishop's company during the night battle on Objective Norfolk. Again, misorientation resulted in a cross-boundary firing, in this case across both its and the brigade's southern boundary (which was also the division's southern boundary). Thinking that they were pointed due east, and engaging from extreme range, the company's gunners had no way of knowing that their targets were outside the battalion's, brigade's and division's boundaries.

In the 2nd Brigade sector, the only major fighting took place when the remnants of an Iraqi armored battalion ran afoul of TF 3-37. The tanks had been assigned to the 30th Infantry Division. The Egyptian 3rd Mechanized Division had smashed through the Iraqi 20th Infantry Division and had continued northward, taking al-Abraq and overrunning one of the 30th Division's infantry brigades. There it had halted. The Iraqi tank battalion, posted to the north of al-Abraq, made its way northward under the command of a brigadier general. As the 1st (U.K.) Armoured Division was still several miles to the west, the Iraqi force was able to pass through the British attack zone without being attacked. The Iraqis' luck soon ran out, however, as their path brought them directly in front of TF 3-37's tanks. Lt.Col. Gross' gunners made the most of the flank shots they were offered, destroying 26 tanks in 17 minutes.

At this point, the 1st Brigade was preparing to take part in its third passage of lines in three days. For the second time in two days, it would be coordinating the passage by radio, on the fly. Unable to make radio contact with 3rd Brigade, Col. Maggart was able to reach Col. Moreno of 2nd Brigade. The two decided that it would be best for Maggart's two lead units, TF 2-34 in the north and 1-34th Armor in the south, to pass through the middle of 2nd Brigade at a spot marked by a burning Iraqi tank. The two battalions made the passage in good order. Because of its mopping-up duties on Norfolk, TF 5-16 had begun refueling late, and had fallen behind. By racing across the desert at speeds of up to 45 mph, Lt.Col. Baker's task force caught up at the passage point and took its place behind the two lead battalions.

As soon as 1st Brigade completed its passage, 1-34th Armor ran into about a dozen T-55 tanks. After Lt.Col. Ritter's battalion destroyed the tanks without breaking stride, the brigade began its turn to the northeast. Within minutes, Col. Maggart's armor ran into a slightly more formidable obstacle, a berm which stretched across most of the brigade's front. After a 30-minute delay, during which several holes were punched in the berm, the two lead battalions advanced directly into another defensive position.

A few short range engagements resulted in the destruction of several Iraqi armored vehicles. As soon as the Iraqi threat to his immediate front had been dealt with, Maggart ordered his brigade to halt. All three brigades of the division were now on line, and there was a good deal of congestion. To press the attack would have risked friendly fire incidents. Maggart decided to wait until the other brigades had moved a comfortable distance from his brigade before continuing the advance.

At about 9:30, after refueling and resupplying, 1-4th Cavalry had continued its screening mission after the fall of Norfolk, picking off Iraqi artillery pieces, fuel and cargo trucks as it advanced. The squadron then overran the last remaining unit of the 12th Armored Division's 46th Mechanized Brigade, a force of 15 tanks and 17 APCs spread widely over a reserve position behind the Tawakalna Line. At around noon, the squadron crossed into Kuwait, where it came upon the positions of what used to be the 10th Armored Division's 17th Armored Brigade. The squadron passed significant numbers of wrecks, the handiwork of Army attack helicopters, and a significant number of abandoned vehicles. Occasionally, crews of individual Iraqi armored vehicles would offer resistance and be destroyed. The squadron added 10 T-62s and 6 BMPs to its tally before it halted at about 12:30, roughly 10 miles inside Kuwait.

At 2:30, the squadron resumed its advance and spent the rest of the afternoon bypassing abandoned positions and disarming surrendering Iraqis on its way to the Basra Highway. Because its mission was to screen the division's left flank, the squadron's path took it to the north of the stretch of mines and quarries which would complicate matters for the 1st and 2nd brigades. With neither defenders nor terrain posing difficulties for the squadron, 1-4th Cavalry made more rapid progress than the rest of the division, and lost contact with 2nd Brigade, the closest unit to it, at about 3:45.

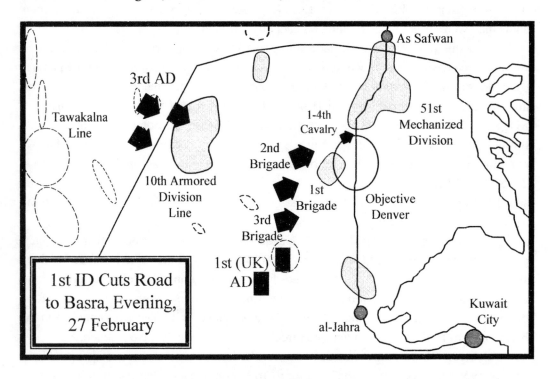

After conferring with his troop commanders, Lt.Col. Wilson decided to keep the squadron moving. Aware that Maj.Gen. Rhame intended for the division to halt on the Kuwait–Basra highway that night, Wilson was confident that contact with the division would soon be reestablished. It seemed unlikely to him that the Iraqis, who seemed more intent on escaping than fighting, would attack his unit before the rest of the division caught up. The squadron reached the highway at about five in the afternoon.

A Troop, leading the squadron, found six T-55 tanks, ten APCs and a ZSU 23-4 self-propelled anti-aircraft gun as well as some 2,000 Iraqi infantrymen on the highway. The Iraqis were taken completely by surprise. Hundreds of Iraqis responded to the approach of the cavalrymen by surrendering. Others attempted to man their armored vehicles and engage the Americans. Within minutes, four T-55s, four APCs and the ZSU 23-4 had been destroyed. The crews of the others surrendered.

The Americans spent the next two hours collecting prisoners and engaging in several spirited firefights. Especially stubborn was a group of Iraqis in a large water pumping station. Unwilling to give the Iraqis an opportunity to inflict casualties by sending his men into the building to conduct room-to-room clearing operations, Wilson had his tanks fire HEAT rounds into the building's concrete walls. After several rounds, its occupants surrendered. By 7:30, Iraqi resistance was broken, although there would be sporadic firefights with small groups of Iraqis throughout the night.

The squadron, now the easternmost unit in the entire VII Corps, would be on its own for the night, even though the 1st ID's 2nd Brigade was only 15 miles from the highway. Lt.Gen. Franks had ordered the rest of the division to stop where it was because it was getting too far ahead of other VII Corps units. Many 1st ID units were also getting critically short on fuel. In its gallop across Iraq, the division's fuel trucks had fallen behind. The halt gave the division's fuel tankers a chance to catch up with the combat elements, but it did not help 1-4th Cavalry. With his squadron isolated, and with over 2,000 prisoners to disarm and process, Lt.Col. Wilson had no choice but to abandon his plan to set a screen line. He pulled his unit into a defensive perimeter astride the highway.

The squadron had arrived at the highway at the best possible time. Shortly after 1-4th Cavalry assumed its thin defensive perimeter, it was shielded from possible Iraqi counterattack by the onset of darkness. Even Iraqi units in an escape posture might have been tempted to attack an isolated cavalry squadron. In the darkness, however, the size and strength of Wilson's force remained a mystery to the Iraqis. Throughout the night, cavalrymen on the east side if the highway would hear Iraqi tanks in the distance, rumbling northward. None of them would test the perimeter.

Though the squadron was not attacked in force, the night was eventful. Among the Iraqi prisoners were about 200 wounded. Most had been wounded in the two hours of fighting which followed 1-4th Cavalry's arrival at the highway, although Iraqis would continue to be wounded in the skirmishes which went on through the night. Responsibility for their care fell to the squadron's medical platoon. Though they were assisted by two doctors, a captured Iraqi and a Kuwaiti, the volume of wounded required squadron medical personnel to work throughout the night.

The 1st Brigade halted in a place its soldiers referred to as the "Valley of the Boogers," a vast mineral mine with pits as deep as 30 feet and high dirt mounds from end to end. Tactical deployment within the mine was impossible and the Iraqis had scores of spots out of which they might spring ambushes. The terrain restricted the brigade to a single road, and limited sight lines to 250–300 meters. The brigade's lead battalion, 1-34th Armor, cautiously entered the valley and halted. Navigation by terrain recognition was impossible, as oily smoke from burning oil wells blotted out moonlight and starlight, rendering night vision devices useless. Since Lt.Col. Ritter's tank was equipped with a Global Positioning System, he took the lead. His crew and the crews of the tanks immediately behind him would spend much of the night fighting off an Iraqi infantry battalion, machine-gunning ground troops and anti-tank teams. During the night, Ritter's tank would expend over 3,000 rounds of 7.62mm coaxial machine-gun ammunition.

Most of Ritter's soldiers had hoped that they would not have to kill any Iraqis that night. During the war's competitive stage they had had a mission to accomplish, so they had eagerly sought Iraqi combat units to destroy in furtherance of that mission. Now, Saddam's forces had been beaten beyond any hope of recovery. The end of the war was now just a matter of time. The only question left was who would or would not be alive to see it. The men of 1st Brigade would therefore have preferred to have been left alone, but since they were not being left alone, they defended themselves violently. Many Americans were actually angry at the stupidity of the Iraqis attacking them after the war's outcome had long since been decided.

The heaviest fighting took place from 10:30 to 2:00, after which the Iraqis became increasingly dispirited. As dawn broke on the 28th, hundreds of Iraqis advanced on the perimeter to surrender. The lack of Iraqi fighting spirit was especially fortunate for the men of 1-34th Armor's support units. The support elements were well behind the battalion's tanks. When dawn broke, they found that they had spent the night near a cluster of Iraqi tanks, which could easily have laid waste their unarmored vehicles.

As 1-34th Armor's battle was at its height, tanks from 3rd Brigade's TF 3-66 were also involved in a bit of drama. Just after nightfall on the 27th, 4-3rd FA Battalion, the artillery battalion supporting 3rd Brigade, reported that it had fallen well behind the brigade and needed tanks to guide it back to the main body. Scattered groups of tanks were fleeing the British, and several had entered the brigade zone behind 3rd Brigade's tanks, but ahead of its artillery. While Iraqi tanks had been no match for Coalition tanks, they were fully capable of destroying thinly armored self-propelled howitzers. Lt.Col. Jones ordered Capt. Ryan's D Company to shepherd the artillery battalion forward.

Ryan brought his company back 15 kilometers, and left it in defensive positions while he led another tank back the remaining 20 kilometers to the artillerymen. Just after midnight, shortly before reaching the positions given by the artillerymen, Ryan and his wing man encountered a small force of Iraqi tanks accompanied by dismounted infantry. Feeling, as Ritter and his men did, that the war was essentially over, Ryan chose to seek the force's surrender rather than immediately annihilating it. A burst of coaxial machine-gun fire over the heads of the Iraqis prompted one of them to move toward Ryan's wingman to discuss surrender. As he did, however, several of the Iraqis attempted to escape, while a few mounted one of the tanks. An American sabot round destroyed the tank, which exploded with sufficient force to blow out the windshield of a Humvee belonging to the nearby artillery unit. While leading the artillery back to the brigade, the two M-1A1s would destroy another two tanks and three BMPs, which would have made life dangerous for the artillerymen had the D Company tanks not been there.

The 2nd Brigade had also been forced to deal with the Valley of the Boogers. Col. Moreno's attack went much more smoothly than Col. Maggart's. The terrain in the 2nd Brigade zone was more trafficable than that in the 1st Brigade zone. Its occupants were also less feisty. The Iraqis in the 2nd Brigade zone made no attempt to obstruct Moreno's brigade, which made steady progress until ordered to halt just after nightfall.

Moreno ordered his battalion commanders to bypass surrendering Iraqis. He knew that securing hordes of surrendering Iraqis would slow his progress. He also knew that his force was not equipped to deal with large numbers of prisoners, since he only had about half of his infantry with him. When the division had headed east on the 25th, TF 2-16 had been left behind to provide security in the breach area. This had left Moreno with only two infantry companies (with TF 3-37).

At first light on the 28th, Col. Moreno received a radio call from Maj.Gen. Rhame informing him that there would be a cease-fire at 8 a.m. Rhame asked how quickly Moreno could get his brigade moving. Moreno replied that he had used the previous evening's halt to refuel, and could move out immediately. Rhame told him to link up with 1-4th Cavalry on the Basra Highway. At six, the brigade moved out. It soon came upon a company of Iraqi tanks on the highway. At 7:30, after destroying the Iraqi armor, 2nd Brigade secured a position on the highway just south of 1-4th Cavalry.

The Big Red One was not finished yet, however. The site chosen for the signing of the armistice which would end the war seemed perfect. As Safwan had an airstrip, so it was convenient. It was also inside Iraq, so there could be no doubt that the Iraqi Army had been defeated. The only problem was that As Safwan had not been captured yet.

About four hours before the cease-fire on 28 February, VII Corps had been ordered to capture As Safwan and the nearby cloverleaf. However, Col. Cherrie, the corps' operations officer, realized that the 1st Infantry Division, the only unit both close enough and with enough fuel to reach the objective within the next few hours, could not get its ground units there by the cease-fire. The best he could do was send Apaches to secure the cloverleaf by destroying or chasing away any Iraqi units located there.

The Apaches found no Iraqi armor at the cloverleaf. About a half-hour before the 8 a.m. cease-fire, as the Apaches were looking for targets, a VII Corps unit reported taking friendly fire. Franks ordered the corps to hold its fire while the reports were sorted out. After only a short pause, Franks determined that the 1st ID was not involved, and gave orders for the division to resume operations. Unfortunately, the Apache unit did not hear the order, and continued to patrol the area without firing in the mistaken belief that the check-fire order was still on.

Since they had heard no report of problems from the Apaches, the VII Corps' staff assumed that they controlled As Safwan. When asked by Third Army for a map overlay indicating the extent of its advance, the corps reported the positions of its lead units. The report showed As Safwan within its lines, since the staff believed that Apaches controlled the area. Third Army passed the information to Gen. Schwarzkopf.

Believing As Safwan to be in American hands, Schwarzkopf had suggested the site to Lt.Gen. Khaled at 11 p.m. on 28 February. Khaled indicated that he was happy with the choice. When Schwarzkopf's staff went to work arranging the talks, they learned that the town was still in Iraqi hands, and reported that fact to Schwarzkopf.

Schwarzkopf exploded. At first he believed that he had been lied to, or, more precisely, that VII Corps had lied to Third Army. He soon found that however embarrassing the mistake had been, it was just that —a mistake. While this realization calmed his fears about the integrity of Lt.Gen. Franks and his staff, he still questioned their judgment. He could not believe that they would send helicopters instead of ground units to seize a vital road junction. As he had not known where many of his ground units were in the closing hours of the war or what their fuel situation was, Schwarzkopf had no appreciation that sending the Apaches had been a necessity, not a choice. Franks accepted blame for the mishap, but replied (correctly) that the helicopters had control of the junction, and but for a communications foul-up would easily have held it.

The mission of capturing As Safwan would fall to the 1st Infantry Division. At 2:40 in the morning on 1 March, Maj.Gen. Rhame called Lt.Col. Wilson, and told him to move 1-4th Cavalry northward at 6:15 and seize As Safwan Airfield. For the mission, the squadron received additional combat power in the form of a company of Apaches, which was kept in a holding area, on call, in case the ground troops needed heavy firepower. Brig.Gen. Carter would accompany the squadron to oversee the operation.

Since speed was of the essence, Wilson kept his unit well to the west of the Basra Highway, where he suspected there might still be viable Iraqi units. As it approached its objective, the squadron would hook to the northeast and split into two prongs at Hill 138, also known as Jabal Sanam, the only piece of commanding terrain for miles. A Troop would sweep to the north of the hill, and B Troop would pass it to the south. At about 8:30, after facing no resistance, the ground troops reached their assigned objectives. Both encountered Iraqis.

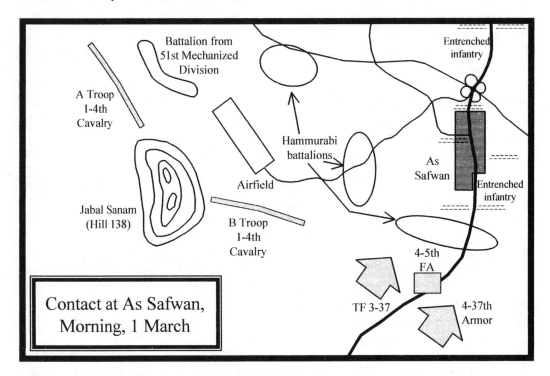

In A Troop's sector, there was a battalion-sized force of T-55 tanks and MTLBs from the 51st Mechanized Division. Capt. Pope told the Iraqi battalion commander that his unit would have to leave. The Iraqi replied that he could not remove his battalion without orders. As the Iraqi turned to leave, he noticed that American soldiers were giving his men MREs. Agitated, he ordered his men to prepare tea and food for A Troop.

At 10:20, the Iraqi battalion commander returned, and told Capt. Pope that he still did not have permission to leave the area. Pope told the Iraqi that he must leave nonetheless if he wished to prevent a confrontation. As if to make the point, an A-10 appeared overhead. Pope told the Iraqi that either his unit would leave, or the A-10 would attack. With that, the commander returned to his unit and led it northward.

A similar encounter took place in B Troop's sector. As the troop arrived at the airfield, the Iraqi anti-aircraft batteries occupying it fled. Leaving the majority of his troop on the airfield, Capt. Bills led a force of two tanks and three Bradleys north of the airfield. Within a few minutes, the small force reached a battalion-sized armored unit from the Republican Guard's Hammurabi Division in defensive positions. Like Pope, Capt. Bills firmly told the Iraqis that they had to leave. Like the commander in A Troop's sector, this Iraqi battalion commander insisted that he needed permission first.

At that point, Lt.Col. Wilson arrived, and forcefully told the Iraqi lieutenant colonel to withdraw his unit. The Iraqi responded by having two of his T-72s drive forward with their main guns pointed at the American vehicles. Wilson calmly countered by calling for Apaches. A few minutes later, with a flight of Apaches hovering overhead, Wilson told the Iraqi commander that if his unit was not withdrawn immediately, the gunships would open fire. The Iraqi relented, and moved his unit out of the area. With the situation in 1-4th Cavalry's sector under control, Brig.Gen. Carter helicoptered to 2nd Brigade's sector, to see how events were unfolding there.

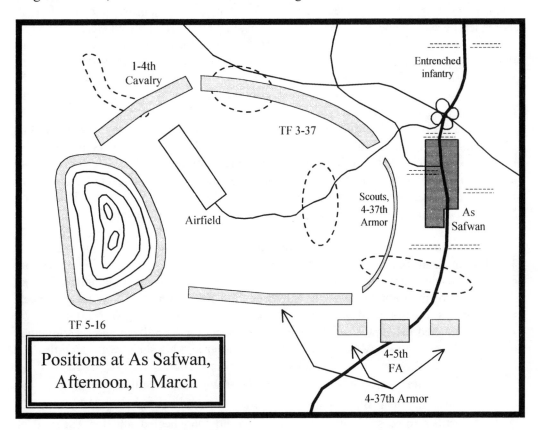

Maj.Gen. Rhame had ordered 2nd Brigade northward shortly after 1-4th Cavalry had arrived at the airfield. The brigade was to join 1-4th Cavalry in the defense of the airfield and secure As Safwan. For the mission, 1st Brigade's TF 5-16 was attached to Col. Moreno's brigade to replace TF 2-16, which was still making its way back to its parent unit after completion of its security duties in the 1st ID breach area. Because it was still to the south with 1st Brigade at that point, TF 5-16 would not be immediately available, however. It would have to catch up with 2nd Brigade at As Safwan.

For the drive to As Safwan, Moreno posted the 4-5th Field Artillery Battalion under the command of Lt.Col. John Gingrich at the front of his brigade, centered on the Basra Highway. Moreno intended to emplace his artillery first, then have TF 3-37 and the 4-37th Armor Battalion roll past it to the left and right, respectively, and secure the town. With artillery already in place, it would be available immediately to the armored units if they needed it in clearing the town. As events unfolded, however, immediately after 4-5th FA took up its positions south of As Safwan, it was approached by Iraqi soldiers. This was the advance guard of a battalion of armor from the Hammurabi Division which was blocking the highway. To the north of the armored battalion were several positions of entrenched infantry on both sides of the road. There was another battalion of Hammurabi armor across the road which ran from the airfield to the cloverleaf north of As Safwan.

Slightly before noon, Col. Moreno arrived to attempt to talk the Iraqis on the highway into leaving. Unfortunately for Moreno, Rhame had told him that because of the cease-fire, his men would not be able to shoot at the Iraqis unless they were fired upon. The discussions quickly broke down, with the commander of the Iraqi force excusing himself to consult with Baghdad. The Americans would later learn that the Iraqi commander originally expected that Moreno's unit was approaching to offer its surrender, because he believed that it was surrounded by the Republican Guard.

He would return to a much different Col. Moreno. During the nearly two hours that the Iraqi was gone, Lt.Gen. Yeosock, the Third Army commander, had relayed Gen. Schwarzkopf's new instructions to Maj.Gen. Rhame. "Tell him that if he doesn't leave by 1600 [4 p.m.]," said Schwarzkopf, "you're going to kill him." Rhame happily passed the new instructions on to Moreno.

On his return, the Iraqi attempted to read a prepared statement. Moreno cut him off and told him that he would be attacking at 4 p.m., and any Iraqi soldiers in front of his brigade would be killed. To drive the point home, Moreno had his tanks roll forward slowly. The previously haughty Iraqi now appeared almost panic-stricken. Claiming that he could not possibly get his troops out by 4 p.m., he begged for an extra 30 minutes. Moreno gave him 20. When the armistice talks were held, the nearest Iraqis would be two miles away.

Moreno's ad hoc unit spent the next day consolidating its hold on the area. TF 5-16 cleared Jabal Sanam. Lt.Col. Baker's men found a significant communications complex, lavishly equipped with Soviet radar, electronics intercept and jamming devices. At the base of the mountain was an extensive network of trenches and bunkers. There were also vast quantities of weapons and tons of ammunition. Lt.Col. Marlin's 4-37th Armor completed the capture of the objective by securing As Safwan and the cloverleaf to the north of the town. Meanwhile, Brig.Gen. Carter and his staff set up facilities and security for the upcoming armistice talks at As Safwan Airfield.

The 1st ID's mission was now complete. With little fanfare, the division had engaged and eliminated all, or parts of, 11 Iraqi divisions, destroying 257 tanks, 173 APCs, 82 artillery pieces, 33 air defense weapons and 206 wheeled vehicles. The division had taken 11,425 prisoners. The Big Red One had lost 19 killed and 67 wounded, as well as five M-1A1s, eight Bradleys and an M-113 APC. The 1st ID had been the only Coalition division to see action on all four days of the campaign. Like other coalition divisions, the 1st ID would be busy after the war, scuttling abandoned Iraqi equipment. During the days after the cease-fire, division soldiers destroyed another 125 tanks, 200 APCs, 130 artillery pieces, 235 AA systems and 435 trucks.

Part IX

Closing Acts and Questions

The Damage

Tanks: 3,200 of 5,000 destroyed

BMPs: 900 of 1,700 destroyed

Other APCs: 1,100 of 2,200 destroyed

Artillery: 200 of 300 MRLs, 200 of 350 SP and 2,300 of 3,500 towed guns destroyed

25

End Game

The war would end as it had begun, with impressive videotapes of a bombing mission. This time the target was a command bunker to the northwest of Baghdad, at al-Taji Airfield. U.S. Air Force planes had destroyed at least three targets during the war that were supposed to contain Saddam Hussein, only to find out in each case that he had been elsewhere. Now, CENTCOM intelligence officers had decided that the bunker at al-Taji was the most likely place Saddam would be hiding, largely because this bunker was one of the most well-protected in Iraq, set beneath 20 feet of reinforced concrete. Thus far, the bunker had stood up against the Coalition's most lethal bombs. It would not withstand the bombs which struck it on the night of 27 February.

The GBU-28 did not exist when the air war began. In the first days of the bombing campaign, conventional bunker penetration bombs worked well enough. However, it soon became apparent that while the Air Force's most effective penetration bomb, the 2,000 lb. GBU-27, could penetrate most Iraqi command bunkers, it could not penetrate all of them. Design was begun on a bomb that could. Manufacture of that bomb began on 25 January.

The first GBU-28 was completed on 17 February. It was 19 feet long and weighed 4,485 lbs. Explosives made up only about 15% (675 lbs.) of the bomb's weight.* Because penetrator bombs are designed to explode in bunkers or other confined spaces, a little explosive goes a long way. Most of the GBU-28's weight came from its casing, a discarded gun barrel from an 8-inch artillery piece. With the addition of a hardened front end, the bomb was complete.

Two prototypes were tested at Holloman Air Force Base in New Mexico. One buried itself 100 feet below the desert surface, earning it the nickname "Deep Throat." The other was mounted on a rocket sled and aimed at a 22 foot thick block of concrete. The sled allowed the bomb to hit the concrete at the same speed it would have if it had been dropped from an aircraft. The bomb sliced through the concrete and traveled an additional half-mile. Several GBU-28s were immediately shipped to Saudi Arabia. In peacetime, the design of a new bomb generally takes about two years. A little over a

---

*By comparison, explosives make up 26% of the GBU-27's total weight.

month had elapsed between the start of the design process and the dropping of the GBU-28s on the bunker at al-Taji.

On the night of 27 February, two F-111Fs, each carrying one GBU-28, dropped their bombs. The first bomb missed. The second hit the bunker's roof, burrowed deep inside the bunker and exploded. Debris shot out of the entrance to the bunker, evidence of an internal explosion. Unfortunately, though several of Saddam's top officers were killed in the raid, once again, Saddam was elsewhere.

At noon on 3 March, the armistice was signed, with Gen. Schwarzkopf and Lt.Gen. Khaled representing the forces of the Coalition. Lt.Gen. Sultan Hashim Ahmad, Chief of Staff of the Ministry of Defense and III Corps' commander, Lt.Gen. Salah Abbud Mahmud represented Iraq.

Schwarzkopf and Khaled found the Iraqis surprisingly compliant. They quickly agreed to repatriate all Allied prisoners of war. After much pressing by Khaled, they also made commitments which led to the return of some 6,500 Kuwaiti civilians who had been taken to Iraq during the occupation.* The Iraqis then handed over maps showing the locations of minefields they had laid during the war, both in Kuwait and in the waters off the coast.

Lulled into letting down his guard by Iraqi cooperation, Schwarzkopf made a concession that he would later regret. Hashim claimed that since so many bridges and roads had been destroyed, the Iraqi government would need to be allowed to fly helicopters so that they could ferry government officials around Iraq. Schwarzkopf told Hashim that he would instruct his forces not to fire upon any Iraqi helicopters, even military helicopters, flying over territory not occupied by Coalition forces. As to helicopters flying over Coalition units, Schwarzkopf said he would prefer that they not be gunships, but did not prohibit them. Thus, when uprisings took place in Basra and southern Iraq immediately after the armistice, the Iraqis took advantage of these concessions, using helicopter gunships to crush the rebellions. Coalition forces were ordered not to intervene.

The American nonintervention would later be rationalized with claims that having been "snookered" (as Schwarzkopf put it) into agreeing to the helicopter flights, American forces could not intervene. This is nonsense. Gen. Schwarzkopf agreed to allow the Iraqis to use helicopters to ferry officials, not conduct combat operations. In any case, U.N. Resolution 678 authorized the use of "all necessary means" to "restore international peace and security in the area." CENTCOM therefore would have been within its rights not only to shoot down Iraqi helicopter gunships, but to launch an attack on the Republican Guard during the uprisings. The United States did not take action because its government chose not to. The war was over and the Bush administration's first priority was bringing American forces home as quickly as possible. In addition, the idea of intervening in an internal struggle, the dynamics of which it did not fully understand, did not appeal to the administration. As a result, there was no intervention. The notion that the United States could not intervene because its hands had been tied by a tricky Iraqi negotiator is frankly a bit silly.

The end of the Gulf War left many with the impression of a job left unfinished. Saddam Hussein had started the war. He had been portrayed as a modern-day Hitler and

---

*Some 600 are still missing, and the Iraqi government has refused to account for them.

a threat to world peace. Now, Saddam was still in power, but Allied troops were going home. Why did the Coalition go to all of this trouble only to leave Saddam and his regime in place, especially when Coalition forces (in the form of the Daguet and the 82nd Airborne divisions) were within 100 miles of Baghdad?

"I suppose our campaigns are ended, but what an enormous difference a few more days would have made," one American general said. "Had they given us another week, we'd have taught them." These words were spoken not by any of CENTCOM's generals in reference to this armistice. The statement was made by Gen. John J. Pershing in 1918, immediately following the cessation of hostile action against the German Army in World War I. The end point of any war will always be a matter of controversy to some degree.

It is always possible for the victors to inflict more punishment on their foes. Wars end when the leaders of victorious powers decide that their ambitions have been satisfied to such an extent that they deem the continuation of military operations wasteful. The question is not: "Can we kill more of their soldiers?" The answer to that is always "yes." The real question is usually more like: "Since we have gotten 98% of what we wanted, can we justify the losses we would incur to get the remaining 2%?" If the answer to that question is "no," the winners usually stop attacking. It is a subjective call, so there is almost always controversy.

To a large extent, American political and military leaders became victims of their own success. The capture of Baghdad had never been a Coalition objective, but when the success of the ground war made Baghdad's seizure an attractive option, many Americans began to expect it. This is not a new phenomenon. During a war, popular definitions of success change.

In World War II, the United States' objective in Europe was the liberation of Western Europe from German forces and the overthrow of Hitler and his regime. Both of those objectives were satisfied, but some Americans never will be, because they feel that the U.S. Army should have gone on to attack the Soviet Army and drive it out of Eastern Europe, or at very least, Germany.

After North Korea attacked South Korea and pushed the remnants of the U.S. force stationed there into the tiny (roughly 1,200 square mile) "Pusan Perimeter" on the southern tip of the country, most Americans probably would have been satisfied with the restoration of South Korea's pre-war borders. When the counterattack planned and led by Gen. MacArthur caused the collapse of the North Korean Army, and American forces found themselves in control of most of North Korea, the American people adjusted their expectations upward. The Chinese Army counterattacked, and the war ultimately ended at more or less the original North Korea–South Korea border. Most Americans now consider that war a tie, although America's original objective (the restoration of South Korea's pre-war border) had been achieved.

When military analysts were predicting tens, or even hundreds of thousands of American casualties, most Americans would have been happy to see the Iraqi Army get out of Kuwait voluntarily, even if it meant that Saddam stayed in power and his army remained entirely intact. The Iraqi Army did not leave voluntarily, and was virtually destroyed as a fighting force. However, during its destruction, the American people had adjusted their expectations upward.

Not only was the capture of Baghdad (and the overthrow of Saddam) not a Coalition objective, it would have been relatively costly. Western nations prefer fighting on open ground, because the advantages of superior equipment, training and tactics are minimized in city fighting. For example, during the Six Day War in 1967, excluding the Battle for Jerusalem, the Israel Defense Forces inflicted about 15,000 battle deaths on the forces of Egypt, Syria and Jordan and lost 597 men in the process, a ratio of about 25 to 1. In the Battle for Jerusalem, the Israelis inflicted 330 battle deaths on the Jordanians and lost 179 men, about a 1.8 to 1 ratio.

There were four full brigades from the Republican Guard's Baghdad Division near Baghdad. There were also members of Saddam's internal security forces as well as several units of less elite but still reliable troops. Rooting these soldiers out would have been difficult. Baghdad's large civilian population made large scale use of air power impossible. Artillery was of limited value for the same reason. M-1A1s would have been too large to employ effectively, and their accurate, long range main guns would have been no advantage, since there are no long range shots in city fighting. They also would have been at risk. While nothing in the Iraqi arsenal could penetrate an Abrams from the front, an RPG-7 fired from a third story window could penetrate its thinner top armor.

Baghdad would have been taken, and the Iraqis would have lost many more men than the French or Americans, but it would have been a relatively expensive proposition. The battle would have involved a certain amount of street-to-street or house-to-house fighting by infantry, supported by light tanks. Since the Iraqis knew the city and the Americans did not, ambushes would have been likely. Snipers would have been a major problem.

Friendly fire and bad tactical decisions would also have taken their toll. Coalition soldiers were no longer fresh and well-rested. They were filthy and bone-tired. Unit commanders had gotten far less sleep than their men in the previous four days, and were far worse off. Their ability to plan, make complex judgment calls, or even think, had been seriously degraded.

Also, by the time the war ended, President Bush was receiving dire predictions that toppling Saddam would create a power vacuum in Iraq. According to some analysts, provinces with large Shi'ite populations would break off and join Iran (though Iraqi Shi'ites had never shown any yearning for life under the hard-line Iranian mullahs). In addition, the Kurds would try to form an independent state (as indeed they did), then try to take Kurdish provinces from Iran and Turkey (possible, but either the Iranian or the Turkish armies would have made short work of the lightly armed Kurds). Of course, in the provinces that remained, there would be chaos and starvation (speculation). It would have taken a president with far more knowledge about the Middle East to ignore nightmare scenarios from people with Ivy League Ph.D.s.

Of course, a question that could not be ignored was: "After we capture Baghdad, then what?" The problem with taking over countries is that the victors have to run them after they take them over. During World War II, the United States conquered Italy, Japan, and half of Germany. The United States then ended up footing much of the bill for the occupation and reconstruction of the lands it had just conquered. Today's military threat has a way of becoming tomorrow's economic burden. The fact that Saddam is still in power may be irritating to many Americans, but it is nowhere near as irritating as the tax bill for a large scale and prolonged occupation of Iraq might have been.

In any event, the Coalition did not have explicit authority to topple Saddam's regime. U.N. Resolution 660 had demanded the unconditional withdrawal of all Iraqi forces from Kuwait. U.N. Resolution 678 had given the Coalition the authority "to use all necessary means to uphold and implement resolution 660." The recapture of Kuwait completed the implementation of Resolution 660. Resolution 678 did authorize the use of "all necessary means" to "restore international peace and security in the area." However, many nations would have found the use of that language to justify storming Baghdad a stretch. There were no longer Iraqi forces in Kuwait. The job was finished as far as much (if not most) of the world was concerned. American forces could have driven onward, taken Baghdad and overthrown Saddam, but the move would have been controversial and some of the United States' wartime allies (and probably all of its Arab allies) would have refused to have any part of such an operation.

Saddam had been driven out of Kuwait and neutralized. The capture of Baghdad would have been overkill, and losses sustained in the process would have been difficult to justify. Saddam's army, once a major threat to the stability of the region, had been destroyed. Iraq had lost about 3,200 of an estimated force of 5,000 tanks (64%) in the Gulf War. In addition, about 2,000 of an estimated 3,900 BMP, MTLB and Type 63 (51%) armored personnel carriers had been destroyed.*† Iraq also lost about 2,700 of an estimated 4,150 guns and rocket launchers (65%). Finally, Iraq lost about 700 other armored vehicles such as armored scout cars or APCs rigged as command vehicles or used for other purposes, from a fleet of around 1,500 (47%). Most of the equipment that survived did so because it was never deployed. About 86% of the tanks, 92% of the APCs, 94% of the guns and 85% of the other armored vehicles deployed to the combat zone were lost.

The war had cost Iraq dearly. Between the damage done to Iraq by Coalition air power, and the damage done to Kuwait by Iraqi forces, the war left Iraq with at least $100 billion worth of damage to pay for.‡ Iraqi aggression also resulted in an embargo, which placed severe restrictions on Iraqi oil exports, a loss of some $15 billion per year. These costs came in addition to the money Iraq already owed creditors before the war.

Considering the amount of devastation meted out to the Iraqi war machine, losses among Iraqi combat soldiers were surprisingly low, probably around 14,000 killed and 20,000 wounded. There were two major reasons for this. First, there were nowhere near as many Iraqis in the combat zone as had been suspected. Second, the Coalition had shown great restraint in regard to killing.

During the Desert Shield deployments, Gen. Schwarzkopf had intimidated the Iraqis by showing the advanced parties of many divisions on television and allowing the Iraqis to assume that all of the divisions were at more or less full strength. Coalition planners fell victim to much the same tactic. CENTCOM calculated that there were 43 Iraqi divisions facing the Coalition. Therefore, since an Iraqi division was believed to contain about 12,500 men, Iraqi manpower strength should have amounted to some 540,000 troops. However, examination of captured documents and interrogations of captured senior Iraqi officers indicated that before the bombing began, Iraqi divisions

---

*Iraq had a few other types of armored personnel carriers (BTR-50s, BTR-60s, etc.), but they were used as reconnaissance/patrolling or command vehicles, field ambulances, or, in a few instances, were fitted with six 122mm rocket launch rails. Only BMPs, MTLBs and Type 63s were used as true APCs.

†About 185 BMPs, MTLBs and Type 63s were destroyed while serving as reconnaissance or command vehicles, field ambulances, or jerry-rigged rocket launchers. I have therefore included these vehicles in the "other armored vehicle" fleet for statistical purposes.

‡During the war, Iraq blew up 535 of Kuwait's 1,080 oil wells and disabled over 250.

had an average of about 5,300 men. As a result, though there turned out to be 45 Iraqi divisions in the Coalition attack zone, total Iraqi manpower strength there was probably around 240,000 at its height.

These divisions were depleted by desertions before the air war even began. Documents captured by U.S. Marines showed that before the bombing began, Iraqi soldiers enjoyed a fairly liberal leave policy, and that about 20% of the soldiers who went on leave never returned to their units. After the onset of the air war, the rate of desertion picked up. Around 82,000 Iraqis either failed to return from leave or drifted away before the start of the ground war.

Desertion was not punished nearly as severely as some analysts believed at the time. Executions were quite rare. When the order to execute deserters came down from the Revolutionary Command Council, most unit commanders ignored it. The few commanders who implemented the order took a minimalist approach. For instance, the commander of the 17th Armored Division held a public execution of a handful of deserters, which was witnessed by groups of soldiers from each of his subordinate units. Those were the only executions in that division during the war. In all likelihood, about 25 Iraqi soldiers were executed for desertion during the war.

It has become fashionable for analysts to talk about how "Desert Storm ultimately failed, because half of the Republican Guard got away," but this does not square with the facts.

The Tawakalna Mechanized Division had begun the war with an authorized strength of 224 tanks and 252 APCs. It actually had about 215 tanks and 235 APCs. The Medina and Hammurabi armored divisions had begun the war with about 300 tanks and 165 APCs each, out of their authorized strength of 312 tanks and 180 APCs.* Of the roughly 1,380 armored vehicles in these three divisions, only about 400 would be in service at the end of the war.

The U.S. Air Force's claim that over 200 of the Tawakalna Division's armored vehicles were destroyed during the air war proved extravagant. The division actually lost about 50 armored vehicles to air attacks. The rest were smashed by VII Corps. Not one Tawakalna armored vehicle survived the war. The division's artillery was also lost. Most of it was abandoned, and was captured and later destroyed.

The Medina Division only lost about 40 armored vehicles during the air war (though the Air Force claimed to have destroyed over 170), but was wiped out during the ground war. About half of the division's armored vehicles were sent to reinforce the Tawakalna Line, and were destroyed when it was overrun. The rest of the division's armor was destroyed by the 1st Armored Division at Medina Ridge. All of its artillery was lost, either destroyed during the fighting or abandoned, overrun and destroyed by 1st AD.

The Hammurabi Armored Division did escape the war in relatively good shape. It fared well during the air war, losing only about 25 armored vehicles (though the Air Force claimed to have destroyed over 130). Its good fortune continued through the ground war. As the Iraqis' theater reserve, the division was posted about 30 miles

---

*Republican Guard armored battalions had an authorized strength of 44 tanks. There were seven battalions (308 tanks), in an armored division or five battalions (220 tanks) in a mechanized division. The three brigade commanders and the division commander were each authorized their own tanks.

southwest of Basra. There were about 180 miles and several Iraqi divisions between VII Corps and the Hammurabi Division. It is far easier to travel 30 unobstructed miles than it is to fight through 180 miles, so once the Hammurabi Division was ordered to head for Basra, VII Corps was not going to catch it no matter how hard Lt.Gen. Franks drove his men. The division retreated to the Basra Pocket in reasonably good order. There, it sustained two massive artillery barrages, one from the 24th ID and one from the 1st AD. The barrages claimed much of the division's artillery, several of its APCs and a few of its tanks. Then, it attempted to sneak past the 24th ID after the cease-fire. The attempt ended in the destruction of 67 of its armored vehicles. The Hammurabi Division thus ended the war with roughly 365 of its original 465 armored vehicles and about 60 of its 108 assigned artillery pieces.

There were about 300 more armored vehicles in Iraq's four motorized Republican Guard divisions. With only 45 authorized tanks (41 or 42 actual), and a battalion (36 authorized, 33 actual, on average) of APCs and 66 artillery pieces each, these divisions were not priority targets.* These truck-borne divisions were therefore untouched by Allied air power. The 7th (Adnan), 4th (al-Fao) and 6th (Nebuchadnezzar) Motorized divisions had most of their armor and artillery pieces surprised and destroyed during the 24th ID's dash to Basra. The 24th ID destroyed or captured all of the tanks and APCs in these three divisions, with the exception of about a dozen that were destroyed by 1st AD and about 20 which retreated to Basra. The 5th (Baghdad) Motorized Division lost none of its armor because none of its armor had deployed to the combat zone. In total, the motorized divisions of the Republican Guard had lost about 210 of their 300 armored vehicles. The 8th (Special Forces) Division had no armor, so it did not lose any, but it lost virtually all of its 66 guns.

The Republican Guard was stripped of almost 70% of its armor and 79% of its artillery pieces. About 73% of the Republican Guard armored vehicles and 88% of the artillery pieces in the path of Coalition forces on G-Day were destroyed. In addition, the 1st Armored Division overran and destroyed stockpiles containing enough ammunition and supplies for two divisions. The 24th Infantry Division destroyed 4½ divisions' worth of supplies. Though after the war, Iraq would be able to scratch together enough equipment to rebuild the Republican Guard, the fact remains that the Republican Guard was severely mauled during the Gulf War.

The Republican Guard reorganized after the war. It had to. With the regular armored force a shadow of its former self, more of the burden of Iraq's defense fell on the Republican Guard. The regular armored force had been the backbone of the army. The Republican Guard's three heavy divisions had been used to stiffen that backbone. Before the war, the regular army's heavy units added up to the equivalent of about eleven divisions (six armored and three mechanized divisions plus a few independent armored brigades). However, the regular army had seen all six armored divisions, all three mechanized divisions and two armored brigades annihilated. By disbanding the independent brigades, stripping light infantry divisions of their tanks and virtually emptying the reserve stocks, the regular army was able to reconstitute three armored and three mechanized divisions.

---

*Each division's tank battalion had an authorized strength of 44 tanks. The division commander was authorized his own tank.

There had been 815 T-72 tanks in the three pre-war Republican Guard heavy divisions, but Iraq had finished the war with about 650 T-72s in the entire inventory. This was not enough to equip three heavy divisions. As of 1999, the Republican Guard had two (Medina and Hammurabi) armored divisions. The Medina Division had an extra armored brigade. The mechanized Tawakalna Division no longer existed. Thus, between the surviving Hammurabi tanks and those that came from emptying the reserve stocks of T-72s, the Republican Guard heavy establishment was reconstituted with seven heavy (5 armored, 2 mechanized) brigades instead of the nine (5 armored, 4 mechanized) it had before the war. In addition, the 17 modern armored battalions (there were 19 before the war) have an authorized strength of 35 tanks, whereas pre-war Republican Guard armored battalions in the heavy units had an authorized strength of 44 tanks.

There had been 565 BMPs in the 17 mechanized battalions of the three pre-war heavy divisions. As of 1999, there were about 800 in the entire Iraqi inventory, and about 360 of those were in regular army heavy units. Though there were far fewer BMPs available, there were six fewer mechanized battalions in the Republican Guard's heavy establishment. There are now 11 mechanized battalions in the Guard's two remaining heavy divisions, with a total of about 400 BMPs.

Plans to expand the Guard to a force of 13 divisions have been scrapped. The Special Forces Division is gone, although there is a division-sized security force known as the "Special Republican Guard." Within that force are two battalions of T-72 tanks. There are still four motorized divisions, though the Baghdad Division now has three brigades instead of four. Due to the need to provide T-72s to the Guard's remaining heavy units, these divisions no longer have organic tank battalions.

To sum it all up, as of 1999 the Republican Guard had rebounded to about 59% of its pre-war tank strength and 51% of its pre-war BMP strength.

Though he would undoubtedly find it scant consolation, the war ironically solved one of Saddam's pre-war problems. The Iraqi Army had been swollen with units which had to be paid and fed, but were unlikely (as they would subsequently prove) to be of much use in combat. There were nearly four light divisions for each Republican Guard or regular army heavy division. Stocked largely with battle-weary veterans, older men, teenagers, and members of unreliable ethnic groups, they were little more than a drain on the treasury and the military establishment. However, a poor economy had made it virtually impossible for Saddam to demobilize any significant number of these units before the war. The beating inflicted on the Iraqi Army and economy during the Gulf War resulted in a vastly streamlined army. On G-Day, there were 45 (40 regular army, 5 Republican Guard) truck-borne or foot-propelled infantry divisions in the Iraqi order of battle. As of 1999, there were 15 such divisions (11 regular army, 4 Republican Guard). With 30 fewer light divisions to stock, Iraq is no longer forced to rely so heavily on politically unreliable soldiers. As of 1999, Kurds were exempt from military service, as were most Shi'ites.

26

Where Were The Terror Weapons?

A great deal of pre-war hype was centered around Saddam's chemical warfare capability. There are a few basic types of war chemicals. These are grouped based on their function (nerve, blood, blister, vomiting, choking, etc.). There are a few varieties of each type. Some of the varieties evaporate shortly after they are delivered, and are referred to as "nonpersistent" agents. Others are persistent, lingering for days or weeks. Some are lethal, others are not. For every agent there are countermeasures.

Iraq's nerve agents caused the most concern. Some nerve agents are more potent than others, but they all work the same way. The human body produces a chemical called acetylcholine, which causes the natural contraction of muscles within the body. Cholinesterase, also produced by the body, breaks down acetylcholine, regulating its function so that muscles contract only as much and as often as they need to. Nerve agents interfere with the actions of cholinesterase, allowing acetylcholine to build up in the body. When this happens, muscle contraction is not controlled, and muscles go into spasms. If the imbalance between the two chemicals is severe enough, death can result.

There are two basic kinds of nerve agents. "G" agents are nonpersistent. They evaporate quickly, and unless they are delivered in high concentrations, they usually produce casualties only if they are inhaled. "V" agents are persistent. They are delivered as a thick liquid mist (globules, actually), and can be absorbed through exposed skin. Iraq did not have significant quantities of V agents, although it did have about 100 tons of Sarin, a G agent. The United States had large stocks of V agents.

Antidotes to nerve agents were carried by Coalition soldiers in the form of a drug called atropine in a spring-loaded injector. Each soldier carried three injectors. An affected soldier would put the tip of the device on a large muscle, preferably the thigh, and press a button at the top. A needle would then penetrate whatever clothing the soldier was wearing, and inject the drug. Atropine blocks the nerve receptors on the muscles that respond to acetylcholine. In essence, the high concentrations of acetylcholine would try to command the muscles to spasm, but the muscles would be unable to receive the command. Atropine also causes the heart to beat faster and the veins to narrow. The heart therefore pumps blood faster and the blood travels through the veins faster. Thus, the nerve agent is sent through the kidneys and out of the body quickly, limiting the amount of damage it can do. The affected soldier would end up dehydrated, but alive.

Many units also had their soldiers take "oxime pills" in the days preceding the ground war. These tablets assist atropine if its use becomes necessary, but they also have side effects like lethargy, disorientation and diarrhea in some soldiers. During the final days, some commanders, especially in the far west, began to doubt that they would face a serious chemical threat, and discontinued the practice.

Blood agents are inhaled by their victims. They enter the blood stream and make it difficult or impossible for hemoglobin in cells to absorb oxygen. If inhaled in sufficient concentration, a victim can suffocate in 15 minutes.

Blood agents are easier to defend against than almost any other type of chemical agent. They cannot be absorbed through the skin, so masked soldiers are not really in danger. They are delivered in aerosol form, so they evaporate almost instantly. They are lighter than air, so as soon as they hit, the agent rises into the atmosphere.

The Iraqi Army had never shown a real commitment to blood agents, which are almost useless as killing agents. It takes 70–140 times as much blood agent as nerve agent to produce the same effect. If the Iraqi Army wanted to use a non-persistent killing agent, it could just use a G-series nerve agent, which is 70 times more potent than hydrogen cyanide, the most potent blood agent.[*]

As their name implies, blister agents cause large blisters to form on exposed areas of the body. They destroy tissue and leave permanent scarring. If inhaled, they cause extensive irritation and scarring of the lungs and windpipe. Mustard gas (dichloroethylsulphide) is the most well known of these agents. The term is inaccurate, since all blister agents are liquid mists, not gas. Mustard got a sinister reputation during the early stages of the First World War as a killing agent. Soldiers were not equipped with masks at that time, so most soldiers who were hit with mustard inhaled a lethal, or at least serious, dose. Now, Western soldiers are trained to put on masks the second that a chemical attack is suspected. Mustard and other types of blister agents are therefore more harassment than killing agents.

Even huge quantities of blister agent would have done little damage to soldiers of the Coalition. Blister agents work best in areas of lush vegetation. Soldiers walk through the vegetation, get the blister agent on them, and break out in blisters hours later. Needless to say, there was little vegetation in the desert. Blister agents also work best in high humidity. The desert is not such a place.

Vomiting agents were originally developed for use in riot control, but they can be used to harass enemy soldiers, causing them to vomit for several minutes to a few hours. Strong enough concentrations can kill. Though there is no record of it actually

---

[*]Blood agents do have one effective military use. They clog respirator filters (in about 10 minutes in a heavy gassing), so they can be used to make chemical protective masks unserviceable in preparation for attacks with more lethal agents. Even that function requires large quantities, however.

having been employed, Soviet doctrine envisioned the use of vomiting agent in house-to-house fighting. The idea was to lob a canister of vomiting agent (preferably Adamsite, which has an immediate effect if inhaled) into a room or bunker, then shoot the occupant when he ran out vomiting all over himself. Vomiting agents can also be mixed with conventional shells at the beginning of a surprise chemical attack. A soldier who is vomiting will find it impossible to wear his protective mask. This would make him more likely to inhale the more deadly agents that follow. Mixing agents in this fashion is commonly referred to as "chemical cocktailing."

Most of the men who were killed by gas during World War I choked to death. One choking agent, Phosgene, accounted for over two-thirds of the gas casualties sustained during that war. However, for all intents and purposes, choking agents are now obsolete. Their instability in storage is the main reason that these agents are no longer a viable weapon. Phosgene, for instance, must be refrigerated while it is being loaded into shells. Choking agents also have a telltale odor of freshly mown hay, so soldiers have ample warning and time to put their masks on before they have inhaled enough gas to do significant damage.

Before the war, Western intelligence services estimated that Iraq's war chemical stockpile was about 3,000 tons. This was a wild exaggeration, but Iraq did have a fairly large stockpile of chemical weapons for a Third World country. After the war, U.N. inspection teams found 1,000 tons of war chemicals, 46,000 filled, and 79,000 unfilled chemical bombs and shells in Iraq. The use of these chemical agents by Iraq might have ended in war crimes trials for those responsible, but there are many practical reasons why the Iraqis did not employ chemical weapons.

The use of chemical weapons would have been tremendously risky for the Iraqis. The Geneva Protocol of 1925 prohibited the use of poisonous gases in warfare. However, the United States did not ratify the agreement until 1975, and did so only with the understanding that a violation of the Protocol by an enemy nation would relieve the United States of any obligations under the Protocol. In other words, the United States reserves the right to hit back with whatever chemical weapon it chooses to employ, in whatever quantity, if an enemy uses chemical weapons first. The mathematics of a chemical exchange could not have been appealing to the Revolutionary Command Council. Iraq's 1,000 ton stock of war chemicals was dwarfed by the United States' 30,000 tons (by conservative estimate) of far more lethal agents.

Had people known how difficult it is to conduct chemical warfare effectively, they would have been far less worried about chemical weapons. They are so difficult to employ effectively that they usually are not worth the trouble. If chemical weapons were a magical key to success on the battlefield, everyone would be using them. The fact is, chemical weapons are of limited military value. Iraq's use of chemical weapons during the war with Iran had availed her little.[*] Only about 5%–8% of the 45,000 Iranian

---

[*]There were also bad experiences. For instance, in 1983 the Iraqis tried to use mustard agent to dislodge Iranian troops from a mountain top in preparation for an infantry assault. Since the agent was heavier than air, it rolled back down the mountain and into the faces of the Iraqi attackers, who ran for their lives. The assault failed.

soldiers who suffered the effects of chemical agents were killed or seriously wounded.[*] The Iraqi Army could have realized a much greater return had it relied totally on conventional artillery rounds.

Even against unprepared civilians the impact of Iraq's chemical weapons was marginal. The world was horrified to see footage of the dead bodies of the gassed Kurdish residents of the town of Halabja. However, according to the highest estimates, three days of gassing left no more than 5,000 dead out of the town's total population of 45,000.

Iraq's experience was not unique. During World War I, when gas warfare was used extensively, only 2% of American and just over 4% of British and French gas casualties died. Even gas casualties in the woefully unprepared and backward Imperial Russian Army experienced only an 11.8% fatality rate.[†] By contrast, over 25% of World War I soldiers hit by bullets or shrapnel died. Gas wounds were also far less debilitating. Wounds from shell fragments were about six times more likely than gas wounds to send a man home disabled. Of the Americans who sustained nonfatal gas wounds during the war, about 96% were able to return to duty.

That was when chemical warfare was novel. There is now very little mystery left in chemical warfare. There are only a few real war chemicals, and enough is known about them to render them almost useless with a few precautions. Chemical weapons are therefore not very effective against prepared troops, and the troops of the Coalition were prepared. Allied units carried monitoring equipment which would have warned of the presence of such agents long before they became a danger. Coalition tank crews would hardly have been inconvenienced. With hatches closed, air pressure inside modern tanks is kept so high that chemicals from outside are unable to push their way in. This allows the vehicles' occupants to fight without masks or suits in a chemical environment.[‡] Coalition soldiers without the protection of armored vehicles still had protective masks and suits. There were also effective medical treatments for any Coalition soldier who might have been affected by chemical agents.

Chemical weapons have a considerable number of limitations. For instance, chemical weapons must be delivered in almost perfect weather conditions to have a significant impact. Uncooperative weather has plagued users of chemical weapons from the beginning. The first combat employment of chemical weapons took place on 3 January 1915, and was a complete failure due to unfavorable weather conditions. At the Battle of Bolimow, the German Army fired about 18,000 shells filled with xylyl bromide (a tear gas) at Russian soldiers in defensive positions. In below-zero temperatures, the xylyl bromide would not vaporize, so the shells had virtually no effect. The attack had so little impact that the Russians did not even bother to report it to their Western Allies.

Conditions in the Gulf War were far from perfect for chemical warfare. When the ground war kicked off, winds were high and unpredictable. It is almost impossible to

---

[*]There would have been even fewer casualties and fatalities if more Iranians had been equipped with protective masks. In addition, many Iranians with masks refused to shave their beards for religious reasons. Beards do not allow a mask to seal out chemicals properly.

[†]The Russians, virtually defenseless against chemical weapons, sustained over 60% of the war's gas casualties. Gas was far less effective against better-equipped French, British or American soldiers.

[‡]Coalition tankmen nevertheless wore suits and carried masks as a precaution.

employ chemical weapons effectively under those conditions. High winds cause chemical weapons to dissipate too quickly to have the desired effect. Unpredictable winds raise the possibility that chemicals can blow back into the faces of the user's own soldiers. Many senior Iraqi officers stated in prisoner interrogations that they had no intention of using chemical weapons because of their unpredictability.

In addition, unlike conventional artillery rounds, chemical rounds are designed to produce small, concentrated bursts. Muffled pops (instead of loud explosions) are a telltale sign of incoming chemical rounds. In order to disguise the fact that chemical rounds are being delivered, artillerymen must mix in plenty of high explosive shells to drown out the pops. That cuts down the number of chemical rounds that can be delivered on a target in a single barrage.

It also takes a lot of chemicals to have a real impact on the enemy. It always has, even when chemical weapons were novel. On 17 January 1917, Germany used mustard gas for the first time. Roughly 50 tons of the agent killed only 87 British soldiers. Over the next three weeks, about a thousand more tons were dropped on the British, killing about 500 more soldiers. Thus, it took about 1.8 tons of mustard in 1,800 shells, to kill each British soldier. As wasteful as this sounds, by chemical warfare standards, it was a fairly positive result. Effectiveness dropped off sharply later on. On 9 April 1918, 2,000 tons of mustard, phosgene and diphenchlorasine killed only 30 British soldiers. Eleven days later, 2,000 more tons of the same agents killed 43. In these two raids, it took an average of 55½ tons of chemicals to kill each soldier.

Modern chemicals are more potent, but they still do not give users much of a return on their investment. Under prevailing conditions in the desert it would have taken about 12 tons of Sarin, the most powerful nerve agent Iraq had in significant quantities, to have a serious impact on just one American battalion. The 122mm shells fired by most of the artillery units of the Saddam Line could have held just under 3 lbs. of Sarin each. Significant numbers of shells (around 8,400) would have been required to deliver those 12 tons.

This does not mean that if the shells had been available, a hundred guns could have fired 84 rounds each (roughly a half-hour's work) to produce an effective chemical strike. Setting aside Allied artillery-spotting technologies and counterbattery capabilities (a point to which I will return), such an operation would not have produced a worthwhile result. After the first few volleys of a conventional artillery barrage, the amount of damage produced by each additional volley drops off sharply, as the targeted soldiers take cover and become more difficult to hit. In a chemical strike, after the first few volleys, the value of additional volleys drops to almost nothing. After a minute or so of firing (after each gun has fired 3–4 rounds), the targeted soldiers have either gotten their chemical-protective gear on, or they have not. Those who have are probably not going to die. Those who have not are probably going to die. Either way, firing additional chemical rounds will be a waste of time, effort and shells. Effective chemical barrages therefore require that massive numbers of shells be delivered within a very short span. In other words, for the Iraqis, it was not a matter of sneaking a few hundred guns within striking distance of Coalition forces, but a few thousand, an impossibility.

It would have been foolish for Iraq to start a chemical exchange. The chemicals Iraq had were not particularly potent by Western standards. Most of the war chemicals that the Iraqis had were harassing, not killing, agents. Iraq had nerve agents and a small stock of blood agents, but blister agents made up the majority of the stocks. Most of the blister agent in Iraq's arsen̲al̲ was Levinstein mustard, the same type of mustard that was used in World War I.* T̲here̲ were more serious blister agents, but Iraq had insignificant quantities of them.

The Iraqi army also had insignificant numbers of filled chemical shells. First generation chemical weapons are a storage nightmare. Many agents are highly corrosive. After a while, the contents begin to "weep" through the shell. The rounds then become dangerous to handle. The United Nations monitoring teams detailed to destroy stocks of Iraqi chemical weapons found that many of the stocks were contaminated because of leakage. Since storing large quantities at unit-level was impractical and potentially deadly, relatively few rounds were stored at unit-level. The Iraqi Army planned to fill chemical shells in well-guarded facilities as they were needed. This is why the UN found 79,000 unfilled chemical munitions in Iraq after the war. When coalition air power destroyed the facilities, the Iraqi Army's ability to fill shells was seriously compromised.

There are also potency problems with "unitary" warheads like those in the Iraqi stockpile. Unitary chemical shells contain the agent in its final, poisonous form. Such munitions, especially those containing nerve agent, have an extremely limited storage life. After about six weeks the agent loses much of its potency. When the ground war began, the most recently filled Iraqi chemical rounds had been sitting for almost two months.

A few years before the war, the United States developed a second generation of chemical weapons, called "binary" chemical munitions. Two chemical agents are held in different compartments within each munition. The two chemicals mix after it is fired (or dropped, in the case of bombs) to form a poisonous agent. Since each compartment holds relatively harmless chemicals, these rounds never become a safety problem. In addition, since the chemical agent is produced only seconds before the impact of the munition, loss of potency is not a worry. As a result, Western armies can fill as many bombs and shells as they want with chemical agents and store them at unit-level if they need to. Iraq could not.

It would have been almost physically impossible for the Iraqis to deliver chemical munitions on Coalition troops even if they had been available at unit-level. The ability to launch effective chemical strikes is tied directly to the abilities of the delivery systems. The most effective method of delivering chemical agents is from the air, by spraying. Aerial spraying was out of the question for the Iraqis since Iraqi planes could not fly without being shot down. Chemical bombs were out of the question for the same reason. Scud missiles could not deliver a militarily significant payload of chemicals.†

Artillery and multiple rocket launchers were the next best way to deliver chemical agents, but Coalition air power and counterbattery fire foreclosed this option as well. When using artillery to deliver them, agents can only be delivered as far as the launching system in question can hurl them. If the Iraqis had used chemical agents, they would have had to rely on their standard 122mm piece with its range of just over 9½ miles. Getting within 9½ miles of Coalition lines would have been suicidal and almost impossible in the face of the most powerful air armada in history. Iraq's multiple rocket launchers could have delivered chemical agents, but they were inaccurate, had short

---

*Levinstein mustard is named after the man who invented the process by which it was first produced.

†An al-Hussein could carry about 620 lbs. of Sarin. The UN found 28 filled Sarin warheads after the war.

ranges (about 10 miles), and were in short supply. Even if the Iraqis could have gotten significant numbers of guns and launchers to within 10 miles of the breach, they could not have delivered a militarily significant number of chemical shells when Coalition counterbattery fire could have located and destroyed their artillery after just one or two salvos. Finally, many of the guns or rocket launchers that could have delivered chemical munitions had been destroyed or abandoned by the time the ground offensive began.

The United States, on the other hand, had a variety of ways to deliver chemicals. A single aircraft can lay a carpet of 1,300 lbs. of VX, which is twice as deadly as Sarin, crop-duster style. Three volleys from an MLRS battery can deliver more than 13 tons of VX. No one in the Iraqi government was prepared to ignore the possibility of chemical or even nuclear retaliation by the United States.

Iraq's soldiers were not equipped to deal with American chemical retaliation. They were particularly vulnerable to nerve agents, because the Iraqi Army was desperately short on nerve agent antidote. Before the war, when Iraq was still on friendly terms with the United States, the Iraqi government attempted to purchase 1.5 million atropine injectors from an American company. An official at the Defense Department, whose job it was to review foreign sales of items with potential military applications, denied the company permission to make the deal.

The majority of the Iraqi soldiers in Kuwait and southern Iraq did not even have masks. Against soldiers without masks, even non-lethal gases would have been tremendously effective. The retaliatory employment of vomiting agents or even tear gas could have caused significant problems for Iraqi field units.

When the subject of biological warfare comes up, many people get the mental image of something like the Andromeda Strain. As usual, fiction was a lot scarier than fact. First, the use of biological weapons on the battlefield is not particularly practical. Chemicals and artillery are more predictable in their effects. The attacker employing chemicals or artillery has some idea how many casualties will be inflicted. One using biological agents can never predict how many enemy soldiers will be infected. Chemicals and artillery are also more immediate in their effects. Biological agents are a long term proposition, designed for use against civilian populations. Long incubation periods maximize an agent's destructive potential. A really effective biological weapon strike would depend on people getting infected, not knowing it for a certain period of time, and spreading the disease to other people. The longer the incubation period of the disease in question, the more people could be infected before the initial victims started developing symptoms and the target country realized that it had a problem on its hands. Those calculations might be valid for planning a strike on a civilian target, but no attacker wants to employ a weapon on a battlefield and wait a week for it to start working.

There are basically three classes of biological warfare agents: micro-organisms (which are living organisms), toxins (which are essentially nonliving poisons), and viruses (which are somewhere in between). Their characteristics define their strengths and weaknesses.

Living biological agents are similar to chemical agents in that it would take a large quantity of them to do any appreciable damage to an enemy unit. As with chemical weapons, a significant portion of the agent's total volume would never reach the enemy. Chemicals dissipate or degrade. Micro-organisms die. Iraq had only one live agent sturdy enough to survive the delivery process: anthrax spores. Anthrax spores can be deadly if even a small number are inhaled. Anthrax is an ugly weapon because anthrax spores can be carried by the wind over a large area and can survive in soil for a long time. Territory infected by anthrax would remain contaminated literally for generations, so using it on your own soil is not a realistic option. Using it on someone else's territory would not be much smarter. Though every major participant on both sides produced it during World War II and developed contingency plans for its use, it was never employed. Some violations of the laws of war are more serious than others. It is universally understood that a nation which introduces anthrax onto the territory of another nation can expect no mercy. In any case, most or all of Iraq's anthrax production facilities were destroyed by bombing.

After the war, when Saddam's son-in-law defected, he revealed that during the war, Iraq had stocks of biological warfare toxins. Toxins are poisons produced by living organisms (venom is a toxin). Since toxins are not living, the illnesses they produce are not contagious. Nevertheless, some can be lethal. One of Iraq's toxins was a myco(meaning from a fungus)toxin called T-2, better known as "Yellow Rain."

The last deliberate use of a virus in war was in 1763, when a British general gave a peace offering of blankets to an American Indian tribe with which he had been fighting. The blankets were infected with the smallpox virus and the recipient tribe was virtually wiped out. Since then, viruses have not been employed for the same reason that anthrax has not been employed. A nation caught using one in warfare could expect no mercy.

Coalition troops would have been relatively well-protected had Iraq used biological weapons. A protective mask and suit will keep out virtually all spores or toxins. Furthermore, effective treatment and decontamination procedures had been developed.

The Iraqi Army, on the other hand, was in too vulnerable a position to have seriously considered exchanging biological warfare strikes with the Coalition. While the Allies lived largely on sealed, prepackaged combat meals, the Iraqi Army lived largely on animals. One of the primary ways in which a biological agent enters the body is through the consumption of infected animals. In addition, unlike the Coalition, the Iraqi Army did not have the medical wherewithal to stop an epidemic. There were already overwhelming hygiene problems in the Iraqi front lines. The retaliatory introduction of even a relatively mild biological agent by the Allies would have been catastrophic for the Iraqi Army.

As with chemical weapons, Iraq was not prepared to risk Coalition retaliation. Iraq would undoubtedly have gotten the worst of a biological exchange and Iraq's military leadership knew it. The United States stopped producing biological weapons in the 1970s and has agreed not to employ them. The United States probably would not have resorted to the use of biological weapons even if the Iraqis had used them, but the Iraqis had no way to be sure about that. As was the case with chemical agents, while Iraqi agents could have been delivered in insignificant amounts, by artillery rounds, the United States could have delivered (if it chose to resume manufacture of them) tons of biological agents over a wide area by aerial spraying. And, of course, there was always the possibility that an Iraqi biological attack might bring an American nuclear response.

Artillery is scary. An exploding shell sends out thousands of fragments at speeds of anywhere from 1,600 to 5,500 feet per second, and artillery has accounted for the majority of casualties in each of the two world wars. So, many were haunted by the prospect of Iraqi artillery slaughtering American soldiers picking their way through the Saddam Line, but the slaughter never materialized.

Iraq's artillery corps had been one of the few bright spots in an otherwise lackluster effort against Iran, but the success of Iraqi artillery was deceptive. Iraqi artillery and artillery tactics were relatively primitive, but since Iran possessed no real counterbattery threat, they were effective.

Almost any Iraqi ground activity during the Iran–Iraq War was preceded by an intense artillery barrage, usually lasting between 30 minutes and an hour. Iraqi artillery doctrine placed more emphasis on massed fire than on accuracy. Iraqi guns did not attack pinpoint targets, they saturated areas. Their relatively light 122mm standard artillery gave them the advantage of a relatively high rate of fire, since smaller shells are easier to load, but in the Gulf War Iraqi artillery could not sustain fire. Iraqi batteries which opened fire were usually punished immediately by Allied counterbattery fire. The lives of Iraqi gun crews in action were measured in minutes rather than hours or days. Under such conditions, many Iraqi artillerymen decided that discretion was the better part of valor and stopped firing altogether. Many ran. There were significant rates of desertion among artillerymen. Allied air attacks had also destroyed large stocks of artillery ammunition in Kuwait. Iraq's front line forces were left with few rounds to fire, few serviceable artillery pieces with which to fire them, and few artillerymen to man the serviceable guns. Coalition forces also advanced quickly, never stopping long enough to become artillery targets.

Before the war, there was concern in the West about Iraq's long range guns. Iraq had purchased over a hundred G-5 155mm field guns from South Africa, and another hundred or so Austrian GH N-45s, each with a maximum range of 24 miles. The ammunition for these guns was state-of-the-art. The revolutionary ERFB (Extended Range Full Bore) round travels some 15%–20% farther than standard 155mm rounds, with almost no reduction in accuracy.

A standard shell is the same diameter through most of its length, with only a small tapering section at the front of the round. This shape allows the round to fit snugly in the gun barrel, but does not allow it to travel through the air very efficiently. ERFB rounds, on the other hand, were designed with aerodynamics in mind. The ERFB round is longer, and tapers almost from base to nose. Fitting the round in the gun barrel was a secondary consideration, achieved by adding four short nubs made of softer metal to the front of the round. The nubs, which are spaced to fit into the rifling of the gun barrel, hold the round in place as it goes down the barrel.

When an artillery round flies through the air, it creates a backwash of air behind it. That backwash creates a slight vacuum at the back end of the round. The vacuum, known as "base drag," slows the round down and limits the shell's range. The ERFB round has a hollow, tapered, aluminum cap screwed onto the back of each round before firing to give it more of a boat shape. This cuts down on base drag, but does not eliminate it completely.

A "base bleed" round virtually eliminates base drag. It has a small gas generator in the aluminum cap, which sends enough flammable gas into the shell's wake to eliminate the vacuum, but not enough to affect the path of the round the way a rocket booster would. Combining the aerodynamic shell design with the gas generator resulted in the ERFB-BB round, which carries about five miles farther than standard shells.

There is nothing mystical about these rounds. The United States was developing them at the time of the Gulf War, but it was not a priority program. These rounds are expensive. Because of the expense, the U.S. Army relied on more conventional designs for the bulk of its inventory. There was no pressing need to spend the extra money for the extra range. If a target was past the range of conventional shells, and was too small to be engaged effectively by longer range but less accurate Rocket Assisted Projectiles, the Army could send Apaches after it.

The G-5s that Iraq had were not the same systems that South Africa has. South Africa wanted a weapon that had both range and accuracy. To ensure accuracy, South African G-5s have their own muzzle velocity analyzers and a computerized fire control system. These are not unnecessary extras, they are vital components. Every gun performs a little differently, and the analyzer and computer measure the differences and compensate. South African G-5s even have their own meteorological station to measure such things as air moisture. The Iraqi Army could not afford these components, and probably would not have been able to use them effectively if it had them.

The G-5 batteries also had the same problem the rest of Iraq's artillery had. They were operating without spotters, essentially firing blind. Artillery is useless if it cannot be delivered accurately and effectively under combat conditions.

The G-5 was also not the standard Iraqi field gun. Iraqi long range guns were few in number. The 122mm was Iraq's main artillery piece. The 155mm guns of the Coalition fired shells about 2½ times as powerful as those fired by the Iraqi 122mm pieces.* They also fired them much more accurately and twice as far.†

The timing of the war was fortuitous for Allied soldiers. Iraq invaded Kuwait before the completion of three artillery projects which could have made life more difficult for Coalition forces.

Dr. Gerald Bull, the renegade Canadian scientist who had been instrumental in developing the technology which led to the G-5, had been working with the Iraqis on a project code named "Babylon." Babylon involved the design of super guns capable of firing shells over 100 miles. Four guns (two of 1,000mm and two of 350mm) had reportedly been planned. Bull had been assassinated, but work on the project continued after his death.‡ The project ended with the post-war dismantling of the unfinished components of the gun under U.N. supervision.

Iraq had a relatively high number of artillery pieces for a Third World army. The lower grade units on the Saddam Line generally had 54 towed 122mm guns each. Regular army heavy units typically had 12 self-propelled (usually 122mm) guns, 18

---

*A 155mm shell contains about twice as much explosive as a 122mm shell. In addition, the explosive inside American shells was Composition B, which was about 33% more explosive than the TNT in Iraqi shells.

†Before the war, a magazine "revealed" that Iraqi G-5s could fire shells more than twice as far as the M-114, their "American counterpart." In fact, the M-114 was first produced in 1939, has a range of just over 9 miles and has not seen service in the Army for years. It has been replaced by the 155mm self-propelled howitzer, which has a range of almost 19 miles.

‡Many suspect Israel's Mossad of carrying out the assassination, although nothing has been proven.

multiple rocket launchers, 18 heavy (130mm, 152mm or 155mm) towed guns and 18 towed 122mm guns each. Each motorized Republican Guard division had 12 multiple rocket launchers, 18 heavy and 36 122mm towed pieces. There was no typical Republican Guard heavy division. The three divisions differed widely in terms of organic artillery, though each division had 84–90 artillery pieces and most were heavy guns. Regular and Guard divisions in critical sectors were also reinforced by corps-controlled artillery units. This brought the artillery complements of some of these divisions to over 100 pieces. Things could have been worse. Saddam had planned to purchase enough guns to equip all of his divisions with 144 guns each. This would have been the largest division-level artillery element in the world.

Not only was Saddam planning to purchase new guns, he was preparing to upgrade the ones he already had. His inventory of roughly 400 Soviet-built 130mm guns was to be upgraded to 155mm using a Yugoslav conversion kit. This would have allowed these guns to fire the same high-tech ammunition as his South African G-5 and Austrian GH N-45 field guns. This would have roughly tripled Saddam's complement of long range guns had the war not intervened.

27

Our Equipment Worked. Theirs Blew Up. Why Were We Surprised?

The First Amendment to the U.S. Constitution guarantees that the press will be free. There is no constitutional requirement for it to be accurate. Much of the public worry which preceded the Gulf War was a result of two factors: reporters in the United States did not always ask the right questions about our equipment, and they did not ask any questions at all about the equipment the Iraqis were using.

During the war, the Apache showed that it could withstand a remarkable amount of punishment. On several occasions, Apaches were badly damaged but were able to return to base. In one case, a gunship took two 57mm anti-aircraft rounds through the engine, and had a fist-sized hole in the fuselage, but made it back to base. That particular Apache was repaired, and later returned to action.

Before the war, much was made of Iraq's long range artillery. However, while the South African-built G-5 outranged American guns, it could not outrange Apaches, which the Army used as long range artillery. In the Apache, the Allies had aerial artillery that was both devastating and highly mobile. Apaches could deliver barrages accurately and instantly, day or night, since the Apache is fully equipped with night vision devices. Each gunship mounted a 30mm rapid fire chain-gun, capable of firing as many as 625 rounds per minute. If configured with rocket pods, it could put seventy-six 2.75-inch rockets on a target in a matter of seconds, with the effect of an instant and accurate mortar barrage. Of course, no artillery could match the Apache (when equipped with guided anti-tank missiles) in terms of armor killing capability.

The public now knows of the Apache's stellar performance during the Gulf War. Apaches were combat-ready 86% of the time during Desert Shield and Desert Storm, even though they were being maintained in the open desert without the benefit of hangars and machine shops. Before the war, however, there had been some concern about the Apache. Most of this concern stemmed from a particularly alarming "60 Minutes" segment. The report relied heavily on the recollections of a retired first sergeant who had served in an air cavalry unit. After telling the interviewer how few of his unit's attack helicopters were combat-ready at any given time, he said that "they would just sit on the tarmac and break."

The first sergeant's statements alarmed the public, but CENTCOM was not worried. The unit in question had a reputation as an underachiever. It was called to action for Desert Shield, but its poor state of readiness had caused the Army to send another unit in its place. That unit had no major problems with its Apaches.

To any officer who has ever been responsible for the maintenance of military equipment, the first sergeant's words had a familiar ring to them. Soldiers are lax about maintenance, but swear that they have performed it thoroughly. Their NCOs and officers are too lazy to check their men's work, but these supervisors swear that they have checked the work. Many even sign official documents to that effect. Then, when the piece of equipment fails, "it" broke. The failure never seems to be anyone's fault, and never stems from shoddy maintenance or inadequate supervision, "it just broke." This is why such misfortune descends upon far more bad units (like the first sergeant's) than good ones.

Occasionally, Sheridan tanks in the 82nd Airborne Division would develop electrical problems, seemingly out of nowhere. However, those tanks had been dropped out of airplanes for an average of 26 years. Even so, these instances (referred to as "gremlin attacks" by tank crews) were rare. Claims from a senior NCO that brand new helicopters "just broke," while they were sitting on the tarmac are therefore exceptionally hard to swallow.

Some equipment is badly designed, but in a case like this, the facts did not support the contention. Most units had no problem with the Apache. When several units are using the same design, and all of the units except one or two have their equipment running most of the time, one cannot blame the design or attribute the problems to bad luck. It is usually bad maintenance.

The report also pointed out that Apaches seemed to have an inordinate number of problems with their 30mm guns jamming. Jamming had been a problem, but it was solved by the time the war broke out. The Apache's 30mm chain-gun is designed to be fired in ten round bursts. Weapons operators are supposed to pull the trigger and hold it until the gun's automatic interrupter kicks in. However, some WOs were firing in bursts of fewer than ten rounds. That threw the gun's timing off and caused it to jam. By the time Apaches started flying combat missions, most WOs had been taught better, and there were far fewer jammed guns as a result.

A cautionary note about the Apache's capabilities is in order. Armed with gun camera footage of Apaches running riot over dug-in battalions of Iraqi tanks and APCs or butchering armor columns on the roads, some analysts were prepared to argue that the tank had lost its place as "King of Battle." In the future, they believed, much of the work which had been traditionally assigned to tank units could be done by helicopter gunships. Tanks were therefore far less important than they used to be, and far fewer would be necessary to conduct future wars. So the argument went. Since top-of-the-line main battle tanks are expensive (by the late-1990s costing more than $4.4 million a copy), there are always government officials willing to listen to such arguments.

As is often the case, however, video fails to tell the whole story. Many of the dug-in units attacked by Apaches were fighting with American heavy units at the time. This meant that the Apaches were attacking units which had already been hit by massive artillery barrages, and had lost most of their anti-aircraft weapons. In other words, heavy units (and their MLRS batteries) paved the way for the Apaches. The 10th Armored Division was not engaged with ground forces at the time it was attacked, and had not been hit by MLRS strikes, but that Apache attack took place at a time when the Iraqi Army was in the advanced stages of disintegration. The division's anti-aircraft weapons had not been destroyed, but most had been abandoned. In any event, without the benefit of refueling points close to the targets, the attacks never would have taken place. Without major ground units fighting their way close to the targets, the refueling points never would have been established. Whatever the Apache's performance proved during the war, to say that Apaches proved that they could destroy viable units with viable anti-aircraft defenses on their own is a stretch.

Units on roads are relatively easy targets. No artillery preparation is necessary for these targets because their heavy anti-aircraft weapons are not a factor. They are in travel mode, with their radars off. When a convoy is jumped by helicopter gunships, there is no time to bring heavy AA weapons into action before the damage is done and the gunships are gone. The crucial question here is not whether Apaches needed help from ground forces in attacking these targets, however. The question is why the units were on the roads (and vulnerable) in the first place. In most instances, it was because they were moving either to attack or run away from Allied heavy units in the area.

Because of their firepower, Apaches can add punch to a heavy unit attack. Because of their mobility, they can exploit opportunities and can help turn an opponent's defeat into a rout. However, like any other weapons system, the Apache has its limitations. Obviously, Apaches cannot physically secure terrain the way ground units can. And, though they are harder to shoot down than helicopters of the past, they are still vulnerable to heavy ground fire. They also cannot go very far on a tank of gas. As a result of these limitations, for the foreseeable future, helicopter gunships will be limited to supporting (albeit important, active) roles. Wars will still be won and lost by heavy ground units.

In the weeks before the ground campaign began, the American public was deluged with inaccurate information regarding Iraq's army and its equipment. One national publication claimed that "much of Iraq's equipment is as good or better than that of the Allied forces." It further claimed that "Iraq has some smart weapons that may be better than their U.S. counterparts." In fact, Iraq's military equipment was woefully inadequate. How could so many bright people so badly overestimate Iraqi equipment and so badly underestimate our own?

Western equipment is thoroughly tested before it is fielded. In democracies, safe and effective weapons are everything, since they keep casualties down. This is important when the relatives of dead and wounded soldiers are allowed to vote. More testing uncovers more defects. The defects then get corrected, most of the time.

Dictators are not pressured to produce effective equipment or test designs thoroughly. They do not have to worry about keeping casualties down. They can just throw men at the other side until the other side breaks. Troop safety is not a top priority. In a dictatorship, when a group of soldiers burns to death in a substandard vehicle, the government can just draft another group of soldiers to replace them.

Dictatorships also do not have to worry about the press. Democracy, through a free press, guarantees that weapons defects will be made public. Unfortunately, the defects tend to get more press coverage than the corrections. Freedom of the press and an active media ensure that every time a weapon falls short of expectations in the United States, the entire country hears about it. There was no such freedom in the Soviet Union and China, producers of most of Iraq's military hardware.

The Soviet Union and China intentionally designed equipment that was cheap and shoddy.* This is almost impossible for Americans to understand, but it made perfect sense to the Soviets and the Chinese.

The Soviets always felt that if a major war broke out with the United States, large numbers of their tanks would be destroyed in combat. Their own experience had led them to that conclusion. Very few Soviet tanks built before the German invasion in June 1941 were still in service a year later. It therefore made no sense to the Soviets to design expensive, long lasting tanks when most of them would probably be destroyed by enemy fire in the first few months of a major war.

The Soviets also recognized that while in peacetime some tank designs have lasted for twenty years, in a major war a good design might be obsolete in six months. In wartime, the best scientists and engineers from each combatant nation shift their focus from civilian pursuits to the war effort. Government spending on the military increases dramatically. Battlefield experience drives technology forward.

The Germans began World War II with tanks protected by armor 1.2 inches thick and with a 37mm tank gun which fired 7 lb. steel shots at just over 1,000 feet per second. Their last tank was protected by 10 inches of armor, and had a 128mm tank gun which fired 58 lb. projectiles at over 3,000 feet per second. Just over five years separated the two tank models, and several other models had come and gone in between.

This is why Western design philosophy puzzled the Soviets. The Abrams was the most technologically advanced tank in the world. Yet, the Soviets believed, if World War III had broken out, within three years there probably would have been no M-1A1s on the battlefield. Those that had not already been destroyed would have been obsolete. This was not an unreasonable assumption. The first Abrams model, the M-1, had come and gone in less than a decade, and that was in peacetime. For that reason, the Soviets saw $4 million a copy as too much to pay for any tank. Soviet tanks were designed to be simple and inexpensive to mass produce, with few frills (again, Lenin's dictum: "Quantity has a quality all its own."). Those they exported to countries like Iraq had even fewer frills. This design philosophy might have paid off in World War III, but in the Gulf War, these designs were just embarrassingly inadequate, and Iraqi tank crewmen paid the price.

The Chinese had an additional concern. The hard currency that comes from the sale of weaponry to the Third World is important to China's economy. Even if China's industry had the technology to produce an Abrams, at more than $4 million a copy, the Chinese would not be able to find Third World buyers. So China turns out relatively unsophisticated but affordable imitations of Soviet designs. The down side is that buyers get what they pay for. When a Type 59 costing less than a million dollars runs into a $4 million Abrams, the outcome is predictable.

---

*Contrary to popular belief, Iraq got almost nothing from the United States. Iraq got some older equipment from France, but basically this was a war between Communist and Western weaponry.

Since Soviet- and Chinese-built tanks don't last as long as Western tanks, the Iraqi Army was forced to severely restrict the use of tanks in training in order to preserve them. Just as pilots need to fly, tank crews need to operate their tanks. Lack of practice meant deficiencies in basic driving skills. That meant that in combat, each Iraqi tank was more likely to get hit.

That lack of durability also made large scale training operations a problem. Major tank exercises, which are common in Western nations, were impossible under the constraints faced by the Iraqi Army. Commanders who have not practiced maneuvering large tank units in peacetime can hardly be expected to display a high degree of proficiency under the pressure of combat. So, neither individual tanks nor tank units were as mobile as they should have been.

Chinese and Soviet tank designers also did not worry as much as they should have about main gun effectiveness. They reasoned that since World War II, most tanks had fought each other at ranges of 500 meters or less, so tank guns did not need to be high-tech or long range. Both nations had planned largely for an outdated type of warfare and their tanks reflected it, but the Iraqis did not know it yet. Most of the tank engagements of the Iran–Iraq War had followed the earlier close range pattern. Weak tank guns had not cost the Iraqis any battles against the Iranians, but in the long range encounters of the Gulf War, many Iraqi tank crews undoubtedly cursed their inadequate guns in the seconds before they died.

The Soviet Union and China also manufactured tanks with low profiles to give enemy tank gunners less to shoot at. That requires very low turret roofs. Low turret roofs make for cramped tank turrets. This is why there were few Soviet tankmen over 5'6" tall. Cramped conditions make crew fatigue more of a factor. A cramped turret also reduces the tank's rate of fire. The main guns on Iraq's tanks had to be elevated after each shot to give the loader enough room to reload the gun. This took time, and hampered the gunner's ability to track enemy tanks.

With a low turret roof, a gunner also cannot depress the gun very far. A tank gun is like a see-saw. When the gun barrel points down, the breech at the back of the gun rises up. A low turret roof limits how much a breech can rise. This has major practical consequences. In defensive positions, a tank "hides" in a "defilade" position (parked on an upward slope). This allows most of the tank to be hidden behind berms or below ground, with only the main gun visible. The more a main gun can depress, the more of a slope the tank can fire from, and the more of the tank can remain hidden. This is why most Allied main guns have a maximum depression of ten degrees. Iraq's tanks had a maximum depression of about five degrees.

Unable to hide effectively, Iraq's tanks provided big targets for Coalition gunners. The Soviets always admitted that their tanks were not particularly well-suited for defensive warfare. By all accounts, they told the Iraqis this when they sold them the tanks. But, like every other piece of equipment it got from the Soviet Union, the Iraqi Army insisted on using the tanks in roles for which they were never intended.

Throughout the Cold War, Western governments had chosen quality in weaponry over quantity. In the years before the war, many of these governments had been tormented by the press on the subject of expensive weaponry, but the Gulf War vindicated this policy. Inexpensive, Communist-designed and built equipment proved not only inadequate, but impotent. The war proved that at a certain level of disparity, quality can render quantity virtually irrelevant.

28

Friendly Fire and Gulf War Syndrome

O ne of the more disappointing aspects of the war was "friendly fire." Friendly fire is a feature of every war. Because the destruction of the Iraqi Army cost the U.S. Armed Forces only 148 combat deaths, the number of fratricides in this war appeared abnormally high. Of 148 American combat deaths, 35 were listed as fratricides. Thus, 24% of all Americans killed in the conflict were killed by their countrymen. Of the 496 wounded, 72 (15%) were friendly fire casualties.

The 24% statistic, though eye catching, is misleading as a measure of military performance. Had American commanders been less skilled, the friendly fire percentages would have looked much better. For instance, if Maj.Gen. Rhame had thrown his 1st ID troops into the Iraqi trenches with pistols, grenades and bayonets as much of America and many analysts expected him to, he would have lost 2–400 more men to hostile fire. The total percentage of friendly fire fatalities would then have been 6%–10% instead of 24%. Likewise, the fact that nine of the twelve Britons killed in the ground assault (75%) were killed by their American allies is not necessarily an indictment of American military competence. It is more a tribute to the military efficiency of the British 1st Armoured Division in losing only three men to hostile fire. Statistically, the fact that Allied forces killed around 14,000 Iraqi soldiers and lost 47 (35 American, 9 British and 3 Saudi) to friendly fire (a 298:1 ratio) paints a more favorable and more accurate picture.

Another useful statistic is the number of enemy targets hit divided by the total number of friendly targets hit. For example, Coalition ground forces destroyed some 3,550 armored vehicles in combat. Forty-eight Allied vehicles were accidentally engaged by ground units. Thus, there was only one accidental engagement for every 74 Iraqi armored vehicles destroyed in combat. About 15% of the Iraqi vehicles that were engaged were abandoned at the time, so only around 3,000 of those vehicles would have been crewed, but that is still a roughly 62½:1 ratio.

Of course, this does not mean that Allied leaders were happy with the friendly fire statistics. While a 62½:1 ratio may indicate that the friendly fire problem was not as bad as it had first appeared, it does not change the fact that there were too many friendly fire incidents during the war. The U.S. Army has spent a great deal of effort in the years since the war trying to find ways to reduce the incidence of friendly fire.

Advanced technology, specifically the Abrams' advanced gunnery system, may have been a major contributor to the problem. American leaders were not certain whether or not the Abrams' armor would stand up to Iraqi main gun rounds at the time of the war. They therefore sought to minimize the possibility of Iraqi hits by having their units engage Iraqi tanks from extended ranges. Unfortunately, at these ranges, while the gunnery system could score hits, it was often difficult to distinguish friend from foe. A substantial majority of the fratricidal Abrams engagements took place at extended range. In war, the old adage: "better safe than sorry" does not always hold true. Going to extreme lengths to avoid one danger can open one up to other dangers.

Nowhere was this fact more evident than in the area of air-to-ground friendly fire incidents. In the face of what were expected to be potent anti-aircraft defenses, Allied pilots bombed from relatively high altitudes. Not only did this limit the capacity of bombers to score hits on Iraqi armor, it made vehicle identification more difficult, dramatically increasing the risk of accidentally hitting Coalition troops. Six friendly fire vehicle destructions by fixed-wing aircraft were more than might have been expected, in view of how few ground attack sorties were flown in proximity to Allied troops. This will pose a dilemma for planners in the future. If attack aircraft drop their ordinance from such high altitudes that they leave significant numbers of enemy tanks intact and pose an unnecessarily high friendly fire threat, ground unit leaders will be hesitant to call upon them. However, to raise their kill-to-friendly fire loss ratio to a level acceptable to ground commanders, bombers will have to bomb from lower altitudes. This will dramatically increase the risk of aircraft loss to enemy anti-aircraft fire, possibly to a level that air commanders find unacceptable. No action in combat can ever be made risk-free. Every person who sets foot on or over a battlefield runs the risk of losing his or her life one way or another.

Friendly fire was a common occurrence in World War II. During the fighting in Europe, American soldiers were often bombed by their own aircraft. During the breakout from the Normandy beachhead (Operation Cobra), heavy bombers pounded the U.S. 30th Infantry Division on successive days, killing 111 (including Lt.Gen. Leslie McNair, the operation's commander), wounding 490 and causing over 160 battle fatigue cases.

The fratricide was not always air-to-ground. In Italy, American anti-aircraft batteries fired on a formation of transport planes carrying units of the 82nd Airborne Division, inflicting severe losses. Of the 144 transports in the flight, 23 were shot down and 37 were damaged. A total of 141 paratroops and aircrew members were killed.

The censorship regulations of the time kept incidents like these from becoming general knowledge. This was probably for the best, since about 15,000 Americans (the equivalent of a large division) were killed or wounded by their fellow Americans during the war.

While armies may be able to reduce the number of friendly fire incidents, eliminating fratricide entirely is impossible. Human beings make mistakes. Human beings who are fatigued and under pressure (like men in combat) are more likely to make mistakes, and those mistakes are more likely to be really bad ones.

Attempts to eliminate friendly fire completely can even be counterproductive. An army obsessed with eliminating friendly fire may place so many restrictions on its forces that it will lose more lives to enemy fire than it saves by reducing fratricides. For example, soldiers attacking certain targets must follow artillery barrages and air strikes closely, before the enemy has a chance to recover. Unfortunately, the occasional bomb or shell may fall on the lead elements. The only way to avoid that possibility is to insist that the attackers wait until well after the bombing or barrage is over to close with the enemy. That way, there will not be any worry about bombs or shells accidentally falling on the first assault wave. What will be a worry is the enemy, who will have been given time to rush out of his bunkers, man his heavy weapons and spray death into the onrushing infantrymen. A slight risk of friendly fire is better than a hail of shells or machine-gun bullets coming at your infantrymen. Again, in war, going to extremes to avoid one danger invariably opens one up to other dangers.

The most baffling mystery to come out of the Gulf War has been "Gulf War Syndrome." Though it will probably be years before the cause of this series of maladies has been identified, enough is known to separate the promising theories from the dead-ends.

One of the hottest theories is one that is almost certainly wrong. At some points between the start of the air war and the start of the ground war, chemical alarms were going off in American positions south of the Iraqi–Saudi border. As a result, there has been speculation that bombing strikes against chemical weapons plants in the vicinity of Baghdad produced a huge cloud of chemical agents which wafted southward and reached American positions in sufficient concentration to produce delayed health problems. Some have even produced computer models to support the assertion. There are a few problems with that theory, however.

The most obvious problem is that the vast majority of soldiers experiencing symptoms were stationed elsewhere. If a cloud of chemicals was causing sickness, then there should be sick people. In fact, the heavy units in this area, the 1st and 3rd Armored and the 1st and 24th Infantry divisions experienced virtually no problems with Gulf War Syndrome. Most of the sufferers have been reservists or members of the 82nd Airborne Division, who spent most of this period in bases well to the east.

The question of why all of those chemical alarms went off remains, however. What might explain it is the fact that one of the first things most of these units did after they were set in their positions was spray pesticide to rid themselves of the millions of flies which were tormenting them. Pesticides are essentially extremely mild, nonpersistent nerve agents. They can therefore set off chemical alarms. There was some record of soldiers getting headaches or upset stomachs during the spraying, but these symptoms went away within days after the units stopped spraying.

American artillery was also causing false chemical alarms. When artillery bombardments began in earnest along the border, there was a wave of false alarms. Escaping gases from the propellant charges which blow the projectiles out of the gun barrels were being carried southward over the armor and infantry units, setting off the alarms.

These explanations make a good deal more sense than the chemical cloud theory. Most war chemicals, and all killing agents, are heavier than air. That was one of the reasons chemical weapons were so attractive to First World War planners. Chemicals would sink into enemy trenches. Being heavier than air, clouds of these chemicals do not go very high and do not drift very far, computer models notwithstanding.

Even if a cloud could drift that far and still reach American lines in sufficient concentration to cause sickness, we would expect to find Iraqi casualties all along its path. At its origin we would expect to find hundreds, or even thousands, of dead Iraqis in a scene similar to that in the vicinity of the Union Carbide plant in Bophal, India. No such carnage was encountered.

However exciting the media might find the chemical weapons angle, the fact is, the soldiers who have developed permanent problems have not shown symptoms consistent with chemical poisoning. Instead, we have seen a wide variety of opportunistic diseases, affecting people whose immune systems had been compromised. Even in the one case where chemical munitions were blown up at a bunker complex, the symptoms shown by the soldiers who later became sick were not consistent with chemical poisoning. More striking is the fact that the soldiers in question (paratroops from an XVIII Airborne Corps combat engineer brigade from Fort Bragg) became sick while soldiers in other nearby units (from the 24th ID) did not. This would appear to be a very strong indication that whatever made the soldiers sick happened earlier.

A few possibilities have been largely overlooked in the search for answers regarding Gulf War Syndrome. One has to do with immunity. There are three basic kinds of immunity. Natural immunity is when the body gets a disease and develops defenses against that disease. Artificial immunity is created when an extremely weak form of a pathogen is introduced into the body in the form of a vaccination. This prompts the immune system to develop a defense to the pathogen. The third, and most overlooked, form of immunity is hereditary immunity. It is overlooked because most natives of a given region are born with it. People who are hypersensitive to whatever milder pathogens are floating around in their environment tend to die early or not reproduce. The people who are not hypersensitive thrive. So, most of us have little to worry about in our native regions. However, if we go somewhere else, all bets are off regarding hereditary immunity. If 600,000 Saudis came to the United States, a few of them would come down with mystery illnesses. When 600,000 Americans go to Saudi Arabia, a few of them are going to get sick.

This does not provide a complete answer to the problem, however. First, there were many more cases of illness than environmental hypersensitivity would have produced. In addition, hypersensitivity cases would have occurred fairly evenly from division to division. A few units suffered an inordinate number of mystery illness cases, though. There is no reason to expect that there would have been several times more hypersensitive people in the 82nd Airborne Division than in the 1st Armored Division. Hypersensitivity probably accounted for a few cases of illness in each Allied division. However, to explain the majority of cases, and the uneven distribution of cases, we will have to look elsewhere.

One place we might look is to port facilities. One cannot help but notice that the units which spent the most time in the desert had the lowest incidence of Gulf War Syndrome and that a lot of the soldiers who got sick had spent a lot of time at port facilities. Ports are unhealthy places. Goods come into countries through ports. Countries do not want pests coming into their countries on these goods, so there is a lot of pesticide spraying done at ports. There are also petroleum fumes and other unhealthy things. In 1989, the 82nd Airborne Division sent a team from a transportation unit to the Port of Wilmington, North Carolina, to look into deployment contingencies. Most of the soldiers had no problems. However, the officer in charge of the team developed a disease of the bone marrow called aplastic anemia and died a few months later. The officer had the flu when she went, then had a bad reaction to an insect bite when she got there. Apparently, these two combined factors compromised her immune system enough for the more serious malady to develop. True, this is one anecdote, but it makes one think.

Another possibility was proximity to industrial establishments. Many of the U.S. Marine Gulf War Syndrome sufferers have exhibited symptoms consistent with heavy metal poisoning (metallic taste in the mouth, etc.). Since some Marine units were stationed in defensive positions near Saudi industrial enterprises during the Desert Shield deployment, it is not illogical to suspect that there may be a link. Again, however, this is anecdotal. I do not have the resources to gather and compile empirical data.

The United States government, on the other hand, does. The main reason this issue is still a mystery is that investigations have not been very systematic or coordinated. As suspicious incidents are reported, investigators look into them. As simplistic as it might sound, the cause of Gulf War Syndrome will be found when a responsible authority in the U.S. government tells his or her staff the following:

1. "Don't tell me whether or not you believe they're really sick. Just tell me who reported diseases, what the symptoms were and what units they were in."

2. "The vast majority of mystery illnesses occurred in a very few units. Compile the data and tell me which units had the most soldiers reporting such illnesses."

3. "Tell me where those units were, from the time they left the United States (mystery illnesses have not been a major problem for the soldiers who had been stationed in Germany) until the time they returned after the war."

4. "Retrace the paths of those units and tell me what their living conditions were. Where did the soldiers live? What did they eat? What was happening in those areas which might have caused large numbers of soldiers to get sick?"

These four logical steps, pursued vigorously, will almost certainly reveal the cause of most of the illnesses and provide an answer to this mystery.

Gen. John Yeosock (Former Commander, 3rd Army)
Gen. Gary Luck (Former Commander, XVIII Airborne Corps)

Lt.Gen. Walter Boomer (Former Commander, I Marine Expeditionary Force)
Lt.Gen. William Carter (Former Assistant Division Commander, 1st Infantry Division)
Lt.Gen. Paul Funk (Former Commander, 3rd Armored Division)
Lt.Gen. L.D. Holder (Former Commander, 2nd Armored Cavalry Regiment)
Lt.Gen. Randolph House (Former Commander, 2nd Brigade, 1st Cavalry Division)
Lt.Gen. Paul Kern (Former Commander, 2nd Brigade, 24th Infantry Division)
Lt.Gen. William Keys (Former Commander, 2nd Marine Division)
Lt.Gen. Thomas Rhame (Former Commander, 1st Infantry Division)
Lt.Gen. Jerry Rutherford (Former Commander, 2nd Armored Division (Fwd),
Assistant Division Commander for Support, 1st Infantry Division)
Lt.Gen. David Weisman (Former Commander, 3rd Brigade, 1st Infantry Division)

Maj.Gen. John Admire (Former Commander, Task Force Taro, 1st Marine Division)
Maj.Gen. Robert Clark (Former Commander, 3rd Brigade, 101st Airborne Division)
Maj.Gen. Leroy Goff III (Former Commander, 3rd Brigade, 3rd Armored Division)
Maj.Gen. Harry Jenkins (Former Commander, 4th Marine Expeditionary Brigade)
Maj.Gen. John Landry (Former Chief-of-Staff, VII Corps)
Maj.Gen. John Leide (Former Intelligence Officer [Bomb Damage Assessment],
CENTCOM)
Maj.Gen. John LeMoyne (Former Commander, 1st Brigade, 24th Infantry Division)
Maj.Gen. Lon E. Maggart (Former Commander, 1st Brigade, 1st Infantry Division)
Maj.Gen. William Nash (Former Commander, 1st Brigade, 3rd Armored Division)
Maj.Gen. Ronald Richard (Former Operations Officer, 2nd Marine Division)
Maj.Gen. Robert Shadley (Former Commander, Division Support Command, 1st
Infantry Division)
Maj.Gen. John Stewart (Former Chief Intelligence Officer, 3rd Army)
Maj.Gen. Dan Zanini (Former Commander, 3rd Brigade, 1st Armored Division)

Brig.Gen. Frank Akers (Former Operations Officer, XVIII Corps)
Brig.Gen. Keith Alexander (Former Chief Intelligence Officer, 1st Armored Division)
Brig.Gen. Raymond Barrett (Former Commander, 3-15th Infantry Battalion, 24th
Infantry Division)
Brig.Gen. John Brown (Former Commander, 2-66th Armor Battalion, 2nd Armored
Division (Fwd), [Attached to the 1st Infantry Division])
Brig.Gen. Mike Burke (Former Commander, Aviation Brigade, 3rd Armored Division)
Brig.Gen. Stan Cherrie (Former Operations Officer, VII Corps)
Brig.Gen. James Cooke (Former XVIII Airborne Corps Liaison Officer to *Daguet*
Division)

Brig.Gen. B.J. Craddock (Former Commander, 4-64th Armor Battalion, 24th Infantry Division)

Brig.Gen. Ed Dyer (Former Commander, 1-37th Armor Battalion, 1st Armored Division)

Brig.Gen. Arnold Fields (Former Commander, 3rd Battalion, 6th Marine Regiment, 2nd Marine Division)

Brig.Gen. Patrick Garreau (Former French Liaison to NATO)

Brig.Gen. Thomas Goedkoop (Former Commander, 4-66th Armor Battalion, 1st Armored Division)

Brig.Gen. Keith Holcomb (Former Commander, 2nd LAI Battalion, 2nd Marine Division)

Brigadier Alwin Hutchinson (Former Commander, Route Development Battle Group, 1st [UK] Armoured Division)

Brig.Gen. Thomas Jones (Former Commander, 1st Battalion, 6th Marine Regiment, 2nd Marine Division)

Brig.Gen. James Mattis (Former Commander, 1st Battalion, 7th Marine Regiment, 1st Marine Division)

Brig.Gen. Eric Olson (Former Commander, 2-18th Infantry Battalion, 197th Infantry Brigade [Attached to the 24th Infantry Division])

Brig.Gen. Ronald Rokosz (Former Commander, 2nd Brigade, 82nd Airborne Division)

Brig.Gen. Ricardo Sanchez (Former Commander, 2-69th Armor Battalion, 197th Infantry Brigade [Attached to the 24th Infantry Division])

Brig.Gen. Henry Stratman (Former Commander, 2-29th Field Artillery Battalion, 8th Infantry Division)

Brig.Gen. Terry Tucker (Former Commander, 4-7th Cavalry Squadron, 3rd Armored Division)

Brig.Gen. John Vines (Former Commander, 4-325th Infantry Battalion, 82nd Airborne Division)

Brig.Gen. Robert Wilson (Former Commander, 1-4th Cavalry Squadron, 1st Infantry Division)

Brig.Gen. Walter Wojdakowski (Former Commander, 3-41st Infantry Battalion, 2nd Armored Division [Attached to the 2nd Marine Division])

Col. David Abrahamson (Former Commander, 1-325th Infantry Battalion, 82nd Airborne Division)

Col. Mark Adams (Former Commander, 3rd Battalion, 11th Marine Regiment, 1st Marine Division)

Col. Roy Adams (Former Operations Officer, 1st Brigade, 1st Armored Division)

Col. Clinton Ancker (Former Operations Officer, 2nd Armored Division (Fwd), [Attached to the 1st Infantry Division])

Col. Robert Arnone (Former Operations Officer, 3-1st Field Artillery Battalion, 1st Armored Division)

Col. Sidney Baker (Former Commander, 5-16th Infantry Battalion, 1st Infantry Division)

Col. Richard Barry (Former Commander, 1st Security Reconnaissance Intelligence Group)

Col. Matthew Belford (Former Commander, 2-325th Infantry Battalion, 82nd Airborne Division)

Col. John Brown (Former Commander, 3-5th Cavalry Battalion, 3rd Armored Division)

Col. Terry Bullington (Former Operations Officer, 1st Infantry Division)

Col. Mike Burton (Former Commander, 4-34th Armor Battalion, 3rd Armored Division)

Col. Bill Chamberlain (Former Commander, 1-18th Infantry Battalion, 197th Infantry Brigade [Attached to the 24th Infantry Division])

Col. Raymond Cole (Former Operations Officer, 1st Marine Division)

Col. Michael Combest (Former Liaison to II Egyptian Corps)

Col. Kevin Conry (Former Commander, 2nd Battalion, 4th Marine Regiment, 2nd Marine Division)

Col. John Counselman (Former Chief Intelligence Officer, 1st Marine Division)

Col. Ward Critz (Former Commander, 7-6th Infantry Battalion, 1st Armored Division)

Col. James Cureton (Historian, 1st Marine Division)

Col. John Davidson (Former Chief Intelligence Officer, VII Corps)

Col. Tom Davis (Former Commander, 4-82nd Field Artillery Battalion, 3rd Armored Division)

Col. Ray Dawson (Former Commander, 3rd Battalion, 23rd Marine Regiment, 2nd Marine Division)

Col. Alphonso Diggs (Former Commander, 3rd Tank Battalion, 1st Marine Division)

Col. Bernard Dunn (Former Liaison to II Egyptian Corps)

Col. Edward P. Egan (Former Commander, 4-7th Infantry Battalion, 1st Armored Division)

Col. Michael Einsidler (Former Operations Officer, 1st Battalion, 1st Marine Regiment, 1st Marine Division)

Col. Daniel Fake (Former Commander, 2-16th Infantry Battalion, 1st Infantry Division)

Col. Michael Fallon (Former Commander, 1st Battalion, 1st Marine Regiment, 1st Marine Division)

Col. William Feyk (Former Commander, 4-70th Armor Battalion, 1st Armored Division)

Col. John Floris (Former Commander, 1-41st Field Artillery Battalion, 24th Infantry Division)

Col. Greg Fontenot (Former Commander, 2-34th Armor Battalion, 1st Infantry Division)

Col. Robert Fulcher (Former Commander, 4-18th Infantry Battalion, 3rd Armored Division)

Col. James Fulks (Former Commander, Task Force Grizzly, 1st Marine Division)

Col. Bruce Gombar (Former Commander, 1st Battalion, 8th Marine Regiment, 2nd Marine Division)

Col. Chris Gregor (Former Chief Intelligence Officer, 2nd Marine Division)

Col. G. Thomas Greco (Former Commander, 3-187th Infantry Battalion, 101st Airborne Division)

Col. David Gross (Former Commander, 3-37th Armor Battalion, 1st Infantry Division)

Col. James Gunlicks (Former Operations Officer, 1st Cavalry Division)

Col. Beaufort Hallman (Former Commander, 4-8th Cavalry Battalion, 3rd Armored Division)

Col. Chesley Harris (Former Operations Officer, 3rd Brigade, 1st Armored Division)

Col. Stephen Hawkins (Former Commander, 1st Engineer Battalion, 1st Infantry Division)

Col. Mark Hertling (Former Operations Officer, 1-1st Cavalry Squadron, 1st Armored Division)

Col. Stuart Herrington (Former Intelligence Officer, 3rd Army)

Col. James Hillman (Former Commander, 1-41st Infantry Battalion, 2nd Armored Division (Fwd), [Attached to the 1st Infantry Division])

Col. Richard Hodory (Former Commander, Task Force Papa Bear, 1st Marine Division)

Col. Tony Isaacs (Former Commander, 1st Squadron, 2nd Armored Cavalry Regiment)

Col. Richard Jemiola (Former Commander, 9th Engineer Battalion, 1st Infantry Division)

Col. Taylor Jones (Former Commander, 3-66th Armor Battalion, 2nd Armored Division (Fwd), [Attached to the 1st Infantry Division])

Col. John Kalb (Former Commander, 4-32nd Armor Battalion, 3rd Armored Division)

Col. Edward Kane (Former Commander, 3-35th Armor Battalion, 1st Armored Division)

Col. Michael Kephart (Former Commander, 1st Tank Battalion, 1st Marine Division)

Col. Yves Kermorvant (French Liaison to U.S. Army Armor Center)

Col. Henry Kinnison (Former Commander, 1-187th Infantry Battalion, 101st Airborne Division)

Col. Scott Knobel (Former Executive Officer, 1-41st Infantry Battalion, 2nd Armored Division (Fwd), [Attached to the 1st Infantry Division])

Col. Michael Kurth (Former Commander, HMLA-369)

Col. Thomas Leney (Former Commander, 2-4th Cavalry Squadron, 24th Infantry Division)

Col. Stephen Lutz (Former Commander, 3-41st Field Artillery Battalion, 24th Infantry Division)

Col. Scott Marcy (Former Commander, 3rd Squadron, 2nd Armored Cavalry Regiment)

Col. David Marlin (Former Commander, 4-37th Armor Battalion, 1st Infantry Division)

Col. Roger Mauer (Former Commander, 2nd Battalion, 7th Marine Regiment, 1st Marine Division)

Col. Dan Magee (Former Operations Officer, 1st Brigade, 1st Infantry Division)

Col. Mike McGee (Former Commander, 6-6th Infantry Battalion, 1st Armored Division)

Col. Daniel Merritt (Former Commander, 2-67th Armor Battalion, 3rd Armored Division)

Col. Dennis Mroczkowski (Historian, 2nd Marine Division)

Col. Clifford Myers (Former Commander, Task Force Shepherd, 1st Marine Division)

Col. Harold Neely (Former Commander, 5-18th Infantry Battalion, 3rd Armored Division)

Col. Mike Parker (Former Commander, 1-5th Cavalry Battalion, 1st Cavalry Division)

Col. Timothy Reischl (Former Commander, 4-67th Armor Battalion, 3rd Armored Division)

Col. Patrick Ritter (Former Commander, 1-34th Armor Battalion, 1st Infantry Division)

Col. Steve Robinette (Former Deputy Commander, 2nd Armored Cavalry Regiment)

Col. Charles Rogers, OBE (Former Commander, Staffordshire Regiment, 1st [UK] Armoured Division)

Col. James Sachtleben (Former Commander, 5th Battalion, 11th Marine Regiment, 1st Marine Division)

Col. Larry Schmidt (Former Commander, 8th Marine Regiment, 2nd Marine Division)

Col. Michael Smith (Former Commander, 3rd Battalion, 9th Marine Regiment, 1st Marine Division)

Col. Stephen Smith (Former Commander, 1-7th Infantry Battalion, 1st Armored Division)

Col. John Sollis (Former Commander, 1st Battalion, 11th Marine Regiment, 1st Marine Division)

Col. Thomas Strauss (Former Operations Officer, 1st Armored Division)

Col. Lynn Stuart (Former Operations Officer, 11th Marine Regiment, 1st Marine Division)

Col. Mark Swanstrom (Former Division Staff Engineer Officer, 2nd Marine Division)

Col. Douglas Tystad (Former Commander, 3-67th Armor Battalion, 2nd Armored Division [Attached to the 2nd Marine Division])

Col. Steve West (Former Deputy Commander, 3rd Brigade, 1st Armored Division)

Col. Steve Whitcomb (Former Commander, 2-70th Armor Battalion, 1st Armored Division)

Col. Michael Vickery, OBE (Former Commander, 14th/20th King's Hussars, 1st [UK] Armoured Division)

Col. Jim Warner (Former Operations Officer, 1st (Tiger) Brigade, 2nd Armored Division [Attached to the 2nd Marine Division])

Col. Robert Williams (Former Operations Officer, 3-67th Armor Battalion, 2nd Armored Division [Attached to the 2nd Marine Division])

Col. Mitch Youngs (Former Commander, 2nd Battalion, 2nd Marine Regiment, 2nd Marine Division)

Lt.Col. Robert Barrow (Former Commander, A Company, 1st Battalion, 1st Marine Regiment, 1st Marine Division)

Lt.Col. Drew Bennett (Former Operations Officer, 1st Battalion, 7th Marine Regiment, 1st Marine Division)

Lt.Col. Roy Bierwirth (Former Operations Officer, 1-67th Armor Battalion, 2nd Armored Division [Attached to the 2nd Marine Division])

Lt.Col. Mike Bills (Former Commander, B Troop, 1-4th Cavalry Squadron, 1st Infantry Division)

Lt.Col. Jerry Bolzak (Former Executive Officer, 3-187th Infantry Battalion, 101st Airborne Division)

Lt.Col. Jack Carter (Former Operations Officer, 1st Battalion, 5th Marine Regiment, 1st Marine Division)

Lt.Col. Kent Cuthbertson (Former Fire Support Officer, 1st Brigade, 24th Infantry Division)

Lt.Col. Robert Dillon (Former Operations Staff Officer, 2nd Armored Division (Fwd), [Attached to the 1st Infantry Division])

Lt.Col. Erik Doyle (Former Operations Officer, 1st Battalion, 8th Marine Regiment, 2nd Marine Division)

Lt.Col. David Estes (Former Operations Officer, 4-32nd Armor Battalion, 3rd Armored Division)

Lt.Col. Thomas Fluker (Former Commander, D Company, 3-67th Armor Battalion, 2nd Armored Division [Attached to the 2nd Marine Division])

Lt.Col. John Garrity (Former Executive Officer, 4-37th Armor Battalion, 1st Infantry Division)

Lt.Col. Timothy Hannigan (Former Commander, 3rd Battalion, 7th Marine Regiment, 1st Marine Division)

Lt.Col. William Hedges (Former Commander, B Company, 3-66th Armor Battalion, 2nd Armored Division (Fwd) [Attached to the 1st Infantry Division])

Lt.Col. John Hemleben (Former Operations Officer, 1st Tank Battalion, 1st Marine Division)

Lt.Col. Bart Howard (Former Commander, B Company, 3-67th Armor Battalion, 2nd Armored Division [Attached to the 2nd Marine Division])

Lt.Col. Kevin Huddy (Former Operations Officer, 1st Brigade, 1st Infantry Division)

Lt.Col. Michael Johnson (Former Commander, 1-67th Armor Battalion, 2nd Armored Division [Attached to the 2nd Marine Division])

Lt.Col. Michael Kershaw (Former Commander, A Company, 3-41st Infantry Battalion, 2nd Armored Division [Attached to the 2nd Marine Division])

Lt.Col. Peter Kinney (Former Operations Officer, 3rd Brigade, 101st Airborne Division)

Lt.Col. Richard Lake (Former Intelligence Officer, 1st Marine Division)

Lt.Col. Chad Lienau (Former Operations Officer, 2nd Battalion, 2nd Marine Regiment, 2nd Marine Division)

Lt.Col. Timothy Lupfer (Former Commander, 3-8th Cavalry Battalion, 3rd Armored Division)

Lt.Col. Roger Mauer (Former Commander, 2nd Battalion, 7th Marine Regiment, 1st Marine Division)

Lt.Col. H.R. McMaster (Former Commander, E Troop, 2nd Armored Cavalry Regiment)

Lt.Col. Joseph Musca (Former Commander, Engineer Detachment, Task Force Papa Bear, 1st Marine Division)

Lt.Col. Jeff Powers (Former Operations Officer, Task Force Shepherd, 1st Marine Division)

Lt.Col. Jean-Robert Richard (Former Staff Officer, 3rd Helicopter Regiment, Daguet [France] Division)

Lt.Col. Victor Riley III (Former Operations Officer, 1st Battalion, 6th Marine Regiment, 2nd Marine Division)

Lt.Col. Joseph Sartiano (Former Commander, G Troop, 2nd Armored Cavalry Regiment)

Lt.Col. Martin Stanton (Former Senior Advisor, 2nd Saudi Arabian National Guard Mechanized Brigade)

Lt.Col. Terry Stanger (Former Commander, 3-69th Armor Battalion, 24th Infantry Division)

Lt.Col. John Terrell (Former Commander, TOW Company, 1st Tank Battalion, 1st Marine Division)

Lt.Col James Trahan (Former Commander, B Company, 1st Battalion, 1st Marine Regiment, 1st Marine Division)

Lt.Col. Douglas Trenda (Former Liaison to Group East, Joint Forces Command-North)

Lt.Col. Michael Tucker (Former Operations Officer, 1-35th Armor Battalion, 1st Armored Division)

Lt.Col. John Turner (Former Operations Officer, Task Force Papa Bear, 1st Marine Division)

Lt.Col. Bryan Watson (Former Combat Engineer Advisor to II Egyptian Corps)

Maj. Louis Abraham (Former Commander, A Company, 3rd Marine Engineer Battalion, 1st Marine Division)

Maj. Ken Amidon (Former Commander, C Company, 2nd Light Armored Infantry Battalion, 2nd Marine Division)

Maj. Greg Balzar (Former Commander, C Company, 1st Battalion, 1st Marine Regiment, 1st Marine Division)

Maj. Garry Bishop (Former Commander, A Company, 3-66th Armor Battalion, 2nd Armored Division (Fwd) [Attached to the 1st Infantry Division])

Maj. John Bushyhead (Former Commander, D Company, 5-16th Infantry Battalion, 1st Infantry Division)

Maj. Kelvin Davis (Former Operations Officer, 1st Light Armored Infantry Battalion, 1st Marine Division)

Maj. Todd Day (Former Assistant Operations Officer, 1-41st Field Artillery Battalion, 24th Infantry Division)

Maj. Brad Dick (Former Commander, A Company, 2-66th Armor Battalion, 2nd Armored Division (Fwd) [Attached to the 1st Infantry Division])

Maj. David Erickson (Former Commander, B Company, 1-35th Armor Battalion, 1st Armored Division)

Maj. Mike Glenn (Former Operations Staff Officer, 2nd Armored Cavalry Regiment)

Maj. Dennis Greene (Former Commander, A Company, 2nd Light Armored Infantry Battalion, 2nd Marine Division)

Maj. Oscar Hall (Former Supply Officer, 4-37th Armor Battalion, 1st Infantry Division)

Maj. Ashley Haszard (Former Commander, K Troop, 2nd Armored Cavalry Regiment)

Maj. Greg Heck (Former Commander, B Troop, 1-1st Cavalry Squadron, 1st Armored Division)

Maj. David Houston (Former Adjutant, 1-187th Infantry Battalion, 101st Airborne Division)

Maj. Mike Hussey (Former Commander, A Company, 8th Tank Battalion [Attached to 2nd Marine Division])

Maj. Kevin McCall (Former Intelligence Officer, 3-8th Cavalry Battalion, 3rd Armored Division)

Maj. John McCombs (Former Scout Platoon Leader, 2-34th Armor Battalion, 1st Infantry Division)

Maj. Marvin Meek (Former Operations Officer, 1-34th Armor Battalion, 1st Infantry Division)

Maj. Dan Miller (Former Commander, I Troop, 2nd Armored Cavalry Regiment)

Maj. Joseph Pacileo (Former Intelligence Staff Officer, 1st Armored Division)

Maj. Phil Patch (Former Commander, C Company, 1st Tank Battalion, 1st Marine Division)

Maj. Joseph Paydock (Former Platoon Leader, I Troop, 2nd Armored Cavalry Regiment)

Maj. Jeff Phillips (Former Public Affairs Officer, 1st Cavalry Division)

Maj. Craig Platel (Former Platoon Leader, TOW Platoon, 24th Marine Regiment [Attached to 2nd Marine Division])

Maj. Mark Porter (Former Supply Officer, 3-37th Armor Battalion, 1st Infantry Division)

Maj. Thomas Protzeller (Former Commander, C Company, 1st Light Armored Infantry Battalion, 1st Marine Division)

Maj. Eddie Ray (Former Commander, B Company, 3rd Light Armored Infantry Battalion [Attached to 1st Marine Division])

Maj. Tim Ryan (Former Commander, D Company, 3-66th Armor Battalion, 2nd Armored Division (Fwd) [Attached to the 1st Infantry Division])

Maj. Wayne Sinclair (Former Platoon Leader, 1st Platoon, A Company, 3rd Marine Engineer Battalion, 1st Marine Division)

Maj. Cecil Turner (Former Forward Air Controller, 1st Tank Battalion, 1st Marine Division)

Maj. David Undeland (Former Commander, D Company, 1st Battalion, 1st Marine Regiment, 1st Marine Division)

Maj. Floyd Usry (Former Air Officer, 2nd Light Armored Infantry Battalion, 2nd Marine Division)

Maj. Mark Winstead (Former Operations Staff Officer, 1-41st Infantry Battalion, 2nd Armored Division (Fwd), [Attached to the 1st Infantry Division])

Maj. Johnny Womack (Former Commander, A Company, 5-16th Infantry Battalion, 1st Infantry Division)

Capt. Glen Burnham (Former Scout Platoon Leader, 1-34th Armor Battalion, 1st Infantry Division)

Capt. Ed Chesney (Former Platoon Leader, A Company, 2-66th Armor Battalion, 2nd Armored Division (Fwd) [Attached to the 1st Infantry Division])

Capt. Greg Cleary (426th Support and Transportation Battalion, 101st Airborne Division)

Capt. Robert Finnegan (Former Executive Officer, B Company, 3-66th Armor Battalion, 2nd Armored Division (Fwd) [Attached to the 1st Infantry Division])

Capt. Robert Langol (Former Platoon Leader, B Company, 3-66th Armor Battalion, 2nd Armored Division (Fwd) [Attached to the 1st Infantry Division])

Capt. Marty Leners (Former Platoon Leader, C Company, 3-5th Cavalry Battalion, 3rd Armored Division])

Capt. Robert Manning (Former Commander, C Company, 2-66th Armor Battalion, 2nd Armored Division (Fwd) [Attached to the 1st Infantry Division])

Capt. Marcus Nerone (Former Operations Staff Officer, 197th Infantry Brigade, [Attached to the 24th Infantry Division])

Capt. Mark Overberg (Former Platoon Leader, B Troop, 1-1st Cavalry, 1st Armored Division)

Capt. David Viggers (Former Operations Staff Officer, 2nd Armored Division (Fwd), [Attached to the 1st Infantry Division])

Lt. Brian Hatheway (Former Fire Support Officer, 4-34th Armor Battalion, 3rd Armored Division)
Lt. John Hillen (Former Platoon Leader, E Troop, 2nd Armored Cavalry Regiment)

CSM Johnny Cameron (Former Platoon Sergeant, B Company, 1-34th Armor Battalion, 1st Infantry Division)
CSM Vincent Conway (Former Battalion Sergeant-Major, 2-66th Armor Battalion, 2nd Armored Division (Fwd) [Attached to the 1st Infantry Division])
CSM Phillip Toms (Former Battalion Sergeant-Major, 1-41st Infantry Battalion, 2nd Armored Division (Fwd) [Attached to the 1st Infantry Division])
CSM David Williams (Former First Sergeant, B Company, 1-41st Infantry Battalion, 2nd Armored Division (Fwd) [Attached to the 1st Infantry Division])

SSG Elias Chavez (Former Scout, 1-34th Armor Battalion, 1st Infantry Division)
SSG Rex Pentland (Former Scout, 2-34th Armor Battalion, 1st Infantry Division)
SSG James Wagner (Former Scout, 1-34th Armor Battalion, 1st Infantry Division)

Dr. Robert Wright (Former XVIII Corps Historian)
Mr. William Schneck (Analyst, U.S. Army Mine-Countermine Systems Directorate)
Mr. James Dillon (Analyst, U.S. Army Mine-Countermine Systems Directorate)

Bibliography

7th (UK) Intelligence Company and the Deputy Chief of Staff, Intelligence, Headquarters, U.S. Military Community, Berlin. *The Gulf Crisis: Iraqi Military Capabilities,* Berlin, 1990.

Adkin, Maj. Mark. *Urgent Fury: The Battle for Grenada.* Lexington, Massachusetts: Lexington Books, 1989.

Adkins, Lt.Col. Ronald A. *Iron Sappers Lead the Way: The 16th Engineer Battalion's Support of 1st Armored Division in Southwest Asia.* Carlisle Barracks: Army War College Study Project, March 1993.

Allen, Brad. "Star Wars in the Gulf." *International Military Review.* July/August 1992, pp. 18–21.

Antal, Maj. John F. "Iraq's Mailed Fist." *Infantry.* January–February 1991, pp. 27–30.

Atkinson, Rick. *Crusade: The Untold Story of The Persian Gulf War.* Boston: Houghton Mifflin, 1993.

Baram, Amatzia. *Building Toward Crisis: Saddam Husayn's Strategy For Survival.* Washington, D.C.: The Washington Institute For Near East Policy, 1998.

Belvoir Research, Development and Engineering Center. *Desert Storm Countermine Equipment.* Ft. Belvoir, Virginia, 1992.

Bennett, Maj. Drew. "Minefield Breaching: Doing the Job Right." *Armor.* July–August 1992, pp. 19–21.

Benson, Nicholas. *Rats' Tails: The Staffordshire Regiment at War.* London: Brassey's, 1993.

Biddle, Stephen. "Victory Misunderstood: What the Gulf War Tells Us About the Future of Conflict." *International Security.* Fall 1996, pp. 139–179.

———. "The Gulf War Debate *Redux.*" *International Security.* Fall 1997, pp. 163–174.

Bigelow, Capt. Michael. "The Faw Peninsula: A Battle Analysis." *Military Intelligence.* April/June 1991, pp. 13–18.

bin Sultan, HRH General Khaled, with Patrick Seale. *Desert Warrior: A Personal View of the Gulf War by the Joint Forces Commander.* New York: HarperCollins, 1995.

Blackwell, James. "Georgia Punch: 24th Mech Puts the Squeeze on Iraq." *Army Times.* December 2, 1991, pp. 12–14, 20, 22, 61–77.

———. *Thunder in the Desert: The Strategy and Tactics of the Gulf War.* New York: Bantam, 1991.

Breitenbach, Col. Daniel L. *Operation Desert Reckoning: Operational Deception in the Ground Campaign.* Newport, Rhode Island: Naval War College Study Project, 19 June 1991.

Brown, Lt.Col. John. *Desert Reckoning: Historical Continuities and the Battle For Norfolk.* Newport, Rhode Island: Naval War College Study Project, 19 June 1992.

———. *The Hundred Hour End Point: An Operational Assessment.* Newport, Rhode Island: Naval War College Study Project, 19 June 1992.

Brown, Russell. "Saddam Hussein's Army Was Devastated in Only 100 Hours of Combat." *Rakkasan Shimbun*, Spring 1991.

Budiansky, Stephen with Bruce Auster and Peter Cary. "Preparing the Ground: U.S. Commanders are Counting on Mobility, Air Support and New Ways to Find the Enemy." *U.S. News & World Report*. February 4, 1991, pp. 32–41.

Burton, Col. James. "Pushing Them Out the Back Door." *Proceedings*. June, 1993, pp. 37–43.

Carlson, Col. Douglas M. *Joint Stars: Success in the Desert, what next?* Maxwell Air Force Base, Alabama: Air War College Research Report, April 1992.

Casualty Data Assessment Team, Operation Desert Storm, Division of Military Trauma Research, Letterman Army Institute of Research. *Final Report*. Presidio of San Francisco, California, January 1992.

CIA Directorate of Intelligence. *Operation Desert Storm: A Snapshot of the Battlefield*. Washington, D.C. September 1993.

Chadwick, Frank. *Desert Shield Fact Book*. Bloomington, Illinois: GDW, 1991.

———. *Desert Storm Fact Book*. Bloomington, Illinois: GDW, 1991.

Chesnoff, Richard. "Behind the Lines: A Car Trip Through Iraq on the Eve of Peace Shows the Hell of War." *U.S. News & World Report*. March 11, 1991, pp. 47–48.

Clancy, Tom and Gen. Fred Franks, Jr. (Ret.). *Into the Storm: A Study in Command*. New York: G. P. Putnam's Sons, 1997.

Cooke, James J. *100 Miles from Baghdad: With the French in Desert Storm*. Westport, Connecticut: Praeger, 1993.

Cooper, Dale. "Young Guns: The Harrier the Better for Marine Jet Jocks." *Soldier of Fortune*. August 1991, pp. 52–57.

———. "Cobra Cowboys: Killer Marine Copters Ride Low in the Sky, High in the Saddle, Over Kuwait." *Soldier of Fortune*. August 1991, pp. 64–67.

———. "Semper Fatal: Yakima Yank Marine Reservists Kick, Bash and Take Names." *Soldier of Fortune*. August 1991, pp. 68–75.

———. "Task Force Ripper: U.S. Marines Go For Iraq's Throat." *Soldier of Fortune*. August 1991, pp. 86–91.

———. "Apaches Draw First Blood: Choppers Blast Corridor to Baghdad." *Soldier of Fortune*. June 1992, pp. 32–37.

Cordesman, Anthony and Ahmed Hashim. *Iraq: Sanctions and Beyond*. Boulder, Colorado: Westview Press, 1997.

Cordesman, Anthony and Abraham R. Wagner. *The Lessons of Modern War, Volume II: The Iran–Iraq War*. Boulder, Colorado: Westview Press, 1991.

Cordesman, Anthony. *The Iran–Iraq War and Western Security 1984–87: Strategic Implications and Policy Options*. New York: Jane's Publishing Inc., 1987.

Cordingley, Maj.Gen. Patrick. "The Gulf War: Operating With Allies." *RUSI Journal*. April 1992, pp. 17–20.

———. *In the Eye of the Storm: Commanding the Desert Rats in the Gulf War*. London: Hodder & Stoughton, 1996.

Coyne, James P. *Airpower in the Gulf*. Arlington, Virginia: Air Force Association, 1992.

Crawley, Vince. "Ghost Troop's Battle at the 73 Easting." *Armor*. May–June 1991, pp. 7–12.

Cureton, Lt.Col. Charles H. *U.S. Marines in the Persian Gulf, 1990–1991, With the 1st Marine Division in Desert Shield and Desert Storm*. Washington, D.C.: History and Museums Division, Headquarters, U.S. Marine Corps, 1993.

Cushman, Lt.Gen. John H. "Desert Storm's End Game." *Proceedings.* October, 1993, pp. 76–80.

Danis, Capt. Aaron. "Iraqi Army Operations and Doctrine." *Military Intelligence.* April/June 1991, pp. 6–12, 48.

Davis, M. Thomas. "After the Friendly Fire." *Washington Post.* May 30, 1993, pg. C5.

de la Billiere, General Sir Peter. *Storm Command: A Personal Account of the Gulf War.* London: Motivate Publishing, 1993.

Department of Defense. *Conduct of the Persian Gulf War: Final Report to Congress Pursuant to Title V of The Persian Gulf Conflict Supplemental Authorization and Personnel Benefits Act of 1991 (Public Law 102–25).* Washington, D.C.: U.S. Government Printing Office, April 1992.

———. *Emergency War Surgery.* Washington, D.C.: U.S. Government Printing Office, 1988.

Dietrich, Lt.Col. Steve E. "From Valhalla With Pride." *Proceedings.* August, 1993, pp. 59–60.

Donnelly, Tom. "The Generals' War, How Commanders Fought the Iraqis." *Army Times.* March 2, 1992, pp. 8, 12, 14–15.

———. "...and Among Themselves." *Army Times.* March 2, 1991, pp. 8, 16, 18, 61–77.

Dugan, General Michael. "First Lessons of Victory." *U.S. News & World Report.* March 18, 1991, pp. 32–36.

Dunnigan, James F., and Austin Bay. *From Shield to Storm.* New York: William Morrow and Company, Inc., 1992.

Dunnigan, James F., and Albert Nofi. *Dirty Little Secrets: Military Information You're Not Supposed to Know.* New York: William Morrow and Company, Inc., 1990.

Dunnigan, James F. *How to Make War: A Comprehensive Guide to Modern Warfare.* New York: Quill, 1992.

Eisenstadt, Michael. *Like a Phoenix From the Ashes?: The Future of Iraqi Military Power.* Washington, D.C.: The Washington Institute For Near East Policy, 1993.

Enders, Lt.Col. G.W. and Maj. J.P. Carothers. *Marine Expeditionary Force Breaching Operations in Southwest Asia.* Camp Lejeune, North Carolina, July 1991.

Englehardt, Lieutenant Colonel Joseph P. *Desert Shield and Desert Storm: A Chronology and Troop List for the 1990–1991 Persian Gulf Crisis.* Carlisle Barracks: Strategic Studies Institute, U.S. Army War College, 1991.

Epkins, Colonel Steven A. *A Division G-2's Perspective on Operations Desert Shield and Desert Storm.* Carlisle Barracks: Army War College Study Project, 15 April 1992.

Eschel, David. *Chariots of the Desert: The Story of the Israeli Armored Corps.* New York: Brassey's 1989.

Evans, Michael. "SAS Mission to Cripple Scuds Earns 41 Awards." *The Times of London.* June 29, 1991, pp. 1, 12.

Floris, Lieutenant Colonel John P. *1-41st Field Artillery in Operation Desert Storm.* Carlisle Barracks: Army War College Study Project, 19 May 1992.

Fontenot, Col. Gregory. "Fright Night: Task Force 2/34 Armor." *Military Review.* January 1993.

———. "The 'Dreadnoughts' Rip the Saddam Line." *Army.* January 1992.

Foss, Christopher and Terry J. Gander, Editors. *Jane's Military Vehicles and Logistics.* Alexandria, Virginia: Jane's Information Group, 1992.

Foss, Christopher, Editor. *Jane's Armour and Artillery, 13th Edition*. Alexandria, Virginia: Jane's Information Group, 1991.

Foss, Christopher. *Artillery of the World*. New York: Charles Scribner's Sons, 1981.

Fox, Robert. "British Role in the Final Liberation of Kuwait." *London Daily Telegraph Magazine*. March 3, 1991 pp. 2–11.

G-2, VII Corps. *The 100 Hour Ground War: How the Iraqi Plan Failed*. Stuttgart, Germany: April 20, 1991.

Galloway, Joseph L. "The Point of the Spear: The U.S. 24th Infantry Division (Mechanized) Broke the Back of Iraq's Army on the Ground." *U.S. News & World Report*. March 11, 1991, pp. 32–43.

Gander, Terry J. *NBC: Nuclear Biological & Chemical Warfare*. New York: Hippocrene, 1987.

Gander, Terry J., Editor. *Jane's NBC Protection Equipment, 5th Edition*. Alexandria, Virginia: Jane's Information Group, 1992.

Gellman, Barton. "Felled by Friendly Fire." *The Washington Post National Weekly Edition*. November 11–17, 1991.

General Accounting Office. *Operation Desert Shield/Desert Storm: Observations on the Performance of the Army's Hellfire Missile*. Washington, D.C. March 30, 1993.

———. *Operation Desert Storm: Investigation of a U.S. Army Fratricide Incident*. Washington, D.C. April 7, 1995.

Gilbert, Martin. *The First World War: A Complete History*. New York: Henry Holt and Company, 1994.

Gill, Capt. Kirk. *3rd Brigade, 101st Airborne Division (Air Assault) "Rakkasans" in Desert Shield and Desert Storm*. Paducah, Kentucky: Turner Publishing Company, 1992.

Gordon, Michael R., and Gen. (Ret.) Bernard E. Trainor. *The Generals' War: The Inside Story of the Conflict in the Gulf*. Boston/New York: Little, Brown Company, 1995.

Gravlin, Maj. Steve. *Second Armored Cavalry Regiment: Operation Desert Storm 1990–1991*. Nuremburg, Germany, 1991.

Griffith, Lt.Gen. Ronald. "Mission Accomplished —In Full." *Proceedings*. August, 1993, pp. 63–65.

Gross, Lt.Col. David. *The Breach of Saddam's Defensive Line: Recollections of an Armored Task Force Commander*. Carlisle Barracks: Army War College Study Project.

Halberstadt, Hans. *Desert Storm Ground War*. Osceola, Wisconsin: Motorbooks, 1991.

———. *Desert Rats: The British 4 and 7 Armored Brigades, WWII to Today*. Osceola, Wisconsin: Motorbooks, 1993.

Hammick, Murray. "A Divisional Commander's View." *International Defense Review*. September 1991, pp. 979–980.

———. "A Battlegroup Commander's View." *International Defense Review*. September 1991, pp. 983–985.

———. "Iraqi Obstacles and Defensive Positions." *International Defense Review*. September 1991, pp. 989–991.

Harris, Chesley. "Operation Desert Storm: Armored Brigade in Combat." *Infantry*. May–June 1992, pp. 13–19.

Headquarters, 1st Infantry Division. *Big Red One: 1st Infantry Division Combat Operations in Operation Desert Storm*. Ft. Riley, Kansas, 1991.

Headquarters, 3rd Armored Division. *Historical Overview of the 3rd Armored Division in the Persian Gulf War.* Frankfort, Germany, 1991.

Headquarters, 3rd Squadron, 2nd Armored Cavalry Regiment. *Memorandum For Record: Operation Desert Storm.* Amberg, Germany, 1991.

Headquarters, 197th Infantry Brigade. *Operation Desert Storm: Summary of Operations, 17 January–10 March 1991.* Ft. Benning, Georgia, 1991.

Henscheid, Maj. Mark R. *Chemical Weapons: The Legacy of Operation Desert Storm.* Newport, Rhode Island: Naval War College Study Project, 21 June 1991.

Hertling, Maj. Mark, Editor. *Collected Vignettes, 1st Squadron, 1st Cavalry (1st Regiment of Dragoons).* April, 1991.

Herwig, Holger H. *The First World War: Germany and Austria-Hungary, 1914–1918.* London: Arnold, 1997

Herzog, Chaim. *The Arab–Israeli Wars: War and Peace in the Middle East from the War of Independence through Lebanon.* New York: Random House, 1984.

Hillman, Lt.Col. James. *Task Force 1-41 Infantry: Fratricide Experience in Southwest Asia.* Carlisle Barracks: Army War College Study Project, April 1993.

Hiro, Dilip. *The Longest War: The Iran–Iraq Military Conflict.* New York: Routledge, 1991.

History and Museums Division, Headquarters, U.S. Marine Corps. *U.S. Marines in the Persian Gulf, 1990–1991: Anthology and Annotated Bibliography.* Washington, D.C., 1992.

Hoyt, Timothy D. "Iraq's Military Industry: A Critical Strategic Target." *National Security Studies Quarterly.* Spring 1998, pp. 33–50.

House of Representatives, Oversight and Investigations Committee, Committee on Armed Services. *Intelligence Successes and Failures in Operations Desert Shield/Storm.* Washington, D.C.: U.S. Government Printing Office, August 16, 1993.

Inbar, Colonel Giora. *Decisive Factors in the Gulf War From the IDF Lessson Learning Perspective.* Carlisle Barracks: Army War College Study Project, 1 April 1993.

Jacobsmeyer, Maj. Paul and Capt. Guy Swann III. "Operation Desert Storm." *Ironsides.* Ansbach, Germany, April 22, 1991.

Jacobson, Michael. "Iraqi Infantry." *Infantry.* January–February 1991, pp. 33–37.

———. "Armor in Desert Shield." *Infantry.* November–December 1990, pp. 32–37.

Jemiola, Lt.Col. Richard W. *The 9th Engineer Battalion in Operation Desert Storm.* Carlisle Barracks: Army War College Study Project, 22 March 1993.

Jones, Maj. John R., Capt. Everett McDaniel and Capt. Stephen Zeltner. "Training and Fighting With the Saudis" *Engineer.* July 1991, pp. 9–13.

Jones, Capt. Robert A. "Firefight at Hamaltyat." *Marine Corps Gazette.* June 1991, pp. 30–32.

Kamiya, Maj. Jason K. "A History of the 24th Mechanized Infantry Division Combat Team During Operation Desert Storm: The Attack to Free Kuwait (January through March 1991)." *The Victory Book.* Ft. Stewart, Georgia, 1992.

Karsh, Efraim. "In Baghdad, Politics is a Lethal Game." *New York Times Magazine.* September 30, 1990, pp. 38–42, 100.

Keany, Thomas. "The Linkage of Air and Ground Power in the Future of Conflict." *International Security.* Fall 1997, pp. 147–150.

Kelly, Michael. *Martyr's Day.* New York: Random House, 1993.

Klemencic, Maj. John and Cpt. John Thomson. *Fire Support for the Corps Covering Force: A Desert Storm, Perspective.* Nuremburg Germany, 1991.

Kindsvatter, Lt.Col. Peter S. "VII Corps in the Gulf War: Ground Offensive." *Military Review.* February 1992, pp.16–37.

———. "VII Corps in the Gulf War: Post Cease–Fire Operations." *Military Review.* February 1992, pp.3–19.

Kinsey, Bert. U.S. Aircraft & Armament of Operation Desert Storm. Waukesha, Wisconsin: Kalmbach Publishing, 1993.

Kurth, Lt.Col. Michael M. "Whiskey With a Kick." *Amphibious Warfare Review.* Summer 1991, pp. 33–34.

Lacquement, Capt. Richard. *Overview of the 1st Armored Division Field Artillery's Participation in Operation Desert Shield/Storm.* Germany, 1991.

Latremoliere, Olivier. "Objectif White: La Bataille D'As-Salman." *Terre Magazine.* Mars–Avril 1991.

Lennox, Duncan, Editor. *Jane's Air Launched Weapons, 6th Edition.* Alexandria, Virginia: Jane's Information Group, 1992.

MacGerrcin, Munremur. "Eyes of the Storm: Gulf War Special Ops." *Soldier of Fortune.* August 1991, pp. 59, 116.

MacKenzie, Richard. "Stormin' Norman Schwarzkopf: Genius of Desert Storm." *Soldier of Fortune.* August 1991, pp. 46–51.

Macksey, Kenneth. "Tank v. Missile." *War Monthly.* Issue 5, August 1974, pp. 39–48.

———. "The Tanks." *History of the Second World War.* Issue 96, January 30, 1975, pp. 2633–2641.

———. "The Men." *History of the Second World War.* Issue 96, January 30, 1975, pp. 2653–48.

Maggart, Col. Lon E. "A Leap of Faith." *Armor.* January–February 1992.

Maggart, Brig.Gen. Lon E. and Col. Gregory Fontenot. "Breaching Operations: Implications for Battle Command and Battle Space." *Military Review.* February 1994.

Mahnken, Thomas G. and Barry D. Watts. "What the Gulf War Can (and Cannot) Tell Us About The Future of Warfare." *International Security.* Fall 1997, pp. 151–162.

Marlin, Lt.Col. David. *History of the 4th Battalion, 37th Armored Regiment in Desert Shield and Desert Storm Vol. 1.* Carlisle Barracks: Army War College Study Project, 15 April 1992.

———. *History of the 4th Battalion, 37th Armored Regiment in Desert Shield and Desert Storm Vol. 2.* Carlisle Barracks: Army War College Study Project, 15 April 1992.

Mathews, Tom. "The Secret History of the War: Prodigious Planning and Unshakable Will Produced a Famous Victory." *Newsweek.* March 18, 1991, pp. 28–39.

———. "The Path to War: How President Bush and His Inner Circle Recovered From a Series of Major Errors to Organize Total Victory Against Saddam Hussein." *Newsweek.* Spring/Summer 1991, pp. 32–48.

Mazaar, Michael J. with Don M. Snyder and James A. Blackwell, Jr. *Desert Storm: The Gulf War and What We Learned.* Boulder, Colorado: Westview Press, 1993.

McIntire, Katherine. "Speed Bumps, 82d Airborne's Shaky Line in the Sand." *Army Times.* October 21, 1991, pp. 12–14, 18, 76–77.

Merritt, Lt.Col. Daniel A. *The "Iron Duke" World Tour: A Personal Experience.* Carlisle Barracks: Army War College Study Project, 31 May 1994.

Military History Magazine Editors. *Desert Storm.* Leesburg, Virginia: Empire Press, 1991.

Miller, David and Christopher Foss. *Modern Land Combat.* New York: Portland House, 1992.

Milner, Laurie. *Royal Scots in the Gulf.* London: Leo Cooper, 1994.

Morningstar, Maj. James. "Points of Attack: Lessons from the Breach." *Armor.* January–February 1998, pp. 7–13.

Mroczkowski, Lt. Col. Dennis P. *U.S. Marines in the Persian Gulf, 1990–1991, With the 2d Marine Division in Desert Shield and Desert Storm.* Washington, D.C.: History and Museums Division, Headquarters, U.S. Marine Corps, 1993.

Mumford, 1LT. Jay C. *Rangers in Iraq: Task Force Ranger, 2nd Battalion, 16th Infantry in the Persian Gulf War.* Ft.Riley, Kansas: Headquarters, 2nd Battalion, 16th Infantry Regiment, August 31, 1991.

Naylor, Sean D. "Flight of Eagles: 101st Airborne Division's Raids Into Iraq." *Army Times.* July 22, 1991, pp. 8–12, 14.

———. "Home of the Brave" *Army Times.* January 27, 1992, pp. 8, 12–14, 16, 58.

Nelan, Bruce W. "Revolution at Defense: After Absorbing the Hard Lessons of Vietnam, the Pentagon Revised its Strategy, Modernized its Methods, and Turned Itself into an Awesome Juggernaut." *Time.* March 18, 1991, pp. 25–26.

O'Ballance, Edgar. *No Victor, No Vanquished: The Yom Kippur War.* Novato, CA: Presidio Press, 1978.

Oakley, John B. "Iraq: An Historical Perspective." *Military Intelligence.* April/June 1991, pp. 19–23.

Office of Technology Assessment, United States Congress. *Proliferation of Weapons of Mass Destruction: Assessing the Risks.* Washington, D.C.: U.S. Government Printing Office, 1994.

———. *Who Goes There: Friend or Foe.* Washington, D.C.: U.S. Government Printing Office, 1993

Ogorkiewicz, R. M. "Interview With Israel's Major General Tal." *International Defense Review.* September 1991, pp. 977–978.

Operations Staff, 1-4th Cavalry. "Riders on the Storm: A Narrative History of the 1-4 Cav's Campaign in Iraq and Kuwait, 24 January–March 1991." *Armor.* May–June 1991, pp. 13–20.

———. *Operations Summary, 1st Squadron, 4th Cavalry Regiment in Desert Shield and Desert Storm,* Fort Riley, Kansas, 1991.

Operations Staff, Task Force Papa Bear. *Summary of Action for Operation Desert Storm (24–27 February 1991).* Camp Pendleton, California, 1991.

Operations Staff, 1st Battalion, 7th Marine Regiment. *Operation Desert Storm: 1st Battalion, 7th Marines Maneuver Synopsis.* Camp Pendleton, California, 1991.

Operations Staff, 1st Tank Battalion. *Operation Desert Storm: Combat Action Summary of 1st Tank Battalion.* Camp Pendleton, California, 1991.

Operations Staff, 2nd Armored Cavalry Regiment. *Operation Desert Storm: 2 ACR Operations Summary, 23 Feb.–1 Mar. 91.* Nuremburg, Germany, 1991.

Operations Staff, 2nd Battalion, 29th Field Artillery. *Desert Storm: Combat Historical Summary, 15 January–16 April 91.* Baumholder, Germany, 1991.

Operations Staff, 2nd Brigade, 3rd Armored Division. Operation *Desert Shield: December 1990 thru 27 February 1991.* Gelnhausen, Germany, 1991.

Operations Staff, 2nd Light Armored Infantry Battalion. *Operation Desert Storm: Operations Summary.* Camp Pendleton, California, 1991.

Operations Staff, 4th Squadron, 2nd Armored Cavalry Regiment. *Fourth Squadron Operations Log, Operation Desert Storm, 31 Dec. 1990–23 Mar. 1991.* Feucht, Germany, 1991.

Operations Staff, 11th Marine Regiment. *11th Marines Operation Desert Storm Summary of Significant Events.* Camp Pendleton, California, 1991.

Ottaway, David and Patrick Bishop. "Slowly But Surely, Egyptians Topple Iraqi Troops." *Washington Times.* February 26, 1991, pp. A14–15.

Paydock, 2Lt. Joseph. *Iron Troop History.* Amberg, Germany, 1991.

Paulsen, Captain Pat. "Depleted Uranium Without the Rocket Science." *Armor.* July–August 1995.

Pearce, Nigel. *The Shield and the Sabre: The Desert Rats in the Gulf.* London, HMSO, 1992.

Pelletiere, Stephen C. and Johnson, Douglas V. *Lessons Learned: The Iran–Iraq War.* Carlisle Barracks: Strategic Studies Institute, U.S. Army War College, 1991.

Phillips, Maj. Jeff and Robyn Gregory. *America's First Team in the Gulf.* Dallas: Taylor Publishing Company, 1992.

Powell, Gen. (Ret.) Colin L. *My American Journey.* New York: Random House, 1995.

Poyer, Joe. "Air Force's Report Card From the Gulf." *International Military Review.* Spring 1992, pp. 40–45.

Press, Daryl G. "Lessons From Ground Combat in the Gulf." *International Security.* Fall 1997, pp. 137–146.

Public Affairs Office, Fort Hood. *Press Packet.* Ft. Hood, Texas, 1991.

Public Affairs Office, VII Corps. *The Desert Jayhawk.* Stuttgart, Germany, 1991.

Quilter, Lt.Col. Charles J. *U.S. Marines in the Persian Gulf, 1990–1991, With the I Marine Expeditionary Force in Desert Shield and Desert Storm.* Washington, D.C.: History and Museums Division, Headquarters, U.S. Marine Corps, 1993.

Reischl, Lieutenant Colonel Timothy J. *Crossing the Line in the Sand: 4th Battalion, 67th Armor in Southwest Asia.* Carlisle Barracks: Army War College Study Project, 5 April 1993.

Reid, Maj.Gen. P.M. "Tanks in the Gulf." *Army Quarterly and Defense Journal.* April 1991, pp. 184–192.

Ritter, Maj. William S. "Operation Tiger: Amphibious Operations in the Northern Persian Gulf Revisited." *Marine Corps Gazette.* July 1996, pp. 62–70.

Rothwell, S.K. "Medium Reconnaissance in the Gulf." *Army Quarterly and Defense Journal.* July 1995, pp. 308–313.

Ryan, John T. "War!: Soldier's Diary Describes Storm of Desert Tanks." *Asheville (N.C.) Citizen Times.* May 19, 1991, pp. D-1, D-8.

———. *The Battle for Objective Norfolk: 2nd Armored Division (FWD), 26–27 February 1991.* Battlefield Reconstruction, 15 January 1999.

Scales, Brig.Gen. Robert H., Jr. *Certain Victory: The U.S. Army in the Gulf War.* Washington, D.C.: Office of the Chief of Staff, United States Army, 1993.

Scales, Col. Robert H., Jr. "Accuracy Defeated Range in Artillery Duel." *International Defense Review.* May 1991, pp. 473–481.

Schmitt, Eric. "U.S. Army Buried Soldiers Alive in Gulf War." *New York Times.* September 15, 1991, pg. A8.

Schwarzkopf, Gen. (Ret.) H. Norman. *It Doesn't Take a Hero: The Autobiography.* New York: Bantam, 1992.

Sciccitano, J. Paul. "Eye of the Tiger." *Army Times.* June 10,1991, pp.12–13, 16, 18, 61.

———. "Night Strikes: The Secret War of the 1st Cavalry Division." *Army Times.* September 23,1991, pp. 8, 14–16.

Schwartz, John and Douglas Waller. "Bringing Them Back Alive: High-Tech Retrieval Teams Take to the Skies When Pilots Bail Out Over Enemy Territory." *Newsweek.* February 4, 1991, pg. 55.

Sloyan, Patrick J. "Desert Scars." *Sunday Newsday.* November 10, 1991, pp. 4–6.

———. "Anger in the Ranks: Friendly Fire Deaths Set Soldier Against Soldier." *Sunday Newsday.* November 10, 1991, pp. 7, 23.

Smallwood, William L. *Strike Eagle: Flying the F–15E in the Gulf War.* Washington, D.C.: Brassey's, 1994.

Smith, Maj.Gen. Rupert. "The Gulf War: The Land Battle." *RUSI Journal.* February 1992, pp. 1–5.

Stanton, Lt.Col. Martin. "The Saudi Arabian National Guard Motorized Brigades: Wheeled Armor Plays a Big Role in the Kingdom's Internal Security Mission." *Armor.* March–April 1996, pp. 6–11.

Steele, Dennis and Eric C. Ludvigsen. "Down in the Sand: The First Brushes." *Army.* March 1991, pp. 33–38.

Stewart, Brig.Gen. John. "Desert Storm: A 3rd U.S. Army Perspective." *Military Intelligence.* October/December 1991, pp. 22–31.

Stockmore, Capt. James. *The History of the 1st Brigade [1st Infantry Division] in Desert Shield and Desert Storm.* Ft. Riley, Kansas, 1991.

Swain, Richard M. *"Lucky War": Third Army in Desert Storm.* Ft. Leavenworth, Kansas: U.S. Army Command and General Staff College Press, 1995.

Swain, Col. Richard. "Compounding the Error." *Proceedings.* August, 1993, pp. 61–62.

Swanstrom, Lt.Col. Mark. *2D Marine Division Breaching Operations During Desert Storm.* Camp Lejeune, North Carolina, April 1991

Taylor, Thomas. *Lightning in the Storm: The 101st Air Assault Division in the Gulf War.* New York: Hippocrene, 1994.

Tice, Jim. "Coming Through: The Big Red Raid." *Army Times.* August 26, 1991, pp. 12–13, 16, 18, 20.

———. "Taking a Town by Shooting the Breeze." *Army Times.* August 26, 1991, pg. 18.

Trummer, Lt.Cdr. Frederick G. and Maj. Bruce L. Twining. *Chemical Warfare: Implications for Operation Desert Storm and Beyond.* Newport, Rhode Island: Naval War College Study Project, 11 February 1991.

Turner, Lt.Col. John. *Counterattack: The Battle at Al Burqan.* Unpublished Article, March 1993.

U.S. Army Armor Center. *Desert Shield and Desert Storm Emerging Observations.* Ft. Knox, Kentucky, October 1991.

U.S. News & World Report Staff. *Triumph Without Victory: The Unreported History of the Persian Gulf War.* New York: Random House, 1991

Vogel, Steve. "A Swift Kick: 2d ACR's Taming of the Guard." *Army Times.* August 5, 1991, pp. 10–13, 18, 28, 30, 61.

————. "Fast and Hard: The Big Red One's Race Through Iraq." *Army Times.* March 25, 1991, pp. 12–13.

————. "Hell Night: For the 2d Armored Division (Forward) It Was No Clean War." *Army Times.* October 7, 1991, pp. 8, 14–15, 18, 24, 61.

————. "Metal Rain: 'Old Ironsides' and the Iraqis Who Wouldn't Back Down." *Army Times.* September 16, 1991, pp. 8, 12–13, 16, 22, 61.

————. "Killer Brigade: 3d Infantry Division 'Phantoms' Hunt the Enemy." *Army Times.* November 11, 1991, pp. 10, 14–16, 22, 69.

————. "Tip of the Spear." *Army Times.* January 13, 1992, pp. 8, 10, 12–13, 16, 54, 69.

Walker, Greg. "From Refugees to Liberators: U.S. Special Forces Turn Demoralized Kuwaitis Into Fighting Force." *Soldier of Fortune.* June 1992, pp. 62–65, 70.

Waller, Douglas. "Architect of the Air War." *Newsweek.* January 28, 1991, pg. 24.

————. "Secret Warriors." *Newsweek.* June 17, 1991, pp. 20–28.

Watson, Bruce W. with Bruce George, MP, Peter Tsouras and B.L. Cyr. *Military Lessons of the Gulf War.* Novato, California: Presidio Press, 1993.

Weber, Maj. K. and Capt. J. Aiello. *History of the Ready First Combat Team, First Brigade 3rd Armored Division, Nov. 1990 Thru 22 March 1991.* Frankfort, Germany, 1991.

Woodmansee, Maj.Gen. John W. "Blitzkrieg and the AirLand Battle." *Military Review.* August 1984, pp. 21–34.

Woodward, Bob. *The Commanders.* New York: Simon & Schuster, 1991.

World Air Power Journal Editors. *Gulf Air War Debrief.* Westport, Connecticut: Airtime Publishing, 1992.

Zumwalt, Lt.Col. J.G. "Tanks! Tanks! Direct Front!" *Proceedings.* July, 1992, pp. 73–80.

————. "Braving the Breach." *Proceedings.* July, 1992, pp. 75–77.